WORLD POLITICS

Trend and Transformation

Twelfth Edition
2009–2010 Update

Charles W. Kegley, Jr.
Carnegie Council for Ethics in International Affairs
with
Shannon Lindsey Blanton
The University of Memphis

WADSWORTH
CENGAGE Learning

Australia • Brazil • Japan • Korea • Mexico • Singapore • Spain • United Kingdom • United States

**World Politics: Trend and Transformation,
Twelfth Edition 2009–2010 Update**
Charles W. Kegley, Jr., Shannon Lindsey Blanton

Executive Editor: Carolyn Merrill

Development Editor: Rebecca Green

Assistant Editor: Katherine Hayes

Marketing Manager: Amy Whitaker

Marketing Communications Manager: Heather
    Baxley

Print Buyer: Judy Inouye

Permissions Editor: Bob Kauser

Production and Composition Services: GEX
    Publishing Services

Photo Manager: Dean Dauphinais

Photo Researcher: Jaime Jankowski

Cover Designer: Blue Bungalow Design

Cover Image: © Fotolia

Internal Designer: Ke Design

For product information and technology assistance, contact us at
Cengage Learning Customer & Sales Support, 1-800-354-9706

For permission to use material from this text or product, submit all requests online at **www.cengage.com/permissions**
Further permissions questions can be emailed to
permissionrequest@cengage.com

Library of Congress Control Number: 2009921390

Student Edition:

ISBN-13: 978-0-495-56569-7

ISBN-10: 0-495-56569-5

Wadsworth
20 Channel Center Street
Boston, MA 02210
USA

Cengage Learning products are represented in Canada by Nelson Education, Ltd.

For your course and learning solutions, visit **www.cengage.com**.

Purchase any of our products at your local college store or at our preferred online store **www.ichapters.com**.

Printed in the United States of America
1 2 3 4 5 6 7 12 11 10 09 08

DEDICATION

To my loving wife Debbie

and

the Carnegie Council for Ethics in International Affairs,
in appreciation for its invaluable contribution to building through
education a more just and secure world
– Charles W. Kegley, Jr.

To my husband Rob

and

our sons Austin and Cullen,
in appreciation of their patience, love, and support
– Shannon Lindsey Blanton

brief contents

contents

CHAPTER 8

CHAPTER 9

CHAPTER 10

PART 7 ENVISIONING YOUR ALTERNATIVE GLOBAL FUTURES AND PREDICTING GLOBAL TRANSFORMATIONS 549

maps

controversy boxes

PREFACE

Understanding twenty-first century world politics requires accurate and up-to-date information, intellectual analysis, and interpretation. In a globe undergoing constant and rapid change, it is imperative to accurately describe, explain, and predict the key events and issues unfolding in international affairs. These intellectual tasks must be performed well so that world citizens and policy makers can harness this knowledge and ground their decisions on the most pragmatic approaches to global problems available. Only informed interpretations of world conditions and trend trajectories and cogent explanations of why they exist and how they are unfolding can provide the tools necessary for understanding the world and making it better. By presenting the leading ideas and the latest information available, *World Politics: Trend and Transformation* provides the tools necessary for understanding world affairs in our present period of history, for anticipating probable developments, and for thinking critically about the potential long-term impact of those developments on countries and individuals across the globe.

World Politics: Trend and Transformation aims to put both changes and continuities into perspective. It provides a picture of the evolving relations among all transnational actors, the historical developments that affect those actors' relationships, and the salient contemporary global trends that those interactions produce. The major theories scholars use to explain the dynamics underlying international relations—realism, liberalism, and constructivism, as well as feminist and radical interpretations—frame the investigation. That said, this book resists the temptation to oversimplify world politics with a superficial treatment that would mask complexities and distort realities. Moreover, the text refuses to substitute mere subjective opinion for information based on evidence and purposefully presents clashing and contending views so that students have a chance to critically evaluate the opposed positions and construct their own judgments about key issues. It fosters critical thinking by repeatedly asking students to assess the possibilities for the global future and its potential impact on their own lives.

OVERVIEW OF THE BOOK

Part 1 introduces the central concepts essential to understanding world politics, global trends, and their meaning. It introduces the leading theories used to interpret international relations and now also includes an overview of international decision making—the processes and procedures by which all transnational actors (and especially states) make foreign policy choices about their goals and the means they use to realize them.

Part 2 identifies the transnational actors in the global arena—the great powers, the less developed countries of the "Global South," the rising powers of the "Global East," intergovernmental organizations (IGOs), and nongovernmental organizations (NGOs). It covers these multiple transnational actors' relationships and patterns of interaction, and also how their actions affect individual citizens and their human rights.

Part 3 looks at the economic, demographic and cultural dimensions of cascading globalization. Initial chapters provide separate treatments of the internationalization of finance and trade, followed by survey chapters examining the global impact of migration, labor, educational trends, the new "slave trade," and health issues—and how global communications are transforming cultures in the so-called "information age."

Part 4 examines two kinds of threats to world security—ecological and military—and places particular emphasis on international warfare, internal or civil wars, terrorism, and their multiple causes.

Part 5 covers the realist roads to national and international security, with attention to the military pursuit of power, national security strategies, coercive diplomacy, alliances, and the balance of power.

In contrast, Part 6 traces the liberal paths to world order through negotiation of international crises, international law, arms control and disarmament, collective security through global and regional international organizations, and the promotion of international morality through the spread of democratization and free trade.

The book concludes with Part 7, which surveys scenarios about the likely future of world politics and poses seven questions raised by prevailing trends in order to stimulate further thinking about the global future.

The updated twelfth edition of the book retains the following highly praised features from the previous edition:

■ **Controversy Boxes.** Long a mainstay of the book, each Controversy box examines the opposing positions on a major issue under debate in international relations. The essays, revised to bring the latest spectrum of opinion about each issue into view, encourage students to think critically about rival viewpoints and to develop their own opinions. Addressing both classic dilemmas in international affairs and the most heated current debates, Controversy boxes offer excellent starting points for class debates or research papers.

- **Expanded, Up-to-date Map and Illustration Program.** One of the most popular pedagogical features of the text, the illustration program—which includes more than three dozen new photographs, maps, tables, and figures—has been expanded and revised to broaden the book's coverage, provoke interest, and enable students to visualize the central developments and data. The new photographs and illustrations have been selected to introduce the timeliest topics and include detailed captions that explain their relevance to the larger issues discussed in the text. Students today are often woefully uninformed about world geography, and the extensive map program helps remedy this problem.

CHANGES IN THE TWELFTH EDITION

Changes to Structure and Presentation

In order to keep you and your students abreast of the latest developments, World Politics has always changed in response to the unfolding developments across our world. Since the publication of the twelfth edition of this book in February 2008, numerous changes have taken place. This updated twelfth edition has been prepared to incorporate the latest developments in global events and scholarly research findings so that students will have access to the most current information. The twelfth edition, in particular, represents a sweeping revision of the book, as instructors familiar with past editions will quickly note. Changes to this edition include:

- *A significant reorganization of the material that consolidates coverage of previously dispersed topics and breaks the chapters into more manageable portions.* As a result, there are now seven parts and eighteen chapters, although the overall length and depth of coverage remains unchanged. Some topics, such as military power and arms control and disarmament, have been repositioned to better fit the way in which instructors conventionally treat them.

- *An all-new design that makes the book easier and more attractive to use.* New streamlined chapter-openers begin with traditional chapter outlines so that students can preview and review the material presented, and thought-provoking quotations there—and now throughout each chapter—have been provided to broaden and deepen awareness of competing ideas and to stimulate interest in the insightful opinions of authors and policy makers on past and present global issues.

▪ ***Revised treatment of key terms.*** Key terms continue to be highlighted with bold faced text and glossed definitions in margins where the terms are first introduced. Now, however, each term is glossed only the first time it is introduced, and a single definition is used to familiarize students with the broadest and most common meaning of the term. If a term is used again in subsequent chapters in a more specific context, the term is identified in *italics* and its more particular meaning is presented in the text itself and does not appear in the marginal glossary.

▪ ***An all-new glossary of key term definitions.*** This new reference tool appears at the end of the text, so students can more easily access terms they may not remember from previously assigned or unassigned chapters.

▪ ***More streamlined end-of-chapter coverage.*** "Suggested Readings" and "Where on the World Wide Web" sections have been removed from the text and are now provided on the book's companion Web site (see below). A list of the key terms introduced in each chapter continues to be provided.

Changes to Content by Chapter

The changes above highlight only the most salient structural modifications in the updated twelfth edition of *World Politics*. Needless to say, this text continues to take pride in identifying and reporting the most recent developments in international affairs and in providing the latest data on the most significant related trends. This updated twelfth edition includes eight new maps, figures, and tables, in addition to 2008 updates to most of the existing ones, and thirty-six new pictures as well as the accompanying background information. The twelfth edition now includes new coverage of negotiation in international bargaining, the Prisoner's Dilemma, the fallout of the war in Iraq, and other topics as described in more detail below. The updated version builds upon these changes and addresses the most important issues on the global agenda, from human rights and human development to the resurgence of Al Qaeda in the border regions of Pakistan and Afghanistan, from the pressing challenges posed by global warming to the oil crisis and the debate surrounding the development of alternative energy sources, and from changes in the globalized political economy to military developments such as private military services and U.S. missile defense. The twelfth edition included three new Controversy boxes, and this updated edition adds two more. As always, this leading text incorporates many thematic shifts in emphasis that capture the latest changes in the way scholars and policymakers understand the key issues and problems in our world, and the entire text has been updated to address the most important changes since the twelfth edition was released in February 2008. The following descriptions pinpoint the most important revisions to each chapter:

- In previous editions, Chapter 1 dealt exclusively with the way individual perceptions and preconceptions influence understanding of world events. In this edition, the scope of the chapter has been expanded by consolidating coverage that was previously scattered among multiple chapters. A new section called "Keys to Understanding World Politics" provides an overview of what is critical to consider when interpreting world politics. The new section discusses the importance of understanding (1) the existing vocabulary for interpreting international affairs; (2) the primary transnational actors (and the historical emergence of the nation state system and the more recent rise of nonstate actors); (3) the distinctions among "foreign policy," "international relations," and "international politics;" (4) the differences of (three) "levels of analysis" and their usefulness in interpreting global trends and issues; and (5) the distinctions between "change," "cycles," "continuities," and "transformations" in world politics. Also more clearly presented is the book's approach and new organization. The chapter has been retitled "Interpreting World Politics" to better reflect the focus of the new material.

- Chapter 2, "Theories of World Politics," now places greater emphasis on constructivism, and feminist as well as radical theory as compelling alternatives to the two major traditional theoretical interpretations of world politics (the realist and liberal traditions).

- Chapter 3, now retitled "International Decision Making" and repositioned in Part 1, has been reorganized by placing first the abstract major models that have been constructed to describe and explain the processes and procedures by which *all* transnational actors (and not just states) go about making choices about priorities in the global arena. First introducing the influences on the making of foreign policy decisions at three levels of analysis, the chapter covers (1) decision-making as rational choice, (2) the bureaucratic politics of decision-making, and (3) the leverage of leaders in making international decisions on behalf of the actors they head. The global and domestic factors shaping international decision making are now illuminated with a discussion of the global and domestic determinants of states' decision-making practices (rather than using the example of states to introduce this general dimension of international relations).

- Chapter 4, "Great-Power Rivalries and Relations," places new emphasis on the probable "power transition" that is unfolding, giving increased attention to the strategic implications of the rise of China and the reemergence of Russia as rivals to the United States. A new controversy box exploits both the "levels of analysis" and the realist, liberal, and constructivist bodies of theory to link the topics to the frameworks provided in Chapter 1 and 2. Moreover, the chapter now includes a discussion of the great powers' current national security strategies.

- Chapter 5, "The Global South in a World of Powers," has been thoroughly updated to capture the changes brought about by the escape from poverty by a number of countries formerly identified with the countries at the bottom of the global hierarchy, especially the rising economic powerhouses of the "Global East." Trends in trade, aid, and investments in the Global South are traced in a fresh consideration of the Global South's changing foreign policy relations with the great powers.

- Chapter 6, which formerly covered all types of non-state actors, now deals exclusively with IGOs and has been retitled "Intergovernmental Organizations and the Quest for Global Governance" to reflect that change. The discussion of the European Union and its origins here now consolidates material from Chapter 15 of the previous edition, covering the topic more conveniently in a single chapter, and places the functionalist and neofunctionalist theories about the political integration of independent states into an amalgamated organization of "pooled sovereignty."

- A new Chapter 7, "Nongovernmental Organizations and the Shape of the Global Future," highlights the new transnational activism by not only nonprofit NGOs but also by the nonstate nations of the Fourth World, "clashing civilizations" of global reach, transnational religious movements, transnational terrorist groups, and multinational corporations. The treatment of international terrorism examines the definitional dilemmas in placing terror NGOs in this chapter rather than in the chapter dealing with armed aggression and violence.

- Chapter 8 has been retitled "People Power and the Promotion of Human Rights," and moved to Part 2 in order to classify individuals as a type of transnational actor in their own right and to be more consistent with the level of analysis distinction used throughout the book. The treatment of "human development" and "human security" has been updated and expanded, with increased attention paid to causes of changes in the human condition. Gender inequalities and the status of women also receive more attention, with greater reliance on developments in feminist theories of international relations. Finally, the global community's response to the global refugee crisis and indigenous peoples are given expanded attention, and the chapter introduces two new controversies dealing with the meaning of "security" and the use of humanitarian intervention to police human rights violations.

- A new Part 3 on "The Economic and Demographic Dimensions of Globalization" includes Chapter 9, now titled "The Globalization of International Finance," which opens with an introduction to both theories of international political economy (IPE) and to the debate about the meaning of "globalization" and where the economic dimensions of globalization fit into the equation. The chapter then proceeds to capture the processes and regulatory procedures governing the transnational exchange of money, the nature of exchange rates, and the "crisis" facing today's international currency system. A brand new controversy box is included to highlight the economic impact of IMF and World Bank policy reforms on countries in the Global South.

- Chapter 10, also included in Part 3 and now titled "International Trade in the Global Marketplace," gives the place of trade in the global economy a new self-contained discussion. The chapter stresses the contest between liberal and mercantilist economic philosophies, the role of multinational corporations' foreign direct investments, and the threat to the free trade regime presented by protectionist barriers.

- Chapter 11 rounds out the discussion in Part 3. Now titled "The Demographic and Cultural Dimensions of Globalization," the new chapter examines the coverage of trends in population changes that are becoming an increasingly global challenge. New sections have been added that deal with global migration flows on three levels: "the globalization of labor," "college goes global," and "the new global slave trade." The chapter also covers the spread of diseases throughout the globe and concludes with an analysis of the growth of communications across borders that is creating the global "information age."

- A new Part 4 has been created to cover two major "Threats to the World." Chapter 12 deals with "Threats to the Preservation of the World's Common Ecology" and puts into perspective the entire range of global ecological issues and debates about planetary environmental dangers, including revised discussions of climate change and global warming, ozone depletion, deforestation, and biodiversity. Moreover, a new section on the sources of ecological dangers places "the tragedy of the commons" and the global politics of energy supplies and consumption, which were previously treated in other chapters, in their proper context here. New discussions of both "global solutions" and "national and local solutions" to environmental sustainability have been added, buttressed by new trend data on international treaties for environmental protection and the prospects for greater reliance on renewable sources for energy. The updated twelfth edition also introduces a new controversy that investigates the debate over the sources of the global food crisis that threatens the well-being of much of the planet's population.

- Environmental threats are next juxtaposed to the threat of violence in a reorganized Chapter 13, "The Threat of Armed Aggression to the World." This chapter compares the latest trends in the incidence of interstate wars between states, armed aggression within states (including the changing characteristics of civil wars, enduring internal rivalries, and new profiles of "failed states") and international terrorism. The chapter now provides consolidated coverage of the causes of armed aggression instead of examining the causes for each of various types of warfare (interstate wars, civil wars, and terrorism) in turn as in previous editions.

- A new Part 5, "Realist Roads to National and International Security," provides two chapters on the subject. Chapter 14, now titled "The Military Pursuit of Power Through Arms and Military Strategy," first introduces the core premises and policy prescriptions underlying realist approaches to war and peace in general. It then focuses on the search for power by states seeking security through the acquisition of arms. Changes in military capabilities are captured by the latest evidence regarding international trends in military spending, the weapons trade, and developments in new weapon technologies. The chapter concludes with a discussion and comparison of "compellence," "deterrence," and "preemption" as military strategies, and a new analysis of "coercive diplomacy through military intervention" illuminated by new data is provided to cover the military roads to national security emphasized by realist theory.

- Chapter 15, titled "Alliances and the Balance of Power," provides a now abridged discussion of realist interpretations about the stabilizing influence of arms control on the preservation of the balance of power, and concludes by comparing interpretations that proclaim the continuation of U.S. global domination with those that describe the United States as a "hobbled hegemon." A new controversy box asks the question, "Why Do Countries Compete When They Could Cooperate? Arms Races and the Prisoner's Dilemma."

- A new Part 6, "Liberal Paths to World Order," begins with Chapter 16, now titled "Negotiated Conflict Resolution and International Law," which includes an entirely new section dealing with "International Crises and the Negotiated Settlement of Disputes" that advances new trend data on the frequency of serious international crises and a new discussion of the role of negotiations in the diplomatic management of disputes. This is followed by an overview of the characteristics, principles, and sources of international law as well as the prospects for the legal control of armed aggression. A new controversy box is included dealing with just war theory as it pertains to the U.S. war in Iraq.

- Chapter 17, "Liberal Approaches to Collective Security," examines the use of arms control and disarmament agreements, the approach to international security most strongly advocated by liberals (and far less so by realist policy makers). A new look at collective security through international organizations is provided, with emphasis on both UN peacekeeping operations and regional security organizations for collective defense. Another new section probes the potential for global consensus built around shared moral values for free trade and "a democratic peace pact" to bind countries together. The concluding section assessing "Liberal Institutions and World Order" is strengthened by another new controversy box ("How Should the World's Problems Be Prioritized?").

- Part 7, "Envisioning Your Alternative Global Futures and Predicting Global Transformations," includes only Chapter 18, "Thinking About Global Trends, Transformations, and the Future of World Politics." That chapter provides a new introductory section that compares analysts' predictions in "Global Trends and Forecasts" and another called "How to Think About How People Think About the World" that inventories insights from philosophers and policy makers about the interpretation of the global condition. A final new section on "The Global Predicament: Key Questions About a Turbulent World," introduces seven of the leading issues being debated about the global future. The chapter concludes with an inspiring and provocative challenge for readers about the posture they might assume when thinking about their future, in "A New World Order, or New World Disorder?"

SUPPLEMENTS

The publisher proudly offers the following state-of-the art supplements prepared specifically for the updated twelfth edition of *World Politics: Trend and Transformation*, many of them available with the book for the first time.

All-new CengageNOW!

The first assessment-centered student tutorial system for International Relations, this powerful and interactive resource helps students gauge their unique study needs, then gives them a Personalized Study Plan that focuses their study time on the concepts they most need to master. **CengageNOW** allows students to study more effectively by providing a personalized learning plan based on their needs in the course. Students are directed to read where they need help, and exercises are provided that help students master concepts and think critically about the material in the course. **Efficient paths to success:** Time-saving and efficient for instructors, **CengageNOW** makes the path from assignment through grading and reporting quick and easy. Student personalized study plans lead them efficiently through textbook material, focusing on what each student still needs to learn—making every minute of study pay off!

Seamlessly tied to the new edition of this text through an eBook as well as detailed chapter quizzing, this learning tool is Web-based and FREE with every new copy of the book. It provides access to all the study resources available for the book within a single framework. These resources include chapter outlines and reviews, suggested readings, annotated web links, all-new simulations, case studies, test questions, and mapping exercises. These resources have been thoroughly expanded and updated as necessary. The case studies now include learning objectives and critical thinking questions. Seven all-new simulations have been added covering The Prisoner's Dilemma, The War in Iraq, Weapons of Mass Destruction, Genocide in Rwanda, Methodologies for Ranking the Development Status of Countries Around the World, the Kyoto Treaty, and International and National Security Policy.

PowerLecture with JoinIn

This one-stop lecture and class preparation tool makes it easy for you to assemble, edit, publish, and present custom lectures for your course, using Microsoft PowerPoint. PowerLecture is the fastest way to build powerful, customized, media-rich lectures. The CD-ROM also contains a full Instructor's Manual, Test Bank in Microsoft Word and ExamView Computerized Testing, JoinIn which features instant classroom assessment and learning, video clips, blank maps you can print or use online to test your students' knowledge of important geography, and a Resource Integration Guide.

Web site

www.cengage.com/politicalscience

Select *Introduction to International Relations: Comprehensive* and follow the 12e Update link. Adopting Kegley and Blanton's book gives you access to an unparalleled array of teaching resources. This outstanding site features chapter-by-chapter outlines and reviews, annotated web links and suggested readings for each chapter. For students it provides online tutorial quizzes, flash cards, crossword puzzles and other useful study aids.

WebTutor™ for WebCT™ and Blackboard

Leverage the power of the Internet and bring your course to life with this course management program. You or your students can use this wealth of interactive resources with those on the text's companion Web site to supplement the classroom experience and ensure students acquire the resources to succeed in today's business world. Instructors can even use this effective resource as an integrated solution for distance learning or a Web-enhanced course.

International Relations: An Introduction Using MicroCase ExplorIt

Authors James C. Roberts of Towson University and Alan Rosenblatt of Stateside Associates created this workbook to explore important concepts, theories, and phenomena in international relations using real data sets. Each chapter is organized around examples that focus on a set of concepts or theories. The workbook contains twelve computer-based assignments and includes software and nine data sets.

Wadsworth Atlas of International Relations

Fifty-one maps chosen by the authors of our texts reflect major topics covered in the course.

ACKNOWLEDGMENTS

Many people — in fact, too many to identify and thank individually — have contributed to the development of this leading textbook in international relations (including especially Eugene R. Wittkopf, who served as coauthor of the first six editions of *World Politics* and to whom the eleventh edition was dedicated following his tragically premature death). Those who made the greatest contributions to making this, the twelfth edition, better include the following, whose assistance is most appreciatively acknowledged.

In the first category are the constructive comments and suggestions offered by reviewers. In particular, gratitude is hereby expressed to the professional scholars who provided blind reviews, including:

Yan Bai, Grand Rapids Community College

George Belzer, Johnson County Community College

John H. Calhoun, Palm Beach Atlantic University

Gregory Domin, Mercer University

Giovanna Gismondi, University of Oklahoma

Kelly A. McCready, Maria College, Albany, New York

Robert Morin, Western Nevada Community College

Anthony Perry, Henry Ford Community College

Deborah Tompsett-Makin, Riverside Community College, Norco Campus

Denise Vaughan, Bellevue Community College

In a second category are scholars who provided advice and data. These include:

Larry Amick, Federal Judge in Indianapolis;

Ruchi Anand at the American Graduate School of International Relations and Diplomacy in Paris;

Osmo Apunen at the University of Tampere;

Chad Atkinson at the University of Illinois;

Andrew J. Bacevich at Boston University;

George Belzer at Webster University and Johnson County Community College;

John Boehrer at the University of Washington;

Robert Blanton at the University of Memphis;

Linda P. Brady at the University of Oregon;

Leann Brown at the University of Florida;

Dan Caldwell at Pepperdine University;

John Candido at La Trobe University;

Greg Carlson at Kimberly Clark in Atlanta;

Roger A. Coate at Georgia College & State University;

Jonathan E. Colby at the Carlyle Group in Washington, D.C.;

Phyllis D. Collins at Keswick Management Inc. in New York City;

George Crow at Northeast Presbyterian Church;

Jonathan Davidson at the European Commission;

Philippe Dennery of the J-Net Ecology Communication Company in Paris;

Thomas Donaldson at the Wharton School of the University of Pennsylvania;

Mary Douglas at Rogue Valley Publications in Ashland Oregon;

Ayman I. El-Dessouki and Kemel El-Menoufi of Cairo University;

Robert Fatton at the University of Virginia;

Matthias Finger at Columbia University;

Marilea Polk Fried of Kluwer Academic Publishers;

Eytan Gilboa at Bar-Ilan University in Israel;

Srajan Gligorijevic at the Defense and Security Studies Centre of the G-17 Plus Institute in Belgrade Serbia;

Richard F. Grimmett at the Congressional Research Office, Ted Robert Gurr at the University of Maryland;

Russell Hardin at New York University;

James Harf at the University of Tampa;

Jonah Heilman at the University of Pennsylvania;

Charles Hermann at Texas A&M University;

Margaret G. Hermann at Syracuse University;

Stephen D. Hibbard at Shearman & Sterling LLP;

Steven W. Hook at Kent State University;

Llewellyn D. Howell at the Thunderbird School of International Management;

Jack Hurd at the Nature Conservancy;

Dorothy V. James at the Newberry Library in Evanston, Illinois;

Patrick James at the University of Southern California;

Loch Johnson at the University of Georgia;

Christopher M. Jones at Northern Illinois University;

Christopher Joyner at Georgetown University;

Michael D. Kanner at the University of Colorado;

Mahmoud Karem of the Egyptian Foreign Service;

William R. Keylor at Boston University;

John Kinnas at the Greek Embassy in Geneva;

Lidija Kos-Stanišić at the University of Zagreb in Croatia;

Matthias Kranke at the University of Tier;

Imtiaz T. Ladak of Projects International in Washington D.C.;

John David Lenoir at New York District of the U.S. Attorney Office;

Jack Levy at Rutgers University;

Kristin M. Lipke at Syracuse University;

Urs Luterbacher of the Graduate Institute of International and Development Studies in Geneva;

Mamdouh Mansour at Alexandria University in Egypt;

Gen. Jeffrey D. McCausland at the U.S. Army War College in Carlisle, Pennsylvania;

Susan McChucheon at the U.S. Department of State;

Jeffrey Pickering at Kansas State University;

James McCormick at Iowa University;

Karen Ann Mingst at the University of Kentucky;

James A. Mitchell at California State University;

Desley Sant Parker at the United States Information Agency;

Rodger A. Payne at the University of Louisville;

Albert C. Pierce at the U.S. Naval Academy;

Alex Platt at the Carnegie Council for Ethics in International Affairs;

Ignacio de la Rasilla at the Université de Genèvee James Ray at Vanderbilt University;

Gregory A. Raymond at Boise State University;

Joseph Reap at the U.S. Department of State;

Leigh Richardson, President of the Richardson Group in Madison, Wisconsin;

Neil R. Richardson at the University of Wisconsin;

Peter Riddick at Berkhamsted Collegiate;

Charles D. Robinson at Northwestern Mutual Life in Milwaukee;

James N. Rosenau at George Washington University;

Joel Rosenthal at the Carnegie Council for Ethics in International Affairs;

Tapani Ruokanen at Suomen Kuvalehti, Finland;

Alpo Rusi at the Finnish Diplomatic Delegation to the United Nations;

Jan Aart Scholte at University of Warwick, U.K.;

Rebecca R. Sharitz at International Association for Ecology;

Shalendra D. Sharma at the University of San Francisco;

Richard H. Shultz at the Fletcher School of Law and Diplomacy, Tufts University;

Dragan R. Simić at the Centre for the Studies of the USA in Belgrade Serbia;

Harriet Stanley at Path;

Michael J. Siler at the University of California;

Walter Stager in Mürren, Switzerland;

Bengt Sundelius at the National Defense College in Stockholm;

Rieky Stuart at Sympatico;

Landon K. Thorne of the Midas Advisory Group Inc. in Beaufort South Carolina;

David Sylvan of the Graduate Institute of International and Development Studies in Geneva;

Rodney Tomlinson at the U.S. Naval Academy;

William R. Thompson of Indiana University;

Blair P. Turner at Virginia Military Institute;

Rob Verhofstad at Radmoud University in Nijmegen the Netherlands;

Jonathan Wilkenfeld at the University of Maryland;

Samuel A. Worthington at InterAction;

and Prince Nicholas Zu at Syracuse University.

Also helpful in a third category was the input provided by our graduate students, Young-Hoon Song at the University of South Carolina, and Jon Stanford and Maggie Sommer at The University of Memphis, who provided invaluable research assistance. Thanks are also given to the insights and advice of professorial colleagues in the Fulbright American Studies Institute, which Kegley co-directed with Don Puchala in 2003, 2004, and 2005.

The always helpful and accommodating project manager Patricia Shogren and GEX Publishing Services in Atkinson, New Hampshire; Photo Researcher Jaime Jankowski with Pre-Press PMG made valuable contributions to this book. In addition, also deserving of special gratitude are our highly skilled, dedicated, and helpful editors at Wadsworth: Executive Editor Carolyn Merrill and Development Editor Rebecca Green, who exercised extraordinary professionalism in guiding the process that brought this edition into print, assisted by the project management of Josh Allen of Wadsworth and Heather Hogan (who patiently and diligently complied the revised master set of references, the Glossary, and the conversion of the first draft revisions to digital files in preparation for copyediting) and Permissions Editors Dean Dauphinais and Bob Kauser. Gratitude is also expressed to the always instructive advice of Amy Whitaker, Wadsworth's skilled Political Science Marketing Manager.

Charles W. Kegley, Jr.
Shannon Lindsey Blanton

ABOUT THE AUTHORS

CHARLES W. KEGLEY is currently the Vice Chair of the Board of Trustees of the Carnegie Council for Ethics in International Affairs. The Distinguished Pearce Professor of International Relations, Emeritus at the University of South Carolina, Kegley is also a past President of the International Studies Association (1993–1994). A graduate of the American University (B.A.) and Syracuse University (Ph.D.) and a Pew Faculty Fellow at Harvard University, Kegley has held faculty appointments at Georgetown University, the University of Texas, Rutgers University, the People's University of China, and the Institut Universitaire de Hautes Études Internationales Et du Développement in Geneva, Switzerland. A founding partner of Kegley International, Inc., a publishing, research, and consulting foundation, Kegley is a recipient of the Distinguished Scholar Award in Foreign Policy of the International Studies Association, and he has widely published his primary research in the leading scholarly journals. Among his more than fifty books, Kegley has recently published *The New Global Terrorism* (2003); *Controversies in International Relations Theory* (1995); and, with Gregory A. Raymond, *The Multipolar Challenge* (2008), *After Iraq: The Imperiled American Imperium* (2007); *The Global Future* (2nd edition, 2007); *From War to Peace* (2002); *Exorcising the Ghost of Westphalia* (2002); *How Nations Make Peace* (1999); *A Multipolar Peace? Great-Power Politics in the Twenty-First Century* (1994); and *When Trust Breaks Down: Alliance Norms and World Politics* (1990). Kegley has also coauthored and edited with Eugene R. Wittkopf a number of leading texts, including *American Foreign*

Policy: Pattern and Process (seventh edition, 2007, with Christopher Jones); *The Global Agenda* (sixth edition, 2001); *The Future of American Foreign Policy* (1992); *The Nuclear Reader* (second edition, 1989); and *The Domestic Sources of American Foreign Policy* (1988).

Kegley has also published widely in leading scholarly journals, including *Armed Forces* and *Society, Asian Forum, Brown Journal of International Affairs, Comparative Political Studies, Conflict Management and Peace Science, Cooperation and Conflict, Ethics and International Affairs, Fletcher Forum of World Affairs, Futures Research Quarterly, Harvard International Review, International Interactions, International Organization, International Politics, International Studies Quarterly, Jerusalem Journal of International Relations, Journal of Conflict Resolution, Journal of Peace Research, Journal of Politics, Korean Journal of International Studies, Orbis,* and the *Western Political Quarterly.*

SHANNON LINDSEY BLANTON is Professor of Political Science at The University of Memphis, where she is also the Vice Provost for Undergraduate Programs. She oversees all undergraduate programs and provides leadership in curriculum planning, general education, the Center for International Programs and Services, the Honors Program and the Learning Communities. She is a past department chair and undergraduate coordinator, and has served nationally as a facilitator for leadership development in higher education. A graduate of Georgia College, the University of Georgia, and the University of South Carolina, she has received numerous research awards and was named in 2007 as the recipient of The University of Memphis' prestigious *Alumni Association Distinguished Research in the Social Sciences and Business Award.* She specializes in the areas of international relations and foreign policy, with an emphasis on human rights, democracy, international political economy and the arms trade. She has served on a number of editorial boards, including those for two of the discipline's foremost journals, *International Studies Quarterly* and *International Studies Perspectives.* Her work has been published extensively in leading scholarly journals, including the *American Journal of Political Science, Journal of Politics, International Studies Quarterly, Journal of Peace Research, International Interactions, Social Science Journal, Journal of Third World Studies, Journal of Political and Military Sociology, Business and Society, Conflict Quarterly* and *Leadership.*

Together Kegley and Blanton have coauthored publications appearing in *The Brown Journal of World Affairs, Futures Research Quarterly, Mediterranean Quarterly,* and *Rethinking the Cold War.*

WHAT FUTURE FOR HUMANKIND? Many global trends are sweeping across a transforming planet. One of many that are threatening is the heatwaves and droughts that have spread across the globe, such as that pictured here in Allahabud, India. Arresting global warming is a global challenge, among many others, that faces humanity.

Part 1

TREND AND TRANSFORMATION
IN WORLD POLITICS

"There is no scientific antidote [to the atomic bomb], only education. You've got to change the way people think. I am not interested in disarmament talks between nations. . . . What I want to do is to disarm the mind. After that, everything else will automatically follow. The ultimate weapon for such mental disarmament is international education."

—Albert Einstein, Nobel Peace Prize physicist

THESE ARE TURBULENT TIMES, INSPIRING BOTH ANXIETY AND HOPE. What lies ahead for the world? What are we to think about the global future? Part 1 of this book introduces you to the study of world politics in a period of rapid change. It opens a window on the many trends that are unfolding, some of them in contrary directions. The combined force of these trends may transform many aspects of international relations, even though they may persist.

There are obstacles that prevent us from understanding world politics accurately. Chapter 1 explains how our perceptions of global realities can lead to distortions, and suggests how to get beyond these barriers by providing five keys to understanding world politics as well as an outline of the book's thematic approach and organization. Chapter 2 introduces the major rival theories (realism, liberalism, and constructivism) that scholars have developed to help policy makers and citizens better describe, explain, and predict the evolving nature of international relations. It also illuminates two powerful critiques of these mainstream theories: radicalism and feminism. Such theories are important tools that can help you construct more accurate images of the complexity of world politics and better interpret emerging trends and transformations. Chapter 3 then moves from theory to practice, and explains how states and all other transnational actors go about the task of making foreign policy decisions. It also identifies the intellectual and political barriers that often reduce the ability of transnational actors to make rational choices about their interests, policy goals, and workable paths for promoting them.

CHAPTER 1
INTERPRETING WORLD POLITICS

The world is at a critical juncture, and so are you. . . . Go ahead and make your plans . . . and don't stop learning. But be open to the detours that lead to new discoveries.

—Kofi Annan, former UN Secretary General

As viewed from outer space, planet Earth looks as if it has oceans without pollution and continents without borders separating states and people. As viewed from newspaper headlines, "world politics" looks much different.

I magine yourself returning home from a two-week vacation on a tropical island where you had no access to the news. The trip gave you a well-deserved break before starting a new school term. But now you are curious about what has happened when you were away. As you glance at a newspaper, headlines catch your eye. They indicate that the insurgency in Iraq persists with no end to the bloodshed in sight. As you ride home from the airport, you hear a radio broadcast that describes the renewed strength and violence of Al Queda and the Taliban in Afghanistan and parts of Pakistan. Glancing at service station signs along the highway, you notice that gasoline prices have climbed sharply, which will make your daily commute to and from your university more expensive. Shortly after arriving at home, you connect to the Internet and find that the value of the euro continued to rise relative to that of the U.S. dollar, making you worry about the higher cost of the study tour you had planned to take in Europe next summer. Finally, when listening to CNN later that evening, you hear several other reports: the summer heat wave has taken global warming of Earth's temperature to record levels, bringing drought and wildfires to many areas and catastrophic floods to others. Moreover, U.S. mortgage delinquencies have shaken global credit markets and caused a massive fall in stock prices worldwide, and further volatility in global financial markets. In addition, CNN shows footage of the flight of refugees from Zimbabwe as they try to escape the violence and instability surrounding an illegitimate presidential election. CNN's report concludes with an announcement that the United States has removed North Korea from its terrorist blacklist and there are signs that North Korea is cooperating with the international community in dismantling its nuclear capabilities. Yet controversy continues about Iran's plans to development its nuclear program.

The scenario just described is not hypothetical. The events identified above record what actually occurred during the month of June 2008.

Undoubtedly, many individuals experienced fear and confusion during this turbulent period. But it is uncomfortably not so different from others. Putting this information about unfolding events together, you cannot help but be reminded that the world matters and that those changes in it affect your circumstances and future powerfully. The "news" you received is not really new, because it echoes many old stories from the past about the growing sea of turmoil sweeping contemporary world circumstances. Nevertheless, the temptation to wish that this depressing kind of chaotic world would just go away is overwhelming. If only the unstable world would stand still long enough for a sense of predictability and order to prevail. Alas, that does not appear likely. You cannot escape the world or control its turbulence, and you cannot single-handedly alter its character.

We are all a part of this world, and this world is an integral part of each of us. Hence, if we are to live adaptively amid the fierce winds of global change, we must face the challenge of discovering the dynamic properties of world politics.

Great things are achieved by guessing the direction of one's century.
—Giuseppe Mazzini, Italian political leader

Because every person is influenced increasingly by world events, all can benefit by investigating how the global system works and how changes are remaking our political and economic world. Only through learning how our own decisions and behavior contribute to the global condition, as well as those of powerful state governments and nonstate transnational actors, and how all people and groups in turn are heavily conditioned by changes in world politics, can we address what former U.S. President Bill Clinton defined as "the question of our time—whether we can make change our friend and not our enemy."

THE CHALLENGE OF INVESTIGATING WORLD AFFAIRS

The American poet Walt Whitman wrote in 1888, "I say we had best look at our times and lands searchingly, like some physician diagnosing some deep disease." His advice is as timely today as it was then. We must perceive our times accurately in order to best understand the political convulsions that confront the globe's 6.7 billion people.

Interpreting the world in which we now live and anticipating what lies ahead for the globe's future—and yours—presents formidable challenges. We are constantly bombarded with a bewildering amount of new information and new developments. Forging a meaningful understanding of the messages about world affairs we receive every day could be the *most* difficult task you will ever face. Why? Partly because the study of international relations requires taking account of every factor that influences human behavior. This is a task that, as the seminal scientist Albert Einstein believed, is extremely challenging. He once hinted at how big the challenge of explaining world politics was when he was asked, "Why is it that when the mind of man has stretched so far as to discover the structure of the atom we have been unable to devise the political means to keep the atom from destroying us?" He replied, "This is simple, my friend; it is because politics is more difficult than physics."

Another part of the challenge stems from the tendency of people to resist unfamiliar information and ideas that undermine their habitual ways of viewing and thinking about world affairs. We know from repeated studies that people do not want to accept ideas that do not conform with their prior beliefs.

A purpose of this book is to help you to cultivate a questioning attitude about your preexisting beliefs about world affairs and about the many actors on the world stage. To that end, we will ask you to evaluate rival perspectives on global issues, even if

> *It is the tragedy of the world that no one knows what he doesn't know—and the less a man knows, the more sure he is that he knows everything.*
>
> —Joyce Carey, English author

they differ with your current images. Indeed, we will expose you to schools of thought prevailing today that you may find unconvincing, and possibly repugnant. Why are they included? Because many other people make these views the bedrock of their interpretations, and these viewpoints accordingly enjoy a popular following.

(For this reason, this text will describe some visions of world politics with which even your authors may not agree, so that you may weigh the wisdom or foolishness of contending perspectives.) The interpretive challenge, then, is to try to observe unfolding global realities objectively, in order to describe and explain them accurately.

To appreciate how our images of reality shape our expectations, we begin with a brief introduction to the role that subjective images of reality play in understanding world politics. This will be followed by a set of analytic tools that this book will use to help you overcome perceptual obstacles to understanding world politics, and to empower you to more capably interpret the forces of change and continuity that affect our world.

HOW PERCEPTIONS INFLUENCE IMAGES OF INTERNATIONAL REALITY

We already hold mental images of world politics, although we may not have attempted to explicitly define our perceptions about the world in our subconscious. But whatever our levels of self-awareness, our images perform the same function: they simplify "reality" by exaggerating some features of the real world while ignoring others. Thus, we live in a world defined by our images.

These mental pictures, or perceptions, are inevitably distortions as they cannot fully capture the complexity and configurations of even physical objects, such as the globe itself (see Controversy: Should We Believe What We See?).

Many of our images of the world's political realities may be built on illusions and misconceptions. Even images that are now accurate can easily become outdated if we fail to recognize changes in the world. Indeed, the world's future will be determined not only by changes in the "objective" facts of world politics but also by the meaning that people ascribe to those facts, the assumptions on which they base their interpretations, and the actions that flow from these assumptions and interpretations —however accurate or inaccurate they might be.

The Nature and Sources of Images

The effort to simplify one's view of the world is inevitable and even necessary. Just as cartographers' projections simplify complex geophysical space so that we can better understand the world, each of us inevitably creates a "mental map"—a habitual way of organizing information—to make sense of a confusing abundance of information. Although mental maps are neither inherently right nor wrong, they are important because we tend to react according to the way the world appears to us rather than the way it is. How we *view* the world (not what it is really like) determines our attitudes, our beliefs, and our behavior. Political leaders, too, are captives of this tendency (Kirkpatrick 2007). As Richard Ned Lebow (1981) warns, "Policymakers are prone to distort reality in accord with their needs even in situations that appear . . . relatively unambiguous."

CONTROVERSY:

CONTROVERSY: SHOULD WE BELIEVE WHAT WE SEE?

Many people assume that "seeing is believing" without questioning whether the ways they have organized their perceptions are accurate. But is there more to seeing than meets the eye? To view and interpret reality, do we perceive in ways that may produce a biased distortion? Students of perceptual psychology think so. They maintain that seeing is not a strictly passive act: what we observe is partially influenced by our preexisting values and expectations (and by the visual habits reinforced by the constructions society has inculcated in us about how to view objects). Students of perception argue that "what you see is what you get" and that two observers looking at the same object might easily see different realities. To illustrate this, perceptual psychologists are fond of displaying the drawing below, which, depending on how the viewer looks at it, can be seen as either a goblet or two faces opposing each other. Both images are possible.

This principle has great importance for investigation of international relations, where, depending on one's perspective, people can vary greatly on how they will view international events, actors, and issues. Intense disagreements often arise from competing images.

To appreciate the controversies that can result when different people (with different perspectives) see different realities even though they are looking at the same thing, consider something as basic as objectively viewing the location and size of the world's continents. There exists a long-standing controversy among cartographers about the "right" way to map the globe, that is, how to make an accurate projection. The accuracy of their rival maps matters politically because they shape how people view what is important. All maps of the globe are distorted because it is impossible to perfectly represent the three-dimensional globe on a two-dimensional piece of paper. The difficulty cartographers face can be appreciated by trying to flatten an orange peel. You can only flatten it by separating pieces of the peel that were joined when it was spherical. Cartographers who try to flatten the globe on paper, without "ripping it" into separate pieces, face the same problem. Although there are a variety of ways to represent the three-dimensional object on paper, all of them involve some kind of distortion. Thus cartographers must choose among the imperfect ways of representing the

globe by selecting those aspects of the world's geography they consider most important to describe accurately, while making adjustments to other parts.

Cartographers' ideas of what is most important in world geography have varied according to their own global perspectives. These four maps (Maps 1.1, 1.2, 1.3, and 1.4) depict the distribution of the Earth's land surfaces and territory, but each portrays a different image. Each is a model of reality, an abstraction that highlights some features of the globe while ignoring others. In examining these four ways of viewing and interpreting the globe, evaluate which projection you think is best. Which features of global reality are most worthy of emphasizing to capture an accurate picture? What does your answer reveal about your values and view of the world?

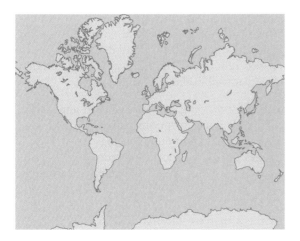

MAP 1.1

MERCATOR PROJECTION This Mercator projection, named for the Flemish cartographer Gerard Mercator, was popular in sixteenth-century Europe and presents a classic Eurocentric view of the world. It mapped the Earth without distorting direction, making it useful for navigators. However, distances were deceptive, placing Europe at the center of the world and exaggerating the continent's importance relative to other landmasses. Europe appears larger than South America, which is twice Europe's size, and two-thirds of the map is used to represent the northern half of the world and only one-third the southern half. Because lines of longitude were represented as parallel rather than convergent, this projection also greatly exaggerates the size of Greenland and Antarctica.

MAP 1.3

ORTHOGRAPHIC PROJECTION The orthographic projection, centering on the mid-Atlantic, conveys some sense of the curvature of the Earth by using rounded edges. The sizes and shapes of continents toward the outer edges of the circle are distorted to give a sense of spherical perspective.

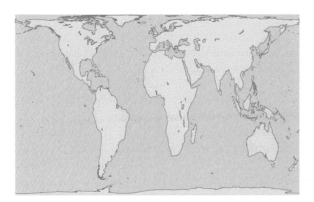

MAP 1.2

PETER'S PROJECTION In the Peter's projection, each landmass appears in correct proportion in relation to all others, but it distorts the shape and position of the Earth's landmasses. In contrast with most geographic representations, it draws attention to the less-developed countries of the Global South, where more than three-quarters of the world's population lives today.

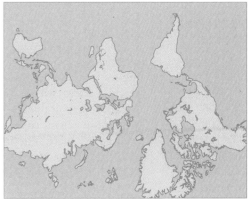

MAP 1.4

"UPSIDE DOWN" PROJECTION This projection gives a different perspective on the world by depicting it upside down, with the Global South positioned above the Global North. The map challenges the modern "Eurocentric" conceptual-ization of the positions of the globe's countries and peoples by putting the Global South "on top."

Most of us—policy makers included—look for information that reinforces our preexisting beliefs about the world, assimilate new data into familiar images, mistakenly equate what we believe with what we know, and deny information that contradicts our expectations. We also rely on our intuitions without thinking and emotionally make snap judgments (Gladwell 2005; Weston 2007).

In addition, we rely on learned habits for viewing new information and for making judgments, because these "schema" guide our perceptions and organize information for us. Research in cognitive psychology shows that human beings are "categorizers" who match what they see with images in their memories of prototypical events and people when attempting to understand the world by **schematic reasoning**. The absentminded professor, the shady lawyer, and the kindly grandmother are examples of "stock" images that many of us have of certain types of people. Although the professors, lawyers, and grandmothers that we meet may bear only a superficial resemblance to these stereotypical images, when we know little about someone our expectations will be shaped by presumed similarities to these characters.

■ **schematic reasoning**

the process of reasoning by which new information is interpreted according to a memory structure, a schema, which contains a network of generic scripts, metaphors, and simplified characterizations of observed objects and phenomena.

Many factors shape our images, including how we were socialized as children, traumatic events we may have experienced growing up that shape our personalities and psychological needs, exposure to the ideas of people whose expertise we respect, and the opinions about world affairs expressed by our frequent associates such as close friends and co-workers. Once we have acquired an image, it seems self-evident. Accordingly, we try to keep that image consistent with our other beliefs and, through a psychological process known as **cognitive dissonance** (Festingner 1957), reject information that contradicts how it portrays the world. In short, our minds select, screen, and filter information; consequently, our perceptions depend not only on what happens in daily life but also on how we interpret and internalize those events.

■ **cognitive dissonance**

the general psychological tendency to deny discrepancies between one's preexisting beliefs (cognitions) and new information.

The Impact of Perceptions on World Politics

We must be careful not to assume automatically that what applies to individuals applies to entire countries, and we should not equate the beliefs of leaders, such as heads of states, with the beliefs of the people under their authority. Still, leaders have extraordinary influence, and leaders' images of historical circumstances often predispose them to behave in particular ways toward others, regardless of "objective" facts. For instance, the loss of twenty-six million Soviet lives in the "Great Patriotic War" (as the Russians refer to World War II) reinforced a long-standing fear of foreign invasion, which caused a generation of Soviet policy makers to perceive U.S. defensive moves with suspicion and often alarm. Similarly, the founders of the United States viewed eighteenth-century European power politics and its repetitive wars as corrupt, contributing to two seemingly contradictory tendencies later evident in U.S. foreign policy: (1) America's impulse to isolate itself (its disposition to withdraw from world affairs), and (2) its determination to reform the world in its own image whenever global circumstances become highly threatening. The former led the country to reject membership in the League of Nations after World War I; the latter gave rise to the U.S. globalist foreign policy since World War II, which committed the country to active involvement nearly everywhere on nearly every issue. Most Americans, thinking of their country as virtuous, have difficulty understanding why others sometimes regard such far-reaching international activism as arrogant or threatening; instead, they see only

We are not afraid to entrust the American people with unpleasant facts, foreign ideas, alien philosophies, and competitive values. For a nation that is afraid to let its people judge the truth and falsehood in an open market is a nation that is afraid of its people.

—John F. Kennedy, U.S. President

good intentions in active U.S. interventionism. As former President Jimmy Carter once lamented, "The hardest thing for Americans to understand is that they are not better than other people."

Because leaders and citizens are prone to ignore or reinterpret information that runs counter to their beliefs and values, mutual misperceptions often fuel discord in world politics, especially when relations between countries are hostile. Distrust and suspicion arise as conflicting parties view each other in the same negative light—that is, as **mirror images** develop.

This occurred in Moscow and Washington during the Cold War. Each side saw its own actions as constructive but its adversary's responses as hostile, and both sides erroneously assumed that their counterparts would misinterpret the intentions of their own policy initiatives. When the psychologist Urie Bronfenbrenner (1961) traveled to Moscow, for example, he was amazed to hear Russians describing the United States in terms that were strikingly similar to the way Americans described the Soviet Union: Each side saw itself as virtuous and peace-loving, whereas the other was seen as untrustworthy, aggressive, and ruled by a corrupt government.

Mirror-imaging is a property of nearly all **enduring rivalries**—long-lasting contests between opposing groups. For example, in rivalries such as Christianity against Islam during the Crusades in the Middle Ages, Israel and Palestine since the birth of the sovereign state of Israel in 1948, and the United States and Al Qaeda today, both sides demonize the image of their adversary while perceiving themselves as virtuous. Self-righteousness often leads one party to view its own actions as constructive but its adversary's responses as negative and hostile. When this occurs, conflict resolution is extraordinarily difficult. Not only do the opposing sides have different preferences for certain outcomes over others, but they do not see the underlying issues in the same light. Further complicating matters, the mirror images held by rivals tend to be self-confirming. When one side expects the other to be hostile, it may treat its opponent in a manner that leads the opponent to take counteractions that confirm the original expectation, therein creating a vicious circle of deepening hostilities that reduce the prospects for peace (Deutsch 1986; Sen 2006). Clearing up mutual misperceptions can facilitate negotiations between the parties, but fostering peace is not simply a matter of expanding trade and other forms of transnational contact, or even of bringing political leaders together in international summits. Rather, it is a matter of changing deeply entrenched beliefs.

Although our constructed images of world politics are resistant to change, change is possible. Overcoming old thinking habits sometimes occurs when we experience punishment or discomfort as a result of clinging to false assumptions. As Benjamin Franklin once observed, "The things that hurt, instruct." Dramatic events in

■ **mirror images**
the tendency of states and people in competitive interaction to perceive each other similarly—to see others the same hostile way others see them.

■ **enduring rivalries**
prolonged competition fueled by deep-seated mutual hatred that leads opposed actors to feud and fight over a long period of time without resolution of their conflict.

particular can alter international images, sometimes drastically. The Vietnam War caused many Americans to reject their previous images about using military force in world politics. The defeat of the Third Reich and revelations of Nazi atrocities committed before and during World War II caused the German people to confront their past as they prepared for a democratic future imposed by the victorious allies. The use of atomic bombs against Japan in the waning days of World War II caused many to confront the horrors of modern warfare and the immorality of weapons of mass destruction. More recently, the rising human and financial costs of the prolonged U.S. war in Iraq have led many policy makers and political commentators to reexamine their assumptions about foreign policy priorities. Often, such jolting experiences encourage us to construct new mental maps, perceptual filters, and criteria through which we may interpret later events and define situations.

As we shape and reshape our images of world politics and its future, we need to think critically about the foundations on which our perceptions rest. Are they accurate? Are they informed? Should they be modified to gain greater understanding of others? Rethinking our images is one of the major challenges we face to avoid prejudice—prejudging what we see in world affairs based on misguided opinions, like a person with his or her nose pressed against the mirror trying to see his or her own body. Questioning our images is one of the major challenges we all face in confronting contemporary world politics.

KEYS TO UNDERSTANDING WORLD POLITICS

If we exaggerate the accuracy of our perceptions and seek information that confirms what we believe, how can we escape the biases created by our preconceptions? How can we avoid overlooking or dismissing evidence that runs counter to our intuition?

There are no sure-fire solutions to accurate observations, no ways to guarantee that we have constructed an impartial view of international relations. However, there are a number of tools available that can improve our ability to interpret world politics. As you undertake an intellectual journey of discovery, a set of intellectual roadmaps will provide guidance for your interpretation and understanding of past, present, and future world politics. To arm you for your quest, *World Politics: Trend and Transformation* advances five keys to aid you in your inquiry.

Terminology

A primary goal of this text is to introduce you to the vocabulary used by scholars, policy makers, and the "attentive public" who routinely look at international developments. You will need to be literate and informed about the shared meaning of common words used worldwide to discuss and debate world politics and foreign policy. Some of this language has been in use since antiquity, and some of it has only recently become part of the terminology employed in diplomatic circles, scholarly research and the media—television, newspapers, and the Internet. These words are the kind of vocabulary you are likely to encounter long after your formal collegiate education (and the course in which you are reading *World Politics*) has ended. It is also the terminology your future employers and educated neighbors will expect you to know. Some of these words are already likely to be part of your working vocabulary, but others may look new, esoteric, pedantic, and overly sophisticated. Nonetheless, you need to know their meaning—immediately and forever. Your use of them will facilitate your ability to analyze and discuss world affairs and mark you hereafter as a knowledgeable, educated person. So take advantage of this "high definition" feature of *World Politics*. Learn these words and use them the rest of your life—not to impress others, but to understand and communicate intelligently.

To guide you in identifying these terms, as you may already have noticed, certain words are printed in **boldface** in the text and a broad definition is provided in the margins. Many repeated terms have a more specific meaning in other contexts, and in cases when a word is used again in a different context, it will be highlighted in *italics* and the more specialized definition will be provided within the text, although the marginal definition will *not* be repeated. In all cases, the primary definition will appear in the Glossary at the end of book, now provided for the first time in this edition.

> *The ability to learn how to learn will be the only security you have.*
> — Thomas L. Friedman, political journalist

Who Are the Primary Transnational Actors?

The globe is a stage, and the players in the drama are many. It is important to identify and classify the major categories of actors (sometimes called *agents*) who take part in international activities. The actions of each transnational **actor**, individually and collectively at various degrees of influence, shape the trends that are transforming world politics. But how do scholars conventionally break the types of actors into categories and structure thinking about the classes of players?

■ **actor**
an individual, group, state, or organization that plays a major role in world politics.

World Politics follows accepted legal conventions about distinctions. The essential building-block units, of course, are individual people—all 6.7 billion of us. Every day, whether each of us choose to litter, light a cigarette, or parent a child, affects in small measure how trends in the world will unfold. Humans, however, join in various groups. All these combine people and their choices in various collectivities and thereby aggregate the power of each expanding group (such as the size of a national army or terrorist movement). Such groups often compete with one another because frequently they have divergent interests and goals.

> *The history of the world is the verdict of the world.*
> —German author Friedrich Von Schiller

For most periods of world history, the prime actors were individual groupings of religions, tribes whose members shared ethnic origins, and empires or expansionist centers of power. When they came into contact, they sometimes collaborated with each other for mutual benefit; more often they competed and fought over valued resources.

The Emergence of the Nation-State System The more than eight thousand years of recorded international relations between and among these groups provided the precedent for the formation of today's system of interactions. As a network of relationships among independent territorial units, the modern state system was not born until the Peace of Westphalia in 1648, which ended the Thirty Years' War in Europe. Thereafter, rulers refused to recognize the secular authority of the Roman Catholic Church, replacing the system of papal governance in the Middle Ages with geographically and politically separate states that recognized no superior authority. The newly independent states all gave to rulers the same legal rights: territory under their sole control, unrestricted control of their domestic affairs, and the freedom to conduct foreign relations and negotiate treaties with other states. The concept of **state sovereignty**—that no other actor is above the state—still captures these legal rights and identifies the state as the primary actor today.

The Westphalian system continues to color every dimension of world politics and provides the terminology used to describe the primary units in international affairs. Although the term *nation-state* is often used interchangeably with "state" and "nation," technically the three are different. A **state** is a legal entity that enjoys a permanent population, a well-defined territory, and a government capable of exercising sovereignty. A **nation** is a collection of people who, on the basis of ethnic, linguistic, or cultural commonality, so construct their reality as to primarily perceive themselves to be members of the same group, which defines their identity. Thus, the term *nation-state* implies a convergence between territorial states and the psychological identification of people within them. However, in employing this familiar terminology, we should exercise caution because this condition is relatively rare; there are few independent states comprising a single nationality. Most states today are populated by many nations, and some nations are not states. These "nonstate nations" are ethnic groups—such as Native Americans in the United States, Sikhs in India, or Basques in Spain—composed of people without sovereign power over the territory in which they live.

The Rise of Nonstate Actors The history of world politics ever since 1648 has largely been a chronicle of interactions among *states* that remain the dominant political organizations in the world. States' interests, capabilities, and goals are the most potent shaping forces of world politics.

However, the supremacy of the state has been severely challenged in recent years. Increasingly, world affairs are also influenced by the new, big players on international affairs: "intergovernmental organizations" (IGOs) that transcend national boundaries, such as global international organizations whose members are states like the United Nations (UN) and regional organizations such as the European Union (EU). Such international organizations carry out independent foreign policies and therefore can be considered global actors in their own right. In addition, as noted, individual people band together to form coalitions of private citizens in order to participate in international affairs. Multinational corporations are an example of "nongovernmental organizations" (NGOs). Diverse in scope and purpose, these *nonstate actors* also push their own agendas and increasingly exert global influence.

In thinking about world politics and its future, we shall probe *all* these "units" or categories of actors. The emphasis and coverage will vary, depending on the topics under examination in each chapter. But you should keep in mind that *all* actors

state sovereignty
a state's supreme authority to manage internal affairs and foreign relations.

state
an independent legal entity with a government exercising exclusive control over the territory and population it governs.

nation
a collectivity whose people see themselves as members of the same group because they share the same ethnicity, culture, or language.

(individuals, states, and nonstate organizations) are simultaneously active today, and their importance and power depends on the trend or issue under consideration. So, ask yourself, continuously, now and in the future, the question: Which actors are most active, most influential, on which issues and under what conditions? That probing should cast doubt on outdated images of international relations.

Distinguishing Foreign Policy, International Relations, and International Politics

All types of transnational actors (individual people, groups, states, and nonstate international organizations) play roles in world politics. Their power, level of activity, and size vary, of course. But *all* take positions on international issues, which are reflections of their value preferences. Hence, all transnational actors operate from a *foreign policy*. When we speak about **foreign policy**, therefore, we refer to the goals that a transnational actor seeks abroad, the values that underlie those goals, and the means used to pursue them.

■ **foreign policy**
the decisions governing authorities make to realize international goals.

When actors take actions, they make pronouncements to communicate to others what their objectives are and the means that will be used to achieve those goals. As Valerie Hudson (2007, 6) elaborates from the perspective of foreign policy analysis, "the source of all international politics and all change in international politics is specific human beings using their agency and acting individually or in groups."

Inspect Figure 1.1. It illuminates how foreign policies relate to the larger realm of relations between and among actors. In the first (1) case, a transnational actor articulates a general statement about its goals with respect to all other actors including, for example, a state's own citizens or a multinational corporation's

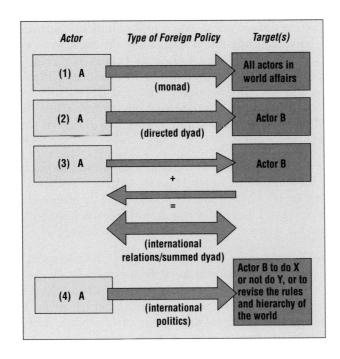

FIGURE 1.1

PICTURING TYPES OF FOREIGN POLICY AND ACTOR RELATIONSHIPS **To study world politics, four major components should be differentiated to break the subject into parts: foreign policy (1), actor policies toward other actors (2), international relations (3), and international politics (4).**

■ monad

a conception of foreign policy that the political actor's foreign policy is undifferentiated to the target, and that it acts under a presupposed generalized characteristic.

■ directed dyadic

a perception of foreign policy in which the actor's foreign policy refers to specific goals with respect to another actor or target in particular.

■ international relations

relationships that exist between pairs or among groups of global actors.

■ summed dyads

the dyadic relationships between various actors that is based upon their foreign policies and toward each other and the acts that are a result of those relationships.

■ politics

to Harold Lasswell, the study of "who gets what, when, how, and why."

employees and investors. This is sometimes called a **monad** because this conception of foreign policy implies that an actor's foreign policy is, to a very large degree, undifferentiated as to the target. The underlying assumption is that the actor is presupposed to act on a general principle in some characteristic way (for example, country A is "imperialistic," aiming to expand its power, or country B is a "status quo" power, aiming to preserve, not overturn, existing international circumstances).

Monadic foreign policy pronouncements communicate signals to all other actors external to itself as well as to internal actors, such as when leaders seek to influence public opinion within a country's domestic environment. Such foreign policy declarations announce what the actor intends to concentrate on globally (for instance, economic prosperity and development, or the promotion of democracy and human rights).

In the second (2) case, the actor's foreign policy refers to its specific goals with respect to another particular actor or target. Such a **directed dyadic** conception addresses the relational attributes of inter-actor exchanges. It captures the policy of one actor as it is directed toward another actor; the policy is target-specific rather than generalized. Here, for example, Canada's policies toward the United States and not the world at large is the object of observation. In this case, we may think of foreign policy by focusing our attention on an actor's particular target (or issue).

A third (3) way of organizing perceptions is to inspect *relations* between two (or more) actors. The nature of the exchange becomes the object of observation. So here we study **international relations** or the kind of relationships that exist between pairs of actors. For instance, how would you characterize the relationship between China and the United States, between the European Union and Russia, or between the United Nations and Iran? Are these exchanges cooperative or conflictual? Are diplomatic relations between the parties to the relationship improving or deteriorating?

When we look at these so-called **summed dyads**, we estimate how the parties to the relationship are acting toward one another. In the study of international relations, the object of analysis frequently draws attention to the question of whether, and to what extent, actor A is cooperating with actor B, and vice versa: will behavior (words and deeds) directed to a foreign target be reciprocated? Will the behavior sent be responded to, and will such actions be returned in kind? This is the stuff of international relations, which is a product of the various actors' foreign policies toward each other. The dyadic relationship is thus a sum of the acts sent and received between the interacting parties.

Relational properties of transnational exchanges are central to the study of world politics because they require us to adopt an interactive perspective. This includes observing both an actor's policies toward a target and the response of that target. When A➡B is investigated in terms of B➡A, we leave the domain of foreign policy analysis and enter the realm of international relations analysis.

Where, then, does **politics** enter the scope of inquiry? Following analytic practice, *World Politics: Trend and Transformation* defines **politics** by the principal purpose behind an actor's transnational policies and activities. Accordingly, still another way of viewing the world (4) is to look at **international politics**. At the broadest level, international political activities entail the exercise of influence to achieve and defend an actor's goals, such as when one country takes action to get another actor to do something it would not otherwise do or to prevent it from doing something against the target's preferences. International politics is aimed at controlling outcomes to one's own advantage, to shape the way of things of value (such as power, prestige, or wealth) are divided. World politics, it follows, is what we will be investigating on our journey when we look at the political activities of transnational actions individually and collectively which are aimed at shaping the course of world history.

It will be helpful as you read this book to keep these distinctions in mind. As different chapters introduce different dimensions of world politics, your understanding will improve if you ask yourself what type of interaction—foreign policy, international relations, or international politics—does this material illustrate?

Distinguishing Levels of Analysis

When we *describe* international phenomena, we answer a "what" question. What is happening? What is changing? When we move from description to *explanation*, we face the more difficult task of answering a "why" question. Why did event X happen? Why is global warming occurring? Why is the gap between rich and poor widening?

One key useful for addressing such puzzles is to visualize an event or trend as part of the end result of some unknown process. This encourages us to think about the causes that might have produced the phenomenon we are trying to explain. Most events and developments in world politics and its future are undoubtedly influenced simultaneously by many determinants, each connected to the rest in a complex web of causal linkages.

To make interpretive sense of the multiple causes that explain why international events and circumstances occur, *World Politics* provides an analytic set of categories that suggest where to look for information about a puzzle by organizing it in terms of an inventory of possible explanatory causes. This analytic distinction conforms to a widespread scholarly consensus that international events or developments can best be understood by first separating the multiple pieces of the puzzle into different categories, or levels, for analytic purposes. Most conventionally, investigators focus on one (or more) of *three* levels. Known as **levels of analysis**, as shown in Figure 1.2, this classification distinguishes: (1) individuals, (2) states as global actors, and (3) the entire global system.

To predict which forces will dominate the future, we also must recognize that many forces are operating at the same time. No trend or trouble stands alone; all interact simultaneously. The future is influenced by many determinants, each connected to the rest in a complex web of linkages. Collectively, these may produce stability by limiting the impact of any single disruptive force. If interacting forces converge, however, their combined effects can accelerate the pace of change in world politics, moving it in directions not possible otherwise.

The **individual level of analysis** refers to the personal characteristics of humans, including those responsible for making important decisions on behalf of state and nonstate actors, as well as ordinary citizens whose behavior has important political consequences. Here, for example, we may properly locate the impact of individuals'

■ international politics
The study of how global actors' activities entail the exercise of influence to achieve and defend their goals and ideals, and how it affects the world at large.

■ levels of analysis
the different aspects of and agents in international affairs that may be stressed in interpreting and explaining global phenomena, depending on whether the analyst chooses to focus on "wholes" (the complete global system and large collectivities) or on "parts" (individual states or people).

■ individual level of analysis
an analytical approach that emphasizes the psychological and perceptual variables motivating people, such as those who make foreign policy decisions on behalf of states and other global actors.

■ **state level of analysis**

an analytical approach that emphasizes how the internal attributes of states influence their foreign policy behaviors.

perceptions on their political attitudes, beliefs, and behavior. We may also explore the question of why each person is a crucial part of the global drama and why the study of world politics is relevant to our lives and future.

The **state level of analysis** consists of the authoritative decision-making units that govern states' foreign policy processes and the internal attributes of those states (e.g., their type of government, level of economic and military power, and number of nationality groups), which both shape and constrain leaders' foreign policy choices. The processes by which states make decisions regarding war and peace and their capabilities for carrying out those decisions, for instance, fall within the state level of analysis.

■ **global level of analysis**

an analytical approach that emphasizes the impact of worldwide conditions on foreign policy behavior and human welfare.

The **global level of analysis** refers to the interactions of states and nonstate actors on the global stage whose behaviors ultimately shape the international political system and the levels of conflict and cooperation that characterize world politics. The capacity of rich states to dictate the choices of poor states falls properly within the global level of analysis. So does the capacity (or incapacity) of the UN to maintain peace.

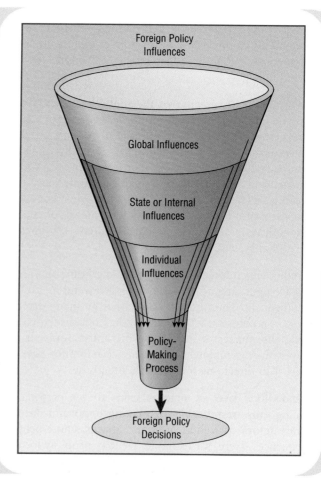

FIGURE 1.2

THE MAJOR FACTORS AFFECTING FOREIGN POLICY DECISIONS AND INTERNATIONAL RELATIONS: INFLUENCES AT THREE LEVELS

The factors that shape states' foreign policies and the decisions of all other global actors can be categorized at three basic levels. At the global level are those structural features of the international system such as the prevalence of civil wars and the extent of trade interdependence. At the state level are internal or domestic influences such as the state's type of government or the opinions of its citizens. At the individual level are the characteristics of leaders— their personal beliefs, values, and personality. All three levels simultaneously affect decisions, but their relative weight usually depends on the issues and circumstances at the time of decision.

Examples abound of the diverse ways in which global trends and issues are the product of influences at each level of analysis. Protectionist trade policies by an importing country increase the costs to consumers of clothing and cars and reduce the standard of living of citizens in the manufacturing states. Such policies are initiated by a state government (national level) but diminish the quality of life of people living both within the protectionist country and those living abroad (individual level) and reduce the level of global trade while threatening to precipitate retaliatory trade wars (global level). Of course, for some developments and issues, factors and forces emanating primarily from one or two particular levels provide more analytical leverage than do those from the other level(s). Accordingly, as we confront specific global issues in subsequent chapters, we emphasize those levels of analysis that provide the most informative lens for viewing them.

Distinguishing Change, Cycles, and Continuities

Once we have identified factors from different levels of analysis that may combine to produce some outcome, it is useful to place them in a chronological sequence. Anyone who owns a combination lock knows that the correct numbers must be entered in their proper order to open the lock. Similarly, to explain why something happened in world politics, we must determine how various individual-, state-, and global system–level factors fit together in a configuration that unfolds over time.

One key to anticipating probable human destiny is to look beyond the confines of our immediate time. It is important to appreciate the impact of previous ideas and events on current realities. As the philosopher George Santayana cautioned, "Those who cannot remember the past are condemned to repeat it." Similarly, former British Prime Minister Winston Churchill advised, "The farther backward you look, the farther forward you are likely to see." Thus, to understand the dramatic changes in world politics today and to predict how they will shape the future, it is important to

> *Not to know what happened before one was born is always to be a child.*
>
> —Cicero, historian and political leader at the height of the Roman Empire

view them in the context of a long-term perspective that examines how transnational patterns of interaction among actors have changed and how some of their fundamental characteristics have resisted change. What do evolving diplomatic practices suggest about the current state of world politics? Are the episodic shock waves throughout the world clearing the way for a truly new twenty-first-century world order? Or will many of today's dramatic disruptions ultimately prove temporary, mere spikes on the seismograph of history?

We invite you to explore these questions with us. To begin our search, we explore how the differences between continuities, changes, and cycles in world history can help you orient your interpretation.

Every historical period is marked to some extent by change. Now, however, the pace of change seems more rapid and its consequences more profound than ever. To many observers, the cascade of events today implies a revolutionary restructuring of world politics. Numerous *integrative* trends point to that possibility. The countries of the world are drawing closer together in communications and trade, producing a globalized market. Yet at the same time, *disintegrative* trends paint a less promising picture. Weapons proliferation, global environmental deterioration, and the resurgence of ethnic conflict all portend a restructuring fraught with disorder.

To predict which forces will dominate the future, we must recognize that no trend stands alone, and that divergent trends may produce stability by limiting the impact of any single disruptive force. It is also possible for converging trends to accelerate the pace of change, moving world politics in directions not possible otherwise.

It appears that the world is now going through a transition period in world politics. The opposing forces of integration and disintegration point toward the probable advent on the horizon of a **transformation,** but distinguishing true historical

■ **transformation**

a change in the characteristic pattern of interaction among the most active participants in world politics of such magnitude that it appears that one "global system" has replaced another.

> *Today many things indicate that we are going through a transitional period, when it seems that something is on the way out and something else is painfully being born. It is as if something were crumbling, decaying, and exhausting itself, while something else, still indistinct, were arising from the rubble.*
>
> —Vaclav Havel, dramatist and former President of the Czech Republic

watersheds from temporary change is difficult. The moment of transformation from one system to another is not immediately obvious. Nevertheless, another useful key for students of world history is to recognize that certain times are especially likely candidates. In the past, major turning points in world politics usually have occurred at the conclusion of wars with many participants, which typically disrupt or destroy preexisting international arrangements. In the twentieth century, World Wars I and II and the Cold War caused fundamental breaks with the past and set in motion major transformations, providing countries with incentives to rethink the premises underlying their interests, purposes, and priorities. Similarly, many people concluded that the terrorist attacks on September 11, 2001 (9/11) produced a fundamental transformation in world affairs. Indeed, 9/11 seemed to change everything: In former U.S. President George W. Bush's words, "Night fell on a different world."

To analyze change in world politics, it is equally important to look also for the possibility of *continuity* amidst apparent transformation. Consider how, despite all that may appear radically different since the 9/11 terrorist attacks, much also may remain the same. As William Dobson (2006) wrote on the eve of the fifth anniversary of 9/11, "what is remarkable is how little the world has changed." "The massive forces of international trade and globalization were largely unaffected by the attacks," notes the historian Juan Cole (2006) in a similair vein. "China's emergence

Carmen Taylor/AP Photo

WAS 9/11 A GLOBAL TRANSFORMING EVENT? **The terrorist attack on the World Trade Center's Twin Towers on 9/11 is widely regarded as a revolutionary date in world history, producing a sea change in world politics. Time will tell whether this event will rank alongside the birth of the nuclear age on August 6, 1945, when the United States bombed Hiroshima, or the November 1989 dismantling of the Berlin Wall, which signaled the end of the Cold War, as events that truly changed the world.**

No idea is so antiquated that it was not once modern. No idea is so modern that it will not someday be antiquated.

—Ellen Glasgow, American author

as an economic giant continues with all its economic, diplomatic, and military implications." Decades-old flash points remain, including the conflicts between India and Pakistan, North Korea and the United States, and Israel and militants in southern Lebanon and the Palestinian territories. "For all their visibility and drama," concludes Cole, "the 9/11 attacks left untouched many of the underlying forces and persistent tensions that shape international politics."

We often expect the future to bring changes automatically, and later are surprised to discover that certain patterns from the past have reappeared. Headlines are not trendlines. Given the rapid changes that are occurring alongside enduring continuities, it is dangerous to assume that a major transformation in world politics is underway.

What criteria can help determine when an existing pattern of relationships gives way to a completely new global system?   Follow Stanley Hoffmann (1961), who argues that we can identify a new global system when we have a new answer to one of three questions: (1) *What are the system's basic units?* (e.g., states or supranational institutions for global governance); (2) *What are the predominant foreign policy goals that these units seek with respect to one another?* (e.g., territorial conquest or material gain through trade); and (3) *What can these units do to one another with their military and economic capabilities?*

These criteria might lead us to conclude that a new system has now emerged. First, new trade partnerships have been forged in Europe, the cone of South America, North America, and the Pacific Rim, and these trading blocs may behave as unitary, or independent, nonstate actors as they compete with one another. Moreover, international organizations such as the European Union (EU) now flex their political muscles in contests with individual states, and transnational religious movements such as Islamic extremist groups challenge the **global system** itself. International law still defines this system as being composed primarily of each *state* consisting of various nationality groups who perceive themselves as unified by a common language, culture, or ethnic identity. At the same time, some states have disintegrated into smaller units.

Second, territorial conquest is no longer states' predominant foreign policy goal. Instead, their emphasis has shifted from traditionally military methods of exercising influence to economic means. Meanwhile, the ideological contest between democratic capitalism and the Marxist-Leninist communism of the Cold War era no longer comprises the primary cleavage in international politics, and a major new axis has yet to become clear.

Third, the proliferation of weapons technology has profoundly altered the damages that enemies can inflict on one another. Great powers alone no longer control the world's most lethal weapons. Increasingly, however, the great powers' prosperity depends on economic circumstances throughout the globe, reducing their ability to engineer growth.

The profound changes in recent years of the types of actors (units), goals, and capabilities have dramatically altered the hierarchical power ranking of states, but the hierarchies themselves endure. The *economic hierarchy* that divides the rich from the poor, the *political hierarchy* that separates the rulers from the ruled, the *resource hierarchy* that makes some suppliers and others dependents, and the *military asymmetries* that pit the strong against the weak—all still shape the relations among states, as they have in the past. Similarly, the perpetuation of international **anarchy**, in the absence of institutions to govern the globe, and continuing national insecurity still encourages preparations for war and the use of force without international mandate. Thus, change and continuity coexist, with both forces simultaneously shaping contemporary world politics.

■ global system
the predominant patterns of behaviors and beliefs that prevail internationally to define the major worldwide conditions that heavily influence human and national activities.

■ anarchy
a condition in which the units in the global system are subjected to few if any overarching institutions to regulate their conduct.

The interaction of constancy and change will determine future relations among global actors. This perhaps explains why **cycles** so often appear to characterize world politics: periodic sequences of events occur that resemble patterns in earlier periods. Because the emergent global system shares many characteristics with earlier periods, historically minded observers may experience déjà vu—the illusion of having already experienced something actually being experienced for the first time.

■ **cycles**
the periodic reemergence of conditions similar to those that existed previously.

PREPARING FOR YOUR JOURNEY INTO WORLD POLITICS

World Politics warns about the obstacles to accurate perceptions of international relations and then provides some guideposts to help you travel on your journey to discovery. This introduction concludes with a brief outline of the book's thematic approach and organizational roadmap.

The Book's Approach

Because world politics is complex and our images of it are often dissimilar, scholars differ in their approaches to understanding world politics. Some take a *macro political* perspective that looks on the global system with a bird's-eye view as a totality and explains the behavior of the actors within it by emphasizing how they are positioned. Other scholars adopt a *micro* political perspective that looks from the ground on the characteristics of individual actors and extrapolates from their behavior to describe the global system as an aggregate whole. Both approaches make important contributions to understanding world politics: the former reveals how the global environment sets limits on political choice; the latter draws attention to how every transnational actors' preferences, capabilities, and strategic calculations influence global conditions. By looking at world politics from a macropolitical perspective, we can see why actors that are similarly situated within the system may behave alike, despite their internal differences. By taking a micropolitical perspective, we can appreciate why some actors are very different or behave differently, despite their similar placement within the global system (see Waltz 2000).

From this analytic point of departure, *World Politics* will accordingly inspect (1) the major macro *trends* in world politics that set the boundaries for action, (2) the values, interests, and capabilities of the individual *actors* affected by these global trends, and (3) the ways these actors interact in their individual and collective efforts to modify existing global circumstances and how these interactions shape the ultimate trajectories of global trends.

This analytic approach looks at the dynamic interplay of actors and their environment as well as how the actors respond and seek to influence each others' behavior.

The approach outlined here can open a window for you not only to understand contemporary world politics but also to predict the likely global future. The approach has the advantage of taking into account the interplay of proximate and remote explanatory factors at the individual, state, and global levels of analysis while avoiding dwelling on particular countries, individuals, or transitory events whose long-term significance is likely to decrease. Instead, *World Politics* attempts to identify behaviors that cohere into general patterns that measurably affect global living conditions. Thus, you will explore the nature of world politics from a perspective that places historical and contemporary events into a larger, lasting theoretical context, to provide you with the conceptual tools that will enable you to interpret subsequent developments later in your lifetime.

The Book's Organization

Part 1 of this book introduces the world of politics as it changes rapidly and sets the stage for the constantly changing aspects of international relations. Chapter 1 explains how our perceptions of global events and realities lead to distorted views, and suggests how to move beyond the limited scope of those views by providing five keys to understanding world politics. The chapter also provides an outline of the book's organization and thematic approach. Your journey continues in Chapter 2 with an overview of the realist, liberal, and constructivist theoretical traditions that scholars and policy makers use most often to interpret world politics. It also considers the radical and feminist critiques of these mainstream traditions. The comparison of these contending theories provides the intellectual roadmap for the description and explanation of the issues and developments treated in the remaining chapters. Your understanding of world politics is further strengthened in Chapter 3, which introduces three ways of looking at international decision-making processes by all transnational actors. It concludes by focusing on the global and domestic determinants of states' international behavior, because states remain the principal actors in world politics.

■ **great powers**

the most powerful countries, militarily and economically, in the global system.

Part 2 turns attention to each of the various types of transnational actors and examines how their characteristics and capabilities affect their interests and influence in the world. Chapter 4 covers the **great powers** (those wealthy countries with the biggest militaries) and their current national security strategies and relationships. Chapter 5 incorporates into the picture the place of the weaker states, that is, the less-developed countries of the Global South, and explains how the fate of this group of states is shaped by their relations with great powers, the rising "Global East" emerging economic powerhouses, as well as the most powerful nonstate actors and international institutions active in world politics. Chapter 6 expands the account to cover intergovernmental organizations (IGOs) such as the United Nations and the European Union. Chapter 7 then captures the impact on world politics of such transnational nongovernmental organizations (NGOs) as the indigenous ethnic groups of the Fourth World, clashing civilizations, transnational religious movements and terrorist groups, and multinational corporations. This coverage describes how IGO and NGO actors interact with states and increasingly challenge the supremacy of all states, including even the great powers, by either transcending or subverting states' sovereign control over their destinies. In Chapter 8, the role of individuals, their relative levels of human security, the status of women, and the global refugee crisis are considered. The chapter thus puts people, and the individual level of analysis, into the equation of actors engaging in international activity, and examines efforts to protect peoples' human rights.

The next group of chapters in Part 3 properly falls within the global level of analysis. Here attention shifts to the economic and demographic dimensions of globalization. Chapter 9 explores the globalization of finance through the lens of theories of international political economy. Chapter 10 follows with a discussion of "International Trade in the Global Marketplace." Chapter 11 completes the coverage by looking at "The Demographic and Cultural Dimensions of Globalization," inspecting population change, migration patterns, the global health crisis, and the global information age as agents of global transformation.

Part 4, "Threats to the World," compares two types of very different but interconnected dangers at the top of the global agenda of international issues. Chapter 12 probes the multiple "Threats to the Preservation of the World's Common Ecology." Chapter 13 looks at changes in violence involving wars between states, civil wars within states, and global terrorism, and considers causes of these three forms of armed aggression at three levels of analysis: human nature, the internal characteristics of countries, and changes in global circumstances.

Part 5, "Realist Roads to National and International Security," unpacks the major realist approaches to war and peace. Chapter 14, "The Military Pursuit of Power through Arms and Military Strategy," reviews realist theoretical accounts of power in world politics, trends in military spending and capabilities, military strategies, and coercive diplomacy through military intervention abroad. The picture is completed in Chapter 15, which explores "Alliances and the Balance of Power" in the realist accounts.

Part 6 compares this set of realist policy postures to international threats with those emphasized by "Liberal Paths to World Order." Chapter 16 puts into the overview, as liberal responses to international crises, both the negotiated settlement of disputes through diplomacy and the legal control of armed aggression. Chapter 17 focuses on arms control and disarmament, the maintenance of collective security through international organizations, and the creation of a shared international moral consensus through the expansion of free trade and democratic institutions.

In Part 7, the major changes and issues surveyed throughout the book are revisited. Drawing on the ideas and information presented in earlier chapters, Chapter 18 places into consideration contending perspectives about the probable shape of the global future by focusing on seven of the most hotly debated questions on the global agenda most likely to dominate political discussion during the next decade.

We live in a moment of history where change is so speeded up that we begin to see the present only when it is disappearing.
—Scottish psychiatrist R. D. Laing

Courtesy of Carla Martinez

IT'S A SMALL WORLD As you begin your journey of discovery to extend your knowledge of world politics, it is important to be aware of the images that you hold and be open to new experiences and interpretations of the world around you. Take full advantage of all of your opportunities to study and learn about the global community. Shown here are U.S. students from The University of Memphis enjoying their study abroad program in San Jose, Costa Rica.

| *Key Terms* |

schematic reasoning	foreign policy	individual level of analysis
cognitive dissonance	monad	state level of analysis
mirror images	directed dyadic	global level of analysis
enduring rivalries	international relations	transformation
actor	summed dyads	global system
state sovereignty	politics	anarchy
state	international politics	cycles
nation	levels of analysis	great powers

CHAPTER 2
THEORIES OF WORLD POLITICS

There is an inescapable link between the abstract world of theory and the real world of policy. We need theories to make sense of the blizzard of information that bombards us daily. Even policy makers who are contemptuous of "theory" must rely on their own (often unstated) ideas about how the world works in order to decide what to do. . . . Everyone uses theories—whether he or she knows it or not.

—Stephen M. Walt, *political scientist*

Theoretical Challenges. An author of your text, Charles Kegley, is a Faculty Fellow teaching for the Maxwell School of Syracuse University's Moynihan Global Affairs Institute. Shown here he lectures at the European Parliament in Strasbourg France on the theoretical study of world politics. His challenge is the same as yours—interpreting theoretically the meaning of a changing world.

I magine yourself the newly elected president of the United States. You are scheduled to deliver the State of the Union address on your views of the current global situation and your foreign policy to deal with it. You face the task of both defining those aspects of international affairs most worthy of attention and explaining the reasons for their priority. To convince citizens these issues are important, you must present them as part of a larger picture of the world. Therefore, based on your perceptions of world politics, you must think *theoretically*. At the same time, you must be careful, because your interpretations will necessarily depend on your assumptions about international realities that your citizens might find questionable. The effort to explain the world, predict new global problems, and sell others on a policy to deal with them is bound to result in controversy because even reasonable people often see realities differently.

When leaders face these kinds of intellectual challenges, they fortunately benefit from various theories of world politics from which they can draw guidance. A **theory** is a set of conclusions derived from assumptions (axioms) and/or evidence about some phenomenon, including its character, causes and probable consequences, and their ethical implications. Theories provide a map, or frame of reference, that makes the complex, puzzling world around us intelligible.

■ **theory**

a set of hypotheses postulating the relationship between variables or conditions advanced to describe, explain, or predict phenomena and make prescriptions about how positive changes ought to be engineered to realize particular goals and ethical principles.

THEORIES AND CHANGE IN WORLD POLITICS

Choosing which theory to heed is an important decision, because each rests on different assumptions about the nature of international politics, each advances different claims about causes, and each offers a different set of foreign policy recommendations. Indeed, the menu of theoretical choice is large. Rival theories of world politics abound, and there is no agreement about which one is the most useful. The reason is primarily because the world is constantly undergoing changes, and no

What is going on? This is the big question that international relations pundits, both academics and practitioners, have scrambled to answer, apparently with little success so far, concerning the reconfiguration of the international system after [2001].

—Cornelia Bjola, Canadian political scientist

■ **paradigm**

derived from the Greek *paradeigma*, meaning an example, a model, or an essential pattern; a paradigm structures thought about an area of inquiry.

single theory has proven capable of making international events understandable for every global circumstance. So there are fads and fashions in the popularity of international theories; they rise and fall over time in popularity and perceived usefulness, depending on the global conditions that prevail in any historical period.

The history of the world is the history of changes in the theoretical interpretation of international relations. In any given era, a **paradigm**, or dominant way of looking at a particular subject, such as international relations, has arisen to influence judgments regarding which characteristics of the subject are most important, what puzzles need to be solved, and what analytic criteria should govern investigations. These paradigms, or "fundamental assumptions scholars make about the world they are studying" (Vasquez 1997), tend eventually to be revised in order to explain new developments. *Cycles* are embedded in history, and theory is forever evolving in an effort to stay in sync with history's pendulum.

Throughout history, paradigms have been revised or abandoned when their assertions have failed to mirror the prevailing patterns of international behavior. Major wars have been especially potent in bringing about significant changes in the theoretical interpretation of world affairs. "Every war . . . has been followed in due course by skeptical reassessments of supposedly sacred assumptions" (Schlesinger 1986) and has influenced "what ideas and values will predominate" (Gilpin 1981). Three such system-transforming wars dominated the twentieth century: World War I, World War II, and the Cold War; and likewise, the 9/11 terrorist attacks in 2001 shattered the preexisting international order. Each shaped policy makers' perceptions of world politics, and each provided lessons critical to developing policies to best preserve world order. Thus, the theories that guide the thinking of policy makers and scholars in different historical circumstances tell us much about world politics itself.

The purpose of this chapter is to compare the assumptions, causal claims, and policy prescriptions of realism, liberalism, and constructivism—the most common theoretical perspectives policy makers and scholars use to interpret international relations. Moreover, the chapter broadens coverage of the range of contemporary international theorizing by introducing you also to the radical and feminist critiques of these three dominant schools of thought.

Realism is the oldest of these three contending schools of thought, so *World Politics* opens a window to theoretical thinking with an overview of realist theory.

REALIST THEORY

Political **realism** has a long, distinguished history that dates back to the writings of Thucydides about the Peloponnesian War in ancient Greece. Other influential figures that contributed to realist thought include the sixteenth-century Italian philosopher Niccolò Machiavelli and the seventeenth-century English philosopher Thomas Hobbes. Realism deserves careful examination because its worldview continues to guide much thought about international politics.

The Realist Worldview

Realism, as applied to contemporary international politics, views the state as the most important actor on the world stage because it answers to no higher political authority. States are sovereign: they have supreme **power** over their territory and populace, and no other actor stands above them wielding the legitimacy and coercive capability to govern the global system. Given the absence of a higher authority to which states can turn for protection and to resolve disputes, realists depict world politics as a ceaseless, repetitive struggle for power where the strong dominate the weak. Because each state is ultimately responsible for its own survival and feels uncertain about its neighbors' intentions, realism claims that prudent political

■ **realism**
a paradigm based on the premise that world politics is essentially and unchangeably a struggle among self-interested states for power and position under anarchy, with each competing state pursuing its own national interests.

■ **power**
the factors that enable one actor to manipulate another actor's behavior against its preferences.

■ self-help

the principle that because in international anarchy all global actors are independent, they must rely on themselves to provide for their security and well-being.

■ relative gains

conditions in which some participants in cooperative interactions benefit more than others.

■ national interest

the goals that states pursue to maximize what they perceive to be selfishly best for their country.

■ balance of power

the theory that peace and stability are most likely to be maintained when military power is distributed to prevent a single superpower hegemon or bloc from controlling the world.

leaders seek arms and allies to enhance national security. In other words, international *anarchy* leads even well-intentioned leaders to practice **self-help**, increase their own military strength and opportunistically align with others to deter potential threats. Realist theory does not preclude the possibility that rival powers will cooperate on arms control or on other security issues of common interest. Rather, it asserts that cooperation will be rare because states worry about the unequal distribution of **relative gains** that can result from cooperation to the disadvantage of one of the parties and the possibility that the other side will cheat on agreements.

At the risk of oversimplification, realism's message can be summarized in the form of ten assumptions and related propositions:

■ People are by nature narrowly selfish and ethically flawed and cannot free themselves from the sinful fact that they are driven to watch out for themselves and to compete with others for self-advantage.

■ Of all humans' evil ways, none are more prevalent, unchangeable, or dangerous than their instinctive lust for power and their desire to dominate others.

■ The possibility of eradicating the instinct for power is a hopeless utopian aspiration.

■ International politics is—as Thomas Hobbes put it—a struggle for power, "a war of all against all."

■ The primary obligation of every state—the goal to which all other national objectives should be subordinated—is to promote its **national interest** and to acquire power for this purpose.

■ The anarchical *global system* dictates that states acquire sufficient military capabilities to deter attack by potential enemies and to exercise influence over others; hence, states should acquire arms and "prepare for war to keep peace," and not be hesitant to use arms, since "might makes right."

■ Economics is less relevant to national security than is military might; economic growth is important primarily as a means of acquiring and expanding state power and prestige.

■ Allies might be sought to increase a state's ability to defend itself, but their loyalty and reliability should not be assumed, and commitments to allies should be repudiated if it is no longer in a state's national interests to honor them.

■ States should never entrust the task of self-protection to international security organizations or international law, and should resist efforts to regulate international behavior through global governance.

■ If all states seek to maximize power, stability will result by maintaining a **balance of power**, lubricated by shifts in the formation and decay of opposing alliances that counter each other's expansionist motives.

Scala/Art Resources, Inc.

Thomas Hobbes (1588-1679), Fuller, Isaac (1606-72)/©Burghley House Collection, Lincolnshire, UK/ The Bridgeman Art Library

REALIST PIONEERS OF POWER POLITICS In *The Prince* (1532) and *The Leviathan* (1651), Niccolò Machiavelli (left) and Thomas Hobbes (right), respectively, argued for basing international decisions on self-interest, prudence, power, and expediency above all other considerations. This formed the foundation of what became a growing body of modern realist thinking that accepts the drive for power over others as necessary and wise statecraft.

With their emphasis on the ruthless nature of international life, realists often question letting ethical considerations enter foreign policy deliberations. As they see it, some policies are driven by strategic imperatives that may require national leaders to disregard moral norms. Embedded in this "philosophy of necessity" is a distinction between private morality, which guides the behavior of ordinary people in their daily lives, and reason of state (*raison d'état*), which governs the conduct of leaders responsible for the security and survival of the state. Whatever actions that are in the interest of state security must be carried out no matter how repugnant they might seem in the light of private morality. "Ignoring one's interests, squandering one's resources in fits of altruism," argues a prominent realist, "is the fastest road to national disaster." For a national leader, "thinking with one's heart is a serious offense. Foreign policy is not social work" (Krauthammer 1993).

The Evolution of Realist Thought

We have seen how the intellectual roots of realism reach back to ancient Greece. They also extend beyond the Western world to India and China. Discussions of "power politics" abound in the *Arthashastra*, an Indian treatise on statecraft written during the fourth century BCE by Kautilya, as well as in works written by Han Fei and Shang Yang in ancient China.

Modern realism emerged on the eve of World War II, when the prevailing belief in a natural harmony of interests among states came under attack. Just a decade earlier, this belief had led numerous countries to sign the 1928 Kellogg-Briand Pact, which renounced war as an instrument of national policy. Now, with Nazi Germany, Fascist Italy, and Imperial Japan all violating the treaty, the British historian and diplomat E. H. Carr (1939) complained that the assumption of a universal interest in peace had allowed too many people to "evade the unpalatable fact of a fundamental divergence of interest between nations desirous of maintaining the status quo and nations desirous of changing it."

In an effort to counter what they saw as a utopian, legalistic approach to foreign affairs, Reinhold Niebuhr (1947), Hans J. Morgenthau (1948), and other realists painted a pessimistic view of human nature. Echoing the seventeenth-century philosopher Baruch Spinoza, many of them pointed to an innate conflict between passion and reason; furthermore, in the tradition of St. Augustine, they stressed that material appetites enabled passion to overwhelm reason. For them, the human condition was such that the forces of light and darkness would perpetually combat for control.

The realists' picture of international life appeared particularly persuasive after World War II. The onset of rivalry between the United States and the Soviet Union, the expansion of the Cold War into a wider struggle between East and West, and the periodic crises that threatened to erupt into global violence all supported the realists' emphasis on the inevitability of conflict, the poor prospects for cooperation, and the divergence of national interests among incorrigibly selfish, power-seeking states.

Whereas these so-called classical realists sought to explain state behavior by examining assumptions about peoples' motives at the *individual level of analysis*, the next wave of realist theorizing emphasized the *global level of analysis*. Kenneth Waltz (1979), the leading proponent of **neorealism** (sometimes called "structural realism") proposed that international anarchy—not some allegedly evil side of human nature—explained why states were locked in fierce competition with one another. The absence of a central arbiter was the defining structural feature of international politics. Vulnerable and insecure, states behaved defensively by forming alliances against looming threats. According to Waltz, balances of power form automatically in anarchic environments. Even when they are disrupted, they are soon restored (see Controversy: Neorealism versus Neoliberalism, page 35).

■ **neorealism**

a theoretical account of states' behavior that explains it as determined by differences in their relative power within the global hierarchy, defined primarily by the distribution of military power, instead of by other factors such as their values, types of government, or domestic circumstances.

There are several members of the Realist family. Structural realism as envisioned by Kenneth Waltz is often referred to as defensive realism to distinguish it from the more recent variant, offensive realism. While both are structural realist theories, defensive realism sees states as focused on maintaining security by balancing others and essentially preserving the status quo, while offensive realism sees states as seeking to ensure security by aggressively maximizing their power (Mearsheimer 2001). Classical realism (now often referred to as neoclassical realism) differs from both in that it assumes "states differ with regard not only to their relative power but also their

Table 2.1   Comparing Variants of Contemporary Realism

Variant	Primary State Objective	Systemic Pressure	Rational State Preference
Defensive realism	Survival	Defensive	Status quo
Offensive realism	Survival	Offensive	Revisionist (hegemons excepted)
Classical realism	Varies (e.g. security, power, or glory)	Defensive or Offensive	Status quo or revisionist

Source: Rynning and Ringsmose 2008, p. 28.

primary motivation... (and) its emphasis on how systemic-level variables are 'translated through unit-level intervening variables such as decision-makers' perceptions and domestic state structure'" (Rynning and Ringsmose 2008, 27: Rose 1998).

The Limitations of Realism

However persuasive the realists' image of the essential properties of international politics, their policy recommendations suffered from a lack of precision in the way they used such key terms as power and national interest. Thus, once analysis moved beyond the assertion that national leaders should acquire power to serve the national interest, important questions remained: What were the key elements of national power? What uses of power best served the national interest? Did arms furnish protection or provoke costly arms races? Did alliances enhance one's defenses or encourage threatening counteralliances? From the perspective of realism's critics, seeking security by amassing power was self-defeating. The quest for absolute security by one state would be perceived as creating absolute insecurity for other members of the system, with the result that everyone would become locked in an upward spiral of countermeasures that jeopardized the security of all (Vasquez 1998).

Because much of realist theorizing was vague, it began to be questioned. Realism offered no criteria for determining what historical data were significant in evaluating its claims and what epistemological rules to follow when interpreting relevant information (Vasquez and Elman 2003). Even the policy recommendations that purportedly flowed from its logic were often divergent. Realists themselves, for example, were sharply divided as to whether U.S. intervention in Vietnam served American national interests and whether nuclear weapons contributed to international security. Similarly, whereas some observers used realism to explain the rationale for the 2003 U.S. invasion of Iraq (Gvosdev 2005), others drew on realist arguments to criticize the invasion (Mansfield and Snyder 2005a; Mearsheimer and Walt 2003).

A growing number of critics also pointed out that realism did not account for significant new developments in world politics. For instance, it could not explain the, creation of new commercial and political institutions in Western Europe in the 1950s

The most fatal illusion is the settled point of view. Since life is growth and motion, a fixed point of view kills anybody who has one.

—Brooks Atkinson, American drama critic

and 1960s, where the cooperative pursuit of mutual advantage led Europeans away from the unbridled power politics that brought them incessant warfare since the birth of the nation-state some three centuries earlier. Other critics began to worry about realism's tendency to disregard ethical principles and about the material and social costs that some of its policy prescriptions seemed to impose, such as retarded economic growth resulting from unrestrained military expenditures.

Despite realism's shortcomings, many people continue to think about world politics in the language constructed by realists, especially in times of global tension. A recent example can be found in the comments by former Bush administration adviser Michael Gerson (2006) about how the United States should deal with Iran's nuclear ambitions. Arguing from the realist assumption that "peace is not a natural state," he called for a robust American response based on a steely-eyed focus on preventing the proliferation of weapons of mass destruction in the Middle East. "There must be someone in the world capable of drawing a line—someone who says, 'This much and no further.'" Peace, he concluded, cannot be achieved by "a timid foreign policy that allows terrible threats to emerge." Unless those who threaten others pay a price, "aggression will be universal."

LIBERAL THEORY

■ **liberalism**

a paradigm predicated on the hope that the application of reason and universal ethics to international relations can lead to a more orderly, just, and cooperative world; liberalism assumes that anarchy and war can be policed by institutional reforms that empower international organization and law.

Liberalism has been called the "strongest contemporary challenge to realism" (Caporaso 1993). Like realism, it has a distinguished pedigree, with philosophical roots extending back to the political thought of John Locke, Immanuel Kant, and Adam Smith. Liberalism warrants our attention because it speaks to issues realism disregards, including the impact of domestic politics on state behavior, the implications of economic interdependence, and the role of global norms and institutions in promoting international cooperation.

The Liberal Worldview

There are several distinct schools of thought within the liberal tradition. Drawing broad conclusions from such a diverse body of theory risks misrepresenting the position of any given author. Nevertheless, there are sufficient commonalities to abstract some general themes.

Liberals differ from realists in several important ways. At the core of liberalism is a belief in reason and the possibility of progress. Liberals view the individual as the seat of moral value and assert that human beings should be treated as ends rather

> *The fundamental character of regimes matters more today than the international distribution of power.*
> —Condoleezza Rice, U.S. Secretary of State

than means. Whereas realists counsel decision makers to seek the lesser evil rather than the absolute good, liberals emphasize ethical principle over the pursuit of power, and institutions over military capabilities (see Doyle 1997; Howard 1978; Zacher and Matthew 1995). Politics at the global level is more of a struggle for consensus and mutual gain than a struggle for power and prestige.

Several corollary ideas give definition to liberal theory. These include (1) the need to substitute attitudes that stress the unity of humankind for those that stressed parochial national loyalties to independent sovereign states; (2) the importance of individuals—their essential dignity and fundamental equality throughout the course of history, and the corollary need to place the protection and promotion of human rights and freedom ahead of national interests and state autonomy; and (3) the use of the power of ideas through education to arouse world public opinion against warfare.

Instead of blaming international conflict on an inherent lust for power, liberals fault the conditions under which people live. Reforming those conditions, they argue, will enhance the prospects for peace. The first element common to various strands of liberal thought is an emphasis on undertaking political reforms to establish stable democracies. Woodrow Wilson, for example, proclaimed that "democratic government will make wars less likely." Franklin Roosevelt later agreed, asserting "the continued maintenance and improvement of democracy constitute the most important guarantee of international peace." Based on tolerance, compromise, and civil liberties, democratic political cultures are said to shun lethal force as a means of settling disagreements. Politics is not seen as a **zero-sum** game, so that the use of persuasion rather than coercion, and a reliance on judicial methods to settle rival claims are the primary means of dealing with conflict.

■ zero-sum
an exchange in a purely conflictual relationship in which what is gained by one competitor is lost by the other.

According to liberal theory, conflict-resolution practices used at home can also be used when dealing with international disputes. Leaders socialized within democratic cultures share a common outlook. Viewing international politics as an extension of domestic politics, they generalize about the applicability of norms to regulate international competition. Disputes between democratic governments rarely escalate to war because each side accepts the other's legitimacy and expects it to rely on peaceful means of conflict resolution. These expectations are reinforced by the

> *Men are more apt to be mistaken in their generalizations than in their particular observations.*
>
> —Niccolò Machiavelli, realist political philosopher

transparent nature of democracies. The inner workings of open polities can be scrutinized by anyone; hence, it is difficult to demonize democratically ruled states as scheming adversaries.

The second thrust common to liberal theorizing is an emphasis on free trade. The idea that commerce can reduce conflict has roots in the work of Immanuel Kant, Charles de Secondat Montesquieu, Adam Smith, and various Enlightenment thinkers. "Nothing is more favourable to the rise of politeness and learning," noted liberal philosopher David Hume (1817), "than a number of neighboring and independent states, connected by commerce." This view was later embraced by the Manchester School of political economy and formed the basis for Norman Angell's (1910) famous rebuttal of the assertion that military conquest produces economic prosperity.

The doctrine that unfettered trade helps prevent disputes from escalating to wars rests on several propositions. First, commercial intercourse creates a material incentive to resolve disputes peacefully: War reduces profits by interrupting vital economic exchanges. Second, cosmopolitan business elites who benefit most from

Christie's Images/CORBIS

The Granger Collection

0004078   IMMANUEL KANT (1724-1804).
Credit: The Granger Collection, New York

PIONEERS IN THE LIBERAL QUEST FOR WORLD ORDER **A product of the Enlightenment, Scottish philosopher David Hume (left) tried to temper his realist concern that reason is a "slave of the passions" by embracing the liberal faith in wealth-generating free markets and free trade that could cohesively bind people together to create a peaceful civil society. Influenced by David Hume and Jean-Jacques Rousseau, Immanuel Kant (right) in *Perpetual Peace* (1795) helped to redefine modern liberal theory by advocating global (not state) citizenship, free trade, and a federation of democracies as a means to peace.**

these exchanges comprise a powerful transnational interest group with a stake in promoting amicable solutions to festering disagreements. Finally, the web of trade between countries increases communication, erodes national selfishness, and encourages both sides to avoid ruinous clashes. In the words of Richard Cobden, an opponent of the protectionist Corn Laws that once regulated British international grain trade: "Free Trade! What is it? Why, breaking down the barriers that separate nations; those barriers, behind which nestle the feelings of pride, revenge, hatred, and jealousy, which every now and then burst their bounds, and deluge whole countries with blood."

Finally, the third commonality in liberal theorizing is an advocacy of global institutions. Liberals recommend replacing cutthroat, balance-of-power politics with organizations based on the principle that a threat to peace anywhere is a common threat to everyone. They see foreign policy as unfolding in a nascent global society populated by actors who recognize the cost of conflict, share significant interests, and can realize those interests by using institutions to mediate disputes whenever misconceptions, wounded sensibilities, or aroused national passions threaten peaceful relations.

The Evolution of Liberal Thought

Contemporary liberal theory rose to prominence in the wake of World War I. Not only had the war involved more participants over a wider geographic area than any previous war, but modern science and technology made it a war of machinery: Old weapons were improved and produced in great quantities; new and far more deadly weapons were rapidly developed and deployed. By the time the carnage was over, nearly twenty million people were dead.

For liberals such as U.S. President Woodrow Wilson, World War I was "the war to end all wars." Convinced that another horrific war would erupt if states resumed practicing power politics, liberals set out to reform the global system. These "idealists," as they were called by hard-boiled realists, generally fell into one of three groups (Herz 1951). The first group advocated creating global institutions to contain the raw struggle for power between self-serving, mutually suspicious states. The League of Nations was the embodiment of this strain of liberal thought. Its founders hoped to prevent future wars by organizing a system of **collective security** that would mobilize the entire international community against would-be aggressors. The League's founders declared that peace was indivisible: an attack on one member of the League would be considered an attack on all. Because no state was more powerful than the combination of all other states, aggressors would be deterred and war averted.

A second group called for the use of legal procedures to adjudicate disputes before they escalated to armed conflict. Adjudication is a judicial procedure for resolving conflicts by referring them to a standing court for a binding decision. Immediately after the war, several governments drafted a statute to establish a Permanent Court of International Justice (PCIJ). Hailed by Bernard C. J. Loder, the court's first president, as the harbinger of a new era of civilization, the PCIJ held its inaugural public meeting in early 1922 and rendered its first judgment on a contentious case the following year. Liberal champions of the court insisted that the PCIJ would replace military retaliation with a judicial body capable of bringing the facts of a dispute to light and issuing a just verdict.

A third group of liberal thinkers followed the Biblical injunction that states should beat their swords into plowshares and sought disarmament as a means of avoiding war. Their efforts were illustrated between 1921 and 1922 by the Washington Naval Conference, which tried to curtail maritime competition among the United States, Great Britain, Japan, France, and Italy by placing limits on battleships. The ultimate goal of this group was to reduce international tensions by promoting general disarmament, which led them to convene the 1932 Geneva Disarmament Conference.

Although a tone of idealism dominated policy rhetoric and academic discussions during the interwar period, little of the liberal reform program was ever seriously attempted, and even less of it was achieved. The League of Nations failed to prevent the Japanese invasion of Manchuria (1931) or the Italian invasion of Ethiopia (1935); major disputes were rarely submitted to the Permanent Court of International Justice; and the 1932 Geneva Disarmament Conference ended in failure. When the threat of war began gathering over Europe and Asia in the late 1930s, enthusiasm for liberal idealism receded.

The next surge in liberal theorizing arose decades later in response to realism's neglect of **transnational relations** (see Keohane and Nye 1971). Although realists continued to focus on the state, the events surrounding the 1973 oil crisis revealed that nonstate actors could affect the course of international events, and occasionally compete with states. This insight led to the realization that **complex interdependence**

■ **collective security**

a security regime agreed to by the great powers that sets rules for keeping peace, guided by the principle that an act of aggression by any state will be met by a collective response from the rest.

■ **transnational relations**

interactions across state boundaries that involves at least one actor that is not the agent of a government or intergovernmental organization.

■ **complex interdependence**

a model of world politics based on the assumptions that states are not the only important actors, security is not the dominant national goal, and military force is not the only significant instrument of foreign policy; this theory stresses cross-cutting ways in which the growing ties among transnational actors make them vulnerable to each other's actions and sensitive to each other's needs.

(Keohane and Nye 1977) sometimes offered a better description of world politics than realism, especially on international economic and environmental matters. Rather than contacts between countries being limited to high-level governmental officials, multiple communication channels connect societies. Instead of security dominating foreign policy considerations, issues on national agendas do not always have a fixed priority, and although military force often serves as the primary instrument of statecraft, other means frequently are more effective when bargaining occurs between economically interconnected countries. In short, the realist preoccupation with government-to-government relations ignored the complex network of public and private exchanges crisscrossing state boundaries. States were becoming increasingly interdependent, that is, mutually dependent on, sensitive about, and vulnerable to one another in ways that were not captured by realist theory.

Although interdependence was not new, its growth during the last quarter of the twentieth century led many liberal theorists to challenge the realist conception of *anarchy*. Although they agreed that the global system was anarchic, they also argued that it was more properly conceptualized as an "ordered" anarchy because most states followed commonly acknowledged normative standards, even in the absence of hierarchical enforcement. When a body of norms fosters shared expectations that guide a regularized pattern of cooperation on a specific issue, we call it an **international regime** (see Hansenclever, Mayer, and Rittberger 1996). Various types of regimes have been devised to govern behavior in trade and monetary affairs, as well as to manage access to common resources such as fisheries and river water. By the turn of the century, as pressing economic and environmental issues crowded national agendas, a large body of liberal "institutionalist" scholarship explored how regimes developed and what led states to comply with their injunctions.

Fueled by the recent history that suggested that international relations can change and that increased interdependence can lead to higher levels of cooperation, **neoliberalism** emerged in the last decade of the twentieth century to challenge realism and *neorealism*. This new departure goes by several labels including "neoliberal institutionalism" (Grieco 1995), "neoidealism" (Kegley 1993), and "neo-Wilsonian idealism"(Fukuyama 1992a).

Like realism and neorealism, neoliberalism does not represent a consistent intellectual movement or school of thought. Whatever the differences that divide them, however, all neoliberals share an interest in probing the conditions under which the convergent and overlapping interests among otherwise independent transnational actors may result in cooperation. Neoliberalism departs from neorealism on many assumptions (see Controversy: Neorealism versus Neoliberalism). In particular, neoliberalism focuses on the ways in which influences such as democratic governance, public opinion, mass education, free trade, liberal commercial enterprise, international law and organization, arms control and disarmament, collective security, multilateral diplomacy, and ethically inspired statecraft can improve life on our planet. Because they perceive change in global conditions as progressing over time, haltingly but still in the same trajectory through cooperative efforts, neoliberal theorists maintain that the ideas and ideals of the liberal legacy could describe, explain, predict, and prescribe international conduct in ways that they could not during the conflict-ridden Cold War.

■ **international regime**

embodies the norms, principles, rules, and institutions around which global expectations unite regarding a specific international problem.

■ **neoliberalism**

the "new" liberal theoretical perspective that accounts for the way international institutions promote global change, cooperation, peace, and prosperity through collective programs for reforms.

CONTROVERSY:

NEOREALISM VERSUS NEOLIBERALISM

Which Theory Makes the Most Reasonable Assumptions?

The issues dividing neoliberal and neorealist theorizing center on the different assumptions they make about the following six topics (Baldwin 1993). Looking at the world, which set of assumptions do you think is the most accurate for interpreting twenty-first-century world politics?

- **The Nature and Consequences of Anarchy.** Whereas everyone recognizes that the global system is anarchical because effective institutions for global governance are lacking, neorealists argue that anarchy does not matter much and in fact may be preferable to the restraints of world government. Neoliberals see anarchy as a big problem that can be reformed through the creation of strong global institutions.

- **International Cooperation.** Although neorealists and neoliberals agree that international cooperation is possible, neorealists think cooperation is difficult to sustain whereas neoliberals believe cooperation can be expected because collaboration produces rewards that reduce the temptation to selfishly compete.

- **Relative versus Absolute Gains.** Both neorealists and neoliberals are concerned with relative gain as well as absolute gain. Neorealists believe that the desire to get ahead of their competitor by obtaining *relative gains* is the primary motive, whereas neoliberals believe that states are motivated by the search for opportunities to cooperate that will produce **absolute gains** for all parties to the cooperative exchange.

- **Priority of State Goals.** Both national security and national economic prosperity are seen as important state goals by neorealists and neoliberals. However, neorealists stress security as the most important, and neoliberals believe states place a greater priority on economic welfare.

- **Intentions versus Capabilities.** Contemporary neorealists maintain that the distribution of states' capabilities is the primary determinant of their behavior and international outcomes. Neoliberals maintain that states' intentions, interests, information, and ideals are more influential than is the distribution of capabilities.

- **Institutions and Regimes.** Both neorealists and neoliberals recognize that states have created a variety of new international **regimes** and institutions to regulate their relations since World War II. Neoliberals believe that institutions such as the World Trade Organization create norms that are binding on their members and that change patterns of international politics. By contrast, neorealists emphasize that organizations such as the United Nations are arenas where states carry out their traditional competition and political rivalry for influence.

■ absolute gains

conditions in which all participants in exchanges become better off.

■ regimes

the rules agreed upon by states to work together to manage shared problems, because long-term benefits to all are expected even though short-term relative losses may ·be encountered.

The Limitations of Liberalism

Liberal theorists share an interest in probing the conditions under which the convergent and overlapping interests among otherwise sovereign national actors may result in cooperation. Taking heart in the international prohibition, through community consensus, of such previously entrenched practices as slavery, piracy, dueling, and colonialism, they emphasize the prospects for progress through institutional reform. Studies of European integration during the 1950s and 1960s paved the way for the liberal institutionalist theories that emerged in the 1990s. The expansion of trade, communication, information, technology, and migrant labor led Europeans to sacrifice portions of their sovereign independence to create a new political and economic union out of previously separate units. These developments were outside of realism's worldview, creating conditions that made the call for a

If you can talk brilliantly about a problem, it can create the consoling illusion that it has been mastered.

—Stanley Kubrick, American movie director

theory grounded in the liberal tradition convincing to many who had previously questioned realism. In the words of former U.S. president Bill Clinton, "In a world where freedom, not tyranny, is on the march, the cynical calculus of pure power politics simply does not compute. It is ill-suited to the new era."

Yet, as compelling as contemporary liberal institutionalism may seem at the onset of the twenty-first century, many realists complain that it has not transcended its idealist heritage. They charge that just like the League of Nations and the Permanent Court of International Justice, institutions today exert minimal influence on state behavior. International organizations cannot stop states from behaving according to balance-of-power logic, calculating how each move they make affects their relative position in a world of relentless competition.

■ low politics

global issues related to the economic, social, demographic, and environmental aspects of relations between governments and people.

■ high politics

geostrategic issues of national and international security that pertain to matters of war and peace.

Critics of liberalism further contend that most studies supportive of international institutions appear in the **low politics** arena of commercial, financial, and environmental affairs, not in the **high politics** arena of national defense. Although it may be difficult to draw a clear line between economic and security issues, some scholars note that "different institutional arrangements" exist in each realm, with the prospects for cooperation among self-interested states greater in the former than the latter (Lipson 1984). National survival hinges on the effective management of security issues, insist realists. Collective security organizations naïvely assume that all members perceive threats in the same way, and are willing to run the risks and pay the costs of countering those threats (Kissinger 1992).

Because power-lusting states are unlikely to see their vital interests in this light, global institutions cannot provide timely, muscular responses to aggression. On security issues, conclude realists, states will trust in their own power, not in the promises of supranational institutions.

*It's important that we take a hard clear look . . . not at some
simple world, either of universal goodwill or of universal hostility,
but the complex, changing, and sometimes dangerous world that
really exists.*

—Jimmy Carter, U.S. President

A final realist complaint lodged against liberalism is an alleged tendency to turn foreign policy into a moral crusade. Whereas realists claim that heads of state are driven by strategic necessities, many liberals believe moral imperatives can guide and constrain leaders. Consider the 1999 war in Kosovo, which pitted the North Atlantic Treaty Organization (NATO) against the Federal Republic of Yugoslavia. Pointing to Yugoslav leader Slobodan Milosevic's repression of ethnic Albanians living in the province of Kosovo, NATO Secretary General Javier Solana, British Prime Minister Tony Blair, and U.S. President Bill Clinton all argued that humanitarian intervention was a moral necessity. Although nonintervention into the internal affairs of other states had long been a cardinal principle of international law, they saw military action against Yugoslavia as a duty because human rights were an international entitlement and governments that violated them forfeited the protection of international law. Sovereignty, according to many liberal thinkers, is not sacrosanct. The international community has an obligation to use armed force to stop flagrant violations of human rights.

To sum up, realists remain skeptical about liberal claims of moral necessity. On the one hand, they deny the universal applicability of any single moral standard in a culturally pluralistic world. On the other hand, they worry that adopting such a standard will breed a self-righteous, messianic foreign policy. Realists embrace **consequentialism**. If there are no universal standards covering the many situations in which moral choice must occur, then policy decisions can be judged only in terms of their consequences in particular circumstances. Prudent leaders recognize that competing moral values may be at stake in any given situation, and they must weigh the trade-offs among these values, as well as how pursuing them might impinge on national security and other important interests. As the former U.S. diplomat and celebrated realist scholar George Kennan (1985) once put it, the primary obligation of government "is to the interests of the national society it represents, not to the moral impulses that individual elements of that society may experience."

CONSTRUCTIVIST THEORY

Since the end of the Cold War, many students of international relations have turned to social constructivism in order to understand world politics. Although constructivism is "a loose paradigm of related interpretations [that] share certain assumptions with realists and liberals" (Steele 2007), constructivism is different. In contrast to realism and liberalism, which emphasize how material factors such as military power and economic wealth affect the relations among states, **constructivist theory** emphasizes how the world revolves around social ideas and shared understandings whose impact on world politics is huge. As discussed in the previous

■ **consequentialism**
an approach to evaluating moral choices on the basis of the results of the action taken.

■ **constructivist theory**
a theoretical approach advocated by Alexander Wendt that sees self-interested states as the key actors in world politics; their actions are determined not by anarchy but by the ways that states socially construct and then accept images of reality and later respond to the meanings given to power politics; as consensual definitions change, it is possible for either conflictual or cooperative practices to evolve.

chapter, international reality is defined by our images of the world. Constructivists stress the intersubjective quality of these images—how perceptions are shaped by prevailing attitudes. All of us are influenced by collective conceptions of world politics that are reinforced by social pressures from the reference groups to which we

> *People make society, and society makes people.*
>
> —Nicholas Onuf, constructivist theoretician

belong. Awareness of how our understandings of the world are socially constructed, and of how prevailing ideas mold our beliefs about what is unchangable and what can be reformed, allow us to see world politics in a new, critical light.

The Constructivist Worldview

As shown in Table 2.1, constructivists differ from realists and liberals most fundamentally by insisting that world politics is socially constructed. That is to say, material conditions acquire meaning for human action only through the shared knowledge that circulating ideas ascribe to them. Socially popular visions of realities provide transnational actors with certain identities and interests, and material capabilities with certain meanings (see Hopf 1998; Smith and Owens 2005; Onuf 1989). Hence, the meaning of a concept such as "anarchy" depends on underlying shared knowledge. An anarchy among allies, for example, holds a different meaning for the states in question than an anarchy composed of bitter rivals. Thus, British nuclear weapons are less threatening to the United States than the same weapons in North Korean hands, because shared Anglo-American expectations about one another differ from those between Washington and Pyongyang. The nature of international life within an anarchy, in other words, is not a given. Anarchy, as well as other socially constructed concepts like "sovereignty" and "power," are simply what states make of them (Wendt 1995).

The Evolution of Constructivist Thought

The intellectual roots of constructivism extend from the work of the twentieth-century Frankfurt School of critical social theory to more recent research by Peter Berger and Thomas Luckmann (1967) on the sociology of knowledge and by Anthony Giddens (1984) on the relationship between agency and social structure. Sometimes described as more of a philosophically informed perspective than a fully fledged general theory (Ruggie 1998), constructivism includes diverse scholars who agree that the international institutions most people take for granted as the natural and inevitable result of world politics need not exist (Hacking 1999). Like the institutions of slavery and even war, these practices are mere social constructs that depend on human agreement for their existence. They are therefore changeable.

The unraveling of the Warsaw Pact and subsequent disintegration of the Soviet Union stimulated scholarly interest during the 1990s in constructivist interpretations of world politics. Neither realism nor liberalism foresaw the peaceful end to the Cold

Table 2.2   A Comparison of Realist, Liberal, and Constructivist Theories

Feature	Realism	Liberalism	Constructivism
Core Concern	War and security How vulnerable, self-interested states survive in an environment where they are uncertain about the intentions and capabilities of others	Institutionalized peace How self-serving actors learn to see benefits to coordinating behavior through rules and organizations in order to achieve collective gains	Social groups' shared meanings and images How ideas, images and identities shape world politics
Key actors	States	States, international institutions, global corporations	Individuals, nongovernmental organizations, transnational networks
Central concepts	Anarchy, self-help, national interest, relative gains, balance of power	Collective security, international regimes, complex interdependence, transnational relations	Ideas, shared knowledge, identities, discourses and persuasion leading to new understandings and normative change
Approach to peace	Protect sovereign autonomy and deter rivals through military preparedness and alliances	Institutional reform through democratization, open markets, and international law and organization	Activists who promote progressive ideas and encourage states to adhere to norms for appropriate behavior
Global outlook	Pessimistic: great powers locked in relentless security competition	Optimistic: cooperative view of human nature and a belief in progress	Agnostic: global prospect hinges on the content of prevailing ideas and values

War and both theories had difficulty explaining why it occurred when it did (see Chapter 4 Controversy: Why Did the Cold War End Peacefully?). Constructivists pointed to the challenge that Mikhail Gorbechev's "new thinking" posed to traditional ideas about national security. New thinking, they suggested, led to the rise of new **norms** governing the relations between Moscow and Washington.

Norms can be the sources of action in three ways: They may be constitutive in the sense that they define what counts as a certain activity; they may be constraining in that they forbid an actor from behaving in a particular way; or they may be enabling by allowing specific actions. In American football, for instance, there are constitutive rules that give meaning to action on the field by defining what counts as a touchdown, a field goal, or a safety. There also are two kinds of regulative rules that guide play: constraining rules prohibit things like clipping and holding, whereas

■ **norms**
generalized standards of behavior that, once accepted, shape collective expectations about appropriate conduct.

PIONEERING INFLUENCES ON CONSTRUCTIVIST THOUGHT **Many constructivists have been influenced by critical theory, especially as it was developed by Max Horkheimer (1947), left, and Jurgen Habermas (1984), right. The roots of critical theory can be traced to the Frankfurt School in Germany during the 1920s. The aims of critical theory were to critique and change conditions, not merely understand them. Rather than viewing the world as a set of neutral, objective "facts" that could be perceived apart from the situation in which observation occurred, critical theorists saw all phenomena embedded within a specific sociohistorical context ascribing normative meaning to information (Price and Reus-Smit 1998; also see Cox 1996).**

enabling rules permit players to throw laterals and forward passes. Similarly, in international relations, constitutive norms of sovereignty define what counts as statehood, whereas regulative norms that either constrain or enable specify how sovereign states ought to conduct themselves.

For constructivists, the game of international power revolves around actors' abilities through debate about values to persuade others to accept their ideas. People and groups become powerful when their efforts to proselytize succeed in winning converts to those ideas and norms they advocate, and a culture of shared understandings emerges. The capacity of some activist transnational nongovernmental organizations, such as Human Rights Watch or Greenpeace, to promote global change by convincing many people to accept their ideas about political liberties and environmental protection, are examples of how shared conceptions of moral and legal norms can change the world. Consensual understandings of interests, self-identities, and images of the world—how people think of themselves, who they are, and what others in the world are like—demonstrably can alter the world when these social constructions of international realities change (Barnet 2005; Adler 2002; Onuf 2002).

The Limitations of Constructivism

The most common criticism of constructivism concerns its explanation of change. If changes in ideas through discussions and discourses lead to behavioral changes within the global system, what accounts for the rise and fall of different ideas and discourses over time? How, when, and why do changes in shared knowledge emerge? "Constructivists are good at describing change," writes Jack Snyder (2004), "but they are weak on the material and institutional circumstances necessary to support the emergence of consensus about new values and ideas." Moreover, critics charge that constructivists remain unclear about what factors cause particular ideas to become dominant whereas others fall by the wayside. "What is crucial," asserts Robert Jervis (2005), "is not people's thinking, but the factors that drive it." Constructivists, he continues, have excessive faith in the ability of ideas that seem self-evident today to replicate and sustain themselves; however, future generations who live under different circumstances and who may think differently could easily reject these ideas. For constructivists, socially accepted ideas, norms, and values are linked to collective identities—stable, role-specific understandings and expectations about self (Wendt 1994). Although constructivists recognize that shared identities are not pregiven and can change over time, critics submit that constructivists cannot explain why and when they dissolve.

A related concern is that constructivism overemphasizes the role of social structures at the expense of the purposeful agents whose practices help create and change these structures (Checkel 1998). According to Cynthia Weber (2005), constructivism as exemplified in the work of Alexander Wendt (2000) reifies states by picturing these collectives like individuals whose decisions become the authors or producers of international life; that is, it treats them as objects that already exist and says little about the "practices that produce states as producers." Although constructivism calls our attention to the importance of the intersubjectively constituted or shared characterizations of the identities and interests that influence how all transnational actors see themselves and behave, it does not offer an account of the practices that the actors themselves construct as producers of global anarchy and other features of world politics.

Despite these criticisms, constructivism is a very popular theoretical approach in world politics. By highlighting the influence that socially constructed images of the world have on your interpretations of international events, and by making you aware of their inherent subjectivity, constructivism can remind you of the contingent nature of all knowledge and the inability of any theory of world politics to fully capture global complexities.

WHAT'S MISSING IN THEORIES OF WORLD POLITICS?

Although realism, liberalism, and constructivism dominate thinking about international relations in today's academic and policy communities, these schools of thought have been challenged. Two of the most significant critiques have come from radicalism and feminism.

> *The very idea that there is another idea is something gained.*
> —Richard Jeffries, English author

The Radical Critique

For much of the twentieth century, socialism was the primary radical alternative to mainstream international relations theorizing. Although there are many strands of socialist thought, most have been influenced by Karl Marx's argument that explaining events in world affairs requires understanding capitalism as a global phenomenon. Whereas realists emphasize state security, liberals accentuate individual freedom, and constructivists highlight ideas and identities, socialists focus on class conflict and the material interests of each class (Doyle 1997).

"The history of all hitherto existing society," proclaimed Marx and his coauthor Friedrich Engels (1820–1895) in the *Communist Manifesto*, "is the history of class struggles." Capitalism, they argued, has given rise to two antagonistic classes: a ruling class (bourgeoisie) that owns the means of production, and a subordinate class (proletariat) that sells its labor, but receives little compensation. According to Marx and Engels, "The need of a constantly expanding market for its products chases the bourgeoisie over the whole surface of the globe." By expanding worldwide, the bourgeoisie gives "a cosmopolitan character to production and consumption in every country."

KARL MARX CHALLENGES INTERNATIONAL THEORETICAL ORTHODOXY **Pictured here is the German philosopher Karl Marx (1818–1883). His revolutionary theory of the economic determinants of world history inspired the spread of communism to overcome the class struggles so pronounced in most countries. The target of his critique was the compulsion of the wealthy great powers to subjugate foreign people by military force and to create colonies for purposes of financial exploitation. Imperial conquest of colonial peoples could only be prevented, Marx warned, by humanity's shift from a capitalist to a socialist economy and society.**

© INTERFOTO Pressebildagentur / Alamy Limited

Vladimir Ilyich Lenin (1870–1924) in the Soviet Union extended Marx's analysis to the study of imperialism, which he interpreted as a stage in the development of capitalism when monopolies overtake free-market competition. Drawing from the work of British economist John Hobson (1858–1940), Lenin maintained that advanced capitalist states eventually face the twin problems of overproduction and underconsumption. They respond by seeking foreign markets and investments for their surplus goods and capital, and by waging wars to divide the world into spheres of influence that they can exploit. Though his assertions have been heavily criticized on conceptual and empirical grounds (see Dougherty and Pfaltzgraff 2001), the attention given to social classes and uneven development stimulated several new waves of theorizing about capitalism as a global phenomenon.

One prominent example is **dependency theory**. As expressed in the writings of André Gunder Frank (1969), Amir Samin (1976), and others (Dos Santos 1970; see Chapter 5), dependency theorists claimed that much of the poverty in Asia, Africa, and Latin America stemmed from the exploitative capitalist world economy. As they saw it, the economies of less developed countries had become dependent on exporting inexpensive raw materials and agricultural commodities to advanced industrial states, while simultaneously importing expensive manufactured goods from them. Raúl Prebisch, an Argentinian economist who directed the United Nations Economic Commission for Latin America, feared that these producers of primary products would find it difficult to escape poverty, because the price of their products would fall over time relative to the price of manufactured goods. Dependency theory was criticized for recommending withdrawal from the world economy (Shannon 1989), and eventually theoretical efforts arose to trace the economic ascent and decline of individual countries as part of long-run, systemwide change (Clark 2008).

World-system theory, which was influenced by both Marxist and dependency theorists, represents the most recent effort to interpret world politics in terms of an integrated capitalist division of labor (see Wallerstein 2005 and 1988; Chase-Dunn and Anderson 2005). The capitalist world economy, which emerged in sixteenth-century Europe and ultimately expanded to encompass the entire globe, is viewed as containing three structural positions: a *core* (strong, well-integrated states whose economic activities are diversified and centered on possession and use of capital), a *periphery* (areas lacking strong state machinery and engaged in producing relatively few unfinished goods by unskilled, low-wage labor), and a *semiperiphery* (states embodying elements of both core and peripheral production). Within the core, a state may gain economic primacy by achieving productive, commercial, and financial superiority over its rivals. Primacy is difficult to sustain, however. The diffusion of technological innovations and the flow of capital to competitors, plus the massive costs of maintaining global order, all erode the dominant state's economic advantage. Thus in addition to underscoring the exploitation of the periphery by the core, world-system theory calls attention to the cyclical rise and fall of hegemonic superpowers at the top of the core hierarchy.

Whereas the various radical challenges to mainstream theorizing enhance our understanding of world politics by highlighting the roles played by corporations, transnational religious movements, and other nonstate actors, they overemphasize economic interpretations of international events and consequently omit other potentially important explanatory factors. According to feminist theorists, one such factor is gender.

■ **dependency theory**
a theory hypothesizing that less developed countries are exploited because global capitalism makes them dependent on the rich countries that create exploitative rules for trade and production.

■ **world-system theory**
a body of theory that treats the capitalistic world economy originating in the sixteenth century as an interconnected unit of analysis encompassing the entire globe, with an international division of labor and multiple political centers and cultures whose rules constrain and share the behavior of all transnational actors.

The Feminist Critique

During the last quarter of the twentieth century, feminism began challenging conventional international relations theory. In particular, feminist theory attacked the exclusion of women in discussions about international affairs as well as the injustice and unequal treatment of women this prejudice caused. The mainstream literature on world politics dismissed the plight and contributions of women, treating differences in men's and women's status, beliefs, and behaviors as unimportant. As feminist theory evolved over time, it moved away from focusing on a history of discrimination and began to explore how gender identity shapes foreign policy decision making and how gendered hierarchies reinforce practices that perpetuate inequalities between men and women (see Tickner 2005 and 2002; Enloe 2004; Beckman and D'Amico 1994; Peterson and Runyan 1993).

Although all feminists stress the importance of gender in studying international relations, there are several contending schools of thought within feminist scholarship. Some feminists assert that on average there are no significant differences in the capabilities of men and women; others claim differences exist, with each gender being more capable than the other in certain endeavors; still others insist that the meaning ascribed to a person's gender is an arbitrary cultural construct that varies from one time or place to another (Goldstein 2002). Regardless of the position taken on the issue of gender differences, as leading feminist scholars Francine D'Amico and

■ **feminist theory**

body of scholarship that emphasizes gender in the study of world politics.

©Pedro Ugarte/AFP/Getty Images

FREE AT LAST? For most of recorded history, women were deprived of the basic human right of voting in elections, as is explained by feminist theory, an extension of neoliberal theorizing. With recent reforms, that situation has begun to change, as shown in this photo of Somaliland women singing as they line up to cast their ballots for the first time on May 31, 2001, at a polling station in Hargeisa, Somalia, during a referendum on the constitution.

Peter Beckman (1995) convincingly demonstrate, many women have proven to be very capable leaders who have left deep footprints on international affairs. More than simply acknowledging the impact of female leaders such as Britain's Margaret Thatcher, Indonesia's Megawati Sukarnoputri, Israel's Golda Meir, the Philippine's Corazón Aquino, Pakistan's Benazir Bhutto, Germany's Angela Merkel, Argentina's Christina Fernandez de Kirchner, or Chile's Michelle Bachelet, they urge us to examine events from the personal perspectives of the countless women who have been involved in international affairs as caregivers, grassroots activists, and participants in the informal labor force. "Women have never been absent in world politics," writes Franke Wilmer (2000). They have, for the most part, remained "invisible within the discourse conducted by men."

THEORIZING ABOUT THEORY

To understand our changing world and to make reasonable prognoses about the future, we must begin by arming ourselves with an array of information and conceptual tools, entertain rival interpretations of world politics in the global marketplace of ideas, and question the assumptions on which these contending worldviews rest. Because there are a great (and growing) number of alternative, and sometimes incompatible, ways of organizing theoretical inquiry about world politics, the challenge of capturing the world's political problems cannot be reduced to any one simple yet compelling account (Chernoff 2008). Each paradigmatic effort to do so in the past has ultimately lost advocates as developments in world affairs eroded its continuing relevance.

Although grand theories fade with the passage of time, they often regain their attractiveness when global transformations make them useful once again. In fact, world politics is so resistant to clear, comprehensive, and convincing analysis that some advocates of so-called **deconstructivism** contend that international change and complexity defy description, explanation, and prediction. Deconstructionists share the philosophical view that all peoples' conceptions of global realities are relative to their understandings. Thus, biased interpretation is inevitable and "objectivity" a myth, so that the validity of all conceptions is dependent on one's own personal point of view (any interpretation is as valid as any other), and there is no point in attempting to develop a shared conception of the world. At the extreme, the nihilistic

■ **deconstructivism**
the postmodern theory that the complexity of the world system renders precise description impossible and that the purpose of scholarship is to understand actors' hidden motives by deconstructing their textual statements.

History cannot be seen, just as one cannot see grass growing.

—Boris Pasternak, Russian author

advocates of deconstructivism maintain that theories of international relations grounded in behavioral science to understand or discover objective truths about the world are meaningless creations of the methods on which they are built (see Controversy: Can Behavioral Science Advance the Study of International Relations?). "Perspectivism," or the claim that any account of international reality can be only given from personal perspectives, rejects the application of reason to interpret evidence because no "facts" can be taken as really true (Behe 2005).

CONTROVERSY:

CAN BEHAVIORAL SCIENCE ADVANCE THE STUDY OF INTERNATIONAL RELATIONS?

How should scholars construct theories to interpret international behavior? The answer to that question has never been satisfactorily resolved, and the long-standing debate about how best to construct theories of international relations continues today. Some scholars, known as advocates of "postmodern deconstructivism," challenge the ability of intellectuals to provide a satisfactory theoretical account of why states and people act as they do in international relations. These scholars devote their efforts to criticizing and "deconstructing" the theories of world politics to expose their inherent limitations.

Most scholars remain motivated by the theoretical quest to interpret and comprehend the complexities of international relations, and they challenge the pessimistic view that world politics defies meaningful understanding, despite the obstacles and limits to knowledge. What do you think? Is the scientific analysis of patterns of international relations a reasonable undertaking? Or, as deconstructionists argue, are explanations of international relations impossible? In formulating your opinion, take into consideration the progression of this intellectual debate over the past six decades.

This evolving epistemological controversy took an important step in the 1960s and early 1970s when dissatisfaction with realism's shortcomings intensified and a movement known as **behavioralism** arose to challenge realism and liberalism, which the behavioralists called "traditionalism," as well as other speculative interpretations of international relations not based on systematic evidence. Behavioralism was not a new theory of international relations so much as a new method of studying it, based largely on the application of scientific methods to the study of global affairs (Knorr and Rosenau 1969; Knorr and Verba 1961).

Behavioralism advances principles and procedures for formulating and stringently testing **hypotheses** inferred from theories to reach generalizations or statements about international regularities that hold true across time and place. Science, the behavioralists claim, is primarily a generalizing activity. From this perspective—a view consistent with that of many "traditional" realists and liberals—a theory of international relations should state the relationship between two or more variables that specifies the conditions under which the relationship(s) hold and explain why the relationship(s) should hold. To uncover such theories, behavioralists lean toward using comparative cross-national analyses rather than case studies of particular countries at particular times. Behavioralists also stress the need for data about the characteristics of transnational actors and how they behave toward one another. Hence, the behavioral movement encourages the comparative and quantitative study of international relations (see, for example, Rosenau 1980; Singer 1968).

What makes behavioralism innovative is its attitude toward the purposes of inquiry: replacing subjective beliefs with verifiable knowledge, supplanting impressions with testable evidence, and substituting data and reproducible information for mere opinion or the assertions of politicians claiming to be authorities. Behavioralism is predicated on the belief that the pursuit of knowledge about the world through systematic analytic methodologies is possible and productive. The behavioral research agenda is based on the conviction that, although laws of international behavior cannot be proven outside the approach used to uncover them, Albert Einstein was correct in arguing that there exists a world independent of our minds, and that this world is rationally organized and open to human understanding (Holt 2005). In this sense, behavioralists embrace liberalism's "high regard for modern science" and its "attacks against superstition and authority" (J. Hall 2001). In place of the self-proclaimed and often mistaken opinions of "experts" (Tetlock 2006), behavioral scientists seek to acquire knowledge cumulatively by suspending judgments about truths or values until they have sufficient evidence to support them. They attempt to overcome the tendency of traditional inquiry to select facts and cases to fit preexisting hunches. Instead, *all* available data, those which contradict as well as those which support existing theoretical hypotheses, are to be examined. Knowledge, they argue, would advance best by theorists assuming a cautious, skeptical attitude toward any empirical statement. The slogans "Let the data, not the armchair theorist, speak," and "Seek evidence, but distrust it" represent the behavioral posture toward the acquisition of knowledge.

The vast majority of scholars reject this defeatist deconstructivist posture to understanding and continue to struggle in the pursuit of theory and knowledge about international affairs. However, because no single general-purpose theory exists that is able to account for all questions regarding international relations, a number of scholars have returned to reconsider the basic questions of **epistemology** that are fundamental to evaluating the relative value and validity of rival theoretical frameworks (see Agnew 2007). How do we know what to believe? What principles of analysis can lead us to recognize the strengths and weaknesses of various theories?

■ **behavioralism**
the methodological research movement to incorporate rigorous scientific analysis into the study of world politics so that conclusions about patterns are based on measurement, data, and evidence rather than on speculation and subjective belief.

> *Thinkers who ponder the meaning of global events often speak of some kind of big social process being at work—a revolution or a wave of change or the emergence of something new—but what is really going on remains a mystery. Where are all these changes leading? What do they mean?*
>
> —Edward Cornish, futurist

How do we separate fact from fiction and sense from nonsense? What is the relative descriptive accuracy and explanatory power of different theories, and how much confidence should be placed in their explanations of world politics? As you review various theoretical interpretations of global circumstances, it is important to evaluate the premises on which each contending account is based.

■ **hypotheses**
speculative statements about the probable relationship between independent variables (the presumed causes) and a dependent variable (the effect).

INTERNATIONAL THEORY AND THE GLOBAL FUTURE

As you seek to understand changing global conditions, it is important to be humble in recognizing the limitations of our understandings of world politics and at the same time inquisitive about its character. The task of interpretation is complicated because the world is itself complex. Donald Puchala theoretically framed the challenge in 2008 by observing:

■ **epistemology**
the philosophical examination of the ways in which knowledge is acquired and the analytic principles governing the study of phenomena.

> Conceptually speaking, world affairs today can be likened to a disassembled jigsaw puzzle scattered on a table before us. Each piece shows a fragment of a broad picture that as yet remains indiscernible. Some pieces depict resurgent nationalism; others show spreading democracy; some picture genocide; others portray prosperity through trade and investment; some picture nuclear disarmament; others picture nuclear proliferation; some indicate a reinvigorated United Nations; others show the UN still enfeebled and ineffective; some describe cultural globalization; others predict clashing civilizations.
>
> How do these pieces fit together, and what picture do they exhibit when they are appropriately fitted?

All theories are maps of possible futures. Theories can guide us in fitting the pieces together to form an accurate picture. However, in evaluating the usefulness of any theory to interpret global conditions, the historical overview in this chapter suggests that it would be wrong to oversimplify or to assume that a particular theory will remain useful in the future. Nonetheless, as the American poet Robert Frost observed, any belief we cling to long enough is likely to be true again someday because "most of the change we think we see in life is due to truths being in and out of favor." So in our theoretical exploration of world politics, we must critically assess the accuracy of our impressions, avoiding the temptation to embrace one worldview and abandon another without any assurance that their relative worth is permanently fixed.

Although realism, liberalism, and constructivism are the dominant ways of thinking about world politics today, none of these theories is completely satisfactory. Recall that realism is frequently criticized for relying on ambiguous concepts, liberalism is often derided for making naïve policy recommendations based on idealistic assumptions, and constructivism is charged with an inability to explain change. Moreover, as the challenges mounted by radicalism and feminism suggest, these three mainstream theories overlook seemingly important aspects of world politics, which limits their explanatory power. Despite these drawbacks, each has strengths for interpreting certain kinds of international events and foreign policy behaviors.

When I was working in Washington and helping formulate American foreign policies, I found myself borrowing from all three types of thinking: realism, liberalism, and constructivism. I found them all helpful, though in different ways and in different circumstances.

—Joseph S. Nye, international relations scholar and U.S. policy maker

Because we lack a single overarching theory able to account for all facets of world politics, we will draw on realist, liberal, and constructivist thought in subsequent chapters. Moreover, we will supplement them with insights from radicalism and feminism, where these theoretical traditions can best help to interpret the topic covered.

| *Key Terms* |

theory	zero-sum	consequentialism
paradigm	collective security	constructivist theory
realism	transnational relations	norms
power	complex interdependence	dependency theory
self-help	international regime	world-system theory
relative gains	neoliberism	feminist theory
national interest	absolute gains	deconstructivism
balance of power	regimes	behavioralism
neorealism	low politics	hypotheses
liberalism	high politics	epistemology

CHAPTER 3
INTERNATIONAL DECISION MAKING

Decisions and actions in the international arena can be understood, predicted, and manipulated only in so far as the factors influencing the decision can be identified and isolated.

—Arnold Wolfers, political scientist

"How Are Foreign Policy Decisions Reached?" That was the question put to former U.S. Secretary of State Henry A. Kissinger in an interview with one of your text's authors, Charles Kegley. Kissinger has observed that "Much of the anguish of foreign policy results from the need to establish priorities among competing, sometimes conflicting, necessities."

Y ou have completed your higher education degrees in international studies. Next, you have embarked on your career. Your employment steps allowed you to apply your acquired knowledge to help make the world a better place. As a result of your wise and efficient use of your analytic capabilities in your work with the World Health Organization (WHO), you now find that you have earned a very important appointment: to head and lead an established nongovernmental organization (NGO) in your area of expertise. In that role, you are expected to construct your NGO's *foreign policy*. Your challenge is to make decisions, based on your organization's values, about the foreign policy goals your NGO should pursue as well as the means by which those international goals might best be realized.

Congratulations! You have unprecedented power. Now your task is to make critical choices that are destined to determine whether or not your foreign policies will succeed. How are you, as a governing authority of a transnational *actor* on the world stage, to make decisions that will best serve your organization's interest and the world at large?

As an international decision maker, your approach will partly depend on your preferences and priorities. But there is no sure path as to how to make foreign policy decisions that are workable, moral, and successful. You will face many obstacles and constraints on your ability to make informed choices. As a former U.S. Secretary of State, Henry Kissinger, warns, foreign policy decisions are rarely made by people having all the facts: "Usually decisions are made in a very brief time with enormous pressure and uncertain knowledge." What is more, any choice you might make is certain to carry with it costs that compromise some values you hold dear and undermine some of the other goals you would like to pursue. So you now face the kind of challenge that throughout history has befuddled every decision maker who has had the power to make foreign policy decisions on behalf of the transnational actor he or she led.

FOREIGN POLICY MAKING IN INTERNATIONAL AFFAIRS

The purpose of this chapter is to introduce you to the lessons that history provides about the patterns, pitfalls, and payoffs that surround alternative approaches for making international decisions. This introduction opens a window to rival ways of describing the processes by which transnational actors make foreign policy decisions.

Transnational Actors and Decision Processes

The chapter, which is derived from historical experience and *theories* of *international relations* that scholarship has constructed about this topic, will look at patterns of international decision making by all transnational actors—the individuals, groups, states, and organizations that play a role in world politics. Thus, it will cover not only countries (for example, Japan) but also take into view at the same time the decision making practices of international organizations such as the Nordic Council; nongovernmental organizations or NGOs such as the World Wildlife Federation; multinational corporations such as Wal-Mart; indigenous nationalities such as Kurds in Iran, Iraq, and Turkey; and terrorist networks such as Al Qaeda. In addition, it is important to reflect on how each and every one of us—all individual people—are part of the equation because we are all in a sense a transnational actor capable of making free choices that contribute in countless ways to the direction of trends in world politics. When mobilized and inspired by a sense of agency, individuals can make a difference in the course of world history; indeed, the decisions that we make every day and the groups that we join are reflections of our own personal "foreign policy," whether or not we are aware of the consequences of our daily choices. Every person matters. As the American anthropologist Margaret Mead advised, "Never doubt that a small group of thoughtful, committed citizens can change the world. Indeed, it is the only thing that ever has."

To stimulate your thinking about international decision making by all types of transnational actors, *World Politics* provides a framework for analyzing and explaining the processes by which foreign policies are made.

Influences on the Making of Foreign Policy Decisions

To structure theoretical thinking about international decision making, it is useful to think in terms of the factors or causes that influence the ways in which foreign policy decisions are made by all transnational actors. What variables or causal influences impact foreign policy decision making?

For starters, it would be an error to assume that international decisions and behaviors are influenced solely by the choices of global leaders. This kind of single factor explanation will not work because no decision maker (not even the most authoritarian in a dictatorship) can act alone in terms of his or her whims and fancies. The leaders of all groups are constrained by various pressures and circumstances that restrict free choices. Speaking on the making of American foreign policy decisions, former U.S. Secretary of State Henry Kissinger pointed out that "One of the most unsettling things for foreigners is the impression that our foreign policy can be changed by any new president on the basis of the president's personal preference." "To some extent," former U.S. presidential adviser Joseph A. Califano said, "a president is a prisoner of historical forces that will demand his attention whatever his preference in policy objectives."

So to cut into the question of how international decision making unfolds, we must go beyond a single factor explanation and think in terms of multiple causes.

For that, it is useful to identify the various clusters of variables that exert an influence on the choices that all types of transnational actors make when they seek to formulate a foreign policy to foster desired relations with another transnational actor or to take a position toward a particular global issue (recall the distinctions among *foreign policy*, *international relations*, and *international politics* as described in Chapter 1). No single category of causation can fully explain foreign policy decisions; rather, a number converge to codetermine the decisions that produce foreign policy "outputs." Like the *level-of-analysis* distinction introduced in Chapter 1 (see Figure 1.2), so, too, can we construct an image of the determinants of international decision making in the foreign policy making process by reference to three major sets of causal variables that impact the policy making process on international decision making. These are the (1) global conditions that prevail at the time of decision, (2) the internal characteristics of the transnational actor making foreign policy choices, and (3) the leaders who head the transnational actor making the decision.

This framework groups the factors that shape international decision making into three broad categories. The three-part organization for inquiry encourages you to think in causal terms about classes of phenomena that explain why particular decisions are made. Each category encompasses a large number of factors, which, together with the influences grouped in the other two categories, tell you what to observe when you construct an explanation as to why a particular decision by a particular transnational actor was taken.

Each of the three categories of influences are connected to each other, in an increasingly larger set of factors that define the sources of foreign policy choices (see "inputs" on the left in Figure 3.1). The characteristics of the *leaders* of transnational actors making decisions are always important, because their individual values, personalities, beliefs, intelligence, and prior experiences can always be assumed to not only define the kind of people they are but also to predispose them to take certain kinds of positions on global issues. That said, the range of choice is also heavily constrained by the *internal characteristics* of the transnational actor the individual decision maker leads. How unified is the membership of the actor about foreign policy issues? What are the processes by which foreign policy decisions are made

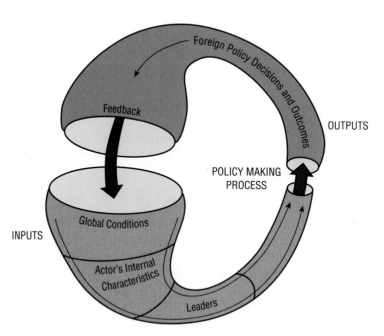

FIGURE 3.1

A "FUNNEL VISION" OF THE INFLUENCES ON INTERNATIONAL DECISION MAKING The determinants or the factors that influence the foreign policy choices of transnational actors are shown here as a "funnel of causality." This construction classifies three categories of influence in the foreign policy making process, whereby policy "inputs" shape the decisions that produce policy "outputs."

within the group? What governing institutions operate to carry out foreign policy decisions? Such factors limit the number of workable options available for foreign policy choice. Moreover, the *global conditions* at the time of decision color both the potency of the influence of the actor's internal attributes and the degree to which leader preferences can account for the choices made. Let's take a closer look at these three categories of causation, beginning with the most comprehensive, global conditions, and working to the most specific, individual leaders.

Global Conditions What is happening in world politics provides the setting for international decision making. The changing state of the world—everything that occurs beyond the actor—affects the decisions of transnational actors. The global circumstances prevailing in effect define the decisional situation, and provoke the need to make decisions (and restrict the actor's freedom to undertake policy initiatives). Take any global trend highlighted in *World Politics* and we can easily visualize how changes in the state of the world condition the issues on the global agenda addressed in international decision making: global warming, nuclear proliferation, the cascading integration of trade fueling interdependent globalization, the AIDS/HIV crisis, rising international terrorism, and civil wars— you name it. All shifts in global circumstances give rise to crucial decisions by transnational actors. As the political scientist George Modelski (1962) observed,

I know of no change in policy, only of circumstances.
—John Quincy Adams, U.S. Secretary of State

"Foreign policy is the system of activities evolved by communities for changing the behavior of other [transnational actors] and for adjusting their own activities to the international environment." That view of changes of global circumstances serving as a catalyst for international decision making was captured by the former U.S. President Richard Nixon when he declared, "The world has changed. Our foreign policy must change with it."

Internal Characteristics As important as the global environment is, it would be mistaken to think it alone is the sole source driving international decision making. Every actor on the global stage is defined by their own attributes, which also act to determine the actor's foreign policy choices.

In the episodic and visual comprehension of our foreign policy, there is serious danger that the larger significance of developments will be lost in a kaleidoscope of unrelated events. Continuities will be obscured, causal factors unidentified.
—George W. Ball, U.S. Under Secretary of State

All transnational actors organized to take action abroad are composed of a collection of individuals. How these group actors are governed, and the processes and procedures they follow to reach foreign policy decisions, are forces on their own that structure and determine the *kinds* of decisions that are reached. The size of the organization, its power relative to the other actors with which it interacts, and the financial resources and the distribution of opinion within the actor all affect the capacity of the actor to make foreign policy choices in response to changes in global circumstances. With respect to states, for example, the rise of "bureaucratic politics" among competing agencies seeking to direct the course of a country's foreign policy now heavily influences the choices that will be made. This is illustrated by former U.S. Under Secretary of State George W. Ball's warning that the nature of the institutional machinery produced the decisions that led to America's failed war in Vietnam: "The process was the author of the policy." Choices about ends and means in foreign policies, therefore, are molded by transformations in international relations *and* by the impact of these global changes on the characteristics of transnational actors.

Actor Leadership   The personal characteristics of the leaders heading transnational actors assume great importance in the making of international decisions. Leaders are influential because "factors external to the actor can become determinants only as they affect the mind, the heart, and the will of the decision maker. A human decision to act in a specific way necessarily represents the last link in the chain of antecedents of any act of policy. A geographical set of conditions, for instance, can affect the behavior of a nation only as specific persons perceive and interpret these conditions" (Wolfers 1962). Thus, changes in global conditions and actors' collective internal characteristics may influence the costs and benefits of particular foreign policy options and stimulate the need for choice. However, these are mediated by leaders' perceptions. As *constructivist theory* argues, ideas and expectations within the heads of leaders are the intellectual filters through which objective realities are interpreted. Therefore, in any explanation of why any international decision is made, it is imperative to take into account how leaders' ideas and images influence the choices taken.

Again inspect this threefold set of influences on international decision making in Figure 3.1. Note that this organization for interpretation is *explanatory*. The framework provides clues as to where to look when asking *why* a foreign policy decision has been reached. Each policy decision can be viewed as the result of the multiple prior causal events taking place in the funnel. Thus, the model stipulates the conditions that precede and promote policy decisions (bearing in mind that frequently it is difficult to distinguish decision making itself from its prior conditions). Policy outcomes depend on the prior conditions in the funnel and are explained by the combined impact of the input factors on the output or outcome (the policy decision).

Observe as well that our framework implies a temporal or time sequence in the transition from inputs to outputs in the foreign policy making process. That is, changes in the determinants of foreign policy occurring at time *t* produce decisions at a later time (*t+1*), which lead to policy outcomes that impact on all the causal factors at a still later time (*t+2*). Moreover, these policy outcomes have consequences for the input factors themselves at a later (*t+3*) time because they exert "feedback" on these causal factors as the foreign policy decisions alter the conditions that influence subsequent (*t+4*) policy making. For example, a cluster of factors at some point in time (*t*) led the United States to make the decision in March 2003 (*t+1*) to invade Iraq (*t+2*), but this decision exerted a painfully negative "feedback" influence on public opinion within America and abroad when that invasion increased the level of international terrorism the invasion was designed to terminate, and this reaction in turn five years later (*t+3*) transformed global conditions as well as attitudes within American society which then began to galvanize revisions (*t+4*, or in 2007) of the original policy decision. Thus, the model advanced here is dynamic. It can be used to account for past policy decisions and behaviors as well as for the effects of those outcomes on later policy decisions. This feature of this way of tracing the determinants and consequences of international decisions provides you the analyst with a lens with which to view and explain theoretically the foreign policy of transnational actors in historical perspective, because the model is not tied analytically to any one time period or actor.

The best way to use the framework is as a guide to developing *hypotheses* about the roots from which a foreign policy decision has been made. Historians often approach such questions by using what is known as **counterfactual reasoning**. "Counter-factuals are essential for prediction, answering 'what if' questions and estimating causal effects" (King and Zeng 2007). This research strategy "poses a series of questions that effectively drop a key variable from the equation and then asks us to speculate about what might have been. Regardless of how we respond to the counterfactual questions, the simple act of posing them facilitates appreciation of the numerous forces shaping foreign policy" (Wittkopf, Jones, and Kegley 2008). Use our framework to frame possible hypothetical answers to questions about *why*

■ **counterfactual reasoning**

speculations about historical events and developments that ask how the world might have changed had certain momentous foreign policy choices not been taken or had other conditions prevailed by inquiring "what would have happened if . . . "

CHOICE AND CONSEQUENCE The Bush administration's March 2003 decision to invade Iraq generated a hostile public reaction on the four-year anniversary of that decision. Shown here on March 17, 2007, are thousands of protestors voicing their rage against the war near the Pentagon, the headquarters and symbol of U.S. military power.

some international decisions were taken and others rejected, and you will have a powerful interpretative tool for analyzing the causes that lead to the decisions that determine the trends in world politics.

With this analytic framework in mind, you are armed intellectually to probe international decision making in greater depth. Or are you? To better inform your analyses of the causes of international decision making, let us inspect three models of decision making formulated by scholars of this topic: rational choice, bureaucratic politics, and the political psychology of leaders and leadership.

DECISION MAKING BY TRANSNATIONAL ACTORS: THREE PROFILES

Realism assumes that foreign policy making consists primarily of adjusting a *transnational actor* to the pressures of an anarchical global system whose essential properties will not vary. Accordingly, it presumes that all decision makers are essentially alike in their approach to foreign policy making:

> If they follow the [decision] rules, we need know nothing more about them. In essence, if the decision maker behaves rationally, the observer, knowing the rules of rationality, can rehearse the decisional process in his own mind, and, if he knows the decision maker's goals, can both predict the decision and understand why that particular decision was made. (Verba 1969, 225)

Because realists believe that leaders' goals and their corresponding approach to foreign policy choices are the same, the decision making processes of each actor can be studied as though each were a **unitary actor**—a homogeneous or monolithic unit with few or no important internal differences that affect its choices. From this assumption can be derived the expectation that transnational actors can and do make decisions by rational calculations of the costs and benefits of different choices.

Decision Making as Rational Choice

The decision making processes of unitary actors that determine national interests are typically described as rational. We define rationality or **rational choice** here as purposeful, goal-directed behavior exhibited when "the individual responding to an international event . . . uses the best information available and chooses from the universe of possible responses that alternative most likely to maximize his [or her] goals" (Verba 1969). Scholars describe rationality as a sequence of decision making activities involving the following intellectual steps:

1   *Problem Recognition and Definition.* The need to decide begins when policy makers perceive an external problem and attempt to define objectively its distinguishing characteristics. Objectivity requires full information about the actions, motivations, and capabilities of other actors as well as the character of the global environment and trends within it. The search for information must be exhaustive, and all the facts relevant to the problem must be gathered.

■ **unitary actor**

a transnational actor (usually a sovereign state) assumed to be internally united, so that changes in its domestic opinion do not influence its foreign policy as much as do the decisions that actor's leaders make to cope with changes in its global environment.

■ **rational choice**

decision making procedures guided by careful definition of situations, weighing of goals, consideration of all alternatives, and selection of the options most likely to achieve the highest goals.

2   *Goal Selection.* Next, those responsible for making foreign policy choices must determine what they want to accomplish. This disarmingly simple requirement is often difficult. It requires the identification and ranking of *all* values (such as security and economic prosperity) in a hierarchy from most to least preferred.

3   *Identification of Alternatives.* Rationality also requires the compilation of an exhaustive list of *all* available policy options and an estimate of the costs associated with each alternative.

4   *Choice.* Finally, rationality requires selecting the single alternative with the best chance of achieving the desired goal(s). For this purpose, policy makers must conduct a rigorous means-ends, cost-benefit analysis guided by an accurate prediction of the probable success of each option.

Policy makers often describe their own behavior as resulting from a rational decision making process designed to reach the "best" decision possible, which employs the logic of *consequentialism* to estimate the results that can be expected from the decision taken.

The quest for rational decision making was illuminated, for example, in the crises that the closed circle of George W. Bush's U.S. advisers faced in September 2001. They claimed that they were faithfully following the rules for rational choice in their declared war against "global terrorism" following 9/11 and in their decision to attack the dictator Saddam Hussein's Iraq. The administration launched a campaign in public diplomacy to persuade all states that it was in their best interest to recognize the danger posed by the high probability that Iraq had illegally obtained weapons of mass destruction, and it took its argument to the UN. The message was clothed in the language of deliberate logical choice to convince skeptics that the costs and benefits of all options had been carefully weighed.

However, like beauty, rationality often lies in the eye of the beholder, and reasonable, clear-thinking people can disagree and often do disagree about the facts and about the wisdom of foreign policy goals. Note that counterarguments against Bush's war plans also were couched in terms of rationality—criticisms that attacked the premises on which Bush's big plans for a major war were based. For example, one Australian observer complained that "unless Bush can mount a more persuasive case that Saddam is uniquely dangerous, Iraq's overthrow by force would send a powerful message that might is right and that the United States alone determines the rules of the game. This would be a repudiation of norms that have governed the conduct of international relations for the past half-century" (Dupont 2002). At home, critics also questioned the rationality of the decision process.

Republican Senator Chuck Hagel in 2002, for instance, worried that Bush failed to address the important questions required of a rational choice: "If we invade Iraq, what allies will we have? Who governs after Saddam? What is the objective? Have we calculated the consequences, particularly the unintended consequences? What does [a war with Iraq] mean for the unfinished work with Afghanistan? For the Israeli-Palestinian conflict? For the tenuous truce between nuclear-armed India and Pakistan? . . . We must recognize there are no easy, risk-free options. . . . Sending young men and women into war should never be taken lightly. Elected leaders should ask tough questions before sending them into a situation that may result in the ultimate sacrifice." To many throughout the world, these critical concerns voiced in March 2002 later proved prophetic, as the cost in lives and money mounted and public support for the U.S. intervention in Iraq declined (despite the dramatic capture of Saddam Hussein and the end of his tyranny).

This debate demonstrated (as constructivism warns) that rationality is a decision-making goal to which all transnational actors aspire but that it is difficult to determine when the criteria for rational choice have been met. This raises the question: What are the barriers to rationality?

Impediments to Rational Choice   Despite the apparent application of rationality in these crises, rational choice is often more an idealized standard than an accurate description of real-world behavior. Theodore Sorenson—one of President Kennedy's closest advisers and a participant in the Cuban missile deliberations—has written not only about the steps that policy makers in the Kennedy administration followed as they sought to follow the process of rational choice but also about how actual decision making often departed from it. He described an eight-step process for policy making that is consistent with the rational model we have described: (1) agreeing on the facts; (2) agreeing on the overall policy objective; (3) precisely defining the problems; (4) canvassing all possible solutions; (5) listing the consequences that flow from each solution; (6) recommending one option; (7) communicating the option selected; and (8) providing for its execution. But he explained how difficult it is to follow these steps, because:

> . . . each step cannot be taken in order. The facts may be in doubt or dispute. Several policies, all good, may conflict. Several means, all bad, may be all that are open. Value judgments may differ. Stated goals may be imprecise. There may be many interpretations of what is right, what is possible, and what is in the national interest. (T. Sorensen 1963, 19–20)

Despite the virtues rational choice promises, the impediments to its realization in foreign policy making are substantial. In fact, **bounded rationality** is typical (Simon 1997; Kahneman 2003).

■ bounded rationality

the concept that decision maker's capacity to choose the best option is often constrained by many human and organizational obstacles.

> *A phenomenon noticeable throughout history regardless of place or period is the pursuit by governments of policies contrary to their own interests.*
> —Barbara Tuchman, diplomatic historian

Some of the barriers that make errors in foreign policy so common are human, deriving from deficiencies in the intelligence, capability, and psychological needs and aspirations of foreign policy decision makers.

> *Once we've perceived a situation and construed it so that it fits one of the patterns we carry in our memory, we've pretty much rigged how we're going to react.*
> —David Brooks, political journalist

Others are organizational, because most decisions require group agreement about the actor's best interests and the wisest course of action. Reaching agreement is not easy, however, as reasonable people with different values often disagree about goals, preferences, and the probable results of alternative options. Thus, the impediments to rational policy making are not to be underestimated.

Scrutiny of the actual process of decision making reveals other hindrances. Available information is often insufficient to recognize emergent problems accurately, resulting in decisions made on the basis of partial information and vague memories. As the U.S. Commander in the Iraq war, General David H. Petraeus, quoted Charles W. Kegley and Eugene Wittkopf (1982) in his 1987 Princeton University Ph.D. dissertation, "Faced with incomplete information about the immediate problem at hand, it is not surprising that decision makers turn to the past for guidance" and rely on historical analogies. Moreover, the available information is often inaccurate because the bureaucratic organizations that political leaders depend upon for advice screen, sort, and rearrange it. Compounding the problem is decision makers' susceptibility to *cognitive dissonance*—they are psychologically prone to block out dissonant, or negative, information and perceptions about their preferred choice and to look instead for information that conforms to their preexisting beliefs to justify their choice. On top of that, they are prone to make decisions on the basis of "first impressions, or intuition, or that amorphous blending of 'what is' with 'what could be' that we call imagination [even though] there is a great body of data suggesting that formal statistical analysis is a much better way of predicting everything . . . than the intuition even of experts" (Brooks 2005; but see also Gladwell 2005, who argues that snap judgments and "rapid cognition can be as good as decisions made cautiously and deliberately"). Those who see themselves as "political experts" are habitually mistaken in their judgments and forecasts (Tetlock 2006), and leaders are prone to place faith in their prior prejudices and to draw false analogies with prior events (Brunk 2008) and to make decisions on emotion (Westen 2007). As so-called "behavioral international relations" research on decision making and **game theory** shows (Mintz 2007), leaders are limited in their capacity to process information and avoid biases; preoccupied with preventing losses, leaders are also prone to "wishful thinking" and "shooting from the hip," which results in frequently making irrational decisions. These intellectual propensities explain why policy makers sometimes pay little heed to warnings and overlook information about dangers, and repeat their past intellectual mistakes.

■ **game theory**
mathematical model of strategic interaction where outcomes are determined not only by a single actor's preferences, but also by the choices of all actors involved.

[It is doubtful that] decision makers hear arguments on the merits and weigh them judiciously before choosing a course of action.
—Daniel Kahneman and Jonathan Renshon, decision making theorists

In addition, determining what goals best serve an actor's interests is difficult, especially in the realm of foreign policy, where risk is high and there is much uncertainty. Decision making often revolves around the difficult task of choosing among values, so that the choice of one option means the sacrifice of others. Furthermore, there is seldom a sufficient basis for confidently making choices, which is why so many decisions seem to produce unintended negative consequences.

A NEW ROLE FOR ROAD-TRIP DIPLOMACY? **U.S. President Barack Obama** has emphasized a willingness to engage in dialogue with leaders of all nations as a key component of his commitment to diplomacy, with a pledge to "personally lead a new chapter of American engagement." Pictured here with Afghan President Hamid Karzai, President Obama views Afghanistan as a top priority in the fight against terrorism.

Xinhua/Landov Media

How can we best choose the maximum alternative rationally, so that we can be certain that we have the best option, until we have considered all the options? Simply put, we cannot, which is why we seldom consider each and every possible choice when making decisions. As an alternative, we irrationally figure **opportunity costs.** "Instead of calculating opportunity cost as the value of the single most attractive foregone alternative, we seem to assemble a negative composite of all the foregone [because] a wider range of slightly inferior options can make it harder to settle for the one you're happy with" (C. Caldwell 2004). People tend to avoid the challenge of searching for options to realize priority goals. This accounts for the tendency for after-the-fact decisions to frequently require later reevaluation. Decision makers are then disappointed to discover that what they thought they wanted was not nearly as valuable as other things they had not even considered.

■ **opportunity costs**

the kinds of sacrifices that sometimes result when the decision to select one option means that the opportunity to realize gains from other options is lost.

> *Being a good decision maker means you're good at making decisions, but it doesn't mean you make good decisions.*
>
> —Christopher Caldwell, political journalist

■ **externalities**

the negative side effects that result from choices, such as inflation resulting from runaway government spending.

There seldom exists a confident basis for making foreign policy decisions. Alongside uncertainty, many decisions tend to produce negative unintended consequences—what economists call **externalities.** Furthermore, decision makers' inability to rapidly gather and digest large quantities of information constrains their capacity to make informed choices. Because policy makers work with an overloaded **policy agenda** and short deadlines, the search for policy options is seldom exhaustive. "There is little time for leaders to reflect," observed Henry Kissinger (1979). "They are locked in an endless battle in which the urgent constantly gains on the important. The public life of every political figure is a continual struggle to rescue an element of choice from the pressure of circumstance." In the choice phase, then, decision makers rarely make value-maximizing choices. Instead of selecting the option with the best chance of success, they typically end their evaluation as soon as an alternative appears that seems superior to those already considered. Herbert Simon (1957) describes this as **satisficing** behavior. Rather than "optimizing" by seeking the best alternative, decision makers are routinely content to choose the first option that meets minimally acceptable standards. Because they frequently face such difficult decisions where it is not possible to make a choice without compromising competing preferences, they often select an option that appears "good enough"—costs and benefits are not carefully calculated. In short, decision makers are prone to rapidly estimate whether rival options are good or bad, react to these hastily constructed classifications, and then are content to settle with the relatively good alternative as opposed to the best.

Studies from psychology and economics have furthered our understanding of the decision making process. These fields conduct experiments in behavioral science (remember Chapter 2) to discover how people perceive and misperceive risks when making choices under conditions of uncertainty. Daniel Kahneman (2003), who won the 2002 Nobel Prize in economics, and Amos Tversky demonstrated that decision makers usually do not behave rationally, contrary to conventional wisdom. Moreover, there are consistent and predictable biases in the way that people depart from rational decision making. Providing a core contribution to **prospect theory**, they posited that the way in which people perceive alternatives is shaped by their sense of potential gains and losses—individuals are risk adverse when in a position of gains, but risk acceptant when in a situation of loss. Indeed, "evidence suggests that individuals value losses twice as much as they value gains" (Elms 2008, 245). One implication for decision making is that people tend to gravitate toward the "status quo." Like people everywhere, leaders tend to overvalue certainty and "peace of mind," even to their detriment. They don't calculate the consequence of choices, and are more concerned with the potential losses that may result from a change than with the potential gains. This problematic outcome is compounded by another common decision making error—the tendency to myopically frame decisions by focusing on short-term choices rather than long-term ones (Elms 2008).

Another implication of prospect theory is that when leaders take risks to initiate bold new foreign policy directions, they will have great difficulty admitting and correcting those choices if they later prove mistaken (Bostdorff 1993). As critics lament of George W. Bush's refusal to acknowledge decision making failures regarding the Iraq war (Draper 2008; Goldsmith 2008), leaders are prone to cling to failed policies long after their deficiencies have become apparent.

The dilemma, of course, is that "if people can't be trusted to make the right choices for themselves how can they possibly be trusted to make the right decisions for the rest of us?" (Kolbert 2008). Yet while decision making that departs from rationality can be problematic, irrationality can still produce "good" decisions. Along these lines, experimental literature indicates that people tend to incorporate a sense of fairness into their decision making even if it is contrary to their own rational self-interest. As economic behaviorist Dan Ariely's (2008) work demonstrates, "People, it turns out, want to be generous and they want to retain their dignity—even when it doesn't really make sense" (Kolbert 2008, 79).

■ policy agenda

the changing list of problems or issues to which governments pay special attention at any given moment.

■ satisficing

the tendency for decision makers to choose the first satisfactory option rather than searching further for a better alternative.

■ prospect theory

the social psychological theory that international decision making is constrained by formed opinions and tendencies to overreact in crises, that decisions tend to be made based on the perceived prospects of choices to fulfill objectives, and that for policy makers, a crucial consideration in taking risks is the perceived prospects for avoiding losses and realizing big gains.

■ two-level games

a concept referring to the growing need for national policy makers to make decisions that will meet both domestic and foreign goals.

To better capture the way most leaders make policy decisions, Robert Putnam coined the phrase **two-level games.** Challenging the assumptions of realism, he asserted that leaders should formulate policies simultaneously in both the diplomatic and domestic arenas and should make those choices in accordance with the rules dictated by the "game."

> At the national level, domestic groups pursue their interests by pressuring the government to adopt favorable policies, and politicians seek power by constructing coalitions among these groups. At the international level, national governments seek to maximize their own ability to satisfy domestic pressures, while minimizing the adverse consequences of foreign developments. Neither of the two games can be ignored by central decision makers so long as their countries remain interdependent, yet sovereign (Putnam 1988, 434).

Most leaders must meet the often incompatible demands of internal politics and external diplomacy, and it is seldom possible to make policy decisions that respond rationally to both sets of goals. Policies at home often have many consequences abroad. Foreign activities usually heavily influence an actor's internal condition. This is why many leaders are likely to fuse the two sectors in contemplating policy decisions.

■ muddling through

the tendency for leaders to make foreign policy decisions by trial-and-error adjustments in an attempt to cope with challenges.

States are administered by individuals with varying beliefs, values, preferences, and psychological needs, and such differences generate disagreements about goals and alternatives that are seldom resolved through orderly, rational processes. These procedures may be better described as **muddling through**, or making incremental policy changes through small steps (Lindblom 1979). As one former U.S. policy maker put it, "Rather than through grand decisions or grand alternatives, policy changes seem to come through a series of slight modifications of existing policy, with new policy emerging slowly and haltingly by small and usually tentative steps, a process of trial and error in which policy zigs and zags, reverses itself, and then moves forward" (Hilsman 1967).

Despite the image that policy makers seek to project, often the degree of rationality "bears little relationship to the world in which officials conduct their deliberations" (Rosenau 1980). Indeed, *constructivism* advances a concept of decision makers as those individuals greatly shaped by the socially accepted shared understandings within their own policy making community and culture, and, furthermore, that these dominating ideas inevitably reduce their capacity to make fully rational choices.

Although rational foreign policy making is more an ideal than a reality, we can still assume that policy makers aspire to rational decision making behavior, which they may occasionally approximate. Indeed, as a working proposition, it is useful to accept rationality as a picture of how the decision process *should* work as well as a description of key elements of how it *does* work (see Table 3.1).

Table 3.1   Foreign Policy Decision Making in Theory and Practice

Ideal Rational Process	Actual Common Practice
Accurate, comprehensive information	Distorted, incomplete information
Clear definition of national interests	Personal motivations and organizational interests shape choices about national goals
Exhaustive analysis of all options	Limited number of options considered; none thoroughly analyzed
Selection of optimal course of action for producing desired results	Courses of action selected by political bargaining and compromise
Effective statement of decision and its rationale to mobilize domestic support	Confusing and contradictory statements of decision, often framed for media consumption
Careful monitoring of the decision's implementation by foreign affairs bureaucracies	Neglect of the tedious task of managing the decision's implementation by foreign affairs bureaucracies
Instantaneous evaluation of consequences followed by correction of errors	Superficial policy evaluation, uncertain responsibility, poor follow-through, and delayed correction

The Bureaucratic Politics of Foreign Policy Decision Making

To make the right choices, leaders must seek information and advice, and must see that the actions their decisions generate are carried out properly. Who can assist in these tasks? Out of necessity, leaders must turn to those with the expertise they lack.

In today's world, leaders must depend on large-scale organizations for information and advice as they face critical foreign policy choices. Even transnational actors without large budgets and complex foreign policy bureaucracies seldom make decisions without the advice and assistance of many individuals and administrative agencies to cope with changing global circumstances.

Bureaucratic Efficiency and Rationality   Bureaucracies, according to the theoretical work of the German social scientist Max Weber, are widely believed to increase efficiency and rationality by assigning responsibility for different tasks to different people. They define rules and standard operating procedures that specify how tasks are to be performed; they rely on record systems to gather and store information; they divide authority among different organizations to avoid duplication of effort; and they often lead to meritocracies by hiring and promoting the most capable individuals. Bureaucracies also permit the luxury of engaging in forward planning to

■ **bureaucracies**
the agencies and departments that conduct the functions of a central government or of a nonstate transitional actor.

determine long-term needs and the means to attain them. Unlike leaders, whose roles require attention to the crisis of the moment, bureaucrats are able to consider the future as well as the present. The presence of several organizations also can result in **multiple advocacy** of rival choices (George 1972), thus improving the chance that all possible policy options will be considered.

■ multiple advocacy

the concept that better and more rational choices are made when decisions are reached in a group context, which allows advocates of differing alternatives to be heard so that the feasibility of rival options receives critical evaluation.

The Limits of Bureaucratic Organization What emerges from our description of bureaucracy is another idealized picture of the policy making process. Before jumping to the conclusion that bureaucratic decision making is a modern blessing, however, we should emphasize that the foregoing propositions tell us how bureaucratic decision making *should* occur; they do not tell us how it *does* occur. The actual practice and the foreign policy choices that result show that bureaucracy produces burdens as well as benefits.

Consider the 1962 Cuban Missile Crisis, probably the single most threatening crisis in the post–World War II era. The method that U.S. policy makers used in orchestrating a response is often viewed as having nearly approximated the ideal of rational choice. From another decision making perspective, however, the missile crisis reveals how decision making by and within organizational contexts sometimes compromises rather than facilitates rational choice.

■ bureaucratic politics model

a description of decision making that sees foreign policy choices as based on bargaining and compromises among competing government agencies.

In Graham Allison's well-known book on the missile crisis, *Essence of Decision* (1971), he advanced what is widely known as the **bureaucratic politics model** (see also Allison and Zelikow 1999; D. Caldwell 1977; C. Hermann 1988). This model of decision making highlights the constraints that organizations and coalitions of organizations in **policy networks** place on decision makers' choices and the "pulling and hauling" that occurs among the key participants and **caucuses** of aligned bureaucracies in the decision process.

The bureaucratic politics model emphasizes how large-scale bureaucratic organizations contribute to the policy making process by devising **standard operating procedures (SOPS)**—established methods to be followed in the performance of designated tasks. Not surprisingly, participants in the deliberations that lead to policy choices also often define issues and favor policy alternatives that serve their organization's needs. "Where you stand depends on where you sit" is a favorite aphorism reflecting these bureaucratic imperatives. Consider why professional diplomats typically favor diplomatic approaches to policy problems, whereas military officers routinely favor military solutions.

■ policy networks

leaders and organized interests (such as lobbies) that form temporary alliances to influence a particular foreign policy decision.

The consequence is that "different groups pulling in different directions produce a result, or better a resultant—a mixture of conflicting preferences and unequal power of various individuals—distinct from what any person or group intended" (Allison 1971). Rather than being a value-maximizing process, then, policy making is itself an intensely competitive game of *politics*. Rather than presupposing the existence of a *unitary actor*, "bureaucratic politics" shows why "it is necessary to identify the games and players, to display the coalitions, bargains, and compromises, and to convey some feel for the confusion" (Allison 1971).

Fighting among insiders and the formation of factions to carry on battles over the direction of foreign policy decisions are chronic in nearly every transnational actor's administration (but especially in democratic actors' accepting of participation by many people in the policy making process). Consider the United States. Splits among key advisers over important foreign policy choices have been frequent. For example, under Presidents Nixon and Ford, Secretary of State Henry Kissinger fought often with James Schlesinger and Donald Rumsfeld, who headed the Department of Defense, over strategy regarding the Vietnam War; Jimmy Carter's national security adviser, Zbigniew Brzezinski, repeatedly engaged in conflicts with Secretary of State Cyrus Vance over the Iran hostage crisis; and under Ronald Reagan, Caspar Weinberger at Defense and George Shultz at State were famous for butting heads on most policy issues. Such conflicts are not necessarily bad because they force each side to better explain its viewpoint, and this allows heads of state the opportunity to weigh their competing advice before making decisions. However, battles among advisers can lead to paralysis and to rash decisions that produce poor results. That possibility became evident in the fall of 2002, when serious divisions within George W. Bush's own administration developed over how and why the president's goal was to wage war against Saddam Hussein in Iraq. Fissures became transparent as key officials publicly debated the wisdom of continuing the current policy of containment through diplomacy versus invasion, and then moved abruptly forward to consider how best to conduct the invasion.

In addition to their influence on the policy choices of political leaders, bureaucratic organizations possess several other characteristics that affect decision making. One view proposes that bureaucratic agencies are parochial and that every administrative unit within a transnational actor's foreign policy making bureaucracy seeks to promote its own purposes and power. Organizational needs, such as large staffs and budgets, come before the actor's needs, sometimes encouraging the sacrifice of group interests to bureaucratic interests, as bureaucrats come to see their own interests as the same as the group's.

The growth and thickening of bureaucratic government is associated with competition among the growing number of overlapping agencies charged with foreign policy responsibilities. Far from being neutral or impartial managers, desiring only to carry out orders from the leaders, bureaucratic organizations frequently take policy positions designed to increase their own influence relative to that of other agencies. Characteristically, they are driven to enlarge their prerogatives and expand the conception of their mission, seeking to take on other units' responsibilities and powers.

The tragic surprise terrorist attack on September 11, 2001, provides a telling example of these ascribed characteristics of bureaucratic politics. The attacks on 9/11 were regarded by many as the worst intelligence failure since Pearl Harbor. Alarmed U.S. citizens asked why, with an enormous army of agencies gathering intelligence, weren't the multitude of messages and warnings about the attack on the World Trade Center and the Pentagon translated in time to prevent the disaster? Why weren't those dots connected? Why were the warnings ignored?

The answer at first accepted by most analysts was that America's chaotic system of intelligence was paralyzed by the morass of cross-cutting bureaucracies responsible. They engaged in turf battles with one another and did not share the vital information that arguably could have identified the Al Qaeda plot and prevented it. The problem was miscommunication and noncommunication; the signals about the attack were not forwarded to the executive branch in time. Why? Morton Abramowitz (2002), a

■ caucuses
informal groups that individuals in governments and other groups join to promote their common interests.

■ standard operating procedures (SOPS)
rules for reaching decisions about particular types of situations.

former Assistant Secretary of State in the Reagan administration, voiced his explanation when he wrote "Three features pervade the making of foreign policy in Washington today: massive overload, internal warfare, and the short term driving out the long term. These problems exist in every administration [but they have become worse in George W. Bush's where internal battles have been] fought daily in the high-level bureaucratic trenches and ideology has been much in play."

As the horror of 9/11 persisted, so did interest in and concern about what became a key issue in the 2004 presidential campaign: Who did what before September 11, 2001, to disrupt the Al Qaeda terrorist network operation? A congressional bipartisan commission was created to investigate what had gone wrong, in order to make needed corrections in the way the U.S. government makes decisions for national security and counterterrorism. The 9/11 Commission (2004) produced a new set of explanations for why so many opportunities to head off the 9/11 disaster were missed.

The Commission did not center blame on the inadequacies and infighting of the country's "alphabet soup" of agencies fighting terror, such as the CIA and FBI. Instead, the commission pointed its criticism at the growing complaints (J. Mann 2004; Woodward 2004) about the inaction of the Bush administration and on the White House's pre–9/11 downplaying or ignoring of the loud and clear warnings submitted by U.S. intelligence bureaucracies of the true, imminent dangers of a likely terrorist attack. In this case, the failure of the U.S. government to protect its citizens might have been more due to the unwillingness of American leadership to listen to the warnings of its national security bureaucracies than to the crippling effects of bureaucratic struggles.

Still, consider the problems faced by every U.S. president who must seek to manage hundreds of competing agencies and subagencies, each of which are habitually loath to share information with one another for fear of compromising "sources and methods." Each agency competes with its rivals and engages in finger-pointing and scapegoating as a blood sport. Moreover, as FBI Special Agent Coleen Rowley testified, "There's a mutual-protection pact in bureaucracies. Mid-level managers avoid decisions out of fear a mistake will sidetrack their careers while a rigid

> *Ninety-nine percent of failures come from people who have the habit of making excuses.*
> —George Washington Carver, African-American botanist

■ **groupthink**
the propensity for members of a group to accept and agree with the group's prevailing attitudes, rather than speaking out for what they believe.

hierarchy discourages agents from challenging superiors. There is a saying: 'Big cases, big problems; little cases, little problems; no cases, no problems.' The idea that inaction is the key to success manifests itself repeatedly" (Toner 2002).

We can discern still another property of bureaucratic politics: the natural inclination of professionals who work in large organizations is to adapt their outlook and beliefs to those prevailing where they work. As *constructivist theory* explains, every bureaucracy develops a shared mind-set, or dominant way of looking at reality, akin to the **groupthink** characteristic that small groups often develop (Janis 1982). Groupthink is often also cited by scholars as a process governing policy decision making that leads to riskier choices and more extreme policies (that ultimately fail miserably) than likely would have been made by individuals without the pressures in peer groups. An institutional mind-set, or socially constructed consensus, also discourages creativity, dissent, and independent thinking: it encourages reliance on standard operating procedures and deference to precedent rather than the exploration of new options to meet new challenges. This results in policy decisions that rarely deviate from conventional preferences.

This accounts for why "organizational routines favor continuity over change because information is processed in certain ways and certain sources of information are privileged" (Garrison 2007). These propensities in bureaucratic decision making suggest why "social scientists have in an increasing degree considered indifference and not rationality as the hallmark of bureaucracy" (Neumann 2007).

In your future employment, you are likely to directly observe the efforts of your employer to make rational decisions. You also are bound to notice firsthand within your organization both the advantages of bureaucratic administration and its liabilities. Many students before you have entered the workforce and found that the payoffs of rational choice and the pitfalls of bureaucratic politics surrounding actual practice described here were *not* figments of scholars' imagination. Rather, these properties and propensities of decision making speak to the real experiences of professionals who have entered into policy making

Jae C. Hong/AP Photo

COLLECTIVE DECISION MAKING Policy decisions are often made in small groups. Pictured here is Barack Obama with a group of his economic advisors in Washington in July 2008 discussing the problems with the U.S. economy, which have global implications in terms of both cause and consequence. From left are former Treasury Secretary Paul O'Neill; AFL-CIO President John Sweeney, former Federal Reserve Board Chairman Paul Volker, Obama, Service Employees International Union Chair Anna Burger, former Treasury Secretary Robert Rubin and New Jersey Governor Jon Corzine.

positions. (Many a student reader of previous editions of *World Politics* has later reported that these interpretations prepared them well for what they encountered later in their careers and helped them overcome some naïve expectations that governments, and nonstate actors, stand united, when most of the effort *within* them centers on debate and dispute among participating factions within their decision making unit.) And keep in mind that Harvard University's John F. Kennedy School of Government bases its entire curriculum on the conviction that the essence of national and international service requires awareness of interagency bureaucratic bargaining and the contribution and impediments that competition makes to rational decision making.

The Leverage and Impact of Leaders

The course of history is determined by the decisions of political elites. Leaders and the kind of leadership they exert shape the way in which foreign policies are made and the consequent behavior of the actors in world politics. "There is properly no history, only biography" is how Ralph Waldo Emerson encapsulated the view that individual leaders move history.

Leaders as Movers of World History
This **history-making individuals model** of policy decision making perceives world leaders as the people whose initiatives create global changes. We expect leaders to lead, and we assume new leaders will make a difference. We reinforce this image when we routinely attach the names of leaders to policies—as though the leaders were synonymous with major international developments—as well as when we ascribe most successes and failures in foreign affairs to the leaders in charge at the time they occurred. The equation of U.S. foreign policy with the **Bush Doctrine** in the 2000s is a recent example.

Citizens are not alone in thinking that leaders are the decisive determinants of states' foreign policies and, by extension, world history. Leaders themselves seek to create impressions of their own self-importance while attributing extraordinary powers to other leaders. The assumptions they make about the personalities of their counterparts, consciously or unconsciously, in turn influence their own behavior (Wendzel 1980), as political psychologists who study the impact of leaders' perceptions and personalities on their foreign policy preferences demonstrate (see, for example, the journal *Political Psychology*). Moreover, leaders react differently to the positions they occupy. All are influenced by the **roles** or expectations that by law and tradition steer the decision maker to behave in conformity with prevailing expectations about how the role is to be performed. Most people submissively act in accordance with the customary rules that define the positions they hold, behaving as their predecessors tended to behave when they held the same position. Others, however, are by personality or preference more bold and ambitious, and they seek to decisively escape the confines of their new role by redefining how it will be performed.

One of the difficulties of leader-driven explanations of international decision making is that history's movers and shakers often pursue decidedly irrational policies. The classic example is Adolf Hitler, whose ruthless determination to seek military conquest of the entire European continent proved disastrous for Germany. How do

■ history-making individuals model
an interpretation that sees foreign policy decisions that affect the course of history as products of strong-willed leaders acting on their personal convictions.

■ Bush Doctrine
the unilateral policies of the George W. Bush administration proclaiming that the United States will make decisions only to meet America's perceived national interests, not to concede to other countries' complaints or to gain their acceptance.

■ roles
the constraints written into law or custom that predispose decision makers in a particular governmental position to act in a manner and style that is consistent with expectations about how the role is normally performed.

we square this kind of behavior with the logic of realism? That theory says that survival is the paramount goal of all states and that all leaders engage in rational calculations that advance their countries' aspirations for self-advantage. But this theory can't account for the times when the choices leaders make ultimately prove counterproductive. If the realists are correct, even defects in states' foreign policy-making processes cannot easily explain such wide divergences between the decisions leaders sometimes make and what cold cost-benefit calculations would predict.

Realism discounts leaders by assuming that global constraints "limit what leaders can do. Because the [global] systemic imperatives of anarchy or interdependence are so clear, leaders can only choose from a limited range of alternatives. If they are to exercise rational leadership and maximize their state's movement toward its goals, only certain actions are feasible" (Hermann and Hagan 2004). However, so-called **instrumental rationality** is another matter. It pictures leaders as powerful decision makers who are able, "based on their perceptions and interpretations, [to] build expectations, plan strategies, and urge actions on their governments about what is possible" (Hermann and Hagan 2004). In this respect, leaders do actually lead and are important. They are instrumentally rational because they have preferences on which they choose. When faced with two or more alternative options, they can rationally make the choice that they believe will produce their preferred outcome.

The idea of instrumental rationality demonstrates that rationality does not "connote superhuman calculating ability, omniscience, or an Olympian view of the world," as is often assumed when the rational-actor model we have described is applied to real-world situations (Zagare 1990). They also suggest that an individual's actions may be rational even though the process of decision making and its product may appear decidedly irrational. Why did Libya's leader, the mercurial Muammar Qaddafi, repeatedly challenge the United States, almost goading President Ronald Reagan into a military strike in 1986? Because, we can postulate, Qaddafi's actions were consistent with his preferences, regardless of how "irrational" it was for a fourth-rate military power to take on the world's preeminent superpower. This and many other examples serve as a reminder of the importance of the human factor in understanding how decisions are made. Temptation, lack of self-control, anger, fear of getting hurt, religious conviction, bad habits, and overconfidence all play a part in determining why people make the kinds of decisions they do.

■ instrumental rationality
a conceptualization of rationality that emphasizes the tendency of decision makers to compare options with those previously considered and then select the one that has the best chance of success.

Factors Affecting Leadership Despite the popularity of the *history-making individuals model,* we must be wary of ascribing too much importance to individual leaders. Their influence is likely to be subtler, a probability summarized by U.S. President Bill Clinton in 1998 when he observed, "Great presidents don't do great things. Great presidents get a lot of other people to do great things." Henry Kissinger urged against placing too much reliance on personalities:

> [There is] a profound American temptation to believe that foreign policy is a subdivision of psychiatry and that relations among nations are like relations among people. But the problem [of easing protracted conflicts] is not so simple. Tensions . . . must have some objective causes, and unless we can remove these causes, no personal relationship can possibly deal with them. We are [not] doing . . . ourselves a favor by reducing the issues to a contest of personalities.

Most leaders operate under a variety of political, psychological, and circumstantial constraints that limit what they can accomplish and reduce their control over events. In this context, Emmet John Hughes (1972), an adviser to President Dwight D.

> *I have not controlled events, events have controlled me.*
> —Abraham Lincoln, U.S. President

Eisenhower, concluded that "all of [America's past presidents] from the most venturesome to the most reticent have shared one disconcerting experience: the discovery of the limits and restraints—decreed by law, by history, and by circumstances—that sometimes can blur their clearest designs or dull their sharpest purposes."

The question at issue is not whether political elites lead or whether they can make a difference. They clearly do both. But leaders are not in complete control, and their influence is severely constrained. Thus, personality and personal political preferences do not determine foreign policy directly. The relevant question, then, is not whether leaders' personal characteristics make a difference, but rather under what conditions their characteristics are influential. As Margaret G. Hermann has observed, the impact of leaders is modified by at least six factors:

> (1) what their world view is, (2) what their political style is like, (3) what motivates them to have the position they do, (4) whether they are interested in and have any training in foreign affairs, (5) what the foreign policy climate was like when the leader was starting out his or her political career, and (6) how the leader was socialized into his or her present position. World view, political style, and motivation tell us something about the leader's personality; the other characteristics give information about the leader's previous experiences and background. (M. Hermann 1988, 268)

The impact of leaders' personal characteristics on foreign policy decisions generally increases when their authority and legitimacy are widely accepted or when leaders are protected from broad public criticism. Moreover, certain circumstances enhance individuals' potential influence. Among them are new situations that free leaders from conventional approaches to defining the situation; complex situations involving many different factors; and situations without social sanctions, which permit freedom of choice because norms defining the range of permissible options are unclear (DiRenzo 1974).

■ political efficacy

the extent to which policy makers' self-confidence instills in them the belief that they can effectively make rational choices.

A leader's **political efficacy** or self-image—that person's belief in his or her own ability to control events politically—combined with the citizenry's relative desire for leadership, will also influence the degree to which personal values and psychological needs govern decision making (DeRivera 1968). For example, when public opinion strongly favors a powerful leader, and when the head of state has an exceptional need for admiration, foreign policy will more likely reflect that leader's inner needs. Thus, Kaiser Wilhelm II's narcissistic personality allegedly met the German people's desire for a symbolically powerful leader, and German public preferences in turn influenced the foreign policy that Germany pursued during Wilhelm's reign, ending in World War I (Baron and Pletsch 1985).

Other factors undoubtedly influence how much leaders can shape their states' choices. For instance, when leaders believe that their own interests and welfare are at stake, they tend to respond in terms of their private needs and psychological drives. When circumstances are stable, however, and when leaders' egos are not entangled with policy outcomes, the influence of their personal characteristics is less apparent.

The timing of a leader's assumption of power is also significant. When an individual first assumes a leadership position, the formal requirements of that role are least likely to restrict what he or she can do. That is especially true during the "honeymoon" period routinely given to newly elected leaders, during which time they are relatively free of criticism and excessive pressure. Moreover, when a leader assumes office following a dramatic event (a landslide election, for example, or the assassination of a predecessor), he or she can institute policies almost with a free hand, as "constituency criticism is held in abeyance during this time" (M. Hermann 1976).

A national crisis is a potent circumstance that increases a leader's control over foreign policy making. Decision making during crises is typically centralized and handled exclusively by the top leadership. Crucial information is often unavailable, and leaders see themselves as responsible for outcomes. Not surprisingly, great leaders (e.g., Napoleon Bonaparte, Winston Churchill, and Franklin D. Roosevelt) customarily emerge during periods of extreme tumult. A crisis can liberate a leader from the constraints that normally would inhibit his or her capacity to control events or engineer foreign policy change.

History abounds with examples of the seminal importance of political leaders who emerge in different times and places and under different circumstances to play critical roles in shaping world history. Mikhail Gorbachev dramatically illustrates an individual's capacity to change the course of history. Many experts believe that the Cold War could not have been brought to an end, nor Communist Party rule in Moscow terminated and the Soviet state set on a path toward democracy and free enterprise, had it not been for Gorbachev's vision, courage, and commitment to engineering these revolutionary, system-transforming changes.

Having said that the history-making individuals model may be compelling, we must be cautious and remember that leaders are not all-powerful determinants of states' foreign policy behavior. Rather, their personal influence varies with the context, and often the context is more influential than the leader (see Controversy: Policy and Personality: Do Leaders Make a Difference?). The "great person" versus zeitgeist ("spirit of the times") debate is pertinent here, as constructivist theorists like to observe. At the core of this enduring controversy is the question of whether certain times are conducive to the emergence of leaders or whether famous leaders would have an impact whenever and wherever they lived (see Greenstein 1987). That question may be unanswerable, but at least it reminds us that multiple factors affect states' foreign policy decisions. The *history-making individuals model* alone appears too simple an explanation of how transnational actors react to external challenges.

■ **zeitgeist**
the "spirit of the times," or the dominant cultural norms assumed to influence the behavior of people living in particular periods.

CONTROVERSY:

POLICY AND PERSONALITY

Do Leaders Make a Difference?

Some theorists, such as proponents of *neorealism*, embrace the assumption of rationality and assume that any leader will respond to a choice in the same way: the situation structures the reaction to the existing costs and benefits of any choice. But does this assumption square with the facts? What do we know about the impact of people's perceptions and values on the way they view choices? Political psychology and constructivism tell us that the same option is likely to have different value to different leaders. Does this mean that different leaders would respond differently to similar situations?

Consider the example of Richard Nixon. In 1971, Americans took to the streets outside the White House to protest the immorality of Nixon's massive bombing of Vietnam. His reaction to this perceived threat was to shield himself from the voice of the people, without success, as it happened. Nixon complained that "nobody can know what it means for a president to be sitting in that White House working late at night and to have hundreds of thousands of demonstrators charging through the streets. Not even earplugs could block the noise."

Earlier, on a rainy afternoon in 1962, John F. Kennedy faced a similar citizen protest. Americans had gathered in front of the White House for a "Ban the Bomb" demonstration. His response was to send out urns of coffee and doughnuts and invite the leaders of the protest to come inside to state their case, believing that a democracy should encourage dissent and debate.

Nixon saw protesters as a threat; Kennedy saw them as an opportunity. This comparison suggests that the type of leader can make a difference in determining the kinds of choices likely to be made in response to similar situations. More important than each president's treatment of the protesters, however, was whether he actually changed his policy decisions based on the protests. Although Kennedy was hospitable to protesters, he did not ban nuclear weapons; in fact, military spending under Kennedy grew to consume half of the federal budget. Many would protest that Kennedy alone could not be expected to eliminate nuclear weapons—that the *zeitgeist* was dominated by fear of the Soviet Union and intense concern for national security. The protesters in 1971, however, were more in keeping with the spirit of the times. Although they alone may not have persuaded

Nixon to alter his policies in Vietnam, widespread protest and discontentment with the war, as well as America's inability to win, eventually prompted Nixon to order the gradual withdrawal of U.S. troops, ending American participation in the Vietnam war. These outcomes suggest that leaders are captive to *zeitgeist*, or larger forces that drive international relations in their times.

What do you think? Did Kennedy and Nixon choose courses of action that reflected who they were as individuals? Or would any president in their respective eras have made similar choices?

AP Photo

THE GLOBAL AND DOMESTIC DETERMINANTS OF STATES' INTERNATIONAL DECISIONS

We have discussed alternative ways of thinking about international decision making, and it is very important now to look at the factors that apply exclusively to the most important actors—states. States have the most power, and by international law are the only transnational actors with the capacity to possess territory, to exercise control over activities within borders, and to monopolize the use of military force. States comprise a special category of player on the world stage and respond to global trends and transformations in ways that are arguably unique. States' foreign policy decisions are the most consequential, and the factors that influence their capacity to make decisions to adapt to changes in world politics are different from many of those that impact other transnational actors' decisions. Therefore, to place states' decision making into proper perspective, this chapter will conclude with insights from "the comparative study of foreign policy" (see Hermann 2008) that help us better appreciate how foreign policy decision making by states is shaped.

Geostrategic location, military might, economic prowess, and system of government are all variables that affect state foreign policy choices. Still, because of the diversity of states as well as their different locations and positions within the contemporary global system, it is difficult to generalize about the influence of any one factor or combination of factors. In classifying the determinants not only of states' foreign policies but also of trends in world politics generally, *the levels-of-analysis framework* introduced in Chapter 1 (see Figure 1.2) helps to describe the multiple influences on decision making processes. Recall that states and the global system make up two distinct levels: the state level encompasses domestic characteristics, and the global or international system level encompasses all actors' relationships and the changes in these relations over time.

Global or "external" influences on foreign policy include all activities occurring beyond a state's borders that affect the choices its officials and the people they govern make. Such factors as the number of military alliances and the changing levels of international trade sometimes profoundly affect the choices of decision makers. Internal or "domestic" influences, on the other hand, are those that exist at the level of the state, not the global system. Here, attention focuses on variations in **states' attributes**, such as military capabilities, level of economic development, and types of government, that may influence different countries' foreign policy choices. Examples of both types of influences are discussed in the sections that follow.

International Influences on Foreign Policy Choice

The global environment within which states operate shapes opportunities for action. It sets an ecological context that limits some foreign policy choices but facilitates others (Sprout and Sprout 1965; Starr 1978). Among the most significant factors of the international environment that make possible certain courses of action but not others are the distribution of power among states and the pattern of the alliances around the most powerful.

■ **states' attributes**
state characteristics that shape foreign policy behavior, such as its size, wealth, and the extent to which its leaders are accountable to its citizens in comparison with other states.

Polarity and Polarization   Power can be distributed in many ways. It can be concentrated in the hands of one preponderant state, as in the ancient Mediterranean world at the zenith of the Roman Empire, or it may be diffused among several rival states, as it was at the birth of the state system in 1648 following the Thirty Years' War, when a handful of great power rivals possessed approximately equal strength. Scholars use the term **polarity** to describe the distribution of power among members of the global system. As explained in Chapter 4, unipolar systems have one dominant power center, bipolar systems contain two centers of power, and multipolar systems possess more than two such centers.

■ **polarity**

the degree to which military and economic capabilities are concentrated in the global system that determines the number of centers of power, or "poles."

Closely related to the distribution of power is the pattern of alignments among states. The term **polarization** refers to the degree to which states cluster around the powerful. For instance, a highly bipolarized system is one in which small and medium-size states form alliances with one of the two dominant powers. The network of alliances around the United States and Soviet Union during the Cold War exemplified such a system.

■ **polarization**

the formation of competing coalitions or blocs composed of allies that align with one of the major competing poles, or centers, of power.

Polarity and alliance *polarization* influence foreign policy by affecting the decision latitude possessed by states. To illustrate this point, let's consider two examples of how these global properties influence the freedom that states have in their international behavior. Our first example pertains to polarity and great powers. As we shall see in Chapters 4 and 15, when power is concentrated in the hands of a single state in a unipolar system, it can more easily choose to use military force and intervene in the affairs of others than it would in a system characterized by a distribution of shared power, where rivals might obstruct its actions. Our second example focuses on polarization and smaller states. When alliances are tight military blocs, the members of each alliance will feel compelled to conform to the dictates of the alliance's leader. Conversely, when alliances are loosely shifting with fluid membership, smaller states can more readily choose to craft foreign policies that are independent of the wishes of the powerful. Of course, you could think of other examples to show how the structural properties of the global system affect decision latitude. What they would show is that the foreign policy impact of *polarity* and *polarization* hinges on the geostrategic position of a given state.

Geostrategic Position   Some of the most important influences on a state's foreign policy behavior are its location and physical terrain. The presence of natural frontiers, for example, may profoundly guide policy makers' choices (see Map 3.1). Consider the United States, which was secure throughout most of its early history because vast oceans separated it from potential threats in Europe and Asia. The advantage of having oceans as barriers to foreign intervention, combined with the absence of militarily powerful neighbours, permitted the United States to develop into an industrial giant and to practice safely an isolationist foreign policy for more than 150 years. Consider also mountainous Switzerland, whose easily defended topography has made neutrality a viable foreign policy option.

Similarly, maintaining autonomy from continental politics has been an enduring theme in the foreign policy of Great Britain, an island country whose physical detachment from Europe long served as a buffer separating it from entanglement in major power disputes on the Continent. Preserving this protective shield has long been a priority for Britain, and it helps to explain why London has been so hesitant in the past twenty years to accept full integration in the European Union (EU).

Most countries are not insular, however; they have many states on their borders, denying them the option of noninvolvement in world affairs. Germany, which sits in the geographic center of Europe, historically has found its domestic political system and foreign policy preferences shaped by its geostrategic position. In the twentieth century, for example, Germany struggled through no less than six major radical changes in governing institutions, each of which pursued very different foreign policies: (1) the empire of Kaiser Wilhelm II; (2) the Weimar Republic; (3) Adolf Hitler's dictatorship; its two post–World War II successors, (4) the capitalist Federal Republic in West Germany and (5) the communist German Democratic Republic in East Germany; and, finally, (6) a reunited Germany after the end of the Cold War, now committed to liberal democracy and full integration in the European Union. Each of these governments was preoccupied with its relations with neighbors but responded to the opportunities and challenges presented by Germany's position in the middle of the European continent with very different foreign policy goals. In no case, however, was isolationistic withdrawal from involvement in continental affairs a practical geostrategic option.

History is replete with other examples of geography's influence on states' foreign policy goals. This is why geopolitical theories are valuable. The **geopolitics** school of realist thought and political geography generally stress the influence of geographic factors on state power and international conduct (S. Cohen 2003). Illustrative of early geopolitical thinking is Alfred Thayer Mahan's *The Influence of Sea Power in History* (1890), which maintains that control of the seas shaped national power and foreign policy. States with extensive coastlines and ports enjoyed a competitive advantage. Later geopoliticians, such as Sir Halford Mackinder (1919) and Nicholas Spykman (1944), argued that not only location but also topography, size (territory and population), climate, and distance between states are powerful determinants of individual countries' foreign policies. The underlying principle behind the geopolitical perspective is self-evident: leaders' perceptions of available foreign policy options are influenced by the geopolitical circumstances that define their state's place on the world stage.

■ **geopolitics**
the theoretical postulate that states' foreign policies are determined by their location, natural resources, and physical environment.

Geopolitics is only one aspect of the *global* environment that may influence foreign policy. In later chapters, we will discuss additional global factors. Here, we comment briefly on three *internal* attributes of states that influence their foreign policies: military capabilities, economic conditions, and type of government.

The Domestic Sources of Foreign Policy Decisions

Various domestic factors and national attributes affect the capacity of states to act when foreign policy decisions must be made (East 1978). To illustrate the impact of internal factors, consider next the three regarded by scholars as the most influential.

Military Capabilities   The realist proposition that states' internal capabilities shape their foreign policy priorities is supported by the fact that states' preparations for war strongly influence their later use of force (Levy 2001). Thus, although most states may seek similar goals, their ability to realize them will vary according to their military capabilities.

Because military capabilities limit a state's range of prudent policy choices, they act as a mediating factor on leaders' national security decisions. For instance, in the 1980s, Libyan leader Muammar Qaddafi repeatedly provoked the United States through anti-American and anti-Israeli rhetoric and by supporting various terrorist activities. Qaddafi was able to act as he did largely because neither bureaucratic organizations nor a mobilized public existed in Libya to constrain his personal whims. However, Qaddafi was doubtlessly more highly constrained by the outside world than were the leaders in the more militarily capable countries toward whom his anger was directed. Limited military muscle compared with the United States precluded the kinds of belligerent behaviors he threatened to practice.

Conversely, Saddam Hussein made strenuous efforts to build Iraq's military might (partly with the help of U.S. arms sales) and by 1990 had built the world's fourth-largest army. Thus, invading Kuwait to seize its oil fields became a feasible foreign policy option. In the end, however, even Iraq's impressive military power proved ineffective against a vastly superior coalition of military forces, headed by the United States. The 1991 Persian Gulf War forced Saddam Hussein to capitulate and withdraw from the conquered territory. Twelve years later, the United States invaded Iraq and finally ousted Saddam Hussein from office. The lessons: what states believe about their own military capabilities and those of their adversaries (and their enemies' intentions) guide their decisions about war and peace.

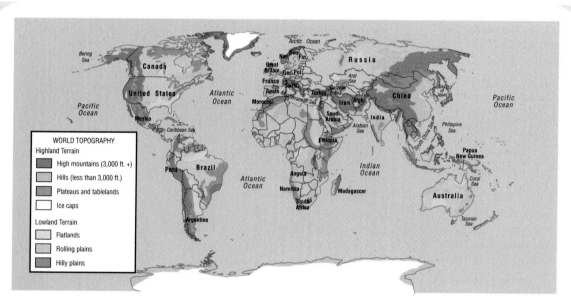

MAP 3.1

GEOGRAPHIC INFLUENCES ON FOREIGN POLICY How countries act towards others is shaped by the number of neighboring states on their borders and whether they are protected from invasion by natural barriers such as mountains and oceans. This map suggests how, until recently, the separation of the United States from Eurasia encouraged an isolationist policy during many periods in U.S. history. Note also how topography, location, and other geopolitical factors may have influenced the foreign policy priorities of Great Britain, Germany, China, Finland, and states in South America—hypotheses advanced by the geopolitics approach to international politics.

Economic Conditions The level of economic and industrial development a state enjoys also affects the foreign policy goals it can pursue. Generally, the more economically developed a state, the more likely it is to play an activist role in the global political economy. Rich states have interests that extend far beyond their borders and typically possess the means to pursue and protect them. Not coincidentally, states that enjoy industrial capabilities and extensive involvement in international trade also tend to be militarily powerful—in part because military might is a function of economic capabilities.

Although economically advanced states are more active globally, this does not mean that their privileged circumstances dictate adventuresome policies. Rich states are often "satisfied" ones that have much to lose from revolutionary change and global instability (Wolfers 1962). As a result, they usually perceive the status quo as serving their interests and often forge international economic policies to protect and expand their envied position at the pinnacle of the global hierarchy.

Levels of productivity and prosperity also affect the foreign policies of the poor states at the bottom of the global hierarchy. Some economically weak states respond to their situation by complying subserviently with the wishes of the rich on whom they depend. Others rebel defiantly, sometimes succeeding (despite their disadvantaged bargaining position) in resisting the efforts by great powers and powerful international organizations to control their behavior.

Thus, generalizations about the economic foundations of states' international political behavior often prove inaccurate. Although levels of economic development vary widely among states in the global system, they alone do not determine foreign policies. Instead, leaders' perceptions of the opportunities and constraints that their states' economic resources provide may more powerfully influence their foreign policy choices.

Type of Government A third important attribute affecting states' international behavior is their type of political system. Although realism predicts that all states will act similarly to protect their interests, a state's type of government demonstrably constrains important choices, including whether threats to use military force are carried out. Here the important distinction is between **constitutional democracy** (representative government), at one end of the spectrum, and **autocratic rule** (authoritarian or totalitarian) at the other.

In neither democratic (sometimes called "open") nor autocratic ("closed") political systems can political leaders survive long without the support of organized domestic political interests, and sometimes the mass citizenry. But in democratic systems, those interests are likely to spread beyond the government itself. Public opinion, interest groups, and the mass media are a more visible part of the policy making process in democratic systems. Similarly, the electoral process in democratic societies more meaningfully frames choices and produces results about who will lead than the process used in authoritarian regimes, where the real choices are made by a few elites behind closed doors. In a democracy, public opinion and preferences may matter and, therefore, differences in who is allowed to participate and how much they exercise their right to participate are critical determinants of foreign policy choices.

■ **constitutional democracy**
government processes that allow people, through their elected representatives, to exercise power and influence the state's policies.

■ **autocratic rule**
a system of authoritarian or totalitarian government in which unlimited power is concentrated in a single leader.

The proposition that domestic stimuli, and not simply international events, are a source of foreign policy is not novel. In ancient Greece, for instance, the realist historian Thucydides observed that what happened within the Greek city-states often did more to shape their external behavior than what each did to the others. He added that Greek leaders frequently concentrated their efforts on influencing the political climate within their own polities. Similarly, leaders today sometimes make foreign policy decisions for domestic political purposes—as, for example, when bold or aggressive acts abroad are intended to influence election outcomes at home or to divert public attention from economic woes. This is sometimes called the "scapegoat" phenomenon or the **diversionary theory of war** (Levy 1989b).

■ diversionary theory of war

the hypothesis that leaders sometimes initiate conflict abroad as a way of increasing national cohesion at home by diverting national public opinion away from controversial domestic issues and internal problems.

The impact of government type on foreign policy choice has taken on great significance following the rapid conversion of many dictatorships to democratic rule. These liberal government conversions have occurred in three successive "waves" since the 1800s (Huntington 1991). The first wave occurred between 1878 and 1926, and the second between 1943 and 1962. The third wave began in the 1970s when a large number of nondemocratic countries began to convert their governments to democratic rule. In a remarkable global *transformation* from past world history, the once radical idea that democracy is the ideal form of decision making has triumphed. According to Freedom House, three-fourths of the world's countries are now fully or partially democratic (see Map 3.2).

THE BURDEN OF FOREIGN POLICY CHOICE FOR GLOBAL LEADERSHIP **The United States is called upon to provide visionary leadership for the world, and this entails a careful assessment of priorities and strategies. Barack Obama declared that "I will strengthen our common security by investing in our common humanity. Our global engagement cannot be defined by what we are against; it must be guided by a clear sense of what we stand for. We have a significant stake in ensuring that those who live in fear and want today can live with dignity and opportunity tomorrow" (Obama 2007, 14).**

This recent growth of democracy has emboldened many liberals to predict that the twenty-first century will be safer than its predecessor. Their reasons for predicting the onset of a **democratic peace** vary, but rely on the logic that Immanuel Kant outlined in his 1795 treatise *Perpetual Peace*. Kant believed that because democratic leaders are accountable to the public, and that because ordinary citizens have to supply the soldiers and bear the human and financial cost of aggressive policies, they would constrain leaders from initiating foreign wars (especially against other liberal democracies similarly constrained by norms and institutions that respect compromise and civil liberties).

A considerable body of empirical evidence supports the proposition that democracies do not wage war against each other (Rasler and Thompson 2005; Russett 2001; Ray 1995). The type of government and, more specifically, whether leaders are accountable to opposition groups through multiparty elections, strongly influence foreign policy goals. Although liberals generally emphasize the pacifying effects of democracy, research findings on the democratic peace have led some political conservatives to advocate a policy called "democratic realism" (Yang 2005), which would promote democracy through targeted interventions into regions where the advance of freedom is deemed critical in the struggle against Al Qaeda and other radical groups that threaten the United States (Krauthammer 2004).

■ **democratic peace**

the theory that although democratic states sometimes wage wars against nondemocratic states, they do not fight one another.

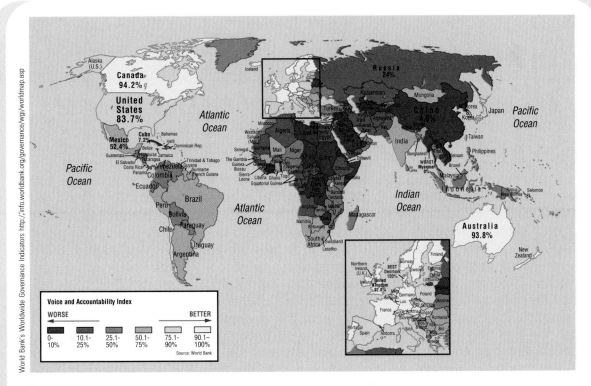

World Bank's Worldwide Governance Indicators http://info.worldbank.org/governance/wgi/worldmap.asp

MAP 3.2

HOW FREE IS YOUR COUNTRY? **The World Bank's Worldwide Governance Indicators ranks countries by the level of freedom citizens have to voice opinions and choose their government. Liberal democratic peace theory predicts that as freedom across countries increases, so will peaceful relations among these democracies. The United States rank fell to 35th "because of a decreased trust in public officials and restrictions on the freedom of the press"** (*Time*, September 17, 2007, p.16).

Some see the intrusion of domestic politics into foreign policy making as a disadvantage of democratic political systems that undermines their ability to deal decisively with crises or to bargain effectively with less democratic adversaries and allies (see Controversy: Are Democracies Deficient in Foreign Affairs?). Democracies are subject to inertia. They move slowly on issues, because so many disparate elements are involved in decision making and because officials in democracies are accountable to public opinion and must respond to pressure from a variety of domestic interest groups (groups mobilized to exercise influence over the future direction of their country's foreign policies, especially on issues highly important to them). A crisis sufficient enough to arouse the attention and activity of a large proportion of the population may need to erupt in order for large changes in policy to come about. As the French political sociologist Alexis de Tocqueville argued in 1835, democracies may be inclined to "impulse rather than prudence" because they overreact to perceived external dangers once they recognize them. "There are two things that a democratic people will always find difficult," de Tocqueville mused, "to start a war and to end it." In contrast, authoritarian governments can "make decisions more rapidly, ensure domestic compliance with their decisions, and perhaps be more consistent in their foreign policy" (Jensen 1982). But there is a cost: nondemocracies "often are less effective in developing an innovative foreign policy because of subordinates' pervasive fear of raising questions." In short, the concentration of power and the suppression of public opposition can be both advantageous and disadvantageous.

CONTROVERSY:

ARE DEMOCRACIES DEFICIENT IN FOREIGN AFFAIRS?

History suggests that democracies enjoy faithful allies and lose fewer wars than do nondemocracies, but, despite these achievements, democracies may make foreign policy choices in ways that are less rational and efficient than autocracies (Siverson and Emmons 1991). One realist thesis argues that democracies are decidedly inferior to nondemocratic governance. Dictators and despots such as Adolf Hitler, Joseph Stalin, and Mao Zedong can embark as warmongers on grand international missions and be hailed as great unifiers and the builders of grandiose projects, whereas democratic politicians are "by nature mediocre. The great dictators . . . give the people a destiny, whereas democrats can only promise happiness. [Some realists fall] under the spell of absolute power. It is a fatal romanticism that justifies unlimited murder" (Buruma 2005). Because classical realism follows Machiavelli by honoring strong rulers who are able to convince subjects of their need to be ruled by them for the glory of the state, these realists prefer the capacity of nondemocratic governments to forge foreign policies freely in pursuit of national interests.

Does the nature of democratic rule help or hinder those governments' capacities to realize their goals under anarchy? In evaluating this controversy, consider that view by a leading realist American policy maker, George F. Kennan, who advanced the following thesis:

I sometimes wonder whether a democracy is not uncomfortably similar to one of those prehistoric monsters with a body as long as this room and a brain the size of a pin. He lies there in his comfortable primeval mud and pays little attention to his environment; he is slow to wrath—in fact, you practically have to whack his tail off to make him aware that his interests are being disturbed; but, once he grasps this, he lays about him with such blind determination that he not only destroys his adversary but largely wrecks his native habitat. You wonder whether it would not have been wiser for him to have taken a little more interest in what was going on at an earlier date and to have seen whether he could not have prevented some of these situations from arising instead of proceeding from an undiscriminating indifference to a holy wrath equally undiscriminating (Kennan 1951, 59).

Against this criticism of democratic governments' tendency to react without foresight or moderation in foreign policy, defenders of liberal democratic governance such as Immanuel Kant, Thomas Jefferson, and Woodrow Wilson have argued just the opposite: that giving people power through the ballot and a voice in the making of foreign policy decisions restrains leaders in those countries from extreme or excessive choices, such as initiating a war of choice rather than necessity on a whim. To liberals, democratization also enables the leader of a democracy to bargain successfully with nondemocracies, because nondemocratic states know that democratic governments are likely to have the support of their people and to honor their agreements.

What do you think? Are democratic procedures for making foreign policy decisions an aid or a handicap? What arguments and evidence can you provide to support your general conclusion about this timeless controversy?

The trends and transformations currently unfolding in world politics are the products of countless decisions made daily throughout the world. Some decisions are more consequential than others. Throughout history, great powers such as the United States today have at times stood at the center of the world political stage, possessing the combination of natural resources, military might, and the means to project power worldwide that earned them great-power status. How such major powers have responded to one another has had profound consequences for the entire drama of world politics. To better understand this, Part II begins in Chapter 4 by inspecting this set of transnational actors and to the dynamics of great-power rivalry on the world stage, and other categories of transnational actors follow in Chapters 5–8.

Key Terms

counterfactual reasoning	bureaucracies	political efficacy
unitary actor	multiple advocacy	zeitgeist
rational choice	bureaucratic politics model	states' attributes
bounded rationality	policy networks	polarity
game theory	caucuses	polarization
opportunity costs	standard operating procedures	geopolitics
externalities	(SOPS)	constitutional democracy
policy agenda	groupthink	autocratic rule
satisficing	history-making individuals model	diversionary theory of war
prospect theory	Bush Doctrine	democratic peace
two-level games	roles	
muddling through	instrumental rationality	

MARCHING FOR CHANGE Protest demonstrations have become an everyday event by mobilized publics seeking to draw global attention to their cause. People, like states and international organizations, are transnational actors. Shown here: About 100,000 Buddhist monks march to protest Myanmar's (Burma) military government, which has crushed pro-democracy uprisings and neglected the welfare of its people. As British Prime Minister Gordon Brown lamented, the ruling junta exacerbated the human suffering wrought by Cyclone Nargis in 2008 by resisting outside aid. "It is being made into a man-made catastrophe by the negligence, the neglect and the inhuman treatment of the Burmese people by a regime that is failing to act and to allow the international community to do what it wants to do."

Part 2
THE GLOBE'S ACTORS AND THEIR RELATIONS

"Everybody has accepted by now that change is unavoidable. But that still implies that change is like death and taxes—it should be postponed as long as possible and no change would be vastly preferable. But in a period of upheaval, such as the one we are living in, change is the norm."

— *Peter Drucker, American futurologist*

SHAKESPEARE WROTE THAT "ALL THE WORLD'S A STAGE AND ALL THE MEN AND WOMEN MERELY PLAYERS." When it comes to world politics, not just people but also organizations, groups, and countries have a variety of roles to play on the global stage. Part 2 identifies the major actors in world politics today and describes the roles they perform, the policies they pursue, and the predicaments they face.

Each chapter in Part 2 focuses on a prominent type of global actor. Chapter 4 opens by giving you a view of the great powers—the actors with the greatest military and economic capabilities—and a profile of their current national security strategies. Chapter 5 compares the great powers with the weaker, economically less-developed countries now known as the Global South, whose fates are powerfully shaped by others. The rise of the Global East to its new status as rivals to the traditional great powers is also covered. Chapter 6 examines the impact of intergovernmental organizations such as the United Nations and the European Union as institutions seeking to strengthen global and regional governance. Chapter 7 takes a look at nongovernmental organizations of private actors such as Greenpeace and Amnesty International whose members actively work for global change. A window is opened for you to also explore the activities of other nonstate global actors, including multinational corporations, ethnic groups, and religious movements. Finally, Chapter 7 puts into the picture the more than 6.7 billion human beings struggling throughout the world to obtain the human rights promised in the U.S. Declaration of Independence: life, liberty, and happiness for all humanity.

CHAPTER 4
GREAT POWER RIVALRIES AND RELATIONS

Great powers fear each other. They regard each other with suspicion, and they worry that war may be in the offing. They anticipate danger. There is little room for trust. . . . From the perspective of any one great power, all other great powers are potential enemies. . . .The basis of this fear is that in a world where great powers have the capability to attack each other and might have the motive to do so, any state bent on survival must be at least suspicious of other states and reluctant to trust them.

—John Mearsheimer, realist political theorist

FDR Library

Allies or New Rivals? The "Big Three" (Winston Churchill, Franklin Roosevelt, and Joseph Stalin) meet at Yalta as victorious great power allies to establish rules for all states to follow in the post–World War II global order, but that cooperation would soon be replaced by bitter competition.

W ho's number one? Who's gaining on the leader? What does it mean for the future if the strongest is seriously challenged for the predominant position?

These are the kinds of questions sports fans often ask when the rankings of the top teams are adjusted after the preceding week's competition. World leaders also adopt what former U.S. Secretary of State Dean Rusk called a "football stadium approach to diplomacy." And many people throughout the world habitually make comparisons of countries, asking which states are the biggest, strongest, wealthiest, and most militarily powerful and evaluating which states are rising and which are falling relative to one another.

When making such rankings, both groups are looking at world politics through the lens of realism. They see a globe of competitors, with winners and losers in an ancient contest for supremacy. And they look most closely at the shifting rankings at the very top of the international hierarchy of power—at the rivalry and struggle among the "great powers." Moreover, they picture this conflict as perpetual. As Arnold J. Toynbee's (1954) famous cyclical theory of history explains: "The most emphatic punctuation in a uniform series of events recurring in one repetitive cycle after another is the outbreak of a great war in which one power that has forged ahead of all its rivals makes so formidable a bid for world domination that it evokes an opposing coalition of all the other powers."

Toynbee's conclusion lies at the center of realism. The starting point for understanding world politics, elaborates Hans J. Morgenthau (1985), the leading post–World War II realist theorist, is to recognize that "all history shows that nations active in international politics are continuously preparing for, actively involved in, or recovering from organized violence in the form of war."

There is a strong probability that this historical pattern is cyclical and unfolds through a series of distinct phases. According to **long-cycle theory**, over the past five centuries periods of global war have been followed by periods of international rule-making and institution building. Shifts in the cycle have occurred alongside changes in the major states' relative power, changing their relations with one another (see Chase-Dunn and Anderson 2005). Each past global war led to the emergence of a **hegemon**. With its unrivaled power, the hegemon has reshaped the rules and institutions of the global system to preserve its preeminent position. However, the ascendancy of one superpower relative to its principal rivals eventually prompted in following phases first questions of the leader's authority, and then organized opposition from the rest. This hegemonic struggle has escalated to global war, and at its painful conclusion the victors have then tried to create a set of rules to contain the recurrence of another catastrophic conflict and to prevent future challenges to the new international order they have constructed.

This general pattern colored twentieth-century world politics, with three global wars breaking out. World Wars I and II were fought with fire and blood; the Cold War was fought without the same magnitude of destruction but with equal intensity. Each of these wars triggered major transformations in world politics.

■ **long-cycle theory**
a theory that focuses on the rise and fall of the leading global power as the central political process of the modern world system.

■ **hegemon**
a preponderant state capable of dominating the conduct of international political and economic relations.

This chapter explores the causes and consequences in order to uncover the underlying dynamics of great power rivalries. By understanding the origins and impact of these three struggles over world leadership, you will be better positioned to anticipate whether the great powers will be able to avoid yet another global war in the twenty-first century.

LONG CYCLES OF WORLD LEADERSHIP

The entrenched pattern of great-power rivalry shows that once a single power gains a hold as the dominant hegemonic power, it has soon learned that global leadership carries with it many problems.

Hegemony always imposes an extraordinary burden on the world leader. A hegemon must bear the costs of maintaining political and economic order while protecting its position and upholding its dominion. Over time, as the weight of global engagement

The price of greatness is responsibility.
—Winston Churchill, British prime minister

takes its toll, every previous hegemon has overextended itself. As challengers have arisen, the security agreements so carefully crafted after the last global war have come under attack. Historically, this struggle for power has set the stage for another global war, the demise of one hegemon and the ascent of another. Table 4.1 summarizes five hundred years of the cyclical rise and fall of great powers, their global wars, and their subsequent efforts to restore order.

Table 4.1   The Evolution of Great-Power Rivalry for World Leadership, 1495–2025

Dates	Preponderant State(s) Seeking Hegemony	Other Powers Resisting Domination	Global War	New Order After Global War
1495–1540	Portugal	Spain, Valois, France, Burgundy, England	War of Italy and the Indian Ocean, 1494–1517	Treaty of Tordesillas, 1517
1560–1609	Spain	The Netherlands, France, England	Spanish-Dutch Wars, 1580–1608	Truce of 1860; Evangelical Union and the Catholic League formed

(continues)

Table 4.1 The Evolution of Great-Power Rivalry for World Leadership, 1495–2025 *(continued)*

Dates	Preponderant State(s) Seeking Hegemony	Other Powers Resisting Domination	Global War	New Order After Global War
1610–1648	Holy Roman Empire (Hapsburg dynasty in Spain and Austria-Hungary)	Shifting ad hoc coalitions of mostly Protestant states (Sweden, Holland) and German principalities as well as Catholic France against remnants of papal rule	Thirty Years' War, 1618–1648	Peace of Westphalia, 1648
1650–1713	France (Louis XIV)	The United Provinces, England, the Hapsburg Empire, Spain, major German states, Russia	War of the Grand Alliance, 1688–1713	Treaty of Utrecht, 1713
1792–1815	France (Napoleon)	Great Britain, Prussia, Austria, Russia	Napoleonic Wars, 1792–1815	Congress of Vienna and Concert of Europe, 1815
1871–1914	Germany, Turkey, Austria-Hungary	Great Britain, France, Russia, United States	World War I, 1914–1918	Treaty of Versailles creating the League of Nations, 1919
1933–1945	Germany, Japan, Italy	Great Britain, France, Soviet Union, United States	World War II, 1939–1945	Bretton Woods, 1944; United Nations, Potsdam, 1945
1945–1991	United States, Soviet Union	Great Britain, France, China, Japan	Cold War, 1945–1991	NATO/Partnerships for Peace, 1995; World Trade Organization, 1995
1991–2025?	United States	China, European Union, Japan, Russia, India	A cold peace or hegemonic war, 2010–2025?	A new security regime to preserve world order?

Critics note that long-cycle theorists disagree on whether economic, military, or domestic factors produce these cycles. They also express frustration with the deterministic tone of the theory, which to them implies that global destiny is beyond policy makers' control. Must great powers rise and fall as if by the law of gravity—what goes up must come down? Still, *long-cycle theory* suggests you should consider

■ **hegemonic stability theory**

a body of theory that maintains that the establishment of hegemony for global dominance by a single great power is a necessary condition for global order in commercial transactions and international military security.

how shifts in the relative strength of great powers affect world politics. It rivets attention on hegemonic transitions, the rise and fall of leading states in the global system, and in so doing provokes questions about whether this long cycle can be broken in your future. *Long-cycle theory* also forces you to evaluate **hegemonic stability theory** and that theory's predictions. Is the theory correct that a future stable world order will require a sustained global leader dominant enough to punish aggressors who challenge the global status quo in their pursuit of hegemony?

To underscore the importance of struggles over world leadership and their impact on trends and transformations in world politics, this chapter accordingly asks you to inspect the three great power wars of the twentieth century, as well as the lessons these clashes suggest for the twenty-first century.

THE FIRST WORLD WAR

World War I rumbled onto the global stage when a Serbian nationalist seeking to free his ethnic group from Austrian rule assassinated Archduke Ferdinand, heir to the Hapsburg throne of the Austrian-Hungarian Empire, at Sarajevo in June 1914. This assassination sparked a series of great power actions and reactions in the five weeks that followed, shattering world peace.

Karim Kadim/AP Photo

MIGHT MAKES FRIGHT Shown here is one example of resistance to U.S. global preeminence: In September 2008, protesters in Sadr City in Baghdad held "Go Out USA" signs. Home to two million Shia and the anti-American cleric Muqtada al-Sadr, Sadr City had been one of the most dangerous areas of Iraq and was the site of intense fighting between the United States and insurgents earlier in the year. Following American construction of a wall across the district, a tenuous calm emerged that was nonetheless regularly interrupted by protests and bombings.

By the time the first major European war in the previous century had ended, nearly ten million people had died, three empires had crumbled, new states had been born, seven decades of communist rule in Russia had begun, and the world geopolitical map had been redrawn in ways that paved the way for the rise of Adolf Hitler in Nazi Germany.

The Causes of World War I

How can such a catastrophic war be explained? Multiple answers are possible.

Most popular are structural neorealist explanations, which hold that World War I was inadvertent, not the result of anyone's master plan. Neorealists believe that it was a war bred by uncertainty beyond the control of those involved, one that people neither wanted nor expected: "a tragic and unnecessary conflict . . . because the train of events that led to its outbreak might have been broken at any point during the five weeks of crisis that preceded the first clash of arms, had prudence or common goodwill found a voice" (Keegan 1999).

Structuralism Structuralism, framed at the *global level of analysis*, postulates that the changing distribution of power within the global system is the primary factor determining states' behavior. The power distribution determines whether coalitions will form and peace will prevail. Looking at the circumstances on the eve of World War I, these historians hypothesize that the great powers' prior rearmament efforts, as well as their alliances and counteralliances, created a momentum that, along with the pressures created by the mobilization of armies and arms races, dragged European statesmen toward war (Tuchman 1962).

This structural explanation concentrates attention on the nineteenth century, when Britain dominated world politics. Britain was an island country isolated by temperament, tradition, and geography from continental affairs. Britain's sea power gave it command of the world's shipping lanes and control of a vast empire stretching from the Mediterranean to Southeast Asia. This dominance helped to deter aggression. However, Germany would mount a challenge to British power.

After becoming a unified country in 1871, Germany prospered and used its growing wealth to create a formidable army and navy. With this strength came ambition and resentment of British preeminence. As the predominant military and industrial power on the European continent, Germany sought to compete for international position and status. As Kaiser Wilhelm II proclaimed in 1898, Germany had "great tasks outside the narrow boundaries of old Europe." With Germany ascendant, Germany's rising power and global aspirations altered the European geopolitical landscape.

Germany was not the only newly emergent power at the turn of the century, however. Russia was also expanding and becoming a threat to Germany. The decline in power of the Austrian-Hungarian Empire, Germany's only ally, heightened Germany's fear of Russia.

Here we observe, again at the *global level of analysis*, the dynamics of shifts in the *balance of power* as a causal factor: the historic tendency for opposed conditions to form so that the distribution of military power is "balanced" to prevent any single

■ structuralism
the neorealist proposition that states' behavior is shaped primarily by changes in the properties of the global system, such as shifts in the balance of power, instead of by individual heads of states or by changes in states' internal characteristics.

power or bloc from seriously threatening others. And that is what *did* happen in the decade prior to Franz Ferdinand's assassination. European military alignments had become polarized, pitting the Triple Alliance of Germany, Austria-Hungary, and the Ottoman Empire against the Triple Entente of Britain, France, and Russia. According to this structural interpretation, after Russia mobilized its armies in response to Austria's attack on Serbia, cross-cutting alliance commitments pulled one European great power after another into the war.

Nationalism   Another interpretation contends with this structural explanation of the origins of World War I. At the *state level of analysis,* many historians view the growth of **nationalism**, especially in southeastern Europe, as having created a climate of opinion that made war likely. Groups that glorified the distinctiveness of their national heritage began championing their own country above all others (Woodwell 2008). Long-suppressed ethnic prejudices soon emerged, even among leaders. Russia foreign minister Sergei Sazonov, for example, claimed to "despise" Austria, and Kaiser Wilhelm II of Germany asserted: "I hate the Slavs" (Tuchman 1962).

■ **nationalism**

a mind-set glorifying a particular state and the nationality group living in it, which sees the state's interest as a supreme value.

Domestic unrest inflamed these passions, making it hard to see things from another point of view. Believing that they were upholding their national honor, the Austrians could not comprehend why Russians labeled them the aggressors. German insensitivity to others' feelings prevented them from understanding "the strength of the Russians' pride, their fear of humiliation if they allowed the Germans and Austrians to destroy their little protégé, Serbia, and the intensity of Russian anger" (White 1990). With each side belittling the national character and ethnic attributes of the other, diplomatic alternatives to war evaporated.

Rational Choice   *Rational choice*—when decision makers choose on the basis of what they perceive to be the best interests for themselves and their states, based on their expectations about the relative usefulness of alternative options for realizing goals—provides still a third alternative interpretation of World War I. From this perspective, framed at the *individual level of analysis,* the war's outbreak was a result of German elites' preference for a war with France and Russia in order to consolidate Germany's position on the continent, confirm its status as a world power, and divert domestic attention from its internal troubles (Kaiser 1990). The people gathered at the Imperial Palace in Berlin are seen as having pushed Europe over the brink.

The rational choice model of decision making suggests that World War I is best seen as a consequence of the goal purposely chosen by rival great powers to compete against one another for global power. This is a drive that realists believe is an "iron law of history." It resulted from "an attempt by Germany to secure its position before an increasingly powerful Russia had achieved a position of equality with Germany (which the latter expected to happen by 1917)" (Levy 1998b).

As these rival interpretations suggest, the causes of World War I remain in dispute. Structural explanations emphasize the global distribution of power, domestic interpretations look at causal factors *within* states, and rational choice explanations direct attention to the calculations and goals of particular leaders. All partially help us to understand the sequences that produced the world's first truly global war.

The Consequences of World War I

World War I destroyed both life and property and changed the face of Europe (see Map 4.1). In its wake, three empires—the Austrian-Hungarian, Russian, and Ottoman (Turkish)—collapsed, and in their place the independent states of Poland, Czechoslovakia, and Yugoslavia emerged. In addition, the countries of Finland, Estonia, Latvia, and Lithuania were born. The war also contributed to the overthrow of the Russian czar in 1917 by the Bolsheviks. The emergence of communism under the leadership of Vladimir Lenin produced a change in government and ideology that would have geopolitical consequences for another seventy years.

Despite its costs, the coalition consisting of Britain, France, Russia, and (later) the United States and Italy defeated the threat of domination posed by the Central powers (Germany, Austria-Hungary, Turkey, and their allies). Moreover, the war set the stage for a determined effort to build a new global system that could prevent another war.

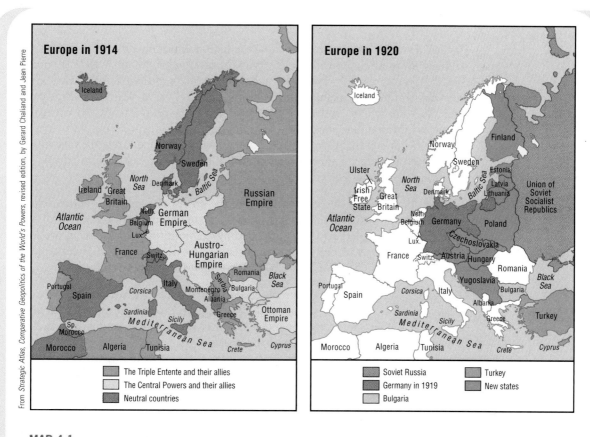

From *Strategic Atlas, Comparative Geopolitics of the World's Powers*, revised edition, by Gerard Chaliand and Jean Pierre

MAP 4.1

TERRITORIAL CHANGES IN EUROPE FOLLOWING WORLD WAR I **The map on the left shows state boundaries on the eve of war in 1914, as well as the members of the two major opposing coalitions that formed. The map on the right shows the new borders in 1920, with the nine new states that emerged from the war.**

For most Europeans, the Great War had been a source of disillusionment. . . . When it was all over, few remained to be convinced that such a war must never happen again. Among vast populations there was a strong conviction that this time the parties had to plan a peace that could not just terminate a war, but a peace that could change attitudes and build a new type of international order. . . .

For the first time in history, broad publics and the peacemakers shared a conviction that war was a central problem in international relations. Previously, hegemony, the aggressive activities of a particular state, or revolution had been the problem. In 1648, 1713, and 1815, the peacemakers had tried to resolve issues of the past and to construct orders that would preclude their reappearance. But in 1919 expectations ran higher. The sources of war were less important than the war itself. There was a necessity to look more to the future than to the past. The problem was not just to build a peace, but to construct a peaceful international order that would successfully manage all international conflicts of the future. (K. Holsti 1991, 175–176; 208–209)

World War I evoked revulsion for war and theories of realism that justified great power competition, armaments, secret alliances, and balance-of-power politics. The staggering human and material costs of the previous four years led many of the delegates to the 1919 peace conference convened at Versailles, outside Paris, to reevaluate their convictions about statecraft. The time was ripe for a new approach to building world order. Disillusioned with realism, many turned to liberalism for guidance on how to manage the global future.

The decade following World War I was the high point of liberal idealism. Woodrow Wilson's ideas about world order, as expressed in his January 1917 "Fourteen Points" speech, were anchored in a belief that by reordering the global system according to liberal principles, the "Great War" (as World War I was then called) would be "the war to end all wars." Wilson's chief proposal was to construct a League of Nations that allegedly would guarantee the independence and territorial integrity of all states. His other recommendations included strengthening international law, settling territorial claims on the basis of self-determination, and promoting democracy, disarmament, and free trade.

However, once the peace conference began, the knives of parochial national interest began whittling away at the liberal philosophy underpinning Wilson's proposals. Many European leaders had been offended by the pontificating American president. "God was content with Ten Commandments," growled Georges Clemenceau, the cynical realist French prime minister. "Wilson must have fourteen."

As negotiations at the conference proceeded, hard-boiled power politics prevailed. Ultimately, the delegates were only willing to support those elements in the Fourteen Points that served their national interests. After considerable wrangling, Wilson's League of Nations was written into the peace treaty with Germany as the first of 440 articles. The rest of the treaty was punitive, aimed at stripping the country of its great power status. Similar treaties were later forced on Austria-Hungary and Germany's other wartime allies.

The Treaty of Versailles grew out of a desire for retribution. In brief, Germany's military was drastically cut; it was forbidden to possess heavy artillery, military aircraft, or submarines, and its forces were banned from the Rhineland. Germany also lost territory in the west to France and Belgium, in the south to the new state of Czechoslovakia, and in the east to the new states of Poland and Lithuania. Overseas, Germany lost all its colonies. Finally, in the most humiliating clause of the treaty, Germany was assigned responsibility for the war and charged with paying heavy financial reparations for the damages. On learning of the treaty's harsh provisions, the exiled German Kaiser is said to have declared that "the war to end wars has resulted in a peace to end peace."

THE SECOND WORLD WAR

Germany's defeat in World War I and its humiliation under the Treaty of Versailles did not extinguish its hegemonic aspirations. On the contrary, they intensified them. Thus conditions were ripe for the second great-power war of the twentieth century, which pitted the Axis trio of Germany, Japan, and Italy against an unlikely "grand alliance" of four great powers who united despite their incompatible ideologies— communism in the case of the Soviet Union and democratic capitalism in the case of Britain, France, and the United States.

The world's fate hinged on the outcome of this massive effort to defeat the Axis powers. The Allied powers achieved success, but at a terrible cost: twenty-three thousand lives were lost each day, and at least fifty-three million people died during six years of fighting. To understand the origins of this devastating conflict, we will once again examine how causal factors operating at different levels of analysis fit into a time sequence.

The Causes of World War II

Following Germany's capitulation in 1918, a democratic constitution was drafted by a constituent assembly meeting in the city of Weimar. Many Germans had little enthusiasm for the Weimar Republic. Not only was the new government linked in their minds to the humiliating Versailles Treaty, but it also suffered from the 1923 French occupation of the industrial Ruhr district, various political rebellions, and the ruinous economic collapse of 1929. By the parliamentary elections of 1932, over half of the electorate supported extremist parties that disdained democratic governance. The largest of these was the Nazi, or National Socialist German Workers, party. This was to be the start of a tragic path.

The Chronological Road to War   On January 30, 1933, the Nazi leader, Adolf Hitler, was appointed chancellor of Germany. Less than a month later, the Reichstag (Parliament) building burned down under mysterious circumstances. Hitler used the fire to justify an emergency edict allowing him to suspend civil liberties and move against communists and other political adversaries. Once all meaningful parliamentary opposition had been eliminated, Nazi legislators passed an enabling act that suspended the constitution and granted Hitler dictatorial power.

In his 1924 book *Mein Kampf* ("My Struggle"), Hitler urged Germany to recover territories taken by the Treaty of Versailles, absorb Germans living in neighboring lands, and colonize Eastern Europe. During his first year in power, however, he cultivated a pacific image, signing a nonaggression pact with Poland in 1934. The following year, the goals originally outlined in *Mein Kampf* climbed to the top of Hitler's foreign policy agenda as he ignored the **Kellogg-Briand Pact** (prohibiting the

■ **Kellogg-Briand Pact**

a multilateral treaty negotiated in 1928 that outlawed war as a method for settling interstate conflicts.

Europe in 1945 from *Strategic Atlas, Comparative Geopolitics of the World's Powers,* revised edition, by Gerard Chaliand and Jean-Pierre Rageau. Copyright 1990 by Gerard Chaliand and Jean-Pierre Rageau. Reprinted by permission of HarperCollins Publishers, Inc.

MAP 4.2

WORLD WAR II REDRAWS THE MAP OF EUROPE **The map on the left shows the height of German expansion in 1943, when it occupied Europe from the Atlantic Ocean and the Baltic Sea to the gates of Moscow in the Soviet Union. The map on the right shows the new configuration of Europe after the "Grand Coalition" of Allied forces—Great Britain, the United States, and the Soviet Union—defeated the Axis's bid for supremacy.**

■ **appeasement**

a strategy of making concessions to another state in the hope that, satisfied, it will not make additional claims.

■ **colonialism**

the rule of a region by an external sovereign power.

use of force). In 1935, he repudiated the military clauses of the Versailles Treaty; in 1936, he ordered troops into the demilitarized Rhineland; in March 1938 he annexed Austria; and in September 1938, he demanded control over the Sudetenland, a region of Czechoslovakia containing ethnic Germans. To address the Sudeten German question, a conference was convened in Munich, attended by Hitler, British prime minister Neville Chamberlain, and leaders of France and Italy (ironically, Czechoslovakia was not invited). Convinced that **appeasement** would halt further German expansionism, Chamberlain and the others agreed to Hitler's demands.

Rather than satisfying Germany, appeasement whetted its appetite and that of the newly formed fascist coalition of Germany, Italy, and Japan, which aimed to overthrow the international status quo. Japan, disillusioned with Western liberalism and the Paris settlements, and suffering economically from the effects of the Great Depression of the 1930s, embraced militarism. In the might-makes-right climate that Germany's imperialistic quest for national aggrandizement helped to create, Japanese nationalists led their country on the path to imperialism and **colonialism.** Japan's invasions of Manchuria in 1931 and China proper in 1937 were followed by

Italy's absorption of Abyssinia in 1935 and Albania in 1939, and both Germany and Italy intervened in the 1936–1939 Spanish civil war on the side of the fascists, headed by General Francisco Franco, whereas the Soviet Union supported antifascist forces.

After Germany occupied the rest of Czechoslovakia in March 1939, Britain and France formed an alliance to protect the next likely victim, Poland. They also opened negotiations with Moscow in hopes of enticing the Soviet Union to join the alliance, but the negotiations failed. Then, on August 23, 1939, Hitler, a fascist, and the Soviet dictator, Joseph Stalin, a communist, stunned the world with the news that they had signed a nonaggression pact, promising not to attack one another. Now confident that Britain and France would not intervene, Hitler invaded Poland. Britain and France, honoring their pledge to defend the Poles, declared war on Germany two days later. World War II began.

The war expanded rapidly. Hitler next turned his forces to the Balkans, North Africa, and westward, as the mechanized German troops invaded Norway and marched through Denmark, Belgium, Luxembourg, and the Netherlands. The German army swept around the Maginot line, the defensive barrier on the eastern frontier that France boasted could not be breached. Within six weeks France surrendered, even though Germany's forces were measurably inferior to those of France and its allies. The alarming and nearly bloodless German victory forced the British to evacuate a nearly 340,000-strong expeditionary force from the French beaches at Dunkirk. Paris itself fell in June 1940. Meanwhile, to deter the United States from participating in the looming war, in September 1940 Japan forged the Tripartite Pact with Germany and Italy that pledged the three Axis powers to come to one another's aid if attacked by another nonbelligerent great power, such as the United States.

In the months that followed, the German air force, the Luftwaffe, pounded Britain in an attempt to force it into submission as well. Instead of invading Britain, however, the Nazi troops launched a surprise attack on the Soviet Union, Hitler's former ally, in June 1941. On December 7, 1941, Japan launched a surprise assault on the United States at Pearl Harbor. Almost immediately, Germany also declared war on the United States. The unprovoked Japanese assault and the German challenge ended U.S. aloofness and **isolationism**, enabling President Franklin Roosevelt to forge a coalition with Britain and the Soviet Union to oppose the fascists.

Underlying Causes at Three Analytic Levels Many historians regard the reemergence of **multipolarity** in the global power distribution as a key factor in the onset and expansion of World War II. The post–World War I global system was precarious because the number of sovereign states increased at the same time the number of great powers declined. In 1914, Europe had only twenty-two key states, but by 1921 the number had nearly doubled. When combined with resentment over the Versailles treaty, the Russian Revolution, and the rise of fascism, the increased number of states and the resurgence of nationalistic revolts and crises made "the interwar years the most violent period in international relations since the Thirty Years' War and the wars of the French Revolution and Napoleon" (K. Holsti 1991).

■ **isolationism**
a policy of withdrawing from active participation with other actors in world affairs and instead concentrating state efforts on managing internal affairs.

■ **multipolarity**
the distribution of global power into three or more great-power centers, with most other states allied with one of the rivals.

■ political economy

a field of study that focuses on the intersection of politics and economics in international relations.

■ imperialism

the policy of expanding state power through the conquest and/or military domination of foreign territory.

The 1930s collapse of the global economic system also contributed to the war. Great Britain found itself unequal to the leadership and regulatory roles it had performed in the world **political economy** before World War I. Although the United States was the logical successor, its refusal to exercise leadership hastened the war. The 1929–1931 Depression was followed in 1933 "by a world Monetary and Economic Conference whose failures—engineered by the United States—deepened the gloom, accelerated protectionist barriers to foreign trade such as tariffs and quotas, and spawned revolution" (Calvocoressi, Wint, and Pritchard 1989). In this depressed global environment, heightened by deteriorating economic circumstances at home, Germany and Japan sought solutions through **imperialism** abroad.

At the *state level of analysis,* psychological forces also led to World War II. These included "the domination of civilian discourse by military propaganda that primed the world for war," the "great wave of hypernationalism [that] swept over Europe [as] each state taught itself a mythical history while denigrating that of others," and the demise of democratic governance (Van Evera 1990–1991).

THE RISE OF HITLER AND GERMAN NATIONALISM
Consistent with the realist view that states have an inherent right to expand, Adolf Hitler's propaganda experts staged dramatic political rallies to glorify the German Fuhrer, "leader" (shown here at a fascist rally with Italy's Benito Mussolini), persuade the German people of the need to persecute the Jews, and expand German borders by armament and aggression.

Topham/Image Works

For example, domestically, German nationalism inflamed latent **irredentism** and rationalized the expansion of German borders both to regain provinces previously lost in wars to others and to absorb Germans living in Austria, Czechoslovakia, and Poland. The rise of **fascism**—the Nazi regime's **ideology** championing anti-Semitic racism against the Jews, flag, fatherland, nationalism, and imperialism—animated this renewed imperialistic push and preached the most extreme version of realism, **matchpolitik** (power politics), to justify the forceful expansion of the German state and other Axis powers that were aligned with Germany. "Everything for the state, nothing outside the state, nothing above the state" was the way Italy's dictator, Benito Mussolini, constructed his understanding of the fascist political philosophy, in a definition that embraced the extreme realist proposition that the state was entitled to rule every dimension of human life by force.

The importance of leaders at the *individual level of analysis* stands out. The war would not have been possible without Adolf Hitler and his plans to conquer the world by force. World War II arose primarily from German aggression. Professing the superiority of Germans as a "master race" along with virulent anti-Semitism and anticommunism, Hitler chose to wage war to create an empire that he believed could resolve once and for all the historic competition and precarious coexistence of the great powers in Europe by eliminating Germany's rivals.

> The broad vision of the Thousand-Year Reich was . . . of a vastly expanded—and continually expanding—German core, extending deep into Russia, with a number of vassal states and regions, including France, the Low Countries, Scandinavia, central Europe, and the Balkans, that would provide resources and labor for the core. There was to be no civilizing mission in German imperialism. On the contrary, the lesser peoples were to be taught only to do menial labor or, as Hitler once joked, educated sufficiently to read the road signs so they wouldn't get run over by German automobile traffic. The lowest of the low, the Poles and Jews, were to be exterminated. . . .To Hitler . . . the purpose of policy was to destroy the system and to reconstitute it on racial lines, with a vastly expanded Germany running a distinctly hierarchical and exploitative order. Vestiges of sovereignty might remain, but they would be fig leaves covering a monolithic order. German occupation policies during the war, whereby conquered nations were reduced to satellites, satrapies, and reservoirs of slave labor, were the practical application of Hitler's conception of the new world order. They were not improvised or planned for reasons of military necessity (Holsti 1991, 224–25).

The Consequences of World War II

Having faced ruinous losses in Russia and a massive Allied bombing campaign at home, Germany's Thousand-Year Reich lay in ruins by May 1945. By August, the U.S. atomic bombing of Hiroshima and Nagasaki forced Japan to end its war of conquest as well, and brace itself, after its shattering defeat followed by six years of U.S. military occupation, to meet the challenge of socially constructing acceptance of new values.

The Allied victory over the Axis redistributed power and reordered borders, resulting in a new geopolitical terrain. The Soviet Union absorbed nearly 600,000 square kilometers of territory from the Baltic states of Estonia, Latvia, and Lithuania, and from Finland, Czechoslovakia, Poland, and Romania—recovering what Russia had lost in the 1918 Treaty of Brest-Litovsk after World War I. Poland, a victim of Soviet expansionism, was compensated with land taken from Germany. Germany itself was

■ irredentism
a movement by an ethnic national group to recover control of lost territory by force so that the new state boundaries will no longer divide the group.

■ fascism
a far-right ideology that promotes extreme nationalism and the establishment of an authoritarian society built around a single party with dictatorial leadership.

■ ideology
a set of core philosophical principles that leaders and citizens collectively construct about politics, the interests of political actors, and the ways people ought to behave.

■ matchpolitik
the German realist philosophy in statecraft that sees the expansion of state power and territory by use of armed force as a legitimate goal.

divided into occupation zones that eventually provided the basis for its partition into East and West Germany. Finally, pro-Soviet regimes assumed power throughout Eastern Europe (see Map 4.2). In the Far East, the Soviet Union took from Japan the four Kurile Islands—or the "Northern Territories," as Japan calls them, and Korea was divided into Soviet and U.S. occupation zones at the Thirty-Eighth Parallel.

With the defeat of the Axis, one global system ended, but the defining characteristics of the new system had not yet become clear. Although the United Nations was created to replace the old, discredited League of Nations, the management of world affairs still rested in the hands of the victors. Yet victory only magnified their distrust of one another.

■ **Yalta Conference**

the 1945 summit meeting of the Allied victors to resolve postwar territorial issues and voting procedures in the United Nations to collectively manage world order.

The "Big Three" leaders—Winston Churchill, Franklin Roosevelt, and Joseph Stalin —met at the **Yalta Conference** in February 1945 to design a new world order. But the vague compromises they reached concealed the differences percolating below the surface. Following Germany's unconditional surrender in May, the Big Three (with the United States now represented by Harry Truman) met again in July 1945 at Potsdam. The meeting ended without agreement, and the facade of Allied unity began to crumble.

After the war, the United States and the Soviet Union remained the two great powers that were still strong and had the capacity to impose their will. The vanquished, Germany and Japan, fell from the ranks of the great powers. The other major-power victors, especially Great Britain, had exhausted themselves and also slid from the apex of the world-power hierarchy. Thus, as Alexis de Tocqueville had foreseen in 1835, the Americans and Russians now held in their hands the destinies of half of mankind. In comparison, all other states were dwarfs.

■ **bipolarity**

a condition in which power is concentrated in two competing centers so that the rest of the states define their allegiances in terms of their relationships with both rival great-power superstates, or "poles."

In this atmosphere, ideological debate arose about whether the twentieth century would become "the American century" or "the Russian century." Thus, perhaps the most important product of World War II was the *transformation* it caused, after a short interlude, in the distribution of global power from *multipolarity* to **bipolarity**. In what in 1949 became known as the Cold War, Washington and Moscow used the fledgling United Nations not to keep the peace but to pursue their competition with each other. As the third and last hegemonic struggle of the twentieth century, the Cold War and its lessons still cast shadows over today's geostrategic landscape.

THE COLD WAR

The second great war of the twentieth century, without parallel in the number of participants and destruction, brought about a global system dominated by two superstates whose nuclear weapons radically changed the role that threats of warfare would play in world politics. Out of these circumstances grew the competition between the United States and the Soviet Union for hegemonic leadership.

The Causes and Evolutionary Course of the Cold War

The origins of the twentieth century's third hegemonic battle for domination are debated because the historical evidence lends itself to different interpretations (see Gaddis 1997). Several postulated causes stand out. The first is advanced by realism: the **Cold War** resulted from the **power transition** that propelled the United States and the Soviet Union to the top of the international hierarchy and made their rivalry inescapable. Circumstances gave each superpower reasons to fear and to struggle against the other's potential global leadership and encouraged each superpower competitor to carve out and establish dominant influence in its own **sphere of influence,** or specified area of the globe.

A second interpretation holds that the Cold War was simply an extension of the superpowers' mutual disdain for each other's professed beliefs about politics and economics. U.S. animosity toward the Soviet Union was stimulated by the 1917 Bolshevik Revolution, which brought to power a government that embraced the radical Marxist critique of capitalistic imperialism (recall the discussion in Chapter 2 of this body of theory). U.S. fears of Marxism stimulated the emergence of anticommunism as an opposing ideology. Accordingly, the United States embarked on a missionary crusade of its own to contain and ultimately remove the atheistic communist menace from the face of the earth.

Similarly, Soviet policy was fueled by the belief that capitalism could not coexist with communism. The purpose of Soviet policy, therefore, was to push the pace of the historical process in which communism eventually would prevail. However, Soviet planners did not believe that this historical outcome was guaranteed. They felt that the capitalist states, led by the United States, sought to encircle the Soviet Union and smother communism in its cradle, and that resistance by the Soviets was obligatory. As a result, ideological incompatibility may have ruled out compromise as an option (see Controversy: Was Ideology the Primary Source of East West Conflict?).

A third explanation sees the Cold War as rooted in the superpowers' misperceptions of each other's motives. In this (constructivist) view, conflicting interests were secondary to misunderstandings and ideologies. Mistrustful actors are prone to see only virtue in their own actions and only malice in those of their adversaries. When such *mirror images* exist—the tendency of competitive states to see enemies as being opposite of the favorable way that they see themselves—hostility is inevitable. Moreover, when perceptions of an adversary's evil intentions are socially constructed and become accepted as truth, a **self-fulfilling prophecy** can develop. Prophecies are

> *Those who foresee the future and recognize it as tragic are often seized by a madness which forces them to commit the very acts which makes it certain that what they dread shall happen.*
>
> —Dame Rebecca West, Irish author and journalist

sometimes self-fulfilling because the future can be affected by the way it is anticipated. Viewing each other suspiciously, each rival giant acted in hostile ways that encouraged the very behavior that was suspected.

■ **Cold War**

the 42-year (1949-1991) rivalry between the United States and the Soviet Union, as well as their competing coalitions, which sought to contain each other's expansion and win worldwide predominance.

■ **power transition**

a narrowing of the ratio of military capabilities between great-power rivals that is thought to increase the probability of war between them.

■ **sphere of influence**

a region of the globe dominated by a great power.

■ **self-fulfilling prophecy**

the tendency for one's expectations to evoke behavior that helps to make the expectations become true.

Additional factors, beyond those rooted in divergent interests, ideologies, and images, undoubtedly combined to produce this explosive Soviet-American hegemonic rivalry. For example, the Truman-Stalin contest over jointly occupied Germany that culminated in the 1948–1949 Berlin airlift swept the two superpowers in unforeseen directions they could not manage: "conditions in the international system created risks that Truman and Stalin could not accept and opportunities they could not resist" (Leffler 2007).

To sort out the relative causal influence of contributory causes, evaluate how, once it erupted after the 1945–1948 gestation period, the Cold War changed over its forty-two-year duration. The character of the Cold War shifted in three phases over its long history (see Figure 4.1 p.105), and in that chronology are conspicuous patterns that illustrate the properties of other great-power rivalries:

■ Periods of intense conflict alternated with periods of relative cooperation; reciprocal, action-reaction exchanges were also evident (friendly U.S. initiatives toward the Soviet Union were reciprocated in kind).

■ **security regime**

norms and rules for interaction agreed to by a set of states to increase security.

■ For reasons of expediency, both rivals were willing to disregard their respective professed ideologies whenever their perceived national interests rationalized such inconsistencies; for example, each backed allies with political systems antithetical to its own when the necessities of power politics seemed to justify doing so.

■ Both rivals consistently made avoidance of all-out war their highest priority. Through a gradual learning process involving push and shove, restraint and reward, tough bargaining and calm negotiation, the superpowers created a **security regime**.

LOST OPPORTUNITIES?
The U.S. thermonuclear standoff that became the Cold War might not have occurred had the two rivals made other choices: "The Cold War was not predetermined," argues Melvyn Leffler (2007). "These leaders made choices." Shown here are Harry Truman (left) and Joseph Stalin (right).

Bettmann/CORBIS

CONTROVERSY:

WAS IDEOLOGY THE PRIMARY SOURCE OF EAST-WEST CONFLICT?

Cold War America was gripped by a "great fear" not simply of the Soviet Union but of communism. Senator Joseph McCarthy led the most infamous hunt for communist sympathizers in government, Hollywood production companies blacklisted supposed communist sympathizers, and average American citizens were often required to take loyalty oaths at their offices. Everywhere, communism became synonymous with treasonous, un-American activity. As the nuclear arms race escalated and the U.S. government took military action to contain the Soviet Union, its justification was almost always expressed in terms of ideology. The threat, as the population learned to perceive it, was that of an atheistic, communistic system that challenged the fundamental American principles of democratic capitalism. Also, according to the **domino theory**, which states that communism was driven to knock over one country after another, Soviet communism was inherently expansionistic. The other side also couched its Cold War rhetoric in terms of ideology, objecting to the imperialistic, capitalist system that the Soviets said America planned to impose on the whole world.

Some would argue that fear of the other side's world dominance may have been more important in the Cold War than pure ideology. Both the American and the Soviet governments may have entered the Cold War to secure their relative power in the world order as much as to protect pure principles. After all, the United States and the Soviet Union had managed to transcend differing ideologies when they acted as allies in World War II. After World War II, however, a power vacuum created by the demise of Europe's traditional great powers drew them into conflict with each other, and as they competed, ideological justifications surfaced.

All people have a psychological need to clarify their values and define them through the lens of an *ideology* or a belief system that expresses their convictions and enables them to explain what is of interest to them. Realism, liberalism, and Marxism-Leninism are all examples of such ideologies of international politics. Ideologies help us to interpret life and its meaning and are for that reason indispensable for organizing thought and values. But commitment to an ideology may at times cause hatred and hostility. Institutional proponents of particular ideologies are prone to perceive other ideologies competitively—as challenges to the truth of their own ideology's core beliefs. However, ideology can also become an excuse for armed violence. Although scholars are still debating the causes of the Cold War, we need to ask whether it was, in fact, an ideological contest over ideas, or a more general contest for power.

What do you think? Was the Cold War really an ideological contest between international communism and the free-market capitalism espoused by the liberal democracies, or were there other, deeper conflicts of interest involved? In considering your opinion, take into account the end of the Cold War, in which the Soviet communistic system crumbled. Communist theoretician Vladimir Lenin described the predicament that he perceived to underlie the Cold War—prophetically, it turned out—when he predicted: "As long as capitalism and socialism exist, we cannot live in peace; in the end, either one or the other will triumph—a funeral dirge will be sung either over the Soviet Republic or over world capitalism."

■ **domino theory**

a metaphor popular during the Cold War that predicted that if one state fell to communism, its neighbors would also fall in a chain reaction, like a row of falling dominoes.

■ **unipolarity**

a condition in which the global system has a single dominant power or hegemon capable of prevailing over all other states.

■ **Truman Doctrine**

the declaration by President Harry S Truman that U.S. foreign policy would use intervention to support peoples who allied with the United States against communist external subjugation.

■ **containment**

a strategy to prevent a great power rival from using force to alter the balance of power and increase its sphere of influence.

The Seedbed of the Cold War, 1945–1948   Prior to the Cold War's onset, a brief period of wary Soviet-American cordiality prevailed, when U.S. power enjoyed uncontested supremacy because it alone possessed the capacity to devastate any adversary with the atomic bomb. This was an interlude period of **unipolarity,** with the United States

> *The United States should take the lead in running the world in the way that the world ought to be run.*
>
> —Harry S Truman, U.S. President

clearly dominant; in this uncustomary preeminent position of preeminent military strength, the United States could afford to experiment with cooperation with the Soviets as it began its drive to manage global affairs.

Goodwill in the U.S.–U.S.S.R. bilateral relationship rapidly vanished as the two giants' vital interests collided outside their clearly defined by agreement *spheres of influence.* At this critical juncture, George F. Kennan, then a diplomat in the American embassy in Moscow, sent to Washington his famous "long telegram" assessing the sources of Soviet conduct. Kennan's ideas were publicized widely in 1947, when the influential journal *Foreign Affairs* circulated his views in an article he published that was signed "X" to conceal his identity as its author. In this article, Kennan argued that Soviet leaders would forever feel insecure about their political ability to maintain power against forces both within Soviet society and in the outside world. Their insecurity would lead to an activist—and perhaps aggressive—Soviet foreign policy. However, the United States had the power to increase the strains under which the Soviet leadership would have to operate, which could lead to a gradual mellowing or final end of Soviet power. Kennan concluded: "In these circumstances it is clear that the main element of any United States policy toward the Soviet Union must be that of a long-term, patient but firm and vigilant *containment* of Russian expansive tendencies" (Kennan 1947, emphasis added).

Soon thereafter, President Harry S Truman made Kennan's assessment the cornerstone of American postwar foreign policy. Provoked in part by violence in Turkey and Greece, which Truman and others believed to be communist inspired, Truman declared, "I believe that it must be the policy of the United States to support free peoples who are resisting attempted subjugation by armed minorities or by outside pressures." Eventually known as the **Truman Doctrine,** this statement defined the strategy that the United States would pursue for the next forty years, over Kennan's (1967) objections. This strategy, called **containment,** sought to prevent the expansion of Soviet influence by encircling the Soviet Union and intimidating it with the threat of a military attack.

Confrontation, 1949–1962   A seemingly endless series of new Cold War crises soon followed. They included the communist coup d'état in Czechoslovakia in 1948; the Soviet blockade of West Berlin in June of that year; the communist acquisition of power on the Chinese mainland in 1949; the outbreak of the Korean War in 1950; the Chinese invasion of Tibet in 1950; and the on-again, off-again Taiwan Straits crises. The Soviets finally broke the U.S. atomic monopoly in 1949. Thereafter, the risks of massive destruction necessitated restraint and changed the terms of the great powers' rivalry.

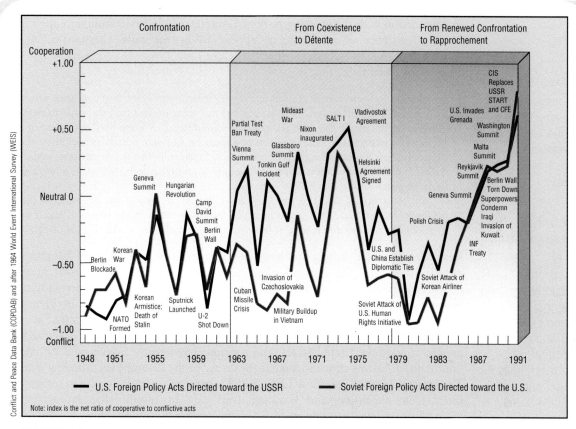

FIGURE 4.1

KEY EVENTS IN THE EVOLUTION OF THE U.S.–SOVIET RELATIONSHIP DURING COLD WAR, 1949–1991
The evolution of U.S.–Soviet relations during the Cold War displays a series of shifts between periods of conflict and cooperation. As this figure shows, each superpower's behavior toward the other tended to be reciprocal, and, for most periods before 1983, confrontation prevailed over cooperation.

Because the Soviet Union remained strategically inferior to the United States, Nikita Khrushchev (who succeeded Stalin upon his death in 1953) pursued a policy of **peaceful coexistence** with capitalism. Even so, the Soviet Union at times cautiously sought to increase its power in places where opportunities appeared to exist. As a result, the period following Stalin's death saw many Cold War confrontations, with Hungary, Cuba, Egypt, and Berlin becoming the flash points.

As the arms race accelerated, the threats to peace multiplied. In 1962, the surreptitious placement of Soviet missiles in Cuba set the stage for the greatest test of the superpowers' capacity to manage their disputes—the Cuban Missile Crisis. The superpowers stood eyeball to eyeball. Fortunately, one (the Soviet Union) blinked, and the crisis ended. This painful learning experience both reduced enthusiasm for waging the Cold War by military means and expanded awareness of the suicidal consequences of a nuclear war.

■ **peaceful coexistence**

Soviet leader Nikita Krushchev's 1956 doctrine that war between capitalist and communist states is not inevitable and that inter-bloc competition could be peaceful.

■ **détente**

in general, a strategy of seeking to relax tensions between adversaries to reduce the possibility of war.

■ **Strategic Arms Limitation Talks (SALT)**

two sets of agreements reached during the 1970s between the United States and the Soviet Union that established limits on strategic nuclear delivery systems.

■ **Carter Doctrine**

President Jimmy Carter's declaration of U.S. willingness to use military force to protect its interests in the Persian Gulf.

■ **"linkage" strategy**

a set of assertions claiming that leaders should take into account another country's overall behavior when deciding whether to reach agreement on any one specific issue so as to link cooperation to rewards.

From Coexistence to Détente, 1963–1978 The growing threat of mutual destruction, in conjunction with the growing parity of American and Soviet military capabilities, made coexistence or nonexistence appear to be the only alternatives. At the American University commencement exercises in 1963, U.S. President John F. Kennedy warned that

... should total war ever break out again—no matter how—our two countries would become the primary targets. It is an ironical but accurate fact that the two strongest powers are the two in the most danger of devastation. . . . We are both caught up in a vicious and dangerous cycle in which suspicion on one side breeds suspicion on the other and new weapons beget counterweapons. In short, both the United States and its allies, and the Soviet Union and its allies, have a mutually deep interest in a just and genuine peace and in halting the arms race. . . .

So let us not be blind to our differences, but let us also direct attention to our common interests and to the means by which those differences can be resolved. And if we cannot end now our differences, at least we can help make the world safe for diversity.

Kennedy signaled a shift in how the United States hoped thereafter to bargain with its adversary, and the Soviet Union reciprocally expressed its interest in more cooperative relations. That movement took another step forward following Richard Nixon's election in 1968. Coached by his national security adviser, Henry A. Kissinger, President Nixon initiated a new approach to Soviet relations that in 1969 he officially labeled **détente**. The Soviets also adopted this term to describe their policies toward the United States, and relations between the Soviets and Americans "normalized." Arms control stood at the center of the dialogue surrounding *détente*. The **Strategic Arms Limitation Talks (SALT)**, initiated in 1969, sought to restrain the threatening, expensive, and spiraling arms race by limiting the deployment of antiballistic missiles. As Figure 4.1 shows, cooperative interaction became more commonplace than hostile relations. Visits, cultural exchanges, trade agreements, and joint technological ventures replaced threats, warnings, and confrontations.

From Renewed Confrontation to Rapprochement, 1979–1991 Despite the careful nurturing of détente, its spirit did not endure. When the Soviet invasion of Afghanistan in 1979 led to détente's demise, President Jimmy Carter defined the situation as "the most serious strategic challenge since the Cold War began." In retaliation, he advanced the **Carter Doctrine** declaring America's willingness to use military force to protect its access to oil supplies from the Persian Gulf. In addition, he attempted to organize a worldwide boycott of the 1980 Moscow Olympics and suspended U.S. grain exports to the Soviet Union.

Relations deteriorated dramatically thereafter. President Ronald Reagan and his Soviet counterparts (first Yuri Andropov and then Konstantin Chernenko) exchanged a barrage of confrontational rhetoric. Reagan asserted that the Soviet Union "underlies all the unrest that is going on" and described the Soviet Union as "the focus of evil in the modern world." The atmosphere was punctuated by Reagan policy adviser Richard Pipes's bold challenge in 1981 that the Soviets would have to choose between "peacefully changing their communist system . . . or going to war." Soviet rhetoric was equally unrestrained and alarmist.

As talk of war increased, preparations for it escalated. The arms race resumed feverishly, at the expense of addressing domestic economic problems. The superpowers also extended the confrontation to new territory, such as Central

Biber/SIPA Press

EASING TENSIONS: U.S.–SOVIET DÉTENTE Pictured here, President Richard Nixon, one of the architects of the U.S. "linkage" strategy along with Secretary of State Henry Kissinger, toasts Soviet Premier Leonid Brezhnev and fellow dignitaries at their meeting to discuss approaches to relaxing tensions between the superpowers.

America, and renewed their public diplomacy (propaganda) efforts to extol the virtues of their respective systems throughout the world. The **Reagan Doctrine** pledged U.S. support for anticommunist insurgents who sought to overthrow Soviet-supported governments in Afghanistan, Angola, and Nicaragua. In addition, American leaders spoke loosely about the "winability" of a nuclear war through a "prevailing" military strategy that included the threat of a "first use" of nuclear weapons in the event of conventional war. Relations deteriorated as these moves and countermoves took their toll. The new Soviet leader, Mikhail Gorbachev, in 1985 summarized the alarming state of superpower relations by fretting that "The situation is very complex, very tense. I would even go so far as to say it is explosive."

However, the situation did not explode. Instead, prospects for a more constructive phase improved greatly following Gorbachev's advocacy of "new thinking" in order to achieve a **rapprochement**, or reconciliation, of the rival states' interests. He sought to settle the Soviet Union's differences with the capitalist West in order to halt the deterioration of his country's economy and international position. Shortly thereafter, Gorbachev embarked on domestic reforms to promote democratization and the transition to a market economy, and proclaimed his desire to end the Cold War contest. "We realize that we are divided by profound historical, ideological, socioeconomic, and cultural differences," he noted during his first visit in 1987 to the United States. "But the wisdom of politics today lies in not using those differences as a pretext for confrontation, enmity, and the arms race." Soviet spokesperson Georgi Arbatov elaborated, informing the United States that "we are going to do a terrible thing to you—we are going to deprive you of an enemy."

■ **Reagan Doctrine**

a U.S. promise to support anticommunist insurgents attempting to overthrow governments backed by the Soviet Union.

■ **rapprochement**

in diplomacy, a policy seeking to reestablish normal cordial relations between enemies.

Surprisingly, to many adherents of *realism* who see great-power contests for supremacy as inevitable and strategic surrender or acceptance of defeat an impossibility, the Soviets did what they promised: they began to act like an ally instead of an enemy. The Soviet Union agreed to end its aid to and support for Cuba, withdrew from Afghanistan and eastern Europe, and announced unilateral reductions in military spending. Gorbachev also agreed to two new disarmament agreements: the START (Strategic Arms Reduction Treaty) treaty for deep cuts in strategic arsenals and the Conventional Forces in Europe (CFE) treaty to reduce the Soviet presence in Europe. In addition, the Soviet Union liberalized its emigration policies and permitted greater religious freedom.

The pace of steps to rapprochement then accelerated, and the "normalization" of Soviet–American relations moved rapidly. The Cold War—which began in Europe—began to crumble in 1989 when the Berlin Wall came down and truly ended there in 1991 when the Soviet Union dissolved, accepted capitalist free-market principles, and initiated democratic reforms. To nearly everyone's astonishment, the Soviet Union acquiesced in the defeat of communism, the reunification of Germany, and the disintegration of its east European bloc of allies, the Warsaw Pact (see Controversy: Why Did the Cold War End Peacefully?). The conclusion of the enduring rivalry between East and West, and with it the end of the seventy-year ideological dispute as well, was such a history-transforming event that, without serious opposition to liberal capitalism, the **end of history** was proclaimed by Francis Fukuyama (1992b). "Liberalism seemed to have triumphed—not merely capitalism but democracy and the rule of law, as represented in the West, and particularly in the United States" (Keohane and Nye 2001a).

The collapse of the Cold War suggested something quite different from the lesson of the twentieth century's two world wars, which had implied that great-power rivalries are necessarily doomed to end in armed conflict. The Cold War was different; it came to an end peacefully, as a combination of factors contributed at various stages in the Cold War's evolution to transform a global rivalry into a stable, even cooperative, relationship. This suggests that it is sometimes possible for great-power rivals to reconcile their competitive differences without warfare.

■ end of history
Francis Fukuyama's thesis that an end-point in the ideological debate about the best form of government and economy had been reached, with liberal capitalism and democracy prevailing throughout the world without serious competition from advocates of either communism or autocracy.

CONTROVERSY:

WHY DID THE COLD WAR END PEACEFULLY?

How history is remembered is important because those memories shape future decisions about the management of great-power rivalries. Why did the Cold War end without the use of armed force? That question remains a puzzle that still provokes much controversy, in part because the Cold War's abrupt end came as such a surprise to most observers. Also, the unanticipated outcome undermined confidence in the adequacy of conventional realist theories—which argued that no great power would ever accept the loss of position to another hegemonic rival without a fight.

What do you think? What was the cause of the Cold War's collapse? In considering your view on this issue, consider the diversity of opinions, at three *levels of analysis*, reflective of realist, liberal and constructivist theorizing:

Contending Interpretations of the Causes of the Cold War's End

Level of Analysis	Theoretical Perspective		
	Realism	Liberalism	Constructivism
Individual	*Hardball Power Politics*	*Leaders as Movers of History*	*External Influences on Leadership*
	"The people who argued for nuclear deterrence and serious military capabilities contributed mightily to the position of strength that eventually led the Soviet leadership to choose a less bellicose, less menacing approach to international politics."—Richard Perle, U.S. presidential adviser	"[The end of the Cold War was possible] primarily because of one man— Mikhail Gorbachev. The transformations . . . would not have begun were it not for him."—James A. Baker III, U.S. Secretary of State	"Reagan's 'tough' policy and intensified arms race [did not persuade] communists to 'give up.' [This is] sheer nonsense. Quite the contrary, this policy made the life for reformers, for all who yearned for democratic changes in their life, much more difficult. . . The [communist hard-line] conservatives and reactionaries were given predominant influence. . . . Reagan made it practically impossible to start reforms after Brezhev's death (Andropov had such plans) and made things more difficult for Gorbachev to cut military expenditures."—Georgi Arbatov, Director of the USSR's Institute for the USA and Canada Studies

(continues)

Level of Analysis	Theoretical Perspective		
	Realism	Liberalism	Constructivism
State	*Economic Mismanagement*	*Grassroots Movements*	*Ideas and Ideals*
	"Soviet militarism, in harness with communism, destroyed the Soviet economy and thus hastened the self-destruction of the Soviet empire."—Fred Charles Iklé, U.S. Deputy Secretary of Defense	"The Soviet Union collapsed at the hands of its own people."—Thomas L. Friedman, political journalist	"[The many Russian demonstrators] who sought to reject communist rule looked to the American system for inspiration. But the source of that inspiration was America's reputation as a haven for the values of limited government, not Washington's [huge and unsurpassed annual] military budget and its network of global military bases."—Ted Galen Carpenter, policy analyst
Global	*Containment*	*International Public Opinion*	*Cross-Border Contagion Effects*
	"The U.S. and our allies deserve great credit for maintaining the military and economic power to resist and turn back Soviet aggression."—Richard M. Nixon, U.S. president	"The changes wrought by thousands of people serving in the trenches [throughout the world] were at least partially responsible [for ending the Cold War]."—David Cortright, political scientist	"The acute phase of the fall of communism started outside of the Soviet Union and spread to the Soviet Union itself. By 1987, Gorbachev made it clear that he would not interfere with internal experiments in Soviet bloc countries. . . . Once communism fell in Eastern Europe, the alternative in the Soviet Union became civil war or dissolution."—Daniel Klenbort, political journalist

Evaluate the validity of these contending hypotheses about the causes of the Cold War's peaceful end. They can't all be correct. So act like a detective looking for clues about causation. And keep in mind the epistemological warning about approaches to analysis voiced by the fictional mastermind detective Sherlock Holmes: "It is a capital mistake to theorize before one has data. Insensibly one begins to twist facts to suit theories, instead of theories to suit facts" (Borer and Bowen 2007).

As constructivism warns, the lessons drawn from this forty-two-year Cold War drama remain important because they affect how leaders are likely to manage new great-power rivalries throughout the twenty-first century.

The Consequences of the Cold War

Although they were locked in a geostrategic rivalry made worse by antagonistic ideologies and mutual misperceptions, the United States and the Soviet Union avoided a fatal showdown. In accepting the devolution of their empire, Russian leaders made the most dramatic peaceful retreat from power in history. The end of the Cold War altered the face of world affairs in profound and diverse ways. With the dissolution of the Soviet Union in 1991, no immediate great-power challenger confronted American hegemonic leadership. However, a host of new security threats emerged, ranging from aspiring nuclear powers such as North Korea and Iran to terrorist networks such as Al Qaeda. As the turbulent twentieth century wound down, the simple Cold War world of clearly defined adversaries gave way to a shadowy world of elusive foes.

THE FUTURE OF GREAT POWER POLITICS: A COLD PEACE?

Rapid, unanticipated changes in world politics create uncertainty about the global future. To optimists, the swift transformations following the collapse of communism signalled "the end of mankind's ideological evolution and the universalization of Western liberal democracy as the final form of government" (Fukuyama 1989). To pessimists, these sea changes suggested not history's end but the resumption of contests for hegemonic domination and opposition over contested ideas and ideologies.

Both groups recognized that Cold War bipolarity had been superseded by *unipolarity*—a hegemonic configuration of power with only one predominant superstate. This presents new and difficult challenges.

America's Unipolar Moment in History

Unipolarity refers to the concentration of power in a single preponderant state. At present, in a historical "moment" in world history (Krauthammer 2003), the United States now stands alone at the summit of the international hierarchy. It is the only country with the military, economic, and cultural assets to be a decisive player in any part of the world it chooses. Its military is not just stronger than anybody else's, it is stronger than everybody else's, with defense expenditures in 2009 larger than nearly all other countries combined. Complementing America's military might is its awesome economic strength. With less than 5 percent of the global population, the United States accounts for a fifth of global income and two-fifths of the entire world's combined spending on research and development. Further, America continues to wield enormous **soft power** (Nye 2008) because it is the hub of global communications and popular culture, through which its values spread all over the world (Galeota 2006). In the words of former French Foreign Minister Hubart Vedrine, the United States is not simply a superpower, it is a "hyperpower."

■ soft power
the capacity to co-opt through such intangible factors as the popularity of a state's values and institutions, as opposed to the "hard power" to coerce through military might.

> *When you can get others to admire your ideals and to want what you want, you do not have to spend as much on sticks and carrots.*
> —Dan Caldwell, foreign policy expert

This rare confluence of military, economic, and cultural power gives the United States what might appear to be an extraordinary ability to shape the global future to its will. This is why America's unique superpower position atop the global pyramid of power seemingly allows it to act independently without worries about resistance from weaker powers. Rather than working in concert with others, a strong and dominant hegemon can address international problems without reliance on global organizations and can "go it alone," even in the face of strident foreign criticism.

Unilateralism has its costs, however. Acting alone may appear expedient, but it erodes international support on issues such as combating terrorism on which the United States is in strong need of cooperation from others. Overwhelming power, observes Henry Kissinger, "evokes nearly automatically a quest by other societies to achieve a greater voice . . . and to reduce the relative position of the strongest." In the wake of the 2003 invasion of Iraq, Washington's neglect of the politics of compromise and consensus building has "reduced America's standing in the world and made the United States less, not more, secure" (Freedland 2007). As former Reagan policy maker Clyde Prestowitz laments, by abusing its power through defiant unilateralism the United States has become a hated and feared "rogue nation" acting as an international outlaw playing by its own rules. Confronted by a wave of "anti-Americanism" abroad, the American empire has grown weaker (Johnson 2007). America finds itself isolated at the very time it most needs friends.

The status of being a superpower, the single "pole," or center, of power without a real challenger has fated the United States with heavy and grave responsibilities. Although the United States may hold an unrivaled position in the world today, in the long run *unipolarity* is very unlikely to endure. No previous *hegemon* has maintained primacy indefinitely. As Map 4.3 and Figure 4.2 show, the long-term economic trajectories based on differential national growth rates point to a world in which China is likely to overtake the United States, followed by another day when a united Europe and perhaps other great powers, such as India, will eventually also challenge American financial preeminence. At the same time, the United States will find it costly to maintain military dominance. Aside from major deployments in Afghanistan and Iraq, U.S. forces are positioned in 737 U.S. military bases in 132 foreign countries (Freedland 2007, 18) along an arc of global instability reaching from the Balkans to the Caucasus, through the Gulf of Arden to the Korean Peninsula in Asia, and in Haiti. Restraints on U.S. hegemonic leadership abound. As Richard Haass, in charge of U.S. policy in 2003, warns: "America remains the world's preeminent actor, but it is also stretched militarily, in debt financially, divided domestically, and unpopular internationally." Diplomatic historian Paul Kennedy (2006) agrees that there are growing limits on American domination: "The United States possesses the world's single largest national economy but faces huge trade and budget deficits and economic rivalries from an equally large European Union and a fast-growing China. Its armed forces look colossal, but its obligations look even larger."

Imperial overstretch, the gap between internal resources and external commitments, has bedeviled every previous leading great power (Kennedy 1987). Throughout history, *hegemons* repeatedly have defined their security interests more broadly than other states, only to slip from the pinnacle of power by reaching beyond their grasp. Excessive costs to preserve America's empire by military means could prove to burst "the bubble of American supremacy" (Soros 2003; Sanger 2005); as shown in Figure 4.2, by 2020 China's economy is expected to surpass America's.

■ **imperial overstretch**

the phrase coined by Paul Kennedy to capture the historic tendency for past hegemons to sap their own strength through costly imperial pursuits and military spending that weaken their economies in relation to the economies of their rivals.

World Development Report 2008, pp. 334–335.

MAP 4.3

EMERGING CENTERS OF POWER IN THE TWENTY-FIRST CENTURY GLOBAL HIERARCHY **To estimate which countries are the most powerful and which are relatively weak, analysts frequently rely on the size of states' economies because that measure predicts the *power potential* of each state (that is, their relative capacity to project power and exercise global influence). This map pictures the proportionate economic clout of the leading great powers (measured by purchasing power parities), showing the United States, China, Japan, India, and Germany as today's leading economic powerhouses.**

> *The problem in defense spending is to figure out how far you should go without destroying from within what you are trying to defend from without.*
>
> —Dwight David Eisenhower, U.S. President

From Unipolarity to Multipolarity

If some combination of U.S. imperial overstretch alongside rising economic and military expense by America's chief challengers transforms the current distribution of global power, many scholars and policy makers predict that a *multipolar* global system with more than two dominant centers of power will emerge. Some of the states frequently mentioned as potential members of a future **power balance** known as multipolarity will include the United States, China, the European Union, Japan, India, and a reinvigorated Russia. Because multipolar systems include several comparatively equal great powers, they are complex. When we take into account the interplay of military and economic factors, such circumstances of great powers competing as equals are also fraught with uncertainty. Differentiating friend from foe becomes especially difficult when allies in military security may be rivals in trade relationships.

■ **power balance**

a division of global military and economic capabilities among more than one center or dominant superpower.

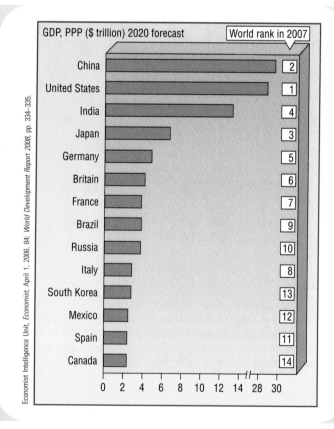

FIGURE 4.2

PROJECTION OF THE LARGEST GLOBAL ECONOMIES BY 2020 (Index, United States = 100) **Using purchasing power parities (PPPs) to remove differences in countries' price levels, the** *Economist* **forecasts the probable size of the largest economies in 2020. The projections show that the rank order of the largest economic powerhouses by 2020 will be substantially different from today's with China narrowly overtaking the United States. The political and military consequences are not predicted, but** *long-cycle theory* **postulates that the economic changes will breed political and even military conflict, because "major shifts of power between states not to mention regions ... occur infrequently and are rarely peaceful" (Hoge 2006).**

Predicting what cleavages and partnerships will develop among the great powers in the future twenty-first-century multipolar system will be difficult because it will be hard to foresee what will become the next major axis of conflict. Competition could emerge from any pair of great powers, but it may be restricted to one sphere of interaction. For example, the United States, Japan, China, and India are highly competitive in their commercial relations, but nevertheless they also display continuing efforts to manage their security relations collaboratively, as shown by their cooperation in fighting terrorism (Mead 2006).

Such cross-cutting axes of conflict and cooperation will affect the stability of any future multipolar system. Throughout history, different types of multipolar systems have existed, some of which have experienced more stability than others. The most unstable have possessed rigid, polarized alignments, such as during the period prior to the outbreak of World War I (Kegley and Raymond 1994). *Polarization*—the formation of competing coalitions or blocs composed of allies that align with one of the major competing poles, or centers, of power—is dangerous because it usually focuses attention on a single threat, making it more likely that minor disagreements will become magnified into larger tests of will. When great powers compete in one sphere of activity but cooperate elsewhere, the potential increases that any given issue will divide them in opposing coalitions. Great-power conflict would be frequent, but as long as security and economic disputes did not overlap, they would not necessarily divide the system into two antagonistic camps. Under these circumstances, the danger of polarization could be managed if the great powers develop international rules and institutions to manage their fluid, mixed-motive relationships.

The diffusion of wealth predicts the likely intensification of great-power political competition. Throughout history, changes in comparative economic advantage have preceded political competition. When multipolarity has existed, economic rivals have struggled to protect their wealth and have competed politically for economic position. Military conflict often has followed a major **power transition** When a great power successfully challenges a hegemon's world leadership, the new leader is likely to pursue changes in the global status quo, even though some newly dominant powers may be interested primarily in conservatively maintaining the new global hierarchy that now works to their benefit (Palmer and Morgan 2007). Power transitions can be either destabilizing or stabilizing depending on the construction that a hegemon makes of the new strategic circumstances. As Monica Toft (2007) observes, "Power matters and so shifts in power matter; but what matters most is how relevant actors perceive the consequences of shifts in power."

■ power transition

a narrowing of the ratio of military capabilities between great-power rivals that is thought to increase the probability of war between them.

A "new cold war" could emerge between any pair of great powers, such as between the globe's two major contenders for supremacy, the United States and China, if their competition escalates and they practice containment to prevent their rival's quest for hegemony. However, this kind of armed rivalry need not develop; cooperation could increase instead. Quite different and inconsistent political types of great-power relations could emerge in the economic and military spheres. There is the probability of economic rivalry growing as global trade expands the integration of states' economies in a ever-tightening web of interdependence. However, the likelihood of security cooperation for many of these same relationships is also high. For example,

Stephen Shaver/AFP/Getty Images

A NEW GLOBAL HEGEMON? China's status as an economic powerhouse has generated fears elsewhere that as China becomes a modern military power it will seek hegemony and eventually use force to cause trouble abroad. In Beijing, China's rise to great power status is seen as helpful to maintaining peace. Shown here are Chinese People's Liberation Army soldiers marching with bayoneted rifles while performing official honor guard duties at a welcoming ceremony in Beijing— a show of strength at Tiananmen Square by the Chinese army, and a symbol of China's potential to project power.

the United States, Japan, and China exhibit intensely competitive commercial relations but nevertheless cooperate to manage their security relations (as shown by their collaboration in fighting terrorism).

Tables 4.2a and 4.2b present a projection of the kind of cross-cutting bilateral relationships that could develop among the great powers throughout the twenty-first century. It estimates the probability of military cooperation and economic conflict between any pair of the five major powers.

Awareness of these different possibilities of cross-cutting axes of conflict and cooperation may have been behind former U.S. Secretary of State Lawrence Eagleburger's warning about the best way to steer the great powers through the ocean of perils:

> The issue: . . . is how well the United States accomplishes the transition from overwhelming predominance to a position more akin to a "first among equals" status, and how well America's partners—Japan and Western Europe—adapt to their newfound importance. The change will not be easy for any of the players, as such shifts in power relationships have never been easy.

The New Great-Power Chessboard: Simultaneously Unfolding Military and Economic Rivalries

Table 4.2a Military Rivalry	United States	Japan	European Union	Russia	China
United States	—				
Japan	L	—			
European Union	M	M	—		
Russia	H	H	H	—	
China	H	H	H	M	—

Table 4.2b Economic Rivalry	United States	Japan	European Union	Russia	China
United States	—				
Japan	H	—			
European Union	H	H	—		
Russia	L	L	M	—	
China	H	H	M	M	—

Note: The symbols H=high, M=medium, and L=low predict the probability of increasing future rivalries in various bilateral relationships.

Today the paradox prevails that many pairs of great powers that are the most active trade partners are also the greatest military rivals, but the key question is whether economic cooperation will help to reduce the potential for military competition in the future. Of course, we have no way of knowing whether the future will resemble the gloomy history of multipolar systems. Patterns and practices can change, and it is possible for policy makers to learn from previous mistakes and avoid repeating them. What is crucial is how the great powers react to the eventual emergence of a new multipolar global system. As Michelle Benson (2007) argues, to understand great power relations it is important to rely upon *power transition theory* because "this theory has proven itself to be the most successful structural theory of war [suggesting] that three simple conditions—power transition, relative power parity, and a dissimilarity of preferences for the status quo—are necessary for great power war." The grand strategies each of the powers forge to adapt to such new circumstances of shared power will be critical. Depending on the national security policies they embrace, they could shape a peaceful future. What are the options in the menu of choice?

Options for Responding to Multipolarity's Challenge

What, then, can the great powers do to prevent the resumption of their rivalry? What security policies should they pursue to avoid the dangers of shared power and rapid transitions in their position and strength in the great-power hierarchy?

Consensus about strategic choices does not exist and is hard to achieve because strategic priorities are not mere products of strategic circumstances (Legro 2007). Debate about foreign policy goals and means in Washington, Beijing, Tokyo, Brussels, and Moscow today revolves around four basic options. Each is actively under consideration, and each will become more or less practical, prudent, or problematic for each great power depending on the circumstances that materialize in tomorrow's multipolar world.

Unilateralism is an especially attractive option for a self-confident *hegemon* that can be self-reliant. Unilateralism can involve isolationism; an attempt to exert hegemonic leadership; a strategy of **selective engagement** that concentrates external involvements on vital national interests; or an effort to play the role of a "balancer" that skillfully backs one side or another in a great-power dispute (but only when necessary to maintain a military equilibrium between the other great-power disputants). At the extreme, unilateralism can lead the global leader to play the role of international bully, seeking to run the world. More commonly, unilateralism derives from the desire for control over the flexible conduct of a great power's foreign relations, independent of control by or pressure from other great powers.

Cultivation of a specialized relationship with another great power, similar to that between Great Britain and the United States, illustrates a second approach that some pairs of great powers might pursue. Many kinds of strategic bilateral partnerships can develop in a climate of fear, even between powers that have suffered from frosty relations in the recent past. For example, asserting that "no country should claim hegemony for itself or pursue policy from positions of strength and monopolize international affairs," Moscow and Beijing announced their agreement to warm relations by joining together to counterbalance the United States as the world's lone superpower. China also strengthened its new alliance with Russia to counterbalance the perceived threat of a U.S.-EU-Japanese attempt to squeeze the country from both east and west. Such dances among global giants, with the rapid formation and expansion of short-term specialized relationships among pairs of great powers in a climate of suspicion, is exactly the kind of national security maneuvering many expect to occur in the twenty-first century under conditions of *multipolarity* (Mearsheimer 2004). Still other types of specialized relations between pairs of great powers could follow, at various levels of mutual support and commitment. Among the several variants of this strategic option are cordial, informal understandings (sometimes termed an **entente**) and alliances formalized by treaties.

A third strategy under consideration is construction of a **concert**, or a cooperative agreement among the great powers to manage the global system jointly and to prevent international disputes from escalating to war. The Concert of Europe, at its apex between 1815 and 1822, is the epitome of previous great-power efforts to pursue this path to peace. The effort to build a great power coalition to wage a war against global terrorism following 9/11 is a more recent example of **multilateralism** to construct a concert through collective approaches.

■ **unilateralism**

an approach that relies on self-help, independent strategies in foreign policy.

■ **selective engagement**

a great power grand strategy using economic and military power to influence only important particular situations, countries, or global issues by striking a balance between a highly interventionist "global policeman" and an uninvolved isolationist.

■ **entente**

an agreement between states to consult one another and take a common course of action if one is attacked by another state.

■ **concert**

a cooperative agreement in design and plan among great powers to manage jointly the global system.

Finally, some policy makers recommend that today's great powers unite with the lesser powers in constructing a true system of *collective security*. The principles rationalizing the formation of the League of Nations in 1919 is the best example of this multilateral approach to peace under conditions of *multipolarity,* and some believe Russia's pledge to cooperate with NATO is representative of a collective security quest to maintain peace through an alliance of powerful countries.

> ■ **multilateralism**
> cooperative approaches to managing shared problems through collective and coordinated action.

Whichever combination of approaches predominates in the strategies forged to prevent great-power rivalries from escalating to war in a multipolar future, it is clear that the choices the great powers make about war and peace will determine the fate of the world.

The future is largely in the hands of the great powers because "powerful states make the rules" (Keohane and Nye 2001a). A look at their current strategies provides a glimpse into how the great powers are constructing new approaches to adapt to changing global circumstances.

THE GREAT POWERS' CONTEMPORARY NATIONAL SECURITY STRATEGIES

For the great powers to forge adaptive strategies, they will have to make hard choices to honor ideals without undermining self-interests: in short, to reconcile *liberalism* and *realism*. This is how the major players are now proceeding.

America's Strategic Initiatives

In 2009, as Barack Obama became the new U.S. President, he faced immediate challenges posed by an array of formidable threats to U.S. security. His administration pledged a change from the "unapologetic and implacable demonstrations of will" (Krauthammer 2001) that had characterized the preemptive and unilateral policies of the prior administration. Instead, he called for a foreign policy that maintained America's military strength but also sought to move beyond a single-minded focus on Iraq and broaden engagement with the global community.

As highlighted by his "Blueprint for Change," President Obama's national security strategy and identification of U.S. priorities reflects a mix of *realpolitik* and *liberalism*:

■ Ending the war in Iraq with a phased withdrawal of U.S. troops, leaving only a small force for training and counter-terrorism purposes, increased political pressure on the Iraqi government to stabilize their political system, and humanitarian assistance for Iraqi refugees

■ Refocusing the fight against Al Qaeda by allocating more U.S. troops and resources to Afghanistan and the tribal regions of Pakistan

■ Reducing the threat of nuclear proliferation, securing all nuclear weapons and materials from terrorists and rogue states, and developing new defenses to protect against the threat of cyber-terrorism and biological weapons

- Renewing American diplomacy, with a willingness to engage in dialogue with friend and foe without precondition in order to advance U.S. interests

- Rebuilding U.S. alliances to usher in a new era of international cooperation, such as the Shared Security Partnership Program that aims to bring together the world's nations in a strengthened effort to destroy global terrorist networks

- Engaging in tough diplomacy with Iran, with incentives such as membership in the World Trade Organization offered if it abandons its nuclear program and increased economic sanctions and political isolation if it does not

- Engaging a resurgent Russia on issues of mutual interest such as nuclear proliferation and the expansion of trade and investment, while providing proactive diplomacy to mitigate conflicts between Russia and its neighboring countries

- Declaring that "one of the most dangerous weapons in the world today is the price of oil," President Obama seeks to achieve energy security by ending American dependence on foreign oil

- Developing a new Global Energy Forum that, as a multilateral initiative, will provide a framework for new international protocols on climate change

China's Ascendance and Global Clout

China's economy has grown since its economic reforms in the 1980s at a compound annual rate of about 10 percent. This has made China one of the world's wealthiest countries. These resources have positioned China, formerly regarded as a sleeping giant, to awaken and play an increasingly active role on the global stage. To convert economic power into geostrategic power, China has implemented an aggressive military modernization program on a crash basis, and has steadily increased its

> *Let China sleep. When it awakens, the world will tremble.*
>
> —Napoleon Bonaparte, French emperor

defense spending. At the same time, Chinese leaders have repeatedly asserted that China seeks peaceful relations with all the great powers (while condemning the United States for pursuing the singular goal of "hegemonic domination of the world").

To find a safe place in the sun, where it feels it belongs, China has defined its national security priorities through a strategy that seeks to

- Deter a large-scale conventional or nuclear attack on China by any other great power, such as the United States

- Develop the military force required to successfully invade Taiwan should negotiations fail to integrate with the mainland what China sees as a renegade province

- Lobby to see that traditional international legal rules prohibiting external interference in sovereign states' domestic affairs is respected, to safeguard against further foreign intervention to punish China for disregard of its citizens' human rights

- View globalization more as an opportunity than a threat (Deng and Moore 2006) by enthusiastically participating in trade and investment overseas

- Maintain a lid on internal rebellion by alleviating the suffering of the 35 percent of its 1.4 billion people below the $2 a day poverty line (WDR 2008, 336). Income inequality within China is growing, and that is leading to dangerous citizen unrest that must be contained for stability. The Chinese "government has acknowledged that more than 50,000 demonstrations take place each year—many of them large and violent" (Keidel 2005, A11)

- Undertake bold reforms to curtail extreme water pollution and land degradation —an environmental crisis that threatens China's quest for global preeminence (Economy 2007)

The European Union's Search for a Strategic Vision

Germany leads and dominates the twenty-seven-member European Union (EU), and what happens in Germany is critical for the rest of Europe. There is no other EU country capable of balancing the power of Germany. "Too big for Europe, too small for the world" describes Germany's place in continental affairs.

A strong German EU aversion to militarism underpins the EU emphasis on nonmilitary approaches to global security. The continent is an enthusiastic supporter of integration and institutional approaches to the preservation of peace, and Europe's security strategy unflinchingly embraces the principles of *neoliberal institutionalism*: the spread of international organizations, European unification, international law, disarmament, and the promotion of democracy and human rights alongside free markets and free trade as the most effective strategy for ensuring that a twenty-first-century peace will prevail. Germany and the European Union share a consensus about the dangers of making war and the kinds of conflicts between allies that, if mismanaged, can lead to warfare. "Their solution is 'anything but war,'" realist political journalist Fareed Zakaria observes, but the European Union spends less than a fifth of what America spends on defense and "no European politician of note has urged large increases in defense spending" that may be necessary to deter another large-scale war. Instead EU countries "spend lavishly on aid and send negotiation teams around the globe pedaling their kinder, gentler power." It may be true that the European Union has aspirations to become a new superpower (Leonard

2005), but that is unlikely to be a realistic aim as long as the European countries remain challenged by the need to reach agreement in their security institutions in order to forge a coordinated approach to foreign policy.

Japan's Strategic Posture

An emerging economic superpower in the 1990s and proudly the third richest country, Japan has recently struggled to keep pace economically and has been overlooked by China, the most expanding economy in the world. The future is clouded by Japan's aging and shrinking population and high national debt.

■ **Yoshida Doctrine**

Japan's traditional security policy of avoiding disputes with rivals, preventing foreign wars by low military spending, and promoting economic growth through foreign trade.

In the aftermath of World War II, Japan strictly adhered to the guidelines of the **Yoshida Doctrine**, in which Prime Minister Shigeru Yoshida argued that Japanese security policy should avoid international disputes, keep a low profile on divisive global issues, and concentrate on economic pursuits. That doctrine remains timely, given the 1990s' "lost decade" in which the Japanese economy actually declined, undermining the country's ability to play a more active global role. Japan continues to stress words over deeds and to advocate a neoliberal foreign policy philosophy.

Despite economic restraints, Japan is expanding its global involvement, Prime Minister Kiichi Miyazawa won passage of the Peacekeeping Operations Bill, which enabled Japan to deploy a self-defense military force to participate in UN peacekeeping operations in Cambodia in 1992—the first use of Japanese armed forces abroad since World War II. Japan's reluctant acceptance of a large increase in its previous UN dues (currently the second largest contributor), its push for inclusion as a permanent member of the UN Security Council, and its rise to become the world's second largest foreign aid donor, also suggest growing Japanese international activism. Such policies continue.

Japan still adheres to the policy of spending no more than 1 percent of its gross national product on defense and remains committed to its postwar constitution, which forbids remilitarization. However, after a half-century of strict pacifism, Japan is alarmed that its neighbors' arms races are disrupting the Asian balance of power, and it is jittery over North Korea's launches of three-stage long-range missiles over Japan in 1998 and again in 2006. In response to China's increase in military expenditures, in 2008 Japanese Defense Minister Shigeru Ishiba called on China to be more transparent about its motives and its military capabilities, including ballistic missiles and nuclear weapons. Japan is reconsidering how military might can contribute to national security and global standing. Japan's Self-Defense Force is impressive, with 272,000 soldiers in uniform and the Pacific's largest navy. Although it does not have advanced offensive weapons such as long-range bombers and aircraft carriers, Japan has some of the most sophisticated submarines in the world. Japan's air force and navy may still be numerically fewer than China's, but they are more advanced and are likely to remain so for a long time.

This shift in strategy worries Japan's neighbors, who remember well Japan's history as a feared military power. Postwar Japanese pacifism could, with this military clout, give way to resurgent militarism aimed at its simmering territorial disputes with both Russia and China. From the Japanese perspective, the country faces growing security concerns, which have intensified in troubled northeast Asia (especially North Korea) because the United States abruptly announced in 2004 its cut of its military presence in Asia by a third so that those troops could be deployed elsewhere.

Japan has sought to adapt the country's national security policies in several ways. First, Japan's security strategy seeks to further tie the country into the web of multilateral global institutions (the UN, the WTO, the G-8) on which it increasingly depends for preservation of the world order that has made possible Japan's post–World War II prosperity. Second, Japan has stepped up its efforts to lead in foreign assistance to developing Global South countries; it perceives advancing the poor a profitable investment in its own advancement. Third, Japan seeks to tie its security closer to America's and to beef up the Japanese-American military alliance treaty by giving Japanese forces new authority to provide logistic support to U.S. combat forces in the vaguely defined "area around Japan." Combinations of bilateralism and multilateralism have replaced Japan's traditional preference for unilateralism in foreign affairs.

However, with its neighbors arming to the teeth, Japan has begun to have second thoughts about nuclear weapons. Alarmed by the rising power of China and the threat it poses to Asian domination and anxious about the sincerity of U.S. security guarantees, some of Japan's most powerful politicians have begun to consider breaking with a half-century-old policy of pacifism by acquiring nuclear weapons. This potential reversal of traditional Japanese doctrine—the three nonnuclear principles never to own, produce, or allow nuclear weapons on Japanese territory—signals the possibility of a radical departure in Japan's posture toward its future military role in the world.

Russia's Quest for Strategic Revival

For Russia, the most important challenge is American dominance, power and policy. However, confronting the United States as an adversary is a fight Russia does not want and could not win. Russia hopes to be recognized as a great power once again, but even with burgeoning revenues from oil exports Russia does not yet have the resources to be an active global power. "Russia's GDP is not much bigger than the economic product of Los Angeles county" (Will 2005, 72). Russia's strategic priority is centered on regaining its former superpower status with the windfall of oil and natural gas profits that are filling the Kremlin's coffers. At the same time, Russia is also pursuing the goals of cementing its fledging alliance with China (as illustrated by the Sino-Russian joint military exercises) as well as alliances with its European allies and even the United States on some issues. Russia's strategy is rapidly adapting to changes underway in world politics, and for this purpose has now set the following priorities:

- Reclaim the former Soviet Union's status as a global military power by undertaking a major rearmament plan to purchase a new generation of missiles, planes and aircraft carriers – with defense spending set to increase to $45 billion by 2010

- Creating with Russia's 1,452,000 military personnel smaller, more mobile and technologically capable fighting forces to manage civil rebellions within Russia as well as along Russia's troubled southern borders in the "near abroad" and with neighbors such as the Ukraine

■ Preserving the boundaries of Russia's sphere of influence, to hold them firmly at Ukraine's western border, or expanding Russian borders by reuniting with former Soviet Republics

■ no first use

the doctrine that a nuclear state would not be the first to use its strategic weapons in the event of a military attack by another state.

■ Repealing Mikhail Gorbachev's **no first use** pledge that Russia would not be the first to use nuclear weapons in the event of an adversary's attack—because Russia relies on its remaining nuclear warheads to repel a foreign aggressor

■ Seeking to resurrect Russia's capabilities and empire by laying claims to vast portions of the resource-rich melting Arctic ice cap

■ Ensure the direct continuation of Putin's power, beliefs, and policy priorities through the election of his close associate, Dmitry Medvedev, as his successor to the presidency and the subsequent appointment of Putin as prime minister and head of Russia's largest political party

[The most significant global] challenge emanates from the rise of nondemocratic great powers: the West's old Cold War rivals China and Russia, now operating under authoritarian capitalist, rather than communist, regimes.

—Azar Gat, Israeli national security scholar

PUTIN'S PUPPET?
In March 2008, Dmitry Medvedev won Russia's presidential election as Putin's hand-picked like-minded successor, and subsequently appointed Putin as prime minister. Though barred by the constitution to a third consecutive presidential term, this role allows Putin to remain a strong leader in the Russian government. Many speculate that Medvedev serves only as a figurehead. Shown here, Putin and Medvedev enjoy the Victory Day military parade through Moscow's Red Square on May 9, 2008 to celebrate Russia's victory over Nazi Germany during World War II.

Grigory Dukor/Reuters/Landov Media

The history of world politics is written largely in terms of the rise to global dominance of hyperpowers and empires, their relations with new great power rivals, and their eventual collapse as they failed to adapt to transformations in global circumstances (Chua 2008; Mead 2008). The same dynamics are evident today. Changes in the global distribution of power are unfolding that are certain to require the great powers to make further adjustments in their national security strategies. Critical as a catalyst to change is the dominant position of the United States *hegemon* and the probability that the global balance of power is likely to shift from a unipolar to a multipolar system. The great powers are in the driver's seat, and it will be the kinds of roles and institutions that they create that will most affect the prospects for global security and prosperity.

What kinds of diplomacy will the great powers practice, and what will be the impact of those practices and norms on all other states? To explore these questions, Chapter 5 turns your attention from the rich powerful and commercially active great powers at the center of the world system to the poorer, weaker, and economically dependent states in the Global South that lie along its periphery and the rising powers in the Global East that have emerged as rivals to Global North dominance.

Key Terms

long-cycle theory
hegemon
hegemonic stability theory
structuralism
nationalism
Kellogg-Briand Pact
appeasement
colonialism
isolationism
multipolarity
political economy
imperialism
irredentism
fascism
ideology
matchpolitik

Yalta Conference
bipolarity
Cold War
power transition
sphere of influence
self-fulfilling prophecy
security regime
domino theory
unipolarity
Truman Doctrine
containment
peaceful coexistence
détente
Strategic Arms Limitation Talks (SALT)
Carter Doctrine

"linkage" strategy
Reagan Doctrine
rapprochement
end of history
soft power
imperial overstretch
power balance
power transition
unilateralism
selective engagement
entente
concert
multilateralism
Yoshida Doctrine
no first use

CHAPTER 5
THE GLOBAL SOUTH IN A WORLD OF POWERS

A global human society based on poverty for many and prosperity for a few, characterized by islands of wealth surrounded by a sea of poverty, is unsustainable.

—Thabo Mbeki, president of South Africa

A Poor Country Amidst the Rich. At the 2007 World Economic Forum in Davos, Switzerland, world leaders met to define the global agenda. A number of Global South leaders were included to give them a voice in Global North deliberations about how to improve the world.

Michel Euler/AP Photo

E arth is divided into two hemispheres, north and south, at the equator. This artificial line of demarcation is, of course, meaningless except for use by cartographers to chart distance and location on maps. However, this divide also represents a popular way of describing the inequalities that separate rich and poor states. By and large, these two groups are located on either side of the equator (see Map 5.1).

■ **Global North**

a term used to refer to the world's wealthy, industrialized countries located primarily in the Northern Hemisphere.

> *All history is only one long story to this effect: Men have struggled for power over their fellow men in order that they might win the joys of Earth at the expense of others, and might shift the burdens of life from their own shoulders upon those of others.*
>
> —William Graham Summer, American realist economic-sociologist

Life for most people in the Northern Hemisphere is very different from that in the Southern Hemisphere. The disparities are profound, and in many places appear to be growing. The division in power and wealth comprising the **Global North** and **Global South** poses both moral and security problems. As the philosopher Plato in fifth-century BCE Greece counseled, "There should exist neither extreme poverty nor excessive wealth, for both are productive of great evil;" his contemporary philosopher Aristotle warned that "wide differences in income are a source of war."

■ **Global South**

a term now often used instead of "Third World" to designate the less-developed countries located primarily in the Southern Hemisphere.

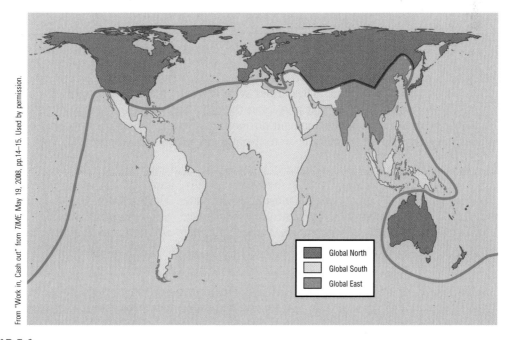

From "Work in, Cash out" from *TIME*, May 19, 2008, pp.14–15. Used by permission.

Legend:
- Global North
- Global South
- Global East

MAP 5.1

THE GLOBAL NORTH, GLOBAL SOUTH (AND GLOBAL EAST) **Global North countries are wealthy and democratic. In contrast, according to the World Bank, the Global South countries are home to 85 percent of the world's population but the impoverished people living there possess only 20 percent of the globe's wealth. As shall be seen, into this picture should now be placed "the Global East" countries that have arisen from the former Global South and are now positioned to rival the levels of prosperity that the Global North has enjoyed in the last two decades.**

Poverty and inequality have existed throughout recorded history. But today the levels have reached extremes. The poor countries find themselves marginalized, in a subordinate position in the global hierarchy.

What are the causes and consequences of the pronounced inequalities between the great powers and the disadvantaged countries trapped in poverty? That is the central question that you will be considering in this chapter.

As a preface to your inquiry, it is important to understand that this chapter investigates the question of international inequalities of the poor *states* as transnational *actors*—that is, at both the *global* and the *state levels of analysis*. Later, in Chapter 7, *World Politics* will look at the human dimensions of international politics by inspecting *peoples'* inequalities at the *individual level of analysis* in order to cover individual people as actors or agents on the international stage; that subsequent treatment will examine the inequalities among people that are evident both across the entire globe as well as within particular states, where the focus will shift to humanitarian concerns and the barriers to human development and human rights.

THE COLONIAL ORIGINS OF THE GLOBAL SOUTH'S CURRENT CIRCUMSTANCES

Many analysts trace the roots of today's inequalities among states at the *global level of analysis* because they believe that the global system has properties built into it that account for the inability of most poor countries to close the gap with the wealthy countries. Taking their hypothesis that prevailing worldwide conditions are part of a much longer historical pattern, they note that the rules governing international politics today were constructed in the 1648 Peace of Westphalia following Europe's Thirty Years' War. These rules were crafted by the most powerful actors on the world stage—the great powers at the time—to serve their parochial self-interests in preserving their predominant positions at the top of the global pyramid of power by preventing less-powerful states from joining them (see Kegley and Raymond 2002).

The origins and persistence of the inequalities of states stem in part from the fact that today's modern global system was initially, and remains, a socially constructed reality *by, of, and for* the most powerful states. The powerful did not design a global system for equals; the great powers followed the prescription of realist thought to always seek self-advantage. Accordingly, they did not build the global system with an eye to preventing the victimization of the weak and the disadvantaged.

■ **indigenous peoples**

the native ethnic and cultural inhabitant populations within countries ruled by a government controlled by others, referred to as the "Fourth World."

So, a good starting place is to begin your inquiry by taking into consideration the legacy of this seedbed for today's global system. Many analysts see the history of *colonialism*, the European conquest of **indigenous peoples** and the seizure of their territory for exclusively European gain, as the root source of the problem. They note that almost all of the independent sovereign states in the Southern Hemisphere were at one time colonies. These analysts argue that today's inequalities are a product of this past colonization.

During the Cold War, the term **Third World** was used to distinguish the growing number of newly independent but economically less-developed states that, for the most part, shared a colonial past with those states that aligned with either the communist East or the capitalistic West. However, the "Third World" soon was used to refer to those countries that had failed to grow economically in a way that was comparable to countries of the **First World** industrialized great powers such as Europe, North America, and Japan. The so-called **Second World**, consisting of the Soviet Union and its allies in other communist countries, was distinguished by a communist ideological commitment to planned economic policies rather than reliance on free-market forces to determine the supply and demand for goods and services. Today, the states comprising the former Second World have almost totally vanished, including "communist" China, with nearly all states now committed to free-market capitalism. The Second World describes the handful of "countries in transition" that have yet to join the World Trade Organization (WTO) and accept its free-market rules.

The term *Third World* carries obsolete Cold War baggage and is most useful to describe the constructed self-image and attitudes that give identity to many living in the Global South. Today the term Global North, which refers to what was previously known as the First World, and Global South, which refers to the less-developed countries in the Southern Hemisphere, are now commonplace.

The placement of particular states within these categories is not easy. Although journalists, policy makers, and scholars frequently generalize about the Global South, considerable diversity exists within this grouping of states. For example, it includes low-income countries such as Ghana and Haiti, where a majority of the population tries to survive through subsistence agriculture; middle-income countries such as Brazil and Malaysia, which produce manufactured goods; and some countries such as Kuwait and Qatar, whose petroleum exports have generated incomes rivaling Global North countries.

Global South countries are different in other ways as well. Included among their ranks is Indonesia, an archipelago of more than seventeen thousand islands scattered throughout an oceanic expanse larger than the United States, and Burundi, a landlocked state slightly smaller than Maryland. Also included is Nigeria, with over 138 million inhabitants, and Belize, with under three hundred thousand people. In addition to these geographic and demographic differences, Global South countries also vary politically and culturally, ranging from democratic Costa Rica to autocratic Myanmar. Also included in this mix are a set of **least developed of the less developed countries (LLDCs)** that are sometimes described as the "Third World's Third World." They are the poorest with little economic growth, experiencing rapid population growth that is increasingly straining their overtaxed society and environment. Many, but not all, are in Africa, south of the Sahara Desert.

Global North countries are wealthy and democratic. In contrast, according to the World Bank, the Global South countries are home to 85 percent of the world's population but possess only 20 percent of the globe's wealth. As we shall see, a new contingent of countries called "the **Global East**" has arisen from the former Global South and is now positioned to rival the levels of prosperity that the Global North has enjoyed in the last two decades.

■ **Third World**
a Cold War term to describe the less-developed countries of Africa, Asia, the Caribbean, and Latin America.

■ **First World**
the relatively wealthy industrialized countries that share a commitment to varying forms of democratic political institutions and developed market economies, including the United States, Japan, the European Union, Canada, Australia, and New Zealand.

■ **Second World**
during the Cold War, the group of countries, including the Soviet Union, its (then) Eastern European allies, and China, that embraced communism and central planning to propel economic growth.

■ **least developed of the less developed countries (LLDCs)**
the most impoverished countries in the Global South.

Global East

the rapidly growing economies of East and South Asia that have made those countries competitors with the traditionally dominant countries of the Global North.

decolonization

the achievement of sovereign independence by countries that were once colonies of the great powers.

nonstate nations

national or ethnic groups struggling to obtain power and/or statehood.

neocolonialism (neoimperialism)

the economic rather than military domination of foreign countries.

mercantilism

a government trade strategy for accumulating state wealth and power by encouraging exports and discouraging imports.

The Global South has the most people but commands little of the world's wealth. These disparities, illustrated in Map 5.2, underlie the long-festering "North–South conflict" more than do political and technological differences. Relations between the wealthy Global North and the poor Global South are governed by struggle because of the fears and resentments that differences in status and unequal opportunities to compete economically naturally arouse. These conflicts are likely to intensify if globalization does not reduce the rich–poor gap.

The emergence of the Global South as an identifiable group of states is a distinctly contemporary phenomenon. Although most Latin American countries were independent before World War II, not until then did other countries of the Global South gain that status. In 1947, Great Britain granted independence to India and Pakistan, after which decolonization—the freeing of colonial peoples from their dependent status—gathered speed. Since then, a profusion of new sovereign states has joined the global community, nearly all carved from the British, Spanish, Portuguese, Dutch, and French empires built under colonialism four hundred years ago.

Today, few colonies exist, and the decolonization process is almost complete. However, the effects persist. Most of the ethnic national conflicts that are now so prevalent have colonial roots, as the imperial powers drew borders within and between their domains with little regard for the national identities of the indigenous peoples. (The divisions among these **nonstate nations** to this day undermine the sense of solidarity so important to the political stability of many multiethnic Global South countries.) Similarly, although European powers no longer lay claim to their former colonies, the Global North maintains an active economic presence in many Global South countries. Thus, as viewed through the eyes of nationalist Global South leaders, the disparity between the rich North and the poor South is the consequence of **neocolonialism** (**neoimperialism**), unequal trade exchanges through which the advantaged exploit the disadvantaged by penetrating the latter's markets and by institutionalizing economic processes for this purpose.

The First Wave of European Imperialism

The first wave of European empire building began in the late fifteenth century, as the Dutch, English, French, Portuguese, and Spanish used their naval power to militarily conquer territories for commercial gain. As scientific innovations made the European explorers' adventures possible, merchants followed in their wake, "quickly seizing upon opportunities to increase their business and profits. In turn, Europe's governments perceived the possibilities for increasing their own power and wealth. Commercial companies were chartered and financed, with military and naval expeditions frequently sent out after them to ensure political control of overseas territories" (Cohen 1973).

The economic strategy underlying the relationship between colonies and colonizers during this era of "classical imperialism" is known as **mercantilism**—an economic philosophy advocating government regulation of economic life to increase state power. European rulers believed that power flowed from the possession of national wealth measured in terms of gold and silver, and that cultivating mining and industry to attain a favorable balance of trade (exporting more than they imported) was the best way to become rich. "Colonies were desirable in this respect because they

Gross National Income

Population

Adapted from data collected by the World Bank in its *World Development Report 2008*, pp. 334–335.

MAP 5.2

THE GREAT NORTH–SOUTH DIVIDE IN WEALTH AND POPULATION **If the countries around the globe were redrawn to reflect the size of their economies and populations, as shown here, huge differences would be visible. Most of the wealth is in the Global North, and most of the people are in the Global South. If prevailing trends persist as expected, the disparities will continue to preserve the existing division between rich and poor.**

afforded an opportunity to shut out commercial competition; they guaranteed exclusive access to untapped markets and sources of cheap materials (as well as, in some instances, direct sources of the precious metals themselves). Each state was determined to monopolize as many of these overseas mercantile opportunities as possible" (Cohen 1973). States wedded to realist justifications of the competitive drive for global power saw the imperial conquest of foreign territory by war as a natural by-product of active government management of the economy.

■ **classical liberal economic theory**

a body of thought based on Adam Smith's ideas about the forces of supply and demand in the marketplace, emphasizing the benefits of minimal government regulation of the economy and trade.

■ **laissez-faire economics**

the philosophical principle of free markets and free trade to give people free choices with little governmental regulation.

By the end of the eighteenth century, the European powers had spread themselves, although thinly, throughout virtually the entire world. But the colonial empires they had built began to crumble. Britain's thirteen North American colonies declared their independence in 1776, and most of Spain's possessions in South America won their freedom in the early nineteenth century. Nearly one hundred colonial relationships worldwide were terminated in the half-century ending in 1825 (Bergesen and Schoenberg 1980).

As Europe's colonial empires dissolved, belief in the mercantilist philosophy also waned. As the liberal political economist Adam Smith argued in his 1776 treatise, *The Wealth of Nations,* national wealth grew not through the accumulation of precious metals but rather from the capital and goods they could buy. Smith's ideas about the benefits of the "invisible hand" of the unregulated marketplace laid much of the intellectual foundation for **classical liberal economic theory**. Following Smith and other liberal free-trade theorists, faith in the precepts of **laissez-faire economics** (minimal government interference in the market) gained widespread acceptance (see also Chapter 9). Henceforth, European powers continued to seek colonies, but the rationale for their imperial policies began to lose supporters at home.

The Second Wave of European Imperialism

From the 1870s until the outbreak of World War I, a second wave of imperialism washed over the world as Europe, joined later by the United States and Japan, aggressively colonized new territories. The portion of the globe that Europeans controlled was one-third in 1800, two-thirds by 1878, and four-fifths by 1914

Rene Burri/Magnum Photos New York

NEW STATES After the decolonization process runs its complete course, more new countries can be expected because many existing states are fragmenting. For example, in 2006, Montenegro voted to sever itself from Serbia and became a newly sovereign independent state. When World War I broke out, only sixty-two independent countries existed; now there are more than two hundred. Many new sovereign states are very small. Pictured here is the "micro" state of Nauru, which has a president, a supreme court, and the full apparatus of government to rule its tiny population. Half the globe's countries have populations smaller than the U.S. state of Massachusetts.

(Fieldhouse 1973). As illustrated in Map 5.3, in the last twenty years of the nineteenth century Africa fell under the control of seven European powers (Belgium, Britain, France, Germany, Italy, Portugal, and Spain), and in all of the Far East and the Pacific, only China, Japan, and Siam (Thailand) were not conquered. But China was divided into **spheres of influence** by the foreign great powers that carved China into separate zones of commerce, which the great powers individually controlled and exploited for profit. Japan itself also imperialistically occupied Korea and Formosa (Taiwan). Elsewhere, the United States expanded across its continent, acquired Puerto Rico and the Philippines in the 1898 Spanish-American War, extended its colonial reach westward to Hawaii, leased the Panama Canal Zone "in perpetuity" from the new state of Panama (an American creation), and exercised considerable control over several Caribbean islands, notably Cuba. The preeminent imperial power, Great Britain, in a single generation expanded its empire to cover one-fifth of the earth's land area and comprised perhaps one-fourth of its population (Cohen 1973). As British imperialists were proud to proclaim, it was an empire on which the sun never set.

Why did most of the great powers—and those that aspired to great-power status—engage in this expensive and often vicious competition to control other peoples and territories? What explains the new imperialism? The answers are rooted in economies and politics.

■ **spheres of influence**

an area dominated by a great power.

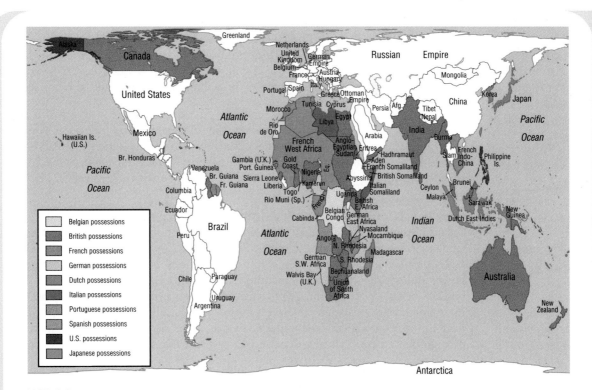

MAP 5.3

GLOBAL IMPERIALISM 1914 **The ten major imperial powers competed for colonies throughout the globe in the present-day Global South, and on the eve of World War I, their combined territories covered much of the world.**

Economic Explanations for the New Imperialism With the Industrial Revolution, capitalism grew—emphasizing the free market, private ownership of the means of production, and the accumulation of wealth. Radical theorists following Karl Marx (see Chapter 2), who called themselves adherents of communism, saw imperialism's aggressive competition as caused by capitalists' need for profitable overseas outlets for their surplus ("finance") capital. One of those adherents was the Soviet leader Vladimir Lenin, who made distinctive contributions to the communist thinking later described as Marxist-Leninism.

In his famous 1916 monograph *Imperialism, The Highest Stage of Capitalism,* Lenin argued that military expansion abroad was produced by the "monopoly stage of capitalism." Lenin concluded that the only way to end imperialism was to abolish capitalism. Classical or liberal economists, by contrast, regarded the new imperialism not as a product of capitalism but, rather, as a response to certain maladjustments that, given the proper will, could be corrected. What the two perspectives shared was the belief that economics explained the new imperialism: It was rooted in the material needs of advanced capitalist societies for cheap raw materials, additional markets to consume growing production, and places for the investment of new capital. Thus, from both the Marxist and classical liberal perspectives, the material needs of capitalist societies explained their imperial drive.

World-system analyses, like Marxist theories, also embrace an economic explanation. World-system theory hypothesizes that a single capitalist world economy emerged during the "long 16th century" from 1450 to 1640 which created a world division of labor separating "core" (industrial) areas from those in the globe's (nonindustrial) "periphery" (see Wallerstein 2005). Northwest Europe first emerged as the core. As the Industrial Revolution proceeded, the core states exchanged manufactured goods for raw agricultural and mineral materials secured at bargain prices by taking advantage of willing sellers and cheap labor in the colonial territories at the periphery.

This perspective emphasizes colonization as the principal method for imperial control over foreign lands. After 1870, colonies effectively became occupation zones abroad in which a small number of temporary European residents coerced indigenous populations into production for the national economy at home (Boswell 1989).

Political Explanations for the New Imperialism Disagreeing with the view that financial motives underpinned the second wave of imperialism, other scholars emphasized purely political factors. For example, in his seminal 1902 book, *Imperialism,* the liberal British economist J. A. Hobson argued that jockeying for power and prestige between competitive empires had always characterized the great powers' behavior in the European balance-of-power system. Hobson also believed that imperialism through overseas expansion was simply a global extension of this inter-European competition for dominance inspired by the realpolitik theoretical premise that all states have an unquenchable thirst for more and more power.

By the 1800s, Britain emerged from Europe's perpetual conflict as the world's leading power. By 1870, however, British hegemony began to decline. Germany emerged as a powerful industrial state, as did the United States. Understandably, Britain tried to protect its privileged global position in the face of growing

Leslie Mazoch/AP Photo

MOUTH OF GLOBAL SOUTH SOCIALISM Reelected in 2007 for another six-year term to the Venezuelan presidency, Hugo Chávez announced that a "new era has begun for twenty-first century socialism." "Jesus Christ was an authentic Communist, anti-imperialist and enemy of the oligarchy," Chávez declared. A self-described communist, Chávez pledged to use Venezuela's huge oil revenues to help his friend, Cuba's communist President Fidel Castro, lead in implementing the radical theories of *Marxist-Leninism* in order to end the long, sad history of class struggles.

competition from the newly emerging core states. Its efforts to maintain the status quo help to explain the second wave of imperial expansion, especially in Africa, where partition served the imperial powers at the expense of local populations.

The British-sponsored *laissez-faire* system of free trade promoted rapid economic growth in a number of colonial territories, but economic development elsewhere proceeded even more rapidly. Western Europe, North America, Australia, and New Zealand were able to complete their industrial revolutions during this period and to rapidly advance. Nonetheless, the gap between the world's rich and poor countries began to widen.

■ **realpolitik**
the theoretical outlook prescribing that countries should increase their power and wealth in order to compete with and dominate other countries.

Self-Determination and Decolonization in the Twentieth Century

The climate of opinion turned decidedly against imperialism when the 1917 Versailles peace settlement that ended World War I embraced *liberalism*—the body of theoretical thought that stresses the importance of ideas, ideals, and institutions to generate progress, prosperity, and peace. Part of that reform program was the

■ **self-determination**

the liberal doctrine that people should be able to determine the government that will rule them.

principle of national **self-determination** championed by U.S. President Woodrow Wilson. Self-determination advocated that indigenous nationalities should have the moral right to decide which authority would rule them. Wilson and other *liberal theorists* (see Chapter 2) reasoned that freedom would lead to the creation of states and governments that were content with their territorial boundaries and therefore less inclined to make war. In practice, however, the attempt to redraw states' borders to separate nationality groups was applied almost exclusively to war-torn Europe, where six new states were created from the territory of the former Austrian-Hungarian Empire (Austria, Czechoslovakia, Hungary, Poland, Romania, and the ethnically divided Yugoslavia). Other territorial adjustments also were made in Europe, but the proposition that self-determination should be extended to Europe's overseas empires did not receive serious support.

Still, the colonial territories of the powers defeated in World War I were not simply parceled out among the victorious allies, as had typically happened in the past. Instead, the territories controlled by Germany and the Ottoman Empire were transferred under League of Nations auspices to countries that would govern them as "mandates" until their eventual self-rule. Many of these territorial decisions gave rise to subsequent conflicts such as in the Middle East and Africa. For example, the League of Nations called for the eventual creation of a Jewish national homeland in Palestine and arranged for the transfer of control over South-West Africa (called Namibia) to what would become the white minority regime of South Africa.

The principle implicit in the League of Nations mandate system gave birth to the idea that "colonies were a trust rather than simply a property to be exploited and treated as if its peoples had no rights of their own" (Easton 1964). This set an important precedent after World War II, when the defeated powers' territories placed under the United Nations (UN) trusteeship system were not absorbed by others but were promised eventual self-rule. Thus, support for self-determination gained momentum. The decolonization process accelerated in 1947, when the British consented to the independence of India and Pakistan. War eventually erupted between these newly independent states as each sought to gain control over disputed territory in Kashmir in 1965, in 1971, and again as the nuclear-armed states clashed in 2002. Violence also broke out in Vietnam and Algeria in the 1950s and early 1960s when the French sought to regain control over their pre-World War II colonial territories. Similarly, bloodshed followed closely on the heels of independence in the Congo when the Belgians granted their African colony independence in 1960, and it dogged the unsuccessful efforts of Portugal to battle the winds of decolonization that swept over Africa as the 1960s wore on.

Despite these political convulsions, decolonization for the most part was not only extraordinarily rapid but also remarkably peaceful. This may be explained by the fact that World War II sapped the economic and military vitality of many of the colonial powers. World-system analysts contend that a growing appreciation of the costs of empire also eroded support for colonial empires (Strang 1990, 1991). Whatever the underlying cause, colonialism became less acceptable. In a world increasingly dominated by rivalry between East and West, Cold War competition for political allies gave both the superpower rivals incentives to lobby for the liberation of overseas empires. Decolonization "triumphed," as Inis Claude (1967) explains, "largely because the West [gave] priority to the containment of communism over the perpetuation of colonialism."

The UN also contributed to the "collective delegitimization" of colonialism. In 1960, with colonialism already in retreat, Global South states took advantage of their growing numbers in the UN General Assembly to secure passage of the historic *Declaration on the Granting of Independence to Colonial Countries and Peoples.* "The General Assembly proclaimed that the subjection of any people to alien domination was a denial of fundamental human rights, contrary to the UN Charter, and an impediment to world peace and that all subject peoples had a right to immediate and complete independence. No country cast a vote against this anticolonial manifesto. . . . It was an ideological triumph" (Riggs and Plano 1994).

As the old order crumbled—and as the leaders in the newly emancipated territories discovered that freedom did not translate automatically into autonomy, economic independence, or domestic prosperity—the conflict between the rich Global North and the emerging states of the Global South began.

NORTH AND SOUTH TODAY: WORLDS APART

The Global South is sometimes described today as a "zone of turmoil" in large measure because, in contrast with the peaceful and democratic Global North, most of the people in the Global South face chronic poverty amidst war, tyranny, and anarchy. In the poorest countries of the Global South where preexisting conditions of dictatorships and dismal financial prospects persist, the odds increase that these countries will experience civil wars and armed conflicts with each other (Collier 2005).

Democracy has spread rapidly and widely since the 1980s, becoming the preferred mode of governance throughout much of the Global South as a means of promoting both economic development and peace. However, some of the Global South's recent additions to the liberal democratic community have governments weakly committed to regular elections and human rights. Furthermore, many Global South countries lack well-developed domestic market economies based on entrepreneurship and private enterprise. Nonetheless, because the Global North's history suggests that free markets spawn the large middle class that is a precondition for free governments (Norberg 2006), the continuing expansion of Global South market economies under capitalism appears likely to hasten democratization. Even so, the continued enlargement of the liberal democratic community is not guaranteed.

Differences in technological capabilities also separate the Global North and Global South. Typically, Global South countries have been unable to evolve an indigenous technology appropriate to their own resources and have been dependent on powerful Global North multinational corporations (MNCs) (see Chapter 7) to transfer technical know-how. This means that research and development expenditures are directed toward solutions of the Global North's problems, with technological advances seldom meeting the needs of the Global South. And in the information age, technology has not been distributed equally geographically: the lowest density of computer connections to the Internet is in the Global South.

The fact that 85 percent of the world's population is poor is both a reflection and cause of these unequally distributed resources. To measure the disparities, the World Bank differentiates the "low-income" and "low- and middle-income," economies in **developing countries,** whose **gross national income (GNI)** average $10,998 billion,

■ developing countries

a category used by the World Bank to identify low income Global South countries with a 2008 GNI per capita below $905 and middle income countries with a GNI per capita of more than $905 but less than $11,116.

■ gross national income (GNI)

a measure of the production of goods and services within a given time period, which is used to delimit the geographic scope of production. GNI measures production by a state's citizens or companies, regardless of where the production occurs.

■ developed countries

a category used by the World Bank (WDR 2008; WDI 2008) to identify Global North countries, with a GNI per capita of $11,116 or more annually.

■ barter

the exchange of one good for another rather than the use of currency to buy and sell items.

from the "high-income" **developed countries**, which average $37,732 billion for each state (WDI 2008, 16). Among the developed countries, wide variations in economic performance (growth and inflation rates, debt burdens, and export prices, for example) and international circumstances (such as the availability of oil and other fuels) are evident.

Numbers paint pictures and construct images, and the data on the division between the Global North and Global South point to brutal disparities and inequalities. When we compare the differences on some key indicators differentiating low- and middle-income countries from high-income countries (at the peak of development), we discover huge gaps (see Table 5.1).

This picture darkens even more when the focus shifts to the plight of the poorest in the low-income developing countries. More than 2.4 billion people (37 percent of humanity) live in one of the fifty-three countries at the bottom of the global hierarchy, the LLDCs, where, typically, **barter** of one agricultural good for another (rather than money) is used for economic exchanges (WDR 2008, 333, 335). These countries are not emerging or reemerging to break the chains of their destitution; they are falling behind the other Global South countries.

Table 5.1 Two Worlds of Development: An International Class Divide

Characteristic	Developing Global South	Developed Global North
Number of countries/economies	150	60
Population (millions)	5,507	1,031
Average annual population growth rate, 2005–2015	1.2%	0.4%
Population density (people for each sq km)	57	31
Women in policy positions	16%	23%
Land area (thousands of km^2)	99,332	34,614
GNI ($ billions)	$10,998	$37,732
Gross national income for each person	$1,997	$36,608
Average annual % growth of GDP per person, 2005–2006	6.0%	2.2%
Net foreign direct investment inflows ($ millions)	$367,492,000	$984,950,000

(continues)

Table 5.1   Two Worlds of Development: An International Class Divide *(continued)*

Characteristic	Developing Global South	Developed Global North
Net foreign direct investment inflows (% of GDP)	3.2%	2.7%
Exports ($ billions)	$4,281	$10,422
Exports (% of GDP)	35%	26%
Imports ($ billions)	$3,837	$10,616
Taxes on international trade (% of government revenue)	8%	1%
Workers' remittances received	$221,912,000	$74,844,000
Refugees received for asylum	11,544,600	2,781,900
Access to improved sanitation (% of population)	51%	100%
HIV prevalence (% of adults)	1.1%	0.4%
Prevalence of undernourishment (% of population)	16%	3%
Public health expenditure (% of GDP)	5.6%	11.4%
Primary pupil/teacher ratio	33%	16%
Primary education completion rate (%)	85%	97%
Daily newspapers for each 1,000 people	67	263
Internet users for each 100 people	8	59
Aircraft departures	6,426,000	18,417,000
Electric power consumption for each person (kwh)	1,290	9,760
Life expectancy at birth	66	79
International tourists (inflow)	332,275,000	510,271,000
Population living in cities (%)	44	78
Number of motor vehicles for each 1,000 people	39	600

(continues)

Table 5.1   Two Worlds of Development: An International Class Divide *(continued)*

Characteristic	Developing Global South	Developed Global North
Personal computers for each 100 people	4	57
Households with television (%)	60%	98%
Research and development (R&D) expenditure (% of GNP, 2000–2004)	0.83%	2.38%
Energy use for each person (kg of oil equivalent)	1,071	5,498
Net energy imports (% of energy use)	23	19
Armed forces	21,431,000	5,599,000
Military expenditures (% of GDP)	2.1%	2.6%
Arms imports	$14,042,000	$12,199,000
Arms exports	$7,728,000	$15,176,000
Arms exports (% of world)	34%	66%

Where people live on the earth influences how they live. As this information shows, the situation is much more favorable—and the quality of life is relatively advantageous—in the developed countries of the Global North than it is in the Southern Hemisphere, where nearly all the Global South countries are located. The World Bank predicts that the discrepancy between the rich and the poor will continue through the year 2050.

World Bank, *2008 World Development Indicators.*

The low-income LLDCs are not participants in the global market: they account for less than 3.3 percent of world trade, and their meager exports are largely confined to inexpensive primary products, including food stuffs (cocoa, coffee, and tea), minerals (copper), hides, and timber. Because these low-income countries consume most of what they produce, theirs is typically a subsistence economy. The prospects for change are dim, because most of these least-developed countries have been bypassed by direct foreign investment and ignored by foreign aid donors (WDI 2008).

High rates of population growth since 1990 have contributed to the widespread poverty of LLDCs. Likewise, it will take only twenty-five years for the LLDCs' total population to double, compared with 250 years for the Global North. LLDCs' economic growth rates in the recent past have averaged less than 0.1 percent each year. Growth rates elsewhere have almost uniformly been higher. This is a powerful reason for why the rich minority gets richer, while the poorest of the poor will likely become even poorer.

Despite wide differences, a daunting scale of misery and marginalization is thus evident across the Global South, from which only a fraction of its countries have begun to escape. For most Global South countries, the future is bleak, and the opportunities and choices most basic to freedom from fear and poverty are unavailable. The aggregate pattern underlying global trends in the last twenty years shows that more than sixty countries today are worse off than they were and are falling ever further behind the levels achieved by the countries in the Global North. When we consider that nearly all the population growth in the twenty-first century will occur in the Global South, the poorest countries cut off from circulation in the globalized marketplace, it is hard to imagine how the gap can close and how the soil of poverty can be prevented from producing terrorism and civil war.

This tragic portrayal of unspeakable despair for so many Global South states raises the basic theoretical question: Why does the Global South, at this historical juncture, suffer from such dismal destitution?

THEORETICAL EXPLANATIONS OF UNDERDEVELOPMENT

Why has the Global South lagged far behind the Global North in its comparative level of well-being and **development**? And why have the development experiences even within the Global South differed so widely?

The diversity evident in the Global South invites the conclusion that under-development is explained by a combination of factors. Some theorists explain the underdevelopment of most developing economies by looking primarily at *internal* causes within states. Other theorists focus on *international* causes such as the position of developing countries in the global political economy. We will take a brief look at each of these schools of thought.

Internal Factors: Classical Economic Development Theory's Interpretation

Based on the definition of development (as constructed in the West) as "increases in income," liberal economic development theories of **modernization** first emerged in the early post–World War II era. They argued that the major barriers to development were posed by the Global South countries' own internal characteristics. To overcome these barriers, most classical theorists recommended that the wealthy countries supply various "missing components" of development, such as investment capital through foreign aid or private foreign direct investment.

Once sufficient capital was accumulated to promote economic growth, these liberal theorists predicted that its benefits would eventually "trickle down" to broad segments of society. Everyone, not just a privileged few, would begin to enjoy rising affluence. Walt W. Rostow, an economic historian and U.S. policy maker, formalized this theory in *The Stages of Economic Growth* (1960). He predicted that traditional societies beginning the path to development would inevitably pass through various stages by means of the free market and would eventually "take off" to become similar to the mass-consumption societies of the capitalist Global North. Even though the rich are

■ **development**
the processes, economic and political, through which a country develops to increase its capacity to meet its citizens' basic human needs and raise their standard of living.

■ **modernization**
a view of development popular in the Global North's liberal democracies that wealth is created through efficient production, free enterprise, and free trade, and that countries' relative wealth depends on technological innovation and education more than on natural endowments such as climate and resources.

likely to get richer, it was argued, as incomes in the world as a whole grow, the odds increase that a preindustrialized economy will grow faster and eventually reduce the gap between it and richer countries.

The Global South rejected that prognosis and the premises on which it was based. Leaders there did not accept the classical liberal argument that the Global North became prosperous because they concentrated on hard work, innovative inventions of new products, and investments in schooling. Instead, they were persuaded by the rival theory that attributed the Global South's plight to the international links between developing countries and the Global North's leadership in the global political economy.

International Factors: Dependency Theory's Interpretation

Whereas classical theory locates the causes of most developing countries' under-development to internal conditions within states, **dependency theory** emphasizes international factors in general and the Global South's dependence on the dominant great powers in particular.

Although the dependency literature is large and diverse (see Caporaso and Levine 1992; Packenham 1992), all dependency theorists reject Rostow's stages-of-growth thesis, arguing that underdevelopment "is not a stalled stage of linear development" (Shannon 1989). As noted in Chapter 2, dependency theory builds on Vladimir Lenin's radical critique of imperialism, but it goes beyond it to account for changes that have occurred in recent decades. Its central proposition is that the structure of the capitalist world economy is based on a division of labor between a dominant core and a subordinate periphery. As a result of colonialism, the Global South countries that make up the periphery have been forced into an economic role whereby they export raw materials and import finished goods. Whereas classical liberal theorists submit that specialization in production according to comparative advantage will increase income in an unfettered market and therein help close the gap between the world's haves and have-nots, dependency theorists maintain that global inequalities cannot be reduced so long as developing countries continue to specialize in producing primary products for which there are often numerous competing suppliers and limited demand.

Dependency theorists also argue that countries in the Global South are vulnerable to cultural penetration by MNCs and other outside forces, which saturate them with values alien to their societies. Once such penetration has occurred, the inherently unequal exchanges that bind the exploiters and the exploited are sustained by elites within the penetrated societies, who sacrifice their country's welfare for personal gain.

The argument that a privileged few benefit from **dependency** at the expense of their societies underscores the dual nature of many developing countries. **Dualism** refers to the existence of two separate economic and social sectors operating side by side. Dual societies typically have a rural, impoverished, and neglected sector operating alongside an urban, developing, or advanced sector—but with little interaction between the two. Thus, whatever growth occurs in the industrial sector in dual societies "neither initiates a corresponding growth process in the rural sector nor generates sufficient employment to prevent a growing population in the stagnant

■ **dependency theory**

a theory that less-developed countries are exploited because global capitalism makes them dependent on the rich countries that create exploitative rules for trade production.

■ **dependency**

a condition of retarded economic growth believed to result from the Global South's subordination and structural exploitation by the Global North's advanced capitalistic market economies, making the Global South especially vulnerable to the Global North's business cycles of expansion and contraction.

■ **dualism**

the separation of a country into two sectors, the first modern and prosperous centered in major cities, and the second at the margin, neglected and poor.

sectors" (Singer and Ansari 1998). MNCs contribute to dualism by favoring a minority of well-compensated employees over the rest that increases gaps in pay and by widening differences between rural and urban economic opportunities. Because MNCs locate their operations primarily in urban areas, they facilitate population flow from the countryside to cities.

Although dependency theory has great appeal within the Global South, it cannot easily explain the emergence of what many people call **newly industrialized countries (NICs)**, members of the Global South that have begun exporting manufactured goods to the Global North. To explain this phenomenon, dependency theorists sometimes use the term **dependent development** to describe the industrialization of the peripheral areas in a system otherwise dominated by the Global North. The term suggests the possibility of either growing or declining prosperity, but *within* the confines of a continuing dominance-dependence relationship between North and South.

Closing the Gap? The Global South's Prospects

Is it possible for the Global South to escape poverty? Look at the situation from the perspective of the poorest of the poor countries. The prospects appear dismal. However, a basis for optimism can be found when you broaden the picture and see the conspicuous exceptions to the general pattern of persistent poverty. Destitution is not necessarily permanent. Although many Global South countries appear to be mired in persistent poverty, some Global South countries have managed to break the chains of underdevelopment and are entering the ranks of the advanced Global North economies. The ability for these rapidly developing countries to escape the syndrome that still affects the rest of the Global South suggests that others can succeed as well.

Fueling Growth Through Oil Consider one category of Global South states whose relative wealth contrasts sharply with the LLDCs' poverty: those Global South states that have fossil fuels to consume and export. The sixteen developing-country exporters of oil and other fuels, and especially the twelve members of the Organization of Petroleum Exporting Countries (OPEC), have escaped the LLDCs' grim fate. Notably, OPEC members Kuwait, Qatar, and the United Arab Emirates have risen to the high-income group's standards of living, rivaling or exceeding some Global North countries.

The Global East Another group of countries that inspire hope and awe are the "middle income" and rapidly rising **newly industrialized countries** in East and Southern Asia. They are experiencing even greater success than the oil-exporting countries. Their achievement lies in moving beyond the export of simple unfinished goods such as crude oil to the export of manufactured goods and to providing service and expertise in the digital revolution of the information age. Today, the NICs are among the largest exporters of manufactured goods and are leaders in the information processing industry. They have climbed from the periphery into the **semiperiphery** and beyond to rival the Global North.

The pace was set by the so called **Asian Tigers**. South Korea, Singapore, Taiwan, and Hong Kong engineered export-led growth through aggressively so-called *neomercantilist* policies aimed at protecting infant industries from foreign competition and subsidizing

■ newly industrialized countries (NICs)
the most prosperous members of the Global South, which have become important exporters of manufactured goods as well as important markets for the major industrialized countries that export capital goods.

■ dependent development
the industrialization of peripheral areas within the confines of the dominance-dependence relationship between the Global North and the Global South, which enables the poor to become wealthier without ever catching up to the core Global North countries.

■ semiperiphery
to world-system theorists, countries midway between the rich "core" or center, and the poor "periphery" in the global hierarchy, at which foreign investments are targeted when labor wages and production costs become too high in the prosperous core regions.

FROM RAGS TO RICHES **A number of formerly poor Global South countries have catapulted to affluence, either through free markets and aggressive trade, or by capitalizing on abundant natural resources. Dubai, shown here (left), is a prime example of the latter. Rising oil prices have created a boom that is transforming this Arab Kingdom into a zone of prosperity, as exemplified by the 2008 construction of the world's largest shopping mall with the world's largest aquarium within it, and a five-story *underwater* hotel. Not to be outdone, Saudi and Kuwaiti investors have bought a large plot of land in war-torn but oil-rich Sudan, Africa's largest country, where the huge financial center shown here (right) is under construction.**

■ Asian Tigers

the four Asian NICs that experienced far greater rates of economic growth during the 1980s than the more advanced industrial societies of the Global North.

■ outsourcing

the transfer of jobs by a corporation usually headquartered in a Global North country to a Global South country able to supply trained workers at lower wages.

their manufacturers. Following the lead paved by Japan in developing new products for export, China, India, Malaysia, and Thailand next followed this route toward joining the ranks of the wealthiest states. Their growth has been energized by the **outsourcing** of jobs from the labor-costly Global North to the skilled Asian workers capable of performing the same labor at less expense to the multinational corporations headquartered in the Global North. What *World Politics* now labels the Global East is the new global success story that is transforming the world (see Map 5.1). A loose definition of the Global East would include not only the long leading economy of Japan and the four Asian Tigers (South Korea, Singapore, Taiwan, and Hong Kong), but also China, India, Malaysia, and Thailand. Together, these nine Asian economies account for almost one-third of the total world PPP gross national income (WDR 2008, 334–335). The spillover from these Global East powerhouses to the other thirty-five still-developing countries throughout Asia is reflected in the projected fast-paced 8.3 percent regional growth rate in 2008—far better than that of the rest of the world (*Economist*, September 22, 2007). This remarkable trend provoked the political journalist Thomas L. Friedman to conclude, "When the history of this era is written, the trend that historians will cite as the most significant . . . will be the rise of China and India." He added, "How the world accommodates itself to these rising powers, and how America manages the economic opportunities and challenges they pose, is the most important global trend to watch." Both China and India are already commercial giants and have set their sights on being the globe's next great powers.

Geography does not identify the Global South countries with the greatest economic potential to escape poverty. The most important precondition for success has proven to be the ability of Global South governments to stabilize the value of their currencies, bring inflation under control, and privatize the businesses once owned by the government. In addition, recent experience shows that the high achievers were able to open themselves to foreign investment.

*Emerging multinational corporations in China and India
are no longer satisfied with imitating. Instead, they seek to convert
cost advantages to more sustainable competitive advantages—often
through innovation.*

—Dan Steinbock, research director of the India,
China, and America Institute

This change in philosophy about the causes of and cures for underdevelopment formerly prevalent throughout the Global South was a concession in Global South thinking stimulated in part by pressures for reform by such powerful institutions as the World Bank and the International Monetary Fund.

The success of the free-market practices of the NICs in elevating themselves above the rest of the Global South has inspired faith in the neoclassical theorists' export-led strategies and now encourages other Global South countries to copy them by removing still other obstacles standing in the way of economic growth, such as speeding up transitions toward fuller economic liberalization and democratic governance.

The NICs' achievements alongside the stagnant financial fates of the poorest Global South's countries raise questions for evaluation. Despite these differences and the inequalities between Global South countries, does there exist a consensus that still unites them as a group? Does the Global South share a socially constructed collective vision around which they can build a common posture? What strategies are the Global South countries forging to deal with their perceived exploitation resulting from having a position of weakness in a world of powers?

THE GLOBAL SOUTH'S FOREIGN POLICY RESPONSE TO A WORLD RULED BY THE GREAT POWERS

The vast political, economic, and social differences separating the Global North (and Global East) and the Global South suggest that the remaining countries in the Global South are increasingly vulnerable, insecure, and defenseless, and that these conditions are products of both internal and international factors. Coping with these challenges continues to bring the Global South into contested debate with the Global North. The globalization of finance and trade (see Chapters 9 and 10) threatens to expand many poor Global South countries' economic vulnerabilities.

Given the multiple problems standing in the way of Global South security and prosperity, ask yourself how you, were you to become a head of state of a Global South country, would approach these awesome challenges. Your choices would undoubtedly benefit by considering the different approaches Global South countries have taken to pursue their objectives, particularly in their relationships with the Global North.

■ **nonalignment**

a foreign policy posture that rejects participating in military alliances with rival blocs for fear that formal alignment will entangle the state in an unnecessary involvement in war.

■ **nonaligned states**

countries that do not form alliances with opposed great-powers and practice neutrality on issues that divide great powers.

■ **Nonaligned Movement (NAM)**

a group of more than one hundred newly independent, mostly less-developed, states that joined together as a group of neutrals to avoid entanglement with the superpowers' competing alliances in the Cold War and to advance the Global South's primary interests in economic cooperation and growth.

■ **failed states**

countries whose governments have so mismanaged policy that their citizens, in rebellion, threaten revolution to divide the country into separate independent states.

> *Wars on nations change maps. War on poverty maps change.*
>
> —Muhammad Ali, American boxing champion

In Search of Power

The Global South countries emerging after World War II struggled on separate tracks to find a foreign policy approach that could provide them with the security they lacked. The paths they have taken fall into four major categories.

Nonalignment   Many Global South countries feared becoming entrapped in the Cold War and adopted foreign policies based on **nonalignment**. The strategy energized both the United States and the Soviet Union to renew their efforts to attract the uncommitted Global South countries to their own network of allies, often offering economic and military aid as an inducement. Some states aligned themselves with either the United States or Soviet Union; others avoided taking sides in the Cold War. The latter approach gathered momentum in 1955, when twenty-nine **nonaligned states** from Asia and Africa met in Bandung, Indonesia to construct a strategy to combat colonialism. Six years later, leaders from twenty-five countries met in Belgrade, Yugoslavia and created the **Nonaligned Movement (NAM)**. The membership of this coalition would later grow to more than one hundred countries.

The Cold War's end eroded the bargaining leverage nonalignment had provided the Global South. As a strategy, nonalignment "died" with the Cold War. But the passion of Global South leaders to eradicate global inequities lives on, as can be seen in the 2003 *Non-Aligned Kuala Lumpur Summit Declaration*, which raised questions about the inability of many Global South countries to advance.

The challenge facing the nonaligned states today is how to promote their interests in a world where few listen to their voices. The nonaligned Global South can complain, but its bargaining power to engineer institutional reforms is limited. This weakness is displayed in the UN, where the most influence the Global South has mustered has symbolically been to delay serious proposals to make Germany and Japan permanent members of the Security Council by insisting that a nonaligned state or one of the larger rising NICs (such as Brazil, India, Indonesia, Mexico, or South Africa) also be given a seat among the mighty. Weak states have some vocal power in numbers, but no clout or control. Thus, the Global South worries that in the future even newer forms of great power imperialism might continue to destroy any Global South hopes for progress.

National Security   These concerns are rooted in past experience: Many developing countries felt betrayed and invaded when they became the battleground on which the superpowers conducted covert activities, paramilitary operations, and proxy wars. The Global South became the world's killing fields; more than 90 percent of the inter- and intrastate conflicts and 90 percent of the casualties in the past sixty years occurred within it (see Chapter 13). The large "zone of turmoil" has swept the Global South. Rebellion and anarchy has spread in many **failed states** whose governments were not strong enough to preserve domestic order. Understandably, national security is now a Global South policy priority.

"Poverty and conflict are not unrelated," warn UN Under Secretaries Nitin Desai and Jayantha Dhanapala. "They often reinforce each other ... particularly when poor countries and people are increasingly aware of the relative affluence of others." In our information age where knowledge of vast differentials in wealth is in the news everywhere, this awareness is unavoidable.

Global South countries must face the fateful question of whether they dare to call for help from the great powers and dominating international organizations when violence, terrorism, and anarchy prevail and their collapsing countries require external **military intervention** to restore order. The cry for assistance poses risks, because where there is outside involvement there tends to follow outside influence, some of which may be unwelcome. There is a fine line between external involvement and interference. On top of this concern is another: the threat of great power indifference or inability to agree about when, where, why, and how they should collectively become involved within Global South borders where violence, ethnic cleansing, and terrorism occur.

■ military intervention
overt or covert use of force by one or more countries that cross the borders of another country in order to affect the target country's government and policies.

Arms Acquisitions   Faced with seemingly endless conflict at home or abroad, it is not surprising that the Global South has joined the rest of the world's quest to acquire modern weapons of war—including, in some cases (China, India, Iran, and Pakistan), nuclear weapons. As a result, the burden of military spending (measured by the ratio of military expenditures to GNP) is highest among those least able to bear it (SIPRI 2008). In the Global South, military spending typically exceeds expenditures on health and education; impoverished states facing ethnic, religious, or tribal strife at home are quite prepared to sacrifice expenditures for economic development in order to acquire weapons.

Few Global South states produce their own weapons. Weak Global South governments, paralyzed by fears of separatist revolts, have invested increased proportions of their country's modest national budgets in arms rather than seek to reduce poverty by reallocating scarce revenues from the military to social and economic development. Most Global South countries have increased their military spending to purchase arms produced in the Global North at higher rates than do their Global North counterparts (SIPRI 2008). Thus, in responding to a world of powers, the Global South appears to be increasing its dependence for arms purchases on the very same rich states whose military and economic domination they historically have most feared and resented.

Reducing Vulnerability to Environmental Disasters   Adding to the Global South's instability is still another source of turmoil: developing countries' vulnerability to natural environmental calamities. In 2008 the cyclone in Myanmar, which the UN estimates caused more than 100,000 deaths, and the massive earthquake in China, which China's Information Office of the State Council reports killed almost 70,000 and affected 45.5 million, underscore the magnitude of the threat posed by recurring typhoons, cyclones, earthquakes, and hurricanes. This has made protecting natural environments another Global South priority.

Although the scale of environmental tragedies can be reduced with effective warning and response systems, the economic struggle for survival within the world's poorest countries leaves few resources for investing in the technology needed for disaster preparedness. As a result, the Global South is petitioning the Global North for help to expand its global network of seismometer and tidal monitoring instruments and to share data from weather satellites that can be used to chart dangerous storms and reduce their risks.

In Search of Prosperity

Breaking out of their dependent status and pursuing their own industrial development remains the greatest foreign policy priority for countries in the Global South. To this end, some countries (particularly those in Latin America) have pursued development through an **import-substitution industrialization** strategy designed to encourage domestic entrepreneurs to manufacture products traditionally imported from abroad. Governments (often dictatorships) became heavily involved in managing their economies and, in some cases, became the owners and operators of industry.

■ **import-substitution industrialization**

a strategy for economic development that centers on providing investors at home incentives to produce goods so that previously imported products from abroad will decline.

Import-substitution industrialization eventually fell from favor, in part because manufacturers often found that they still had to rely on Global North technology to produce goods for their domestic markets. The preference now is for **export-led industrialization**, based on the realization that "what had enriched the rich was not their insulation from imports (rich countries do, in fact, import all sorts of goods) but their success in manufactured exports, where higher prices could be commanded than for [Global South] raw materials" (Sklair 1991).

■ **export-led industrialization**

a growth strategy that concentrates on developing domestic export industries capable of competing in overseas markets.

Not all Global South economies are positioned to survive in this highly competitive globalized market. Many of the least-developed countries remain heavily dependent on raw materials and other primary products for their export earnings. Although some benefit from global economic integration and prosper, others remain immune to the alleged benefits of globalization and are especially vulnerable to recessions in the global economy. How to cope with dominance and dependence thus remains a key Global South concern.

A New International Economic Order? The emerging Global South countries were born into a political-economic order with rules they had no voice in creating. In order to gain control over their economic futures, they began coordinating their efforts within the United Nations where their growing numbers and voting power gave them greater influence than they could otherwise command. In the 1960s, they formed a coalition of the world's poor, the **Group of 77 (G-77)** (known in diplomatic circles simply as the G-77) and used their voting power to convene the UN Conference on Trade and Development (UNCTAD). UNCTAD later became a permanent UN organization through which the Global South would express its interests concerning development issues.

■ **Group of 77 (G-77)**

the coalition of Third World countries that sponsored the 1963 *Joint Declaration of Developing Countries* calling for reform to allow greater equality in North–South trade.

A decade later, the G-77 (then numbering more than 120 countries) again used its UN numerical majority to push for a **New International Economic Order (NIEO)** to replace the international economic regime championed by the United States and the other capitalist powers since World War II. Motivated by the oil-exporting countries' rising bargaining power, the Global South sought to compel the Global North to abandon practices perceived as perpetuating their dependence. More specifically, the proposals advanced under the banner of the NIEO included:

- Giving preferential, nonreciprocal treatment to Global South exports to industrialized countries

- Establishing commodity agreements to regulate and stabilize the world market for primary commodities

- Linking the price of Global South exports to the price of imports from industrialized states

- Increasing financial resource transfers to Global South countries

- Reducing the burden of Global South debt through rescheduling, interest subsidization, or cancellation

- Increasing the participation and voting power of Global South countries in international financial institutions

- Regulating the activities of multinational corporations in the Global South to promote the reinvestment of profits earned by MNCs in host country economies

- Expanding technical assistance programs and reducing the cost of transferring technology to the Global South

Not surprisingly, the Global North rebuffed many of the South's proposals, although some of the issues that were raised (such as debt relief) remain on the global agenda. At the 2003 World Trade Organization meeting in Cancún, Mexico, for example,

> *The twenty-first century is going to be about more than great power politics.*
> —Bill Clinton, U.S. president

the poor countries united to demand major concessions from the wealthy countries, especially with regard to foreign subsidies. In 2008 another step was taken when "Banco del Sur" (Bank of the South) was launched by founding members Brazil and Argentina to compete directly with the World Bank and thereby fund big infrastructure projects through the region's new oil wealth to go around Global North interference.

Regional Trade Regimes   With the failure of reform envisioned by the NIEO, the integration of Global South countries into the globalization process will occur according to the rules dictated by the Global North. Are there alternatives? Can regional arrangements enable Global South states to take advantage of growing economic interdependence to achieve their development goals?

■ **New International Economic Order (NIEO)**
the 1974 policy resolution in the UN that called for a North–South dialogue to open the way for the less-developed countries of the Global South to participate more fully in the making of international economic policy.

To promote growth through regional economic agreements, in the 1990s the global economy began to subdivide into three "trade blocs"—one in Europe, with the European Union (EU) as its hub; a second in the Americas, with the United States at the center; and a third in the *Global East*, with Japan and China dominant. Consider some recent developments:

- In the Americas: The Central America-Dominican Republic Free Trade Agreement (CAFTA-DR) aims to emulate NAFTA and create a free-trade zone that includes the United States, Dominican Republic, Guatemala, El Salvador, Nicaragua, Honduras, and Costa Rica. Intent on liberalizing U.S. and Central American markets, the agreement is the first major "sub-regional" agreement between very unequal trading partners—the combined GDP of Central America is equal to 0.5% of the U.S. GDP (Washington Office on Latin America, www.wola.org, June 23, 2008). Mercosur, commonly referred to as the "Common Market of the South," is the largest trading bloc in South America and aims for full economic integration of the region. Full members include Argentina, Brazil, Paraguay, Uruguay and Venezuela, with Bolivia, Colombia, Ecuador, Peru, and Chile holding associate membership status.

- In Asia: The association of Asia-Pacific Economic Cooperation (APEC), an informal forum created in 1989, has committed itself to creating a free-trade zone during the next twenty-five years. In addition, the members of the Association of Southeast Asian Nations (ASEAN), first established in 1967 by Brunei, Indonesia, Malaysia, the Philippines, Singapore, and Thailand and now including Vietnam, agreed to set up a free-trade area.

- In Sub-Saharan Africa: The Southern African Development Community (SADC) is the largest (0.8 percent of world exports) of twelve regional free-trade areas in the region.

Will the lofty expectations of these regional politico-economic groups be realized? In the past, political will and shared visions have proven to be indispensable elements in successful regional trade regimes that set rules for members' collaboration. Economic complementarity is another essential component, as the goal is to stimulate greater trade among the members of the free-trade area, not simply between it and other regions. If one or more members export products that each of the others wants, the chances of the regime's success are greater; if, by contrast, they all tend to export the same products or to have virtually no trade with one another (typically the case in Africa), failure is more likely.

Prospects for the success of regional trade regimes seem greatest when Global South countries cobble their futures to Global North states—but, complain Global South leaders, on terms that the Global North dictates. That conclusion hardly bodes well for regional economic agreements as an effective method for balancing the North–South relationship.

Trade, Aid, Investment, and Debt Relief   The developing countries have long pleaded for "trade, not aid" to improve their global position, turning to the NIC's and the Global East experience to support the view that access to the Global North's markets is critical to Global South economic growth. And those requests for greater trade through reduced barriers has met with success: the number of free-trade agreements between Global South and Global North countries increased to 109, from only 23 in

1990 (*Harper's*, February 2005). But many Global South countries have not improved their lot, often for two major reasons. First, market access remains difficult because domestic pressure groups in these low-growth Global South countries have lobbied their governments to reduce the imports of other countries' products that compete with their own industries. Trade may be preferred to aid, but political barriers often interfere with free trade. Second, the character and distribution of foreign aid have changed as criticism of its effectiveness and effects has risen. Consequently, levels of foreign aid remain moderate.

Foreign aid comes in a variety of forms and is used for a variety of purposes. Some aid consists of outright grants of money, some of loans at concessional rates, and some of shared technical expertise. Although most foreign aid is **bilateral** and is termed **official development assistance (ODA)**—meaning the money flows directly from one country to another—an increasing portion is now channeled through global intergovernmental institutions such as the World Bank, and hence is known as "multilateral aid." Moreover, the purposes of aid are as varied as its forms. Commonly stated foreign aid goals include not only the reduction of poverty through economic development but also human development, environmental protection, reduced military spending, enhanced economic management, the development of private enterprise, increased power for women, the promotion of democratic governance and human rights, and humanitarian disaster relief and assistance to refugees. However, security objectives traditionally have figured

> *The purpose of human life is to serve, and to show compassion and the will to help others.*
>
> —Albert Schweitzer, German Lutheran pastor who helped pioneer in the advocacy and practice of humanitarian deeds

prominently as motives of donors' allocations of both economic aid and military assistance, and still do. For example, the United States continues to target Israel and Egypt as major recipients to symbolize friendship, maintain a balance of power, and tilt the scales toward peace in the Middle East. Also, security was the primary motive behind the doubling of the U.S. foreign assistance budget following 9/11 to provide funds for allies' use in the global war on terrorism.

The assumption that development will support other goals, such as fostering solidarity among allies and promoting commercial advantage, free markets, or democratization, still underpins most donors' assistance programs. The general trend for the past fifteen years in foreign aid allocations has been toward slowly rising increases. In 2006 Global North donors gave $104 billion to poor countries (five percent less than 2005), but at the 2007 G-8 summit in Gleneagles, Scotland the donors promised to increase aid to $130 billion by 2010 (*Economist*, April 7, 2007). Wide variations in the levels and types of aid provided by each Global North donor persist (see Figure 5.1).

Many aid donors have become frustrated with the slow growth rates of many of the Global South recipients and have grown impatient and doubtful of the effectiveness of their aid programs, despite strong evidence that foreign aid has made a positive difference (Easterbrook 2002). Critics particularly resent what they perceive to be an

■ **foreign aid**
economic assistance in the form of loans and grants provided by a donor country to a recipient country for a variety of purposes.

■ **bilateral**
interactions between two transnational actors.

■ **official development assistance (ODA)**
grants or loans to countries from donor countries, now usually channeled through multilateral aid institutions such as the World Bank for the primary purpose of promoting economic development and welfare.

entrenched state of mind in many Global South cultures that stands in the way of development, which—while bemoaning poverty—at the same time condemn the profit motive, competition, and consumerism at the heart of capitalism's spirit. Donors are especially resentful that the countries seeking aid do not value the core Western values of hard work, economic competition, and entrepreneurial creativity believed to be crucial for progress and prosperity.

Most bothersome to "aid pessimists" resisting what they see as a failed "ideology of development" (Easterly 2007) are the failures caused by corrupt and autocratic Global South leaders. Former U.S. Secretary of State Colin L. Powell summarized the prevailing Global North mood when he argued the case for assistance as a provider of market incentives: "Economic systems work best when access to opportunity is fair, when free people can use their talents to help themselves and others to prosper. Aid can be a catalyst for development, but the real engines of growth are entrepreneurship, investment, and trade. They are what produce jobs, and a job is the most important social safety net for any family. If economic aid to developing countries is to succeed, it must be part of an incentive system for good governance. Foreign aid that succeeds is foreign aid that makes itself obsolete. If a country needs aid year after year, decade after decade, it will develop a dependency on outside assistance."

In response to this viewpoint, donors have grown increasingly insistent on "conditionality" or demands that aid recipients must meet to receive assistance. Donors also persist in their habit of making development assistance "tied" to the donors for their benefit, such as requiring purchases from the donors, even though the World Bank estimates this practice reduces the value of aid by 15 to 30 percent, decreases its efficiency, and violates the same free-market principles that the Global North promotes. When donors treat foreign aid as a subsidy for their own domestic corporations to encourage exports, they play a *two-level game* by making decisions aimed at meeting both domestic and foreign policy goals.

On top of this, Global South countries complain that the Global North donors have been promising for the past thirty-five years to allocate 0.7 percent of their gross domestic product to foreign aid, but only a few have kept the promise (or even come close). This is true despite the evidence that more assistance does indeed contribute to development when it is designed properly and is delivered in a sustained way to countries with records of improving democratic governance (Sachs 2005). Global South confusion about the Global North's true motives stems from the fact that 38 percent of aid is distributed to the middle- and high-income countries (WDI 2007, 362). Much more money—more than double the global total in foreign aid—is primarily funneled into Global South economies through the **remittances** that migrant laborers working in the Global North earn each paycheck and faithfully send home to their families. Global remittances rose steadily each year since the 1970s, and reached $318 billion in 2007 from only $170 billion in 2002 (*Economist*, December 15, 2007, p. 106). A feature of globalization, remittances serve as a special kind of "homeland security" because "80 percent of the money or more is immediately spent on food, clothing, housing and education" and has increased the impact on Global South economic growth in the recipient countries because the money sent goes "to small-bank financial institutions which use the resultant capital pool to lend to local entrepreneurs" (DeParle 2007, 3).

■ **remittances**

the money earned by immigrants working in rich countries (which almost always exceeds the income they could earn working in their home country) that they send to their families in their country.

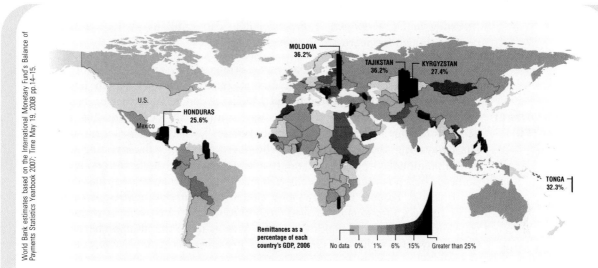

FIGURE 5.1

SENDING MONEY BACK HOME **The billions of dollars that migrant workers send home each year is vital to developing countries. For example, in Tajikistan remittances amount to almost 36% of the gross domestic product. As the global economy continues to experience a slump at the start of 2009, the stream of revenue may slow. This concerns governments such as Mexico's, where fewer Latin American immigrants in the United States are sending money back home.**

An equal indicator of the modest levels of Global North assistance for development is how it compares to charitable contributions from private citizens to humanitarian aid agencies such as CARE, even though in most donor countries their gifts there are income tax write-offs. "About $11.1 billion a year is funneled to poor countries through private charities," some of which is also stimulated by government tax breaks for charitable giving (*Economist*, March 4, 2006, 96).

Recently, however, many Global South leaders have joined Global North critics of foreign aid, interpreting it as an instrument of neocolonialism and neoimperialism and resenting the conditionality criteria for receiving aid imposed by the IMF and other multilateral institutions. They have joined the chorus of experts advocating trade and investment as substitutes for aid. Without lobbying, it appears unlikely that aid from all sources will expand above the current low level of only 0.3 percent of all Global South developing countries' combined gross national income (WDI 2007, 16, 344).

"There is a widely held fiction that masses of money are poured into aid. In fact, industrialized countries spend roughly one quarter of one percent of their gross domestic product for assistance to the world's poor countries," argued James D. Wolfensohn, the World Bank president, when he urged the Global North to recognize that greater foreign aid can contribute directly to the Global North's national security by helping to combat such problems as drug trafficking, climate change, and civil war. But now, after years of neglect, foreign aid may be making a comeback. A *hegemon* can lead, and it did when the United States announced the Millennium Challenge Account (MCA) as a part of the U.S. national security strategy, to provide from 2006 onward at least $5 billion each year in aid to seventeen eligible countries that "govern justly, invest in their people, and encourage economic freedom." This represented the largest increase in U.S. development assistance since the Marshall Plan, and it inspires hope that the 3,000-page UN *Investing in Development: A Practical Plan* can fulfill its goal of ending global poverty though big increases in foreign aid.

In addition to foreign aid, another tactic sitting center stage in the Global South's strategies for escaping destitution and stagnant economic growth has been to encourage multinational corporations (MNCs) to funnel an increasing share of their **foreign direct investment** (FDI) into its countries, thereby increasing its export earnings to gain a greater share of global trade. This strategy for economic growth has always been the target of critics who question whether the investment of capital by multinational corporations (and, to a lesser extent, private investors) into local or domestic business ventures is really a financial remedy. The strategy has always been controversial, because there are many hidden costs, or **externalities**, associated with permitting corporations controlled from abroad to set up business within the host state for the purpose of making a profit. Who is to be the ultimate beneficiary, the foreign investor or the states in which the investments are made? Considerable risks are entailed, as are a number of trade-offs among competing values (see Controversy: Multinational Corporations in the Global South: Do They Help or Hurt?).

The primary danger with this strategy is the potential for foreign investments to lead to foreign control and the erosion of sovereign governments' capacities to regulate the economy within their borders. An additional danger is the probability that the multinational foreign investors will not invest their profits locally but channel them abroad for new investments or disburse them as dividends for their wealthy Global North shareholders. However, despite the risks, many developing countries have relaxed restrictions in order to attract foreign investors, with less emphasis placed on liberalizing investment restrictions and encouraging open domestic economic competition than on offering tax and cash enticements and opportunities for joint ventures. This has stimulated a recent surge in the flow of capital investments to the Global South (see Figure 5.2). However, keep in mind that 71 percent of all FDI is channeled to the Global North, and the poorest Global South countries (the LLCDs) benefit from only 0.2 percent of investments from abroad (WDI 2007, 342). Instructively the United States, Great Britain, and China are expected to attract 30 percent of FDI flows between 2007 and 2011 (*Economist*, September 15, 2007, 121).

The impact of this new infusion of foreign investments in the developing countries has been substantial, given the Global South's relatively small economies. It has paved the way for emerging markets to expand their rates of economic development —despite the resistance of local industries that are threatened by the competition and the critics who complain about the income inequalities that the investments are causing. Such fears and consequences notwithstanding, developing countries are intensifying their competition for foreign investment capital in order to liberate themselves from dependence and destitution. And FDI is the leading cause of the shift from farm work to service jobs in Global South urban areas (now 42 percent of the developing countries' labor force) that is lifting millions of people out of poverty while at the same time *outsourcing* skilled jobs from the Global North (*Christian Science Monitor*, September 4, 2007, 1,10).

The prospects for either foreign aid or for foreign direct investments to contribute to the future development of, and relief of poverty in, the Global South will depend on a number of other factors. Foremost is the extent to which the staggering level of debt facing many Global South countries can be managed.

■ foreign direct investment (FDI)

a cross-border investment through which a person or corporation based in one country purchases or constructs an asset such as a factory or bank in another country so that a long-term relationship and control of an enterprise by nonresidents results.

■ externalities

the unintended side effects of choices that reduce the true value of the original decision, such as trade protectionism against foreign imports increasing the costs of goods to consumers and stimulating inflation.

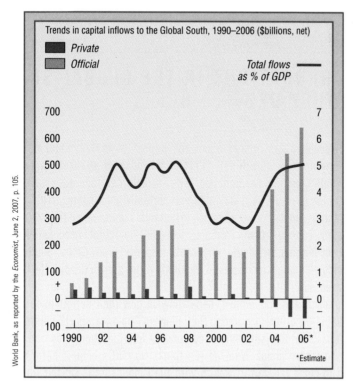

Trends in capital inflows to the Global South, 1990–2006 ($billions, net)

■ Private
■ Official

Total flows ——
as % of GDP

*Estimate

World Bank, as reported by the *Economist,* June 2, 2007, p. 105.

FIGURE 5.2

TRENDS IN CAPITAL INVESTMENTS IN THE GLOBAL SOUTH **Private capital has in recent years increasingly poured into the Global South's developing countries through foreign direct investments and commercial bank loans, accelerating a trend that began in 2002. In 2006, net capital flows climbed to $647 billion, the highest level on record (*Economist,* June 2, 2007, 105). The Asia/Pacific region now accounts for two-fifths of worldwide capital investments. These Global South investment gains notwithstanding, Global South repayments to official lenders are increasing and draining resources; $185 billion was repaid between 2003 and 2006 to lenders such as the International Monetary Fund.**

The IMF estimates that Global South debt in 2006 exceeded $3207 billion for 146 countries and that their debt-service payments were $495.3 billion. This is unsustainable. It accounts for 14 percent of the value of their combined exports of goods, services, and income (WDI 2007, 256). Worse off are the twenty-eight heavily indebted poor countries (HIPCs), with arrears of $782 billion, seeking relief through debt rescheduling or cancellation. A number of multilateral lending institutions created by the Global North great powers have begun to respond to the HIPCs and other Global South countries facing dire financial debts.

■ **heavily indebted poor countries (HIPCs)**

the subset of countries identified by the World Bank's Debtor Reporting System whose ratios of debt to gross national product are so substantial they cannot meet their payment obligations without experiencing political instability and economic collapse.

> *The development of debt means the death of development.*
>
> —*Marie Michael, development economist*

CONTROVERSY:

MULTINATIONAL CORPORATIONS IN THE GLOBAL SOUTH: DO THEY HELP OR HURT?

Within the Global South, widespread concern has existed about the impact of multinational corporations' (MNCs) activities on the local economy and its growth rate. Part of the concern stems from the historic tendency for MNCs to look to Global South countries as production sites so they can take advantage of cheap labor for production and avoid labor-union pressure that for years was virtually nonexistent. MNCs can either promote or inhibit development, depending on how they channel investments and, when they do, how they operate in the host country. Despite these concerns about MNCs as powerful, potentially neocolonial, nonstate actors that may compromise national sovereignty and undermine local prosperity, many Global South countries have overcome their fears and now welcome global companies to stimulate rapid growth despite the many risks and costs that MNCs' penetrations often incur.

MNCs continue to be alternately praised and condemned, depending on how their performance is viewed. The record is mixed and can be evaluated on different criteria. The following "balance sheet" summarizes the major arguments for and against MNCs. Using this summary of contending interpretations, you can easily see why the role and impact of MNCs is so controversial. What do you think? Do MNCs help or harm the Global South's ability to develop rapidly and to close the gap in wealth with the Global North? On the whole, is the impact of multinational corporations constructive or exploitative?

Positive

- Increase the volume of trade

- Assist the aggregation of investment capital that can fund development

- Finance loans and service international debt

- Lobby for free trade and the removal of barriers to trade, such as tariffs

- Underwrite research and development that allow technological innovation

- Introduce and dispense advanced technology to less-developed countries

- Reduce the costs of goods by encouraging their production according to the principle of *comparative advantage*

- Generate employment

- Encourage the training of workers

- Produce new goods and expand opportunities for their purchase through the internationalization of production

- Disseminate marketing expertise and mass advertising methods

- Provide investment income to facilitate less-developed countries' modernization

- Generate income and wealth

- Advocate peaceful relations between and among states to preserve an orderly environment conducive to trade and profits

- Break down national barriers and accelerate the globalization of the international economy and culture and the rules that govern international commerce

Negative

- Give rise to huge merged conglomerations that reduce competition and free enterprise

- Raise capital in host countries (thereby depriving local industries of investment capital) but export profits to home countries

- Breed debtors and make the poor dependent on those providing loans

- Limit the availability of commodities by monopolizing their production and controlling their distribution in the world marketplace

- Create "sanctuary markets" that restrict and channel other investments to give MNCs an unfair advantage

- Export technology ill-suited to underdeveloped economies

- Inhibit the growth of infant industries and local technological expertise in less-developed countries while making Global South countries dependent on Global North technology

- Create monopolies that contribute to inflation

- Curtail employment by driving labor competition from the market

- Limit workers' wages

- Limit the supply of raw materials available in international markets

- Erode traditional cultures and national differences, leaving in their place a homogenized world culture dominated by consumer-oriented values

- Widen the gap between rich and poor countries

- Increase the wealth of local elites at the expense of the poor

- Support and rationalize repressive regimes in the name of stability and order

- Challenge national sovereignty and jeopardize the autonomy of states

- Create cartels with other MNCs that share markets in order to cut competition

These institutions also recognize that debt relief is necessary for arresting the collapse of the HIPCs that could wreck the entire world economy. In 2005, the IMF Steering Committee agreed to forgive $40 billion worth of debt for eighteen of the poorest countries and to consider debt cancellation of another $15 billion for as many as twenty other countries.

This was partly done out of compassion but also was a result of the economic self-interest of the Global North, which sees in debt relief a pragmatic method for preventing an economic collapse that could threaten the entire world economy in the age of interdependent globalization. The World Bank's "Enhanced HIPC Initiative" and the IMF's "Enhanced Structural Adjustment Facility" are the primary products of this attempt to reduce the widening disparities between the Global North and Global South. Whether these programs will succeed, argue their sponsors, will depend on the degree to which developing countries can undertake, with minimal corruption, the often painful liberalizing political and economic reforms that are required for sustained economic growth. This argument reflects what is known as the **Washington consensus**, the view held by numerous U.S. government, World Bank, and IMF officials (all headquartered in Washington, D.C.) that balanced government budgets, the privatization of state-owned enterprises, the reduction of barriers to trade and foreign investment, and the elimination of subsidies to domestic producers are prerequisites for economic growth.

■ **Washington consensus**

the view that Global South countries can best achieve sustained economic growth through democratic governance, fiscal discipline, free markets, a reliance on private enterprise, and trade liberalization.

Scratch a pessimist and you find often a defender of privilege.
—Lord Beveridge, British economist

Yet these reforms may not be as successful as their advocates claim. On the one hand, China and Singapore have enjoyed rapid economic growth without undertaking significant political liberalization. On the other hand, many Global South countries that have implemented economic liberalizing reforms have not experienced growth (Collier 2007). Indeed, Joseph Stiglitz (2003), a Nobel Laureate in economics and former chief economist of the World Bank, complains that the policies emanating from the Washington consensus produce disappointing results because they are anchored in a free-market dogma that ignores the unique sociocultural contexts of the countries where they are applied.

In summary, an unqualified free-market approach to development that minimizes the role of the state may not be sufficient by itself to create rapid economic growth. Other factors, such as fair, effective systems of property and regulatory law, and honest, responsive political institutions, need to augment trade openness. Moreover, under certain circumstances, a stronger role for the state is advantageous, especially in providing a safety net for the most vulnerable members of society and in addressing distributional inequities related to ethnicity, gender, or geographic region (Clemens 2007). Given the diversity of the Global South, development strategies for the future should avoid grandiose claims of universality and one-size-fits-all policies. What works in one country may be impractical or undesirable in another.

THE GLOBAL SOUTH'S FUTURE

It is useful to remember the historical trends underlying the emergence of the Global South as an actor on the global stage, rather than rely on analysts' socially constructed concepts that became popular and shaped its identity. Those states that came to regard themselves as its members share important characteristics. Most were colonized by people of another race, experienced varying degrees of poverty and hunger, and felt powerless in a world system dominated by the affluent countries that once controlled them and perhaps still do. Considerable change occurred among the newly emergent states as post–World War II *decolonization* proceeded, but much also remained the same. Thus, the term *Third World* continues to describe a state of mind that still galvanizes the Global South as it seeks to overcome the disorder and destitution that afflict so many people living there.

The relationships between the world's developed and developing countries will no doubt continue to change. Exactly how remains as uncertain as why it took throughout recorded history until the Industrial Revolution in the early 1800s for the world's standard of living to finally grow, when it suddenly began its march forward toward a growth rate exceeding a factor of at least six times (Clark 2008). The economic history of relations between countries and the forces that allow some to prosper and others to decline remains fraught with puzzles.

In the future, Global South destiny and relations with the cycles of Global North growth and decline are difficult to predict. However, the future of Global South development is certain to depend in the near term on the activities of the Global North. A turn inward toward isolationist foreign policies in the Global North could lead to a posture of "benign neglect" of the Global South. Conversely, a new era of North-South cooperation could commence, dedicated to finding solutions to common problems ranging from commercial to environmental and security concerns. Elements of both approaches are already evident.

The Global South remains a set of global actors dominated by the great powers. That domination is funneled in part through the powerful international organizations like the United Nations and the World Bank that the great powers have created. To understand world politics and the roots of changes in international affairs, it is important to inspect the impact of these influential IGOs as actors in the global arena. To complete the picture, you also need to inspect the thousands of NGOs, whose presence and pressure as nonstate actors are also transforming international politics, for both the Global North and the Global South. We turn to both of these transnational actors in Chapters 6 and 7.

Key Terms

Global North
Global South
indigenous peoples
Third World
First World
Second World
least developed of the less
    developed countries (LLDCs)
Global East
decolonization
nonstate nations
neocolonialism (neoimperialism)
mercantilism
classical liberal economic theory
laissez-faire economics
spheres of influence
communism
Marxist-Leninism
world-system theory

realpolitik
self-determination
developing countries
gross national income (GNI)
developed countries
barter
development
modernization
dependency theory
dependency
dualism
newly industrialized countries
    (NICs)
dependent development
semiperiphery
Asian Tigers
outsourcing
nonalignment
nonaligned states

Nonaligned Movement (NAM)
failed states
military intervention
import-substitution
    industrialization
export-led industrialization
Group of 77 (G-77)
New International Economic
    Order (NIEO)
foreign aid
bilateral
official development assistance
    (ODA)
remittances
foreign direct investment (FDI)
externalities
heavily indebted poor countries
    (HIPCs)
Washington consensus

CHAPTER 6
INTERGOVERNMENTAL ORGANIZATIONS AND THE QUEST FOR GLOBAL GOVERNANCE

Lasting achievements require patience and perseverance, too. They also require [state] partnerships . . . with the relevant international institutions to solve common problems.

—Colin L. Powell, U.S. Secretary of State

United Nations

"The Last Best Hope for Humanity"? That was the view U.S. President John F. Kennedy held about the United Nations, whose headquarters in New York City is pictured here. With many problems populating the global agenda, the question is whether the UN is an IGO adequately empowered by the great powers to lead for effective global governance.

Y ou are a member of the human race, and your future will be determined to a large degree by the capacity of humanity to create effective institutions to manage the many common problems that confront the entire world. How is the world responding to this challenge?

The answer for centuries has been reliance primarily on sovereign territorial states. Countries remain the most influential actors on the world stage, and it is *states'* foreign policy decisions and interactions that, more than any other factors, give rise to trends and transformations in world politics. Today, however, that extraordinary power by states over global destiny is eroding.

A novel redistribution of power among states, markets, and civil society is underway, ending the steady accumulation of power in the hands of states that began with the Peace of Westphalia in 1648.
—Jessica T. Mathews, international relations scholar

If this is so, a critical question to consider is if the predicted decline of states' sovereign authority and independence will ultimately prove to be a cure for global problems, or a curse by reducing states' ability to rely on *self-help* measures to address problems unilaterally as each state seeks solutions that best serve its own self-interests.

This chapter provides information and insight that can help you evaluate this question. More specifically, it will enable you to confront and assess the theoretical hypothesis advanced by two world leaders. The first was posited by UN Secretary General Kofi Annan, when he said, "Globalization is a source of new challenges for humanity. Only a global organization is capable of meeting global challenges. When we act together, we are stronger and less vulnerable to individual calamity." The second is a corollary by World Bank Vice President for Europe Jean-Francois Rischard, who argues, "One thing is sure: global complexity [is creating a] global governance crisis that will have to be solved through new ways of working together globally, and bold departures from old, trusted concepts."

Global problems without a doubt often require global solutions. As yet, global institutions do not exist that can engineer a prosperous and peaceful world order. However, there have arisen an impressive number of nonstate actors on the world stage that are increasingly flexing their political muscle in efforts to engineer adaptive global changes. This chapter will explore the first set—international organizations that carry out independent foreign policies as transnational actors. In Chapter 7, you will have the opportunity to evaluate a second type of nonstate actor— nongovernmental organizations made up of individual people who band together in coalitions of private citizens to exercise international influence. To introduce this, we take a brief look at both types of nonstate actor.

My first axiom: The quest for international security involves the unconditional surrender by every nation, in a certain measure, of its liberty of action, its sovereignty that is to say, and it is clear beyond all doubt that no other road can lead to such security.
—Albert Einstein, leading scientist of the twentieth century

INTERGOVERNMENTAL ORGANIZATIONS (IGOs) AND NONGOVERNMENTAL ORGANIZATIONS (NGOs)

What distinguishes the two principal types of nonstate actors is that **intergovernmental organizations (IGOs)** are international organizations whose members are states, whereas **nongovernmental organizations (NGOs)** are associations comprised of members who are private individuals and groups.

IGOs are purposely created by states to solve shared problems. This gives IGOs whatever authority they possess for the purposes states assign them. But because IGOs are produced by states, they are generally regarded as more important than NGOs.

In part, this is because IGOs are defined by the fact that their members are the governments of states and also by the permanence of their institutions. IGOs meet at regular intervals, and they have established rules for making decisions and a permanent secretariat or headquarters staff.

A global trend in world politics is the spectacular growth of IGOs. As shown in Figure 6.1, their numbers have increased sharply since the nineteenth century, in response to the growth of international commerce and communications alongside industrialization. By 1909, thirty-seven IGOs were in existence. By 1960, there were 154 IGOs, and at the start of 2007 the number had risen to 246. If these definitional criteria for identifying an IGO were relaxed, an additional 5,387 highly active "special type" IGOs would qualify for inclusion, as would another 1,717 "other" international-oriented national IGOs (*Yearbook of International Organizations, 2005/2006*, Vol. 5, 33).

■ **intergovernmental organizations (IGOs)** institutions created and joined by states' governments, which give them authority to make collective decisions to manage particular problems on the global agenda.

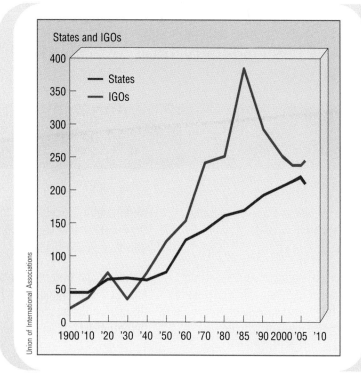

Union of International Associations

FIGURE 6.1

TRENDS IN THE NUMBER OF IGOs AND STATES SINCE 1900 **Since 1900 the number of independent states has increased dramatically, and that growth accelerated especially after World War II when the decolonization movement began. But note that the number of intergovernmental organizations has grown even more rapidly in this period, declining only since the late 1980s when a number of formerly independent IGOs began to merge with one another.**

■ **nongovernmental organizations (NGOs)**

transnational organizations of private citizens maintaining consultative status with the UN; they include professional associations, foundations, multinational corporations, or simply internationally active groups in different states joined together to work toward common interests.

GLOBAL INTERGOVERNMENTAL ORGANIZATIONS

IGOs vary widely in size and purpose. Only thirty-three IGOs qualify as "intercontinental organizations" and only thirty-four are, like the UN, "universal membership" IGOs. The rest, accounting for more than 72 percent of the total, are limited in their scope and confined to particular regions. Table 6.1 illustrates these differences. The variation among the organizations in each subcategory is great, particularly with single-purpose, limited-membership IGOs. The North Atlantic Treaty Organization (NATO), for example, is primarily a military alliance, whereas others, such as the Organization of American States (OAS), promote both economic development and democratic reforms. Still, most IGOs concentrate their activities on specific economic or social issues of special concern to them, such as the management of trade or transportation.

The expansion of IGOs has created a complex network of overlapping international organizations that cooperate with one another to deal with a wide range of global issues. They support one another to work, for example, on issues as varied as trade, defense, disarmament, economic development, agriculture, health, culture, human rights, the arts, illegal drugs, tourism, labor, gender inequality, education, debt, the environment, crime, humanitarian aid, civilian crisis relief, telecommunications, science, globalization, immigration, and refugees.

Begin your analysis of nonstate actors in world affairs by examining the most prominent and representative IGOs: the United Nations, the EU, and various other regional organizations. After benefiting from a description of these IGOs, as noted, your eyes should be directed toward forming your opinion about the extent to which IGOs' activities (1) are adequate for dealing with the pressing threats to human welfare and (2) whether these IGOs are undermining states' continuing autonomy and, if so, whether an erosion of state power will prove helpful or harmful.

Table 6.1 A Simple Classification of Intergovernmental Organizations (IGOs)

Geographic Scope of Membership	Range of Stated Purpose	
	Multiple Purposes	Single Purpose
Global	United Nations, World Trade Organization, UNESCO, Organization of the Islamic Conference	World Health Organization, International Labor Organization, International Monetary Fund, Universal Postal Union
Interregional, regional, subregional	European Union, Organization for Security and Cooperation in Europe, Organization of American States, Organization of African Unity, League of Arab States, Association of Southeast Asian Nations	European Space Agency, Nordic Council, North Atlantic Treaty Organization, International Olive Oil Council, International North Pacific Coffee Organization, African Groundnut Council

The United Nations

The United Nations (UN) is the best-known global organization. What distinguishes it from most other IGOs is its nearly universal membership, including today 192 independent member states from every region (see Figure 6.2). The UN's nearly fourfold growth from the fifty-one states that joined it at the UN's birth in 1945 has been spectacular, but the admission process has from the start been governed by political conflicts that show the extent to which the organization reflects the relationships of the five great powers that created it and govern it through veto authority in the Security Council.

In principle, any sovereign state that accepts the UN's goals and regulations can join, but the great powers have often let *realpolitik*—the belief that countries should put their own national interest above concern for the global community—guide their foreign policy decision making about their votes regarding which new countries should be admitted. This was especially true during the Cold War. Both the United States and the Soviet Union prevented countries aligned with their adversary from joining, and the controversy has continued about Taiwan ever since. In the 1970s, the United States recognized the communist government in China and engineered the transfer of the "China seat" from the so-called Republic of China in Taiwan. Because China insists that Taiwan is not an independent state but instead a rebel province of the mainland, Taiwan cannot rejoin the world organization. Similar political barriers have stood in the way of Palestine being admitted to the United Nations.

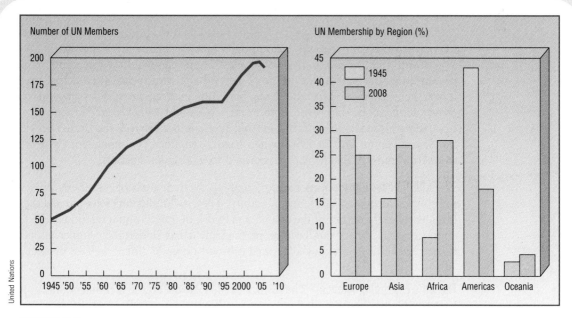

FIGURE 6.2

THE CHANGING MEMBERSHIP OF THE UNITED NATIONS **As the figure on the left shows, the UN's membership has seen episodic bursts of growth from fifty-one states in 1945 to 192 at the start of 2009, with the most recent admission in 2006 of newly independent Montenegro (the world's 212th sovereign state). As shown in the figure on the right, during nearly six decades of expansion, the UN has increasingly included Global South countries. This shift has influenced the kinds of interests and issues the UN has confronted, expanding the global agenda from the priorities of the great powers in the Global North to include those important to the developing states in the Global South.**

The UN's Purposes   In addition to its nearly universal mirroring of world politics, the UN is also a multipurpose organization. Article 1 of the UN Charter defines the UN's objectives as centered on:

- Maintaining international peace and security

- Developing friendly relations among states based on respect for the principle of equal rights and the self-determination of peoples

- Achieving international cooperation solving international problems of an economic, social, cultural, or humanitarian character and in promoting and encouraging respect for human rights and for fundamental freedoms for all

- Functioning as a center for harmonizing the actions of countries to attain these common ends

Peace and security figured prominently in the thinking of the great powers responsible for creating the UN and its predecessor, the League of Nations. Following each twentieth-century global war, world leaders created new institutions to keep peace. These institutional reforms were inspired by the liberal conviction that both war and the management of other global problems can best be controlled by removing global *anarchy*—the absence of supranational authority to regulate relations between states—from the international scene. The League of Nations sought to prevent a reoccurrence of the catastrophic World War I by replacing the balance-of-power system with one based on the construction of a *collective security* regime made up of rules for keeping peace, guided by the principle that an act of aggression by any state would be met by a collective retaliatory response from the rest. When the League failed to restrain expansionistic aggression by Germany, Japan, and Italy during the 1930s, it collapsed. At the start of World War II, the U.S., British, and Russian allies began planning for a new international organization, the United Nations, to preserve the postwar peace after victory because it was believed that peace could not be maintained unilaterally by any one great power acting alone. However, faith in the UN's ability quickly eroded when it soon became paralyzed by the unforeseen Cold War conflict between the United States and the Soviet Union. But, in 1991, when Russia renounced communism, the UN was freed from paralysis and, reborn, returned to its original mission.

The UN has sought from its birth to combine the dual goals of preserving peace and improving the quality of life for humanity. These twin missions have carried the UN into nearly every corner of the complex network of international relations. The UN's conference machinery has become permanent: it has undertaken numerous peace-keeping operations and has addressed a broad range of global welfare problems.

The UN's Expanding Agenda   The history of the UN reflects the fact that countries from both the Global North and the Global South have successfully used the organization to promote their own foreign policy goals, and this record has led to the ratification of more than three hundred treaties and conventions consistent with the UN's "six fundamental values:" international freedom, equality, solidarity, tolerance, respect for nature, and a sense of shared responsibility.

Consider the wide array of world conferences that the organization has been asked to address since the 1970s:

Table 6.2   World Conferences, 1970 – Present

human environment (1972, 2002)	the protection of children (1990, 2004, 2005)
law of the sea (1973)	the environment and economic development (1992, 2002)
population (1974, 1984, 1994, 1999)	transnational corporations (1992, 2004)
food (1974, 1976, 2008)	indigenous peoples (1992, 1994)
women (1975, 1980, 1985, 1995, 2005)	internationally organized crime (1994)
human settlements (1976, 2003)	the human rights responsibilities of transnational corporations (2004)
basic human needs (1976)	social development (1995)
water (1977, 2002)	housing (1996)
desertification (1977, 2006)	human rights (1993, 1997)
disarmament (1978, 1982, 1988)	global warming (1992, 1997, 2002)
racism and racial discrimination (1978, 2002)	international trafficking of children for prostitution and slavery (2000, 2004)
technical cooperation among developing countries (1978)	principles for world order (2000)
agrarian reform and rural development (1974, 1979)	small arms (2005, 2006)
science and technology for development (1979)	Arab-Israeli relations (2005)
new and renewable sources of energy (1981)	climate change (2005, 2007 and 2008)
least-developed countries (1981)	nuclear proliferation (2005)
aging (1982, 2004)	biodiversity (2005)
the peaceful uses of outer space (1982)	information society (2005)
Palestine (1947, 1982)	migration (2006)
the peaceful uses of nuclear energy (1983)	urbanization (2006)
the prevention of crime and the treatment of offenders (1985)	AIDS (2006)
drug abuse and illicit trafficking in drugs (1987, 1990, 1998)	review of the *Millennium Development Goals* (2005)

These conferences provide a summary of the most important problems facing the global community, show how urgent needs compete with one another for attention, and suggest how so many of these global problems are resistant to solution, given the persistance with which most issues resurface.

In response to the demands that have been placed upon it, the United Nations has evolved over time into a vast administrative machinery, with offices and staff not only in the UN headquarters in New York but also in centers throughout the globe (see Map 6.1, p. 169). To estimate the capacity of the United Nations to fulfill its growing responsibilities, we next consider how the United Nations is organized.

Organizational Structure   The UN's limitations are perhaps rooted in the ways it is organized for its wide-ranging purposes. According to the Charter, the UN structure contains the following six major organs:

- **General Assembly.** Established as the main deliberative body of the United Nations, all members are equally represented according to a one-state/one-vote formula. Decisions are reached by a simple majority vote, except on so-called important questions, which require a two-thirds majority. The resolutions it passes, however, are only recommendations.

▨ **Security Council.** Given primary responsibility by the Charter for dealing with threats to international peace and security, the Security Council consists of five permanent members with the power to veto substantive decisions (the United States, the United Kingdom, France, Russia, and the People's Republic of China), and ten nonpermanent members elected by the General Assembly for staggered two-year terms.

▨ **Economic and Social Council.** Responsible for coordinating the UN's social and economic programs, functional commissions, and specialized agencies, its fifty-four members are elected by the General Assembly for staggered three-year terms. This body has been particularly active addressing economic development and human rights issues.

▨ **Trusteeship Council.** Charged with supervising the administration of territories that had not achieved self-rule, the Trusteeship Council suspended operation in 1994, when the last remaining trust territory gained independence.

▨ **International Court of Justice.** The principal judicial organ of the United Nations, the International Court of Justice is composed of fifteen independent judges who are elected for nine-year terms by the General Assembly and Security Council. The competence of the Court is restricted to disputes between states, and its jurisdiction is based on the consent of the disputants. The Court may also give nonbinding advisory opinions on legal questions raised by the General Assembly, Security Council, or other UN agencies.

▨ **Secretariat.** Led by the Secretary-General, the Secretariat contains the international civil servants who perform the administrative and secretarial functions of the UN.

The founders of the UN expected the Security Council to become the organization's primary body, because it was designed to maintain peace and its permanent members were the victorious great powers that had been allied during World War II. The Security Council was crafted by the five great-power members to jointly manage the world and protect their top-dog position within it (Gaddis 2004). It is exclusively permitted by the UN Charter to initiate actions, including especially the use of force. The General Assembly can only make recommendations. The founders of the UN did not foresee that this limited mandate would later be expanded to allow the General Assembly to participate with the Security Council in managing security.

As the General Assembly has grown in numbers and importance, it has assumed wider responsibilities and is now the primary body for addressing security as well as social and economic problems. The growth of the General Assembly's power may not be sufficient, however, and the original five great powers in the Security Council continue to run the show—with the U.S. *hegemon* in a pivotal position of preeminent influence. The United States resisted the 2005 proposal to expand the Security Council to twenty-four members because it would dilute American power, and Washington announced that it would not support extension of the veto power held by the big five permanent members to other members. In a similar move to maintain power within the UN, China surprised India in May 2008 with its refusal to support an Indian bid for a permanent seat.

> *There is a need to adjust this organization to the new historical reality. Who else will take the role of coordinating and organizing global work but the United Nations?*
>
> —Vladimir Putin, Russian Prime Minister

As now configured, the UN is not well organized to control the threats facing humanity which prompted Chinese President Hu Jintao to call for reorganizing the United Nations to put it at the center of efforts to fight terrorism and settle disputes.

The UN's inadequacies are not necessarily permanent. Look at the UN's history. In response to the challenge of managing the seemingly growing number of world problems, the UN has adaptively evolved into an extraordinarily complex network of overlapping institutions, some of which (the UN Children's Fund or UNICEF and the United Nations University, for example) fulfill their mission in part through NGOs. The UN has also increasingly come to rely on the many NGOs that are not under its formal authority. This collaboration blurs the line between governmental and nongovernmental functions, but UN-NGO cooperation has led to the UN becoming not one organization but a decentralized conglomerate of countless committees, bureaus, boards, commissions, centers, institutes, offices, and agencies scattered around the globe, with each of its many specialized activities managed from offices in various cities (see Map 6.1).

If any of these various units in the UN's widespread family occupies a central role in the UN's overall structure, it is the General Assembly. Countries in the Global South —seizing advantage of their growing numbers under the one-state, one-vote rules of

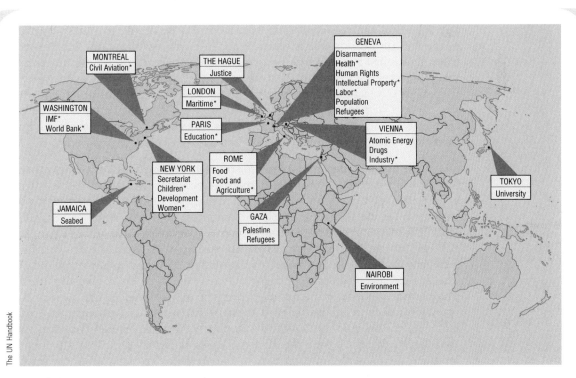

The UN Handbook

MAP 6.1

THE UN'S HEADQUARTERS AND GLOBAL NETWORK Since its creation the UN has sought to address the continuously expanding problems on the global agenda. To reduce the gap between aspiration and accomplishment, the UN (as shown on the map) has spread its administrative arm to every corner of the globe in order to fulfill its primary purpose of spearheading international cooperation. To service its worldwide missions, in 2008 the UN continued its search for additional cheap office space, including islands, cruise ships, and large tents.

the General Assembly—have guided UN involvement in directions of particular concern to them. This explains the enormous growth of diverse affiliated agencies that have been created to address the full array of the world's problems and needs. Today, a coalition of 132 Global South countries constituting three-fourths of the UN and led by the *Group of 77 (G-77)* previously *nonaligned states*, along with the "Fifth Committee" (which deals with the UN budget), seeks to resist domination by the *Global North*. This coalition protests that the UN ignores economic and social needs and fails to respect the Global South's special interests. The Global South's power in numbers gives it enormous clout.

Budget Blues   Differences between the Global North and the Global South over perceived priorities are most clearly exhibited in the heated debate over the UN's budget. This controversy centers on how members should interpret the organization's charter, which states that "expenses of the Organization shall be borne by the members as apportioned by the General Assembly."

The UN budget consists of three distinct elements: the core budget, the peacekeeping budget, and the budget for voluntary programs. States contribute to the voluntary programs and some of the peacekeeping activities as they see fit. The core budget and other peacekeeping activities are subject to assessments.

The precise mechanism by which assessments have been determined is complicated, but, historically, assessments have been allocated according to states' capacity to pay. Although this formula is under attack in many wealthy states, it still governs. Thus, the United States, which has the greatest resources, contributes 22 percent of the UN's core budget (and 27 percent of the peacekeeping budget as well as 37 percent of voluntary contributions for humanitarian programs). In comparison, the poorest 70 percent of the UN's members pay the minimum (0.01 percent), contributing only $13,000 annually. By this agreement the richest states paid more than four-fifths of the UN's 2006–2007 budget.

Resistance to this budgetary formula for funding UN activities has always existed. It has grown progressively worse in large part because when the General Assembly apportions expenses, it does so according to majority rule. The problem is that those with the most votes (the less-developed countries) do not have the money, and the most prosperous countries do not have the votes. Wide disparities have grown, adhering to the principle that UN expenses should be appropriated according to members' capacity to pay—a rule by Resolution 55/B that applied through 2007. The ten largest contributors command only ten votes but pay 82 percent of the cost. The poorest members pay only 18 percent of the UN budget but command 182 votes. This deep imbalance has led to many fierce financial disputes between the more numerous Global South developing countries. These countries wield considerable influence over the kinds of issues on which the UN's attention and resources are focused and contribute to the great powers' concern about the UN's priorities, administrative efficiency, and expenses. The wealthy members charge that the existing budget procedures institutionalize a system of taxation without fair representation. The critics counter with the argument that, for fairness and justice, the great-power members should bear financial responsibilities commensurate with their wealth and influence.

At issue, of course, is not simply money, which is paltry (averaging less than fifty-four cents for each person in the world each year). Differences in images of what is important and which states should have political influence are the real issues. Poor states argue that need should determine expenditure levels rather than rich countries' interests. Major contributors, sensitive to the amounts asked of them and how funds are spent, do not want to pay for programs they oppose. For years, the United States has been the most vocal about its dissatisfaction, and since 2000 has been in arrears an average of $1.35 billion each year.

Even though the Global South countries have usually managed to set the agenda in the General Assembly, like the United States they also are not paying their assessments on time. In January 2008, these other members accounted for a fifth of the total unpaid $80 million owed for the UN's regular budget.

In response to persisting cash flow crises and rising complaints about the UN's "bloated bureaucracy" and inefficient administration, bold "Millennium + 5" reforms were undertaken in 2005 to consolidate programs, reduce costs, correct corruption and waste, and reassign administrative responsibilities in order to make the UN more efficient. These massive reforms cut the Secretariat's administrative costs by one-third, from 38 percent of the core budget to 25 percent, and put the savings into a development fund for poor countries. The assessments of some Global North members were also adjusted. The United States at the start of 2008 was paying 22 percent of the regular budget, and the four other permanent members of the Security Council were scheduled to pay proportionately less (Britain and France, 6.1 percent; China, 2.1 percent; and Russia only 1.1 percent). This formula understandably upsets the other major contributors who pay large sums but are still excluded from Security Council participation as permanent members. Consider Japan, which reluctantly paid 19.5 percent of the UN budget in 2005 but planned on cutting its annual contribution by as much as 5 percent when negotiations begin to determine budget revenues for 2007–2009.

The UN's chronic financial crises leave the organization poorly positioned to carry the burdens assigned to it. Member states responsible for the highest contributions are hesitant to reform financing by accepting proposals such as instituting a global tax on currency transactions or on the arms trade. They fear they might lose their existing political control of the UN's activities. So the UN remains without the resources to combat global problems. Compare these facts. At the start of 2008 all the UN's programs had available only $3.00 to serve each of the world's 6.7 billion people (Global Policy Forum 2008). In contrast, global military spending totaled $1,339 billion, costing each of the world's inhabitants an average of $202 (SIPRI 2008).

Future Challenges   The UN's future remains uncertain. The past ten years have been sobering, reducing confidence in the UN's ability to fulfill its ambitious goals by building global norms and international law to regulate unacceptable state behavior. These doubts were compounded by a string of scandals including charges of mismanagement in the 1990s Iraqi "Oil-for-Food" program, sexual abuse of women in Congo by UN peacekeepers, and inaction until late 2007 in response to years of mass genocide in the Darfur region of Sudan, which left three hundred thousand people dead and two million displaced in the sanctuary of refugee camps. However, given the UN's successful history of organizational adaptation to challenges, supporters have reasons to be optimistic about the organization's long-term prospects to live up to its creators' bold mandate to attack world problems. The UN has undertaken since 2006 a series of reforms to change its management procedures and bring its recruitment, contracting, and training responsibilities into line with its vast new responsibilities. These reforms include protection for "whistleblowers" who report scandals, an antifraud and corruption policy, a unified standard of conduct for peacekeepers to prevent sexual abuse, and expanded financial disclosure requirements for senior officials. However, in 2007 the *Group of 77,* fearing that new Secretary General Ban Ki-moon of South Korea would bend to big-donor pressure, began to resist some of these plans. This suggests that the UN will probably remain an arena for heated jockeying among member states and hemispheric blocs, a fact bound to undermine its capacity to solve new global problems. And, with less money than the annual budget for New York City's police department, financial constraints will impede the UN's ability to engineer progress and meet the needs of 192 states and 6.7 billion people.

Yet supporters counter that the UN is frequently blamed unfairly for failures when the real failure belongs to its members, particularly those of the Global North (Power 2008). "Those powers are seldom willing to give it sufficient resources, attention and boots on the ground to accomplish the ambitious mandates they set for it" (Fukuyama 2008, 14). As one high-level UN civil servant, Brian Urquhart, argues, "Either the UN is vital to a more stable and equitable world and should be given the means to do the job, or peoples and government should be encouraged to look elsewhere."

FILLING THE LEADERSHIP VACUUM South Korea's Ban Ki-moon is the eighth Secretary General in the UN's sixty-year history. Ban was chosen in a selection process marked by unprecedented speed, consensus, and calm. In 2008, he was ranked as the most popular leader in a worldwide poll that "asked respondents whether they trusted international leaders 'to do the right thing regarding world affairs'" (WorldPublicOpinion.org, accessed June 30, 2008).

Timothy A. Clary/AFP/Getty Images

While less than perfect, the United Nations is the only global mechanism for effective collaboration in circumstances where states are reluctant or ill-placed to act alone.

—Robert DeVecchi and Arthur C. Helton, political journalists

In the final analysis, the UN can be no more than the mandates and power that the member states give to it. However, the administrative, political, and financial restraints on the UN do not automatically doom it to failure, as critics predict. Though much maligned, the United Nations is very much needed. "The United Nations is everybody's whipping boy," notes Jonathan Power (2004), "but it is revealing how in a crisis the big powers can run to it and find a solution."

Other Prominent Global IGOs

Beyond the UN, literally hundreds of other IGOs are active internationally. Fewer than 14 percent are truly global, including as members every independent state. Unlike the UN, most IGOs include as members a large but incomplete list of today's sovereign states. In addition, the most influential, visible, and controversial IGOs usually have less formal procedures in place to make policy decisions. To round out the sample, we look briefly at three of the most prominent of these other IGOs, all of which are specialized in their focus on the international political economy: the World Trade Organization (WTO), the World Bank, and the International Monetary Fund (IMF).

In each example, note that these IGOs were created by the great powers for the purposes of their sponsors in response to the great powers' need for a stable international economic order, even at the voluntary sacrifice of sovereignty. Why, one may ask, would states give up some of their own independent autonomy, when that surrender reduces some of their control over their destiny? The primary reason is that multilateral cooperation enables those cooperating states to receive benefits that they would not otherwise receive. The creation of international *regimes* (rules agreed to by a set of states to regulate cooperative ventures) as well as authoritative IGO institutions for global governance can pay dividends. Shared problems often cannot be managed without multilateral cooperation. Unilateral measures on many issues by even the most powerful great power acting independently simply will not work. For example, global warming is commonly cited as a global problem that requires multilateral solutions.

Consider the three economic IGOs that best illustrate how cooperation produces payoffs that compensate for the cooperating states' partial loss of sovereignty.

The World Trade Organization Remembering the hardships caused by the Great Depression of 1929, after World War II the United States sought to create international economic institutions that would prevent another depression by facilitating the expansion of world trade. One proposed institution was the

International Trade Organization (ITO), first conceived as a specialized agency within the overall framework of the UN. While negotiations for the anticipated ITO were dragging on, many people urged immediate action. Meeting in Geneva in 1947, twenty-three states agreed to a number of bilateral tariff concessions between two states. These treaties were written into a final act called the General Agreement on Tariffs and Trade (GATT), which originally was thought of as a temporary arrangement until the ITO came into operation.

When a final agreement on the ITO proved elusive, GATT provided a mechanism for continued multilateral negotiations on reducing tariffs and other barriers to trade. Over the next several decades, eight rounds of negotiations were held to liberalize trade. Under the principle of nondiscrimination, GATT members were to give the same treatment to each other as they gave to their "most favored" trading partner.

On January 1, 1995, GATT was superseded by the World Trade Organization (WTO). Although it was not exactly the ITO envisaged immediately following World War II, it nevertheless represents the most ambitious tariff-reduction undertaking yet. Unlike GATT, the WTO is a full-fledged intergovernmental organization with formal decision-making procedures. Mandated to manage disputes arising from its trading partners, the WTO was given authority to enforce trading rules and to adjudicate trade disputes.

The WTO now seeks to transcend the existing matrix of free-trade agreements between pairs of countries and within particular regions or free-trade blocs, and replace them with an integrated and comprehensive worldwide system of liberal or free trade. This liberal agenda poses a threat to some states. At the heart of their complaint is the charge that the WTO undermines the traditional rule of law prohibiting interference in sovereign states' domestic affairs, including management of economic practices within the states' territorial jurisdiction. However, it should be kept in mind that the WTO developed as a result of voluntary agreements states reached to surrender some of their sovereign decision-making freedom, under the conviction that this pooling of sovereignty would produce greater gains than losses. Nonetheless, the WTO is criticized because "there is little evidence of democracy within the WTO operations" (Smith and Moran 2001). Many of its policies are orchestrated by its most powerful members during informal meetings that do not include the full WTO membership.

The World Bank   Created in July 1944 at the United Nations Monetary and Financial Conference held in Bretton Woods, New Hampshire, attended by forty-four countries, the World Bank (or International Bank for Reconstruction and Development) was originally established to support reconstruction efforts in Europe after World War II. Over the next decade, the Bank shifted its attention from reconstruction to developmental assistance. Because Global South countries often have difficulty borrowing money to finance projects aimed at promoting economic growth, the Bank offers them loans with lower interest rates and longer repayment plans than they could typically obtain from commercial banks. By 2008 the Bank's loans exceeded $600 billion. "It is the Global South's most powerful antipoverty institution" (Pound and Knight 2006).

Beth A. Keiser/AP Photo

RAGE AGAINST INSTITUTIONAL SYMBOLS OF GLOBALIZATION In the recent past, the meetings attended by finance ministers at such powerful IGOs as the World Bank or the IMF drew little interest or publicity. Now, with increasing criticism of the globalization of national economies, these meetings are convenient targets for protesters. Seen here is one recent outburst, when the meeting of the WTO mobilized a broad-based coalition of NGOs to criticize the impact of economic globalization.

Administratively, ultimate decision-making authority in the World Bank is vested in a board of governors, consisting of a governor and an alternate appointed by each of the Bank's 184 member countries. A governor customarily is a member country's minister of finance or an equivalent official. The board meets annually in the Bank's Washington, DC, headquarters to set policy directions and delegate responsibility for the routine operations of the Bank to the twenty-four directors of its executive board. The five countries with the largest number of shares in the World Bank's capital stock (the United States, Germany, Japan, France, and the United Kingdom) appoint their own executive directors, and the remaining executive directors are either appointed (Saudi Arabia), elected by their states (China, Russia, and Switzerland), or elected by groups of countries. This weighted voting system recognizes the differences among members' holdings system and protects the interests of the great powers that make more substantial contributions to the World Bank's resources. If a country's economic situation changes over time, its quota is adjusted and its allocation of shares and votes changes accordingly.

Over the years, both the self-image and operations of the World Bank have changed —from a strictly financial IGO to now assisting states' development planning and training. The World Bank's success in addressing poverty has been attributed in part to the introduction of Poverty Reduction Strategy (PRS) programs that include input from the poor themselves (Blackmon 2008). The World Bank also has participated increasingly in consortium arrangements for financing private lending institutions while insisting that democratic reforms are made a condition for economic assistance. Additionally, with charges of bribery, kickbacks, and embezzlement being levelled against World Bank projects from road building in Kenya to dam construction in Lesotho, the last three bank presidents (James Wolfensohn, Paul Wolfowitz, and Robert Zoellick) have insisted on anticorruption reforms as well.

Despite its increased pace of activity and its goal for members to pledge nearly $20 billion for three years starting in mid-2008 (*Economist*, April 21, 2007, 70), the World Bank is poorly prepared to meet all the needs for financial assistance of developing states. The repayment of loans in hard currencies has imposed serious burdens on impoverished and indebted Global South states. The deficiencies of the World Bank, however, have been partly offset by the establishment of another lending IGO, the International Monetary Fund.

The International Monetary Fund   Before World War II, the international community lacked institutional mechanisms to manage the exchange of money across borders. At the 1944 Bretton Woods Conference, the United States was a prime mover in creating the International Monetary Fund (IMF), a truly global IGO designed to maintain currency-exchange stability by promoting international monetary cooperation and orderly exchange arrangements and by functioning as a lender of last resort for countries experiencing financial crises.

The IMF is now one of the sixteen specialized agencies within the UN system. Each IMF member is represented on its governing board, which meets annually to fix general policy. Day-to-day business is conducted by a twenty-two-member executive board chaired by a managing director, who is also the administrative head of a staff of approximately two thousand employees.

The IMF derives its operating funds from its 185 member states. Contributions are based on a quota system set according to a state's national income, monetary reserves, and other factors affecting each member's ability to contribute. In this way, the IMF operates like a credit union that requires each participant to contribute to a common pool of funds from which it can borrow when the need arises. The IMF's voting is weighted according to a state's monetary contribution, giving a larger voice to the wealthier states.

The IMF attaches strict conditions to its loans, which has led to considerable criticism as IMF loan programs have been linked to slower economic growth (Vreeland 2003), as well as increases in human rights violations (Abouharb and Cingranelli 2007). (See Controversy: The IMF, World Bank, and Structural Adjustment Policies: Is the "Cure" Worse than the "Disease"? in Chapter 9). Push for IMF reform has become prevalent following the Asian financial crisis in the late 1990s, as many argued that IMF intervention was counterproductive. It has also come under fire for implementing "cookie cutter" solutions that did not take into account differences in the political and economic systems of individual countries (Stiglitz 2003).

REGIONAL INTERGOVERNMENTAL ORGANIZATIONS

The tug of war between individual states and groups of states within the UN, the WTO, the World Bank, and the IMF are reminders of an underlying principle that IGOs are run by the states that join them. This severely inhibits the IGOs' ability to rise above interstate competition and independently pursue their own purposes. Because they cannot act autonomously and lack the legitimacy and capability for independent global governance, universal IGOs are often viewed more as instruments of their state members' foreign policies and arenas for debate than as independent nonstate actors.

When states dominate universal international organizations like the UN, the prospects for international cooperation can decline because, as *realism* emphasizes, states are fearful of multilateral organizations that compromise their vital national interests. This limits IGOs' capabilities for multilateral decision making to engineer global change.

The European Union

A rival hypothesis—that cooperation among powerful states is possible and that international organizations help produce it—emerges from neoliberal theory. This viewpoint is especially pertinent to the **European Union (EU)**. The EU is the globe's best success story among the other regional IGOs playing global roles. The EU stands out because it is unique. The EU serves as a model for other regional IGOs to emulate as the globe's greatest example of peaceful cross-border cooperation producing an integrated **security community** with a single economy. In addition, the EU's dedication to liberal democratic governance and capitalistic free markets as well as its emphasis on the search for a **Third Way** to alleviate human suffering is paving an approach that other regional IGOs are pursuing.

The EU, or what has become known as "Euroland," is not, strictly speaking, a freestanding supranational organization for the collective management of European domestic and foreign affairs. The EU coexists with a large number of other European IGOs, in which it is nested and with which it jointly makes decisions. Of these, the Organization for Security and Cooperation in Europe (OSCE) and the Council of Europe stand as regional institutions of equal European partners, free of dividing lines, designed to manage regional security and promote the human rights of minorities through democratization. In this overlapping network of European IGOs, the EU nonetheless is prominent as the primary example of a powerful organization that has transformed itself from a single- to a multiple-purpose nonstate actor.

EU Expansion and Political Integration The process of European integration began with the creation of the European Coal and Steel Community (ECSC) in 1951, the European Atomic Energy Community (Euratom) in 1957, and the European Economic Community (EEC) in 1957. These initiatives initially centered on trade development. Since the late 1960s, the three have shared a common organization, and, through successive steps, have enlarged the EU's mission as they came to be called "the European Community." Its membership grew, and its geographical scope broadened as the EU expanded in a series of waves to encompass 15 countries by

■ **European Union (EU)**

a regional organization created by the merger of the European Coal and Steel Community, the European Atomic Energy Community, and the European Economic Community (called the European Community until 1993) that has since expanded geographically and in its authority.

■ **security community**

a group of states whose high level of institutionalized or customary collaboration results in the settlement of disputes by compromise rather than by military force.

■ Third Way

an approach to governance advocated primarily by many European leaders who, while recognizing few alternatives to liberal capitalism, seek to soften the cruel social impact of free-market individualism by progressively allowing government intervention to preserve social justice and the rights of individuals to freedom from fear of the deprivations caused by disruptions in the global economy.

1997: Belgium, France, Germany, Italy, Luxembourg, and the Netherlands (the original "six"); Denmark, Ireland, and the United Kingdom (which joined in 1973); Greece (1981); Portugal and Spain (1986); and Austria, Finland, and Sweden (1995). In 2004, the EU reached a new milestone in its path toward enlargement when it formally admitted ten new members (the Czech Republic, Slovakia, Estonia, Hungary, Latvia, Lithuania, Malta, Poland, Slovenia, and the Greek-controlled part of Cyprus). This bold enlargement added seventy-five million people to create the globe's biggest free-trade bloc, and it transformed the face of Europe by ending the continent's division. And that enlargement process continued when Bulgaria and Romania joined in 2007, bringing the EU to twenty-seven members (see Map 6.2).

Further expansion is also conceivable because the admission procedures for possible new membership are currently underway for Croatia and Turkey, and other countries in the western Balkans lobbying for future membership. Expansion remains controversial, however. In particular, the prospect of a populous Muslim Turkey joining the EU raises fundamental questions about Europe's identity. As constructivist theorists point out, identities shape how agents envision their interests and, in turn, how they act. The possible entry of Turkey and perhaps more remote and different countries would have major implications for the way many people, especially within the six Western founders of the EU, conceive of Europe. Nevertheless, the idea of a single, integrated Europe is compelling for those who are haunted by the specter of European nationalities and states that have been fighting each other ever since the Pax Romana collapsed eighteen hundred years ago.

The Functionalist Philosophical Rationale for European Integration Ideas have consequences. Big ideas often come from painful experiences and crises, such as devastating wars. And that is what happened after World War II. European leaders

> *War forces men to make moral choices.*
> —James Michener, American historical novelist

■ political integration

the processes and activities by which the populations of many or all states transfer their loyalties to a merged political and economic unit.

conceived of a bold plan to remove the curse of war by attacking the incentives for war. Their reform program aimed at the **political integration** of Europe to build a new supranational institution that transcended individual European states—to seek nothing less than the *transformation* of international relations from instruments *of* states to institutions *over* them.

In the immediate aftermath of World War II, a number of reformers proposed a radical remedy—mounting a frontal attack on independent sovereign states by replacing the state-based global system with a central authority for global governance. This school of thought is known as **world federalism**. Federalists advocate merging previously sovereign states into a global integrated federal union. Federalists follow the liberal conviction of Albert Einstein "that there is no salvation for civilization, or even the human race, other than the creation of a world government."

■ world federalism

a reform movement proposing as a path to peace combining many or all previously independent countries into a single federal institution for global governance.

In contrast to federalism, **functionalism** was directed toward "peace by pieces" through IGOs built around the "sharing of sovereignty" instead of its surrender. Functionalism advocated a "bottom-up" evolutionary strategy for building cooperative ties and unity among states.

The Evolutionary Development of European Union Expansion

Belgium (1); **France** (2); **Germany** (3);
Italy (4); **Luxembourg** (5); **Netherlands** (6)

Denmark (7); **Ireland** (8);
United Kingdom (9)

Greece (10)

Portugal (11); **Spain** (12)

Austria (13); **Finland** (14); **Sweden** (15)

Cyprus (16); **Czech Republic** (17);
Estonia (18); **Hungary** (19); **Latvia** (20);
Lithuania (21); **Malta** (22); **Poland** (23);
Slovakia (24); **Slovenia** (25)

Bulgaria (26); **Romania** (27)

From "Few to Many: The Expansion of the European Union, 1951–2005," Wall St. Journal Europe, May 3, 2004, p.A6. Reprinted by permission.

MAP 6.2

FROM FEW TO MANY: THE EXPANSION OF THE EUROPEAN UNION, 1951–2009 **The European Union is a premier example of the formation and integrative growth of a supranational regional IGO. It has grown in seven expansions from six members in 1951 to twenty-seven in 2009, as shown here, and waiting in the wings are Ukraine, Turkey, and others. Expansion has enabled the EU to position itself to become a true superpower (see Chapter 4).**

■ **functionalism**

the theory advanced by David Mitrany and others explaining how people can come to value transnational institutions (IGOs, integrated or merged states) and the steps to giving those institutions authority to provide the public goods (for example, security) previously, but inadequately, supplied by their own state.

■ **epistemic communities**

scientific experts on a subject of inquiry such as global warming that are organized internationally as NGOs to communicate with one another and use their constructed understanding of "knowledge" to lobby for global transformations.

According to European functionalists, technical experts talking to one another in their area of specialization as members of **epistemic communities**, rather than professional diplomats, were the best agents for building collaborative links across European borders. Diplomats, functionalists saw, were naturally overly protective of their own country's national interest at the expense of collective interests. Transnational cooperation in social and economic technical areas was envisioned as a first step to overcome this obstacle. Habits of cooperation learned in one technical area (such as medicine), they predicted, would "spill over" into others—especially if the cooperative experience proved mutually beneficial and demonstrated the potential advantages of cooperation in other areas (such as transportation and telecommunications). If these collaborative exchanges continued, functionalists predicted that the bonds among European countries would multiply because no state government would dare oppose a web of functional organizations that provided such clear-cut benefits to citizens.

Functionalism's intellectual parent, David Mitrany (1966), argued in *A Working Peace System* (first published in 1943) that functionalism is based on self-interest:

> Functionalism proposes not to squelch but to utilize national selfishness; it asks governments not to give up sovereignty which belongs to their peoples but to acquire benefits for their peoples which were hitherto unavailable, not to reduce their power to defend their citizens but to expand their competence to serve them. It intimates that the basic requirement for peace is that they have the wit to cooperate in the pursuit of national interests that coincide with those of other states rather than the will to compromise national interests that conflict with those of others. (Claude 1971, 386)

Persuaded by the logic of this argument, farsighted liberals such as Jean Monnet applied functionalist theory to begin the process by which war-prone Europe began to form an integrated security community after World War II.

The permanent problem-solving organizations created in the 1800s, such as the Rhine River Commission (1804), the Danube River Commission (1857), the International Telegraphic Union (1865), and the Universal Post Union (1874), suggested a process by which states might cooperate to enjoy mutual benefits and hence to launch the more ambitious experiments that functionalists anticipated.

As convincing as functionalist theory appeared, dissatisfied critics arose, arguing that functionalists were naïve to argue that technical (functional) undertakings and political affairs can be separated. If technical collaboration becomes as important to state welfare as the functionalist argued it would, then states would assume an active role in fostering such transborder cooperative exchanges. But why, then, the skeptics asked, were some states so actively resisting functional integrative momentum? The expansion of transnational institutions' authority and competency at the expense of national governments and state sovereignty was therefore interpreted as unlikely because the solution of economic and social problems are seldom if ever divorced from political motivations (Lentner 2004). Functionalism accordingly began to be seen as an idea whose time had passed, and a new, albeit derivative, theory first arose in the 1950s to question the assumption that ever-expanding functional needs for joint action to address property rights, health, technological change, and other shared problems would force the resolution of political disputes. Termed **neofunctionalism**, the reconstructed liberal theory sought to directly address the political factors that dominate the process of merging formerly independent states:

> *Neofunctionalism* holds that political institutions and policies should be crafted so that they can lead to further integration through the process of ... "the expansive logic of sector integration." For example, [the first] president of the ECSC [European Coal and Steel Community], [Jean] Monnet, sought to use the integration of their social security and transport policies, arguing that such action was essential to eliminate distortions in coal and steel prices. [The] neofunctionalism of Monnet and others [had] as its ultimate goal ... the creation of a federal state. (Jacobson 1984, 66)

Neofunctionalist theory thus proposes to accelerate the processes leading to new supranational communities by purposely pushing for cooperation in politically controversial areas, rather than by avoiding them (Baratta 2005). It advocates bringing political pressure to bear at crucial decision points to persuade opponents of the greater benefits of forming a larger community among formerly independent national members.

In many respects, both the functionalist and neofunctionalist paths to European integration were tried in ways that have led to the unification of most of Europe in a federated political union. The program has worked. However, even though the long-standing goal of European enlargement and institutional federalism has been largely accomplished, those achievements have generated new and continuing problems. The European Union's "agenda is not new—deepen in order to widen, widen in order to deepen, and reform in order to do both—but its scope and urgency are" (Serfaty 2003).

EU enlargement through eastward expansion has presented the organization with a host of troublesome questions, compounded by the fact that the twelve newest members, whose combined economies are less than 10 percent of that of the entire EU, have poorer economies and smaller populations than the previous fifteen EU members. These new members, therefore, have different needs and interests that can make reaching agreement on policy decisions increasingly difficult. The distinction made by former U.S. Defense Secretary Donald Rumsfeld between the "old" Europe (the West) and the "new" Europe (the East) underscored the probability of some EU divisions on the horizon, because the new members supported the American war in Iraq and the Western members, with the exception of Great Britain, opposed the military invasion. If Germany, France, and the other Benelux countries join together to oppose the smaller less-developed new members, a "club within a club" could split the EU into two opposed coalitions. And if East-West frictions coincide with new tensions between the big and small EU members, collective decision making will be immeasurably more complicated. How is the EU organized to avoid this outcome?

EU Organization and Management   As the EU has grown and expanded its authority, its principal institutions for governance have changed. As shown in Figure 6.3, the EU organization includes a Council of Ministers, the European Commission, a European Parliament, and a Court of Justice.

The EU's central administrative unit, the Council of Ministers, consists of cabinet ministers drawn from the EU's member states, who participate when the most important decisions are made.

■ **neofunctionalism**
the revised functional theory explaining that the IGOs created by states to manage common problems provide benefits that exert new pressures by political means for further political integration, the creation of additional IGOs, and the globalization of international relations in an expanding network of independence that reduces states' incentives to wage war.

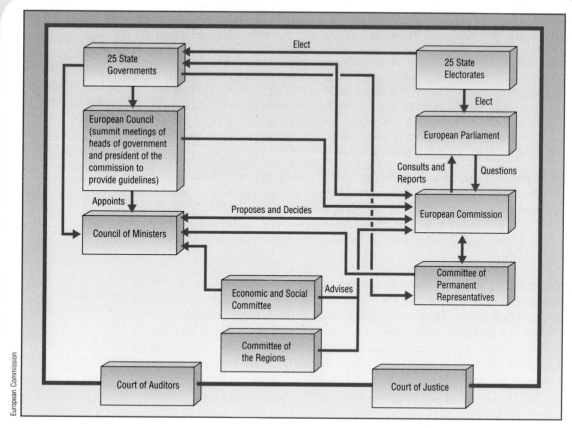

European Commission

FIGURE 6.3

THE EVOLUTIONARY DEVELOPMENT OF THE EUROPEAN UNION'S GOVERNMENTAL STRUCTURE **The EU is a complex organization, with different responsibilities performed by various units. This figure illustrates the principal institutions and the relationships among them that collectively lead to EU decisions and policies.**

■ **European Commission**

The executive organ administratively responsible for the European Union.

The Council of Ministers represents the governments of the EU's member states and retains final authority over the policy-making decisions. The council sets general policy guidelines for the **European Commission**, which consists of thirty-two commissioners (two each from Britain, France, Germany, Italy, and Spain, and one each from the other member states). Commissioners are nominated by EU member governments and must be approved by the European Parliament. Headquartered in Brussels, the primary functions of the European Commission are to propose new laws for the EU, oversee the negotiation of EU treaties, execute the European Council's decrees, and manage the EU's budget (which, in contrast with most international organizations, derives part of its revenues from sources not under the control of member states). A professional staff of eighteen thousand civil service "Eurocrats" assist the commission's administrative bureaucracy in proposing and directing decision making (by majority vote) for the EU and the Council of Ministers.

The European Parliament represents the political parties and public opinion within Europe. It has existed from the beginning of Europe's journey toward political unification, although at its creation this legislative body was appointed rather than elected and had little power. That is no longer the case. The European Parliament is now chosen in a direct election by the citizens of the EU's member states. Its more than six hundred deputies debate issues at the monumental glass headquarters in Brussels and at its lavish Strasbourg palace in the same way that democratic national legislative bodies do. The European Parliament shares authority with the Council of Ministers, but the Parliament's influence has increased over time. The elected deputies pass laws with the council, approve the EU's budget, and oversee the European Commission whose decisions they can overturn. This last element in the Parliament's authority gives it substantial clout, which it has not been hesitant to exercise. For example, in July 1999 the Parliament accused the previous group of commissioners of cronyism and corruption and forced their resignation.

The European Court of Justice in Luxembourg has also grown in prominence and power as European integration has gathered depth and breadth. From the start, the court was given responsibility for adjudicating claims and conflicts among EU governments as well as between those governments and the new institutions the EU created. The court interprets EU law for national courts, rules on legal questions that arise within the EU's institutions, and hears and rules on cases concerning individual citizens. The fact that its decisions are binding distinguishes the European Court of Justice from most other international tribunals. In 2008, the Court rendered a landmark decision widely seen as a victory for the Internet surfer in ruling that EU law does not compel Internet Service Providers to disclose customers' names if subpoenaed in copyright infringement file-sharing cases. Though recognizing the conflict between an individual's right to privacy and a company's right to protect its intellectual property, and allowing member states to interpret EU directives, the "ruling means the right of privacy for the individual has been upheld as the governing legal principle in file-sharing prosecutions that originate in the EU" (Warner 2008).

European Community

IGO GOVERNANCE IN ACTION Shown here is the hemi-cycle of the European Parliament in Brussels, Belgium, where EU Parliament members representing twenty-seven countries make collective decisions.

EU Decision-Making Challenges   Disagreement persists over the extent to which the EU should become a single, truly united superstate, a "United States of Europe." Debate continues also over how far and how fast such a process of **pooled sovereignty** should proceed. In 2008, the controversial Lisbon Treaty was presented as an institutional treaty that would streamline the decision-making process for the twenty-seven member Union by "creating a full-time president to represent EU governments and a single foreign-policy chief to speak for Europe" (Economist June 21, 2008, 61). It would also discard national vetoes in a number of areas, change members' voting weights, and give the European Parliament additional powers. While proponents argued that institutional reform is critical if expansion is to continue and Europe is to be a unified global power that can balance other major powers, resistance within the EU (reflected in Ireland's rejection of the treaty in a national referendum in June 2008) indicated that many are satisfied with the status quo, reluctant to pursue deeper political integration and further constrain the pursuit of individual national self-interest, and are concerned about the extent to which EU decision making is democratic. As essentially the fourth treaty rejection on institutional reform—the French and Dutch rejected the EU Constitution in 2005, the Irish rejected the Nice Treaty in 2001, and the Danes rejected the Maastricht Treaty in 1992—the rejection of the Lisbon Treaty by the Irish calls into question whether there is sufficient popular support for a federal Europe. While some European leaders such as Italian president Giorgio Napolitano have called for a "two-speed Europe" that would leave those who did not agree behind, others such as German chancellor Angela Merkel and French president Nicolas Sarkozy do not support the idea and argue that consensus is needed to proceed.

These issues will be debated in the future and only time will tell how they will be resolved. That said, the EU represents a remarkable success story in international history. Who would have expected that competitive states that had spent most of their national experiences waging war against one another would put their clashing ideological and territorial ambitions aside and construct a "European-ness" identity built on unity and confederated decision making?

Other Regional IGOs

Since Europe's 1950s initiatives toward integration, more than a dozen regional IGOs have been created in various other parts of the world, notably among states in the Global East and Global South. Most seek to stimulate regional economic growth, but many have drifted from that original single purpose to pursue multiple political and military purposes as well. The major regional organizations include:

- The Asia Pacific Economic Cooperation (APEC) forum, created in 1989 as a gathering of twelve states without a defined goal. APEC's membership has grown to twenty-one countries (including the United States). APEC plans to establish free and open trade and investments in the region for developed countries by 2010 and for developing member countries by 2020.

- The North Atlantic Treaty Organization (NATO), a military alliance created in 1949 primarily to deter the Soviet Union in Western Europe. The security IGO has expanded its membership to twenty-six countries and broadened its mission to promote democratization and to police civil wars and terrorism outside its traditional territory within Europe. The United States and Canada are also members.

■ pooled sovereignty

legal authority granted to an IGO by its members to make collective decisions regarding specified aspects of public policy heretofore made exclusively by each sovereign government.

- The Association of Southeast Asian Nations (ASEAN), established in 1967 by five founding members to promote regional economic, social, and cultural cooperation. In 1999, it created a free-trade zone among its ten Southeast Asian members as a counterweight outside the orbit of Japan, China, the United States, and other great powers so that ASEAN could compete as a bloc in international trade. ASEAN's expansion has created an identity crisis, with fears of new divisions between the older and wealthy "haves" and the newer and less-wealthy "have not" members, which include Vietnam, Laos, Cambodia, and Myanmar. ASEAN has negotiated a free merchandise trade agreement with South Korea and opened free-trade talks with the European Union.

- The Caribbean Community (CARICOM), established in 1973 as a common market to promote economic development and integration among its fifteen country and territory members.

- The Council of Arab Economic Unity (CAEU), established in 1964 from a 1957 accord to promote trade and economic integration among its ten Arab members.

- The Economic Community of West African States (ECOWAS), established in 1975 to promote regional economic cooperation among its fifteen members with a much larger agenda today.

- The Organization of the Islamic Conference (OIC) was established in 1969 to promote Islamic solidarity and cooperation by coordinating a large number of activities among fifty-seven Islamic states (plus Palestine). Although not technically a regional IGO, the OIC orchestrates preventive diplomacy, does not condone the use of terrorism, and is not concerned with promoting fundamentalist Islamic religious principles.

- The Latin American Integration Association (LAIA), also known as Asociación Latinoamericana de Integración (ALADI), established in 1980 to promote and regulate reciprocal trade among its twelve members.

- The Southern African Development Community (SADC), established in 1992 to promote regional economic development and integration and to alleviate poverty among its fourteen members.

- The South Asian Association for Regional Cooperation (SAARC), established in 1985 to promote economic, social, and cultural cooperation and respect for sovereign territorial independence and noninterference in states' internal affairs among its seven members.

As these examples illustrate, most IGOs are organized on a regional rather than global basis. The governments creating them usually concentrate on one or two major goals (such as liberalizing trade or promoting peace within the region) instead of attempting to address at once the complete range of issues that they face in common, such as environmental protection, democratization, and economic and security cooperation. Africa illustrates this tendency at the regional level. Within strife-torn Africa, fragile states have created a complex network of regional IGOs, with multiple, cross-cutting memberships. Some are large multipurpose groups such as the Economic Community of Western African States (ECOWAS), the Common Market for Eastern and Southern Africa (COMESA), the Southern African

Development Community (SADC), and the Arab Maghreb Union (AMU). Alongside these are many smaller organizations such as the Economic Community of the Great Lakes Countries and the Mano River Union.

It is hazardous to generalize about organizations so widely divergent in membership and purpose alongside many other, older IGOs whose function is to perform particular missions—such as the International Telecommunication Union founded in 1865, the World Meteorological Organization (1873), the International Labour Organization (1919), and the International Civil Aviation Organization (1944). No regional IGOs have managed to collaborate at a level that begins to match the institutionalized collective decision making achieved by the EU.

The particular reasons why many regional IGOs sometimes fail and are often ineffective vary. Evidence suggests that the factors promoting successful integration efforts are many and their mixture complex. It is not enough that two or more countries choose to interact cooperatively. Research indicates that chances of political integration wane without geographical proximity, steady economic growth, similar political systems, supportive public opinion led by enthusiastic leaders, cultural homogeneity, internal political stability, similar experiences in historical and internal social development, compatible economic systems with supportive business interests, a shared perception of a common external threat, bureaucratic compatibilities, and previous collaborative efforts (Cobb and Elder 1970; Deutsch 1957).

Though not all of these conditions must be present for integration to occur, the absence of more than a few considerably reduces the chances of success. The integration of two or more societies—let alone entire world regions—is, in short, not easily accomplished. Europe's experience indicates that even when conditions are favorable there is no guarantee integration will proceed automatically. Even in Europe high hopes have alternated with periods of disillusionment. When momentum has occurred, **spillover**—involving either the deepening of ties in one functional area of cooperation or their expansion to another to ensure the members' satisfaction with the integrative process—has led to further integration. But there is no sure path to expanding integration efforts once they begin. Thus, **spillback** (when a regional integration scheme fails, as in the case of the East African Community) and **spillaround** (when a regional integration scheme stagnates, or its activities in one area work against integration in another) are also possible.

The substantial difficulty that most regions have experienced in achieving a level of institution building similar to that of the EU suggests the enormity of the obstacles to creating new political communities out of previously divided ones. At the root of the barriers is one bottom line: All IGOs are limited by national leaders' reluctance to make politically costly choices that would undermine their personal popularity at home and their governments' sovereignty. Nonetheless, regional ventures in cooperation demonstrate that many states accept the fact that they cannot individually manage many of the problems that confront them collectively.

Because the state is clearly failing to manage many transnational policy problems, ironically it finds itself acting as the primary agent of the same cooperative management efforts that are eroding the state's power. Collective problem solving through IGOs is likely to continue. Globalization and the force of a shrinking, borderless world are increasing the influence of international institutions; in turn, IGOs' expanding webs of interdependence are infringing on the power of states and

■ spillover

the propensity for successful integration across one area of collaboration between states to propel further integration in other areas.

■ spillback

the reversal of previous steps toward integration, reducing the number of sectors in which integrating states are engaged in cooperative exchanges.

■ spillaround

the stagnation or encapsulation of regional integration as the costs of integration in one cooperative venture reduce efforts to try integration in other spheres of transaction.

changing the ways in which they network on the global stage. These IGOs and processes promise to transform world politics. This is why the thesis that the state is in retreat and its power to govern is eroding is so commonly voiced (Paul, Ikenberry, and Hall 2003). There are many good reasons to see the impact of IGOs as a threat to states' continuing domination of world politics (see Controversy: Will Global IGOs Replace States as the Primary Actor in World Politics?) As one scholar hypothesizes (Falk 2001b), "It is anachronistic to analyze world politics as if territorial supremacy continues to be a generalized condition or a useful fiction. In particular, sovereignty, with its stress on the inside/outside distinction between domestic and international society, seems more misleading than illuminating under current conditions."

CONTROVERSY:

WILL GLOBAL IGOs REPLACE STATES AS THE PRIMARY ACTOR IN WORLD POLITICS?

At the *global level of analysis*, the question at center stage is whether existing territorially defined states can cope with the many challenges they now face in the absence of creating powerful IGOs to manage those problems. The nineteenth-century French political philosopher Auguste Comte argued that all institutions form in order to address problems and meet human needs, and that when those IGOs are no longer able to perform these functions, they disappear. Today, the managerial capabilities of states are failing to inspire confidence. So a controversy has arisen: Do states have a future, and if not, will IGOs become the new primary actors in world politics? Can IGOs assume a capacity for global governance? If so, would this usher into being a *transformation* in world politics of such proportions that future generations will conclude that one global system has ended and a new one has begun?

That question has become a hot topic about which heated controversies now center. What do you think? In formulating your assessment, consider not only what you have learned about IGOs and their power and limits in this chapter, but also the range of theoretical opinion percolating about this question. Consider the differences of opinions reflective of realist and liberal theorizing in this table:

Theoretical Perspective

Realism	Liberalism
"The one trend that is sure to dominate the coming quarter-century is the decline of the power of the state"—Fareed Zakaria, political journalist	"We are at present embarked on an exceedingly dangerous course, one symptom of which is the erosion of the authority and status of world and regional intergovernmental institutions. Such a trend must be reversed before once again we bring upon ourselves a global catastrophe and find ourselves without institutions effective enough to prevent it."—Javier Pérez De Cuéllar, UN Secretary General

(continues)

Theoretical Perspective *(continued)*

Realism	Liberalism
"States retain many of their present functions [even if] effective governance of a partially—and increasingly—globalized world will require more extensive international institutions to promote cooperation and resolve conflict."—Robert O. Keohane, international relations scholar	"A wide variety of forces has made it increasingly difficult for any state to wield power over its peoples and address issues it once considered its sole prerogative."—The Stanley Foundation

The task of inquiry for you to face is to weigh the evidence behind these rival theoretical interpretations. Both perspectives cannot be equally valid. As the Communist President of China, Mao Zedong counseled, "Seek truth through facts."

Some facts speak favorably to the opinion of the renowned international relations scholar James N. Rosenau, who predicts, "While states may not be about to exit from the political stage, and while they may even continue to occupy center stage, they do seem likely to become vulnerable and impotent." Against this is another opinion, summarized by Anne Marie Slaughter (1997): "Liberal internationalists see a need for international rules to solve states' problems, proclaim the end of the nation-state, [and see IGOs] rapidly becoming the most wide-spread and effective mode of international governance." And put into your analysis the views of still others. For example, Howard Lentner (2004) contends that the territorial state is still flourishing because it is needed to provide military security, give people identity, raise taxes, provide safety nets for the needy, protect the environment, and may even be indispensable for the preservation of world order. As the theoretical perspective of constructivism advises, your interpretation of this issue, along with those of billions of other people, will determine how world public opinion will shape the new world in the making.

IGOs are not the only nonstate actors leading the potential *transformation* of world politics. Another set of agents are nongovernmental organizations (NGOs). They include not only transnational humanitarian organizations such as Amnesty International but also multinational corporations, transnational religions and ethnic groups, and global terrorist networks. Such NGOs are growing in number and roaring in voices too loud to ignore, making them increasingly influential in world politics. In Chapter 7, you will evaluate the behavior and global impact of NGOs.

Key Terms

intergovernmental organizations (IGOs)
nongovernmental organizations (NGOs)
European Union (EU)
security community

Third Way
political integration
world federalism
functionalism
epistemic communities
neofunctionalism

European Commission
pooled sovereignty
spillover
spillback
spillaround

CHAPTER 7
NONGOVERNMENTAL ORGANIZATIONS AND THE SHAPE OF THE GLOBAL FUTURE

No reason exists why—in addition to states—nationalities, diasporas, religious communities and other groups should not be treated as legitimate actors. . . . In the emerging global politics, however, state sovereignty and authority are withering and no alternative, such as some system of world government, is about to fill the vacuum.

—Samuel P. Huntington, *realist theoretician*

Rob Elliott/AFP/Getty Images

People Power. Shown here are some of the eighty thousand people who traveled from more than one hundred countries to participate at the "anti-Davos" annual World Social Forum in Bombay, India, to raise their voices in protest against their perception of injustice and inequalities within global capitalism and a long list of other complaints.

I f you are like most people with a heart and interest in making the world a better place, there is at least one problem that crosses national borders of concern to you. You would like to see it resolved. But you probably realize that it would be impossible for you to engineer global changes all by yourself. How should you act on your values to promote the needed transformations in world politics that you would like to see occur?

Recognizing that voices raised collectively in groups are most likely to be heard, many people throughout the world have found that, by joining *nongovernmental organizations (NGOs)*, they can lobby more effectively for the causes they support. Huge numbers of people have done so for these reasons, and their actions and activities are making a difference in international politics.

NGOs are transnational actors whose members are not states, but instead are people drawn from a population of two or more countries who have come together to promote their shared interests and ideals. Your analytic goal in this chapter is to examine the characteristics of NGOs in order to evaluate the impact of NGOs as actors in international affairs.

THE CHARACTERISTICS OF NONGOVERNMENTAL ORGANIZATIONS

One of the most significant trends in international affairs has been the spectacular growth in the last one hundred years in the number of NGOs. In 1909, there were only 176 NGOs worldwide, but by 1954 the number had grown more than sevenfold to 1,255, and at the start of 2007 the number had risen to 27,723 (see Figure 7.1).

Increasing numbers of people have found that through joining private interest groups they can lobby to influence international decision making. They have chosen to become international decision makers themselves by electing to join one or more NGOs, and these tens of thousands of "transitional activists" are influencing the policies of state governments and intergovernmental organizations (IGO's) through a variety of strategies. NGO activism is transcending the traditional distinctions between what is local and what is global (Tarrow 2006).

NGOs differ widely in their characteristics. For example, some are small with membership in the hundreds; others are huge, with the biggest being Amnesty International, which includes 1.8 million members spread across seventy national chapters. Because of their number and diversity, NGOs are even more difficult to classify than IGOs. Like IGOs, some NGOs merge with other NGOs, and about 13 percent have dissolved or become inactive (UIA 2006, 33). Thus, the numbers are constantly changing. At the beginning of 2007, the Union of International Associations categorized the major "conventional" NGOs as split, with 7 percent as "universal," almost 15 percent as "intercontinental," and the vast majority, 78 percent, as "regionally oriented." Functionally, NGOs span virtually every facet of political, social, and economic activity in an increasingly borderless globalized world, ranging from earth sciences to ethnic unity, health care, language, history, culture, education, theology, law, ethics, security, and defense.

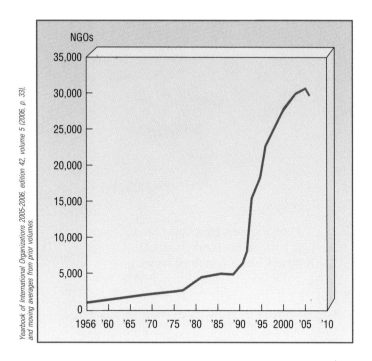

Yearbook of International Organizations 2005-2006, edition 42, volume 5 (2006, p. 33), and moving averages from prior volumes.

FIGURE 7.1

TRENDS IN THE NUMBER OF NGOs SINCE 1956

Participation in the formation of new nongovernmental organizations has been a growth industry. There are now almost twenty-eight thousand NGOs in existence worldwide, and the number of people joining them has grown exponentially.

Nongovernmental organizations are not a homogeneous group. The long list of acronyms that has accumulated around NGOs can be used to illustrate this. People speak of NGOs, INGOs (International NGOs), BINGOs (Business International NGOs), RINGOs (Religious International NGOs), ENGOs (Environmental NGOs), QUANGOs (Quasi-Non-Governmental Organizations—i.e., those that are at least partially created or supported by states), and many others. Indeed, all these types of NGOs and more are among those having consultative status at the UN. Among the NGOs . . . are the Academic Council on the UN System, the All India Women's Conference, the Canadian Chemical Producers Association, CARE International, the World Young Women's Christian Association, the World Wide Fund for Nature International, the Union of Arab Banks, the Women's International League for Peace and Freedom, the World Energy Council, the World Federation of Trade Unions, and the World Veterans Association. Thus, it is difficult to generalize about NGOs at the UN (Stephenson 2000, 271).

In general, the socially constructed image of NGOs widely accepted throughout the world is highly positive—humanitarian movements dedicated to improving the human condition rather than seeking to benefit themselves at the expense of others. An example is the World Bank's definition of NGOs as "private organizations that pursue activities to relieve suffering, promote the interests of the poor, protect the environment, provide basic social services, or undertake community development" (World Bank, http://web.worldbank.org, November 19, 2008). However, some NGOs arguably unite people for collective action in ways that can harm others.

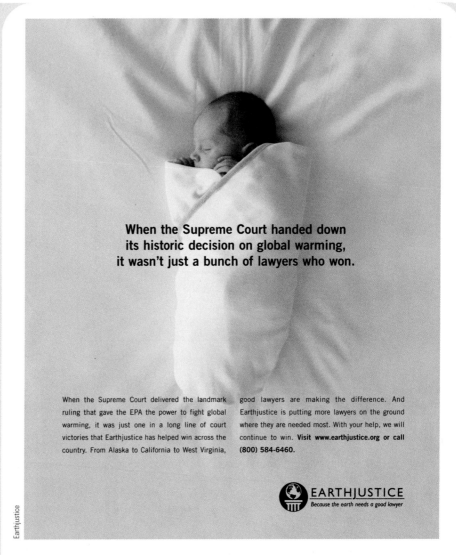

When the Supreme Court handed down
its historic decision on global warming,
it wasn't just a bunch of lawyers who won.

When the Supreme Court delivered the landmark ruling that gave the EPA the power to fight global warming, it was just one in a long line of court victories that Earthjustice has helped win across the country. From Alaska to California to West Virginia, good lawyers are making the difference. And Earthjustice is putting more lawyers on the ground where they are needed most. With your help, we will continue to win. **Visit www.earthjustice.org or call (800) 584-6460.**

EARTHJUSTICE
Because the earth needs a good lawyer

Earthjustice

GRASSROOTS RECRUITMENT FOR GLOBAL CHANGE. **NGOs are advocates of a wide variety of changes in the world. In this advertisement, the Earthjustice Legal Defense Fund promotes the fight against global warming.**

The term *NGO* can be applied to *all* nonstate and nonprofit organizations that operate as intermediaries to build transnational bridges between those with resources and a targeted group in order to address global problems. Thus, it is also customary to think of NGOs as intersocietal organizations that contribute to negotiations between and among states in the hope of reaching agreements for global governance on nearly every issue of international public policy. NGOs link the global society by forming "transnational advocacy networks" working for policy changes (Keck and Sikkink 2004). They are inspired to action by their interests and values.

The mere fact that something is to a man's interest is no guarantee that he will be interested in it.

—Kenneth Burke, American philosopher

For this purpose, note that many NGOs interact formally with IGOs. For instance, more than one thousand NGOs actively consult with various agencies of the extensive UN system, maintain offices in hundreds of cities, and hold parallel conferences with IGO meetings to which states send representatives. Such partnerships between NGOs and IGOs enable both types to work (and lobby) together in pursuit of common policies and programs. That said, many IGOs work for, and are heavily financed by, rich corporations and some state governments, which also fund NGOs that support their interests. Although widespread geographically, NGOs are most active in the wealthy Global North industrial democracies where greater incomes enable greater involvement (Tarrow 2006).

Most NGOs pursue objectives that are highly respected and constructive and therefore do not provoke much opposition. For example, NGOs such as Amnesty International, the International Chamber of Commerce, the International Red Cross, Save the Children, the World Wildlife Federation, and Global Youth Connect (which supports young people who are victims of human rights abuses) enjoy widespread popular support. Others, however, are more controversial because they push for changes that, were they to succeed, would threaten the interests of other groups who have a stake in preserving the status quo. For example, NGOs such as the Union of Concerned Scientists and Doctors Without Borders are among the hundreds of transnational peace activist organizations seeking to reduce military spending (UIA 2006, Vol. 4). Their pressure threatens the budgets of the **military-industrial complex** in many countries where jobs and income depend heavily on high defense expenditures (Markoe and Borenstein 2005). As the transnational activism of Islamic militants, international drug rings, humanitarian relief organizations and environmental protection activists suggest, many NGOs work at cross-purposes in a competitive struggle to redefine the global agenda.

NGOs are increasingly prominent globally because their bargaining has succeeded in creating many international regimes, or new rules, to regulate transnational problems. Powerful NGOs now shape the decisions that alter the global agenda—decisions that only recently were made almost exclusively by states and multinational corporations. NGOs' technical expertise, innovative capacity, rapid response, and connections to and communications with other grass-roots organizations have empowered them to operate as mediators between states and unregulated market freedom. At the same time, NGOs are reducing the significance of borders and making states vulnerable both to external pressures and to challenges from within states' boundaries. NGO demands are shaking state-government authority and control. This is especially evident in autocratic governments, where repression of minority racial or religious NGOs leads to rebellions that are causing a wake of failing states. In democracies, by contrast, the grievances of ethnic groups are better contained through **devolution** of the central government's power (Saxton 2005).

■ **military-industrial complex**

a combination of defense establishments, contractors who supply arms for them, and government agencies that benefit from high military spending, which act as a lobbying coalition to pressure governments to appropriate large expenditures for military preparedness.

■ **devolution**

states' granting of political power to minority ethnic groups and indigenous people in particular national regions under the expectation that greater autonomy will curtail the groups' quest for independence as a new state.

Abid Katib/Getty Images

NGOS: CROSSING BORDERS Members of the International Rescue Committee's emergency response team work with the Myanmar Red Cross Society to provide relief to the 2.4 million people in Myanmar affected by Cyclone Nargis. In the days following the May 2008 catastrophe, the Myanmar junta was condemned by the international community for refusing to allow humanitarian aid organizations into the country. Though eventually granting visas to some aid workers, one reported that "ongoing bureaucracy and restricted access for foreign aid workers make it hard to find out conditions and needs of many people. Getting supplies to them becomes less than straightforward. Still, our team and our local partner have managed to reach close to 25,000 people with medicines as well as common household items like blankets, buckets and lanterns - materials that are critical in emergencies" (International Rescue Committee, http://blog.theirc.org/tag/burma/, July 2, 2008).

As NGOs rise in numbers and influence, a key question to contemplate is whether what may be termed a "nongovernmental global society" will materialize to override the traditional global system centered on sovereign states, and, if so, whether this structural *transformation* will democratize or disrupt global governance.

PROMINENT TYPES OF NONGOVERNMENTAL ORGANIZATIONS

■ nonstate nations

national or ethnic groups struggling to obtain power and/or statehood.

Inspect the major NGOs to evaluate if and how their efforts are contributing to global changes, and, if so, whether their impact spells promise, or peril. Today, a small subset of increasingly active and self-assertive NGOs receives the most attention and provokes the most controversy. To simplify your task, *World Politics* will ask you to examine only five of the most visibly active NGO nonstate actors: **nonstate nations** that include ethnic nationalities and indigenous peoples, clashing civilizations with shared cultural traditions, transnational religious movements,

> *We are now entering a different phase of the relationship of peoples and states.*
>
> —Douglas Hurd, British Foreign Secretary

transnationally active terrorist groups, and multinational corporations. This chapter's purpose is to describe NGOs and to encourage you to examine if, and how, these nonstate actors are gathering sufficient traction to alter global conditions.

Nonstate Nations: The Indigenous Ethnic Groups of the Fourth World

Realists often ask us to picture the all-powerful state as an autonomous ruler of a unified nation, that is, as a *unitary actor*. But, in truth, that construction is misleading. Most states are divided internally and are highly penetrated from abroad, and few states are tightly unified and capable of acting as a single body with a common purpose.

Although the state unquestionably remains the most visible global actor, as constructivism emphasizes, *nationalism* (values within a national group that place the nationality living within a state as the most important for their identity) is a very potent cultural factor that has the most meaning to many peoples. Individuals who think nationalistically are very likely to pledge their primary allegiance not to the state and government that rules them but, rather, to a politically active minority group with which they most associate themselves. One broad category is the **ethnic groups** of a nationality whose members identify with one another because they perceive themselves as bound together by kinship, language, and a common culture. They view themselves as members of their nationality or ethnic group first and of their state only secondarily. **Ethnicity** is socially constructed, in that members of an ethnic or racial group learn to see themselves as members of that group and accordingly perceive their identity as determined by their inherited membership at birth. That perception is likely to be strongly reinforced when recognized by other ethnic groups. Hence, ethnicity is in the eye of the beholder—a constructed identity. "A basic definition might be a group of humans who share significant elements of culture and who reproduce themselves socially and biologically" (T. Hall 2004).

Ethnic nationalism (people's loyalty to and identification with a particular ethnic nationality group) reduces the relevance of the unitary state. Many states are divided, multiethnic and multicultural societies made up of a variety of politically active groups that seek, if not outright independence, a greater level of regional autonomy and a greater voice in the domestic and foreign policies of the state. Three-fourths of the world's larger countries are estimated to contain politically significant minorities, and since 1998, 284 minority groups, comprising one-sixth of the world population, have been classified as "at risk" from persecution by the state in which they resided and had mobilized for collective defense against the government they perceived as perpetuating organized discriminatory treatment (Minorities At Risk, www.cidcm. umd.edu/MAR, January 6, 2008). In 2008, China came under intense international criticism for its crackdown on ethnic Tibetan groups following rioting in Lhasa, the

■ **ethnic groups**

people whose identity is primarily defined by their sense of sharing a common ancestral nationality, language, cultural heritage, and kinship.

■ **ethnicity**

perceptions of likeness among members of a particular racial grouping leading them to prejudicially view other nationality groups as outsiders.

■ **ethnic nationalism**

devotion to a cultural, ethnic, or linguistic community.

Tibetan capital. Representing Tibetan interests, the Dalai Lama sought renewed talks with China in "the interest of stability, unity and harmony of all nationalities in the People's Republic of China." The Chinese, however, see him as a "splittist," with the spiritual leader having fled Tibet in 1959 following a failed armed uprising against Chinese Communist rule (Drew 2008). Ethnic divisions such as these challenge the realist "billiard ball" conception of international relations as homogeneous interactions between unified states. "The multiethnic state is 'normal' in the statistical sense [and] this deepens the puzzle of the chimera of the ethnically homogeneous nation-state" (T. Hall 2004).

Fourth World

a term used to recognize the native national groups residing in many so-called united states who, although often minorities, occupied the state's territory first and refuse to accept domination, seeking instead as noncentral governments (NGCs), regional governments, and subnational entities (SNEs) to govern themselves or to create a new state for themselves by separating from existing states.

The globe is populated by an estimated sixty-eight hundred separate indigenous nations, each of which has a strong, often spiritual, tie to an ancestral homeland. In most cases, indigenous people were at one time politically sovereign and economically self-sufficient. Today an estimated 650 million indigenous people, or about one-tenth of the world's population, are scattered in more than seventy countries (Center for World Indigenous Studies, http://www.halcyon.com, January 17, 2008). To heighten awareness of the poverty, deprivation, and sometimes repression that confront many native tribal or indigenous peoples, they are referred to as the **Fourth World**, following Richard Griggs's (1995) definition as "nations forcefully incorporated into states which maintain a distinct political culture but are internationally unrecognized."

The number of distinct nonstate nations making up the Fourth World's individual indigenous peoples is usually measured by the number of known spoken languages because each language provides an ethnic and cultural identity. As Edward Sapir and Benjamin Lee Whorf hypothesized in the 1930s, different languages reflect different views of the world that predispose their speakers toward different ways of thought. By this index, indigenous cultures are disappearing. "Linguists estimate that 10,000 years ago there were up to 12,000 spoken languages," but now with 6.7 billion people

PROTECTING INDIGENOUS PEOPLES **Warriors from an isolated Amazon basin tribe rainforest on the Brazilian-Peruvian border prepare to defend their homes from the strange "bird" flying above. Dedicated to locating remote tribes and protecting them, this aerial picture was released in 2008 by activists with the *Brazilian Indian Protection Agency, Funai*, and *Survival International* in an effort to generate international concern for the threat posed by the logging industry to "uncontacted" indigenous tribes in the area. Through these actions, these NGOs claimed success in pressuring Peru to re-examine its logging policy.**

Gleison Miranda/Funai/AP Photo

worldwide "the number of unique languages has shrunk to fewer than 7,000 [and] some experts estimate we lose one language every month, while others peg the loss at one every two weeks. Some experts maintain that 90 percent of the world's languages will vanish or be replaced by dominant languages by the end of this century" (*Vital Signs, 2006–2007*, 112). What this means is that indigenous peoples are at risk, with high percentages nearing extinction.

Clashing Civilizations

The Fourth World's indigenous peoples are located *within* many of the globe's pluralistic states. But they also display a transnational face, because they are geographically spread *across* existing state boundaries. This dispersion has increased as indigenous peoples have migrated across borders from their ancestral homelands. Some move in search of employment or farmland and, as they are assimilated in the new country's culture, they begin to lose their original sense of cultural identity. Others depart as refugees, escaping through exodus from state persecution or from devastating epidemic diseases or environmental destruction that has made their homelands incapable of supporting life or liberty. These trans-state dispersions have erased the traditional equation of countries with ethnic nationality (see Map 7.1).

For example, indigenous peoples such as the sizable Kurdish minorities of Turkey, Iraq, Iran, and Syria have members living in more than one of the globe's existing independent states but as yet there is no single sovereign country the Kurds can call their home. Such peoples, linked together by a common ancestry across national borders, also share a common intellectual heritage and culture on which they often place a higher value than patriotic loyalty to a particular state. As a result of these divisions, as many as eleven separate transnational cultural identities, or "civilizations," can be identified across the globe (see Map 7.2). The consequences are not certain, but some possibilities for world politics are alarming. Samuel P. Huntington (1996, 2001a) pessimistically predicts the most troubling outcome: that a **clash of civilizations** is probable between some of these universalistic civilizational identities and that armed conflict is especially likely between the West and Islam.

That prediction proved rather prophetic on September 11, 2001, when the Al Qaeda terrorist network attacked the United States to vent the anger of its extremist Islamic members against the West. "What recent events demonstrate is that ethnicity, and race [and cultural conflict] are issues that are not disappearing and becoming less important. . . . Recent processes of global change, often glossed under the term globalization, are rapidly changing the contexts under which ethnic [and cultural] conflict arises [which] are no longer, if they ever were, entirely local" (T. Hall 2004). For that reason, we now turn from ethnic group NGOs to an examination of the ways religious movements may operate as transnationally active NGOs as well.

Transnational Religious Movements

In theory, religion would seem a natural worldwide force for global unity and harmony. Yet millions have died in the name of religion. The Crusades, which took place between the eleventh and fourteenth centuries, originally were justified by Pope Urban II in 1095 to combat Muslim aggression, but the fighting left millions of

■ **clash of civilizations**
political scientist Samuel Huntington's controversial thesis that in the twenty-first century the globe's major civilizations will conflict with one another, leading to anarchy and warfare similar to that resulting from conflicts between states over the past five hundred years.

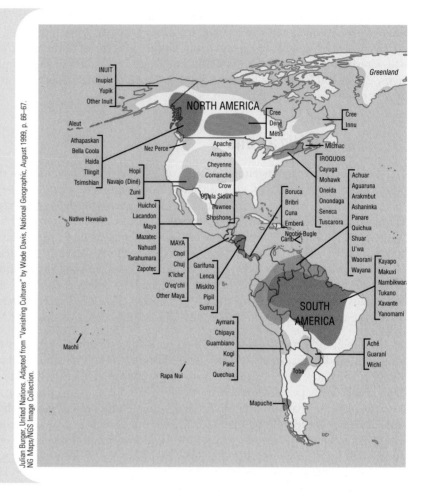

Julian Burger, United Nations. Adapted from "Vanishing Cultures" by Wade Davis. National Geographic, August 1999, p. 66-67. NG Maps/NGS Image Collection.

MAP 7.1

THE INDIGENOUS CULTURES OF THE WORLD **Indigenous peoples are scattered throughout many countries of the world, but as this map shows, their location tends to be concentrated in particular regions.**

Christians and Muslims dead and, "in terms of atrocities, the two sides were about even [as both religions embraced] an ideology in which fighting was an act of self sanctification" (*Economist,* January 5, 1996). Similarly, the religious conflicts during the Thirty Years' War (1618–1648) between Catholics and Protestants killed nearly one-fourth of all Europeans.

■ transnational religious movements

a set of beliefs, practices, and ideas administered politically by religious organizations to promote the worship of their conception of a transcendent deity and its principles for conduct.

Many of the world's more than 6.7 billion people are affiliated at some level with **transnational religious movements**—politically active organizations based on strong religious convictions. At the most abstract level, a religion is a system of thought shared by a group that provides its members an object of devotion and a code of behavior by which they can ethically judge their actions. This definition points to commonalities across the great diversity of organized religions in the world, but it fails to capture that diversity. The world's principal religions vary greatly in the theological doctrines or beliefs they embrace. They also differ widely in the size of their followings, in the geographical locations where they are most prevalent (see Map 7.3, p.201), and in the extent to which they engage in political efforts to direct international affairs.

These differences make it risky to generalize about the impact of religious movements on world affairs (Haynes 2004). Those who study religious movements comparatively note that a system of belief provides religious followers with their

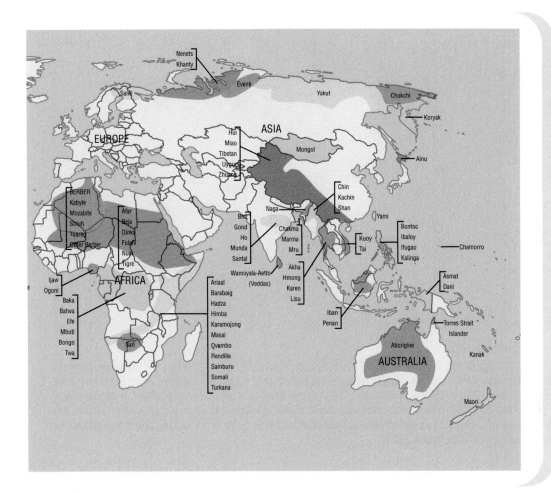

main source of identity, and that this identification with and devotion to their religion springs from the natural human need to find a set of values with which to evaluate the meaning of life and the consequences of choices. This need sometimes leads believers of a religious creed to perceive the values of their own religion as superior to those of others, which sadly often results in intolerance. The proponents of most organized religious movements believe that their religion should be universal —that is, accepted by everyone throughout the world. To confirm their faith in their religious movement's natural superiority, many organized religions actively proselytize to convert nonbelievers to their faith, engaging in evangelical crusades to win over nonbelievers and followers of other religions. Conversion is usually achieved by persuasion through missionary activities. But at times conversion has been achieved by the sword, tarnishing the reputations of some international religious movements (see Controversy: Are Religious Movements Causes of War or Sources of Transnational Harmony?).

In evaluating the impact of religious movements on international affairs, it is important to distinguish carefully the high ideals of doctrines from the activities of the people who head these religious bodies. The two realms are not the same, and each can be judged fairly only against the standards they set for themselves. To condemn what large-scale religious movements sometimes do administratively when

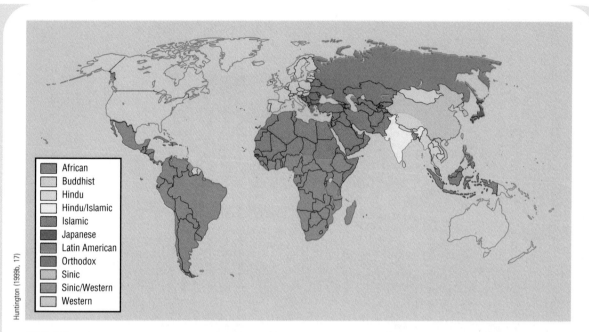

Huntington (1999b, 17)

MAP 7.2

THE WORLD'S MAJOR CIVILIZATIONS: WILL THEIR CLASH CREATE GLOBAL DISORDER? **This map shows the location of the world's major civilizations according to the much-debated thesis of Samuel P. Huntington, who predicts that future global war is likely to result from a "clash of civilizations." Critics of this thesis point out that no "civilization" is homogenous in language or beliefs, that the characteristics of any civilization fail to predict how individual people identified with it will act, and that even identity-creating groups such as distinct cultures have often learned to speak to one another across their differences and to coexist peacefully (Sen 2006; Appiah 2006).**

they abuse their own religion's principles does not mean that the principles themselves deserve condemnation. Moreover, not all religious movements are intolerant of and competitive with other faiths. Consider the Hindu ideology of tolerance of different religions, which teaches that there are many paths to truth and accepts pluralism among diverse populations. Similarly, Buddhism preaches pacifism, as did early Christianity, which prohibited Christians from serving in the armies of the Roman Empire (later, by the fourth century, when church and state became allies only Christians were allowed to join Roman military units).

The relationship between transnational religions and states' governments is a major issue in the global community. In some countries, the two realms are separate politically, with legal protection for freedom of religion and little or no state support for a particular established religion. But in many other countries, religion and state are tightly linked and almost indistinguishable. In such a country, that is, in a **theocracy**, religious institutions submissively subordinate their religion to state control in order to survive, grow, receive state subsidies, and cement political influence. In these countries, crown and church protect and preserve each other through an alliance.

■ **theocracy**

a country whose government is organized around a religious dogma.

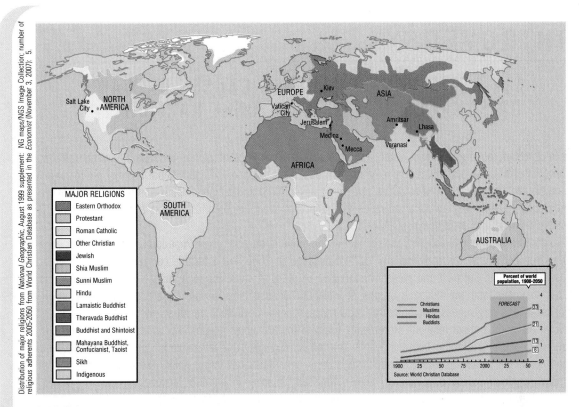

MAP 7.3

MAJOR RELIGIONS OF THE WORLD This map shows where the world's major religious affiliations have attracted a dominant following. The chart on the bottom right predicts the number of people who will adhere to the four largest religious groups by the year 2050.

> *There is growing worry that religion has too much influence on the world around us, from inspiring terrorists to shaping government policy.*
>
> —John Meacham, political journalist

Most troublesome, however, are radical religious movements that are enraged, militant, and fanatically dedicated to promote their cause globally, often through violence and terror (Kifner 2005). The leaders of **extreme militant religious movements** are convinced that those who do not share their convictions must be punished and that compromise is unacceptable.

■ **extreme militant religious movements**

politically active organizations based on strong religious convictions, whose members are fanatically devoted to the global promotion of their religious beliefs.

CONTROVERSY:

ARE RELIGIOUS MOVEMENTS CAUSES OF WAR OR SOURCES OF TRANSNATIONAL HARMONY?

After 9/11, debate about the impact of religion on international conflict intensified because many believed that the terrorist attacks were motivated by religious fanatics in the Islamic Al Qaeda global terrorist organization. As a result, the "religious roots of terrorism" (Juergensmeyer 2003) and religious opposition to democracy in the Global South (Shah 2004) have received much attention, as have religions and religious bodies acting as NGO global actors more generally (Haynes 2004).

"To do harm, to promote violence and conflict in the name of religion," said Pope John Paul II in Egypt after fighting between Christians and Muslims led to bloodshed in 2000, "is a terrible contradiction and a great offense against God. But past and present history give us many examples of such misuse of religion." Yet it is difficult to understand the religious origins of violence because most people equate religion with peace, compassion, and forgiveness, not hatred or intolerance. Indeed, because high ideals inspire the believers of nearly all the world's major religious movements, many of the principles religions espouse are very similar and conducive to peaceful relations between people. They all voice respect and reverence for the sanctity of life and acceptance of all people as equal creations of a deity, regardless of race or color. These are noble ideals. Religions speak to universal principles, across time and place—to enduring values in changing times. Moreover, they recognize no boundaries for their eternal validity—no north, south, east, or west—but only true virtue wherever found and the relevance of moral precepts (e.g., the prohibition of killing and the value of working for the betterment of humankind throughout the world).

If all the world's great religious movements espouse universalistic ideals, why are those same religions increasingly criticized as sources of international conflict—of exclusivism, hatred, terror, and war? This, in the age of religious conflict and political violence, is a boiling controversy. What do you think?

In evaluating the role of religious NGOs in international affairs, consider first the view of sociologists of religion who contend that religious hostility results from the fact that universalistic religions are managed by organizations that often adopt a particularistic and dogmatic outlook (see Juergensmeyer 2003). The virtues that religions uphold ironically can become weapons against those who do not hold such views. Followers of a religion may conceive the world and history through an ideological lens that views one deity protecting a chosen people against inferior others. In an effort to believe in unshakable doctrines, they reject the attempt to separate what they wish to be true from what they or other religions think to be true. This constructed reality inspires an ethic that justifies violence, plunder, and conquest. In part, they tend to see outsiders as threatening rivals whose loyalty and allegiance to other deities represents a challenge to their own religion's claim of universal worldwide applicability. In a word, religious movements often practice intolerance—disrespect for diversity and the right of people to freely embrace another religion's beliefs. The next logical step is for fanatics to paint these imagined enemies as evil, unworthy of mercy, and to justify brutal violence against them.

However, using this violence as an argument against religion is controversial. It is dangerous to accept stereotypes of religious groups as responsible for relentless barrages of terrorism. Paganistic and atheistic societies recognizing no higher deity have equally long histories of waging violent wars against external enemies and their own people. Meanwhile, many religions ably perform the mission of peace making, and in fact most religious bodies have historically coexisted peacefully for centuries.

It is important for you to objectively weigh the evidence about the impact of religious NGOs on world affairs. In so doing, take into account the impact of this controversy on theories of world politics and world order. The inclination of extremist religious movements to evoke prejudice and aggression has led some realist theorists of international politics to conclude that such movements are more a menace than a pacific influence. Observing that most wars (such as the Israel-Lebanon 2006 war) have been fought in the name of religion, these realist critics recommend recognizing the vicious mean-spiritedness of followers who betray their religion's humanistic and global values by championing a style of religious thought that denies that morality is about nourishing life, not destroying it. What do you think?

Radical religious movements involved in world politics share certain similar characteristics:

- Militant religious political movements tend to view existing government authority as corrupt and illegitimate because it is secular and not sufficiently rigorous in upholding religious authority or religiously sanctioned social and moral values.

- They attack the inability of government to address the domestic ills of the society in which the movement exists. In many cases the religious movement substitutes itself for the government at the local level and is involved in education, health, and other social welfare programs.

- They subscribe to a particular set of behaviors and opinions that they believe political authority must reflect, promote, and protect in all governmental and social activities. This generally means that government and all of its domestic and foreign activities must be in the hands of believers or subject to their close oversight.

- They are universalists: unlike ethnic movements, they tend to see their views as part of the inheritance of everyone who is a believer. This tends to give them a trans-state motivation, a factor that then translates their views on legitimacy of political authority into a larger context for action. In some cases, this means that international boundaries are not recognized as barriers to the propagation of the faith, even if this means they resort to violence.

- They are exclusionists: they relegate all conflicting opinions on appropriate political and social order to the margins—if they do not exclude them altogether. This translates as second-class citizenship for any nonbeliever in any society where such a view predominates.

- Finally, they are militant, willing to use coercion to achieve the only true end (Shultz and Olson 1994, 9–10).

Militant religious movements are nonstate actors that tend to stimulate five specific types of international activities. The first is *irredentism*—the attempt by a dominant religion (or ethnic group) to reclaim previously possessed territory in an adjacent region from a foreign state that now controls it, often through the use of force. The second is **secession, or separative revolts**—the attempt by a religious (or ethnic) minority to revolt and break away from an internationally recognized state. Third, militant religions tend to incite migration, the departure of religious minorities from their countries of origin to escape persecution. Whether they move by force or by choice, the result, a fourth consequence of militant religion, is the same: the emigrants create **diasporas,** or communities that live abroad in host countries but

■ secession, or separative revolts
a religious or ethnic minority's efforts, often by violent means, to gain independent statehood by separating territory from an established sovereign state.

■ diasporas
the migration of religious or ethnic groups to foreign lands despite their continuation of affiliation with the land and customs of their origin.

THE FUSION OF CHURCH AND STATE In many countries, religious bodies are supported by the armies of the state, and the state supports the transnational activities of favored religious movements.

Patrick Aventurier/EYEDEA PRESSE

■ **international terrorism**

the threat or use of violence as a tactic of terrorism against targets in other countries.

maintain economic, political, and emotional ties with their homelands (Sheffer 2003). Finally, as we shall see, a fifth effect of militant religions is **international terrorism** in the form of support for radical coreligionists abroad (Homer-Dixon 2005; Sageman 2004).

In sum, transnational religious movements not only bring people together but also divide them. Through globalization, religions are transforming social forces that create transnational communities of believers with "dual loyalties" to more than one country; immigration by adherents to religion brings more faiths into direct contact with one another and forges global networks transcending borders (Levitt 2007). This consequence notwithstanding, transnational religions compete with one another, and this tends to divide humanity and to breed separatist efforts that can tear countries apart.

■ **terrorism**

premeditated violence perpetrated against noncombatant targets by subnational or transnational groups or clandestine agents, usually intended to influence an audience.

Transnational Terrorist Groups

Are terrorist groups correctly seen as a particular category of nonstate actors—as NGOs—on the global stage? Many people now think so, even if these groups can hardly be considered conventional NGOs given their use of violence, because terrorist organizations and networks are very active today throughout the entire world. A contagious disease stalks the face of the earth, because **terrorism** arguably is today much different than in the past. Terrorism now is seen as:

■ global, in the sense that with the death of distance, borders no longer serve as barriers to terrorism

- lethal, because now terrorists have shifted their tactics from theatrical violent acts seeking to alarm for publicity to purposeful destruction of a target's civilian noncombatants, to kill as many as possible for the purpose of instilling fear in as many people as possible

- waged by civilians without state sanction in ways and by means that erase the classic boundaries between terrorism and a declared war between states

- reliant on the most advanced technology of modern civilization to destroy through those sophisticated technological means the modern civilization seen as posing a threat to the terrorists' sacred traditions

- orchestrated by transnational nonstate organizations through global conspiratorial networks of terrorist cells located in many countries, involving unprecedented levels of communication and coordination (Sageman 2004)

The previous reasons for terrorist activity remain as strong as ever, but the **information age** has made transnational networking among terrorist groups easy. Terrorists now have available a variety of new methods, such as the use of electronic "cyberterrorism" and "netwar" strategies. International terrorist organizations are increasingly active as NGOs for many other reasons. One of the most important and potent is the condition that Walter Laqueur terms **postmodern terrorism**. This phrase describes the globalized environment that today makes terrorism easy to practice, in part because it has become so "complex" (Homer-Dixon 2006). So-called postmodern terrorism is likely to expand because the globalized international environment without meaningful barriers separating countries allows terrorists to practice their ancient trade by new rules and methods. At the same time, this new global environment encourages the rapid spread of new weapons and technology transport across borders, which provides unprecedented opportunities for terrorists to commit atrocities and to change their tactics in response to successes in countering them. Another reason is the growing difficulty of detecting and deterring the attacks of disciplined globalized terrorist networks that are generously funded by international organized crime (IOC) syndicates and internationally linked networks of thousands of gangs to facilitate their profit in the narcotics trade.

The activities of nonstate terrorist organizations are likely to remain a troubling feature of world politics also because every spectacular terrorist act always generates a powerful shock effect and gains worldwide publicity through the global news media. Immediate worldwide attention makes it attractive for terrorists to perpetrate new acts. In 2008, Joe Lieberman, Chair of the U.S. Homeland Security and Governmental Affairs Committee in the U.S. Senate, called on Google to remove Internet video content that was produced by terrorist organizations: "Islamist terrorist organizations use YouTube to disseminate their propaganda, enlist followers, and provide weapons training… (and) YouTube also, unwittingly, permits Islamist terrorist groups to maintain an active, pervasive, and amplified voice, despite military setbacks…"

Definitional Dilemmas in Identifying Terror NGOs

A word of caution is in order. Even if you recognize the existence of terrorist groups as a virulent type of NGO conducting its lethal trade across borders, it is very difficult to identify these terrorist groups, and you would make a big mistake if you lumped all terrorist movements together. Today, terrorism is a strategy practiced by a very diverse group of nonstate actors.

- **information age**
the era in which the rapid creation and global transfer of information through mass communication contribute to the globalization of knowledge.

- **postmodern terrorism**
to Walter Laqueur, the terrorism practiced by an expanding set of diverse actors with new weapons "to sow panic in a society to weaken or even overthrow the incumbents and to bring about political change."

This is seen by the fact that in 2009 the U.S. State Department identified dozens of groups as worldwide terrorist organizations. Yet it should be noted that there is no universally accepted list of known terrorist organizations.

Precise definitions and distinctions will be required for your analysis. Take care to consider how your value judgments can affect your image and interpretation of the identity of any group you may believe belongs in this menacing category of NGO

> *Because of the word's pejorative connotation, many people seek to label any use of violence they perceive as illegitimate or with which they disagree as "terrorism."*
>
> —Martha Crenshaw and Maryann Cusimano Love,
> terrorism and international relations experts

actors. Constructing a valid account will be a challenge especially in regard to such a controversial topic. The cliché "one person's terrorist is another person's freedom fighter" springs from the hold of prior and subjective perceptions on many peoples' definitions of objective realities. Moreover, *cognitive dissonance* is likely to be experienced in the evaluation of different groups' motives and activities: Reasonable people, faced with facts leading to an unwanted conclusion, might seek to discredit those very facts or search for competing facts that support their preconceived conclusions. Though terrorists are popularly portrayed as "madmen" bent on death and destruction, as terrorist expert Bruce Hoffman has noted, "Terrorism has a purpose. Writing it off as mindless and irrational is not useful." Table 7.1 identifies some of the known terrorist NGOs. As you can see, there is diversity in the primary goals of various groups. Some, such as FARC and ETA, focus on secular nonreligious objectives such as ethnic self-determination or overthrow of a government. Others, most notably Al Qaeda, are driven by religious convictions and have more sweeping goals. There is also variation in the manner in which their organizations are structured, with some having a hierarchical structure and newer groups tending to favor a networked form with insulated cells dispersed across the globe.

Table 7.1   Some Terrorist NGOs: Primary Location and Goals

Name	Primary Location	Goal
Al Qaeda	A global network with cells in a number of countries and tied to Sunni extremist networks. Bin Laden and his top associates are suspected to reside in Afghanistan or the border region in Pakistan, and the group maintains terrorist training camps there.	To establish pan-Islamic rule throughout the world by working with allied Islamic extremist groups to overthrow regimes it deems "non-Islamic" and expel Westerners and non-Muslims from Muslim countries.
Revolutionary Armed Forces of Colombia (FARC)	Colombia with some activities (extortion, kidnapping, logistics) in Venezuela, Panama, and Ecuador.	To replace the current government with a Marxist regime.

(continues)

Table 7.1 Some Terrorist NGOs: Primary Location and Goals *(continued)*

Name	Primary Location	Goal
Hezbollah (Party of God) a.k.a. Islamic Jihad, Revolutionary Justice Organization, Organization of the Oppressed on Earth, and Islamic Jihad for the Liberation of Palestine.	In the Bekaa Valley, the southern suburbs of Beirut, and southern Lebanon. Has established cells in Europe, Africa, South America, North America, and Asia.	To increase its political power in Lebanon, and opposing Israel and the Middle East peace negotiations.
Hamas (Islamic Resistance Movement)	Primarily the occupied territories, Israel.	To establish an Islamic Palestinian state in place of Israel. In 2008, Hamas entered into a tenuous truce with Israel to bring about a cease-fire in Gaza, which it took over the prior year.
Army for the Liberation of Rwanda (ALIR), a.k.a. Interahamwe, Former Armed Forces (ex-FAR)	Primarily in the Democratic Republic of the Congo and Rwanda, but a few may operate in Burundi.	To topple Rwanda's Tutsi-dominated government, reinstitute Hutu control, and, possibly, complete the genocide begun in 1994.
Revolutionary United Front (RUF)	Sierra Leone, Liberia, Guinea.	To topple the current government of Sierra Leone and retain control of the lucrative diamond-producing regions of the country.
Basque Fatherland and Liberty (ETA), a.k.a. Euzkadi Ta Askatasuna.	Primarily in the Basque autonomous regions of northern Spain and southwestern France.	To establish an independent homeland based on Marxist principles in the Basque autonomous regions.
Al-Jihad a.k.a. Egyptian Islamic Jihad, Jihad Group, Islamic Jihad	Primarily Cairo, but has a network outside Egypt, including Yemen, Afghanistan, Pakistan, Sudan, Lebanon, and the United Kingdom.	To overthrow the Egyptian government and replace it with an Islamic state; attack United States and Israeli interests in Egypt and abroad.
Liberation Tigers of Tamil Eelam	Sri Lanka.	To establish an independent Tamil state.
Aum Supreme Truth (Aum) a.k.a. Aum Shinrikyo, Aleph	Principal membership is located only in Japan, but a residual branch comprising an unknown number of followers has surfaced in Russia.	To take over Japan and then the world.
Sendero Luminoso (Shining Path)	Peru.	To destroy existing Peruvian institutions and replace them with a Communist peasant revolutionary regime.
Abu Sayyaf Group (ASG)	Primarily the southern Philippines with members occasionally traveling to Manila.	To promote an independent Islamic state in western Mindanao and the Sulu Archipelago, areas in the southern Philippines heavily populated by Muslims.

Source: Adapted from the Center for Defense Information, http://www.cdi.org/terrorism/terrorist-groups.cfm (July 3 2008)

The same obstacles to objective interpretation apply to the analysis of another type of NGO, multinational corporations (MNCs). Like transnational terrorist groups, MNCs are both praised and condemned because different people ascribe to them different attributes. In the information age of disappearing borders, money matters, and this makes multinational corporations increasingly influential as nonstate actors, connecting cash flows and people globally in ways that may be eroding the sovereignty that states have previously taken as an unchanging given.

Multinational Corporations and Transnational Banks

■ **multinational corporations (MNCs)**

business enterprises headquartered in one state that invest and operate extensively in many other states.

Multinational corporations (MNCs)—business enterprises organized in one society with activities in others growing out of direct investment abroad—are a fifth major type of NGO. MNCs have grown dramatically in scope and potential influence with the globalization of the world political economy since World War II (see Chapters 9 and 10). As a result of their immense resources and power, MNCs have provoked both acceptance and animosity. As advocates of liberal free trade and as active contributors to the globalization of world politics, MNCs generate both credit for the positive aspects of free trade and globalization as well as blame for their costs.

MNCs cast a shadow over global trade, cross-border investments, and production. One indicator of MNCs' presence on the world stage is that 77,175 of their parent firms together own a total of 773,019 foreign affiliates (OECD 2007b: 260–261) and employ more than ninety-five million people worldwide. Moreover, also consider that the top five hundred MNCs' revenues recently exceeded $21 trillion (*Economist* July 21, 2007, 93), and that the combined sales of the top two hundred MNCs were the equivalent of 28 percent of world gross domestic product (Piasecki 2007, 9). The UN estimates that MNCs account for approximately two-thirds of the world's exports and one-third of the stock of all *foreign direct investment (FDI)*, formally defined by the IMF as "ownership of assets in one country by residents of another for purposes of controlling the use of those assets." The dramatic growth of FDI investments is expanding MNCs' global impact.

This global penetration positions the biggest MNCs to propel changes in relations between countries and within them, as well as in the global marketplace. For example, the MNCs have recently taken steps toward engineering a "social responsibility revolution" by "making products and delivering services that generate profits and also help the world address challenges such as climate change, energy security, healthcare, and poverty. It's not just about public relations any more. Firms see big profits in green solutions" (Piasecki 2007). Consider Wal-Mart, with annual sales of more than $360 billion (larger than Sweden's GDP) and two million employees, which has unveiled its "Sustainability 360" initiative to sell environmentally friendly products in order to increase the 100 million customers throughout the world Wal-Mart currently attracts every week. MNCs in many sectors are also increasingly sensitive to human rights conditions in potential host countries (Blanton and Blanton 2009), as well as the impact MNCs themselves may have upon human rights (Spar 1999).

In the past, MNCs were headquartered almost exclusively in the United States, Europe, and Japan, and their common practice was to make short-term investments in the Global South's plants, sales corporations, and mining operations. At the start of the twenty-first century, about 80 percent of all MNCs' employees worked in the developing countries, where wages were lower, to bolster corporate profits at the parent headquarters. But no longer. "More and more multinationals will shift the operation and control of key business functions away from their home office [to transfer] white-collar professionals. . . . A growing number of companies are setting up regional headquarters or relocating specific headquarter functions elsewhere." (Hindle 2004, 97–98). Such outsourcing of management to locations where wages and costs are lower but skills are substantial is likely to continue, accelerating the consolidation of the global economy into a seamless integrated web. This outsourcing is now eagerly welcomed by the Global South's developing countries as a means to economic growth where once MNC domination was resisted. The spread of digital information technology contributes to this rapid dispersion of MNCs' managers worldwide.

MNC expansion is facilitated by **transnational banks (TNBs)**, another type of global NGO whose revenues and assets are primarily generated by global financial transactions. TNBs have become major forces in the world political economy and dominate in the rankings of the top MNCs (*Economist*, July 21, 2007, 93). They have contributed to worldwide financial integration at the same time that globalization has made international banks critical to global economic stability (as illustrated by the collapse of lending following occasional banking crises and the costs of recapitalizing, reorganizing, or liquidating insolvent banks by countries). In 2006, the world's ten largest banks held a staggering $12.8 trillion in assets (*Economist*, May 20, 2006, 4). This attests to the continuing highly profitable consolidation of global financial resources. The major banks have formed strategic alliances and have been merging rapidly with banks abroad to expand, with an eye toward maximizing their already huge revenues. The mergers and acquisitions among some of the largest TNBs from the United States, the eurocurrency area, and Japan and Britain are a sign of global banking's steady consolidations.

TNBs funnel trade and help to reduce the meaning of states' borders. They make each state's economy dependent on other states' economies by the transfer of capital through international loans and investments. In the era of globalization, coalitions across a broad range of nonstate actors is the norm. Together, TNBs and MNCs redistribute wealth and income in the world economy, contributing to the economic development of some states and the stagnation of others.

One feared consequence in the Global South is that the TNBs advance the rich Global North at the South's expense, because 87 percent of foreign direct investment is funneled into the richest countries (and now especially the rapidly growing economic powerhouses in the Global East). The poorest countries typically receive very little (WDI 2007, 342). Like MNCs, therefore, TNBs spread the rewards of globalization unequally, increasing wealth for a select group of countries and marginalizing the others.

Through their loans to the private sector, TNBs have made capital highly mobile and expanded the MNCs' capacity to lead the way in reducing differences across countries' tastes, lifestyles, and consumer products sold. MNCs have grown in scope, size, and power, fueled by a growing number of mergers and acquisitions that reached 465 deals worth over $1 billion each in the first half of 2007, totaling $2.7 trillion (*Economist* July 7, 2007, 94). With this clout, concern has understandably risen about whether MNCs' efforts to remove state barriers to foreign investments and trade are undermining the ability of seemingly sovereign states to control their own economies and therefore their own fates and cultures.

■ **transnational banks (TNBs)**
the globe's top banking firms, whose financial activities are concentrated in transactions that cross state borders.

The benefits and costs attributed to MNCs as they have risen to a position of prominence have been many and complex. This has made them highly controversial nonstate actors, especially in the Global South where people frequently see MNCs as the cause of exploitation and poverty (see Chapter 5).

MNCs are increasingly influential NGOs because the world's giant producing, trading, and servicing corporations have become the primary agents of the globalization of production. Table 7.2 captures their importance in world politics, ranking firms by annual sales and states by GNI. The profile shows that of the world's top one hundred economic entities, among the top fifty, multinationals account for only fourteen, but in the next fifty, they account for thirty-five. MNCs' financial clout thus rivals or exceeds that of most countries.

Table 7.2   Countries and Corporations: A Ranking by Size of Economy and Revenues

Rank	Country/ Corporation	GNI/Revenues (billions of dollars)	Rank	Country/ Corporation	GNI/Revenues (billions of dollars)
1	United States	12,912.9	16	Russia	638.1
2	Japan	4,976.5	17	Switzerland	411.4
3	Germany	2,835.6	18	Belgium	378.7
4	United Kingdom	2,272.7	19	Sweden	369.1
5	China	2,269.7	20	WAL-MART STORES	351.2
6	France	2,169.2	21	EXXON MOBIL	347.3
7	Italy	1,772.9	22	Turkey	342.0
8	Spain	1,095.9	23	ROYAL DUTCH/SHELL	318.8
9	Canada	1,052.6	24	Austria	306.2
10	India	804.1	25	Saudi Arabia	289.2
11	South Korea	765.0	26	Indonesia	282.2
12	Mexico	753.4	27	Norway	281.5
13	Australia	673.2	28	BRITISH PETROLEUM	274.4
14	Brazil	662.0	29	Poland	273.1
15	Netherlands	642.0	30	Denmark	261.8

(continues)

Table 7.2 Countries and Corporations: A Ranking by Size of Economy and Revenues *(continued)*

Rank	Country/Corporation	GNI/Revenues (billions of dollars)	Rank	Country/Corporation	GNI/Revenues (billions of dollars)
31	South Africa	223.5	53	SINOPEC	131.6
32	Philippines	223.1	54	Israel	128.7
33	Greece	220.3	55	CRÉDIT AGRICOLE	128.5
34	GENERAL MOTORS	207.4	56	Venezuela	128.1
35	TOYOTA MOTOR	204.8	57	Malaysia	125.9
36	CHEVRON	200.6	58	ALLIANZ	125.5
37	Finland	196.9	59	FORTIS	121.2
38	Hong Kong, China	192.1	60	Singapore	119.8
39	DAIMLER CHRYSLER	190.2	61	BANK OF AMERICA	117.0
40	Portugal	181.3	62	HSBC HOLDINGS	115.4
41	Iran	177.3	63	Czech Republic	114.8
42	Thailand	175.0	64	AMERICAN INTERNATIONAL GROUP	113.2
43	Argentina	173.1	65	CHINA NATIONAL PETROLEUM	110.5
44	CONOCOPHILLIPS	172.5			
45	Ireland	171.1	66	BNP PARIBAS	109.2
46	TOTAL	168.4	67	ENI	109.0
47	GENERAL ELECTRIC	168.3	68	UBS	107.8
48	FORD MOTOR	160.1	69	Pakistan	107.3
49	ING GROUP	158.3	70	SIEMENS	107.3
50	CITIGROUP	146.8	71	STATE GRID	107.2
51	AXA	139.7	72	New Zealand	106.3
52	VOLKSWAGEN	132.3	73	Colombia	104.5

(continues)

Table 7.2 Countries and Corporations: A Ranking by Size of Economy and Revenues *(continued)*

Rank	Country/ Corporation	GNI/Revenues (billions of dollars)	Rank	Country/ Corporation	GNI/Revenues (billions of dollars)
74	United Arab Emirates	103.5	87	NIPPON TELEGRAPH & TELEPHONE	92.0
75	ASSICURAZIONI GENERALI	101.8	88	HEWLETT-PACKARD	91.7
76	Hungary	101.6	89	INTERNATIONAL BUSINESS MACHINES	91.4
77	J.P. MORGAN CHASE	100.0	90	VALERO ENERGY	91.1
78	CARREFOUR	99.0	91	HOME DEPOT	90.8
79	BERKSHIRE HATHAWAY	98.6	92	Egypt	90.1
80	PEMEX	97.5	93	Algeria	89.6
81	DEUTSCHE BANK	96.2	94	NISSAN MOTOR	89.5
82	DEXIA GROUP	95.8	95	SAMSUNG ELECTRONICS	89.5
83	Chile	95.7	96	CREDIT SUISSE	89.4
84	HONDA MOTOR	94.8	97	HITACHI	87.6
85	MCKESSON	93.6	98	Romania	84.6
86	VERIZON COMMUNICATIONS	93.2	99	SOCIÉTÉ GÉNÉRALÉ	84.5
			100	AVIVA	83.5

Gross National Income (GNI), World Bank, 2007 *World Development Indicators*, pp.14-16; MNC revenues, *Fortune* (July 23, 2007), pp. 133-140.

Wealth and power remain highly concentrated; the big seem to get bigger and bigger. The fifty largest MNCs account for one-third of the total revenues controlled by the top five hundred MNCs (*Fortune*, July 23, 2007, 133, 140). Equally revealing is the geographical concentration of MNCs' economic resources: the fifty largest MNCs from the Global South control less than ten percent of the assets controlled by the fifty largest Global North MNCs (Oatley 2008, 175).

In addition to their global reach and economic power, MNCs' involvement in the domestic political affairs of local or host countries is also controversial. In some instances this concern has extended to MNCs' involvement in the domestic politics of their home countries, where they actively lobby their governments for more liberal trade and investment policies to enhance the profitability of their business. In turn, both host and home governments have sometimes used MNCs as instruments in their foreign policy strategies. Perhaps the most notorious instance of an MNC's intervention in the politics of a host state occurred in Chile in the early 1970s when International Telephone and Telegraph (ITT) tried to protect its interests in the profitable Chiltelco telephone company by seeking to prevent the election of Marxist-oriented Salvador Allende as president and, once Allende was elected, pressured the U.S. government to disrupt the Chilean economy. Eventually Allende was overthrown by a military dictatorship. More recently, the huge profits and activities of corporate giant Halliburton to rebuild the infrastructure of Iraq after the 2003 U.S. occupation provoked widespread complaints that this MNC was exploiting the circumstances to line its pockets, at U.S. taxpayers' expense. As a sign of the times, in 2007 the corporate giant Halliburton moved its headquarters from Texas to Dubai.

MNCs assist in promoting free trade and are active participants in the process by which governments have reached agreements on rules liberalizing economic transactions in the global marketplace. Thus, it is tempting to conclude that MNCs are a threat to state power. However, this interpretation overlooks the fact that as MNCs have grown in size, the regulatory power of states has also grown.

> Only the state can defend corporate interests in international negotiations over trade, investment, and market access. Agreements over such things as airline routes, the opening of banking establishments, and the right to sell insurance are not decided by corporate actors who gather around a table; they are determined by diplomats and bureaucrats. Corporations must turn to governments when they have interests to protect or advance. (Kapstein 1991–1992, 56)

Still, the blurring of the boundaries between internal and external affairs adds potency to the political role that MNCs unavoidably play as nonstate actors at the intersection of foreign and domestic policy. The symbolic invasion of national borders by MNCs can be expected to arouse the anger of many local nationalists who fear the loss of income, jobs, and control to foreign corporate interests. Because multinationals often make decisions over which leaders of states have little control (such as investments), MNCs' growing influence appears to contribute to the erosion of the global system's major organizing principle—that the state alone should be sovereign. MNC's awesome financial resources are much greater than the official statistics suggest, and this is why many states fear that MNCs, which insist on freedom to compete internationally, are stripping away their sovereign control. And in fact, in some respects states *are* losing control of their national economies as MNCs merge with one another and, in the process, cease to remain tied to any one parent state or region.

A new kind of business organization, the globally integrated enterprise, is emerging that is best understood as 'global' rather than 'multinational' [because] companies are investing more to change the way they supply the entire global market.

—Samuel J. Palmisano, Chief Executive Officer of International Business Machines

■ globally integrated enterprises

MNCs organized horizontally with management and production located in plants in numerous states for the same products they market.

■ strategic corporate alliances

cooperation between multinational corporations and foreign companies in the same industry, driven by the movement of MNC manufacturing overseas.

"Who owns whom?" can no longer be answered. This is because many MNCs are now **globally integrated enterprises** that produce the same goods in different countries so that their horizontal organization no longer ties them to any single country.

"Half of Xerox's employees work on foreign soil, and less than half of Sony's employees are Japanese. More than 50 percent of IBM's revenues originate overseas; the same is true for Citigroup, ExxonMobil, DuPont, Procter & Gamble, and many other corporate giants. Joint ventures are no longer merely a domestic decision. Corning obtains one-half of its profits from foreign joint ventures with Samsung in Korea, Asahi Glass in Japan, and Ciba-Geigy in Switzerland" (Weidenbaum 2004, 26–27). How can any single state manage such multinational giants when no country can claim that an MNC is "one of ours"?

Controlling the resulting webs of corporate interrelationships, joint ventures, and shared ownership for any particular state purpose is nearly impossible. Part of the reason is that 30 to 40 percent of world trade takes place *within* multinationals, from one branch to another (Oatley 2008, 170). Joint production and **strategic corporate alliances** to create temporary phantom "virtual corporations" undermine states' ability to identify the MNCs they seek to control. "There is widespread concern that

The market economy as such does not respect political frontiers. Its field is the world.
—Ludwig von Mises, Austrian-born U.S. economist

MNCs are becoming truly 'stateless' [as] the explosion of strategic alliances is transforming the corporate landscape" with more than 10,000 strategic alliances estimated to be forged each year (Stopford 2001, 74–75). "You can't find targets any more, and if you aim at a target you often find it's yourself," observes Richard J. Barnet, coauthor of *Global Reach* (Barnet and Müller 1974).

The multinationals' potential long-run influence is depicted in *Global Dreams: Imperial Corporations and the New World Order*:

> By acquiring earth-spanning technologies, by developing products that can be produced anywhere and sold everywhere, by spreading credit around the world, and by connecting global channels of communication that can penetrate any village or neighborhood, these institutions we normally think of as economic rather than political, private rather than public, are becoming the world empires of the twenty-first century. The architects and managers of these space-age business enterprises understand that the balance of power in world politics has shifted in recent years from territorially bound governments to companies that can roam the world. As the hopes and pretensions of government shrink almost everywhere, these imperial corporations are occupying public space and exerting a more profound influence over the lives of ever larger numbers of people. (Barnet and Cavanagh 1994, 14)

In the past twenty years the number of MNCs has increased ninefold (Oatley 2008, 189) and MNCs are playing a correspondingly larger and larger role in world politics. This is forcing sovereign states to confront many challenges. How will they respond? Assessing the future requires a theoretical examination of contemporary thinking regarding the MNCs and the other types of NGOs.

ISSUE-ADVOCACY AND GLOBAL CIVIL SOCIETY: CAN NGOS TRANSFORM WORLD POLITICS?

As citizens increasingly participate in NGOs in order to gain a voice in and influence over the institutions that shape the conditions in which they live, interest-group activity on the global stage has risen to unprecedented levels. Many people now see NGOs as a vehicle empowering individuals to engineer transformations in international affairs. The growth of transnational activism by NGOs "is leading to a diffusion of power away from central governments" (Nye 2007). Assuming that this trend persists, the outlines of a future type of dual global system may be coming into view, driven simultaneously by both the continuing importance of relations between states and by the growing impact of multiple cross-border transactions and channels of communication among nonstate actors. To be sure, transnational NGOs are putting increasing pressure on states and, in the process, may truly be paving the path for a possible *transformation* of world politics. This change would lead to a hybrid or two-tiered world in which the clout and authority of the governments that rule countries declines while the relative power of nonstate actors rises.

Is this liberal constructivist image of the processes by which trends in world politics are determined that emphasize the importance of the shared meanings people and groups construct to define their identities and interests realistic? Or is it exaggerated? Are NGOs influential? Or is a rival hypothesis—that NGOs remain relatively powerless in global governance—more accurate?

What is clear is that networks of transnational activists have formed NGOs at an accelerating rate, and through their leverage have performed an educational service that has demonstratively contributed to the emergence of a global civil society.

These networks of transnational social movements are altering international culture by reshaping values about international conduct (Barnett and Finnemore 2004).

> *We're not asking you to put your hand in your pockets, but we are asking people to put their fist in the air. This is your moment. Make history by making poverty history.*
>
> —Bono, lead singer of the rock band U2

■ **civil society**
a community that embraces shared norms and ethical standards to collectively manage problems without coercion and through peaceful and democratic procedures for decision making aimed at improving human welfare.

Furthermore, they have registered some dramatic successes in their efforts to bring about global changes, as seen by the agreements reached (despite U.S. rejection) on the International Criminal Court, the Kyoto Protocol on global warming, and the Landmine Convention. That said, skeptics warn that the NGOs' power has been exaggerated on some issues like the environment and human rights and is very weak on others, such as national security. The tendency for rising reform movements to mobilize groups aimed at countering and resisting their reforms undermines the capacity of a network to push history forward rapidly in a particular direction. But even more striking is the failure of NGOs to become "a serious rival to the power and processes of the state;" their goals of transforming the dominant processes of policy making and corporate capitalism have not met with success (Price 2003). Indeed, it has been argued that it is inaccurate to accept the interpretation often pictured by *neoliberal theory* of NGOs weakening state sovereignty, because instead NGOs (some well-financed by states and IGOs) "have helped states retain—and in some instances even increase—their internal and external control, autonomy and legitimacy" (Weir 2007).

According to this thesis, world politics is still controlled by states—especially the great powers; it is a world ruled by the powerful, in which nonstate actors have little real influence.

Seen through *realist theory*, the critical choices that direct global destiny are made by the most powerful states. Global governance is not a product of the values and interests of the world's 6.7 billion people at large, organized into tens of thousands of nongovernmental organizations; it is dominated by a privileged minority, namely, the great powers, which possess the means to see that the most important global policy decisions are made to protect their national interests.

Juxtaposed to this conclusion is an alternative explanation: Whereas individuals do influence international policy by organizing themselves into groups to petition powerful governments on behalf of their shared interests and values, their individual efforts are compromised by the opposition of other NGOs resisting the first group of NGOs' endeavors to push international relations in a particular direction. Skeptics also point out that many NGOs represent powerful vested interests that work secretly behind the scenes to lobby for global policies that protect the powerful through private commercial interests as well as the great powers (their primary clients) at the expense of collective interests. Thus, the question is raised, precisely how influential and effective are grassroots NGOs in their efforts to lobby the powerful for new global rules and regimes that put human welfare and the collective interests of all humanity above particular, parochial national interests?

Studies of the impact of NGO pressure on global policy making suggest some conclusions that reduce confidence in the expectation that NGO pressure can lead to far-reaching reforms, even transformations, in the conduct of international relations:

- Interest group activity operates as an ever-present, if limited, constraint on global policy making. However, the impact *varies with the issue,* and their influence is weakest on the most important problems on the global agenda.

- Similarly, the occasions when private NGOs are most influential are rare. The influences are greatest with respect to a particular issue—such as nuclear nonproliferation—when in the interest of the great powers.

▪ As a general rule, NGOs are relatively weak in the *high politics* of international security because states remain in control of defense policy and are relatively unaffected by external NGO pressures. Conversely, the NGOs' clout is highest with respect to issues in *low politics*, such as protecting endangered species (e.g., whales) or combating climate change, which are of concern to great and small powers alike.

▪ The influence between state governments and NGOs is reciprocal, but it is more probable that government officials manipulate transnational interest groups than that NGOs exercise influence over governments' foreign policies.

▪ Single-issue NGO interest groups have more influence than large general-purpose organizations.

▪ NGOs sometimes seek *inaction* from governments and maintenance of the status quo; such efforts are generally more successful than efforts to bring about major changes in international relations. For this reason NGOs are often generally seen as agents of policy continuities.

The foregoing characteristics of NGO efforts to redirect global policy suggest that the mere presence of such groups, and the mere fact they are organized with the intent of persuasion, does not guarantee their penetration of the global policy-making process. On the whole, NGOs have participation without real power and involvement without real influence, given that the ability of any *one* to exert influence is offset by the tendency for countervailing powers to materialize over the disposition of any major issue. That is, as any particular coalition of NGOs works together on a common cause and begins to be powerful, other groups threatened by the changes advocated tend to spring up to balance it. When an interest group seeks vigorously to push policy in one direction, other nonstate actors—aroused that their established interests are being disturbed—are stimulated to push policy in the opposite direction. Global policy making consequently resembles a taffy pull: every nonstate actor attempts to pull policy in its own direction while resisting the pulls of others. The result is often that the quest for consensus proves elusive, and the international community's posture toward many global problems fails to move in any single direction.

This balance process between opposing actors helps to account for why so few global issues are resolved. Competition stands in the way of consensus, and contests of will over international issues are seldom settled. No side can ever claim permanent victory, for each decision that takes international policy in one direction merely sets the stage for the next round of the contest, with the possibility that today's losers will be tomorrow's winners. The result is usually a continuous battleground over the primary global issues from which no permanent resolution of the struggle materializes. The debate and contests between those wishing to make environmental protection a global priority and those placing economic growth ahead of environmental preservation provide one example among many.

As the world grows more interdependent and transactions across state borders increase through the movement of people, information, and traded products, it is likely that world politics nonetheless will be increasingly affected by the activities of both IGO and NGO nonstate actors. Even though nonstate actors are unlikely to join together in a common cause to pressure the international community for radical reforms, their activities (however divided) are likely to challenge the ironlike grip that sovereign states have exercised in determining the global system's architecture and rules ever since the 1648 Peace of Westphalia.

Are transnational nonstate actors truly capable of flexing their muscles in ways that can directly challenge states' sovereign control over both their foreign and domestic policies? If so, are the pillars of the Westphalian state system beginning to crumble, as some predict (Falk and Strauss 2001; Kegley and Raymond 2002a)?

As you contemplate these questions, keep in mind one clear lesson: It is misleading to think that politics is only about territorial states in interaction, with each exercising supreme authority within their borders. Given their accountability and abuses of power (Grant and Keohane 2005), are there good reasons to see the challenges of NGOs as a threat to states' continuing domination of world politics? If that is the prevailing trend, as NGOs "multiply the channels of access to the international system and blur the boundaries between states and citizens, are they transforming the practice of state sovereignty" (Keck and Sikkink 2004)?

These speculations by no means prove that the era of state dominance is finished at a time when corporations and other nonstate actors find their clout rising. This is particularly relevant for the mass for all humanity that includes ordinary people everywhere. It is to the circumstances of all individuals—you and all other members of the human race—that we turn to in the next chapter.

Key Terms

military-industrial complex
devolution
nonstate nations
ethnic groups
ethnicity
ethnic nationalism
Fourth World
clash of civilizations

transnational religious movements
theocracy
extreme militant religious
    movements
secession, or separative revolts
diasporas
international terrorism
terrorism

information age
postmodern terrorism
multinational corporations
    (MNCs)
transnational banks (TNBs)
globally integrated enterprises
strategic corporate alliances
civil society

CHAPTER 8
PEOPLE POWER AND THE PROMOTION OF HUMAN RIGHTS

One person with a belief is equal to a force of 99 who have only interests.
—John Stuart Mill, English liberal philosopher

Jerome Delay/AP Photo

Life Without Liberty. "The cost of liberty is less than the price of repression," the African-American sociologist W.E.B. Dubois argued. Shown here are inmates in Iraq's Abu Ghraib prison crying for freedom when dictator Saddam Hussein still ruled. After the 2003 U.S. invasion of Iraq, American occupation forces used the same prison to torture suspected insurgents. Amnesty International condemned this method for fighting terrorism as "atrocious human rights violations."

When we think about international relations, we are inclined to think about the most influential transnational actors—the great powers (Chapter 4), the weaker states of the Global South (Chapter 5), the global institutions or IGOs that states create (Chapter 6), and the NGOs that people join to lobby for global changes (Chapter 7). We tend to view differences in actors' prosperity, power, and capacity to influence global trends as being derived from differences in **agency** or the relative clout of each group of global actors. However, this perspective assigns agency to states and mighty nonstate actors, and discounts everyone else.

■ **agency**

the capacity of actors to harness power to achieve objectives.

The predominant constructed state-centric image of the forces and factors that drive world affairs is helpful in understanding some properties of international relations, such as the dynamics of war and economic conditions that propel the rise and fall of the great powers in their rivalry to attain hegemony. However, such a simplifying construction fails to capture the role played by human agency—by the 6.7 billion people comprising the human race. Peoples' individual choices are consequential because they combine in countless unseen ways to produce global trends. The proportion of people who habitually smoke, litter, break promises, or engage in conspicuous consumption that harms the environment all make a difference and thereby make worse the global condition experienced by all people.

If you, as a student of international affairs, are to develop a more complete comprehension of the forces behind the prevailing trends in world politics, it is important to ask the question, how do humans—that is, ordinary individual people—act as agents of global change? What conception of human agency should be constructed? In short, to borrow the famous phrase in the radical theorist Karl Marx's *Das Capital,* the story of the world is *de te fibula narrator*—"this story is about you."

PUTTING PEOPLE INTO THE PICTURE

Until relatively recently in the unfolding evolution of the theoretical study of world politics, the needs of the faceless billions of everyday people were neglected. That past theoretical legacy, in this tradition, pictured the mass of humanity as marginalized victims or left them invisible by painting peoples' fates as controlled by forces over which hapless people have little influence. The French world-systems historian Fernand Braudel (1973) wrote that "when I think of the individual, I am always inclined to see him imprisoned within a destiny in which he himself has little hand, fixed in a landscape in which the infinite perspectives of the long-term stretch into the distance both behind and before."

■ **ethics**

criteria for evaluating right and wrong behavior and the motives of individuals and groups.

When thinking about world affairs, people—the average person—have long been relegated to a mere "subject" whom rulers were traditionally permitted to manipulate to advance their states' interests. That vision has been rejected throughout the world. A consensus now supports the view that people are important, that they have worth, and therefore, that **ethics** and **morality** belong in the study of international relations. As defined by ethicist Ronald Dworkin (2001), "Ethics includes convictions about what kinds of lives are good or bad for a person

■ **morality**

principles about the norms for behavior that should govern actors' interactions.

For millennia, human beings saw nothing odd about slavery, about selling and disposing of persons as if they were things.

—Michal Ignatieff, ethicist

to lead, and morality includes principles about how a person should treat other people." These principles apply to interstate relations, and they are at the heart of all analyses of human rights in world politics.

That consensus notwithstanding, many observers embrace the traditional assumptions of realism that vast global forces make people powerless. Realists recognize that people participate politically but claim they have no real power because an invisible set of powerful forces described as the "system" gives most human beings only superficial involvement without real influence.

This denial of the importance and influence of individual human agency today seems increasingly strange, because classic thinking about the world has long concentrated on people and on the essential character of human nature. As the anthropologist Robert Redfield (1962) argued, "Human nature is itself a part of the method [of all analysis]. One must use one's own humanity as a means to understanding. The physicist need not sympathize with his atoms, nor the biologist with his fruit flies, but the student of people and institutions must employ [one's] natural sympathies in order to discover what people think or feel." A humanistic interpretation is needed that gives people status and value. Moreover, in the global community there is emerging a **civil society**. A normative consensus has grown about the inherent moral worth and status of humans and the concomitant obligation of states to recognize and protect that status (Fields and Lord 2004).

Morality matters, because most states have publicly proclaimed the ethical standard that states should respect "the universalist claim that all human beings have the same moral status; to accept universal human rights [is to make on states] the moral demand to respect the life, integrity, well-being and flourishing of . . . *all* human beings" (Vandersluis and Yeros 2000a). This claim was expressed in the ringing

■ civil society
a community composed of citizens that create institutions to protect civil liberties (such as free speech and freedom from arbitrary governmental interference) and that use peaceful methods for conflict resolution.

In the idea that those who suffer "no grievance or injury" have the obligation to speak up for those who have suffered them lies the birth of the vision that human rights are universal.

—Adam Hochschild, humanitarian historian

words of the 1948 *Universal Declaration of Human Rights:* "Recognition of the inherent dignity and of the equal and inalienable rights of all members of the human family is the foundation of freedom, justice, and peace in the world." This treaty expressed the hope that people should be empowered and made by global agreement the ultimate concern, and therefore no longer reduced to "simply hapless victims of fate, devoid of any historical agency" (Saurin 2000).

AFP/Getty Images

HUMAN RIGHTS VERSUS STATES' RIGHTS Although eighty-nine countries have now abolished the death penalty for all crimes, thousands of executions of alleged criminals are carried out each year. China carried out 1,010 death sentences in 2006, "though the real number may be near 8,000. China, Iran, Pakistan, Iraq, Sudan and the United States accounted for more than nine out of the ten known executions worldwide" (*Economist*, April 28, 2007, 69–70).

■ **human rights**

the political rights and civil liberties recognized by the international community as inalienable and valid for individuals in all countries by virtue of their humanity.

■ **sanctions**

punitive actions (short of military force) by one global actor against another to retaliate for its previous objectionable behavior.

This chapter introduces information about the human condition to enable you to evaluate the unfolding debate about the human prospect, the role of humans as actors on the global stage, and the ethics of **human rights**. Given "the increasing willingness to regard concern for human rights violations as acceptable justification for various kinds of international intervention in the domestic affairs of states ranging from diplomatic and economic **sanctions** to military action," you have the opportunity to investigate the challenges posed by that lofty humanitarian ideal rooted in liberalism in order to explain why "the doctrine of human rights is a political construction intended for certain political purposes and to be understood against the background of a range of general assumptions about the character of the contemporary international environment" (Beitz 2001).

As described in Chapter 11, there are now 6.7 billion people on the face of the Earth, and world population is growing. Between two and four billion more people will be added to the planet's population between now and the last quarter of the twenty-first century. With these numbers come concerns. Will humanity be valued, and will human welfare and rights be protected?

These are critical questions. Where does humanity fit into the prevailing and most popular *paradigms* or theoretical orientations that policy makers and scholars construct about what matters in world politics, such as neorealism and neoliberalism? For the most part, classical realism worships the state and its ruler's sovereign freedom, and, except for building its image of international reality from a pessimistic conception of human nature, it ignores the role of leaders and the NGOs that people form (see Chapter 2). Liberals attach more importance to humans, following the ethical precept of the German philosopher Immanuel Kant that people should be treated as ends and not means, and that therefore peoples' human rights should be safeguarded. Feminist theory goes further, countering realist logic by making humanity the primary level of analysis (Sylvester 2002; Enloe 2004; D'Amico and Beckman 1995; see Chapter 2).

How Does Humanity Fare? The Human Condition Today

"Man is born free, and everywhere he is in chains," the political philosopher Jean Jacques Rousseau bemoaned in his famous 1762 book, *Social Contract*. Times have since changed. But in many respects Rousseau's characterization of the human condition remains accurate. How should we evaluate the depth of human deprivation and despair against this fact? Can the poorest proportion of humanity sever the chains of their disadvantages to realize their human potential and obtain the high ideals of human security, freedom, and dignity?

The inequalities and disparities evident in people's standards of living cannot help but to evoke sympathy for the difficult conditions faced by many people, especially for those in the less-developed Global South countries. One American graduate student, when working on his Ph.D., painfully learned about the plight of people in the Global South during his field research in South America. Brian Wallace found a reality far different from his own experience of growing up in the southern United States. In 1978 he was moved to write:

> I spent the first 24 years of my life in South Carolina. When I left . . . for Colombia [South America], I fully expected Bogotá to be like any large U.S. city, only with citizens who spoke Spanish. When I arrived there I found my expectations were wrong. I was not in the U.S., I was on Mars! I was a victim of culture shock. As a personal experience this shock was occasionally funny and sometimes sad. But after all the laughing and the crying were over, it forced me to reevaluate both my life and the society in which I live.
>
> Colombia is a poor country by American standards. It has a per capita GNP of $550 and a very unequal distribution of income. These were the facts that I knew before I left.
>
> But to "know" these things intellectually is much different from experiencing first-hand how they affect people's lives. It is one thing to lecture in air conditioned classrooms about the problems of world poverty. It is quite another to see four-year-old children begging or sleeping in the streets.
>
> It tore me apart emotionally to see the reality of what I had studied for so long: "low per capita GNP and maldistribution of income." What this means in human terms is children with dirty faces who beg for bread money or turn into pickpockets because the principle of private property gets blurred by empty stomachs.
>
> It means other children whose minds and bodies will never develop fully because they were malnourished as infants. It means street vendors who sell candy and cigarettes 14 hours a day in order to feed their families.
>
> It also means well-dressed businessmen and petty bureaucrats who indifferently pass this poverty every day as they seek asylum in their fortified houses to the north of the city.

It means rich people who prefer not to see the poor, except for maids and security guards.

It means foreigners like me who come to Colombia and spend more in one month than the average Colombian earns in a year.

It means politicians across the ideological spectrum who are so full of abstract solutions or personal greed that they forget that it is real people they are dealing with.

Somewhere within the polemics of the politicians and the "objectivity" of the social scientists, the human being has been lost.

Despite wide differences that enable a proportion of humanity to enjoy unprecedented standards of living, a daunting scale of poverty and misery is evident throughout the world, from which only a small fraction of people in many countries have begun to escape (see Map 8.1). One indicator is money. According to the World Bank's definition of extreme poverty as income of one dollar or less a day, as 2008 began 1.23 billion people (18.4 percent of the world) were living in extreme poverty and another 3.2 billion (48 percent of world population) were seeking to survive two dollars or less a day (WDI 2007, 16, 63). Income inequality is a serious global problem from which many other difficulties and disputes result. And that problem is entrenched: "In the gross sense of inequality as the gap between the richest and the poorest citizens of the world, global inequality has increased dramatically since World War II, continuing a macro trend of the previous hundred and perhaps thousand years."

> *One-fifth of humanity live in countries where many people think nothing of spending $2 a day on a cappuccino. Another fifth of humanity survive on less than $1 a day and live in countries where children die for want of a simple anti-mosquito bed net.*
>
> — United Nations Development Programme

And "there is some evidence that the forces of globalization in trade, investment and the labor forces are working to increase" the gap between rich and poor people, much as it appears to widen the gap between the wealthy Global North and poor Global South countries (Babones and Turner 2004; see Chapter 5). One estimate calculates that, since 1960, the income of the average person in the Global North grew twenty-seven times that of the average person in the Global South (*Vital Signs 2003*, 88). This trend has produced a world in which the poorest fifth of the global population produce and consume only 2 percent of the world's goods and services, creating huge inequalities: "A homeless person panhandling for two U.S. dollars a day on the streets of Boston would sit in the top half of the world in income distribution" (Dollar 2005, 80).

Against this grim picture are trends that inspire some hope. For some segments of humanity things have improved: "On average, people in developing countries are healthier, better educated, and less impoverished—and they are more likely to live in a multiparty democracy. Since 1990 life expectancy in developing countries has increased by 3 years (WDI 2008). There are 3 million fewer children out of school. More than 130 million people have escaped extreme poverty. These human development gains should not be underestimated. Nor should they be exaggerated.

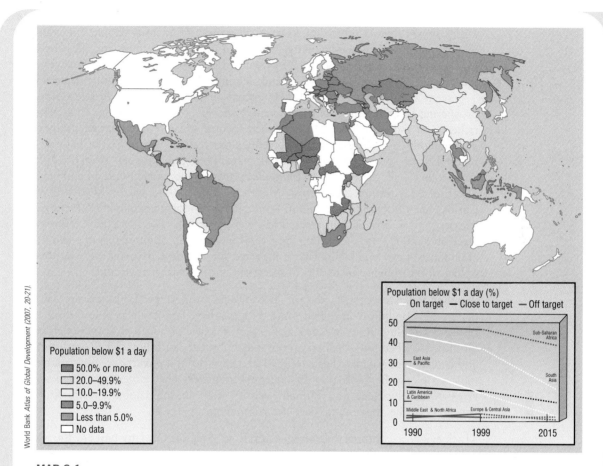

World Bank Atlas of Global Development (2007, 20-21).

MAP 8.1

WHERE POVERTY PREVAILS IN THE WORLD: THE SHARE OF PEOPLE LIVING ON LESS THAN $1 A DAY. **As this map shows, billions of people in a wide range of countries are struggling to exist under conditions of extreme poverty. The most people living in extreme poverty are in Asia, but Africa has the largest number of high-poverty countries. The World Bank (WDR 2008, 1) warns that most Global South countries are not on track to achieve the UN goal of cutting poverty in half by the year 2015.**

In the midst of an increasingly prosperous global economy, 10.7 million children every year do not live to see their fifth birthday, and millions of children have been orphaned" (UNDP 2005, 3). According to the International Labor Organization (ILO), over one million children are sold into labor every year and are faced with brutality and horrific work conditions (Vital Signs 2007–2008, 113). "So if one focuses on the developing world outside China, the number of poor has changed very little. . . . The number of poor has fallen in the Global East, but risen elsewhere. It has roughly doubled in Africa," where one in three of the world's poorest live (Ravallion 2004, 65; see also WDR 2008).

Consumption patterns also show that the division between the rich and the poor is growing. Only about one-fifth of the globe's wealthiest people consume anywhere from two-thirds to nine-tenths of its resources.

The proportions reflect the figures given in the United Nations' annual *Human Development Report,* which shows the richest fifth of humanity having, for example, 90 percent of all Internet accounts, 74 percent of all phone lines, and 82 percent of all export markets. The poorest 20 percent of the world's population receives only 0.2 percent of global commercial bank lending, 1.3 percent of global investment, 1 percent of global trade, and 1.4 percent of global income. A select few are prospering in comparison with the many who are barely surviving: "The world's richest 500 individuals have a combined income greater than that of the poorest 416 million. . . . The richest 10 percent, almost all of whom live in high-income [Global North] countries, account for 54 percent" of global income (UNDP 2005, 4). Put another way, there are 946 *billionaires* around the world, with a combined net worth of $3.5 *trillion* (*Economist*, March 17, 2007, 106), led by Mexican tycoon Carlos Slim who with a $59 billion—and climbing—fortune (equal to 6.6 percent of Mexico's GDP) makes him the world's richest person (*Foreign Policy*, November/ December 2007, 35). Crushing poverty for one-half of humanity against rising abundance for a small minority is a recipe for hopeless desperation and possibly destruction through violent acts of terrorism and suicidal martyrdom.

Another indicator besides the absence of income and available resources is the deplorable conditions in which many humans live. For many people the future is bleak, resembling how in 1651 the realist English political philosopher Thomas Hobbes described life—"solitary, poor, nasty, brutish, and short." The opportunities and choices that are most basic to freedom from fear and poverty are unavailable for most people in the Global South's poorest countries. They experience much slower rates of development and human security than in the Global North, and the prospects of the "have-nots" are not improving.

Much evidence captures the extreme suffering of people in many parts of the world, but especially in the low-income countries of the Global South where life has changed little from that of their ancestors. For example, life expectancy in the Global South averages 64 years, whereas in the Global North it is 76 years (HDR 2008, 232). Human agony is also starkly evident in other respects. In the Global South, infant mortality rates are among the highest in the world; less than half of the adult population is literate (a proportion even lower among women); agriculture remains the dominant form of productive activity; and four out of every five people live in rural areas even as the world is undergoing rapid urbanization. Former World Bank President James Wolfensohn captured the growing threat of global poverty by noting that "2 billion people have no access to clear water; 120 million children never get a chance to go to school; over 40 million people in the developing countries are HIV-positive with little hope of receiving treatment for this dreadful disease. . . . So the world is at a tipping point: either we recommit to deliver on the goals, or the targets will be missed, the world's poor will be left even further behind—and our children will be left to face the consequences."

Given the serious deprivations in many aspects of life facing so many people, there are many reasons for humanitarian concern. The denial to most humans of the inalienable rights to which all humans are presumably entitled—the "life, liberty, and the pursuit of happiness" of which the U.S. Declaration of Independence speaks —attests to the extent to which fundamental human rights are not being met. This problem prompted Mary Robinson, the UN High Commissioner for Human Rights, to "call on global actors—corporations, governments and the international financial organizations—to join with globalized civil society and share responsibility for humanizing **globalization**."

To make the promotion of human rights the globe's major priority, a precise measure of human welfare is needed. How can human welfare—its level and the prospects for humanity's escape from poverty—best be gauged?

Measuring Human Development and Human Security

The human dimension of development first gained attention in the 1970s, partly in response to the growing popularity of dependency theory (see Chapter 5). This theory, advanced by Global South leaders, attributed persistent poverty to exploitation caused by dependent relationships of the less-developed countries with the wealthy Global North. It also reflected the realization that more is not necessarily better. Advocates of a basic **human needs** perspective sought new ways to measure development beyond those focusing exclusively on economic indicators such as the average income for each person in each country.

In 1990, Mahbud ul Haq, a famous social scientist, constructed for the United Nations Development Programme (UNDP) a **Human Development Index (HDI)** to measure states' comparative ability to provide for their citizens' well-being. Successive *Human Development Reports* have provoked fresh debate about the meaning of human development in international forums such as the World Summit for Social Development.

The HDI, as the UNDP most recently defines it, seeks to capture as many aspects of human development as possible in one simple, composite index and to rank human-development achievements. Although no multiple-indicator index (a detailed set of statistical measures) can monitor progress in human development, the HDI comes close as an estimating procedure. It measures three dimensions of human welfare— living a long and healthy life, being educated, and having a decent standard of living.

The HDI is a more comprehensive measure than per capita income and has the advantage of directing attention from material possessions toward human needs. Income is only a means to human development, not an end. Nor is it the sum total of human lives. Thus, by focusing on aspects of human welfare beyond average income for each person—by treating income as a proxy for a decent standard of living—the HDI provides a more complete picture of human life than income does. By this measure, the evidence provides a basic profile of the extent to which humanitarian aspirations are succeeding and failing.

The HDI ranges from 0 to 1. The HDI value for a country shows the distance that it has already traveled toward the maximum possible value of 1 and allows for comparison with other countries. The difference between the value achieved by a country and the maximum possible value shows how far it has to go, and the challenge for every country is to find ways to reduce that discrepancy.

Look at the ability of countries to contribute to the human development of the people living within their borders, as measured by the HDI. We derive a revealing picture of the way personal welfare is provided (see Figure 8.1). These indicators

■ globalization

the integration of states, through increasing contact, communication, and trade, to create a common global culture for all humanity.

■ human needs

those basic physical, social, and political needs, such as food and freedom, that are required for survival and security.

■ Human Development Index (HDI)

an index that uses life expectancy, literacy, average number of years of schooling, and income to assess a country's performance in providing for its peoples' welfare and security.

show that consumption is not the same as human welfare and that economic growth does not automatically produce human development. In fact, if not managed, high consumption can produce inequalities and poverty that erode the capacity of people "to participate in the decisions that affect one's life and to enjoy the respect of others in the community. . . . The HDI can give a more complete picture of the state of a country's development than can income alone [since many countries] highlight the importance of policies that translate wealth into human development. In particular, well designed public policy and provision of services by governments, local communities and civil society can advance human development even without high levels of income or economic growth" (UNDP 2004, 128).

Humanitarian goals for human development vary greatly in the countries of the world. Why is this the case? Let us consider several explanations.

FIGURE 8.1

MEASURING HUMAN DEVELOPMENT: WHAT IS QUALITY OF LIFE? **When using the Human Development Index to measure the human welfare and development of people within various populations, notice how countries can rank somewhat differently than when using an aggregate measure such as the gross domestic product (GDP) per capita—whereas Norway ranks very high and Niger ranks very low on both measures, South Africa's AIDS epidemic has left it in the 121st position on the HDI, despite its relatively high income. Compare the HDI rankings with those recorded for the GDP per person to see how closely the two indicators correspond. All standards of living measures are controversial. Note, for example, another problem with the HDI is that "it does not include measures of the other aspects of human development such as leisure, security, justice, freedom, human rights, and self respect. It would be possible to register a high HDI in a zoo or even in a well-run prison. And, although at low incomes illness often leads to death, the HDI has no independent indicator of morbidity, the absence of which is surely one of the most basic needs. Life can be nasty, brutish, and long" (Streeten, 2001).**

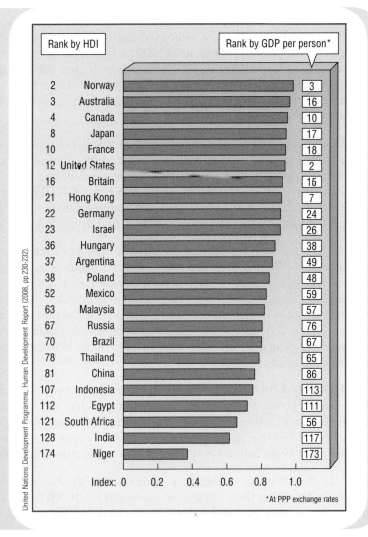

United Nations Development Programme, Human Development Report (2008, pp.230-232).

The Democratic and Economic Underpinnings of Human Development

What factors affect people's human rights to live a good life? Among many, one correlate stands out: political freedom—the degree to which countries rule themselves democratically and protect citizens' civil liberties. This is a potent determinant of human development. Where democracy thrives, there also thrives human rights and human development. Recall the states where democracy and political liberties exist (see Map 3.2, "How Free Is Your Country?," p. 79). That geographical profile supports the conclusion that at the start of 2008 less than half of the countries in the world, 46 percent, were "free," providing their citizens with a broad range of civil liberties in their political, civic, educational, cultural, ethnic, economic, and religious rights. In human terms, these liberties are experienced by 2.8 billion individuals, or 37 percent of the globe's population (Freedom House, http://www.freedomhouse.org). Now compare the location where people benefit from such freedom with Map 8.2, which shows the various levels of human development in countries across the globe. The two go hand in hand: Where democracy flourishes, human development flourishes. But in autocratic governments not ruled by the will of the people, where government policies fail to recognize cultural identities and discourage diversity, human rights are denied and human development fails to occur.

Along with democratization and respect for cultural liberty, rising economic prosperity clearly helps the pace of human development, as shown in Figure 8.1, which indicates the wealth of each person for countries based on **purchasing power parity (PPP)** exchange-rate comparisons. This is why levels of human development are generally highest in the Global North, where economic prosperity on average is also highest (as opposed to the low-income Global South and some countries in the Global East such as China). But the exceptions demonstrate the general rule that how countries organize themselves for governance, and their protection of the civil and cultural liberties of their populations, makes a crucial difference in achieving levels of human development.

Some question the "trickle-down" hypothesis (that if the rich first get richer eventually the benefits will trickle down to help the poor) while accepting the evidence that meeting basic human needs promotes long-term economic growth (WDR 2008). Others maintain that redistributive policies to meet basic human needs or otherwise enhance human welfare, and growth-oriented policies through trickle-down effects work at cross-purposes because the latter can only be attained at the expense of the former. And many now recommend fostering human development through a *"Third Way"* strategy that combines the efficiency of a free enterprise capitalistic market with the compassion of governmental economic planning and regulation in an effort, through a fused administrative system, to cooperatively produce the greatest good for the greatest number. Proponents agree that this mixed approach would enable a free market to generate rapid growth while providing a safety net for those most in need of assistance, and this formula is the best solution for engineering economic growth with a moral human purpose.

■ **purchasing power parity (PPP)**

an index that calculates the true rate of exchange among currencies when parity—when what can be purchased is the same—is achieved; the index determines what can be bought with a unit of each currency.

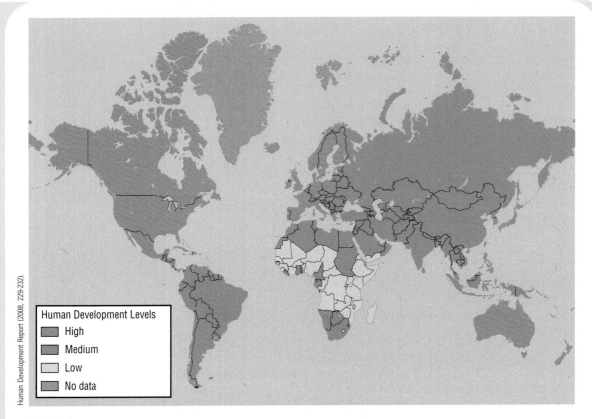

Human Development Report (2008, 229-232).

MAP 8.2

THE MAP OF HUMAN DEVELOPMENT. This map measures the level of human development in the countries of the world, using the HDI scale. Note the wide variation. Although the Global East and some Global South countries have made big gains in the past quarter century (following political reforms leading to greater democracy and economic reforms leading to free markets), a gap in peoples' quality of life and in their levels of human development is apparent and parallels to some degree the gap between the Global North and the Global South.

Human Development in the Age of Globalization

The rapid transfer of global capital and investment across borders is integrating the world's economies and has led to widespread speculation that globalization will provide a cure for the chronic poverty facing the majority of humanity. There exists "a widely shared image of globalization—a worldwide process of converging incomes and lifestyles driven by ever-larger international flows of goods, images, capital, and people as formidable equalizers [because] greater economic openness has made small parts of the changing world full-fledged members of the global village . . . so that globalized islands of prosperity are thriving in many developing nations" (Heredia 1999). Evidence supports the conclusion that those countries that respect human rights also encourage trade that reduces poverty (Blanton and Blanton, 2007).

However, critics of globalization complain that it is the culprit, that relative deprivation is caused by globalization, not cured by it. They see globalization as a part of the problem of human suffering, not the solution. To their constructed image of the consequences of cascading globalization, a more global economy increases inequality in some countries, particularly in the marginalized periphery of the Global South. Other critics decry the "human harms" wrought by globalization, arguing that "nothing is more certain than the inequality and exploitation generated by a totally free market. The inequalities that global capitalism generates are inequities because they violate the principles of egalitarian individualism. . . . This sin of globalization is thus both collective (an assault on the nation) and individual (injuring the nation's citizens), making it a severe violation of the global moral order" by creating "risks of injury and incapacitation that strike at the very being of human beings" (Boli, Elliott, and Bieri 2004).

The fundamental deprivation of human rights [is] first and above all the deprivation of a place in the world.
—Hannah Arendt, German-American philosopher

Complaints about the harmful impact of globalization to humanity often point to the damage caused to individuals by threats to the environment and nature, local culture, jobs and labor, religion, and other values humans hold dear. However most complaints center on economic deprivation and declining standards of living for the poorest. It is argued that globalization is not benefiting the people that most need help.

The poor are paying the price for everyone else's prosperity.
—Rombert Weakland, globalization economist

Capital may flow more freely around the world, but it flows most slowly to the places and people where it is most scarce. A skeptical political economist from Mexico cautions that "More and more people across the planet have become increasingly exposed to the amenities of the global marketplace, although mostly as permanent window shoppers and silent spectators. The large majority of humankind, however, is rapidly being left outside and far behind" (Heredia 1999).

Although progress in human development has occurred and will likely persist, so will trends toward declining human welfare, making the twenty-first century appear to be both the best of times and the worst of times. Thus, the future of world politics will be not only a struggle between the Global North and the Global South but also a contest between those who hopelessly expect continuing human poverty and those who envision as possible further progress in human development.

The great feature of poverty is the fact that it annihilates the future.
—George Orwell, British author

Even as globalization forges greater interdependence, the world seems more fragmented—between rich and poor, between the powerful and the powerless, and between those who welcome the new global economy and those who demand a different course. The September 11, 2001, terrorist attacks on the United States cast new light on these divisions. The United States aggressively sought to counter terrorism. Critics complained that America had in the process compromised its traditional ideals supporting the protection of civil liberties and human rights in the process. Many realists, on the other hand, emphasized the importance of putting national self-interests ahead of liberal values. Liberals responded by arguing the importance of preserving global humanitarian norms and America's reputation for honorable international conduct. The U.S. decision to give primary attention to national security over human rights was questioned by ethicist Michael Ignatieff (2004a) when he attempted to remind the Bush administration that "all the world's national security challenges come from regimes that are also human rights violators."

HUMAN RIGHTS AND THE PROTECTION OF PEOPLE

Rights are entitlements that a person has to something of value. By acknowledging a right, we set limits on the actions of others and empower the right holder to have nullified any encroachments into what is protected. As stated earlier, human rights are entitlements that a person possesses simply because he or she is a human being. As such, they are held equally by all and cannot be lost or forfeited.

Unfortunately, not everyone enjoys all of the human rights recognized by international law. Three areas that remain problematic are the rights of women, refugees, and indigenous peoples.

Gender Inequality and Its Consequences

Over the past three decades, the status of women has become a major human rights concern (see Table 8.1). Increasingly, people have realized that women have an important influence on human development, and that their treatment is an issue that affects everyone.

■ Gender Empowerment Measure (GEM)

the UN Development Programme's attempt to measure the extent of gender equality across the globe's countries, based on estimates of women's relative economic income, high-paying positions, and access to professional and parliamentary positions.

For more than three decades, global conferences have highlighted the critical role of women and how it can be a human rights concern. A global consensus emerged about the need to improve the status of women if human rights and development were to progress. These conferences are signposts that increasingly depict gender equality and empowerment across political, social, and economic arenas as a fundamental right. They have educated the world to the incontrovertible evidence that women's status in society, and especially their education, has an important influence on human development, and that women's treatment is a global rights issue that affects everyone (Pettman 2005).

As measured by the UN's **Gender Empowerment Measure (GEM)**, women throughout the world continue to be disadvantaged relative to men across a broad spectrum (HDR 2008, 326–346). Disparities between men and women persist, for example, in literacy rates, school and college enrollments, and targeted educational resources. Moreover, women enjoy less access to advanced study and training in professional fields, such as science, engineering, law, and business. In addition, within occupational groups, they are almost always in less-prestigious jobs, they face formidable barriers to political involvement, and everywhere they receive less pay than men.

Table 8.1   Important Steps on the Path toward Human Rights and Women's Rights

Year	Conference	Key Passage
1975	World Conference on International Women's Year (Mexico City)	Launched a global dialogue on gender equality and led to the establishment of the United Nations Development Fund for Women (UNIFEM)
1979	Convention on the Elimination of All Forms of Discrimination against Women (Women's Convention, New York)	Article 12 calls on countries to "take all appropriate measures to eliminate discrimination against women in the field of health care in order to ensure, on a basis of equality of men and women, access to health care services, including those related to family planning."
1980	Second World Conference on Women (Copenhagen)	Calls for governments to enact stronger measures that will ensure women's ownership and control of property, improve women's rights to inheritance, child custody, and loss of nationality
1985	Third World Conference on Women (Nairobi)	Recognized the need for governments to bring gender concerns into the mainstream and develop institutional mechanisms to promote broad-based gender equality and empowerment of women
1993	United Nations World Conference on Human Rights (Vienna)	The Vienna Declaration includes nine paragraphs on "The Equal Status and Human Rights of Women," and for the first time recognizes that "violence against women is a human-rights abuse."
1994	International Conference on Population and Development (Cairo)	ICPD Program of Action "reaffirms the basic human rights of all couples and individuals to decide freely and responsibly the number and spacing of children and to have the information, education, and means to do so."
1995	United Nations Fourth World Conference on Women (Beijing)	Sets a wide-ranging, ambitious agenda for promoting human development by addressing gender inequality and women's rights
2001	World Conference Against Racism	Highlights that women and girls may be discriminated against due to their gender and race, addresses the racial dimensions of human trafficking, and calls for states to adopt immigration and refugee policies that afford protection to women subject to domestic violence

(continues)

Table 8.1   Important Steps on the Path toward Human Rights and Women's Rights *(continued)*

Year	Conference	Key Passage
2002	World Summit on Sustainable Development (Johannesburg)	Drafts resolutions to combat abject and dehumanizing poverty, stressing the importance of reform to encourage gender equity and the rights of women in order to stimulate sustainable economic growth
2004	NATO Conference on Trafficking in Humans (Brussels)	Seeks a convention to contain the growing problem of human trafficking and export of people across borders—particularly women and children
2004	United Nations Conference on the Human Rights Obligations of Multinational Corporations (Geneva)	Opens debate to create a new code—the Human Rights Norms for Business—to impose human rights and gender equality obligations on "transnational companies and other businesses."
2004	United Nations Conference on Sexual and Reproductive Rights (New York)	Launches action plan to uphold women's "fundamental human rights including sexual and reproductive rights."
2005	United Nations World Conference on Women (Beijing)	*110 Platform for Action* charts strategies for empowerment of women and girls

■ **gender inequalities**

differences between men and women in opportunity and reward that are determined by the values that guide states' foreign and domestic policies.

Indeed, in most countries, **gender inequalities**—differences in living standards between men and women—remain widespread both within and across states, despite the measurable improvement in the daily lot and future prospects of millions of women during the past several decades. Although many facets of human development

> *A people's condition may be judged by the treatment which women receive under it.*
>
> —Herbert Spencer, American sociologist

are improving, the prevalent worldwide gender gap remains especially wide in three Global South regions: Southern Asia, the Middle East, and Sub-Saharan Africa (HDR 2008, 326–346). Women's share of earned income in developing countries is less than a third of men's. Worse still, women account for a much smaller proportion of the nonagricultural workforce than men, and their pay in that sector for the same work is routinely less. Females hold fewer teaching positions at all levels of education and fewer Ph.D.s, and their share of administrative and managerial jobs is minuscule. Much the same holds true in politics: Since 1900 only 15 percent of the world's countries have had one or more female heads of state (*Harper's*, January 2008, 15) and, in 2008 women accounted for only 14.5 percent of ministerial positions (*Time* May 5, 2008, 14).

HOW TO TRANSCEND THE GENDER GAP? Shown here are examples of how the empowerment of women is changing. Following a traditional medieval ritual that is slowly vanishing, a woman in a clan of Northern Albania could claim the right to live and rule her family as a man only if she forsook her womanhood (left). As the first female Chancellor of Germany (right), Angela Merkel is one of the most powerful women in the world.

Furthermore, gender differences continue at the most basic levels of human development. More girls than boys die at a young age, and females' access to adequate health care is more restricted (Carpenter 2005). Despite the fact that "since the eighteenth century feminists, scholars, and activists have taken up the task of revealing just how much political life has been built on presumptions about femininity and masculinity . . . there is abundant evidence now that regimes and the states beneath them in fact have taken deliberate steps to sustain a sort of hierarchical gendered division of labor that provides them with cheapened, often completely unpaid, women's productive labor" (Enloe 2001). It is therefore easy to conclude that women remain victims of human rights abuse and discrimination nearly everywhere, as reflected in the grim statistics that 70 percent of all refugees are women and their dependent children (Enloe 2001, 313); that 20 percent of women have suffered child abuse as children (Eisler 2007, 9); and that according to the International Labour Organization "between 700,000 and 2 million women and children are trafficked across an international border somewhere in the world every year, feeding an industry with profits at somewhere between $12 billion and $17 billion per year. According to the United Nations, there are currently 127 "source countries" that provide large numbers of prostitutes, mainly in Asia and Eastern Europe, and 137 "destination countries" (Moorehead 2007, 15). It was not until 2001 that "sexual enslavement" was established at The Hague as a war crime, a fact feminists point out as an example of the traditional disregard for women's human rights.

Gender myopia, denying the existence of the many barriers that prevent women equal freedoms and privileges enjoyed by men, is pervasive, although the need to extend women equal human rights for economic growth is clear-cut: "Educating girls is the single most effective way to boost economic progress" (Coleman 2005). What is also clear is that "robust democracy is exceedingly rare in societies that marginalize women" (Coleman 2005). These principles were recognized at the Johannesburg World Summit on Sustainable Development. "The river of thought on human rights and development runs inexorably toward the emancipation of women everywhere, and the equality of men and women," notes the *State of the World*

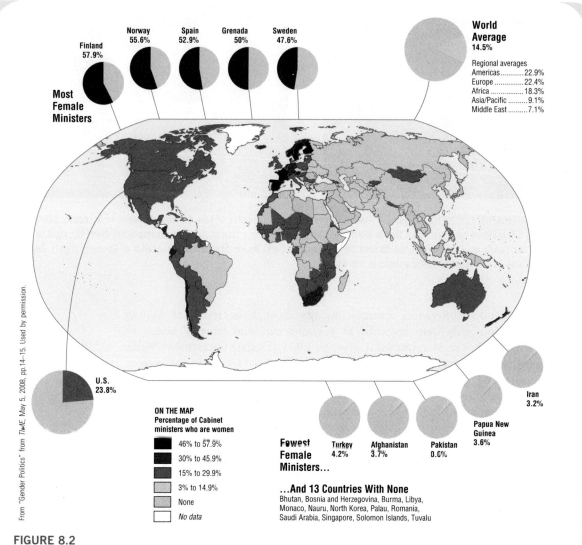

FIGURE 8.2

GENDER POLITICS Spain's Cabinet has more women than men—including Defense Minister Carme Chacón, who gave birth to her first son while serving in office. But worldwide, women fill only 14.5 percent of ministerial positions. Their most common portfolios are in human services and education; defense is one of the rarest.

2002, which warned sadly, "but eddies and rivulets carry the water backwards every day—as when pregnant girls are expelled from school, or when the genitals of young women are cut in a ritual destruction of their capacity for sexual pleasure."

Protecting women's rights is difficult because the issues touch deeply entrenched as well as widely divergent religious and cultural beliefs. In many Islamic countries, for example, women must hide their faces with veils in public, and women and men are often completely separated in social and religious activities. For many in liberal Western countries focused on social, political, and economic equality of the sexes, these traditions are difficult to understand.

In 1995, in Beijing, the UN convened its fourth World Conference on Women, the largest-ever gathering of women. Many of the arguments provoked by differing religious and cultural traditions surfaced during the conference on gender issues. "Gender empowerment" is based on the conviction that only the realization of the full potential of all human beings can enable true human development. Once this concept gained acceptance as an *ideology* or lens through which to construct a view of the core issues on the global agenda, gender issues became a central concern.

Feminist theory, a departure from classical realist theory, seeks to rectify the ways conventional but distorted images of world politics are, as *constructivism* informs us, socially constructed (see Chapter 2; Barnett 2005). The objective is to sensitize the world to the neglect of gender and the place of women in global society and to offer an alternative theoretical vision that empowers women, secures their basic human rights, and challenges realist theories that honor the state and military power (Enloe 2004; D'Amico and Beckman 1995; Hunt and Posa 2005; Sylvester 2002; Tickner 2002).

The Global Refugee Crisis

Another sign of concern about **human security** is expressed by the refugee crisis that now prevails in our "age of migration." Refugees are individuals whose race, religion, nationality, membership in a particular social group, or political opinions make them targets of persecution in their homelands and who, therefore, migrate from their country of origin, unable to return. According to the UN High Commissioner for Refugees (UNHCR), at the start of 2008, the world's refugee population was a staggering 16 million, of whom 11.4 million fell under UNHCR's mandate and 4.6 million Palestinian refugees fell under the responsibility of the United Nations Relief and Works Agency for Palestinian Refugees in the Near East (UNRWA). Also included as "persons of concern" are internally displaced persons (IDPs), which the UNHCR estimated at 51 million worldwide with roughly 26 million displaced as a result of armed conflict and another 25 million displaced by natural disasters (see Figure 8.3). These may be conservative estimates however; they only account for individuals that fell under the UNHCR's mandate, and evidence suggests that at the start of 2008 there may be as many as 67 million displaced persons. Additionally, though not considered displaced *per se*, there are about 12 million stateless people worldwide (UNHCR 2008). This does not include the additional millions of children and women kidnapped by crime rings in the huge sex-trafficking trade and smuggled across borders as captives for prostitution.

Refugees and displaced persons alike are often the victims of war and political violence. For example, **genocide** in Rwanda in 1994 drove more than 1.7 million refugees from their homeland; the persecution, **ethnic cleansing,** and armed conflict that accompanied the breakup of the former Yugoslavia uprooted nearly 3 million victims, moving Europe to the list of continents with large numbers of refugees—over 6 million—for the first time since World War II. More recently, UNHCR estimates that more than 1.2 million Iraqis were displaced within their country between 2006 and 2008. Renewed fighting between government armed forces and militia groups, as well as widespread human rights violations, caused over a half million Congolese to flee their homes. In Somalia, the renewal of armed conflict led to roughly one million IDPs by the start of 2008.

■ **human security**
a measure popular in liberal theory of the degree to which the welfare of individuals is protected and promoted, in contrast to realist theory's emphasis on putting the state's interests in military and national security ahead of all other goals.

■ **refugees**
people who flee for safety to another country because of a well-founded fear of political persecution, environmental degradation, or famine.

■ **genocide**
the attempt to eliminate, in whole or in part, an ethnic, racial, religious, or national minority group.

■ **ethnic cleansing**
the extermination of an ethnic minority group by a state, in violation of international law.

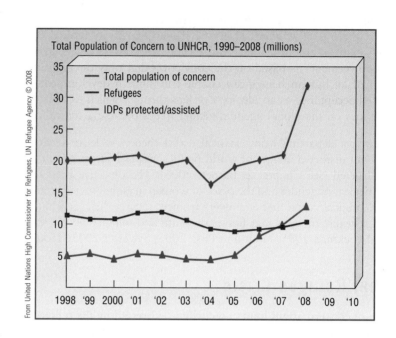

FIGURE 8.3

THE CHRONIC GLOBAL REFUGEE CRISIS **The "persons of concern" to the UN Refugee Agency (UNHCR) includes refugees and internally displaced persons (IDPs). The problem is huge and has become steadily worse since 2004, climbing to over 31.7 million at the start of 2008.**

A large proportion of the world's refugees and displaced people flee their own homelands when ethnic and religious conflicts erupt in failed states without government to preserve domestic law and order. In addition, millions of refugees flee their homelands because when disaster strikes they are denied basic human rights such as police protection, access to fair trials in courts, and public assistance. A combination of push-and-pull forces now propels migration trends (Parker and Brassett 2005). Human rights violations, environmental degradation, unemployment, overpopulation, famine, war, and ethnic conflict and **atrocities** within states—all push millions beyond their homelands. Migrants also are pulled abroad by the promise of political freedom elsewhere, particularly in the democratically ruled Global North countries. "We are now faced with a complex mix of global challenges that could threaten even more forced displacement in the future," explains António Guterres, the UN high commissioner. "They range from multiple new conflict-related emergencies in world hot spots to bad governance, climate-induced environmental degradation that increases competition for scarce resources and extreme price hikes that have hit the poor the hardest and are generating instability in many places" (*International Herald Tribune*, June 19, 2009, 3). While it is commonly assumed that Western states admit the most refugees from conflict, evidence indicates instead that most refugees flee to neighboring countries. Indeed, the UNHCR estimates that between 83 and 90 percent of refugees remain within their region of origin.

■ **atrocities**

brutal and savage acts against targeted citizen groups or prisoners of war, defined as illegal under international law.

Yet today's refugees are not finding safe havens; shutting the door is increasingly viewed as a solution (Parker 2005) and **xenophobia** is on the rise. Among both developed and developing countries, there is a growing unwillingness to provide refuge for those seeking a better life. Construction of a "great wall of America," intended to prevent migration over the U.S.—Mexico border, continues. In 2008, the European Parliament approved controversial immigration rules that provided for illegal immigrants to be detained up to 18 months and then expelled. And developing countries are also imposing tougher standards for admission. Security concerns since

■ **xenophobia**

the suspicious dislike, disrespect, and disregard for members of a foreign nationality, ethnic, or linguistic group.

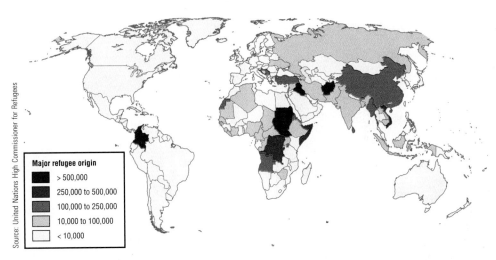

MAP 8.3

FROM WHENCE DO THEY FLEE? Oppressive and violent conditions cause many people to leave their homes in the interest of security and survival. Comprising 27 percent of the global refugee population, Afghanistan continued to be the leading country of origin. At the start of 2008, there were roughly 3.1 million Afghan refugees with 96 percent of them fleeing to Pakistan and Iran. Iraq was the second largest country of origin, responsible for 2.3 million displaced persons. Together, Afghanistan and Iraq accounted for almost half of the global refugee population. Colombia followed as third with over 550,000 refugees.

9/11 have escalated worldwide, and the linkage drawn between refugees and the probability of terrorism has tightened immigration controls. With a weakening global economy, people are ever more resistant to foreigners competing for domestic jobs or resources. And developing countries are increasingly unwilling to bear the burden of hosting refugees. This places blame for insecurity on the victims—refugees seeking refuge—because "as a general rule, individuals and communities do not abandon their homes unless they are confronted with serious threats to their lives and liberty. Flight from one's country is the ultimate survival strategy. . . . Refugees serve both as an index of internal disorder and the violation of human rights and humanitarian standards" (Loescher 2005).

That said, efforts to stem the tide in a borderless world have not reversed the trend of people seeking **sanctuary**. By the start of 2008, a total of 647,200 applications for **asylum** or refugee status were submitted to governments and UNHCR offices in 154 countries. This represented the first increase in 4 years and constituted a 5 percent increase over the prior year, due in part to the large number of Iraqis seeking international protection in Europe.

The ethical issue is whether in the future the wealthy countries will respond to the plight of the needy with indifference or with compassion. How will human security be reconciled with **national security**? The welfare and survival of everyday people are endangered, and the need for their protection is increasing. But that is not the end of the story. Other people suffer as well.

■ **sanctuary**

a place of refuge and protection.

■ **asylum**

the provision of sanctuary to safeguard refugees escaping from the threat of persecution in the country where they hold citizenship.

■ **national security**

a country's psychological freedom from fears that the state will be unable to resist threats to its survival and national values emanating from abroad or at home.

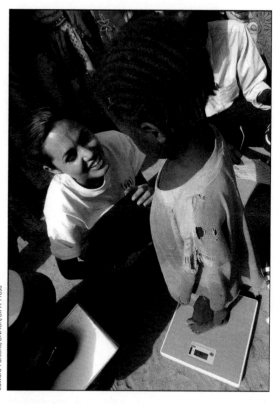

John Moore/Getty Images

Edward Parsons/UNHCR/SIPA Press

DESPERATE REFUGEES ON THE RUN. On average, over the last decade about 15 million refugees *each year* have become homeless people in search of sanctuary. Shown here (left) is one example: immigrants from Zimbabwe that are trying to get into a refugee center in Johannesburg South Africa. Political violence surrounded the illegitimate re-election of President Robert Mugabe in June 2008, with some saying "they had been coerced, fearing punishment or even death unless they could produce a finger colored with red ink as evidence of having cast a ballot" (*International Herald Tribune* June 28–29 2008, 3). Shown to the right is movie star Angelina Jolie, who visited the Oure Cassoni camp in March 2007 "to draw the world's attention to 26,000 refugees residing there in constant danger." "I had to do something to help," Jolie explained.

The Precarious Life of Indigenous Peoples in the Fourth World

As you learned in Chapter 7's introduction to *nonstate actors*, *indigenous peoples* are representative of one type of ethnic and cultural group that were once native to a geographic location now controlled by another state. The globe is populated by an estimated five thousand separate indigenous groups, each of which has a unique language and culture and strong, often spiritual, ties to an ancestral homeland. In most cases indigenous peoples were at one time politically sovereign and economically self-sufficient. Today as many as three hundred seventy million indigenous peoples known as the "Fourth World" are without a homeland or self-rule and live within the borders of about seventy of the globe's independent countries (see Map 7.1, p. 198).

Karel Prinsloo/AP Photo

ETHNIC CLEANSING. In 1994, ethnic conflict escalated to genocide in Rwanda as the Hutu militia attacked the Tutsi, and later as the Tutsi-dominated Rwandan Patriotic Front retaliated against the Hutus. This photo depicts the results of one such bloodbath, where as many as 800,000 Tutsis died.

Many indigenous peoples feel persecuted because their livelihoods, lands, and cultures are threatened. In part, these fears are inspired by the 130 million indigenous peoples who were slaughtered between 1900 and 1987 by state-sponsored violence in their own countries (Rummel 1994). The mass killing of Armenians by Turks, of Jews (and other groups) by Hitler, of Cambodians by the Khmer Rouge, and of the Tutsi of Rwanda by the Hutu exemplify the atrocities committed during the twentieth century. Responding to the tragedy of the Nazi holocaust, the Polish jurist Raphael Lemkin coined the word *genocide* from the Greek word genos (race, people) and the Latin caedere (to kill), and called for it to be singled out as the gravest violation of human rights, a heinous crime the international community would be morally responsible for punishing. In his view, genocide has several dimensions, including physical (the annihilation of members of a group), biological (measures taken to reduce the reproductive capacity of a group), and cultural (efforts to eliminate a group's language, literature, art, and other institutions).

"Brute force realpolitik," concludes Manus Midlarski (2005), "often provides a rationale rooted in **ethnocentrism** for the physical extermination of victim minorities by leaders claiming genocide is a necessary 'altruistic punishment' for the good of the dominant nationality."

Various native peoples are now fighting back across the globe against the injustice they perceive states to have perpetrated against them. This is not to suggest that all indigenous minority groups are bent on using violence to attain power. The members of many such nonstate nations are divided about objectives, and militants who are

■ ethnocentrism
a propensity to see one's nationality or state as the center of the world and therefore special, with the result that the values and perspectives of other groups are misunderstood and ridiculed.

prepared to fight for independence are usually in a minority. In fact, most Fourth World indigenous movements only seek a greater voice in redirecting the policies and allocation of resources within existing states and are eliciting the support of NGOs and IGOs to pressure states to recognize their claims and protect their rights.

A substantial number of indigenous movements in the last decade have successfully negotiated settlements resulting in *devolution*—the granting of regional political power to increase local self-governance. Examples include the Miskitos in Nicaragua, the Gagauz in Moldova, and most regional separatists in Ethiopia and in India's Assam region. Yet, as suggested by the continuing hostilities between the Chechens and the Russian Federation, resolving clashes between aspiring peoples and established states can be extremely difficult.

The goal expressed in the UN Charter of promoting "universal respect for, and observance of, human rights and fundamental freedoms" for everyone is a challenge for many nationally diverse countries, because protecting the human rights and civil liberties of minority populations is inherently difficult. The division of these states along ethnic and cultural lines makes them inherently fragile. Consider the degree to which minority groups compose many states: for example, the share of indigenous populations in Bolivia is 70 percent and Peru, 40 percent. Or consider the number of distinct languages spoken in some countries, with Indonesia's 670 languages, Nigeria's 410, India's 380, Australia's 250, and Brazil's 210 being conspicuous examples (Durning 1993, 83, 86).

Racism and intolerance are hothouses for fanaticism and violence. The belief that one's nationality is superior to all others undermines the concept of human rights (Clapham 2000). Although interethnic competition is a phenomenon that dates back to Biblical times, it remains a contemporary plague. According to The Minorities at Risk Project (MAR, www.cidcm.umd.edu/MAR, January 7, 2008), since 1998, more than 284 politically motivated minority groups throughout the globe suffered in their home countries from organized discriminatory treatment and mobilized in collective action to defend themselves and promote their self-defined interests. Some analysts predict that conflict within and between ethnically divided states will become a major axis on which twenty-first-century world politics revolves.

Efforts to toughen domestic refugee legislation and criteria for granting asylum raise important ethical issues. Where will the homeless, the desperate, the weak, and the poor find *sanctuary*—a safe place to live where human rights are safeguarded? Will the rich countries act with compassion or respond with indifference? And more broadly, what is the best way to view human security and reconcile it with national security? The policy proposals crafted to address these questions may involve controversial trade-offs, and will thus make the global refugee crisis a topic of intense debate for years to come (see Controversy: What Is Security?).

CONTROVERSY:

WHAT IS SECURITY?

How should security be defined? Policy makers disagree. Some see it primarily in military terms; others in human welfare terms. Underlying the disagreement lies a different conception of what is most important on the global agenda. One tradition gives states first priority and assumes that protecting their territorial integrity must be foremost in the minds of national leaders. Others challenge this conception and give primacy to the security of individual people, arguing that social and environmental protection must therefore be seen as a global priority, because all people depend on a clean, healthy environment for survival.

What do you think? To what extent should human and environmental protection be considered security issues? In considering this question, take into consideration the traditional realist view that national security is essentially the freedom from fear of attack by another country or nonstate terrorists. Realists maintain that armed aggression is a paramount security priority and that preparing for war to prevent war is each state's supreme imperative overriding any other security concerns. Safeguarding the state by military means matters most, and therefore "security" must be defined primarily in terms of each country's capacity to resist armed threats to survival and national values by either foreign enemies or by revolting insurgents at home. This definition puts the protection of entire states' interests first above those of individual people.

In contrast, "human security" has risen as a recent concept that focuses on protecting individuals from *any* threat. The Human Security Centre (2006) elaborates this new conception that derives from *liberal theory* and thought, explaining that "secure states do not automatically mean secure peoples. Protecting citizens from foreign attack may be a necessary condition for the security of individuals, but it is not a sufficient one. Indeed, during the last one hundred years far more people have been killed by their own governments than by foreign armies. All proponents of human security agree that its primary goal is a protection of individuals. But consensus breaks down over what threats individuals should be protected from . . . The UN's *Commission on Human Security* argues that the threat agenda should be broadened to include hunger, disease, and natural disasters because these kill far more people than war, genocide and terrorism combined." Extending this perspective, note that so-called "environmental security" is one of the many points of departure in the "human security" approach to national security that stresses the threat of global environmental degradation to human well-being and welfare throughout the planet. That liberal position "rests primarily on evidence that there has been serious degradation of natural resources (fresh water, soils, forests, fishery resources, and biological diversity) and vital life-support systems (the ozone layer, climate system, oceans, and atmosphere) [and that] these global physical changes . . . are comparable to those associated with most military threats that national security establishments prepare for" (Porter 1995).

Ask yourself, to what extent is the "national security" approach emphasized by realists and the "human security" approach favored by liberals a contradiction and in competition with one another? Are they? Might they instead be complementary and mutually reinforcing? What do you think? Can either type of security be achieved in the absence of the other?

RESPONDING TO HUMAN RIGHTS ABUSES

Laws regulating the practices that sovereign states may use have expanded rapidly in recent years. The human rights revolution has advanced moral progress by breaking states' monopoly on international affairs and over citizens (Ignatieff 2004b). In this sense, liberalism triumphed and *realism* was repudiated, for the human rights

> *The human family is a dysfunctional family. What is needed is a network of structures, institutions, principles and elements of law to help manage in the best possible way the world's common good, which cannot be protected only by individual governments.*
>
> —Diarmuid Martin, Archbishop of Dublin, Ireland

movement has rejected the harsh realist vision expressed by Thomas Hobbes, who argued in the seventeenth century that because world politics is "a war of all against all, the notions of right and wrong, justice and injustice have there no place." Moreover, international law has fundamentally revised the traditional realist protection of the state by redefining the relationship of states to humans. As former UN Secretary-General Kofi Annan often notes, "States are now widely understood to be instruments at the service of their people, and not *vice versa*. When we read the Charter today, we are more than ever conscious that its aim is to protect individual human beings, not to protect those who abuse them."

Khaled Fazaa/AFP/Getty Images

Piers Benetar/Panos Pictures

HUMAN RIGHTS VIOLATIONS. Pictured (left) is a young girl whose impoverished family gave her away in marriage, a fate that befalls girls as young as 8 in Yemen where an average marriage age in rural areas is 12 to 13 years old. On the right, a starving farmer in Afghanistan, Akhtar Mohammed, watches his ten-year-old son, Sher, whom he traded to a wealthy farmer in exchange for a monthly supply of wheat. "What else could I do?" he asked. "I will miss my son, but there was nothing to eat." "Since 1817, more than a dozen international conventions have been signed banning the slave trade. Yet, today there are more slaves than at any time in human history" (Skinner 2008, 62), and children are frequent victims.

Internationally Recognized Human Rights

The body of legal rules and norms designed to protect individual human beings is anchored in the ethical requirement that every person should be treated with equal concern and respect. The path-breaking 1948 *Universal Declaration of Human Rights*, is the most authoritative statement of these norms. It "establishes a broad range of civil and political rights, including freedom of assembly, freedom of thought and expression, and the right to participate in government. The declaration also proclaims that social and economic rights are indispensable, including the right to education, the right to work, and the right to participate in the cultural life of the community. In addition, the preamble boldly asserts that 'it is essential, if man is not to be compelled to have recourse, as a last resort, to rebellion against tyranny and oppression, that human rights should be protected by the rule of law'" (Clapham 2001).

These rights have since been codified and extended in a series of treaties, most notably in the *International Covenant on Civil and Political Rights*, and the *International Covenant on Economic, Social, and Cultural Rights*.

There are many ways to classify the rights listed in these treaties. The international ethicist, Charles Beitz (2001, 271), groups them into five categories:

1 **Rights of the person:** "Life, liberty, and security of the person; privacy and freedom of movement; ownership of property; freedom of thought, conscience, and religion, including freedom of religious teaching and practice 'in public and private'; and prohibition of slavery, torture, and cruel or degrading punishment."

2 **Rights associated with the rule of law:** "Equal recognition before the law and equal protection of the law; effective legal remedy for violation of legal rights; impartial hearing and trial; presumption of innocence; and prohibition of arbitrary arrest."

3 **Political rights:** "Freedom of expression, assembly, and association; the right to take part in government; and periodic and genuine elections by universal and equal suffrage."

> *If you are neutral in a situation of injustice, you have chosen the side of the oppressor*
> —Archbishop Desmund Tutu, Nobel Prize winner

4 **Economic and social rights:** "An adequate standard of living; free choice of employment; protection against unemployment; 'just and favorable remuneration'; the right to join trade unions; 'reasonable limitation of working hours'; free elementary education; social security; and the 'highest attainable standard of physical and mental health.'"

5 **Rights of communities:** "Self-determination and protection of minority cultures."

Fred Peer/Camera Press London

CRUEL AND UNUSUAL, OR SIMPLY USUAL? **The UN Human Rights Commission holds annual sessions that deal with accusations that some UN members are violating human rights treaties. This photo shows the kind of human rights abuse that some countries practice: a person being punished according to Saudi Arabia's Islamic laws.**

Although the multilateral treaties enumerating these rights are legally binding on the states ratifying them, many have either not ratified them or done so with significant reservations. When states specify reservations, they are expressing agreement with the broad declarations of principle contained in these treaties while indicating that they object to certain specific provisions and elect not to be bound by them. The United States, for example, ratified the *International Covenant on Civil and Political Rights* with reservations in 1992, but it has not ratified the *International Covenant on Economic, Social, and Cultural Rights*. As this example illustrates, countries who agree with the general principle that all human beings possess certain rights that cannot be withheld may still disagree on the scope of these rights. Thus, some emphasize rights associated with the rule of law and political rights, whereas others stress the importance of economic and social rights.

The Challenge of Enforcement

Once the content of human rights obligations was enumerated in multilateral treaties, international attention shifted to monitoring their implementation and addressing violations. The policy question now facing the world is what steps can and should be taken to safeguard these rights. Agreement has yet to be reached on the extent to which the international community has a responsibility to intervene in order to enforce human rights. As the International Commission on Intervention and State Sovereignty noted in its report, *The Responsibility to Protect*, "If intervention for human protection purposes is to be accepted, including the possibility of military action, it remains imperative that the international community develop consistent, credible, and enforceable standards to guide state and intergovernmental practice."

Agreement about the principles that should guide **humanitarian intervention** has proven elusive, and that is why contemporary debate is so heated (see Controversy: Should Tyranny and Human Rights Violations Justify Humanitarian Intervention?). The issue is not whether there exists a compelling need and moral obligation to express concerns about populations at risk of slaughter, starvation, or persecution; the issue is about how to craft a just response, when any response will comprise an interference in the domestic affairs of a sovereign state.

■ **humanitarian intervention**
the use of peacekeeping troops by foreign states or international organizations to protect endangered people from gross violations of their human rights and from mass murder.

> *For most of the world's people, the glittering opportunities of the new century are beyond reach . . . The problems may seem insurmountable, but they are not. We have the tools; we have brilliant dedicated people to find answers. All we need is a sense of sharing and the will to change. The will can grow from understanding. Once we care, we can change.*
> —Jimmy Carter, U.S. President

William Schultz, Executive Director of Amnesty International, explains by condemning realists who "regard the pursuit of rights as an unnecessary, sometimes even a dangerous extravagance, often at odds with the national interest. What they seem rarely to garner is that in far more cases than they will allow, defending human rights is a prerequisite to protecting that interest." Human rights buttress political and economic freedom "which in turn tends to bring international trade and prosperity. And governments that treat their own people with tolerance and respect tend to treat their neighbors in the same way."

Humanitarian intervention encompasses the international community's actions to assist the population of a state experiencing unacceptable, persistent levels of human suffering caused by natural disaster, political collapse, or deliberate government policy. Humanitarian intervention is controversial because it pits the legal principle of territorial sovereignty against what some see as a moral duty to protect vulnerable populations from egregious violations of human rights. Because concerns for human rights have gained stature under international law and are being monitored more closely by IGOs and NGOs than ever before, we can expect human rights to receive continuing attention, as long as people are caught in emergency situations such as the threat of famine or genocide.

CONTROVERSY:

SHOULD TYRANNY AND HUMAN RIGHTS VIOLATIONS JUSTIFY HUMANITARIAN INTERVENTION?

Imagine yourself an American on a vacation in a foreign country. You find yourself unjustly imprisoned on accusations that you were transporting illegal drugs, spying for your government, trafficking in the practice and sale of children for prostitution, you name it. You are innocent and you are angry! Your human right to basic civil liberties has been violated. To make matters incredibly worse, you discover that the jail in which you are incarcerated is full of thousands of political prisoners held, and abused, by their guards, who are employed by a military dictatorship that claims the sovereign right to treat all accused lawbreakers any way they want. Never in the authorities' explanation is mention made of human rights, such as trial by a jury of peers and prohibition against the cruel punishment of prisoners.

What can you do? You are an innocent victim. Do you, and for that matter the hundreds of other possibly innocent victims in prison with you, have any hope?

For centuries, the answer was that your fate was hopeless. You had no power. Power was monopolized by state governments, which could do anything and everything to protect and promote their self-interests by preempting potential threats to their self-preservation. That code of conduct, enshrined in the 1648 Westphalian treaties drafted by realists, proclaimed that state authority was sacrosanct and that people and their human rights were subservient. For the state and its rulers, anything goes toward subjects within a sovereign country's territory.

However, there is protection: recently, international law has radically changed. "For nearly 60 years after the creation of the Universal Declaration of Human Rights in 1948, there [was] still no international consensus about when [human] rights violations in one state justify other states to interfere" (Ignatieff 2004a). But no longer. Now protecting human rights in foreign states has become legal for the first time under international law. The law has been "updated 'to close the gap between legality and legitimacy' [so that] rules and international law [now have been changed] to permit armed intervention for humanitarian protection" (Slaughter 2004b). This is hope for justice!

Or is there? An ideology that helps to protect your human rights also undermines the national interests of sovereign states. What may be beneficial for you may be harmful to your country. For instance, the United States cited the sovereign right to imprison suspected culprits of the 9/11 terrorist attacks without the right to legal defense or jury in its military prison in Guantánamo, Cuba, and to the imprisonment and (it was later discovered) inhumane treatment of captives in Iraq—to the outrage of the global community. The United States initially claimed a right to indefinitely detain "enemy combatants" on the grounds of "necessity" in times of warfare—this time against faceless terrorists—though the U.S. Supreme Court later ruled in 2008 that detainees had a constitutional right to challenge their detention in federal court.

Here you are forced to ask, Was that right? Moral? Legal? Should you defend the proclaimed might of your country to do as it pleases in times of alleged war, when that defense will compromise your ability to defend your complaint that your imprisonment was an immoral violation of your basic human rights and civil liberties by a sovereign state, and that complaint will undermine the case that your own government has championed?

So you have a tough issue to face: How can you reconcile your understandable love of country and its claimed sovereign national interests against your personal need to be shielded by a global code of state conduct that puts the human rights of all on an equal footing?

This is a major issue on the global agenda. How would you choose? Keep in mind that your choice between the alternatives of external humanitarian intervention to protect human rights and continuing support for the prohibition of intervention in the internal affairs of other states could matter, if many also agree with you. So which do you put first, country or all of humanity? And as you contemplate this hypothetical controversy, keep in mind many countries' entrenched defense of the traditional right of their state to be protected against foreign intervention—even for humanitarian purposes. Consider the globe's reigning hegemon, the United States, which has placed national security ahead of humanitarian protection and has a long history of supporting state terrorists and dictators to protect America's security interests (see Johnson 2007; Goldsmith 2008). Likewise, many other states, especially the weak and relatively defenseless governments in the Global South, also vigorously resist humanitarian interference within their borders. They maintain that opposition to resist humanitarian intervention within their borders is legal and that movement against the nonintervention norm is not in their interests, either. The rising China agrees vehemently with the Global South and the United States on this point as well.

The global community has expanded its legal protection of human rights significantly over the past fifty years. As Table 8.2 shows, a large number of conventions have been enacted that have steadily endowed individuals with rights—asserting that people must be treated as worthy of the freedom and dignity traditionally granted by international law to states and rulers. Contrary to its intent, however, "the deepening international human rights regime creates opportunities for rights-violating governments to display low-cost legitimating commitments to world norms, leading them to ratify human rights treaties without the capacity or willingness to comply with the provisions" (Hafner-Burton et al. 2008, 115). Sadly, there are some countries that endorse human rights treaties as merely a superficial symbolic commitment and continue to repress human rights.

Table 8.2 Some Major Legal Conventions in the Development of International Human Rights Protection

1948	Universal Declaration of Human Rights
1948	International Convention on the Prevention and the Punishment of the Crime of Genocide
1949	Geneva Convention relative to the Treatment of Prisoners of War
1949	Geneva Convention relative to the Protection of Civilian Persons in Time of War

(continues)

Table 8.2   Some Major Legal Conventions in the Development
of International Human Rights Protection *(continued)*

1950	Convention for the Suppression of the Traffic of Persons and the Exploitation of the Prostitution of Others
1951	Convention on the Status of Refugees
1953	Convention on the Political Rights of Women
1954	Convention on the Status of Stateless Persons
1957	Convention on the Abolition of Forced Labour
1959	Declaration of the Rights of the Child
1961	Convention on the Reduction of Statelessness
1965	International Convention on the Elimination of All Forms of Racial Discrimination
1966	International Covenant on Civil and Political Rights
1966	Declaration of the Principles of International Cultural Co-operation
1967	Convention on the Elimination of All Forms of Discrimination against Women
1967	Declaration on Territorial Asylum
1969	Inter-American Convention on Human Rights
1971	Declaration on the Rights of Mentally Retarded Persons
1973	International Convention on the Suppression and Punishment of the Crime of Apartheid
1974	Declaration on the Protection of Women and Children in Emergency and Armed Conflict
1975	Declaration on the Protection of All Persons from Being Subjected to Torture and Other Cruel, Inhumane or Degrading Treatment or Punishment
1975	Declaration on the Rights of Disabled Persons
1978	Convention on the Protection of the Right to Organize and Procedures for Determining Conditions of Employment in the Public Service
1979	Convention on the Elimination of All Forms of Discrimination against Women

(continues)

Table 8.2 Some Major Legal Conventions in the Development of International Human Rights Protection *(continued)*

Year	Convention
1981	Convention on the Promotion of Collective Bargaining
1984	Safeguards Guaranteeing Protection of the Rights of Those Facing the Death Penalty
1985	Declaration of Basic Principles of Justice for Victims of Crime and Abuse of Power
1985	Declaration on the Human Rights of Individuals Who Are Not Nationals of the Country in Which They Live
1988	Body of Principles for the Protection of All Persons under Any Form of Detention or Imprisonment
1989	Convention on the Rights of the Child
1989	Convention on Indigenous and Tribal Peoples in Independent Countries
1990	Basic Principles for the Treatment of Prisoners
1990	Basic Principles on the Role of Lawyers
1990	United Nations Rules for the Protection of Juveniles Deprived of Their Liberty
1990	International Convention on the Protection of the Rights of All Migrant Workers and Members of Their Families
1991	Convention on the Prevention and Suppression of Genocide
1991	Principles for the Protection of Persons with Mental Illness
1992	Declaration on the Rights of Persons Belonging to National or Ethnic, Religious or Linguistic Minorities
1993	Vienna Convention on Human Rights
1993	Declaration on the Elimination of Violence against Women
1997	Universal Declaration on the Human Genome and Human Rights
2000	Convention Prohibiting Trafficking of Women and Children for Prostitution
2002	Protocol to the Convention against Torture and Other Cruel, Inhumane or Degrading Treatment or Punishment
2006	Convention on the Rights of Persons with Disabilities

The old assumption that national sovereignty trumps all other principles in international relations is under attack as never before.

—David Rieff, security analyst

Promoting the rights and dignity of ordinary people around the world is a formidable challenge. Although some individuals believe that everyone, by virtue of being human, has certain inherent and inalienable rights that warrant international protection, others remain skeptical of claims that we all have transcendent moral obligations to humanity as a whole. The idea of a humanitarian imperative—a conviction that human suffering obliges others to respond—has ancient roots. From Zeno (335–263 BCE) and Chrysippus (250–207 BCE) through Seneca (4 BCE–65 CE) and Marcus Aurelius (121–180 CE), Greek and Roman Stoics believed in the equality and unity of humankind. Eleanor Roosevelt was a modern champion of this *cosmopolitan* ideal, and the energetic leadership she displayed was largely responsible for global acceptance in 1948 of the *Universal Declaration of Human Rights*. Her noble pursuit shows that one person can make a difference in transforming world politics. When thinking about the human condition in the early twenty-first century, we can profit by the inspiration of her nightly prayer: "Save us from ourselves and show us a vision of a world made new."

In Part III you will have an opportunity to examine trends in the economic and demographic conditions that prevail as the cascading globalization of world politics accelerates. This survey can aid understanding of the world as it presently exists and allow you to contemplate, as caring global citizens, the prospects for transformations that could create a better world.

Key Terms

agency
ethics
morality
civil society
human rights
sanctions
globalization
human needs

Human Development Index (HDI)
purchasing power parity (PPP)
Gender Empowerment Measure
    (GEM)
gender inequalities
human security
refugees
genocide

ethnic cleansing
atrocities
xenophobia
sanctuary
asylum
national security
ethnocentrism
humanitarian intervention

CULTURE AND COMMERCE IN A GLOBALIZED WORLD The growing
web of globalization is creating an interdependent world. Shown here are the
2008 Beijing Olympics, which opened with a celebration of Chinese culture and
international goodwill. Originally founded to promote peace and bridge cultural
divides, the naissance spirit of the Olympic games was reflected in Chinese
President Hu Jintao's pronouncement that "The world has never needed mutual
understanding, mutual toleration and mutual cooperation as much as it does today."
Yet critics have charged that the Olympics have devolved into "a form of amoral
universalism in which all countries are entitled to take part in the games no matter
how barbaric their leaders may be" (Hoberman 2008, 22). As evidence of this, they
point to crass commercialism, the masking of human rights abuse, and the air of
legitimacy granted to unsavory governments.

Part 3

THE ECONOMIC AND DEMOGRAPHIC DIMENSIONS OF GLOBALIZATION

"The rich and poor worlds are linked as never before—by economics and trade, migration, climate change, disease, drugs, conflict and yes, terrorism. We know that elections are won and lost on local issues—that is true for every country. But it is global issues . . . that will shape the world our children live in."

— *James Wolfenshohn, former World Bank President*

AS MONEY, GOODS, AND PEOPLE TRAVEL ACROSS NATIONAL BORDERS WITH BLINDING SPEED, GLOBALIZATION IS TRANSFORMING WORLD POLITICS. What happens in one place influences what happens every place, just as how people live in any one place affects how people live everywhere else. The chapters in Part 3 portray the ways in which the erosion of national borders is transforming international relations. Chapter 9 inspects how the globalization of finance is altering the international economic landscape, and Chapter 10 inspects how the globalization of international trade is transforming the world. Chapter 11 then examines the demographic dimensions of globalization as well as how the rise of the global information age is shaping perceptions worldwide of culture and identity.

CHAPTER 9
THE GLOBALIZATION OF INTERNATIONAL FINANCE

Globalization is no longer a buzzword: it has arrived. There is substantial evidence for an increasingly globalized marketplace. World trade is expanding much faster than world production and cross-border investments are growing at a more rapid rate than trade. People in one country are more likely to be affected by economic actions in other nations in many capabilities: as customers, entrepreneurs and investors, managers and taxpayers, and citizens.

—Murray Weidenbaum, political economist

Jose Luis Magana/AP Photo

Money Matters. Currency now moves effortlessly across borders, and the globalization of international finance is wrecking havoc on the efforts of state governments to control rapid fluctuations in the rates at which their national currencies are exchanged with those of other countries. Shown here is an example of how monetary policies sometimes unleash hostile feelings: Activists protest during the International Monetary Fund's 2008 spring meetings in Washington, D.C.

"Money makes the world go 'round." "Money is the root of all evil." "All that glitters is not gold." "Money can't buy you happiness." "There's hell in not making money."

You have all heard these old sayings at one time or another. They all contain elements of truth, even though such aphorisms and clichés are somewhat contradictory. Your challenge is to separate fact from fantasy by sorting out the place of money in your life and in the world in which you live. This task will heavily depend on your personal values and preferences. However, the wisdom or folly of your conclusions will depend on your analytic skills in evaluating how money is a factor affecting many dimensions of world politics—and your own personal future financial fate.

Increasingly, this age-old intellectual task is more difficult than in the past. Today, more than ever, money truly *is* moving around the world, and at ever-quickening speed. And the rapidity of the movement of finance capital across borders directly affects your quality of life every day. When you make a purchase, the odds are now very high that the goods have been produced overseas. What is more, when you buy a sandwich, a sweater, a car, or gasoline to make it run, the cost of your payment is very likely to be affected by the rate at which your own country's currency is valued and exchanged for the currency of the producer abroad. Should you have the opportunity to travel overseas for work or for tourism, you will instantly discover how powerfully the global exchange of national currencies will determine whether you can afford to attend a rock concert or buy an extra bottle of wine.

This chapter is about how money markets in the global financial system operate. It looks at the processes governing currency exchanges, concentrating on how the transfer of money across borders affects levels of national prosperity and human security. Note that this topic is part of the larger one of international economics in general, and serves as an introduction to the coverage in Chapter 10 on international trade in the global political economy. Neither dimension of international economics—money and marketplaces for trade—can be considered without the other; the two are tied intimately, and only by looking at both together can you gain an understanding of

> *The importance of money essentially flows from its being a link between the present and the future.*
> —John Maynard Keynes, British economist

how money and markets drive the rise and fall of wealth for individuals and for countries. You therefore will be looking at a phenomenon as old as recorded history, and inspecting how it is influencing life in the twenty-first century.

THE GLOBAL CONTEXT FOR INTERPRETING CONTEMPORARY ECONOMIC CHANGE

When changes occur in the world, they force people to think about and interpret world politics in fresh ways. Of all the many recent changes, perhaps none has been more continually invasive and far-reaching than those occurring in the economic world. This is one of the main playing fields on which the game of world politics is

■ **geo-economics**

the relationship between geography and the economic conditions and behavior of states that define their levels of production, trade, and consumption of goods and services.

■ **geopolitics**

the relationship between geography and politics and their consequences for states' national interests and relative power.

■ **international political economy (IPE)**

the study of the intersection of politics and economics that illuminates why changes occur in the distribution of states' wealth and power.

■ **globalization**

the integration of states through increasing contact, communication, and trade, creating a holistic, single global system in which the process of change increasingly binds people together in a common fate.

played. In fact, to some analysts **geo-economics** (the geographic distribution of wealth) will replace **geopolitics** (the distribution of strategic military and political power) as the most important axis around which international competition will revolve and will determine the globe's future destiny (see Chapter 4). To interpret the dynamics underlying the rules of this geo-economic game, it is helpful to gain perspective by turning to economic *theory* (or a set of propositions that explain why observable repetitions and regularities are evident in some phenomena).

International Political Economy

Fortunately, a large body of theory has been constructed that speaks to the questions about how changes in one country's economics and politics influence trends in world politics. This approach is known as the **international political economy (IPE)**. This area of scholarship investigates a number of topics, such as the political determinants of international economic relations. As Stephen Krasner (2001) elaborates, "International political economy tries to answer such questions as: How have

> *The study of economics is an easy subject,*
> *at which very few excel!*
>
> —John Maynard Keynes, British economist

changes in the international distribution of power among states affected the degree of openness in the international trading system? Do the domestic political economies of some states allow them to compete more effectively in international markets? Is the relative poverty of the [Global South] better explained by indigenous conditions in individual countries or by some attribute of the international economic system? When can economic ties among states be used for political leverage?"

IPE is increasingly important because it is at the vortex of politics and economics that has become so controversial today. Why? Primarily it is because of the **globalization** of world finance and trade. The growth of the interdependence of states' economies can be viewed as the recent culmination of a trend that began more than a century ago, but its current level is without precedent. As states' economies have become more closely linked, basic traditional ideas about states, currency exchange mechanisms, trade, and markets have been reexamined in a new light. The contest between the rich Global North and poor Global South, and supplier and producer, have risen to the top of the global agenda in policy and theoretical debate. The economic game of world politics has assumed increasing importance because the undercurrents in economics are shaping the foundation of international politics. The dramatic growth of international trade and the increasingly interlocked nature of the world's economies have compelled greater and greater attention to economic transactions. Today, high interest rates in one country lead to high interest rates in others. A stock market free fall starting in Asia will spread like wildfire to New York and London. Depression abroad means recession at home. Inflation is shared everywhere, and it now seems beyond the control of any single actor. The balance of fiscal power is now as important to a country's national security as is the global balance of military power. These are some of the consequences of growing international interdependence known as globalization, defined by the International Monetary Fund as "the increasingly close international integration of markets both for goods and services, and for capital."

The Economic Dimensions of Globalization

Globalization has led scholars to rediscover old theories of political economy in order to interpret contemporary world affairs. Scholars and theorists are now reexamining classic mid-nineteenth-century studies such as John Stuart Mill's *Principles of Political Economy* as well as the radical communist theorist Karl Marx's *A Contribution to the Critique of Political Economy*.

This revival has been stimulated by the growing awareness that the conventional categories of politics and economics can no longer be separated into two disciplines. They do not form a meaningful dichotomy. The two realms are now inextricably joined in the era of globalization.

Much of politics is economics, and most of economics is politics.
—Charles E. Lindbolm, political economist

It is important for you to look at globalization in all its dimensions and not just from a single viewpoint. Some regard it as little more than a euphemism for capitalism (Petras and Veltmeyer 2004). But it is more than that. Globalization is a short hand for a cluster of interconnected phenomena and you will find the term used to describe, alternatively, a process, a policy, a predicament, or the product of vast, invisible international forces producing massive changes worldwide. Moreover, most analysts would probably agree that globalization is a permanent trend that has become a global phenomenon leading to the probable *transformation* of world politics—the end of one historic pattern and the beginning of a new one in history.

Perhaps the leading analyst of globalization, political journalist Thomas L. Friedman, thinks this prophecy is accurate: "This new era of globalization will prove to be such a difference of degree that it will be seen, in time, as a difference in kind. . . . The world has gone from round to flat. If I am right about the flattening of the world, it will be remembered as one of those fundamental changes—like the rise of the nation-state or the Industrial Revolution—each of which, in its day, produced changes in the role of individuals, the role and form of governments, the way we innovated [and] the way we conducted business."

What Is Globalization?

Friedman raises the rhetorical question for you to consider in the context of evaluating the financial dimensions of globalization:

> What is globalization? The short answer is that globalization is the integration of everything with everything else. A more complete definition is that globalization is the integration of markets, finance, and technology in a way that shrinks the world from a size medium to a size small. Globalization enables each of us, wherever we live, to reach around the world farther, faster, deeper, and cheaper than ever before and at the same time allows the world to reach into each of us farther, faster, deeper, and cheaper than ever before.

Now is your opportunity to test this proposition with respect to the globalization of international finance and capital. So focus your attention on the dynamics of the floating **international monetary system** through which currencies and credits are calculated in our borderless world when capital moves across national boundaries through investments, trade, foreign aid, and loans.

MONEY MATTERS: THE TRANSNATIONAL EXCHANGE OF MONEY

Part of the equation on which global economic destiny depends is the character of **laissez-faire** capitalism without regulation above states. State governments have taken some tentative steps to create rules for adjusting their currencies with one another and stabilizing wide fluctuations in their exchange rates. However, the process through which money between and among countries is exchanged after financial transactions have been conducted does not have strong supranational regulatory institutions. Those transactions, as noted, are escalating with feverish pitch. What does this trend mean?

The Globalization of Finance

Global finance encompasses "all types of cross-border portfolio-type transactions—borrowing and lending, trading of currencies or other monetary claims, and the provision of commercial banking or other financial services. It also includes capital flows associated with foreign direct investment—transactions involving significant control of producing enterprises" (Cohen 1996; 2005). The **globalization of finance** refers to the increasing transnationalization or centralization of financial markets through the worldwide integration of capital flows. The central characteristic of the emerging consolidated system of financial arrangements is that it is not centered on a single state. Thus, globalization implies the growth of a single, unified *global* market. Whereas telecommunications specialists talk about the "death of distance," financial specialists talk about the "end of geography" because geographic location is no longer important to finance.

Evidence of financial globalization abounds. Although trade has grown dramatically, since World War II the volume of cross-border capital flows has increased even more. The daily turnover in foreign currency markets has more than doubled between 1989 and 2001, and since 1973 has grown a staggering sixty times faster than the value of world trade (McGrew 2005, 212). Another indicator of the expansion of the global capital market is captured by the fact that it has increased at twice the rate of global GDP, fueled in part by the explosion of hedge-fund trading worldwide that reached in the year 2007 $69.8 *trillion* (*Economist*, May 26, 2007, 75).

This flow of capital is not entirely new. In an early form of globalization, a network of financial centers flourished along the Baltic and North Seas, and city-states such as Lübeck, Hamburg and Bergen dominated finance and trading. Since then, major ups and downs have occurred in the major secondary financial centers. At the turn of the nineteenth century, London supplanted Amsterdam as the world's leading financial center, and New York began to rival London in the early twentieth century—antecedents of today's shifting financial hubs to Tokyo, Singapore, and Dubai (see Cassis 2007). These cycles notwithstanding, what is different now is the speed and spread of the movement of finance capital throughout the entire globe. Financial centers are proliferating, and big transactions are made by many participants "sitting in front of computer screens, moving zillions of dollars, pounds, euros and yen around the globe at the flick of a key. Technology, the mobility of capital and the spread of deregulation around the globe have created a vibrant and growing network . . . between financial centers as investors have diversified across regions. Yet interconnectedness has a cost. In an era of greater volatility, the latest market news spreads from one continent to another in an instant" (*Economist*, September 15, 2007). This is today's globalized finance that links the world at unprecedented levels, connecting capital, people and exchanges as these trends expand cross-border consolidation. Next we take a closer look at these global economic dynamics and their consequences for the global future.

The Rising Flow of Capital across Borders

A catalyst to the growth of financial globalization has been the activities of private currency traders. These people speculate on the changing value of different countries' currencies in the hopes that they can reap immediate profits by buying one currency at a lower rate than it can be sold the next day or week. These private currency investors engage in what is known as **arbitrage**. The volume of arbitrage traders routinely exceeds $2 trillion daily, and the level of their transactions has been steadily climbing.

As a result of increasing cross-border capital flows, the global financial market has become increasingly interconnected. This has made imperative the need for a reliable system of money exchange across borders to cope with the broad array of fluctuating national currencies. The daily turnover on the global currency markets often is greater now than the global stock of official foreign exchange reserves, and this has practically eliminated the capacity of government central banks to influence exchange rates by buying and selling currency in those markets.

Globalization has cost states a huge measure of the control that they formerly could exercise over the value of their currencies internationally. The powerlessness of the U.S. government to raise the price of the Chinese yuan against the U.S. dollar between 2005 and 2008 (to reduce the huge U.S. balance-of-trade deficit) speaks volumes to the breakdown of governments' ability to modify the rates at which their currencies are exchanged. "Most central banks are now irrelevant" (Thurow 1998).

The integration of the global economy has also tightened the webs of financial interdependence of states. As the market value of stock transactions increased fivefold between 1980 and 2008, a major change occurred: a rise or fall in the security market of any one state began to immediately cause similar changes in other countries' stock indexes. In addition, "derivatives" emerged, leading to new markets in which stocks are traded. Derivatives combine speculation in options and futures to hedge against volatility in financial markets, but they require no actual purchase of stocks or bonds. Derivatives account for trillions of dollars in cross-border transactions and are now estimated to be the most globalized financial market.

■ **arbitrage**
the selling of one currency (or product) and purchase of another to make a profit on changing exchange rates; traders ("arbitragers") help to keep states' currencies in balance through their speculative efforts to buy large quantities of devalued currencies and sell them in countries where they are more highly valued.

■ **digital world economy**

a system based largely on globalized electronic debt and credit transfers.

■ **commercial liberalism**

an economic theory advocating free markets and the removal of barriers to the flow of trade and capital as a locomotive for prosperity.

■ **capital mobility hypothesis**

the proposition that the massive movement of investment capital across state borders has led to the globalization of finance.

Automated online trading for equity sales on the Internet in the emerging **digital world economy** has lowered the costs and increased the volume of such cross-border exchanges. It also has contributed to the rise of global portfolio equity investments and nonbank credit flows through dedicated bond purchases to their highest levels in the past seven years—$225 billion in 2004—as the Institute of International Finance has reported.

The computerization of financial transactions and contracts occurred at the same time that **commercial liberalism** and its advocacy of state deregulation of global investments and capital movements gained acceptance. States reduced their authority by relaxing their legal control over their economies and by opening their markets to foreign capital.

The predictable result of financial liberalization has been great increases in capital mobility—an exploding expansion of international financial transactions. According to the **capital mobility hypothesis** the free or unregulated flow of money across borders has globalized finance capital. Mobile money in an increasingly open global marketplace translates into financial markets no longer centered within states. This creates a loss of state power to manage the level of finance in their national economies or to contain the increasing power of private markets and corporations. However, there is a payoff: "financial globalization has exerted a disciplinary effect on the conduct of policies, because international capital flows adversely respond to imprudent macroeconomic policies. . . . Similarly, with monetary policy increasingly focused on inflation control, inflation rates have been decreasing across the globe" (IMF 2005). With globalization undermining states' regulatory capabilities, the assumption of realist theory that states are autonomous, unitary actors in control of their own international economic affairs is being undermined: "'realist orthodoxy' . . . has trouble integrating change, especially globalization and the rise of nonstate actors" (Hoffmann 2005).

The lightning speed of capital mobility has made national markets extremely volatile and vulnerable to sudden reversals caused by their dependence on foreign capital and the rapid flight of capital at the first sign of economic trouble. Capital mobility is at historically high levels, having tripled since 1990 as a share of world GDP, with the high-income Global North and Global East economies still accounting for the lion's share of the flow (see Map 9.1). But that distribution is changing, with increasing shares of capital flight directed to the Global South. And now all types of external finance (through banks, portfolio and equity investments, and foreign direct investments) are soaring, especially *foreign direct investments (FDI)* that have increased twelvefold since 1980 (Oatley 2008, 169). The increasing proportion of global finance capital being directed to the Global South and especially the Global East is widely accounted for by these countries' economic liberalization reforms and the falling costs of cross-border transportation and communication.

Nonetheless, the globalization of finance and "capital flight" has resulted in inequalities. True, all countries are mutually vulnerable to rapid transfers of capital in an interdependent, globalized financial world. But the Global South is the most dependent and vulnerable. This circumstance suggests why bankers and economists have called for the creation of more reliable multilateral mechanisms for policy coordination to better manage the massive movement of cross-border capital. For instance, in 2004 Director-General Juan Somavia of the International Labour

Organization called for a new compact of different institutions to steer globalization, which is "changing the policy landscape and distribution of power and gains" in order to better defend "social justice for all seekers of sustainable growth."

As capital has become increasingly mobile under conditions of cascading globalization fueled by the rapid expansion of international trade (see Chapter 10), concern and debate have understandably increased about the monetary factors underlying trade transactions. Controversies have risen over whether the international monetary system in place is causing inequalities or, worse still, reducing growth in international commerce. States' exports and imports depend on many factors, of course, such as changes in global demand for the goods and services that

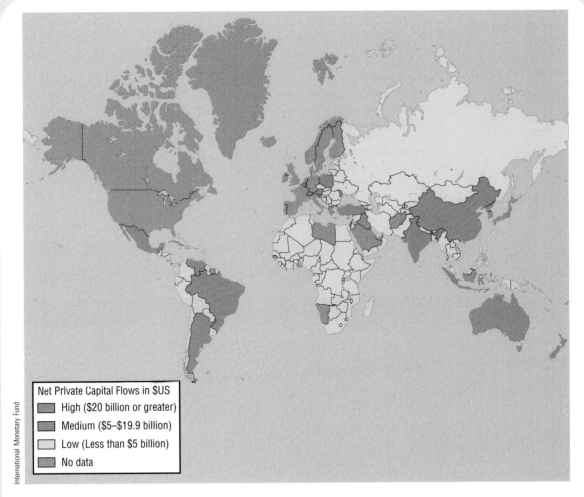

MAP 9.1

THE INTERNATIONAL FLOW OF FINANCE CAPITAL **The movement of capital across borders has expanded greatly since the 1950s. On the eve of World War I, about 25 percent of the world stock of foreign capital was sent equally to both rich and poor countries. Today, however, the Global South receives less than 5 percent of world finance capital. This "financial divide," like the "digital divide" between the Global North and the Global South, makes the international flow of finance capital look less globalized than regionalized.**

■ **monetary system**

the processes for determining the rate at which each state's currency is valued against the currency of every other state, so that purchasers and sellers can calculate the costs of financial transactions across borders such as foreign investments, trade, and cross-border travel.

■ **exchange rate**

the rate at which one state's currency is exchanged for another state's currency in the global marketplace.

countries' producers sell and the prices they charge in the global marketplace. Among these, the mechanisms for setting the currency exchange rate by which goods are priced heavily influence changes in the flow of international trade across borders. Indeed, the **monetary system** is the most critical factor allowing for international trade. Without a stable and predictable method for calculating the value of sales and foreign investments, those transactions would become too risky. Trade in investment activities would fall. Trade requires the transfer of money, and it is supported by a predictable global monetary system to determine the price or **exchange rate** of one national currency in relation to another.

The Nuts and Bolts of Monetary Policy

Monetary and financial policies are woven into a complex set of relationships between states and the global system. Because monetary and currency issues have their own specialized technical terminology (see Table 9.1), they are difficult to understand. However, the essentials are rather basic:

> **Monetary policy** works on two principal economic variables: the aggregate supply of money in circulation and the level of interest rates. The **money supply** (currency plus commercial bank demand deposits) is thought to be directly related to the level of economic activity in the sense that a greater money supply induces expanded economic activity by enabling people to purchase more goods and services. This in essence is the monetarist theory of economic activity. Its advocates argue that by controlling the growth of the money supply, governments can regulate their nations' economic activity and control inflation. (Todaro 2000, 657)

Table 9.1   Understanding Currency: Basic Terms and Concepts

Term	Concept
Balance of Payments	A calculation summarizing a country's financial transactions with the external world, determined by the level of credits (export earnings, profits from foreign investment, receipts of foreign aid) minus the country's total international debts (imports, interest payments on international debts, foreign direct investments, and the like). A favorable balance of payments is achieved when a country's international credits exceed its national debits, as recorded in its current account (the market value of exports and imports with the rest of the world) and its capital account (the ratio of a country's private and foreign investments flowing into and out of the country).
Balance-of-Trade Deficit	A situation that results when a state buys more from abroad than it sells. The balance measures both the value of merchandise goods and services imported and exported. To correct a payments deficit, a country has available three basic but painful options: (1) its government can initiate deflationary policies at home by raising interest rates to tighten budgets; (2) it can restrict the outflow of money by imposing higher tariffs, import quotas, or other restrictions; or (3) it can borrow in capital markets or liquidate its foreign exchange reserves.

(continues)

Table 9.1 Understanding Currency: Basic Terms and Concepts *(continued)*

Term	Concept
Central Bank	A state's major agency in charge of issuing its currency, managing its foreign resources, putting the government's monetary policies into practice, and acting as a bank for the government and for the state's commercial bank.
Devaluation	The lowering of the official exchange rate of one country's currency relative to other currencies. This is generally done to increase exports, as devaluation lowers the relative prices of a country's exports. However, it can also reduce the spending power of citizens within that country.
Exchange Rate	The rate at which one state's currency is exchanged for another state's currency in the global marketplace. For example, on June 28, 2008, for one U.S. dollar you would have received .63 euros or 10.31 Mexican pesos. Exchange rates are subject to constant fluctuations. Daily changes are generally quite small, though they can vary greatly over the long run. For example, on June 28, 2001, the U.S. dollar was worth 1.17 euros and 9.08 Mexican pesos.
External Debt	According to the UN, "Debt owed by a country to nonresidents repayable in foreign currency, goods, and services."
Fixed Exchange Rate	A system in which a government sets the value of its currency at a fixed rate for exchange in relation to another country's currency (usually the U.S. dollar) so that the exchange value is not free to fluctuate in the global money market.
Floating Exchange Rate	The system that replaced the Bretton Woods system of fixed exchange rates in the early 1970s, when the link between the dollar and gold was severed. Market forces, rather than government interventions, are expected to adjust the relative value of states' currencies to reflect the underlying strengths and weaknesses of their economies. In principle, a floating exchange rate is based on the expectation that imbalances in states' payments to one another will more or less automatically adjust themselves in association with changes in supply and demand in foreign exchange markets.
Fixed-but-Adjustable Exchange Rate System	A system in which a government fixes its currency in relation to that of another country's currency, but may still change the fixed price to reflect changes in the underlying strengths and weaknesses of their economies. The general expectation is that such changes are rare and only occur under specially-defined circumstances.

To understand the importance of a state's monetary policy as a determinant of their trade, growth rates, and wealth, consider both why exchange rates fluctuate daily, often widely, and the impact of these currency fluctuations. Money works in several ways and serves different purposes. First, money must be widely accepted, so that people earning it can use it to buy goods and services from others. Second, money must serve to store value, so that people will be willing to keep some of their wealth in the form of money. Third, money must act as a standard of deferred payment, so that people will be willing to lend money knowing that when the money is repaid in the future, it will still have purchasing power.

Governments attempt to manage their currencies to prevent inflation. Inflation occurs when the government creates too much money in relation to the goods and services produced in the economy. As money becomes more plentiful and thus less acceptable, it cannot serve effectively to store value or to satisfy debts or serve well as a medium of exchange; however, a restrictive monetary policy that reduces the amount of money in circulation tends to decrease inflation, but increase unemployment rates.

Movements in a state's exchange rate occur in part when changes develop in peoples' assessment of the national currency's underlying economic strength or the ability of its government to maintain the value of its money. A deficit in a country's balance of payments, for example, would likely cause a decline in the value of its currency relative to that of other countries. This happens when the supply of the currency is greater than the demand for it. Similarly, when those engaged in international economic transactions change their expectations about a currency's future value, they might reschedule their lending and borrowing. Fluctuations in the exchange rate could follow.

Arbitrage speculators who buy and sell money also affect the international stability of a country's currency. Speculators make money by guessing the future. If, for instance, they believe that the Japanese yen will be worth more in three months than it is now, they can buy yen today and sell them for a profit three months later. Conversely, if they believe that the yen will be worth less in three months, they can sell yen today for a certain number of dollars and then buy back the same yen in three months for fewer dollars, making a profit. The globalization of finance now also encourages managers of investment portfolios to rapidly move funds from one currency to another in order to realize gains from differences in states' interest rates and the declining value of other currencies in the global network of exchange rates. Short-term financial flows are now the norm: The International Monetary Fund estimates that more than 80 percent of hedging and arbitrage transactions are to round-trip operations taking a week or less.

In the same way that governments try to protect the value of their currencies at home, they often try to protect them internationally by intervening in currency markets. Their willingness to do so is important to importers and exporters, who depend on orderliness and predictability in the value of the currencies they deal in to carry out transnational exchanges. Governments intervene when countries' central banks buy or sell currencies to change the value of their own currencies in relation to those of others. Unlike speculators, however, governments are pledged not to manipulate exchange rates so as to gain unfair advantages, for states' reputations as custodians of monetary stability are valuable. Whether governments can affect their currencies' values in the face of large transnational movements of capital is, however, increasingly questionable. So is the value of any country's currency in relation to any other's (see Figure 9.1).

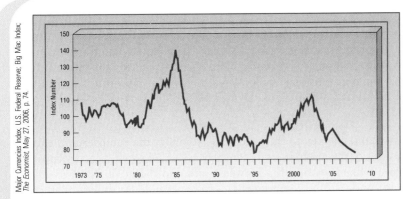

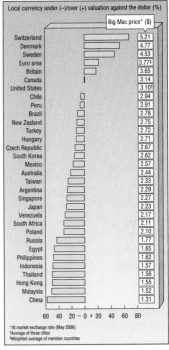

FIGURE 9.1

CALCULATING THE CHANGING COSTS OF GOODS IN THE GLOBE'S CONFUSING CURRENCY EXCHANGE SYSTEM This figure shows changes over time of the weighted average of the foreign exchange values of the U.S. dollar against a subset of the currencies of a large group of major U.S. trading partners. People from the United States who are traveling abroad must use currency exchange rates to convert the price of purchases there to U.S. dollars, and sometimes become alarmed at the higher price (the U.S. dollar has dropped 50 percent against the euro since 2003). An exchange rate is the price someone must pay in one country's currency to purchase one unit of another country's currency. Economists usually calculate currency exchange rates in terms of purchasing power of parity (PPP) because that index of the value of exchange rates measures the cost of identical goods or services in any two countries. On the right this index uses a McDonald's Big Mac which is available for sale in more than 130 countries. The least expensive burger could be purchased in China for $1.31 (10.5 yuan at the May 27, 2006, exchange rate), versus an average price of $3.10 in the United States. To make the two prices equal would require an exchange rate of 3.39 yuan to the dollar, rather than the market rate of 8.03, implying that the yuan was undervalued against the dollar at this point in time, where the euro was 22 percent overvalued and the Swiss franc was 68 percent overvalued.

The Bretton Woods Monetary System

When in 1944 the leaders of the capitalist West met at Bretton Woods, they were acutely aware of the need to create a reliable mechanism for determining the value of countries' currencies in relation to one another. They agreed to a set of concepts to define monetary and currency policy for conducting international trade and finance. Recognizing that a shared system and vocabulary was a necessary precondition for trade, and from it post–World War II economic recovery and prosperity, the negotiating parties agreed that the postwar monetary regime should be based on **fixed exchange rates**, and they assigned governments primary responsibility for enforcing its rules. In addition, they foresaw the need to create what later became the **International Monetary Fund (IMF)** to help states maintain equilibrium in their balance of payments and stability in their exchange rates with one another. The International Bank for Reconstruction and Development, known as the **World Bank**, was also created to aid recovery from the war.

■ **fixed exchange rates**

a system under which states establish the parity of their currencies and commit to keeping fluctuations in their exchange rates within narrow limits.

■ International Monetary Fund (IMF)

a financial agency now affiliated with the United Nations, established in 1944 to promote international monetary cooperation, free trade, exchange rate stability, and democratic rule by providing financial assistance and loans to countries facing financial crises.

■ World Bank

also known as the International Bank for Reconstruction and Development (IBRD), the World Bank is the globe's major IGO for financing economic growth and reducing poverty through long-term loans.

■ international liquidity

reserve assets used to settle international accounts in the form of dollars.

Today the IMF and World Bank are important, if controversial, players in the global monetary and financial systems. Eighty-five percent of their state members belong to both IGO's that serve as "lenders of last resort" to members facing financial crises (providing those seeking assistance meet the often painful conditions requiring domestic adjustments to strengthen their economies). In the period immediately after World War II, these institutions commanded too little authority and too few resources to cope with the enormous devastation of the war. The United States stepped into the breach.

The U.S. dollar became the key to the hegemonic role that the United States eagerly assumed as manager of the international monetary system. Backed by a vigorous and healthy economy, a fixed relationship between gold and the dollar (pegged at $35 per ounce of gold), and the U.S. commitment to exchange gold for dollars at any time (known as "dollar convertibility"), the dollar became a universally accepted "parallel currency." It was accepted in exchange markets as the reserve used by monetary authorities in most countries and by private banks, corporations, and individuals for international trade and capital transactions.

To maintain the value of their currencies, central banks in other countries used the dollar to raise or depress their value. Thus, the Bretton Woods monetary regime was based on fixed-but-adjustable exchange rates and ultimately required a measure of government intervention for its operation.

To get U.S. dollars into the hands of those who needed them most, the Marshall Plan provided Western European states billions of dollars in aid to buy the U.S. goods necessary for rebuilding their war-torn economies. The United States also encouraged deficits in its own balance of payments as a way of providing **international liquidity**.

In addition to providing liquidity, the United States assumed a disproportionate share of the burden of rejuvenating Western Europe and Japan. It supported European and Japanese trade competitiveness, permitted certain forms of protectionism (such as Japanese restrictions on importing U.S. products), and accepted discrimination against the dollar (as the European Payments Union did by promoting trade within Europe at the expense of trade with the United States). The United States willingly agreed to pay these costs of leadership because subsidizing economic growth in Europe and Japan increased the U.S. export markets and strengthened the West against communism's possible popular appeal.

Although at first the United States acting as the world's banker worked well, the costs grew as the enormous number of dollars held by others made the U.S. economy increasingly vulnerable to financial shocks from abroad. As the British had discovered before, U.S. leadership made it difficult to devalue the dollar to manage inflationary or deflationary pressures at home without harming allies abroad. This situation reduced the United States' ability to use the normal methods available to other states for dealing with the disruption caused by deficits in a country's balance of trade, such as adjusting interest and currency exchange rates.

The End of Bretton Woods

As early as 1960 it was clear that the dollar's top currency status could not be sustained by U.S. preeminence as a global *hegemon*. A number of developments in combination lead to a monetary crisis. In a modern version of the **commercial domino theory**, a "fiscal contagion" spread uncontrollably around the world, wreaking havoc on global capitalism. The fall of fiscal dominos rippling through the world economy had become an increasingly common experience. As the international monetary system became more and more interconnected, capital and currency began to instantaneously move outside borders at the slightest sign of fiscal troubles. In these volatile financial circumstances, any imploding national market (such as when one country's currency reserves were depleted), set panic in motion as investors abroad reduced their holdings and the flight of capital brought down other countries in a chain reaction (Sanger 1998).

For the first time in history a single, integrated global economic system had emerged, and this *transformation* exposed the deficiencies of global financial institutions with unstable fixed and floating currencies. But not much was done to revise and reform the shaky existing global financial architecture. In a world of increasingly mobile capital and the absence of global financial regulation, volatility in capital flows threatens world economic growth.

"Much of the international relations literature concerned with prospects for international monetary reform can be read as a search for an alternative to hegemony as a basis for international monetary stability" (Eichengreen 2000). The need for a reformed system stems in large part from the failure of the United States to adjust its policies so it could continue to serve as a hegemonic stabilizing force in international finance or unilaterally regulate international monetary affairs (Underhill and Zhang 2003).

■ **commercial domino theory**
the proposition that under conditions of globalization the depletion of one country's currency reserves panics investors worldwide and spreads like a contagious disease to other countries, which witness the decline of their own currency reserves as the flight of capital also reduces the value of their currency.

Floating Exchange Rates

In 1971, U.S. President Richard Nixon abruptly announced—without consulting with allies—that the United States would no longer exchange dollars for gold. With the price of gold no longer fixed and dollar convertibility no longer guaranteed, the Bretton Woods system gave way to a substitute system based on **floating exchange rates**. Market forces, rather than government intervention, now determine currency values. A country experiencing adverse economic conditions now sees the value of its currency fall in response to the choices of traders, bankers, and businesspeople. This was expected to make its exports cheaper and its imports more expensive, which in turn would pull its currency's value back toward equilibrium—all without the need for central bankers to support the value of its currency. In this way, it was hoped that the politically humiliating devaluations of the past could be avoided.

Those expectations were not met. Beginning in the late 1970s, escalating in the 1980s, and persisting through the 1990s, a rising wave of financial crises, both in currency and banking, occurred. These crises were (and remain) compounded by massive defaults by countries unable to make interest payments on their debts. This chronic problem in the crushing sea of circulating capital flows throughout the globe has strained the international monetary process to the brink of collapse. A third of the

■ **floating exchange rates**
an unmanaged process in which governments neither establish an official rate for their currencies nor intervene to affect the value of their currencies, and instead allow market forces and private investors to influence the relative rate of exchange for currencies between countries.

GROWING FROM ECONOMIC INTEGRATION **New** skyscrapers—a symbol of *Global East* economic growth—dot the skyline of Shanghai, the venue of the ninth Asia Pacific Economic Cooperation (APEC) forum to respond to growing economic and trade interdependence in the region. Shanghai has joined the ranks of the globe's leading financial centers.

Greg Baker/AP Photo

world's countries have foreign debts in excess of $10 billion, and altogether the Global South countries are facing over $2,742 billion of debt owed to foreigners. Worse still, forty-eight countries have external debt service payments that exceed 5 percent of their total GNI, and eighteen are paying for past debts more than 10 percent (WDI 2007, 250–256). Needless to say, this staggering debt load greatly reduces these countries' capability to chart their future by themselves—as sovereign states are supposed to do. Even the most powerful countries are also vulnerable. The United States may be the reigning hegemon with the globe's largest economy, but it is borrowing from foreign creditors about $2 billion every day to sustain its enormous current account deficit (*Foreign Affairs*, May/June 2007, 93). By the start of 2008 the U.S. government's external debt to foreigners had risen to rival an American economy nearing $14 trillion, while a year earlier foreigners had purchased $7.3 *trillion* of U.S. stocks and bonds (Samuelson 2007, A7). The crash of the dollar against other major currencies by 38 percent since 2002 lies behind the financial crisis that has "tarnished America's image as a financial center" (*Economist*, September 15, 2007, 89).

> *The United States risks undermining the faith foreigners have put in its management of the dollar.*
>
> —Benn Steil, international economist

The International Currency System in Crisis

Financial crises have become increasingly frequent throughout the world as a result of the inability of states to manage their debt, inflation, and interest rates and accrue available income by themselves, and the global monetary circulatory system is experiencing wild currency exchange-rate gyrations. In the past forty-five years, more than one hundred major episodes of banking insolvency occurred in nine of ten rapidly growing Global East countries. This financial disease is also spreading to the Global North countries and their banking institutions. The financial cost of these currency crises, in terms of the percentage of GDP lost, has been huge and threatens to increase. The disastrous debts generated by banking and currency disruptions forced governments to suffer, on average between 1970 and 1997, direct losses of nearly 15 percent of their GDP for *each crisis* as well as more than a 5 percent decline in their economic growth rates following each of these crises (World Bank 1999b, 126).

Liberal theorists attribute the many problems in the existing processes by which currencies are exchanged internationally under globalization to the weak and uncoordinated management of the international monetary system, a structural deficiency that they feel amounts to international anarchy. Liberal reformers raise an

> *The architecture of the international finance system must be reformed to reduce the susceptibility to crises. The ultimate key is not economics or finance, but politics—the art of developing support for strong policy.*
> —Robert Rubin, former U.S. Secretary of the Treasury

even more fundamental question: Is the traditional state system of independent countries up to the task of dealing unilaterally with global problems which defy management by each country acting through *self-help* alone? If not, is the 350-year-old domination of world politics by states finally at an end?

In reaction to growing awareness of the extent to which the global prosperity of each country depends on a stable international currency system, the call has risen with increasing voice about the need for the great powers and all others to collectively coordinate, through multilateral agreements, the stabilization of international exchange rates.

Frederick Brown/AFP/Getty Images

Eric Feferberg/Getty Images

THE DOMINO EFFECT IN GLOBAL FINANCE When a country's banks go bankrupt and its economy collapses, foreign capital flees in panic. No worldwide central bank exists to cushion such crashes. Money problems in one country lead to money problems in others, provoking currency depreciations and plunges in stock prices at home and abroad. Here, stunned brokers react to the plummet of Hong Kong stocks that caused the key indexes in Asia, London, Frankfurt, New York, and Paris to fall. Volatile economic conditions on Wall Street in 2008 have affected markets around the world.

CONTROVERSY:

THE IMF, WORLD BANK, AND STRUCTURAL ADJUSTMENT POLICIES: IS THE "CURE" WORSE THAN THE "DISEASE"?

Protests and riots against the IMF and the World Bank have become relatively commonplace. In some instances, such as the 2003 "Black Friday" protests in Bolivia in which thirty-three people were killed, the violence can turn deadly. In the case of Indonesia in 1998, such protests and riots can sometimes help to overturn a government.

Why is there so much controversy surrounding organizations whose primary purpose is to spur development within the Global South, and whose mission statements include such laudable goals as "global poverty reduction and the improvement of living standards" and fostering "economic growth and high levels of employment"?

Of great contention are Structural Adjustment Policies (SAPs), the package of policy reforms that accompany IMF and World Bank financial assistance. The basic goal of SAPs is to help countries repay their foreign debts through a combination of fiscal and monetary policy reforms, as well as increased participation in the global economy. SAPs were first introduced in the early 1980s as a way of helping countries in Latin America recover from the Debt Crisis. Since then, over 100 countries have undertaken some type of SAP (Abouharb and Cingranelli 2007). Though used in a wide variety of countries, there is a common policy "playbook" for SAPs. In particular, they involve the following:

- Fiscal "austerity" (reductions in state spending)

- A decreased role of the state in the economy, including a reduction in the overall size of the public sector as well as the privatization of state-run industries (most commonly utilities)

- Monetary policy changes, including increased interest rates and currency devaluation

- Trade liberalization measures, such as the cessation of tariffs and non-tariff barriers to foreign trade

The overall goal of SAPs is to help a state resolve its balance of payments problems by reducing spending and increasing the flow of capital. Though this "playbook" is in line with basic macroeconomic principles for reducing deficits, the political and economic results of these measures have been subject to a great deal of criticism.

SAPs—which are often enacted very rapidly—are very recessionary, particularly in the short run. Decreases in government spending often translate into decreases in government jobs (thus increased unemployment), as well as decreased levels of support for education, healthcare, and economic welfare. Interest rate increases make it more expensive for citizens to acquire loans, while currency devaluation lowers individual spending power. In many instances, the reduction of state subsidies may result in drastic increases in the prices that citizens pay for basic services, such as electricity and water, or goods that were formerly subsidized, including fuel and food. For example, in 2001 Ghana was forced to increase its water prices by 95 percent, while Nicaragua was forced to increase its water prices by 30 percent (Grusky 2001). These difficulties can be further exacerbated by trade liberalization, as inefficient domestic industries may be incapable of competing with their foreign counterparts. As a result, these industries may be forced to cut jobs or close down entirely.

Politically, participation in SAPs is also problematic. The IMF and World Bank are largely controlled by the states of the Global North—indeed the policy mix represented by the IMF is often referred to as the "Washington Consensus." To the extent that the reforms often override decades of government policy, acceptance of SAPs can readily be interpreted as "surrendering" to the policies of the Global North. Countries in the Global South may view these institutions as another manifestation of "neocolonialism," which serves more to meet the interests of global investors and corporations rather than citizens of the Global South. Indeed, in many instances "privatization" results in many large state-run industries being sold off to multinational corporations from the Global North. For example, when Bolivia was forced to privatize its water industry, the contract was awarded to a company controlled by Bechtel (Forero 2005), while water privatization contracts in Argentina were picked up by Enron (Nichols 2002). Moreover, as SAPs are applied in a very uniform manner, countries resent the "one size fits all" nature of these reforms.

Many of the criticisms against the IMF were primarily from more populist and Marxist sources and focused on individual cases. However, recent studies have begun to systematically examine the impact of SAPs upon their recipient states. The empirical results paint an overwhelmingly negative picture—SAPs have been linked to reductions in social spending, greater income inequality, and lower levels of economic growth (Vreeland 2003). Moreover, the social unrest which can occur due to SAPs is often met with violence by the state. As a result, these programs are associated with greater levels of human rights abuse (Abouharb and Cingranelli 2007).

Though acknowledging an imperfect record, the World Bank and the IMF defend their role in the international financial system. Pointing to successes such as Poland, officials note that the IMF has played a key role in helping countries recover. Moreover, countries only apply for help when they are in financial trouble and thus it is hard to blame these organizations for problems that the country was facing anyway. Put another way, critics are confusing "cause" and "effect." Finally, officials note that political leaders often find it expedient to "scapegoat" the IMF and the World Bank, which can provide them "cover" for enacting necessary, though unpopular, economic policies. Ultimately, as argued by IMF economist Kenneth Rogoff, countries would be much worse off if they isolated themselves from the global economy. "Perhaps poor nations won't need the IMF's specific macroeconomic expertise—but they will need something awfully similar" (Rogoff 2003).

REFORMING THE INTERNATIONAL FINANCIAL ARCHITECTURE?

Hardly anyone is happy with the prevailing chaotic condition of rapidly fluctuating currency values, and the problems of volatile international finance cannot be dismissed. Trends point to their increasing magnitude. Almost no global financial architecture is in place to manage these massive cross-border capital flows, although a set of loosely defined general principles of relatively universal scope are recognized worldwide.

Usually, with the onset of financial crises severe enough to threaten a global recession, pressure mounts to engineer reforms of the international monetary system. Many proposals have been advanced to help cushion the aftershocks of the rapid movement of investment funds among countries that create booms and busts, from the 1980s Latin American debt crisis to the Asian Financial Crises of 1997–98 to the subsequent crises in Russia, Brazil, Argentina, and Turkey. In all, financial crises have swept like a contagious epidemic to over sixty countries between 1973 and 2009 (costing on average 10 percent of each affected state's GNP). The threats that followed these crises —unemployment, rising taxes, crime, and military coups d'etat and dictatorships— precipitated many calls for reform. In response to both national and global panic, these threats galvanized crisis-management efforts at debt rescheduling, control of capital flows, and, most optimistically, cross-national coordination through multilateral regulation to prevent future crises in financial collapse. "After the East Asian crisis,

Muchtar Zakaria/AP Photo

SURRENDERING TO THE IMF? **A controversy surrounding multilateral institutions, such as the IMF, is that their policies are seen as another way in which powerful states of the Global North seek domination over those in the Global South. In this picture, taken on January 15, 1998, Indonesian President Suharto signs an agreement for a $43 billion assistance and reform package, while IMF Managing Director Michel Camdessus looks on. This picture proved damaging for both Suharto and the IMF. Indonesians, who place a great value on symbolism and body language, viewed the picture as a humiliating loss of face for the President, who was forced out of office four months later. It was also an economic and public relations disaster for the IMF. In addition to helping to solidify negative opinions of the IMF within the developing world (Camdessus later apologized for his arm-crossing and his stance), Suharto subsequently reneged on many aspects of the deal, particularly those that called for the dismantling of business monopolies owned by his family members.**

such debates filled library shelves with myriad proposals for a new global financial architecture" (Pauly 2005). Similarly, in the wake of the current global financial crisis that originated largely from multiple bank failures in the United States, the "G-20" (an informal grouping of the 20 largest economies in the world) has begun to consider establishing common sets of guidelines for their financial institutions.

What these and other proposals seek is a mechanism for creating the currency stability and flexibility on which prosperity through trade depends. However, there is little agreement about how to bring about reforms. With the spread of democracy throughout the globe (see Chapter 3), most governments now face increasing domestic pressures to sacrifice such goals as exchange rate stability for unemployment reduction. So it seems likely that floating exchange rates, with all their costs and uncertainties, are here to stay. As one observer notes,

> The . . . leading powers in the world economy have too much of a stake in existing arrangements to show much appetite for reinventing the IMF or for charting a new Bretton Woods. For these actors, the IMF remains a preferred instrument for coping with financial crises. Hence, while the schemes for alternatives proliferate, the prospects are for incremental tinkering rather than wholesale restructuring (Babai 2001, 418).

We are thus left with a troubling situation: Global investment flows continue to proliferate, and there is every reason to expect that the currency dilemmas facing the world will continue to intensify. Yet a fundamental reform of the present international financial system is unlikely.

That conclusion was highlighted by the "solution" to the currency problem the European countries adopted in 2002, which severed dependence on the U.S. dollar in preference for a **regional currency union** to try to stabilize erratic exchange rate fluctuations. To this end, the EU created the euro in the hopes that a single currency would make the EU a single market for business, and that the euro would promote economic growth, cross-border investment, corporate innovation and efficiency, and political integration.

As innovative as the creation of the euro appears, it may not serve as a model for other countries and regions. The euro remains controversial even in Europe, especially among important EU states (Britain, Denmark, and Sweden so far have rejected it). The EU common currency is much more than an economic change; to critics it is an ambitious *political* change designed to create a European superstate and thereby erase the individuality and economic and political sovereignty of European states. This solution through currency integration in Europe is best seen as a response to U.S. domination of the global economy, where the U.S. dollar although under challenge, remains the primary global currency for settling international accounts. To many, globalization really means the "dollarization" of the international political economy. As long as U.S. economic and military supremacy continues, it is unlikely that the present free-floating exchange mechanism for currency exchanges valued in terms of the U.S. dollar will be overturned by creation of new global institutions accepting supranational management.

This means that the debate over currency and monetary policies will remain as intense as ever, particularly in the turbulent arena of international trade. It is that twin dimension of economic globalization that we will next consider in Chapter 10.

■ **regional currency union**
the pooling of sovereignty to create a common currency (such as the EU's euro) and single monetary system for members in a region, regulated by a regional central bank within the currency bloc to reduce the likelihood of large-scale liquidity crises.

Key Terms

geo-economics
geopolitics
international political
    economy (IPE)
globalization
international monetary system
laissez-faire
globalization of finance

arbitrage
digital world economy
commercial liberalism
capital mobility hypothesis
monetary system
exchange rate
monetary policy
money supply

fixed exchange rates
International Monetary Fund (IMF)
World Bank
international liquidity
commercial domino theory
floating exchange rates
regional currency union

CHAPTER 10
INTERNATIONAL TRADE IN THE GLOBAL MARKETPLACE

Under what is rather barrenly termed "globalization," we don't have to shop at the big local company; we can turn to a foreign competitor. We don't have to work for the village's one and only employer; we can seek alternative opportunities.

—Johan Norberg, political economist

Richard Vogel/AP Photo

Producing at Home for Export Sales Abroad. Goods are traded across borders at an escalating rate, and all countries are competing for a share of the global marketplace. Shown here is one example: workers using sewing machines in Vietnam to make sports clothes for sale in European and U.S. markets.

A s you struggle to make payments toward your college tuition, your father calls with some bad news: His employer has decided to move its production to India in order to save money by hiring lower-paid foreign workers without trade unions. Now your father will face unemployment. The downside of globalized international trade has come home to roost, and the quality of your life is declining. Or so it would appear as you contemplate your future clad in Levi jeans no longer produced in the United States and Calvin Klein shirts made in China. Trying to find meaning in the whirlwind of international trade going on around you, you race off to your international economics course, where you hope you can derive some insight. And you are in luck. Your professor hones in on her theme for today's lesson: "The Impact of International Trade on Global and National Circumstances." She introduces her topic by telling you that trade across national borders is the biggest part of the globalization of world politics generally. She begins by quoting former World Bank President Paul Wolfowitz—"I like globalization; I want to say it works, but it's hard to say that when 6,000,000 people are slipping backwards."

> *A world connected by trade and technology must be bound by common values.*
> —Mary Robinson, former president of Ireland

Somehow, your professor's emphasis on globalization does not on the surface appear very helpful. True, international trade is increasing at record speeds, and you can accept readily the hypothesis that the transfer of goods and technology across borders is producing multiple changes. However, you cannot help but feel that looking for globalization is like looking for air. You can't see it because it's everywhere, and it defies precise definition. And you are struck by the admission of your instructor of the ambiguity attached to the term globalization. As she quotes from one authority, the word *globalization* is "the most ubiquitous in the language of international relations and has spawned a new vocabulary: *globaloney* (why all the hype when the global economy was more integrated in the age of Queen Victoria?); *globaphobia* (the new, mainly mistaken, backlash); *globeratti* (the members of the international *nongovernmental organizations (NGOs)* who travel around the world from conference to conference, except when they are on the Internet mobilizing for the next conference), and so on" (Ostry 2001).

As you next learn in your lecture, scholars also hold very competing views about the *consequences* of the globalization of international trade. To construct an objective evaluation of these rival interpretations, begin by stepping backward to understand leading ideas about states' trade policies, which are rooted in past thinking. In this chapter, you will focus on the critical role of the United States as an economic superpower in shaping the contest between liberalism and mercantilism that underlies the different trade strategies states are pursuing in their quest for power and wealth. However, the place to start is with data that describe trends in the globalization of international trade.

THE GLOBALIZATION OF TRADE

■ General Agreement on Tariffs and Trade (GATT)

a UN affiliated IGO designed to promote international trade and tariff reductions, replaced by the World Trade Organization.

After World War II, the victors joined together in their belief that they could stimulate economic growth by removing barriers to international trade. Under the **General Agreement on Tariffs and Trade**, the so-called Geneva Round of negotiations in 1947 reduced tariffs by thirty-five percent. Successive rounds of negotiations in the 1950s, 1960s (the Kennedy Round), 1970s (Tokyo Round), and the 1980s and 1990s (Uruguay Round) virtually eliminated tariffs on manufactured goods. The **World Trade Organization (WTO)**, which succeeded GATT in 1994, enlarged its membership (see Map 10.1), and continued in the Doha Round to seek further reductions in barriers to international trade.

The reduction of tariff rates has permitted international trade and world economic output to grow hand in hand. Since the founding of GATT, the world economy has expanded by a factor of six and global trade has increased twenty times (Samuelson 2006, 89). The impact of the rising volume of goods shipped from producers in one country to consumers in another has been enormous, making trade increasingly important to all states.

Trade Integration

Trade integration is the measure of the extent to which the growth rate in world trade increases faster than does the growth rate of world gross domestic product. As trade integration grows, so does globalization, because states' interdependence

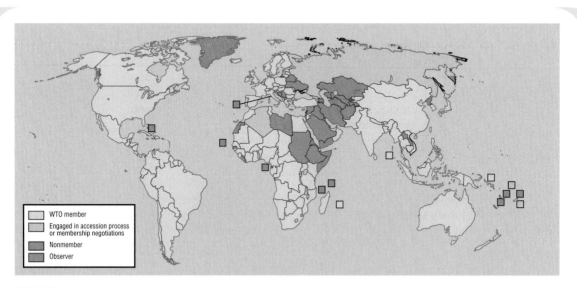

MAP 10.1

THE WORLD TRADE ORGANIZATION GOES GLOBAL **At the start of 2008, 151 countries or seventy percent of the world's 212 states were members of the World Trade Organization. In addition, thirty "observers" are in the process of negotiating to become formal members (such as Russia). Why states seek to join the WTO is puzzling to those who think the WTO undermines states' sovereign independence. But these critiques overlook the fact that the WTO is an IGO within which each member has the power to veto any changes in rules, and that the WTO is more properly seen as a mere referee when members face trade disputes.**

grows when countries' exports account for an increasing percentage of their gross domestic product (GDP). As Michael Mazarr (1999) explains, "Measuring global trade as a percentage of GDP is perhaps the simplest and most straightforward measure of globalization. If trade in goods and merchandise is growing faster than the world economy as a whole, then it is becoming more integrated."

Figure 10.1 records the remarkable speed at which trade integration has progressed since 1970. Countries have become more interdependent, and the world more increasingly globalized because international trade has far outpaced growth in the overall global economy (and in world population as well). Of course, countries differ in the degree to which their economies have become integrated through trade. Trade integration has become most rapid because of the Global East and the Global South, reflecting these countries' rising contribution to world trade and their mounting importance for continued Global North economic growth. The Global South's share of global exports in manufactured products has grown from ten percent in 1980 to thirty percent (WDI 2008, 212), fueled by the Global East's growth in the share of new export products.

■ **World Trade Organization (WTO)**

a multilateral agency that monitors the implementation of trade agreements and settles disputes among trade partners.

■ **trade integration**

the difference between gross rates in trade and gross domestic product.

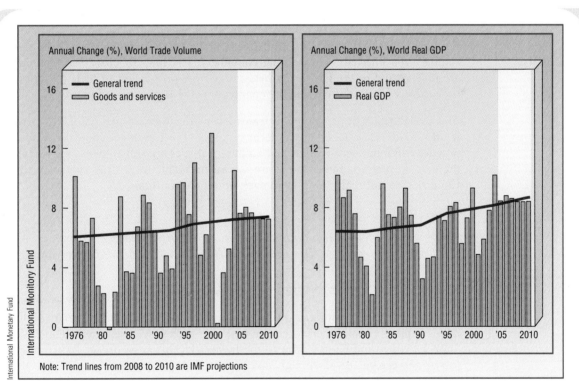

FIGURE 10.1

THE GROWTH OF GLOBAL TRADE INTEGRATION 1976–2010 When the percentage change each year in the volume of world trade grows faster than the annual rate of growth of the combined world economy, "trade integration" increases. Inspect these two figures. Globalization through "trade integration" is indeed occurring; the volume of world trade has been growing on average almost seven percent each year (left) but the yearly increase of the world economy is growing at a much slower pace (right), stimulated in part by the rising level of international trade. This differential was evident in 2006, when "the value of global merchandise trade grew 15 percent, while the world economy grew roughly five percent" (Naím 2007, 95).

A similar pattern may be emerging with regard to trade in services. Because the United States enjoys comparative advantages in this area, it has been a strong advocate of bringing services under the liberalizing rules of the WTO. Trade in services has already expanded more than threefold since 1980, with the Global North reaping most of the benefits. However, the spread of information technology, the ease with which new business software can be used, and the comparatively lower wage costs in developing economies are among reasons why the World Bank predicts that developing countries will capture an increasing share of world trade in services. Global East countries such as India, with significant numbers of educated, English-speaking citizens, are already operating call centers and consumer assistance hotlines for Global North companies.

Multinational Corporations and Their Foreign Direct Investments' Impact

Selling products to consumers in another country often requires companies to establish a presence abroad, where they can produce goods and offer services. Traditionally the overseas operations of *multinational corporations (MNCs)* were "appendages" of a centralized hub. The pattern nowadays is to dismantle the hub by dispersing production facilities worldwide, which was made economically feasible by the revolutions in communication and transportation (including use of the standardized international shipping container). The sales of most large companies are now geared to the global market, and a large proportion of their revenues are now earned from sales outside the countries where they are headquartered.

This globalization of production is transforming the international political economy. It once made sense to count trade in terms of flows between countries, and that practice continues because national account statistics are still gathered with states as the unit of analysis. But that picture increasingly fails to portray current realities. Countries do not really trade with each other; corporations do.

> *The idea of economic competition among nations is flawed. Companies compete. But economically, countries depend on each other.*
>
> —Robert J. Samuelson, political economist

The world's 77,175 multinational corporations and the 73,000 foreign affiliates have steadily increased their foreign investments each year. They climbed in 2007 to $120 billion to the Global South—the highest level ever recorded, accounting for forty-eight percent of all foreign investments that year from all investors (OECD 2007a, 260-261; OECD 2007b, 14). Together MNCs are now responsible for about one-fourth of the world's production and two-thirds of global exports. As much as forty percent of global trade is *between* MNCs' cross-border affiliates (Oatley 2008, 170).

MNCs are now the primary agents in the globalization of production. By increasingly forming strategic corporate alliances with companies in the same industry, and by merging with one another, MNCs have become massive NGOs rivaling states in financial resources (see Table 7.2, pp. 210–212). These global actors have grown in influence also because many MNC parent companies are now linked with one another in **virtual corporations** and alliances of co-ownership and coproduction. These MNC networks pursue truly global strategies for financial gain, often through long-term supplier agreements and licensing and franchising contracts. As they funnel large financial flows across national borders, these global corporate conglomerates are integrating national economies into a worldwide market. In the process, this huge movement of investments across borders is leading to economic convergence by causing "countries to adopt similar institutions and practices to organize economic life. . . . It is important to know not only how much FDI a country receives but from where. The effect of inward FDI needs to be appreciated beyond its

■ **virtual corporations** agreements between otherwise competitive MNCs, often temporary, to join forces and skills to coproduce and export particular products in the borderless global marketplace.

> *There are no longer any national flag carriers. . . . Corporations must serve their customers, not governments.*
>
> —Kenichi Ohmae, Japanese management consultant

usual role of alleviating resource scarcities and creating jobs in host countries. FDI is a conveyor of norms, technologies, and corporate practices" (Prakash and Potoski 2007).

FDI flows throughout the world since 1970 increased one hundredfold by 2000 to $1.4 trillion (after which investments declined until rising in 2008 sixteen percent from that previous 2000 high). The direction of FDI flows is constantly changing, but a trend is the rise of the Global East and the Global South as fully engaged participants in this enormous transnational investment activity. Developing countries are now averaging each year over $135 billion in their overseas investments, or about 17 percent of total outflows (OECD 2007, 14). And the Global South countries are also increasingly the recipients of investments from abroad: "From an initial level of less than $25 billion in 1990, net inflows of FDI to developing countries have increased tenfold" (WDI 2007, 314). However, large differences exist among the companies investing overseas to expand their global financial presence and trade, as well as among the targets of FDI inflows (see Figure 10.2).

Among some of the most ardent advocates of globalization, the progressive integration of national economies into a single world marketplace is seen as a panacea for poverty. Is this accurate? Despite evidence that the widening and deepening of international trade flows have been associated with economic growth, the distribution of these gains has not been uniform. As the UN's annual *Human Development Report* once put it: "A rising tide of wealth is supposed to lift all boats. But some are more seaworthy than others. The yachts and ocean liners are indeed rising in response to new opportunities, but the rafts and rowboats are taking on water—and some are sinking fast." Trade globalization, in other words, is creating winners and losers, both between and within countries. As a result, a backlash of protest against these inequalities is rising among those groups that see themselves as victims of an integrated trade world.

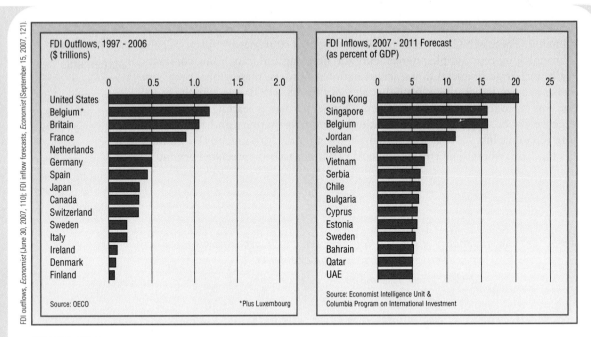

FIGURE 10.2

THE SHIFTING DISTRIBUTION OF FOREIGN DIRECT INVESTMENTS **As the figure (left) demonstrates, the thirty wealthy OECD countries are the biggest overseas investors. Since 1997 their investments outside their borders exceeded $8 trillion, with the U.S. total ($1.58 trillion) the largest source of money. OECD FDI in 2006 rose 29 percent above the previous year to $1.12 trillion. Between 2007 and 2011, the United States, Britain, and China are predicted to remain the top destinations for FDI (30 percent of global inflows), but as the figure (right) predicts, many smaller countries are expected to show the biggest gains as a share of their GDP, a measure of their success in attracting overseas investments.**

CONTENDING TRADE STRATEGIES FOR AN INTERDEPENDENT WORLD

As you have learned, international trade is the most far-reaching dimension of globalization. Accordingly, because so much is at stake, the globalization of trade is one of the most hotly debated global issues. Disputes have intensified because the major participants in international trade are taking opposed foreign economic policy approaches.

To understand the trade strategies different states are pursuing, it is important to understand the economic philosophies of liberalism and mercantilism that guide their international economic decisions.

The Shadow of the Great Depression

In July 1944, forty-four states allied in war against the Axis powers met in the New Hampshire resort of Bretton Woods to devise new rules and institutions to govern international trade and monetary relations after World War II. As the world's preeminent economic and military power, the United States played the leading role.

Iain Masterton/Alamy

CASCADING GLOBALIZATION: COMMUNIST CHINA CHOOSES TO CONVERT TO CAPITALISM AND CONSUMERISM Shown here is one example of China's growing consumerism: a view of the huge South China Mall in Donggum, claimed to be the world's biggest shopping center. "China now has utterly embraced America's 'shop-'til-you-drop' ethos and is in the midst of a buy-at-the-mall frenzy. By 2010 China is expected to be home to at least seven of the world's ten largest shopping malls" (Barboza 2005, 1, 4).

Its proposals were shaped by the perceived causes of the 1930s economic catastrophe and its beliefs about the need for active U.S. leadership. The United States sought free trade, open markets, and monetary stability—all central tenets of what would become the "Bretton Woods system"—based on the theoretical premises of *commercial liberalism*, which advocates free markets with few barriers to trade and capital flows.

Britain also played an important role at the conference. Led by John Maynard Keynes—whose theories about the state's role in managing inflation, unemployment, and growth still influence economic thinking throughout the world—the British delegation won support for the principle of strong government action by states facing economic problems. That ideology conforms less closely with liberalism than with the principles of mercantilism, which assigns states a greater role than markets in managing economic interactions as a strategy for acquiring national wealth.

Despite these differences, the rules established at Bretton Woods reflected a remarkable level of agreement. They rested on three political bases. First, power was concentrated in the rich Western European and North American countries, which reduced the number of states whose agreement was necessary for effective management by restricting the potential challenges from Japan, the Global South, and the then-communist Soviet Union and its sphere of influence in Eastern Europe. Second, the dominant states shared a preference for an open international economy with limited government intervention. The onset of the Cold War helped cement Western unity, because a common external enemy led the West to economically cooperate and share burdens for prosperity and military security. Third, Bretton Woods worked because the United States assumed the burdens of hegemonic leadership and others willingly accepted that leadership.

Commercial liberalism's preference for market mechanisms over government intervention and the urge to privatize and otherwise reduce government regulation of markets has spread worldwide. Thus, it is still useful to characterize the contemporary international economic system as a **Liberal International Economic Order (LIEO)**—one based on such free market principles as openness and nondiscriminatory trade.

Although liberalization has spread worldwide as a policy principle (Simmons and Elkins 2004), not all states consistently support the liberal tenet that governments should not interfere by managing trade flows because they fear the potential costs of free trade. **Commercial liberalism** is under attack in many states, including some of liberalism's unenthusiastic proponents, which are pressured domestically to protect industries and employment at home. Globalization has not eliminated the urge to compete, because states fear that **interdependence** will compromise their sovereignty and security. Interdependence encourages states to maximize their gains through transborder transactions while minimizing their costs. States' trade policies are naturally influenced by the selfish desire to increase the domestic benefits of international economic transactions and to lessen their adverse consequences, even if this undermines the expansion of a global capitalist economy propelled by free trade.

The Clash between Liberal and Mercantilist Values

How should states rationally cope in the globalized political economy to best manage economic change? The choices inspire different philosophies and policies. They force governments to attempt to reconcile the overriding need for states to cooperate in trade liberalization if they are to maximize their wealth with each state's natural competitive desire to put its own welfare first.

> *No science in the world is more elevated, more necessary and more useful than economics.*
>
> —Carl Linnaeus, Swedish inventor of today's method to classify living organisms

Most controversies in *international political economy* are ultimately reducible to differences between liberalism and mercantilism. A comparison of their divergent theoretical positions on five central questions illuminates the issues of debate that divide these schools today: (1) for liberalism economic relations are harmonious, but for mercantilism they are conflictual; (2) to liberalism the major actors are households and business firms, but to mercantilism states are the only important actors; (3) to liberalism the goal of economic activity is to maximize global welfare, but to mercantilism it is to serve the national interest; (4) to liberalism economics should determine politics, but to mercantilism politics determines economics; and (5) liberalism's theory pictures global change in a dynamic ever-adjusting equilibrium,

■ **Liberal International Economic Order (LIEO)**

the set of regimes created after World War II, designed to promote monetary stability and reduce barriers to the free flow of trade and capital.

■ **commercial liberalism**

an economic theory advocating free markets and the removal of barriers to the flow of trade and capital as a locomotive for prosperity.

■ **interdependence**

a situation in which the behavior of international actors greatly affects others with whom they have contact, making all parties mutually sensitive and vulnerable to the others' actions.

whereas mercantilism postulates that world transformations are the products of shifts in the distribution of states' relative power (Gilpin 2004). Let's look deeper at these contending economic perspectives.

Commercial Liberalism A theory advances a set of conclusions derived from assumptions (axioms) and/or evidence about some phenomenon, including its character, causes, and probable consequences and their ethical implications. Commercial liberalism is one such theory that proceeds from the premise that humankind's natural inclination is to cooperate. Thus, progress through mutually beneficial exchanges is possible, both to increase prosperity and to enlarge individual liberty under law. In commercial liberalism, economic activity can lead to global welfare, and the major problems of capitalism (boom-and-bust cycles, trade wars, poverty, and income inequalities) can be managed. One of the globe's "great causes" (Bhagwati 2004) is to promote free international trade to lift the poor from poverty and to expand political liberties.

Adam Smith laid the foundations for commercial liberalism. In 1776, he wrote the now-classic *The Wealth of Nations*. It argued how the "invisible hand" in an unregulated market fueled by humans' natural tendency to "truck, barter, and exchange" in pursuit of private interest could serve the globe's collective or public interest by permitting efficiency and gains. How? By encouraging resources to be directed to their most productive use. As Smith wrote in a widely circulated liberal effort to classify community interests as admirable but best driven by self-interest:

> Every individual necessarily labors to render the annual revenue of the society as great as he can. He generally, indeed, neither intends to promote the public interest, nor knows how much he is promoting it. . . . He intends only his own gain, and he is in this, as in many other cases, led by an invisible hand to promote an end which was no part of his intention. Nor is it always the worse for the society that he was no part of it. By pursuing his own interest he frequently promotes that of the society more effectually than when he really intends to promote it. I have never known much good done by those who affected to trade for the public good.
>
> It is not from the benevolence of the butcher, the brewer, or the baker that we expect our dinner, but from their regard to their own interest. We address ourselves, not to their humanity but to their self-love, and never talk to them of our own necessities but of their advantages.

Another eighteenth-century political economist, David Ricardo, added an important corollary. He demonstrated conclusively that when all states specialize in the production of those goods in which they enjoy a **comparative advantage** and trade them for goods in which others enjoy an advantage, a net gain in welfare for both states, in the form of higher living standards, will result. The principle of comparative advantage is the basis for commercial liberalism's advocacy of free trade for capital accumulation. Material progress is realized and mutual gains are achieved, according to this principle, when countries specialize in the production of what they can produce least expensively, when they are willing to purchase goods from other countries that are costly for them to produce, and when they do not restrict the flow of trade across borders.

Trade competition is beneficial, according to liberalism, because it stimulates technological innovation to improve production efficiency in order to meet the competition for trade by other producers. In the long run the world's output and

■ **comparative advantage**
the concept in liberal economics that a state will benefit if it specializes in those goods it can produce comparatively cheaply and acquires through trade goods that it can only produce at a higher cost.

income will increase and everyone's standard of living will rise, if all countries abide by the rules of free trade and open markets. Commercial liberalism recognizes that in the short run free trade will result in unequal rewards for some and produce inequalities in countries' rate of growth, but it argues that the long-term gains for all in a *laissez-faire* economic system of free markets are most important.

Why does free trade produce benefits for trade partners who specialize in the production of goods for which they each have comparative advantage? Consider a hypothetical illustration of Japan and the United States, each of which produces cameras and computers but with different worker productivity (output per hour) for each country, as shown in the first column of Table 10.1.

Clearly Japan has an absolute advantage in both products, as Japanese workers are more productive in turning out cameras and computers than are American workers. Does this mean the two countries cannot benefit by trading with each other? If trade does occur, should each country continue to allocate its resources as in the past? The answer to both questions is no.

Each country should specialize in producing the item for which it has the greatest cost advantage or least cost disadvantage, and trade for others. Because Japan is three times more productive in cameras than computers, it should direct more of its resources into manufacturing cameras. One cost of doing so is lost computer output, but Japan can turn out three additional cameras for every computer given up. The United States, by contrast, can obtain only two computers. Like their Japanese counterparts, American workers are also more productive in making cameras than computers. Still, U.S. resources should be directed to computers because the United States is at a smaller disadvantage compared with Japan in this area. If the United States specializes in computers and Japan in cameras and they trade with each other, each will benefit. The following scenario shows why.

Begin with one hundred workers in each industry without specialization or trade (second column). Next specialize production by shifting ten Japanese workers from computer to camera production and shifting twenty American workers from camera production to computers (third column). Then permit free trade so that eighty

Table 10.1 Comparative Advantage and the Gains from Free Trade

Country	Work Productivity per Hours		Before Specialization		Specialization, No Trade		Specialization, with Trade	
	Cameras	Computers	Cameras	Computers	Cameras	Computers	Cameras	Computers
Japan	9	3	900	300	990	270	910	300
United States	4	2	400	200	320	240	400	210

Japanese-manufactured cameras are exported to the United States and thirty U.S. computers are exported to Japan. With specialization *and* free trade, the benefits to both countries improve.

By shifting Japanese resources into the production of cameras and U.S. resources into computers and allowing trade, the same total allocations will cause camera and computer output to rise ten units each (fourth column). Resources are now being used more efficiently. Both countries realize benefits when each trades some of their additional output for the others. Japan ends up with more cameras than before specialization and trade and with the same number of computers. The United States finds itself with more computers and the same number of cameras. More output in both countries means higher living standards.

Liberal economists such as Joseph Schumpeter believed that capitalist free enterprise could free entrepreneurs to succeed in generating wealth if politicians would give it a chance to work by staying out of the way. Economics should determine *politics* because markets succeed best without political interference by governments. For liberals, state regulation of the national economy should be minimal to maximize growth and prosperity. The best government is one that stays out of business, and politics should be divorced from the economic market. A free market is the foundation for broad-based, steady economic growth that allows democratic institutions to flourish (Naím 2007).

The basis of liberalism is that trade liberalization produces many economic benefits for the individual states who actively participate in a liberal global marketplace: The removal of trade restrictions generates rapid export and economic growth because it promotes competition, improves resource allocations, reduces production costs,

No nation was ever ruined by trade.

—Benjamin Franklin, American leader in the revolutionary war

generates pressures for increased production efficiencies, attracts foreign capital and expertise, provides foreign exchange needed for imports, and promotes more equal access to scarce resources. Thus, open trade promotes growth in a variety of ways. Entrepreneurs are forced to become increasingly efficient because they must compete against the best in the world to survive. Openness also affords access to the best technology and allows countries to specialize in what they do best rather than produce everything on their own. Liberalism also predicts that free trade produces political payoffs or *externalities* (the side effects produced by choices and behaviors in one activity that alter other conditions). At the *state level of analysis* economic freedom leads to political freedom, because liberal economies increase the probability of democratic governance and the protection of citizens' civil liberties and human rights. At the *global level of analysis*, trade is a source of peace and stability because the benefits of trade interdependence build habits of cooperative relations among trading partners who value the resulting economic advantages and thus seek to avoid political or military confrontation.

There is a fly in this liberal ointment, however. Although commercial liberal theory promises that the "invisible hand" will maximize efficiency so that everyone will gain, it does not promise that everyone will gain equally. Instead, "everyone will gain in accordance with his or her contribution to the whole, but . . . not everyone will gain equally because individual productivities differ. Under free exchange, society as a whole will be more wealthy, but individuals will be rewarded in terms of their marginal productivity and relative contribution to the overall social product" (Gilpin 2001). This applies at the global level as well. The gains from international trade are distributed quite unequally, even if the principle of comparative advantage governs. Globalization has not benefited middle-income countries as much as richer and poorer states (Garrett 2004). Commercial liberal theory ignores these differences, as it is most concerned with *absolute gains* for all rather than **relative gains**. Mercantilist theory, in contrast, is more concerned with the political competition among states in anarchy that determines how economic rewards are distributed.

■ **relative gains**

the benefits some participants in an exchange receive that are larger than the benefits of the other participants.

Mercantilism   An economic extension of realist theorizing, mercantilism sees competition between states as the essence of international life, with pursuit of national self-interests leading naturally to conflict and war to alter the balance of power in one's favor. Accordingly, mercantilism sees power politics determining economics and advocates government regulation of economic life to increase state wealth and security. It is an outlook influenced by the prevailing global conditions at the birth of capitalism in the late 1400s (Wallerstein 2005) and the system of sovereign states. Mercantilism emerged in Europe as the leading political economy philosophy after the decline of feudalism and helped to stimulate the first wave of Europe's imperialist expansion, which began in the fifteenth century. Accumulating gold and silver was seen as the route to state power and wealth, and imperialistically acquiring overseas colonies was seen as a means to that end.

■ **neomercantilism**

a contemporary version of classical mercantilism that advocates promoting domestic production and a balance-of-payment surplus by subsidizing exports and using tariffs and nontariff barriers to reduce imports.

Although states no longer try to stockpile precious metals, many continue to intervene in the marketplace. In the contemporary context, then, **neomercantilism** refers to a state trade policy to maximize exports, minimize imports, and expand the home economy faster than that of foreign rivals. Its advocates are sometimes called "economic nationalists." In their view, states must compete for position and power, and economic resources are the source of state power. From this it follows that "economic activities are and should be subordinate to the goal of state building and the interests of the state. All nationalists ascribe to the primacy of the state, of national security, and of military power in the functioning of the international system" (Gilpin 2001).

Mercantilism shares much in common with realism: Realists and mercantilists both see the state as the principal transnational actor, both view the global system as anarchical, and both dwell on the aggressively competitive drive of people and states for advantage. "Economic nationalists . . . stress the role of power in the rise of a market and the conflictual nature of international economic relations; they argue that economic interdependence must have a political foundation and that it creates yet another arena of interstate conflict, increases national vulnerability, and constitutes a mechanism that one society can employ to dominate another" (Gilpin 2001).

Whereas commercial liberals emphasize the mutual benefits of cooperative economic agreements, mercantilists focus on the likelihood of *zero sum* competition and are therefore more concerned that the gains realized by one party in a trade exchange will come at the expense of the other trade partner. For mercantilists relative gains are more important than both parties' absolute gains. An American economic nationalist, for instance, would complain about a trade agreement that promised the

> *The logical absurdity of all governments seeking a trade surplus at the same time is not perceived [by mercantilists] as a problem. Within a zero-sum world, there has to be winners and losers.*
>
> —James Mayall, political economist

United States a 5 percent growth in income and China 6 percent. Although the bargain would ensure an eventual increase in U.S. living standards, its position compared with China's would erode. Indeed, projected over the long run, such seemingly small differences would eventually lead to China's replacement of the United States as the world's largest economy. This outcome is regarded as highly unacceptable to American economic nationalists.

To look into the future of the global economy, it is important to foresee the parameters of U.S. foreign economic policy for the next decade (Bergsten 2005). America is pivotal because it presently has the world's single largest national economy, and it is therefore capable of practicing **hegemony** by dominating the rules governing the international flow of capital and trade. How, and if, the United States politically chooses to balance commercial liberalism and mercantilism is likely to heavily influence the global economic future.

HEGEMONY: A PRECONDITION FOR ECONOMIC ORDER?

Hegemonic stability theory is based on the proposition that free trade and international peace depend on a single predominant great power that is willing and able to use its economic and military strength to protect rules for international interaction. That theory hypothesizes that when a great power gains supreme military and economic power, a hegemon—a single, overwhelmingly powerful state that can exercise great influence over all other global actors—will emerge. When this happens, international economic stability based on liberal principles can materialize to reduce the fear of nationalistic mercantilist trade protection. Unlike mercantilism, hegemonic stability theory follows the realpolitik logic of long cycle theory (see Chapter 4). It views the maintenance of a global balance of power as necessary to preserve economic order under conditions of global anarchy (without true supranational governance), and postulates that "a liberal economic system cannot be self-sustaining but must be maintained over the long term through the actions of the dominant economy" (Gilpin 2001). This interpretation carries with it the assumption that leading states are and must remain in control of the world economy and use their power to coordinate their economic policies by creating an international regulatory *regime* with rules to regulate international economics (Drezner 2007).

■ **hegemony**
the ability of one state to lead in world politics by promoting its worldview and ruling over arrangements governing international economics and politics.

The most important player in creating international economic stability is the most powerful—a *hegemon*. From its preponderant position, the strongest great power is best prepared to promote liberal rules for the whole global system. This has been the experience of the United States and Britain before it whose domestic economies are based on capitalist principles and who took the lead in championing liberal international economic rules (see Mead 2007). This is because their comparatively greater control of technology, capital, and raw materials gave them more opportunities to profit from a system free of mercantilist restraints. When they have enforced such free-trade rules, the hegemon's economy typically has served as "engines of growth" for others in the "liberal train."

Historically, however, every previous hegemon has also had special responsibilities. They have had to coordinate states' **macroeconomics** policies, manage the international monetary system to enable one state's money to be exchanged for others', make sure that countries facing balance-of-payments deficits (imbalances in their financial inflows and outflows) could find the credits necessary to finance their deficits, and serve as lenders of last resort during financial crises. When the most powerful liberal states could not perform these tasks, they often backtracked toward more closed (protected or regulated) domestic economies, and in doing so they undermined the open trading rules that previously were advantageous to them. Such a departure has historically made tariffs, monetary regulations, and other mercantilist policies more widespread and thereby weakened or destroyed the LIEO regime. In short, a liberal global economy is now widely viewed as a public or **collective good**, because it provides benefits that everyone shares and for which no one can be selectively excluded. That is, an open international economy permitting the relatively free movement of goods, services, and capital is seen today as a desirable collective good. It permits economic benefits for all states that would not be available if the global economy were closed to free trade.

According to hegemonic stability theory, the collective good of an open global economy needs a single, dominant power—a hegemon—to remain open and liberal. If a hegemon does not exist or is unwilling to use its power to provide this collective good, states will be tempted to take selfish advantage of the opportunities provided rather than contribute to maintaining the liberal international economy. A major cost which the hegemon must pay is to open its own market to less-expensive imported goods even if other countries "free-ride" by not opening their own markets. And if enough states take this easy route, the entire free-trade regime could collapse.

The analogy of a public park helps to clarify this principle. If there were no central government to provide for the maintenance of the park, individuals themselves would have to cooperate to keep the park in order (the trees trimmed, the lawn mowed, litter removed, and so on). But some may try to come and enjoy the benefits of the park without pitching in. If enough people realize that they can get away with this—that they can enjoy a beautiful park without helping with its upkeep—it will not be long before the once beautiful park looks shabby. Cooperation to provide a public good is thus hard to sustain.

This is also the case with the collective good of a liberal international economy, because many states that enjoy the collective good of an orderly, open, free market economy pay little or nothing for it. These are known as **free-riders**. A hegemon typically tolerates free-riders, partly because the benefits that the hegemon provides,

macroeconomics
the study of aggregate economic indicators such as GDP, the money supply, and the balance of trade that governments monitor to measure changes in national and global economies such as the rates of economic growth and inflation or the level of unemployment.

collective good
a public good, such as safe drinking water, from which everyone benefits.

free-riders
those who obtain benefits at others' expense without the usual costs and effort.

such as a stable global currency, encourage other states to accept the leader's dictates. Thus, both gain—much as liberalism sees the benefits of cooperation as an absolute gain outcome because all parties to a bargain stand to benefit from their exchanges. If the costs of leadership begin to multiply, however, a hegemon will tend to become less tolerant of others' free riding. In such a situation cooperation will increasingly be seen as one-sided or zero-sum because most of the benefits come at the expense of the hegemon. Then the open global economy will crumble amid a competitive race for individual gain at others' expense.

Charles Kindleberger (1973) first theorized about the need for a preponderant liberal hegemon to maintain order and stability. In his explanation of the 1930s Great Depression, Kindleberger concluded that "the international economic and monetary system needs leadership, a country which is prepared, consciously or unconsciously, . . . to set standards of conduct for other countries; and to seek to get others to follow them, to take on an undue share of the burdens of the system, and in particular to take on its support in adversity." Britain played this role from 1815 until the outbreak of World War I in 1914, and the United States assumed the British mantle in the decades immediately following World War II. In the interwar years, however, Britain was unable to play its previous leadership role, and the United States, although capable of leadership, was unwilling to exercise it. The void, Kindleberger concluded, was a principal cause of the "width and depth" of the Great Depression throughout the world in the 1930s.

At issue is whether the world will once again experience such a catastrophic economic collapse, brought on by another failure of hegemonic leadership to preserve a liberal international economy. The prospects are not favorable given America's temptation to turn to trade protectionism because the United States is by far the globe's greatest importer ($15.5 trillion in 2006) and is facing a trade deficit that has exploded between 1991 and 2007 from $31 billion to $818 billion while America is unprepared to deal with huge debts and unsustainable obligations to pay entitlement commitments exceeding "$43 trillion in unfunded liabilities, or $350,000 for every taxpayer" (Brooks 2007, A7).

"Despite all the misgivings about international trade, the fact remains that countries in which the share of economic activity related to exports is rising grow one and a half times faster than those with more stagnant exports" (Naím 2007, 95). That fact

> *The use of [trade subsidies] has been found almost inseparable from abuse.*
>
> —Thomas Jefferson, U.S. president

accounts for the continuing popularity of the liberal belief that the exponential growth of trade contributes enormously to economic prosperity, as the last sixty years suggest (see Figure 10.3). If further reductions to free-trade barriers accelerate, world trade is certain to continue to rise, by the year 2015 to perhaps 40 percent of world GDP (*Global Trends 2015*, 2002).

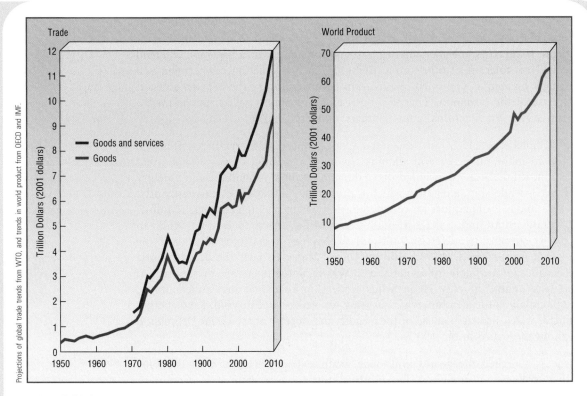

Projections of global trade trends from WTO, and trends in world product from OECD and IMF.

FIGURE 10.3

THE GROWTH OF WORLD TRADE AND WEALTH, 1950–2010 **The figure on the left records the expansion of global trade in goods and services through 2007 (and extends the likely trend projected by the WTO and IMF to 2010). The figure on the right traces trends in the expansion of the entire world economy for the same time span. World economic product is predicted to climb to $66 trillion by 2010, assuming trade growth continues to make its historic contribution to global wealth. Not all are participating equally in this expansion. The United States, with 20 percent of world GDP, commands 9.8 percent of global exports; the Euro area with 14.7 percent captures 29 percent of global trade; and coming on fast are the "emerging economies" with 26.6 percent of world GDP and 24.2 percent of global exports (*Economist*, April 21, 2007, 109).**

■ **most-favored-nation principle (MFN)**

the central GATT principle of unconditional nondiscriminatory treatment in trade between contracting parties underscoring the WTO's rule requiring any advantage given by one WTO member to also extend it to all other WTO members.

It is not surprising that many states today welcome an open trading system. "Commercial common sense supported by evidence show a statistical link between freer trade and economic growth," the WTO summarizes. "Liberal trade policies—policies that allow the unrestricted flow of goods and services—produce the best results." This conclusion accounts for why so many states see advantages in accepting the **most-favored-nation principle** (MFN) (which holds that the tariff preferences granted to one state must be granted to all others exporting the same product) and the **nondiscrimination rule** (goods produced at home and abroad are to be treated the same). However, free trade will only remain popular if everyone can benefit.

These payoffs notwithstanding, there persists many reasons why so many states still attempt to increase their own domestic standard of living through trade protectionism. Some of these feel that free trade is neither free nor fair because it does not benefit everyone equally. Moreover, even though the percentage of countries practicing "domestic economic liberty" has increased throughout the globe

Angel Franco/The New York Times/Redux Pictures

PREPARING THE PATHWAYS TO GLOBAL ECONOMIC RECOVERY **To avert a massive recession in the wake of the September 11, 2001, terrorist attacks, many world leaders gathered for the first time in New York at the World Economic Forum to talk about multilateral plans for recovery. Shown here, New York police practice as bodyguards to protect Forum participants from protestors opposed to free trade.**

for twelve straight years, many states remain unwilling to open their domestic markets to foreign imports because they are also unwilling to undertake reforms at home to create a free domestic economy. According to the Heritage Foundation's *Index of Economic Freedom*, at the start of 2008 only seven countries, or 4 percent, of the world's states were "free." Twenty-three (fifteen percent) were "mostly free," and the remaining countries (81 percent) were "moderately free," "mostly unfree," or "repressed." Economic freedom at home may produce the highest economic growth rates, provide the safest environments with the least risk for investments, and lead to foreign trade, but many non-democratic and repressive governments are unwilling to realize these benefits through the liberalization of their local economies. It is not an accident that such governments rule countries that also tend to be the poorest and the most corrupt (defined by Transparency International as the abuse of public office for private gain). According to Freedom House, Hong Kong, Singapore, and Australia score the highest in encouraging free trade internally and with other countries, and New Zealand, Denmark, and Finland rank as the world's least corrupt countries; they also are among the most democratic and prosperous (see Johnston 2006). In contrast, Somalia, Myanmar, and war-stricken countries like Afghanistan, Iraq, and Sudan are classified among the least free economically and most politically corrupt countries (*Economist*, September 29, 2007, 106), and not by

■ **nondiscrimination rule**

a rule accepting both most-favored-nation and nondiscrimination as principles for free trade, stipulating that goods produced at home and abroad are to be treated the same for import and export agreements.

coincidence, they rank among the poorest with the lowest economic growth rates. This evidence underscores the influence of internal conditions on states' international economic practices. It suggests that the future preservation of the free trade regime is unlikely in the absence of increases in the globe's percentage of free governments and free economies.

> *Trade may be global, but politics is still local.*
> —Ramesh Thakur and Steve Lee, global civil servants

THE FATE OF FREE TRADE

Although many countries have reduced tariff barriers restricting imports from the rest of the world, there is much room for additional reductions. Seventy-three countries still impose tariffs of 10 percent or more, and the Global South average tariff wall (9.2 percent) remains high in comparison to the wealthy Global North's low average (3.8 percent) (WDI 2008, 340–342). Unfortunately for the fate of the existing liberal rules supporting freer trade, the threats to global prosperity are multiplying at the same time that countries' growing dependency on volatile export and import markets is creating a precariously unstable situation. If the entire global economy begins to decline, scores of countries are likely to turn away from the free-trade regime that has engineered their previous period of unprecedented growth. In hard times, people are tempted to build barriers against foreign competitors. Even in many economically open countries, protectionist pressures inevitably increase when jobs are lost.

■ **North American Free Trade Agreement (NAFTA)**

an agreement that brings Mexico into the free-trade zone linking Canada and the United States.

The age-old debate between free traders and mercantilists is likely to persist as a global issue, and the World Trade Organization stands center stage as the major target about which debate centers (see Controversy: Globalization's Growing Pains: Is the World Trade Organization a Friend or Foe?).

The dynamics underlying trends in trade policies are illustrated by the transformations unfolding in trade patterns within and between regions.

An Emerging Regional Tug-of-War in Trade?

■ **Free Trade Area of the Americas (FTAA)**

a set of rules to promote free trade among thirty-four democracies in North and South America.

Another recent trade trend has been the construction of trade partnerships within regions and bilaterally between pairs of countries. The United States first experimented with the former approach in 1984, with the Caribbean Basin Initiative to reduce tariffs and provide tax incentives to promote industrialization and trade. This experiment was soon followed in 1987 with free-trade agreements with Israel and Canada and in 1989 with the **North American Free Trade Agreement (NAFTA)** (signed by Canada, Mexico, and the United States in 1993). NAFTA's purpose was the most ambitious—to integrate the North American region. In addition, in 2001 the United States and thirty-three Western Hemisphere democracies pledged to build the **Free Trade Area of the Americas (FTAA)** in that region. This would create the globe's largest barrier-free trade zone, from the Arctic to Argentina, but in

CONTROVERSY:

GLOBALIZATION'S GROWING PAINS: IS THE WORLD TRADE ORGANIZATION A FRIEND OR FOE?

In late November 1999, the then 135 member countries of the World Trade Organization (WTO) and thirty additional observer states made final preparations to stage in Seattle what was billed as the *Millennium Round* on trade negotiations—the follow-up to the Uruguay Round of trade talks completed in 1993. The mood was optimistic. The meeting promised to celebrate the free-trade regime for the global marketplace and the contributions that lower trade barriers arguably had made to the growth of international exports and, for many members (particularly the United States), their longest and largest peacetime economic expansion in the twentieth century. There appeared to be widespread recognition that a half-century of generally rising prosperity had generated a climate of enthusiasm for the power of free trade. Fears of imports tend to recede in good economic times, and, with the best decade ever, most leaders in the twilight of the twentieth century emphasized the sunnier side of free trade. Advocates share the liberal conviction that countries, companies, and consumers have much to gain by a globalized economy freed from restraints on the exchange of goods across borders. Leaders embrace the liberal belief that a world without walls promotes prosperity and welfare, and in 1999 negotiators expected added benefits from a new trade round that could slash tariffs and other trade barriers in agriculture, manufactured goods, and services.

> *Every country in history that has raised its living standards—including the United States—has done so by hitching its wagon to the world economy. . . . During the past [60] years, the world has seen a massive reduction in trade barriers—and consequently the biggest and longest economic boon in history. Since 1950, world exports of manufactured goods multiplied [twentyfold] and world economic output increased sixfold. All this has meant rising standards of living for people around the world, but most especially those in the West and the United States.*
>
> —Fareed Zakaria, political economist

That mood and the seeming consensus on which it was based was shattered when the Seattle trade talks opened. An estimated fifty thousand to one hundred thousand protesters and grassroots anti-WTO activists, who differed widely in their special interests (the poor, environment, labor, women, indigenous people) joined hands to shout their common opposition to the general idea of globalization and free trade. A plane trailed a banner proclaiming "People Over Profits: Stop WTO" as part of what became known as "The Battle in Seattle" or, alternatively, the "Carnival against Capitalism." A tirade against open trade ensued, fueled by citizen backlash (Weir 2007; Aaronson 2001).

The immediate target of the demonstrations was the WTO; however, the organization itself was simply a convenient symbol of a much larger sea of discontent. The WTO protests (and the failure of the WTO conference attendees to compromise on tightly held positions and agree on even a minimal accord) exposed the deep divisions about the best ways to open global commerce and adopt new rules at a time of rapid change.

Controversies about globalization, free trade, and global governance are multiple. At the core is the question of whether a globalized economy is inevitable and, if so, if it is an antidote to suffering or an enemy of human welfare. The debates are explosive, because everyone is affected, but in quite different ways. Many enjoyed the 1990s boom years under liberalized trade engineered by the WTO's trade agreements. But the celebration is confined largely to the top—the privileged, powerful, and prosperous. Many others see themselves as clear victims of an open global economy, as when a factory closes and workers lose their jobs. Those discontented with globalized free trade include a diverse coalition of protestors, many of whom harbor specific concerns about wages, the environment, and human rights issues. Labor leaders contend that the WTO is sacrificing worker rights; environmental groups complain that when green values collide with world commerce, environmental standards are left out of trade negotiations; and human rights activists accuse the WTO of serving the preferences of MNCs for erasing trade barriers in ways that fail to protect human security. In addition, enraged Global South trade ministers see a Global North conspiracy in the WTO's efforts to adopt core labor standards, because the less-developed Global South views such high-sounding rules as a method to impose high tariffs on their products and take away the comparative advantages Global South nations enjoy with lower wage scales.

These, and other issues, continue and "for more than a decade trade talks have been described as 'acrimonious', 'grid locked' and 'stagnant'. [In June 2007, the trade ministers meeting in Doha, Qatar] denounced each other as 'uncooperative' and departed without agreement—paradoxically while global trade continued to grow at its usual rapid pace" (Naím, 2007)

What do you think? Is the WTO a valuable tool for improving global governance and human welfare, or a threat? Is the WTO and the free-trade practices it promotes too strong or too weak? Does the WTO put corporate greed and profits above human needs and environmental protection, as critics charge? Or do you agree with WTO Director-General Mike Moore's defense of free trade, and his warning against what he called a "false debate" between people and the WTO? He maintained, "Trade is the ally of working people, not their enemy. As living standards improve, so does education, health, the environment and labor standards."

■ **regional trade agreements (RTAs)**

sometimes called preferential trade agreements, RTAs are treaties among members of a trade bloc that establish special advantageous reductions of trade barriers to members but permit discrimination tariffs against nonmembers.

December 2005 negotiations stalled in strong resistance to U.S. pressure for FTAA. The deadlock was fueled by Venezuela's fiery president Hugo Chávéz's opposition to "free trade in any form [because the agreement, he claimed, would] permanently extend American political domination of the region to the economic realm."

The successful Mercosur free-trade zone in South America is another example of a regional regime. Its six member countries—Argentina, Brazil, Paraguay, Uruguay, and later Chile and Bolivia—increased the value of trade within the bloc to $21.1 billion from only $4.1 billion in 1990. The enlarged ten-member Association of Southeast Asian Nations (ASEAN) free-trade region represents yet another among the many multilateral regional trading blocs. Its intrablock trade climbed to $143 billion from less than $23.7 billion in 1990 (WDI 2007, 332).

Many feel that NAFTA and other regional free-trade zones are consistent with the WTO's rules. They see **regional trade agreements (RTAs)** as catalysts to trade because they provide tariff preferences or duty-free treatment to exports originating within the bloc's members. Others worry, however, that a division of the global marketplace into competing regional trade blocs is an obstacle to the integration of the entire global economy, and that RTAs intensify competition between the three major trade blocs, ASEAN, NAFTA, and the EU. If trade-bloc rivalry intensifies, the result would

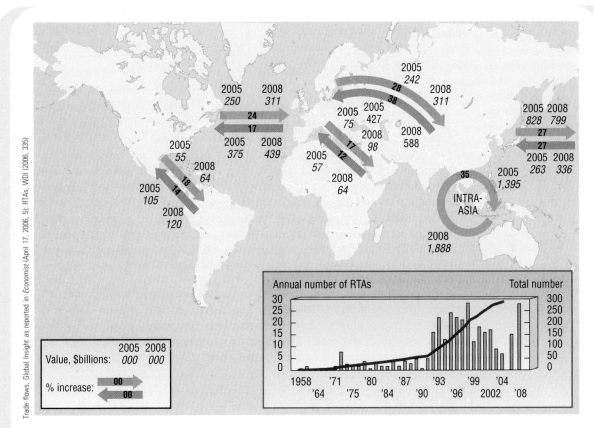

Trade flows, Global Insight as reported in *Economist* (April 17, 2006, 5); RTAs, WDI (2006, 335)

MAP 10.2

THE VOLUME OF TRADE FLOWS BETWEEN MAJOR REGIONS, 2005–2008 The arrows on this map trace the levels of trade volume and increases between the major regions from 2005 to 2008. A telling trend is the continued concentration of world trade between the three major trade blocs in the wealthy Global North—although trade with the Global East and Global South is increasing. Another trend (right) is the growth of regional trade agreements (RTAs).

be a cutthroat mercantile rivalry in which each bloc's fear and exclusion of the others splits the world into three or more competitive economic poles, or regional trade centers, and destroys the benefits that open world trade can provide for all.

Inspect Map 10.2, tracing the levels of trade flowing across and between the globe's regions. Intraregional trade, the growing percentage of trade in exports *within* a trade bloc as a result of the major regional trade agreements, has been a growing trend since 1970. For example, 66 percent of European Union exports are with other EU partners and over 56 percent of NAFTA exports are to other NAFTA partners (WDI 2007, 333). Thus, in general, the fact that trade is increasingly concentrated within regional RTAs is a strengthening trend.

On top of this development has been the rapid emergence of *bilateral* trade deals with both regional trade organizations outside states' own regions as well as with other individual states. Countries are racing to negotiate RTAs in order to cement special trade relationships with countries and regions with which they presently lack access to vigorous trade. This is an entrenched trend: The World Bank in 2008 recorded more than 250 regional trade agreements in force (six times as many as two decades ago) and calculated that about one third of global trade takes place between pairs of countries with reciprocal trade agreements. "If RTAs reportedly planned or under negotiation are concluded, the total number of RTAs in force might well approach three hundred" (www.wto.org, December 4, 2008).

The impact seems destined to be a consequential transformation in global trade integration. "The international trading system is increasingly characterized by a complex network of preferential trade regimes, sitting side-by-side with the WTO multilateral trading system. We see a rise in cross-regional bilateral agreements, the growing involvement of countries that have traditionally remained outside regional agreements, the development of interlinked (overlapping) agreements, and considerable variations in the design and content of RTAs. One-third of the FTAs currently under negotiation are among countries that belong to different geographical areas. All major countries are involved in cross-regional FTAs. . . . Countries that have traditionally remained outside regional agreements are now negotiating and joining RTAs" (WTO 2003, 51). The proliferation of RTAs and increasing bilateral free-trade agreements have meant overlapping membership for many countries.

This trend suggests that the globalization of trade integration throughout the entire world is progressing, even though the expansion of trade within regions is also growing. The removal of trade barriers sharpens competition, and it also increases economic growth. Thus, trade flows reward the competitors that produce the best products at the best price, wherever in the world they are located.

Trade Tricks

Trade liberalization has played a key role in the growth of the global economy since World War II, and there is virtual unanimity among economists regarding the potential benefits of free trade. As economist and columnist Paul Krugman noted, "If there were an Economist's Creed, it would surely contain the affirmations 'I Understand the Principle of Comparative Advantage' and 'I Advocate Free Trade'" (1987: 131).

However, free trade is at a *political* disadvantage to neomercantilism. This is due to the nature of the costs and benefits that accompany free trade. In the aggregate, the societal benefits of free trade greatly outweigh the costs. Yet these benefits, particularly the consumer gains that result from imports, are spread throughout an entire society, and are often not noticed. For example, though foreign trade may enable you to save ten dollars on a sweatshirt, you are probably unaware that imports are the reason behind your savings. There is thus little incentive to politically organize in the interests of imports—if you discovered that the price of sweatshirts had risen by ten dollars, you would probably not take the time to organize "pro-import" protest marches! However, the "costs" of free trade are quite concentrated and visible. It is quite common, for example, to hear of plants being closed and jobs being lost due to the presence of cheaper imports. There are thus greater political incentives to organize against free trade and for these forces to influence the political process. In short, "bad economics is often the cornerstone of good politics" (Drezner 2000: 70).

Given this dilemma, trade squabbles are likely to continue, as states have political incentives to enact neomercantilist policies. This section will explain some of these policy tools, all which fall under the broad rubric of **protectionism**—policies designed to "protect" domestic industries from foreign competition.

- **Tariffs**—a tax placed on imported goods—are the most well-known protectionist policy tool. Though average tariff levels have greatly decreased due to the WTO, they are still occasionally employed. For example, in 2002 President Bush imposed tariffs ranging from 8 percent to 30 percent on steel imports.

- **Import quotas** unilaterally specify the quantity of a particular product that can be imported from abroad. In the late 1950s, for example, the United States established import quotas on oil, arguing that they were necessary to protect U.S. national security. Hence the government, rather than the marketplace, determined the amount and source of imports.

- **Export quotas** result from negotiated agreements between producers and consumers and restrict the flow of products (e.g., shoes or sugar) from the former to the latter. **Orderly market arrangements (OMAs)** are formal agreements through which a country accepts limiting the export of products that might impair workers in the importing country, often under specific rules designed to monitor and manage trade flows. Exporting countries are willing to accept such restrictions in exchange for concessions from the importing countries. The Multi-Fiber Arrangement (MFA) is an example of an elaborate OMA that restricts exports of textiles and apparel. It originated in the early 1960s, when the United States formalized earlier, informal **voluntary export restrictions (VERs)** with Japan and Hong Kong to protect domestic producers from cheap cotton imports. The quota system was later extended to other importing and exporting countries and then, in the 1970s, to other fibers, when it became the MFA.

- As quotas and tariffs have been reduced, a broader category of trade restrictions known as **nontariff barriers (NTBs)** have been created to impede imports without direct tax levies. They cover a wide range of creative government regulations designed to shelter particular domestic industries from foreign competition, including health and safety regulations, government purchasing procedures, subsidies, and antidumping regulations (to prevent foreign producers from selling their goods for less than they cost domestically).

- Among developing countries whose domestic industrialization goals may be hindered by the absence of protection from the Global North's more efficient firms, the **infant industry** argument is often used to justify mercantilist trade policies. According to this argument, tariffs or other forms of protection are necessary to nurture young industries until they eventually mature and lower production costs to successfully compete in the global marketplace. Import-substitution industrialization policies, which were once popular in Latin America and elsewhere, often depended on protection of infant industries (see Chapter 5).

- In the Global North and Global East, creating comparative advantages now motivates the use of what is known as **strategic trade policy** as a neomercantilist method to ensure that a country's industries will remain competitive. Strategic trade targets government subsidies toward particular industries so they gain comparative advantages over foreign producers. One popular protectionist

■ protectionism

barriers of foreign trade, such as tariffs and quotas, that protect local industries from competition for the purchase of products local manufacturers produce.

■ tariffs

tax assessed on goods as they are imported into a country.

■ import quotas

nontariff barriers to free trade that limit the quantity of particular products that can be imported.

■ export quotas

barriers to free trade agreed to by two trading states to protect their domestic producers.

■ orderly market arrangements (OMAs)

voluntary export restrictions through government-to-government agreements to follow specific trading rules.

■ voluntary export restrictions (VERs)

a protectionist measure popular in the 1980s and early 1990s, in which exporting countries agree to restrict shipments of a particular product to a country to deter it from imposing an even more burdensome import quota.

■ nontariff barriers (NTBs)

measures other than tarriffs that discriminate against imports without direct tax levies and are beyond the scope of international regulation.

■ infant industry

newly established industries ("infants") that are not yet strong enough to compete against mature foreign producers in the global marketplace until in time they develop and can then compete.

■ strategic trade policy

government subsidies for particular domestic industries to help them gain competitive advantages over foreign producers.

strategy is **countervailing duties** that impose tariffs to offset alleged subsidies by foreign producers, as seen in the $268 billion the rich OECD countries paid in 2006 in subsidies to their farmers (*Economist*, November 10, 2007, 122). Another strategy is the imposition of **antidumping duties** to counter competitors' sale of products at below the cost of production. In 2006, WTO members launched eighty-seven new investigations of alleged dumping, but members "imposed 71 counter-measures, such as duties on dumped products, to protect their domestic industries" (*Economist*, December 2, 2006, 102).

Realist theory helps to account for states' impulse to practice mercantilist and neomercantilist protectionism. Recall that realism argues that states often compete rather than cooperate because international anarchy without global governance feeds states' distrust of each other. Anarchy encourages states to seek self-advantage and economic primacy—to get ahead. In this sense, neomercantilist strategic trade is a prime example of this realist explanation of states' concern for self-interest. "It focuses on economic development as a matter of strategic significance. It explicitly aims to achieve trade surpluses and large dollar reserves. It's aimed at fostering production and a high savings rate but suppressing consumption" (Prestowitz 2005).

Neomercantilism Ascendant?

The WTO warns that many states are likely to heed the siren call of trade protectionism against competitive imports. Given the political advantages of neomercantilist policies, states often have a hard time resisting the constant demands of domestic industries and interest groups for protection. They do so even if, according to liberalism, their relations with their trade partners will deteriorate and all will suffer in the long run if these trade partners retaliate with clever and innovative new counter-protectionist tariffs, of which there are many. If neomercantilist thinking that "imports are bad but exports are good" spreads, the free-trade regime will lose its momentum.

The simultaneous pursuit of liberalism and mercantilism today shows states' determination to reap the benefits of interdependence while minimizing its costs. It also reveals the tension between states and markets, between the promise that everyone will benefit and the fear that the benefits will not be equally distributed. The absence of world government encourages each state to be more concerned with how it fares competitively in relation to other states—its relative gains—than collectively with its *absolute gains*. U.S. trade policy reflects twin instincts: to push for trade liberalization in foreign markets and to cushion the costs of imports to the U.S. economy and employment rate.

How U.S. trade partners and rivals view the American commitment to free trade will heavily shape their own trade policies and whether they will choose free trade over protectionism. America's trade competitors are upset because the United States, once the principal advocate of free trade in the post-World War II era, has not lived up to its own rhetoric and has increasingly engaged in neomercantilist protectionism.

One illustration: One-fourth of all U.S. foreign aid goes to helping the recipients buy U.S.-provided weapons, equipment, or services (*Harper's*, October 2005, 11). U.S. neomercantilism is undermining the liberal trade regime because the U.S. stature as the globe's leading economic superpower has not been harnessed to take responsibility for setting standards for free trade. "Perhaps the greatest hypocrisy," writes Ian Campbell (2004) "is that the United States, which preaches the merits of free trade more strongly than almost any other country, spends tens of billions of dollars to prevent its own markets from being free and has taken fresh measures to enable its own markets to discriminate against other countries' producers."

To free-trade liberals, the trade game is rigged by the routine and lucrative corruption known as "rent-seeking" (economic interests getting governments to impose handicaps on competitors). **Rents** that create obstacles to participants in the global marketplace harm everyone, but especially the poor (Klein 2007). Even by 2020, however, an intelligence team of forecasting experts (NIC 2004) predicts, "the benefits of globalization won't be global. . . . Gaps will widen between those countries benefiting from globalization economically . . . and those underdeveloped nations or products within nations left behind [despite the likelihood that] the world economy is projected to be about 80 percent larger in 2020 than it was in 2000."

The pressures on free trade notwithstanding, "rapid globalization has done nothing to undermine the confidence liberals have always placed in trade. No serious economist questions the case for international integration through flows of goods and services, though there is a lively argument over how integration through trade can be brought about" (Crook 2003, 3). Will that confidence prevail?

TRIUMPH OR TROUBLE FOR THE GLOBAL ECONOMY'S FUTURE?

The struggle to maintain a liberal trading order, like the global financial struggles (see Chapter 9), is far from over. In assessing future trends and controversies within the global trading order, it is helpful to keep the following parameters in mind:

■ **Though there are problems with the global trading system, it has a better developed "architecture" than the global financial system.** As covered in Chapter 9, the global financial system is prone to "manics, panics, and crashes" (Kindleberger 2000)—currencies fluctuate according to the dictates of the markets, and the IMF merely provides for the monitoring of financial systems and "crisis management" for countries that are in dire financial straits. By contrast, the WTO provides a fairly well-developed global "architecture" for the world trading system. When the GATT evolved into the WTO in 1995, it greatly expanded its mandate, becoming a true rules-based regime that discourages neomercantilist measures and settles trading disputes among states. The WTO can hold even its most powerful members accountable for their trade practices. For example, the WTO played a pivotal role in forcing the United States to rescind its 2002 steel tariffs—according to a WTO ruling, had the United States not ended the protection of its steel markets, the EU would have been able to impose some $4 billion worth of trade sanctions against the United States (Becker 2003).

In addition to having the policy "sticks" to bring member states in line, the "carrot" of WTO membership, which brings with it access to the markets of the 151 member states, can serve to open up societies and improve the quality of state governance. Recent additions to the WTO, China, Saudi Arabia, and Cambodia, were all forced to undergo sweeping reforms of their trading regimes, including increases in the

---

■ **countervailing duties**

government tariffs to offset suspected subsidies provided by foreign governments to their producers.

■ **antidumping duties**

taxes placed on another exporting state's alleged selling of a product at a price below the cost to produce it.

■ **rents**

higher-than-normal financial returns on investments that are realized from governmental restrictive interference or monopolistic markets.

accountability and transparency of their trade policies in order to make it through the "accession process" and join the WTO. According to Peter Sutherland, a Founding Director of the WTO, "Cambodia, China, and Saudi Arabia have changed dramatically—and mostly for the better—in the context of acceding to the WTO" (2008: 127). Moreover, Aaronson and Zimmerman (2007) note that the WTO accession process, as well as the periodic trade policy reviews required of WTO members, may have positive effects for the overall quality of governance within states, including increases in state transparency and levels of political participation.

▓ **However, the WTO is currently a "victim" of its successes.** When the GATT, the precursor to the WTO, was formed it contained twenty-three members and was charged with one central goal—the reduction of tariffs. It has been very successful in lowering tariffs. From the time that GATT was founded in 1947 until the WTO was finalized in 1995, average tariff levels fell from 40 percent to 3 percent. Moreover, the WTO has near–universal membership. Of the 212 states in the world, 151 are WTO members and another 30 are in various stages of negotiating membership.

As tariffs have declined as a policy tool, the WTO has begun to confront a broad variety of issues related to international trade, including agricultural policy, intellectual property rights (see Chapter 11), trade in services, environmental protection measures, labor standards, and government procurement policies. As demonstrated in the "Controversy" section for this chapter (see page 295), as well as the wave of protests in South Korea regarding U.S. beef imports (Sang-Hun 2008), these new issues are much more difficult to resolve than the reduction of tariff levels, in that they tap into key concerns about state sovereignty. The WTO is thus in an interesting dilemma—having largely succeeded in its goal of lowering tariffs, and having attracted almost every state into the organization, they are now tasked with getting an increasing number of states to agree on an increasing number of issues. Indeed, the most recent round of WTO negotiations, the Doha Round, has been ongoing since 2002 and still faces a variety of major obstacles (Lynn 2008). It is commonly argued that the proliferation of regional and bilateral trade agreements is due in no small part to the WTO's lack of progress in recent years.

▓ **The perennial struggle between free trade and protectionism is only part of the current puzzle.** Many of the burgeoning controversies surrounding trade cannot be viewed as only a debate between free trade and protectionism. In particular, many deal with the potential impact of trade on "non-trade" issues, such as labor rights, human rights, and the environment. As trade policy specialist I.M. Destler posits, a "new politics" of international trade is emerging. Key controversies surrounding the WTO, as demonstrated by the 1999 "Battle of Seattle" and the seemingly ubiquitous protests at WTO meetings, concern such issues as the protection of worker rights and the environment. Unlike the traditional trade debates, these new issues involve "not the balance to be struck among economic interests and goals, but rather the proper balance between economic concerns and other societal values." Given the breadth of these issues, they are far more difficult to reconcile, and pose "a challenge that long-standing trade policy institutions were ill-equipped to meet or even to understand" (Destler 2005, 253).

Overall, though the world trading system has certainly evolved since the 1944 meeting at Bretton Woods, it faces a variety of challenges that can greatly undermine the further progression—or even the legitimacy—of the liberal trade order. However, a number of other global trends are also likely to influence the future direction of the world political economy, beyond the policies of the United States. These, in combination, may sustain and strengthen the liberal free-trade regime that has contributed to global economic growth. World commerce has become globalized; global financial flows outstrip trade transactions within countries; and market forces

> *One of the paradoxes of the global economy is that even as trade agreements stumble and protectionism appears strong, international trade is booming.*
> —Carlos Lozada, economics editor at the Washington Post

almost everywhere are now being given a freer reign to determine economic outcomes. With trade growing rapidly in the absence of barriers, and with the expansion of free-trade areas as well as cross-regional trade agreements and states' bilateral open-trade agreements with regional blocs and with one another, pressure to preserve the liberal trade regime is expanding. Multinational corporations are increasingly playing a larger role in the continuing growth of commercial liberalism worldwide. Moreover, India and China, which will emerge as the largest markets in the world over the course of this century, have "converted" to free trade and are opening up their restrictive markets to exports. All of these developments suggest that the prospects for the momentum of commercial liberalism to gain strength are promising.

The world may seem to be spinning out of control in a sea change of rapid globalization that hides the decisions that affect our daily lives. To be sure, the globalization of both international finance and international trade are entangling the functions of governments and markets, and making it difficult to tell the difference between countries and corporations. In the next chapter, you will move to an exploration of *geo-economics*. Here you can examine how changes in world population and global culture are transforming world politics by tearing down the boundaries of national barriers in ways that are creating a global village in a borderless world.

Key Terms

General Agreement on Tariffs and Trade (GATT)
World Trade Organization (WTO)
trade integration
virtual corporations
Liberal International Economic Order (LIEO)
commercial liberalism
interdependence
comparative advantage
relative gains
neomercantilism

hegemony
macroeconomics
collective good
free-riders
most-favored-nation principle (MFN)
nondiscrimination rule
American Free Trade Agreement (NAFTA)
Free Trade Area of the Americas (FTAA)
regional trade agreements (RTAs)
protectionism

tariffs
import quotas
export quotas
orderly market arrangements (OMAs)
voluntary export restrictions (VERs)
nontariff barriers (NTBs)
infant industry
strategic trade policy
countervailing duties
antidumping duties
rents

CHAPTER 11
THE DEMOGRAPHIC AND CULTURAL DIMENSIONS OF GLOBALIZATION

Globalization is a revolutionary change, but it is also a continuation of the conflicts of the past. In some important respects it is leveling the playing field . . . and to that extent it is a force for human advance. At the same time it is inflaming nationalist and religious passions . . . Globalization makes the world smaller. It may also make it, or sections of it, richer. It does not make it more peaceful or more liberal. . . . It turns society upside down, destroying entire ways of life.

—John Gray, political economist

Visions of America LLC/Alamy Limited

The World at One's Fingertips. The revolution in telecommunications has contributed to "the death of distance," as virtually instantaneous communications are possible nearly everywhere. Here, in a remote and desolate region of northern Kenya, a Masai warrior makes a call on his cellular telephone.

Everyone in the world is becoming more alike each and every day. It really is a small world, after all. As you probably already have at one time or another imagined, beneath the skin every human being is essentially similar. We all share the same planet. And we all tend to respond to the same experiences that almost everyone everywhere feels at one time or another—love, fear, alienation or a sense of a common community and destiny. And everyone also certainly shares a similar aspiration for a better world, as expressed by world futurist Rafael M. Salas: "The final binding thought is to shape a more satisfying future for the coming generations, a global society in which individuals can develop their full potential, free of capricious inequalities and threats of environmental degradation."

There is rising expectation that this universal hope will be fulfilled. Why? An answer is that growing numbers throughout the world are pursuing these human goals, because globalization is bringing all of humanity together as never before in bonds of interdependence. Do you, like them, think that breaking down barriers and boundaries can bring people together in a human family that recognizes no East, West, North, or South, but every individual as part of the same human race? Should you therefore practice, not cutthroat politics, but morals? And if that goal is your passion, should you, like many others joining together in NGOs across the globe, promote not partisanship, but the recognition of true merit wherever found?

Is this rising consciousness and global activism warranted? Is the vision on which people are increasingly defining themselves as global citizens realistic? Reasonable? Will a truly global society come into being in your lifetime, propelled by the pressure

We are in the midst of a global "associational revolution."
—Lester M. Salamon, global civil society scholar

of cascading globalization that is tearing down visions of separate states, nations, and races that throughout past history have so divided humanity? This chapter opens a door to evaluating the prospect for such a jaw-dropping development. You will be asked to consider if global trends might transform the world, and the world politics that condition it.

POPULATION CHANGE AS A GLOBAL CHALLENGE

To formulate your interpretation of this human dimension of globalization, it is instructive to first look at how changes in world population are a part of the globalization of world politics.

"Chances are," notes an expert in **demography**, Jeffrey Kluger (2006), "that you will never meet any of the estimated 247 human beings who were born in the past minute. In a population of 6.7 billion, 247 is a demographic hiccup. In the minute before last, however, there were another 247. In the minutes to come, there will be another, then another, then another. By next year at this time, all those minutes will have produced millions of newcomers in the great human mosh pit. That kind of crowd is very hard to miss."

■ demography
the study of population changes, their sources, and their impact.

As the population on this planet increases, globalization is bringing us closer together in a crowded global village. Evidence strongly suggests that unrestrained population growth will result in environmental degradation and strife (see Chapter 12 and 13). Population change also forces consideration of standards for ethics (the criteria by which right and wrong behavior and motives should be distinguished). Some people regard the freedom to parent as a human right. Others claim that controls on family size are necessary because unregulated population will "parent" a crowded and unlivable future world without the resources necessary to sustain life for all people. For this reason, politics—the exercise of influence in an attempt to resolve controversial issues in one's favor—surrounds debate about population policies. To understand why the globalization of population has become such a controversial issue, it is helpful to trace the global trends in population growth that have made this topic so problematic.

World Population Growth Rates

The rapid growth of world population is described by a simple mathematical principle that the Reverend Thomas Malthus noticed in 1798: unchecked, population increases in a geometric or exponential ratio (e.g., 1 to 2, 2 to 4, 4 to 8), whereas subsistence increases in only an arithmetic ratio (1 to 2, 2 to 3, 3 to 4). When population increases at such a geometric rate, the acceleration can be staggering. Carl Sagan illustrated this principle governing growth rates with a parable he termed "The Secret of the Persian Chessboard":

> The way I first heard the story, it happened in ancient Persia. But it may have been India, or even China. Anyway, it happened a long time ago. The Grand Vizier, the principal adviser to the King, had invented a new game. It was played with moving pieces on a board of 64 squares. The most important piece was the King. The next most important piece was the Grand Vizier—just what we might expect of a game invented by a Grand Vizier. The object of the game was to capture the enemy King, and so the game was called, in Persian, shahmat—shah for king, mat for dead. Death to the King. In Russia it is still called shakhmaty, which perhaps conveys a lingering revolutionary ardor. Even in English there is an echo of the name—the final move is called "checkmate." The game, of course, is chess.
>
> As time passed, the pieces, their moves and the rules evolved. There is, for example, no longer a piece called the Grand Vizier—it has become transmogrified into a Queen, with much more formidable powers.
>
> Why a king should delight in the creation of a game called "Death to the King" is a mystery. But, the story goes, he was so pleased that he asked the Grand Vizier to name his own reward for such a splendid invention. The Grand Vizier had his answer ready: He was a humble man, he told the King. He wished only for a humble reward. Gesturing to the eight columns and eight rows of squares on the board he devised, he asked that he be given a single grain of wheat on the first square, twice that on the second square, twice that on the third, and so on, until each square had its complement of wheat.
>
> No, the King remonstrated. This is too modest a prize for so important an invention. He offered jewels, dancing girls, palaces. But the Grand Vizier, his eyes becomingly lowered, refused them all. It was little piles of wheat he wanted. So, secretly marveling at the unselfishness of his counselor, the King graciously consented.

When the Master of the Royal Granary began to count out the grains, however, the King was in for a rude surprise. The number of grains starts small enough: 1, 2, 4, 8, 16, 32, 64, 128, 256, 512, 1,024. . . . But by the time the 64th square is approached, the number becomes colossal, staggering. In fact the number is nearly 18.5 quintillion grains of wheat. Maybe the Grand Vizier was on a high fiber diet.

How much does 18.5 quintillion grains of wheat weigh? If each grain were 2 millimeters in size, then all the grains together would weigh around 75 billion metric tons, which far exceeds what could have been stored in the King's granaries. In fact, this is the equivalent of about 150 years of the world's present wheat production. (Sagan 1989, 14)

To picture in another way how growth rates unfold, consider how money deposited in a savings account grows as it earns interest not only on the original investment but also on the interest payments. If one of your ancestors had saved a mere $10 in the bank for us two hundred years ago, and if it accrued a steady 6 percent annual interest, today you would be a millionaire! Population grows in the same way. It is a function of increases in the original number of people plus those built from past population growth. Thus, a population growing at a 1 percent rate will double in sixty-nine years, whereas a population growing at a 2 percent rate will double in only thirty-five years. (The impact of different growth rates on doubling times can be easily calculated by dividing sixty-nine by the percentage of growth.)

The story of population growth is told in its statistics. The annual rate of population growth in the twentieth century increased from less than 1 percent in 1900 to a peak of 2.2 percent in 1964. It has since dropped to about 1.2 percent. Despite the recent drop in rate, however, the absolute number of people *added* each year expanded, from sixteen million in 1900 to a peak of eighty-eight million in 1989, and thereafter

If one postulates that the human race began with a single pair of parents, the population has had to double only thirty-one times to reach its huge total.

—Robert S. McNamara, former World Bank President

has declined to about an additional seventy-four million new people, when global population expanded by adding the equivalent of another Egypt (WDR 2008, 334). Plainly, the planet is certain to have many people by the mid-twenty-first century, well beyond the 6.7 billion in 2008 (see Figure 11.1). Yet the much-feared "population explosion" is now expected to be much less than previously predicted.

The Demographic Divide between Global North and Global South Population is growing much more rapidly in the developing Global South countries (which are least able to support their existing populations) than in the wealthy Global North, where population is declining gradually despite increasingly longer life spans. This portends fulfillment of the "demographic divide" predicted in Figure 11.2, which is based on the probability that the population of the Global North will fall (from 23 percent of total world population in 1950 and 15 percent in 2007) to only 10 percent by 2050 (WDI 2007, 16).

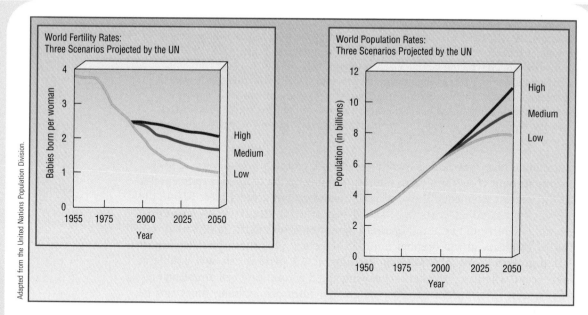

FIGURE 11.1

WORLD POPULATION GROWTH PROJECTIONS TO THE YEAR 2050 By 2050 an additional 2.4 billion people are forecast to be living on the Earth, the UN predicts, raising the total to 9.3 billion because of Global South fertility declines and increasing Global North longevity. Such predictions are uncertain because growth rates depend on a variety of factors. The UN figure on the right displays the range of world population forecasts by the year 2050.

■ **replacement-level fertility**

one couple replacing themselves on average with two children so that a country's population will remain stable if this rate prevails.

■ **fertility rate**

the average number of children born to a woman (or group of women) during her lifetime.

Global population cannot stabilize until it falls below **replacement-level fertility** (each couple replacing itself with 2.1 children). That will not happen until the total **fertility rate**, the worldwide average number of children born to a woman, falls from the rate of 2.7 today to 2.1. This is unlikely to happen because 95 percent of population growth worldwide is centered in the least-developed Global South countries where preferred family size remains far in excess of the replacement level, averaging 4.9 children for each mother in the least-developed countries (HDR 2008, 246).

Almost all the problems in the North–South dispute can be traced to disparities in income and economic growth that are directly linked to the differentials in population growth rates. A brief look at these dynamics completes the picture of ongoing political conflict between the haves and the have-nots.

Population Momentum   Even though birthrates are likely to decline throughout the twenty-first century, world population is projected to continue to surge for decades in the future because of "population momentum" resulting from the large number of women now entering their childbearing years. Like the inertia of a descending airliner when it first touches down on the runway, population growth simply cannot be halted even with an immediate, full application of the brakes. Instead, many years of high fertility mean that more women will be entering their reproductive years than in the past. Not until the size of the generation giving birth to children is no larger than the generation among which deaths are occurring will the population "airplane" come to a halt.

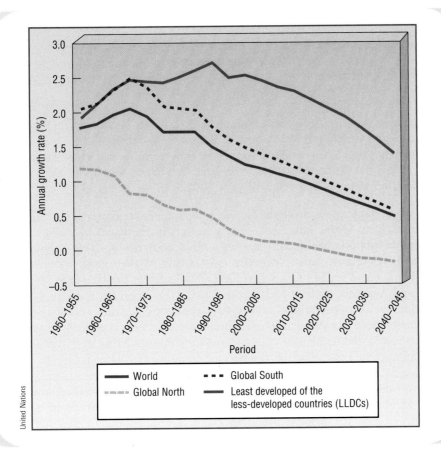

Annual growth rate (%)

World
Global North
Global South
Least developed of the
less-developed countries (LLDCs)

Period

United Nations

FIGURE 11.2

THE GLOBAL NORTH–
GLOBAL SOUTH
POPULATION DIVIDE
China now is home to 20.5
percent of world
population, India 17.4
percent and the Global
South 46.8 percent
(*Economist*, April 21, 2007,
109). By the year 2015, 86
percent of the globe's
population will be living in
the low- and the middle-
income Global South
countries (HDR 2008, 246).
In contrast, as shown in
this figure, a "birth-dearth"
is underway in the Global
North.

Western Europe and sub-Saharan Africa illustrate the force of population momentum. Africa's demographic profile is one of rapid population growth, as each new age group (cohort) contains more people than the one before it. Thus, even if individual African couples choose to have fewer children than their parents, Africa's population will continue to grow because there are now more men and women of childbearing age than ever before. In contrast, Europe's population profile is one of slow growth, as recent cohorts have been smaller than preceding ones. In fact, Europe has moved beyond replacement-level fertility to become a "declining" population with low birthrates and a growing number of people who survive middle age. A product of an extended period of low birthrates, low death rates, and increased longevity, Europe is best described as an aging society, where the low birthrates and aging populations have caused alarm that the number of European newborns will not be sufficient to renew populations.

The Aging and Graying World Population Take a close look at the "graying of the world." It is changing the contours of the global community. A revolution in longevity is unfolding, with life expectancy at birth worldwide at a record-high sixty-eight years, and expected to rise by the year 2015 to seventy-five years. This is creating an increasingly aged world population. By 2015, over nine percent of the globe's expected 7.3 billion people are likely to be sixty-five or older (HDR 2008, 232, 243).

> *The coming death shortage [from] the longevity boom will make us sorry to be alive.*
>
> —Charles Mann, futurist

Global aging is occurring at rates never seen before, in part because of improvements in medicine and health care. "In absolute terms, the number of older persons has tripled over the last 50 years and will more than triple again over the next 50 years. In relative terms, the percentage of older persons is projected to more than double worldwide over the next half century" (UN 2002, 33).

Rapidly aging populations make the "highly vulnerable" economies of Global North countries such as Spain, Italy, and France especially burdened by rising old-age dependency costs compared with less-vulnerable countries such as Belgium, the Netherlands, Germany, Japan, Sweden, and Canada or even those states ranking relatively low on an index of "aging vulnerability" such as the United States, Great Britain, and Australia (Cetron and Davies 2005, 5). In contrast, population trends are heading in the opposite direction in Global South countries. Fertility rates are three times higher there (WDI 2007, 42). Because each cohort is typically larger than the one before it, the number of young men and women entering their reproductive years continues to grow. Though the pace of aging is actually faster in the Global South than in the Global North—in the less-developed countries the population of people over the age of sixty-five will rise to 35 percent by 2050—people between the ages of 15 and 29 comprise more than 25 percent of the population in much of North Africa and the Middle East (Slackman 2008). As the burgeoning youth population in the Global South faces poor economic conditions and a lack of resources to provide for a family, many are turning to religious fundamentalism to counter their frustration and despair and are propelling an Islamic revival. Moreover, youth bulges, particularly in conjunction with economic stagnation, have been linked to a greater propensity for domestic armed conflict (Urdal 2006).

The resulting differences in these demographic momentums are producing quite different population profiles in the developed and the developing worlds. The rich Global North is aging, with falling birth rates and declining populations; the poor Global South is home to a surplus of youth, with rising birth rates and aging people and growing populations. It is not difficult to see how this facet of globalization is *not* making people in the world more alike. Differentials in the geographical distribution of population are increasing differences in the quality of life experienced on the planet.

■ **population density**

the number of people within each country, region or city, measuring the geographical concentration of the population as a ratio of the average space available for each resident.

Urbanization   When interpreting projections in demographics, take into account also the number of people within each country as defined geographically by their concentration. This is known as **population density** to measure how close together people are living. Some countries and regions are very crowded and others are not. For example, Singapore is the most congested country in the world, with 6,508 people for each square kilometer, and people in Mongolia and Namibia are the least likely to bump into one another, with only two people for each square kilometer (WDI 2008, 14–16).

This urbanizing trend is producing a related kind of demographic divide, too: the increasing concentration of population in giant megacities (see Map 11.1). The majority of people live in cities: "There are in the world today some 400 giant cities with more than one million inhabitants. Among them, 120 have more than two million and fifty have more than five million; thirty-seven metropolises have between 8 million and 26 million" (Dogan 2004, 347).

Human history will ever more become urban history.
—John Grimond, demographer

As the percentage of world population residing in urban agglomerations increases worldwide, the "*dualism*" between city dwellers and those living in the rural and poor periphery will make the urbanized core cities more similar to each other in outlooks, values, and lifestyles, with people in megacities communicating and computing with one another at greater rates than they do with people living in the countryside within their own states (Dogan 2004). This trend is producing another form of cultural globalization, and the urbanization of the world is accelerating and spreading. In 2008, "3.3 billion people will be living in urban areas. By 2030, this is expected to swell to almost 5 billion" (UNFPA 2007). What is more, already three-fourths of the populations in the Global North live in these big cities that are getting bigger, but cities are growing fastest in the developing Global South countries.

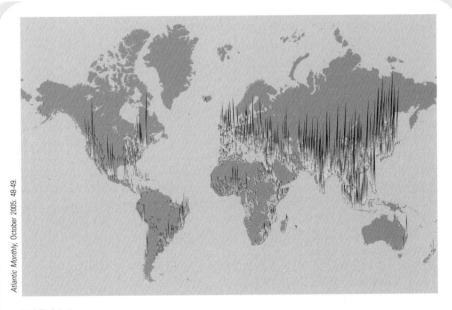

Atlantic Monthly, October 2005: 48-49.

MAP 11.1

A WORLD THAT IS "SPIKY," NOT FLAT As this map shows, "more and more people are clustering in urban areas—the world's demographic mountain ranges, so to speak. The share of the world's population living in urban areas, just 3 percent in 1800, was nearly 30 percent by 1950. Today it stands at about 50 percent; in advanced countries, three out of four people live in urban areas (HDR 2008, 246). This map shows the uneven distribution of the world's population. Five megacities currently have more than twenty million inhabitants each. Twenty-four have more than ten million inhabitants, sixty more than five million, and one hundred fifty more than 2.5 million.

"This will be particularly notable in Africa and Asia where the urban population will double between 2000 and 2030... By 2030, the towns and cities of the developing world will make up 81 per cent of urban humanity" (UNFPA 2007; see also Burdett 2008).

The impact of global urbanization is likely to be the aggravation of health and environmental problems, straining supplies of clean water, shelter, and sanitation. If the urbanization throughout the global community continues at its current pace, which is almost certain, this trend will lead to still another kind of *transformation* in the world. We will consider another example next—the movement of people across borders through migration.

Global Migration Trends

■ global migration crisis

a severe problem stemming from the growing number of people moving from their home country to another country, straining the ability of the host countries to absorb the foreign emigrants.

The movement of populations across frontiers has reached unprecedented proportions, producing a **global migration crisis**. Each year since 1998, on average more than twelve million people qualified for and received refugee assistance (see Figure 8.2, p. 238). As floods of people leave their homeland for another country each year, cross-national migration has become a norm—so common in some places that leaving one's native country has almost become an expectation.

> *The ease of travel and communication, combined with looser borders, gives rise to endless crisscrossing streams of wanderers and guest workers, and international drifters.*
> —Eva Hoffman, demographer

Global travel and emigration have become routine in the global "age of migration" (Castles and Miller 2004). The mass movement by people living abroad has raised a host of moral issues, such as the ethnic balance inside host countries, the meaning of citizenship and sovereignty, the distribution of income, labor supply, *xenophobia*, the impact of multiculturalism, protection of basic human rights and prevention of exploitation, and the potential for large flows of migrants and refugees from *failed states*—countries whose governments no longer enjoy support from their rebelling citizens and from displaced peoples who either flee the country or organize revolts to divide the state into smaller independent units—to undermine democratic governance and state stability (see Chapters 7 and 13). Particularly troubling is the moral inconsistency between liberal democracies that simultaneously defend the fundamental right of refugees to emigrate and the absolute right of sovereign states to control their borders.

The governments of sovereign states are losing their grip on regulating the movement of foreigners inside their borders, and no multilateral IGOs for meaningful global governance exist to deal with the consequences of the escalating migration of people (and labor) around the globe. Porous borders create ambiguous ethics about the theoretical interpretation of mass migration movements (see Parker and Brassett 2005), but one consequence is clear: there are both winners and losers through the globalization of migration. Migration's impact on this dimension is uneven, for while migration has been largely beneficial for both sending and receiving countries, there is a growing backlash. By some estimates, the number of legal and illegal migrants is 200 million (Roberts 2008). For millions, a common approach to recovering hope for a future is to migrate, and this mass movement of people across borders for jobs has had many *externalities*, unintended side effects produced by the choices and behaviors in one activity that alter other conditions, for some beneficially and for others negatively. People most commonly migrate in search of better jobs. For host countries, this can contribute to economic growth. For example, the Hellenic Migration Policy Initiative in Greece attributes 1.5–2.0 percent of the growth in GDP each year to immigration (Roberts 2008, 6). For the home country, many of which are poor Global South countries, the growing flow of *remittances* or money that migrants earn while working abroad and then send to their families in their home countries provides one of the biggest sources of foreign currency. Yet there are worries that migration may reduce the job opportunities for natives and place a strain on public services. In 2008 many countries adopted measures intended to stem the flow of peoples across borders. In the United States, construction continues to extend the line of fences along the border with Mexico (Von Drehle 2008), the "European Parliament approved tough new rules for expelling undocumented immigrants" (Blake 2008, 1), and even countries in the Global South such as Nigeria took steps to counter what it saw as a security threat posed by large flows of illegal immigrants (Ekhoragbon 2008). As money goes around the world at these growing remittance rates, the globalization of migration means the globalization of labor and transfer of money.

The Globalization of Labor

In *Communist Manifesto*, his radical theory on the evils of capitalism, Karl Marx urged the workers of the world to unite and to throw off the chains imposed by the oppressive owners of capital. Marx assumed that workers everywhere were members of the same disadvantaged class who shared a common purpose and vision of their exploitation. But that assumption is not as accurate today. As the liberalization and rapid integration of markets throughout the world proceeded, labor markets were profoundly affected. Alongside the growth of organized labor unions and progressive reforms to protect workers' rights in the Global North industrial world, working conditions improved in the twentieth century.

Today, with the globalization of international trade and finance (see Chapters 9 and 10), interstate competition for workers has grown increasingly more competitive. Because the spread of globalization is uneven, some employees have become winners whereas many others have become losers.

As recently as the 1970s, one-third of the world's workers were insulated from the rest of the world through states committed to centralized economic planning such as the former communist bloc. That is no longer the case. Today, two giant population blocs—China and India, with half the world's labor force between them—are dominating the global labor market. Many other countries, from Mexico to Indonesia, are now capturing an ever-increasing share of the global employment market. The outsourcing of Global North production and employment has brought what the World Bank estimates to be more than 90 percent of the world's work force into the global economic mainstream.

Accommodating the wave of new workers available for employment is proving difficult. The growth of trade has not automatically created more employees and better wages. The prospects for rising wages remain especially grim for women. The lack of jobs is a worldwide problem. For example, even in the Global North sustained economic growth has not reduced Europe's chronic unemployment; for the past two decades about 12 percent of Europe's indigenous labor force has been idle. Unemployment and **underemployment** rates are lower in the United States, but the real wages of most U.S. workers have fallen over the past two decades and companies have been quick to hire legal and illegal migrant workers in huge numbers at lower pay to work for them.

■ **underemployment**
a condition critics trace to trade globalization in which a large portion of the labor force only works part time at low pay in occupations below their skill level.

Mass unemployment describes conditions in most countries today, and throughout much of the Global South employment growth has slowed and wages have fallen. With a world population of 6.7 billion, when "national governments face the daunting task of creating millions of additional jobs each year for the next fifty years in a situation of labor surplus, the quality of jobs suffer. Workers settle for lower wages, longer hours, fewer benefits, and less control over work activities. As global economic integration proceeds, surplus labor anywhere can weaken labor's bargaining power everywhere. Rapid technological developments and globalization have also decreased demand of some kinds of labor" (*Vital Signs 2000*).

The cost of declining employment rates is high. As the United Nations Development Programme has observed, "In both poor and rich countries dislocations from economic and corporate restructuring, and from dismantling the institutions of social protection, have meant greater insecurity in jobs and incomes. For the skilled,

> *Globalization has exposed a deep fault line between groups who have the skills and mobility to flourish in global markets and those who either do not have these advantages or perceive the expansion of unregulated markets as inimical to social stability.*
>
> —Dani Rodrik, development economist

salaries and work styles become similar, and likewise for the unskilled low wages and unemployment are increasingly a shared experience. High levels of joblessness produced by global economic integration result in human suffering and hopelessness, rising inequality within and between countries, and deteriorating social cohesion, domestic disintegration, and corroding democratic institutions." Growing global interdependence in one country affects the economic circumstances of workers in others as well:

> During that first era of openness, labor was more mobile than today (it was a time of mass migration). Now highly skilled and professional workers are mobile, either physically or via computer, but most countries no longer welcome unskilled immigrants.
>
> Meanwhile, companies that once were anchored in their communities can easily pick up and relocate. In fact, companies which do not go where they can manufacture and operate most efficiently will soon be overtaken by those which do. So capital can move, but labor can't; business executives are in a strong bargaining position, but workers aren't; and the result is pretty much what you would expect. (Hiatt 1997, 8)

Frank Fournier/Contact Press Images

CHILD LABOR IN A GLOBAL SYSTEM Globalization is sped not only by the rapid expansion of technology but by the availability of cheap labor in some countries which take advantage of their peoples' low wages to make products highly competitive in the globalized marketplace. Here a child labors at near slave wages in Bangladesh, producing goods that cost less than those made where labor unions protect workers.

Multinational corporations have been a primary vehicle of growing global interdependence that benefits some workers at the relative expense of others' wages. This forecast about the successes of the rich and powerful that makes workers the losers and that makes "the hollowing of the middle class a feature of income distribution in many countries" (Rodrik 1997b), has been fulfilled in the global economy; "wage inequality between skilled and unskilled labor is a global trend." Part of the reason is because MNCs easily move manufacturing sites and technical know-how to developing countries, where labor is cheap and their ability to control wages and move production has been facilitated by cross-border mergers and acquisitions.

> *To understand another human being you must gain some insight into the conditions which made him what he is.*
>
> —Margaret Bourke-White, American photojournalist

The World Bank estimates that since 1985, three-fourths of the jobs created by multinational corporations were in the Global South. Clearly, these workers with new job opportunities are benefiting from the globalization of labor. However, the World Bank warns, "many developing countries fear that increased competition for production by *other* developing countries is leading MNCs to make footloose investments and leave at the slightest shock." Such fears are also very alive in the

Global North because workers there are now fearful of losing their jobs to low-cost production in the Global South. The fear is compounded by the tendency for the companies that employ them to relocate abroad. So one price of the globalization of labor has been "jobless growth." And even if they can keep their jobs, workers site cheap foreign labor for their own lack of pay hikes and stagnating living standards.

Many people believe that globalization is responsible for the widening income gap between the richest and the poorest people and that increased competition from Global South workers is reducing the wages paid to Global North workers and contributing to rising levels of unemployment. However, analysts disagree about how trade competition is producing "work force blues" and income inequalities. Still, the trends underway are unmistakable: the world will have one billion millionaires by 2025 while billions will remain in poverty (*Futurist*, "Outlook 2008," November/December 2007, 2). Controversies about globalization's economic consequences worldwide are not likely to vanish because the *outsourcing* of jobs and workers across borders shows no signs of abating.

Another migration trend is far less controversial and may even be beneficial, because the migrants do so voluntarily by choice and for self-advancement: the spread of students to foreign universities throughout the globe.

College Goes Global   You are already aware of the importance of world affairs and its growing impact on your future. In all probability, you are now taking a course in international relations at your university, and your decision to do that shows your astute wisdom that your education could never be complete without knowledge about the world and how it works. Congratulations! You are on the road to global understanding and citizenship.

This book is designed to open and expand your global vision, so as you read it (happily, your authors hope!), you have begun a journey of lifelong learning. (Thousands of other students worldwide in universities are sharing your experience; *World Politics* has been translated in many languages for instruction throughout the world, including Chinese, Serbo-Croatian, Hebrew, Arabic, and Spanish.) Perhaps this book's introduction to the world also will inspire you to travel as often as possible to the other countries you are reading about—as tourists, students in exchange programs overseas, and maybe someday as an employee.

International education is responding to the need in the age of globalization to meet the demands that people in all countries are making. Throughout the world there is high and growing recognition about the importance of higher education in today's global marketplace. Everyone agrees "that a college degree is an indispensable passport to the globalized knowledge economy of the twenty-first century. Higher education, once the rarified province of the elite, is now viewed by most nations as an indispensable strategic tool for shaping, directing, and promoting economic growth" (Brody 2007).

To seek the best education, many students have gone away from their homeland to study at universities overseas. There are now more than 2.7 million foreign students attending classes in other country's universities. Figure 11.3 provides an account of the percentage of university enrollments in institutions of higher learning within each country that come from abroad. The numbers are growing each year, so the globalization of international education is a growing part of the whole trend toward globalization in general.

"The evolution of the global higher education market, and the U.S. predominant role in the field is of great and increasing consequence both for the United States and abroad. How should institutions of higher learning . . . adapt to this changing environment? Is this field, like so many others in the past, destined to see the emergence of a handful of global players—educational powerhouses—that come to dominate and define it? Will the twenty-first century be the era of the 'Global U'?" These are the questions about the globalization of international education that the president of Johns Hopkins University, William R. Brody, raises to describe this globalization trend and the rising need, as he puts it, for universities "to go far beyond their traditional borders" to find the students and brain power to conduct the research to propel prosperity and growth in the global future. Open borders, jet transportation, and instantaneous global communications are making this search for human resources a growing factor in the globalization of world politics.

The New Global Slave Trade The globalization of higher education signals a potentially helpful trend. It brings people together and elevates their knowledge and appreciation of the value of learning from and about people from other cultures

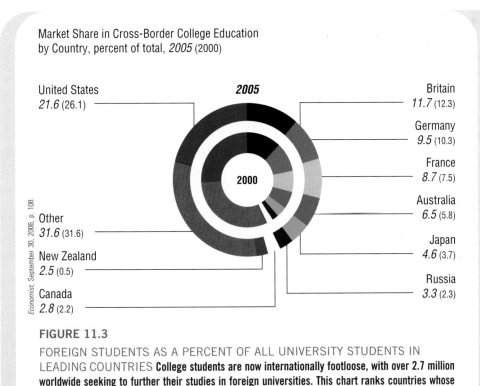

Market Share in Cross-Border College Education by Country, percent of total, *2005* (2000)

United States
21.6 (26.1)

2005

2000

Britain
11.7 (12.3)

Germany
9.5 (10.3)

France
8.7 (7.5)

Australia
6.5 (5.8)

Japan
4.6 (3.7)

Russia
3.3 (2.3)

Other
31.6 (31.6)

New Zealand
2.5 (0.5)

Canada
2.8 (2.2)

Economist, September 30, 2006, p. 108

FIGURE 11.3

FOREIGN STUDENTS AS A PERCENT OF ALL UNIVERSITY STUDENTS IN LEADING COUNTRIES **College students are now internationally footloose, with over 2.7 million worldwide seeking to further their studies in foreign universities. This chart ranks countries whose universities are attracting the highest proportion of students from overseas. The United States now attracts 21.6 percent of the globe's foreign students, but that representation hides the sharp decline of its share of 25.3 percent in 2000 (*Economist*, November 17, 2007, 69).**

with different perspectives. Another demographic trend signals the opposite: hurt and harm. People are being forced to move across borders against their will for very evil purposes: slavery and sexual exploitation.

This face of globalization involves humans, but without respect for humanity and their human rights. And this trend is a dimension of demographic dynamics that is "back with a vengeance." As Ethan Kapstein explains:

> When most people think about slavery—if they think about it at all—they probably assume that it was eliminated during the nineteenth century. Unfortunately, this is far from the truth.
>
> Slavery and the global slave trade continue to thrive to this day; in fact, it is likely that more people are being trafficked across borders against their will now than at any point in the past. This human stain is not just a minor blot on the rich tapestry of international commerce. It is a product of the same political, technological, and economic forces that have fueled globalization. Just as the brutal facts of the Atlantic slave trade ultimately led to a reexamination of U.S. history—U.S. historiography until the 1960s had been largely celebratory—so must growing awareness of the modern slave trade spark a recognition of the flaws in our contemporary economic and governmental arrangements. The current system offers too many incentives to criminals and outlaw states to market humans and promises too little in the way of sanctions. Contemporary slavery typically involves women and children being forced into servitude through violence and deprivation. (Kapstein 2006, 103)

About eight hundred thousand to nine hundred thousand people *each year* are estimated to be victims of forced migration. The trade in humans bought, sold, or forced into a miserable life of subjugation, servitude, and sexual slavery is huge. The UN estimates that 80 percent of today's slaves are women in the illegal trafficking of people across borders. Of these, most are young—very young: at least half are children under the age of eighteen. And this growing slavery trade crisscrosses the entire globe; people are being trafficked from an estimated 127 countries to be exploited in as many as 137 foreign countries (Moorehead 2007, 15). An estimated forty-five thousand to five thousand people are trafficked to the United States every year; the minimum number of persons forced into labor as a result of global trafficking is 2.45 million people annually. This lucrative criminal activity grosses between $12 and $17 billion annually. It is the third largest illicit global business after trafficking in drugs and the arms trade (Obuah 2006, 241; see also Skinner 2008).

The globe on the horizon is, by these accounts, not going to be a better world. Globalization portends many prospects on which people are basing their hopes. But globalization is breeding many countertrends spelling doom and gloom that are provoking peoples' fears about their future. One of the most threatening is the cross-border spread of infectious and deadly diseases. This is another human dimension of globalization that must be factored into your interpretations.

As you build these other projections about the effects of globalization on demographic trends, keep in mind that *all* projections are dangerous. Natural or human-made events can overturn the conditions that are creating today's prevailing globalization trends bringing people and states into ever-closer interdependent ties. For example, almost all predictions can be overturned overnight by a nuclear war or by a terrorist act of mass destruction with biological weapons, rendering obsolete today's life expectancy in the Global North of nearly eighty years (HDR 2008, 232).

Other threats, such as the outbreak of a widespread and deadly disease, could produce a **population implosion**. Next we will look at examples of life-threatening diseases that are sweeping a globe without borders.

NEW PLAGUES? THE GLOBAL IMPACT OF TUBERCULOSIS, HIV/AIDS, AND OTHER DISEASES

Although infant and child mortality rates remain discouragingly high in much of the developing countries, at least they are decreasing. On a global level, life expectancy at birth each year since 1950 has increased, climbing by UN estimates to sixty-eight years (HDR 2008, 232). However, this trend in rising longevity could reverse if globally transmittable diseases cut into the extension of life spans made possible by improvements in health care, nutrition, water quality, and public sanitation. Throughout history, the spread of bacteria, parasites, viruses, plagues, and diseases to various ecospheres, regardless of state borders, has suspended development or brought down once mighty states and empires (Kolbert 2005). In our age of globalization, a disease such as drug-resistant strains of tuberculosis (TB), which is

> *A relationship exists between the health of individuals within a state and that state's national security. A population's health is of utmost importance to the state's ability to survive.*
>
> —Jeremy Youde, global health expert

killing two million worldwide each year (WDI 2006, 12), knows no borders. It can spread with a sneeze or a cough on an international flight. Likewise, there are three hundred million to five hundred million cases of malaria each year, leading to more than one million deaths (WDI 2006, 12). Because communicable diseases cause one third of deaths worldwide (WDI 2007, 110), global health is a concern and a threat to human security.

The grim possibility that virulent disease will decimate the world's population because we all share a common global environment is made nowhere more evident than in the spread of the **human immunodeficiency virus (HIV)** that causes **acquired immune deficiency syndrome (AIDS)**. Since the 1970s onset of the AIDS pandemic, the UN estimates that "every day more than 8,000 people die of AIDS. Every hour almost 600 people become infected. Every minute a child dies of the virus." Today, one of every one-hundred people in the world between the ages of 15 and 49 has HIV (WDI 2007, 293).

> *In the ruthless world of AIDS there is no us and them.*
>
> —Kofi Annan, former UN Secretary General

■ **population implosion**

a rapid reduction of population that reverses a previous trend toward progressively larger populations; a severe reduction in the world's population.

■ **human immunodeficiency virus (HIV)**

a virus that can lead to the lethal acquired immune deficiency syndrome (AIDS).

■ **acquired immune deficiency syndrome (AIDS)**

an often fatal condition that can result from infection with the human immunodeficiency virus (HIV).

CAN AIDS BE STOPPED? **The AIDS epidemic has claimed the lives of millions since HIV was discovered in 1981. Here, South Africans demonstrate outside the South African parliament, demanding antiretroviral drugs for pregnant women to prevent the transfer of HIV from a mother to her child.**

The circumstances are tragic, and stopping the tragedy is "a moral duty" even though the UN estimates that the AIDS pandemic is beginning to lose momentum. In 2008 about 33 million people worldwide were infected with HIV; the number of new infections peaked in 1998 at 3.4 million and deaths peaked in 2005. This does not mean that the epidemic is vanishing: in many of the most seriously AIDS-affected countries, deaths are projected to overtake births and cause population decreases in the next few years.

> *Tackling the world's diseases has become a key feature of many nations' foreign policies.*
>
> —Laurie Garrett, world public health expert

The HIV contagion respects no borders and is a truly global epidemic, killing throughout the world (see Map 11.2). Are world death rates thus destined to rise in the future, reversing the upward trend in world population? The "age of AIDS" is a sobering reminder that population and power are heavily determined by natural phenomena in an era when what occurs anywhere often has consequences everywhere.

Sadly, there are many diseases which pose significant threats to human well-being and remind us of just how permeable are our national borders. Malaria is a major threat to global health, with the World Health Organization reporting 350–500 million cases of malaria annually, of which over one million result in death (Vital Signs 2007–2008). This is tragic as the disease, which is transmitted by mosquitoes to humans, is largely preventable and treatable. Efforts to combat the spread of the disease include the

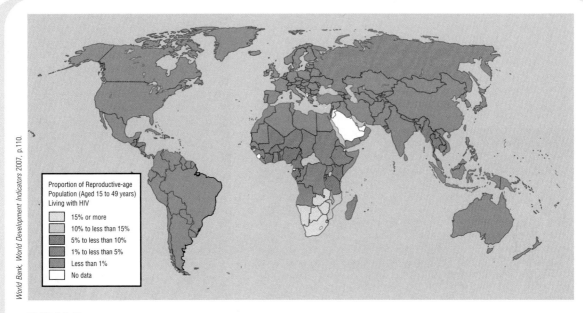

World Bank, World Development Indicators 2007, p.110.

MAP 11.2

DEATH IN THE PRIME OF LIFE: THE MOST SERIOUSLY HIV-AFFECTED COUNTRIES **This map shows the severity of the HIV global health crisis. Worldwide, 31 percent of the female population is infected with HIV. Wealth is not a barrier: on average, one out of every three females in the high-income Global North is infected (WDI 2007, 110).**

distribution of millions of insecticide-treated bed nets. Avian flu, the so-called bird flu, is also of global concern as, according to the WHO, the current outbreak "has been the most deadly of all the influenza viruses that have spread from birds to humans, killing more than half of the people infected" (Vital Signs 2007–2008, 90). Since the outbreak in 2003, at least 170 people have died from the disease and hundreds of millions of chickens, ducks, and other birds have been killed in an effort to curb its spread. Experts believe the disease can be spread through the direct handling of chickens and the processing of meat and are extremely concerned that the disease "will mutate into a virus that can easily spread from person-to-person, sparking a pandemic." In 2008, concern over the spread of mad cow disease led to rioting in South Korea when the government lifted the ban on beef imported from the United States. Mad cow disease, or bovine spongiform encephalopathy (BSE), is a brain-degenerative disease in cattle that may be spread to humans through consumption of infected beef. Many South Koreans felt their sovereignty and public health were being compromised with the agreement to import U.S. beef due to concerns over weak testing for the disease in the United States, the inclusion of beef from older cattle that are believed to be more prone to the disease, and the commitment to continue to import U.S. beef even if there were a recurrence of mad cow disease.

The spread and control of infectious diseases such as AIDS, tuberculosis, malaria, Lassa fever, Ebola, lymphatic filariasis, Avian flu, and mad cow disease have established themselves on the radar screen of policymakers throughout the world. They will not vanish from sight anytime soon. Yet protection is lacking in a borderless world because effective international coordination to combat the disease has not materialized.

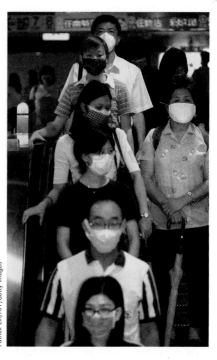

DOES GLOBALIZATION MAKE THE WHOLE WORLD SICK? **The dangerous threat of a global flu pandemic "ranks higher than a major terrorist attack, even one involving weapons of mass destruction"** (*Newsweek*, October 31, 2005). **Shown (left) is a cause for global alarm: at a market in Shanghai, workers sleep with their chickens, and close contact with infected birds is the primary source of deadly hybrids of human and animal viruses.**

Shown (right) is another symptom of globalization's potential dangers: in Taipei, Republic of China, commuters alarmed by the global spread of infectious diseases take care to avoid infection as they travel to work. Another possible health hazard of globalization: breast cancer, now "a global concern because the spread of U.S. and European lifestyles is [suspected to] contribute to the global breast cancer boom" (Kingsbury 2007, 39).

THE GLOBAL INFORMATION AGE

As you conduct your analysis, try to fill in the blanks by constructing a full evaluation of competing views of globalization. You have already been asked to contemplate two very different possible futures for world politics as a result of the acceleration of globalization. That is, you have been asked to compare two forecasts for the global future. On one optimistic scenario, *neoliberal theory* sees sovereignty at bay as the globalization of cultures transcends contemporary geopolitical boundaries and erodes the meaning of national identity, creating "global citizens" who assign loyalty to the common interests of all peoples. In the other, more pessimistic forecast, states will compete with one another to retain the devoted loyalty of the citizens they govern so as to preserve and protect their sovereign independence from the homogenizing forces now sweeping the world. This competition will divide the world even as countries become more alike, making some wealthy and stable but others poorer and fragile.

Such forces imply nothing less than a redistribution of global economic power. Are they bound to increasingly lead to a redistribution of international political power?

So now assess the potential impact of growing cross-border transfers of communications information. Trends in this cultural dimension of globalization are generating changes on culture and how people construct their identities. Such an assessment forces you to consider the prospects for the continuation of states as sovereign and independent actors against the growing tide toward a **cosmopolitan** viewpoint. This puts emphasis on an emergent *civil society*—a "cosmopolitan global culture promising a democratization of world politics" (Jaeger 2007), culminating possibly in the creation of a global polity with strong institutions for global governance. This analysis will also force you to interpret perhaps in novel ways to which you are accustomed to thinking the prospects for global cooperation.

■ **cosmopolitan**
an outlook that values viewing the cosmos or entire world as the best polity or unit for political governance and personal identity, as opposed to other polities such as one's local metropolis or city of residence (e.g., Indianapolis or Minneapolis).

> *The onrush of economic and ecological forces demand integration and uniformity and mesmerize the world with fast music, fast computers, and fast food—with MTV, Macintosh, and McDonald's pressing nations into one commercially homogenous global network: one McWorld tied together by technology, ecology, communications, and commerce.*
> —Benjamin R. Barber, global trends expert

Rapid and unrestrained communication is a hallmark of the **global village**—a metaphor used by many to portray a future in which borders will vanish and the world will become a single community. The major source of this global transformation is the growing speed and flow of communications. In the "age of global television" the meaning of "home" and "abroad" and of "near" and "distant" vanishes, promoting changes in people's images of community and their own identity. Will cellular phones, the World Wide Web, blogs, and other means of transnational communication portend consensus, and, perhaps, an integrated global village? Or is this vision of such a global village, in which shared information breeds understanding and peace, pure mythology? Worse, will the virus of interconnectiveness within globalization do away with private life, erasing what remains of identity, individualism, and independence?

■ **global village**
a popular cosmopolitan perspective describing the growth of awareness that all people share a common fate because the world is becoming an integrated and interdependent whole.

Global Communications

Cellular phones have become available worldwide, with "around 2.8 billion already in use and a further 1.6 million added every day" (*Economist*, April 28, 2007, 3). This has enabled many in the world who have never before made a phone call to communicate instantly with others. The "wireless world" of mobile or cellular phones that use radio waves rather than installed lines is growing, allowing communication between rural areas in developing Global South countries and "wired" Global North countries, where more than one billion fixed-line telephones are already abundant. The globe is also linked by mobile phone subscribers worldwide that enable one of every five people in the world to make wireless connections to the Internet (*Vital Signs 2006-2007*, 70). Broadband links are bridging the communications divide between the rich and the poor. As costs decrease, the volume of international communications is increasing exponentially, causing "the death of distance" and radically altering people's decisions about where to work and to live as well as their images of "us" and "them." As the salience of national borders vanishes with escalating global communication, so, too, do conventional concepts of identity.

Computers are another significant agent of globalization. No area of the world and no arena of politics, economics, society, or culture is immune from the pervasive influence of computer technology. Even victims of ethnic or racial conflict and natural disasters in the most remote corners of the world are connected to others by the laptop computers that relief workers from the International Red Cross and Red Crescent Societies bring with them.

A billion computers are estimated to be in use today, about 95 percent of which are personal computers (PCs). PCs are growing in use by millions each year, and they are growing smaller and more powerful, doubling in capacity every eighteen months (according to "Moore's Law" advanced by Intel founder Gordon Moore). The result of the expanding worldwide use of the Internet is the creation of a **cyberspace**, a global information superhighway allowing people everywhere to communicate freely without constraints as they surf the Web, exchange e-mails, and join Internet chat rooms. The increasing number of Internet users (by about a million *weekly*) is promoting a cultural revolution by giving most of the world access to information for the first time. This creates a single globe, united in shared information. This face of globalization submerges borders and breaks barriers. It lays the foundation for a smaller, shrinking, and flatter world by permitting ideas to move around in the world "farther, further, deeper, and cheaper than ever before and at the same time [allowing] the world to reach into each of us further, farther, deeper, and cheaper than ever before" (Friedman 2007).

The growth of Internet **blogs**, or active diarists known as "bloggers" who share their opinions with a global audience, adds to the influence of what has become known as "the information age." "Nearly 80,000 new blogs are created every day, and there are some 14.2 million in existence already" (*International Herald Tribune*, August 6–7, 2005, 4). Drawing on the content of the international media and the World Wide Web, bloggers weave together an elaborate network with agenda-setting power on issues ranging from human rights in China to the U.S. occupation of Iraq. "What began as a hobby is evolving into a new medium that is changing the landscape for journalists and policymakers alike" (Drezner and Farrell 2006). That trend is accelerating by leaps and bounds with the rapid diffusion of iPods and the enormous popularity of **podcasting**, allowing people to create their own Web site channels and share audio and visual versions of new uploads with anyone throughout the world who signs on.

■ **cyberspace**

a metaphor used to describe the global electronic web of people, ideas, and interactions on the Internet, which is unencumbered by the borders of the geopolitical world.

■ **blogs**

online diaries, which spread information and ideas worldwide in the manner of journalists.

■ **podcasting**

to Thomas Friedman, "the technology that enables individuals to produce their own poetry and songs, videos and photos, and upload them onto a podcasting Web site, and then offer this content to anyone who wants to sample it."

> *People from all over the world will draw knowledge and inspiration from the same technology platform, but different cultures will flourish on it. It is the same soil, but different trees will grow. The next phase of globalization is going to be more 'glocalization'—more and more local content made global.*
>
> —Thomas L. Friedman, international journalist

Futurists predict that rapid information technology development will have staggering consequences. They believe that it will produce **the singularity** or "a point in time when current trends will go widely off the charts" as exponential technological growth makes it impossible to envision the transformations that will result (Bell 2006). Nanotechnology, the building of devices on a scale smaller than atoms, and that merge living tissues with mechanical devices, could speed information transmission and permit technologies to reproduce themselves beyond human capacity to control. And on the horizon are "quantum computers that use spinning electrons rather than silicon based chips to process data to do in seconds what would take a modern computer billions of years, raising the prospect of infinite processing power by the year 2020" (*Futurist*, "Outlook 2008," November/December 2007, 8).

The Internet is an engine for the conduct of business and the transfer of capital through e-commerce across borders. In this sense, although the entire world is being connected, it is at different rates. The ratio of Global North to Global South Internet users is about five to one. Geography still matters. The Internet has not liberated many in the Global South countries from their technological dependence on the places where almost all management of Web sites is located. Even if the Internet has created the worldwide hypermobility of ideas and information, the so-called digital arms race has resulted in the concentration and control of **intellectual property** in the Global North in such leading international Internet bandwidth giants as Singapore and the United States. This is made especially evident with respect to global e-commerce, which raises concerns. Three-quarters of all e-commerce currently takes place in the United States, and the U.S. also accounts for 90 percent of commercial Web sites. What is more, the entire global Internet is coordinated by the California-based, private-sector nonprofit NGO called the *Internet Corporation for Assigned Names and Numbers (ICANN)*. This is criticized as yet another example of U.S. unilateral global dominance. Nonetheless, at the UN Summit on the Information Society in Tunis, one hundred countries reluctantly agreed to allow ICANN to remain in control of the Web address system for users to navigate the Web and send e-mail.

Communication technologies are driving much of the globalization process and are the underlying force in the global race for knowledge in today's "information age" and "knowledge-based economics":

> Communications technology sets this era of globalization apart from any other. The Internet, mobile phones, and satellite networks have shrunk space and time. Bringing together computers and communications unleashed an unprecedented explosion of ways to communicate at the start of the 1990s. Since then tremendous productivity gains, ever-falling costs and rapidly growing networks of computers have transformed the computing and communications sector. If the automobile industry had the same productivity growth, a car today would cost $3. (UNDP 1999, 57–58)

If one constant stands out, it is continuous change in technological innovation. The rapid pace of **information technology (IT)** development drives globalization. It can make today's methods of communicating look ancient in a few years, and in the process is transforming how people communicate as well as which countries lead (and prosper) and which follow. Consider what Thomas Friedman labels "the third great era of globalization":

> the convergence of a variety of software applications—from e-mail to Google, to Microsoft Office, to specially designed outsourcing programs—that, when combined with all those personal computers and bandwidth, made it possible to create global

■ **the singularity**
a future phenomenon that will occur when machine intelligence surpasses human intelligence.

■ **intellectual property**
inventions created by the use of human intelligence in publications, art and design by individuals that are often illegally used for commercial purposes without credits or royalties to their creators in violation of GATT's *Trade Related Intellectual Property Rights* agreement.

■ **information technology (IT)**
the techniques for storing, retrieving, and disseminating through computerization and the Internet recorded data and research knowledge.

work-flow platforms. These work-flow platforms can chop up any service job—accounting, radiology, consulting, software engineering—into different functions and then, thanks to scanning and digitization, outsource each function to teams of skilled knowledge workers around the globe, based on which team can do each function with the highest skill at the lowest price. Then the project is reassembled back at headquarters into a finished product. Thanks to this new work-flow network, knowledge workers anywhere in the world can contribute their talents more than ever before, spurring innovation and productivity. But these same workers will be under more pressure than ever to constantly upgrade their skills. India and China are at the moment the primary beneficiaries of this technological face of globalization, supplying the skilled labor at low costs for services other countries cannot supply competitively and, in the process, creating an explosion of wealth in the middle classes of the world's two biggest nations, India and China, and giving both nations a huge stake in the success of globalization. (T. Friedman 2004b)

To enthusiasts, the advantages of the global communications revolution are a blessing for humanity. When people are connected worldwide through the revolution in digital communications, the shared information propels human development and productivity. Proponents also see the globalized digital revolution as producing many side payoffs: reducing oppressive dictators' authority, allowing small business to successfully compete globally, empowering the globe's transnational activists within nearly 28,000 nongovernmental organizations (NGOs) to exercise more influence, and providing opportunities for a diversity of voices and cultures (see Chapter 7).

On the other hand, there is a "dark side" to the global communications revolution. Critics complain that the growing electronic network has created a new global condition known as **virtuality**. In such a world, one can conceal one's true identity, which threatens to make the activities of international organized crime and terrorist groups easier, as illustrated by the global terrorist network Al Qaeda's use of computers to coordinate the destruction of the World Trade Center towers in New York on September 11, 2001. The specter is raised that "privateness will become passé [through] the spread of surveillance technology and the rise of Websites like YouTube, which receives more than 65,000 video uploads daily and is driving a trend toward cyber-exhibitionism" (*Futurist*, "Outlook 2008," November/December 2007, 6). In the name of national security, governments are also developing extensive surveillance systems that discreetly monitor activities, many in public spaces. One example is the high-tech surveillance program in China, known as "Golden Shield," that will identify dissent and allow the government to address it before it turns into a mass movement. Using people-tracking technology supplied by American corporations like General Electric, IBM, and Honeywell, the goal is to create "a single, nationwide network, an all-seeing system that will be capable of tracking and identifying anyone who comes within its range" (Klein 2008, 60).

Critics also warn that even as Internet use and commerce grow, the communications revolution is widening the gap between the rich and the poor, leading to the globalization of poverty and the destruction of local culture. Noting that access to and use of the Internet is heavily concentrated in the Global North (see Figure 11.4), the critics fear that the advantages of the digital communication for small entrepreneurs in the Global South will not be shared and that the **digital divide** in access to **communications technology** is not closing as rapidly as expected.

■ **virtuality**

imagery created by computer technology of objects and phenomena that produces an imaginary picture of actual things, people, and experiences.

■ **digital divide**

the division between the Internet technology-rich Global North and the Global South in the proportion of Internet users and hosts.

■ **communications technology**

the technological means through which information and communications are transferred, such as through the World Wide Web.

At present, the Global North (and particularly the United States, where the Internet was developed) remains predominant and the primary beneficiary of the IT revolution. However, the growing capacity of many U.S. rivals to excel in IT innovation has rapidly closed the gap (see "Readiness Index," Figure 11.4). This trend suggests that America's domination in technology and information may not endure for long without a revival of U.S. public support for education. The current U.S. education system does not compete with many other countries (T. Friedman 2005b) even though U.S. universities still attract nearly 22 percent of the world's foreign students who study abroad (*Economist*, November 17, 2007, 69). The U.S. decline in spending for education is already creating a U.S. "creativity crisis" (Florida 2007).

The Media: Markets or Monopoly?

Ours is often described as the information age, but a remarkably large portion of the available information is controlled by a cartel of a handful of huge multinational media corporations that are merging to combine their resources and, in the process, expanding their global reach. These media giants keep "us fully entertained and perhaps half-informed, always growing here and shriveling there, with certain of its members bulking up, while others slowly fall apart or get digested whole. But while the players tend to come and go—always with a few exceptions—the overall leviathan itself keeps getting bigger, louder, mightier, forever taking up more time and space, in every street, in countless homes, in every other head" (Miller 2006). The world's population is a captive audience, and the information presented by these telecommunication corporate giants shapes our values and our images of what the world is like.

■ **cartel**
a convergence of independent commercial enterprises or political groups that combine for collective action, such as limiting competition, setting prices for their services, or forming a coalition to advance their groups interests.

Note that the media cartel is headquartered in the rich Global North countries. The behemoths have extraordinary control over the information people receive throughout the world, despite the falling proportion of countries where the media are "not free" to express themselves and annoy rulers, which declined to 22 percent as 2009 started (www.freedomhouse.org, December 17, 2008).

Not surprisingly, the message of international events and ideas projected by the media is highly reflective of Western culture. The handful of news and information agencies operate like a giant circulatory system, pumping ideas, information, and ideals from the wealthy center to the remote periphery in the Global South. The Internet, CNN, and MTV are media channels with global reach centered in the Global North. What Global South opponents of globalization complain about is not so much modernization and trade; rather, they oppose "corporate globalization" dictated by mass media MNCs that, they contend, ignores the values and needs of the vast majority in the developing world. Nonetheless, most of the growth in the media industries is expected to occur in the Global South over the next five years. "The fastest growth is expected in Latin America, with spending set to jump at a 10.6 percent annual rate" followed by the Asia-Pacific region at 8.8 percent, and the Middle East, Africa, and Europe at 6.8 percent (Pfanner 2008, 13).

The type of power the media wield over international affairs is arguably specific and limited. Scholarship shows that the media influence what people *think about* more than what they *think*. In this way, the media primarily function to *set the agenda* of public discussion about public affairs instead of determining public opinion. In the

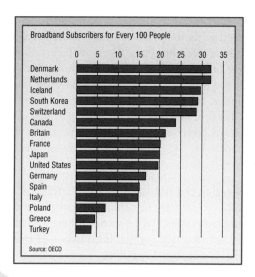

Communications in the Globalized World

Flanagan, Frost and Kugler (2001, 24)

Broadband Subscribers for Every 100 People

Source: OECD

FIGURE 11.4

THE DIGITAL DIVIDE IN INFORMATION AND COMMUNICATION TECHNOLOGIES

This figure on the top illustrates the density of communications flows worldwide and renders the so-called digital divide strikingly evident. The figure on the bottom measures selected countries' relative "network readiness" according to the percent of broadband subscribers in each country. It shows that in 2007 Denmark topped the list of 122 states.

■ **agenda setting**

the thesis that by their ability to identify and publicize issues, the communications media determine the problems that receive attention from governments and international organizations.

process of **agenda setting** the media demonstrably shape international public policy (see Gilboa 2002). For example, global broadcasts of the ruthless repression and illegitimate tactics associated with Mugabe's bid for reelection in Zimbabwe in 2008 ignited a worldwide chain reaction to aid that country's refugees and pressure the government to reform. This example of the power of information technology in international politics aside, some people caution that this kind of "virtual diplomacy," possible because of the development of a "global brain" circulating shared information through hundreds of communications satellites weaving an information web around the globe, has real limitations. One critic has described the impact of CNN and the media this way:

> In foreign policy circles these days one often hears that the advent of instantaneous and global technology has given the news media far greater influence in international relations than ever before, robbing diplomacy of its rightful place at the helm in the process. Observers of international affairs call it the CNN curve. . . . It suggests that when CNN floods the air-waves with news of a foreign crisis, it evokes an emotional outcry from the public to "do something." Under the spell of the CNN curve, goes this

refrain, policymakers have no choice but to redirect their attention to the crisis at hand or risk unpopularity, whether or not such revision is merited by policy considerations. (Neuman 1995–1996, 109)

Control of television and other media sources by the U.S. hegemon and a small number of European countries became a hot dispute with the Global South during the 1980s. Dissatisfied with the media coverage it received from Global North news agencies and resentful of Group of Eight rich states' domination of other forms of communication, Global South leaders demanded a **New World Information and Communication Order (NWICL)** to create a new regime with fair rules to right the imbalance of the information flows from Global North to Global South. The image of the Global South painted by such sources, they believed, promoted Northern values, such as consumerism and conspicuous consumption that perpetuated the South's cultural dependence. As the North–South conflict brewed, the United States angrily withdrew from the United Nations Educational, Scientific, and Cultural Organization (UNESCO), in part as a rejection of its role in promoting the new communications order.

The NWICO has since receded on the global agenda, but the issues remain very much alive in NGOs, concerned about the concentration of so much media power in so few hands. In 1995, Hollywood was able to beam the Academy Awards around the world to over a billion people, and the American evangelist Billy Graham preached via electronic links to a similar number.

■ **New World Information and Communication Order (NWICL)**

the controversial Global South effort to combat what was termed "cultural imperialism" by limiting the news and information disseminated by the Western transnational news agencies.

Jan Bauer/AP Photo

THE INTERNET AND THE EXPORT OF MASS CULTURE THROUGHOUT THE GLOBE **The Internet is the primary information highway leading to the globalization that is erasing national identities and making for a common world culture. Internet usage grew 238 percent globally in 2006 (*Futurist*, March/April 2007, 16). This photo of a Huli tribal chief from Papua New Guinea presenting his new website illustrates the global spread of information technology.**

> *Globalization is just a nice word that multinational corporations use to hide their efforts to infect the entire world with the cultural virus of commercialism.*
>
> —Hamid Mowlana, American-based global communications scholar

Against this interpretation, many, such as the British analyst Philippe Legrain (2003), think that despite America's hegemonic leadership at this point in history, "cultural globalization is *not* Americanization. It is a myth that globalization involves the imposition of Americanized uniformity, rather than an explosion of cultural exchange. . . . If critics of globalization were less obsessed with 'Cola-colonization,' they might notice a rich feast of cultural mixing that belies fears about Americanized uniformity. . . . For all the spread of Western ideas . . . globalization is not a one-way street. . . . Americans are [not] the only players in the global media industry. Of the seven market leaders that have their fingers in nearly every pie, four are American (AOL Time Warner, Disney, Viacom, and News Corporation), one is German (Bertelsmann), one is French (Viendi), and one Japanese (Sony). . . . The biggest publisher in the English-speaking world is Germany's Bertelsmann, which gobbled up America's biggest publisher, Random House. . . . Bertelsmann publishes books by American writers, News Corporation broadcasts Asian news, Sony sells Brazilian music."

Richard Vogel/AP Photo

THE MAKING OF A GLOBAL CULTURE? Some people regard globalization as little more than the spread of values and beliefs of the globe's reigning hegemon, the United States. Shown here is one example that fuels their images—a Santa Claus mannequin with a bicycle "sleigh" attempting to attract customers in downtown Hanoi, Vietnam—a predominantly Buddhist city still subscribing to the communist principles emphasizing the greed of market capitalism and the class divisions it is believed to create. The sale of Christmas trees is rising there, too.

Whatever its true character, the more than $1 trillion global telecommunications industry is without question the major vehicle for the rapid spread of ideas, information, and images worldwide. That impact accelerated after the WTO created in 1997 the World Telecom Pact. This *regime* ended government and private telecommunications monopolies in many states, and the cuts in phone costs were widely seen as a catalyst to the world economy's expansion.

The success of this regime suggests the kinds of financial benefits to business, ordinary people, and the world economy that can result from international cooperation to conduct global transactions by rules. Advocates see global telecommunications as a vehicle for progress, liberating minds, expanding choices, penetrating societies closed to diplomatic communication, and creating a single, more united, homogenized global culture. Others disagree, however. They note that the airwaves can broadcast divisive messages as well as unifying ones, and that what is said is more important than how much is said. A counterpoint, therefore, to the "McWorld" of transnational media consumerism is "Jihad"—a world driven by "parochial hatreds," not "universalizing markets" (Barber 1995). Because globalized communications and information may be used as tools for terrorism and revolution as well as for community and peace, the creation of a world without boundaries, where everybody will know everything about anybody's activities, will not necessarily be a better world. You should ask: Would the world be better or worse if it were to become an increasingly impersonal place, with rootless individuals with declining connections to their own country's culture and history?

GLOBALIZATION AND THE GLOBAL FUTURE

Rapid globalization, propelled in large measure by revolutions in technology, is almost certain to continue. Is globalization desirable, or despicable?

Expect the controversies about globalization's alleged virtues and vices to heighten as finance, trade, population, labor, communications, and cultures continue to converge globally. Whereas globalization has narrowed the distance between the world's people, some have gained and others have lost ground. The *global village* is not proving to be an equally hospitable home for everyone. Indeed, levels of satisfaction with cascading globalization vary widely, as do the levels to which countries and people are linked to globalization's multiple forces (see Figure 11.5). Winners in the game downplay the cost of global integration, and critics deny globalization's benefits. And the debate about globalization's problematic impact is intensifying, but without resolution as the debaters are hardening their positions without listening to the counterarguments.

You have now taken into account a number of dimensions of the trend toward globalization—in international economics, demography, and the potential spread of universal values for the entire world. If the trends you have surveyed actually do culminate for the first time in a global consensus uniting all of humanity, these values and understandings might unify all people on Earth into a common global culture. This could conceivably prepare the way for the advent of a global *civil society*, even with the eventual emergence of supranational institutions to govern all of humanity.

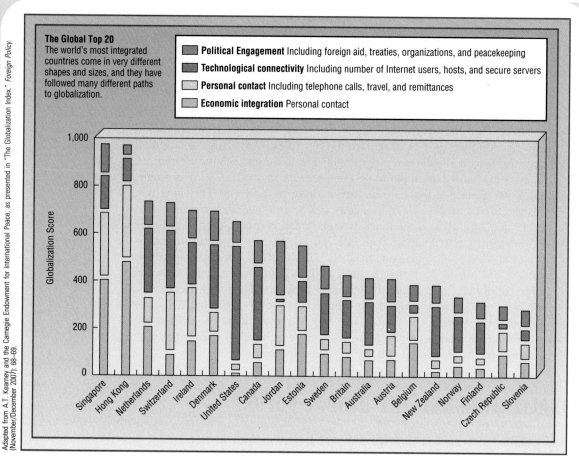

The Global Top 20
The world's most integrated countries come in very different shapes and sizes, and they have followed many different paths to globalization.

■ **Political Engagement** Including foreign aid, treaties, organizations, and peacekeeping
■ **Technological connectivity** Including number of Internet users, hosts, and secure servers
□ **Personal contact** Including telephone calls, travel, and remittances
□ **Economic integration** Personal contact

Globalization Score

(y-axis: 0, 200, 400, 600, 800, 1,000)

(x-axis countries: Singapore, Hong Kong, Netherlands, Switzerland, Ireland, Denmark, United States, Canada, Jordan, Estonia, Sweden, Britain, Australia, Austria, Belgium, New Zealand, Norway, Finland, Czech Republic, Slovenia)

FIGURE 11.5

LEVELS OF GLOBALIZATION In an effort to take stock of globalization's progress, this index examines multiple indicators spanning trade, business, politics, and information technology to determine the rankings of the 72 countries that together account for 97 percent of the world's gross domestic product and 88 percent of the world's population to gauge which countries are globalizing and which are not (*Foreign Policy*, November/December 2007, 68-69).

This worldview and set of predictions strikes fear into the hearts of many people who experience *cognitive dissonance* when they confront a frightening vision that challenges their customary way of thinking about world affairs. These people (and there are multitudes) strenuously reject the radical idea that the traditional system of independent sovereign states can or should be replaced by a global community with strong supranational regulatory institutions for global governance. So conclude your inspection of globalization's influence on world politics by evaluating the available evidence. What do prevailing trends tell you? Is Thomas Friedman's "flat world" concept that globalization has emasculated the state as an "electronic herd" tramples down borders valid? Or is Daniel Drezner (2007) more accurate in arguing that "states make the rules" and that powerful governments are still in control of shaping global destiny because "great powers cajole and coerce those who disagree with them into accepting the same rulebook."

To frame your opinion about the issues in this debate, see Controversy: Is Globalization Helpful or Harmful? Your opinions matter. Globalization is real, for better or for worse. Your actions can make a difference. So choose wisely. The consequences will be monumental. In one vision, the political economist John Gray predicts that as globalization spreads, it will turn society upside down, destroying entire ways of life, and that the future as a consequence will be marked by the current resource wars as the great powers struggle for control. Against this scenario, the political economist Murray Weidenbaum has voiced a contrary view: "Globalization —warts and all—is working [to create] widespread wealth." Both prophecies cannot be correct at the same time. Which is the more accurate?

In the next part of *World Politics*, you will look at two major threats to the global future. The first is the growing danger that the environment of the entire planet may suffer from deterioration and destruction if human choices erode Earth's capability to sustain human life. The second is the threat that armed violence through war or terrorism will end the history of the human story in the annihilation of the human species. Globalization speaks to either outcome. As Pope John Paul II warned, "In the past, it was possible to destroy a village, a town, a region, even a country. Now it is the whole planet that has come under threat. This fact should fully compel everyone to face a basic moral consideration: from now on, it is only through a conscious choice and then deliberate policy that humanity can survive."

CONTROVERSY:

IS GLOBALIZATION HELPFUL OR HARMFUL?

Many people recommend globalization for international public policy, because they believe that its consequences are basically good for humankind. However, critics argue that globalization's costs far outweigh its benefits. As the pace of globalization has become a recognized force in world politics, it also has become a heated topic of debate. Globalization has hit a political speed bump, provoking intense critical evaluation of globalization's causes, characteristics, and consequences and inspiring fresh ethical examination of the elevated interdependence of countries and humans. The uncertain wisdom and morality of globalization may be the most discussed issue on today's global agenda, receiving even more attention even than poverty, disease, urbanization, or the preservation of identity.

To many students of international relations, globalization displays two faces, one positive and the other negative. To those whose perceptions focus on globalization's benefits, globalization is a blessing that should be promoted to deepen and widen its helpful effects. They believe that globalization helps to break down traditional divisions of humanity—between races, nations, and cultures—that are barriers to peace, prosperity, and justice. To others, globalization is a harmful phenomenon, breeding such things as global warming and threats to local job security, and therefore a force to be resisted.

What do you think? Take any issue that is part of the debate and sort out the balance sheet of globalization's costs and benefits. For example, consider the charge that globalization has increased poverty and inequality. Is that true? Examine the evidence presented in Chapter 5 on the Global South and Chapter 7 on the income inequity of human beings on the planet. Consider, too, the differences of opinion by policy makers and scholars and the theories of international relations (recall Chapter 2) that inform these divergent opinions. Conduct the kind of evaluation that the International Labour Organization undertook when it challenged itself to provide "new thinking to break the deadlock and bridge the divide about the globalization debate."

Imagine yourself writing such a report. Do you think your research

Kin Cheung/AP Photo

TRADE AS AID TO HELP THE POOR In April 2002 the aid agency Oxfam International launched an international "Make Trade Fair" campaign with a report on trade, globalization, and the fight against poverty entitled "Rigged Rules and Double Standards." Oxfam argued that the United States and the European Union have betrayed their own free-trade principles by tilting the rules of the global trading system overwhelmingly to their advantage. Here they sail a boat in Hong Kong to urge fair trade rules for rich and poor countries alike, which Oxfam says can fight poverty better than aid or debt relief.

would agree or disagree with the findings of the ILO's World Commission? To frame your analysis, see if your evaluation would support or question the World Commission's conclusion:

> Globalization can and must change. [We acknowledge] globalization's potential for good—promoting open societies, open economies, and freer exchange of goods, knowledge, and ideas. But the Commission also found deep-seated and persistent imbalances in the current workings of the global economy that are ethically unacceptable and politically unsustainable.
>
> These imbalances are reflected in today's global economy. . . . The gap between people's income in the richest and poorest countries has never been wider, having risen from fifty-to-one in the 1960s to more than one hundred twenty-to-one today. Global unemployment is at its highest level ever. More than one billion people are either unemployed, underemployed, or working poor. Clearly, globalization's benefits are out of reach for far too many people. (Somavia 2004, 6)

An alternative exercise would be to make an ethical assessment of the morality or immorality of globalization. This is what the philosopher Peter Singer did in *One World: The Ethics of Globalization* (2004). In it, he applies as a criterion the utilitarian principle that it is a moral duty to maximize the happiness and welfare of all human beings and even animal welfare. Singer sees great benefits to the retreat of the doctrine of state sovereignty and to the advance of the view that the entire world should be the unit of ethical analysis. Global interdependence encourages global thinking and a moral outlook because it promotes one's ethical responsibilities to act from awareness that there is only "one community," "one law," "one economy," and "one atmosphere." This is beneficial, to Singer, because globalization gives all of us great incentives to perform our utilitarian duty toward others. His conclusion springs from a UN report that observed, "In the global village, someone else's poverty very soon becomes one's own problem: illegal immigration, pollution, contagious disease, insecurity, fanaticism, terrorism." Under globalization, altruism and concern for others pay dividends, whereas narrow selfish behavior causes the selfish competitor counterproductive harm. To this logic, globalization is beneficial. What do you think?

Or try one last thought experiment. Think like an economist. This is what the famous Harvard social scientist Jagdish Bhagwati did in writing *In Defense of Globalization* (2004). Would your similar economic analysis of globalization agree with his conclusions? Richard N. Cooper (2004) summarizes Bhagwati's liberal theoretical position and propositions:

Globalization is a buzzword that has no precise definition. It takes on many meanings, drawing both fervent support and fervent opposition. Indeed, the term is so imprecise that it is possible to be simultaneously for and against globalization.

In Defense of Globalization focuses on its economic dimension, defined by Bhagwati as "diverse forms of international integration such as foreign trade, multinational direct foreign investment, movements of 'short-term' portfolio funds, technological diffusion, and cross-border migration." His main thesis is that economic globalization is an unambiguously good thing, with a few downsides that thought and effort can mitigate. His secondary thesis is that globalization does not need to be given a "human face"; it already has one. A thoughtful and objective evaluation, Bhagwati believes, will make this clear, and that is what he sets out to do.

The book addresses a slate of charges against globalization; that it increases poverty, encourages child labor, harms women, threatens democracy, imperils culture, lowers wages, erodes labor standards, worsens the environment, and gives full reign to predatory corporations. Bhagwati also discusses capital market liberalization and international migration before turning to fixes for globalization's downsides: improving governance, accelerating social agendas, and managing the speed of transitions. He concedes a few points to globalization's critics but, wielding logic and fact, demolishes most of the allegations made against it. His conclusion: that the world, particularly its poorest regions, needs more globalization, not less. . . . To the claim that globalization increases poverty, Bhagwati's response is, rubbish. (Cooper 2004, 152–53)

Key Terms

demography
replacement-level fertility
fertility rate
population density
global migration crisis
underemployment
population implosion
human immunodeficiency
  virus (HIV)

acquired immune deficiency
  syndrome (AIDS)
cosmopolitan
global village
cyberspace
blogs
podcasting
the singularity
intellectual property

information technology (IT)
virtuality
digital divide
communications technology
cartel
agenda setting
New World Information and
  Communication Order (NWICL)

WARNINGS ON WARMING AND WAR. Of the thirteen hottest years on record, eleven occurred between 1995 and 2009. On the left is shown one symptom of global warming's threat: A penguin in the Antarctic surveys its shrinking habitat. Shown on the right is one symbol of contemporary violence now permanently etched in people's mind's throughout the world: the 9/11 terrorist attack on the N.Y. World Trade Center.

Part 4

THREATS TO THE WORLD

"Problems will always torment us, because all important problems are insoluble: that is why they are important."

— *Arthur M. Schlesinger, Jr., American historian*

"**WHAT IS THE GREATEST THREAT TO THE WORLD?"** If you were asked to answer in an interview for a public opinion poll, how would you respond? The possibilities are almost limitless. Whatever your answer, it likely would be influenced by many factors. You might answer differently if you are residing in Baghdad instead of Beijing, Bombay, Boston, or Buenos Aires; if you are a woman, not a man; or if you are a Christian and not a Muslim, Jew, or Buddhist.

Part 4 looks at two threats that would today likely rank very high on most people's lists. The two are different, but related. In Chapter 12 you will examine the threats to global environmental protection that many people now see as a serious danger and possibly *the* biggest threat. Chapter 13 looks at the military threats to international security posed by wars between states, wars within states, and international terrorism. Ecological threats and armed aggression are linked, you will discover. Environmental deterioration is a breeding ground for armed conflict, and wars are highly destructive of the environment in which they are fought. So both threats must be managed if either one is to be addressed effectively.

CHAPTER 12
THREATS TO THE PRESERVATION OF THE WORLD'S COMMON ECOLOGY

Today we abuse the Earth's resources. We feed on portions that belong to unborn generations. . . . Protection of the environment is a noble endeavor in itself. But the survival of the environment is also the strategic basis of human survival.

—Thabo Mbeki, Fernando Henrique Cardoso, and Goran Persson, presidents respectively of South Africa, Brazil, and Sweden

Feeling the Heat. The UN's Intergovernmental Panel on Climate Change (IPCC) composed of six hundred scientists from forty countries concluded for the first time that evidence of the Earth's rising temperatures was "unequivocal" and that global warming was more than 90 percent likely to be the product of human activity. Shown here is one symptom: one of the authors of *World Politics*, Charles Kegley, hiking with his wife, Debbie, in the balmy Swiss Alps, following the winter 2007 "snowless" ski season.

"Where you stand depends on where you sit" is an aphorism used to describe the determinants of peoples' positions when they make decisions (recall Chapter 3). Where do you stand on one of the most "hotly" debated issues created by a warming globe and deteriorating environment? You may already have strong feelings about this controversy. Many others do. Whatever your view, there is some scholarly expert and many politicians who agree with you.

Some scientists and politicians reject the view that the planet is really in danger; they claim that there doesn't exist a real problem because technological innovation can reverse the trends in global warming (which they argue may not even be "real" because the long-term cyclical pattern of the Earth's evolution suggests that our present period of rising temperatures is temporary). These people claim that environmental deterioration and resource depletion has many people needlessly alarmed. Other scientists are pessimistic and are now certain that the threats are real.

> *Climate Cassandras say the facts are clear and the case is closed. [It's true that] global warming is happening [but] we do not know the extent to which human activity caused this. The activity is economic growth, the wealth-creation that makes possible improved well-being—better nutrition, medicine, education, etc. How much reduction of such social goods are we willing to accept by slowing economic activity in order to try to regulate the planet's climate?*
>
> —George F. Will, political journalist

They are themselves alarmed by optimists who fail to face the "clear and present danger" of environmental threats and undertake reforms. The ecological threats that rivet the worried scientific community were documented in Al Gore's famous movie and book on global warming, *An Inconvenient Truth*, for which he won a 2007 Nobel Peace Prize. Those frightened climate experts are advocating big changes by governments, and *now*—before it becomes too late to save the human race from certain doom.

In this chapter, you have the opportunity to sharpen your own thinking by weighing the available evidence about prevailing global trends conditioning the environment shared by all on Earth. So take a look at various dimensions of the planet's ecology now in transformation. Then base your stand on this global issue on information that can better ground your existing opinions.

ENVIRONMENTAL SUSTAINABILITY AND HUMAN SECURITY

The population on our planet inexorably continues to increase. The activities of humans on planet Earth are constantly undergoing changes—adapting to changes in the global environment while peoples' customs and choices also continually lead to changes in that environment. These interactive changes are historical constants.

Today, globalization is bringing everyone increasingly together in an emerging global village. One consequence is that rising interdependence is making everyone increasingly influenced by what people and governments everywhere are doing. This means that conditions abroad are affecting more powerfully than ever before conditions at home. Ecologists—those who study the interrelationships of living organisms and the Earth's physical environment—use the term **the global commons** to highlight this interdependence, because they see the Earth as a common environment made up of the totality of organisms. In a world where everything affects everything else, the fate of the global commons is the fate of humanity.

■ **the global commons**

the physical and organic characteristics and resources of the entire planet—the air in the atmosphere and conditions on land and sea—on which human life depends and which is the common heritage of all humanity.

The planet's **carrying capacity**—the Earth's ability to support and sustain life—is at the center of discussion about the future of the global commons. One concerned view about this declining capacity is voiced by Lester R. Brown, the president of the Earth Policy Institute. In 2007, he argued:

> Throughout history, humans have lived on the Earth's sustainable yield—the interest from its natural endowment. Now, however, we are consuming the endowment itself. In ecology, as in economics, we can consume principal along with interest in the short run, but, for the long term, that practice leads to bankruptcy.

This kind of questioning concern has created global alarm about potential food and resource shortages (see Controversy: Why Is There a Global Food Crisis?). As Josette Sheeran, Executive Director of the United Nations World Food Programme lamented in 2008, "If we do not act quickly, the bottom billion will become the bottom two billion virtually overnight as their purchasing power is cut in half due to a doubling in food and fuel prices."

■ **carrying capacity**

the maximum number of humans and living species that can be supported by a given territory.

The pessimists sounding the alarm about the signs of ecological deterioration and the optimists confidently extolling the virtues of free markets and technological innovation in saving the planet paint very different visions of the global future.

> *What man makes, unmakes man.*
> —Norman Cousins, editor and journalist

Whether the world community has the political will and capacity to cope with ecological problems and expand the possibilities for humanity will be critical for *human security*—the extent to which individuals' basic needs such as sufficient food are available for survival and welfare. A paradigm or popular way of organizing thought about international problems is rising among scholars and policy makers who are now convinced that threats to the preservation of the global commons deserves equal attention to the threat of global warfare.

■ **ecopolitics**

how political actors influence perceptions of, and policy responses to, changing environmental conditions, such as the impact of carbon dioxide emissions on the temperature of the Earth.

Forging a Consensus on Ecological Dangers

Global environmental challenges and the study of responses to them is what is termed **ecopolitics**— the causal linkage between ecology and politics. Ecology deals with the relations between people and other living organisms and environmental conditions. Politics is concerned with the exercise of power. Ecopolitics therefore investigates how political actors make choices to manage the harmful impact of human behavior on the environment in which all people on Earth live. Politics underlies all dimensions of environmental and resource issues. These political issues range from the evaluation of scientific evidence to policy prescriptions in dealing with that evidence.

What is not controversial is that the ecological preservation of the global environment is required if any other values are to be achieved. Without the means to a healthy life no other values can be realized. Awareness of the importance of environmental protection has expanded greatly in recent years. When U.S. astronauts first viewed Earth from the Apollo spacecraft, they told millions of listeners about the "big blue marble" planet they saw and how the clouds and continents flowed into one another without regard to the political boundaries humans had imposed on a pristine planet. Those images are still often replayed. However, the improvement in space technology since the 1990s also allows the world to see uncomfortable images—of atmospheric poisons that encircle the globe, of violent winter and summer storms pounding islands and continents with relentless fury, of massive holes in the ozone shield that protects humans from dangerous ultraviolet rays, of vanishing forests and widening deserts.

Environmental issues are linked to other values that states prize, notably, security, and economic and social well-being. "Security" means freedom from fear, risk, and danger. Because fear of a nuclear holocaust and other forms of violence have long haunted the world, security has been conventionally equated with *national security*, the struggle for state power central to *realist theory* and its emphasis on armed aggression. Today, many experts urge people and governments to construct a broader definition of what really constitutes security (as the U.S. Department of Defense did when in April 2007 it warned that global warming should be regarded as a threat to American national security). This reconstruction is compatible with *neoliberal theory*, which emphasizes that security should be defined as the capacity to protect the quality of life. From this transformation in thinking emerges the so-called **politics of scarcity**, which predicts that future international conflict will likely be caused by resource scarcities—restricted access to food, oil, and water, for example—rather than by overt military challenges.

Framing Global Ecological Issues

Environmental security is a useful concept that broadens the definition of national security by pushing visions beyond borders and their protection. It focuses on the transboundary character of challenges to preserving the global environment by recognizing that threats by such phenomena as global warming, ozone depletion, and the loss of tropical forests and marine habitats can threaten the future of humanity as much as the threat of warfare using weapons of mass destruction. Because environmental degradation undercuts states' economic well-being and the quality of life all governments seek for their citizens, *liberalism* informs current thinking about how states can cooperate with international organizations (IGOs) and nongovernmental organizations (NGOs) to preserve the global environment. The neoliberal *epistemic community* has been active sharing their expertise and knowledge to redefine "security" in order to move beyond realism's conventional state-centric portrayal of international politics.

■ **politics of scarcity**
the view that the unavailability of resources required to sustain life, such as food, energy, or water, can undermine security in degrees similar to military aggression.

■ **environmental security**
a concept recognizing that environmental threats to global life systems are as dangerous as the threat of armed conflicts.

CONTROVERSY:

WHY IS THERE A GLOBAL FOOD CRISIS?

You do not have to go far to learn about the impact of the global food crisis. Indeed, a quick trip to the grocery store is revealing—since 2003, bread prices have gone up almost 75 percent, pork prices have more than doubled, and the price of bananas has gone up over 40 percent (Dykman 2008, 35). Globally, increased food prices have created a good deal of civil unrest (including the "tortilla riots" in Mexico and the "pasta riots" in Italy), as well as a wave of humanitarian crises in the developing world. As World Bank President Robert Zoellick concluded, "we are entering a danger zone" that threatens to drive over 100 million additional people into extreme poverty (World Bank 2008).

Examining some of the major factors that are pushing us into this "danger zone" provides insight into the interconnected nature of global threats, the trade-offs inherent in trying to provide for human needs, as well as the ways in which the policies of individual governments and international organizations can influence the international system as a whole. With that in mind, let us briefly touch upon some of the major root causes of the food crisis.

First, *environmental stress*, due to changing demographics and climates, contributes to the crisis. For example, increases in urbanization have resulted in increased stress upon the agricultural sectors—not only is key agricultural land often incorporated into rapidly growing urban areas, but government support formerly targeted at agricultural sectors (such as assistance with irrigation and farm equipment) may be diverted to urban development (Teslik 2008). One of the primary effects of climate change is an increase in "extreme weather" events, and such events have had a key role in damaging agricultural production. For example, droughts in Australia cut its wheat production in half, while flooding in Ecuador played a key role in the recent rise of banana prices.

Government policies have also served to exacerbate the situation. As noted in Chapter 10, governments have traditionally protected their agricultural markets through subsidies and tariffs, which have served to increase the price of many agricultural goods. Moreover, recent food shortages have resulted in a proliferation of another form of government intervention—limits on the export of agricultural products such as wheat and rice. Indeed, the UN World Food Programme found that forty countries were currently engaging in such export bans (Teslik 2008). These bans serve to decrease the world supply of these goods, which thus increases prices. Along these lines, government encouragement of biofuel production has had an impact upon food prices. A World Bank study estimates that biofuel production has accounted for 65 percent of the rise in world food prices; and the IMF cites biofuel production as being responsible for a "significant part of the jump in commodity prices" (Lynch 2008).

Prices of agricultural inputs have risen greatly. Agriculture relies heavily on petroleum for many aspects of production as well as transport, and the sector has thus been hit hard by increases in energy prices. Moreover, fertilizer prices have also risen dramatically. For example, the price of nitrogen fertilizer has increased over 350 percent since 1999 (*Financial Times* 2007).

Finally, *food consumption patterns* in emerging markets, such as China, India, Russia, and Brazil, have changed as their countries have developed. In particular, these countries have greatly increased their consumption of meat and dairy products. For example, meat consumption in China, traditionally a vegetarian

FREAK FOOD OR UNFAIR FOREIGN TRADE? **A Greenpeace activist in France protests the import of genetically modified corn, which the United States produces for export around the globe.**

society, has more than doubled since 1980, and dairy consumption has tripled (Dymkan 2008). Dairy consumption in Brazil doubled from 2005 to 2007 (*Financial Times* 2007). This has contributed to increased demand for these products, as well as the inputs necessary for their production (such as cattle feed).

The food crisis is thus at the "crossroads" of many international phenomena and raises many fundamental issues about the international system. An immediate issue of concern is whether the food crisis will continue into the future. Unfortunately, many of the causes cited above are the result of structural changes that are quite averse to change in the short term. This raises a related issue—how should we respond to this crisis? Most every international organization has begun to articulate some type of response, though maintaining the political will to enact fundamental changes is always difficult. Developed countries, for example, are very resistant to reducing agricultural subsidies. Moreover, some of the suggested solutions, such as the increased use of **genetic engineering** and **transgenetic crops** and livestock, are quite controversial and not supported by a variety of countries and NGOs. Finally, the food crisis raises a question fundamental to our existence—is our world capable of supporting itself? This has been an issue of contention for generations, and arguments generally fall along one of two lines. **Neo-Malthusians** believe that the earth's population is already pushing Earth's resources, and worry that continued levels of population growth and development are unsustainable. This pessimistic view is in contrast to the **cornucopians**, who posit that the overall "condition" of humanity has improved over the past decades, and that new technologies and increased productivity will enable the world to continue these improvements.

The dominant cornucopian social *paradigm* stressing the right to conspicuous consumption is under attack by environmental activists and think-tank experts such as Worldwatch, which question the dubious equation of consumption with happiness, noting that in today's consumer culture peoples' life satisfaction has not risen with their increasing wealth (*State of the World* 2004). Unrestrained consumption is also under attack internationally. **Sustainable development** is now

■ genetic engineering

research geared to discover seeds for new types of plant and human life for sale and use as substitutes for those produced naturally.

popularly perceived as an alternative to the quest for unrestrained growth. The movement began in earnest in 1972, when the UN General Assembly convened the first UN Conference of the Human Environment in Stockholm. Since then, conferences on a wide range of environmental topics have produced scores of treaties and new international agencies to promote cooperation and monitor environmental developments.

The concept of sustainable development is even more directly traceable to *Our Common Future*, the 1987 report of the World Commission on Environment and Development, popularly known as the "Brundtland Commission," after the Norwegian prime minister who chaired it. The commission concluded that the world cannot sustain the growth required to meet the needs and aspirations of the world's growing population unless it adopts radically different approaches to basic issues of economic expansion, equity, resource management, energy efficiency, and the like. Rejecting the "limits to growth" maxim popular among neo-Malthusians,

NASA

ENVIRONMENTAL THREATS ON A PLANETARY SCALE **People on the planet collectively face many threats to survival, one of which is the threat posed by heat-trapping greenhouse gases that contribute to climate change and destructive global warming. Taken from an NASA global satellite surveillance system, this photo shows how the integrated and globalized borderless planet shares a single interconnected ecology. As demographic environmentalist Bill McKibbin warns, "We are heating up the planet, substantially. This is not a problem for the distant future, or even the near future. The planet has already heated up a degree or more. We are perhaps a quarter of the way into the greenhouse era, and the effects are already being felt."**

it emphasized instead "the growth of limits." The commission defined a "sustainable society" as one that "meets the needs of the present without compromising the ability of future generations to meet their own needs."

Another milestone in the challenge to the then–dominant cornucopian social paradigm occurred at the 1992 Earth Summit in Rio de Janeiro, Brazil on the twentieth anniversary of the Stockholm conference. The meeting brought together more than 150 states, 1,400 nongovernmental organizations, and 8,000 journalists. Before the Earth Summit, the environment and economic development had been treated separately—and often regarded as being in conflict with each other because economic growth frequently imperils and degrades the environment. In Rio, the concept of sustainability galvanized a simultaneous treatment of environmental and development issues. That concept was next enthusiastically endorsed at the 2002 UN World Summit on Sustainable Development in Johannesburg. Other international conferences have since punctuated the strong consensus behind the proposition that all politics—even global politics—are local, that what happens any place ultimately affects conditions every place, and accordingly that the protection of Earth's environment is a primary international security issue.

Sustainability cannot be realized without substantial changes. Is that possible? Are individuals willing to sacrifice personal consumption for the common good? Will they sacrifice now to enrich their heirs? To make a prediction, the next step is for you to characterize and estimate the nature and magnitude of environmental threats. Consider next two interrelated clusters of problems on the global ecopolitical agenda: (1) climate change and ozone depletion, and (2) deforestation and biodiversity. The clusters illustrate some of the obstacles to the sustainable development of common properties and renewable resources.

The Ecopolitics of the Atmosphere

The scores of government negotiators and nongovernmental representatives who converged on Rio de Janeiro in 1992 came in the wake of the hottest decade on record. For years, scientists had warned that global warming—the gradual rise in world temperature—would cause destructive changes in world climatological patterns and that rising sea levels, melting glaciers, and freak storms would provoke widespread changes in the globe's political and economic systems and relationships. Perhaps because they had been burned by the chronic heat wave throughout the 1980s, negotiators agreed at Rio to a *Framework Convention on Climate Change.* Since then, fears have increased in conjunction with the continuing rise of planetary temperatures. In response to the series of record-setting global temperatures in the twenty-first century, attention to the pollutants blamed for global warming has risen.

Climate Change and Global Warming Major gaps in knowledge about climate change remain, but the vast majority of climate scientists are now convinced that the gradual rise in the Earth's temperature, especially evident since the late eighteenth century when the invention of power-driven machinery produced the Industrial Revolution, is caused by an increase in human-made gases that alter the atmosphere's insulating effects. The gas molecules, primarily carbon dioxide (CO_2) and chlorofluorocarbons (CFCs), form the equivalent of a greenhouse roof by trapping heat remitted from Earth that would otherwise escape into outer space. As these gases are released into

■ **transgenetic crops**

new crops with improved characteristics created artificially through genetic engineering that combine genes from species that would not naturally interbreed.

■ **neo-Malthusians**

pessimists who warn of the global ecopolitical dangers of uncontrolled population growth.

■ **cornucopians**

optimists who question limits-to-growth analyses and contend that markets effectively maintain a balance between population, resources, and the environment.

■ **sustainable development**

economic growth that does not deplete the resources needed to maintain life and prosperity.

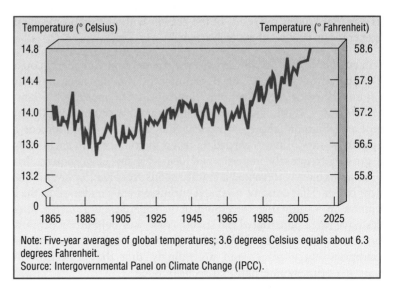

Note: Five-year averages of global temperatures; 3.6 degrees Celsius equals about 6.3 degrees Fahrenheit.
Source: Intergovernmental Panel on Climate Change (IPCC).

FIGURE 12.1

RISING AVERAGE GLOBAL TEMPERATURES AT THE EARTH'S SURFACE SINCE 1867 **The World Meteorological Organization (WMO) monitors average global surface temperatures at thousands of sites around the world. Its records show that so-called global warming is not a myth. For 150 years, the globe's temperature has seesawed up and down, usually by tiny fractions of degrees. However, since the mid-1970s the mercury has been rising, and the 1996–2008 period has been the warmest since reliable measurements began. The ICPP 2008 Report predicts that, depending on greenhouse-gas emissions, global temperature will probably rise about 2 to 12 degrees Fahrenheit by 2100, with longer and more intense heat waves.**

■ **greenhouse effect**

the phenomenon producing planetary warming when gases released by burning fossil fuels act as a blanket in the atmosphere, thereby increasing temperatures.

the atmosphere, they have created a **greenhouse effect**, which has caused global temperatures to rise. As shown in Figure 12.1, the average global temperature on the Earth's surface has increased nearly 1 degree Celsius in the past century and more than half of that warming—a rise of 0.6 degrees—has occurred in the past thirty years, meaning that the warming trend is accelerating (*Vital Signs 2006–2007*, 42).

The globe's temperature is now projected to further increase dramatically by 2100 if aggressive preventive action is not taken. Although CO_2 is the principal greenhouse gas, concentrations of methane in the atmosphere are growing more rapidly. Methane gas emissions arise from livestock populations, rice cultivation, and the production and transportation of natural gas. To many scientists' alarm, the largest concentrations of methane are not in the atmosphere but locked in ice, permafrost, and coastal marine sediments. This raises the probability that warming will cause more methane to be released into the atmosphere, which would then increase global temperatures because of methane's strong warming potential.

Some scientists insist that the rise in global temperature is only part of a cyclical change the world has experienced for thousands of years. They are able to cite evidence of "sudden and dramatic temperature swings over the past 400,000 years, from warm climates to ice ages. [These] global warming skeptics say the climate changes we're seeing today reflect these natural variations" (Knickerbocker 2007).

These skeptics believe that cold water needs to be poured on all the "hot air" because global warming is a climate myth. But "most climate scientists say human-induced greenhouse gases are at work—and note that these temperature changes correlate with levels of carbon dioxide" (Knickerbocker 2007).

The UN team of hundreds of atmospheric scientists from around the world known as the Intergovernmental Panel on Climate Change (IPCC) first conclusively stated in 1995 its belief that global climate trends are "unlikely to be entirely due to natural causes," that humans are to blame for at least part of the problem, and that the consequences are likely to be very harmful and costly. The implications were self-evident: without significant efforts to reduce the emission of greenhouse gases, the increase in global temperatures by the year 2100 could be equivalent to that which ended the last ice age. Even at the lower end of the panel's estimates, the rise would be faster than any experienced in recorded human history.

According to the IPCC, global warming is not coming, it's here, and has led to a rising number of natural disasters (see Figure 12.2).

The most inconvenient truth about global warming is that we cannot stop it. The trouble is, if you accept all the facts and theories about global warming, it is difficult to see how any human response launched today can avert it.

—Fareed Zakaria, political journalist

The IPCC warns that the effects of continued rising temperatures will be both dramatic and devastating:

- Sea levels will rise, mostly because of melting glaciers and the expansion of water as it warms up. This will produce massive floods of vast areas of low-lying coastal lands, especially in Asia and the U.S. Atlantic coast. New York City could be submerged. Millions of people are likely to be displaced by major floods each year.

- Winters will get warmer and heat waves will become increasingly frequent and severe, producing avalanches from melting glaciers in high altitudes.

- Rainfall will increase worldwide, and deadly storms such as the devastating Asian tsunami in December 2004 will become more common. As oceans heat, hurricanes, which draw their energy from warm oceans, will become increasingly stronger and more frequent.

- Because water evaporates more easily in a warmer climate, drought-prone regions will become even drier.

- Up to 30 percent of living species will face an increasing risk of extinction as entire ecosystems vanish from the planet. A hotter Earth will drive some plant life to higher latitudes and altitudes, requiring farmers to change their crops and agricultural practices.

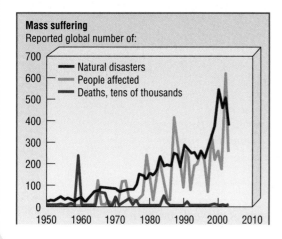

FIGURE 12.2

GLOBAL WARMING, CLIMATIC CATASTROPHES, AND MASS SUFFERING **As the globe heats up, so have the numbers of natural disasters. Indeed, the Centre for Research on the Epidemiology of Disasters predicts that 4,650 natural disasters will occur in the period between 2000 and 2009 (*Economist, The World in 2007*, 63). Shown (left) is the destruction caused in 2008 by a massive earthquake in China and the flooding that followed the tsunami in Myanmar (right).**

- The combination of flooding and droughts will cause tropical diseases such as malaria and dengue fever to flourish in previously temperate regions that were formerly too cold for their insect carriers; "a warmer CO_2-rich world will be very, very good for plants, insects, and microbes that make us sick" (Begley 2007).

- The world will face increased hunger and water shortages, especially in the poorest countries. Africa will be the hardest hit, with up to 250 million people likely to suffer water shortages by 2020.

Ozone Depletion and Protection   The story of climate change is similar to states' efforts to cope with the depletion of the atmosphere's protective **ozone layer** In this case, however, an international regime has emerged, progressively strengthened by mounting scientific evidence that environmental damage is directly caused by human activity.

Ozone is a pollutant in the lower atmosphere, but in the upper atmosphere it provides the Earth with a critical layer of protection against the sun's harmful ultraviolet radiation. Scientists have discovered a marked depletion of the ozone layer—most notably an "ozone hole" over Antarctica that has grown larger than the continental United States. They have conclusively linked the thinning of the layer

■ **ozone layer**

the protective layer of the upper atmosphere over the Earth's surface that shields the planet from the sun's harmful impact on living organisms.

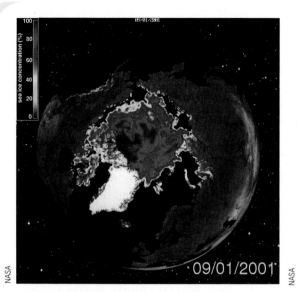 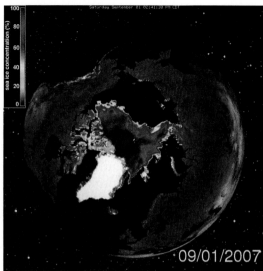

Pictured are NASA satellite images of the Arctic icecap in September 2001 (left) and again in September 2007 (right). As you can see, the Arctic icecap is melting fast and it is "only half the size that it was 50 years ago. For the first time, the Northwest Passage —a fabled sea route to Asia that European explorers sought in vain for centuries—opened for shipping" (Borgerson 2008, 63). Due to the dramatic potential to transform energy markets and global shipping, there are calls for a multilateral Arctic treaty that would address competing claims for resources and prevent global conflict.

to CFCs—a related family of compounds known as halons, hydrochlorofluorocarbons (HCFCs), methyl bromide, and other chemicals. Depletion of the ozone layer exposes humans to health hazards of various sorts, particularly skin cancer, and threatens other forms of marine and terrestrial life.

Scientists began to link halons and CFCs to ozone depletion in the early 1970s. Even before their hypotheses were conclusively confirmed, the **United Nations Environment Programme (UNEP)**, a UN agency created in the aftermath of the 1972 Stockholm conference, sought some form of regulatory action. Despite scientific uncertainty and policy differences, the 1987 landmark *Montreal Protocol on Substances that Deplete the Ozone Layer* treaty was signed by 146 countries, and its acceptance has led to a huge 90 percent reduction since the late 1980s in global atmospheric concentrations of chlorofluorocarbons (WDI 2007, 176–178). The ozone regime was made possible by strong scientific evidence and by having an active NGO epistemic community to actively promote the treaty. International cooperation for the construction of regimes sometimes works. However, in spite of reductions in CFCs over the past twenty years, the ozone hole over Antarctica continues to expand, and depletion of the protective ozone shield is expected to continue before it begins to regenerate itself.

■ **United Nations Environment Programme (UNEP)**

a UN agency that studies environmental deterioration and proposes regulations to protect the global environment.

Production of CFCs in the Global North declined sharply in the 1990s as the largest producers (and consumers) prepared for their complete phase-out. However, production in the Global South surged, and increased demand for refrigerators, air conditioners, and other products using CFCs will offset the gains realized by stopping production in the Global North. Developed countries agreed to provide aid to help the developing countries adopt CFC alternatives, but they have failed to provide all of the resources promised. Without this support, many in the Global South may not be able to keep their end of the global bargain. Meanwhile, a significant illegal trade in both virgin and recycled CFCs has emerged, threatening to further undermine the positive effects of the ozone regime.

Success at containing ozone depletion has raised hopes that other environmental threats also can be given higher priority than vested financial interests. Controlling pollution in the world's mountains provides one example. The UN designated 2002 the International Year of Mountains, highlighting the importance of mountains as the source of rich plant and animal life and more than half the world's freshwater. Mountains and highlands cover about a quarter of the globe and are home to ten percent of the world's population. According to the UN, mountains are the "water towers of the world," supplying more than half of the world's population. But that supply is endangered because about one-fourth of today's armed conflicts around the world are fought in mountainous areas, destroying the environment. Beyond that environmental challenge, efforts to negotiate treaties to protect forests and Earth's biological heritage are critically important.

The Ecopolitics of Forests and Biodiversity

■ **biodiversity**
the variety of plant and animal species living in the Earth's diverse ecosystems.

Forests are critical in preserving the Earth's **biodiversity** and protecting the atmosphere and land resources. For these reasons, they have been a rising ecological issue on the global agenda. Some rules have emerged to guide international behavior in the preservation of biodiversity, but issues concerning forests have proven much more difficult to address.

■ **deforestation**
the process of clearing and destroying forests.

Shrinking Forests and Dust Bowls   Trends since the 1980s point toward considerable **deforestation** throughout much of the world. Over the past eight thousand years, the World Resources Institute estimates that almost half of the forests once covering the Earth have been converted for ranching, farmland, pastures, and other uses, and that "one-fifth of the Earth's original forest remains in large, relatively natural ecosystems—what are known as 'frontier forests.'" Three-fourths of the world's forests are located in the Global South (WDI 2007, 140). Forest loss is most severe in the tropics of Asia (30 percent), and Africa and South America (20 percent), which adds to the total loss for the world (about 22 percent) (*Vital Signs 2006–2007*, 102). Destruction of tropical rain forests in such places as Brazil, Indonesia, and Malaysia is a matter of special concern because much of the world's genetic heritage is found there.

The representatives sent to the 1992 Earth Summit hoped to secure an easy victory on a statement of principle for global forest conservation. But opposition quickly developed to the principle that the global interest makes all countries responsible for protecting national forests. The Global South—led by Malaysia, a principal exporter of tropical wood products—objected especially vigorously to the socially constructed view that the world's forests were a common property resource, the "common heritage of mankind." These developing countries feared that legally accepting this view would enable the Global North to interfere with the local management of their tropical forest resources. As Ogar Assam Effa, a tree plantation director in Nigeria, observes "The developed countries want us to keep the forests, since the air we breathe is for all of us, rich countries and poor countries. But we breathe the air, and our bellies are empty." He asks "Can air give you protein? Can air give you carbohydrates? It would be easy to convince people to stop clearing the forest if there was an alternative" (Harris 2008, A2). In the end, the Earth Summit backed away from the goal of establishing international guidelines for trade in "sustainably managed" forest products, and the situation today remains largely unchanged, with less than 5 percent of the globe's forests sustainably managed (*Economist*, May 27, 2006, 78).

Meanwhile, high population growth rates, industrialization, and urbanization increase pressure to farm forests and marginal land poorly suited to cultivation. This has led to deforestation and **desertification**, which turn an increasing portion of the Earth's landmass into deserts useless for agricultural productivity or wildlife habitats. "The world is running out of freshwater. There's water everywhere, of course, but less than three percent of it is fresh, and most of that is locked up in polar ice caps and glaciers, unrecoverable for practical purposes. Lakes, rivers, marshes, aquifers, and atmospheric vapor make up less than one percent of the Earth's total water, and people are already using more than half of the accessible runoff. Water demand and water use in many areas already exceed nature's ability to recharge supplies, and demand seems destined to exceed supplies since ground water overdraft and aquifer depletion are expected to increase 18 percent between 1995 and 2025" (*Vital Signs 2005–2006*, 104). "By 2025, two out of every three people on the planet will live in a water-stressed area," predicts James Canton (2007). "Water wars are an imminent threat" (Cetron and Davies 2005). Part of the problem is because agriculture, globally, uses more than 70 percent of freshwater which is declining by an average of 3,807 billion cubic meters each year (WDI 2007, 122, 144). With rising population and consumption, in the absence of serious water-conservation measures and cooperation among mutual water users for watershed preservation, water availability will become an ever-growing resource issue.

Soil degradation has stripped billions of acres of the Earth's surface from productive farming. Soil erosion and pollution are problems both in densely populated developing countries and in the more highly developed regions of mechanized industrial agriculture. "Global demand for food is projected to double in the next fifty years as urbanization proceeds and income rises. But arable land per capita is shrinking" (WDI 2007, 124). The threat will surely increase because land degradation is increasing. "Deforestation continues at about 13 million hectares a year," as land degradation has reduced agricultural productivity since 1980 by as much as 8.9 percent (WDI 2007, 124; Harris 2008). Map 12.1 shows the trends across regions where desertification is occurring most rapidly.

In the Global North, reforestation has alleviated some of the danger. This is not the case in many cash-starved Global South countries, where the reasons for rapid destruction vary. South American forests, most notably the Amazon, are generally burned for industrial-scale soybean farming or cattle grazing. In Southeast Asia, forests are burned or cut for large scale planting of palm to obtain the oil that is used in a wide array of products, including cosmetics and food processing. In Africa,

■ **desertification**
the creation of deserts due to soil erosion, overfarming, and deforestation, which converts cropland to nonproductive, arid sand.

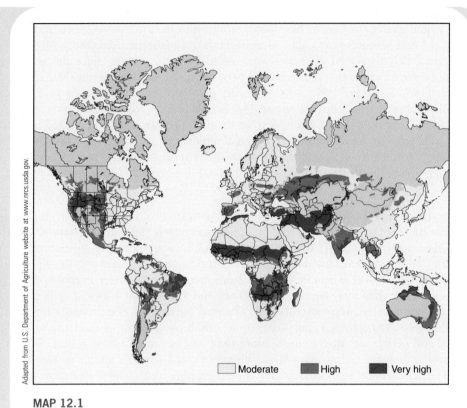

Adapted from U.S. Department of Agriculture website at www.nrcs.usda.gov.

☐ Moderate ■ High ■ Very high

MAP 12.1

LOSS OF FOREST AND GROUND TO DESERTS **This map displays the extent to which certain regions are experiencing desertification or lost, degraded, dry lands as the result of climate change, exploitative agricultural overgrazing, and the lack of conservation efforts. Each year millions of acres of farmland become unproductive deserts.**

individuals hack out small plots for farming (Harris 2008). And most recently, deforestation is being spurred by the global demand for biofuels. "Worldwide investment in biofuels rose from $5 billion in 1995 to $38 billion in 2005 and is expected to top $100 billion by 2010" (Grunwald 2008, 40). In Brazil, deforestation roughly doubled in 2008 alone due in part to the dramatic expansion in agriculture aimed at producing farm-grown fuels. As John Carter, founder of a non-profit that promotes sustainable ranching in the Amazonian region, lamented "You can't protect it. There's too much money to be made tearing it down."

While biofuels such as ethanol are often touted as being eco-friendly, critics point out that ethanol destroys forests, contributes to global warming, and inflates food prices. Moreover, the clearing and burning of tropical rain forests to make room for farms and ranches is doubly destructive because agriculture uses 70 percent of freshwater globally (WDI 2007, 144). From the viewpoint of climate change, green plants remove CO_2 from the atmosphere during photosynthesis. So the natural processes that remove greenhouse gases are destroyed when forests are cut down, and, as the forests decay or are burned, the amount of CO_2 released into the atmosphere increases. The Amazon rain forest is "an incomparable storehouse of carbon, the

Arko Datta/AFP/Getty Images

very carbon that heats up the planet when it's released into the atmosphere. Brazil now ranks fourth in the world in carbon emissions, and most of its emissions come from deforestation" (Grunwald 2008, 40).

The Threat to Global Biodiversity   Biodiversity, or biological diversity, is an umbrella term that refers to the Earth's variety of life. Technically, it encompasses three basic levels of organization in living systems: genetic diversity, species diversity, and ecosystem diversity. Until recently, public attention has been focused almost exclusively on preserving species diversity, including old forests, tall grass prairies, wetlands, coastal habitats, and coral reefs.

Forests, especially tropical forests, are important to preserving biodiversity because they are home to countless species of animals and plants, many of them still unknown. Scientists believe that the global habitat contains between eight and ten million species. Of these, only about 1.5 million have been named, and most of them are in the temperate regions of North America, Europe, Russia, and Australia. Destruction of tropical forests, where two-thirds to three-fourths of all species are believed to live, threatens the destruction of much of the world's undiscovered biological diversity and genetic heritage. Overwhelming, alarming evidence indicates that environmental deterioration is destroying a wide range of living organisms. In

2004, a scientific study predicted that global warming could drive to extinction up to 37 percent of all living species by the mid-twenty-first century (Gugliotta 2004, A6). Another study ominously concluded that "current extinction rates are 100 to 1,000 times higher than prehuman levels, and projected losses of habitat from land conversion . . . will probably push this rate higher still" (WRI, www.wri.org/trends). As the world consumes more fish (and as others perish in pollution), overfishing could soon destroy the seafood supply (Kher 2006).

Many experts worry that the globe is relentlessly heading toward major species extinction. Of the 242,000 plant species surveyed by the World Conservation Union, some 33,000, or 14 percent, are threatened with extinction, mainly as a result of clearing land for housing, roads, and industries. Others doubt the imminence of a massive die-out, estimating that only a small fraction of the Earth's species have actually disappeared over the past several centuries. Indeed, optimistic cornucopians argue that species extinction may not be bad news, as new species may evolve that will prove even more beneficial to humanity (McKibben 2006).

Threats to biodiversity have implications for all species, some of which face increasing competition for survival from nonnative species entering their local habitats through the cross-border transportation facilitated by globalization. The problem parallels other threats to other kinds of shared resources, but biodiversity's distributional characteristics also make it unique. In particular, because so much of the Earth's biological heritage is concentrated in the tropics, the Global South has a special interest in this issue. Moreover, the Global South also has a growing concern about protecting its interest in the face of MNCs' efforts to reap profits from the sale of biologically based products. Concerns are centered on the claim that the genetic character of the many species of plants and animals should be considered a part of the global commons and therefore available for commercial use by all, for their medical benefit.

■ enclosure movement

the claiming of common properties by states or private interests.

The rapid growth of biotechnology has added incentives for preserving the Earth's biological diversity so as to maintain a wide gene pool from which to develop new medical and agricultural products. MNCs in the Global North are major players in the so-called **enclosure movement** geared to privatize and merchandize the products derived from plant and animal genes that are the genetic bases for sustained life. In India, for example, products from the neem tree have been used for medicine, contraception, toiletries, timber, fuel, and insecticides. In 1985, U.S. and Japanese firms began patenting a variety of neem compounds that Indians never patented. Now, local Indian populations must compete with MNCs for neem-derived products, often at sharply higher prices.

Pharmaceutical companies in particular have laid claim to Global South resources. They actively explore plants, microbes, and other living organisms in tropical forests for possible use in prescription drugs. Ten of the globe's twenty-five top-selling drugs are derived from "natural biological sources" (UNEP, www.un.org).

Biogenetical engineering of harvests threatens to disrupt established trade and profits because most transgenetically altered foods and crops (primarily soybeans, beef, corn, and cotton) derived from the Global South are produced in North America and later exported for sale abroad in other countries' grocery stores. For example, food suppliers increasingly must acquire primitive germ plasma (the genetic material containing hereditary information) from the Global South to produce genetically altered seeds for the international market. Such seeds are patented and as private

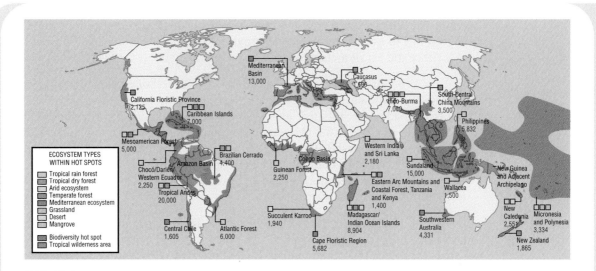

MAP 12.2

LOCATING BIODIVERSITY BASTIONS AND ENDANGERED BIODIVERSITY HOT SPOTS **This map provides a picture of global "danger zones" indentifying the estimated number of plant and animal species that are endangered in these biodiversity "hot spots." German Environment Minister Sigmar Gabriel in 2008 estimated that "up to 150 species become extinct every day."**

property can be sold back to Global South consumers. Most genetically altered seeds require expensive additives such as chemical fertilizers and pesticides that often are environmentally as well as financially costly. To compound the problem, when farmers in the Global South rely on hybrid varieties and genetically altered seeds, it increases the risk that old varieties will disappear.

Biogenetic engineering threatens to escalate the loss of global diversity. Biological resources—animal and plant species—are distributed unevenly in the world. Map 12.2 shows the major "biodiversity bastions" where more than half the Earth's species are found, primarily tropical wilderness territories laden with plant and animal species covering only 2 percent of the land. It also shows the location of "biodiversity hot spots," where human activity threatens to disturb and potentially destroy many species that international law defines as collective goods, a resource for all humanity from which everyone benefits. According to the UN, about fifty thousand plant and animal species become extinct each year as the global community wrestles with the ethics of biodiversity preservation and management policies.

SOURCES OF THE ECOLOGICAL THREATS TO THE GLOBAL COMMONS

Ever notice that people everywhere are remarkably alike? True, people and groups behave very differently. However, there seem to be some values that everyone cherishes that make him or her essentially similar. These values are universals, maintained throughout space and time. No matter what one's religion, nationality, language, country or color of skin, who wants clean air to breath? Who wants to live with access to clean and fresh water? Who wants to have adequate food supplies? Who wants to live where nature has provided a beautiful landscape? Who wants to experience the joy of a climate suitable for human habitation? Everybody!

It also can be said that there are some things that everybody throughout the world wishes to *avoid*. Who wants to live in a crowded city suffocating in smog? Who wants to reside near polluted lakes and streams contaminated with toxic wastes? Who wishes to move to a desert that has become a dust bowl through drought and the destruction of forests? Who desires to live in cities whose zoos now contain fewer and fewer live animals and more and more mere photos of species from the animal kingdom that now are extinct? Nobody. There is not a person on Earth who desires to experience these things; everyone wants to avoid them.

If nearly all people embrace certain values, there is another human commonality that makes all people everywhere alike. Everyone to some degree is a consumer. All people eat food, drink water, and consume energy, although at different rates. So all make demands on resources that can only be provided by the same planet on which we all live. This means people must be put into the ecological picture. How many people live on Earth and what they do while they live and how much they consume while living is a key to the planet's long-term fate.

If all humans desire the same kind of clean and green environment and seek to avoid ones that are polluted, dangerous to health, and prone to floods, hurricanes, tornadoes and typhoons, why, then, have threats to the global ecology increased when this trend is a part of no one's interest or value? Why are people worldwide now so worried about the conditions that are likely to transform planet Earth in ways that no one seeks?

The Tragedy of the Global Commons

The causes of the many growing threats to the preservation of planet Earth are many. No one cause is responsible for the trends in the global environment. Many causes interact with each other to produce the dreaded dangers undermining the preservation of the world's life systems on which human existence depends. But among the ecologists who scientifically study the origins of planetary predicaments and problems, one explanation has become very popular. It is based on further assumptions about universals in human motivations through time that they believe are leading to the dangerous unintended consequences of planetary deterioration. It seems that there is another value that drives many people. As realists, mercantilists, and free-market economists, as well as theologians in every religious tradition, point out, *all* humans seek wealth, comfort, and health that money can help to purchase. Everyone hopes for a better life, most of all for themselves and often, secondarily as an afterthought of less importance, the same advantages for others. This means that people are prone to self-love and self-advancement. As a result, and to the extent that this value priority becomes an overriding motive for human action, bad things occur that sometimes make things worse in the long run for everyone, including the most successful competitors for money and the pleasures that high income can purchase.

Environmental degradation is one such product of the individual pursuit of private gain. At least that is the consensus of many experts who study the environment and are so worried about the potentially dismal prospects for preserving the planet's ecology. The **tragedy of the commons** is a popular term constructed to capture the human roots of the growing threats to the planet's resources and its delicately balanced ecological system. First articulated in 1833 by the English political economist William Foster Lloyd, the concept was later popularized and extended to contemporary global environmental problems by the human ecologist Garrett Hardin, in a famous article published in 1968 in the journal *Science*. "The commons" emphasizes the impact of human behavior driven by the search for personal self-advantage, and although it stresses the importance of individual action and personal motivations, it also ascribes those motives to collectivities or groups such as corporations and entire countries. The central question asked through the "commons" analogy is, what is the probable approach to resources held in common in an unregulated environment? If individuals (and corporations and countries) are interested primarily in advancing their own personal welfare, what consequences should be anticipated for the finite resources held in common and hence for all?

■ **tragedy of the commons**
a metaphor, widely used to explain the impact of human behavior on ecological systems, that explains how rational self-interested behavior by individuals may have a destructive collective impact.

Lloyd and later Hardin asked observers to consider what happened in medieval English villages, where the village green was typically common property on which all villagers could graze their cattle. Freedom of access to the commons was a cherished village value. Sharing the common grazing area worked well as long as usage by individuals (and their cattle) didn't reduce the land's usefulness to everyone else. Assuming that the villagers were driven by the profit motive and that no laws existed to restrain their greed, herders had maximum incentive to increase their stock for gain as much as possible. If pushed, individual herders might concede that the collective interest of all would be served if each contained the size of their herd rather than increasing it, so that the commons could be preserved. But self-restraint— voluntary reductions of the number of one's own cattle to relieve the pressure on the common village green—was not popular. Indeed, there was no guarantee that others would do the same. By contrast, the addition of one more animal to the village green would produce a personal gain whose costs would be borne by everyone. Therefore, economic *rational choice* to pursue wealth encouraged all to increase indiscriminately the size of the herds, and it discouraged self-sacrifice for the common welfare. Ultimately, the collective impact of each effort to maximize individual gain was to place more cattle on the village green than it could sustain. In the long run, the overgrazed green was destroyed. The lesson? "Ruin is the destination toward which all men rush," Hardin (1968) concluded, "each pursuing his own best interest."

The tragedy of the commons has become a standard concept in ecological analysis because it illuminates so well the sources of environmental degradation and many other global problems and predicaments. It is particularly applicable to the debate today about pressures on the global environment because the English common green is very comparable to planetary "common property," such as the oceans and the atmosphere from which individual profit is maximized on the basis of a first-come, first-served principle. Overuse of common property is also highlighted, as when the oceans and atmosphere are used by a few as sinks for environmental pollutants whose costs are borne by many.

Are these dynamics behind global ecological dangers? Many people think so. However, you have probably already guessed that experts disagree about the moral and ethical implications of Hardin's interpretation. Note that the logical conclusion is that reforms are required to save planet Earth. The needed changes will require both some self-restraint on people's freedom of choice as well as a modicum of regulation in order to control the ruinous consequence of the tragedy of an unmanaged global commons.

Theorists adhering to *realism* and free-market *mercantilism* go very far in defending freedom of economic choice without regulation as the best and safest path to realizing the greatest good for the greatest number. Theorists from these traditions believe that the pursuit of self-interest and personal profit will in the long run benefit all, producing more income and technological innovation than would occur by supervisory regulation of corporations, entrepreneurs, and investors given free reign to seek profits. They also feel that minimal interference in the pursuit of personal gain is helpful to the preservation of the Earth's ecological health. To their way of reasoning, the pursuit of private gain with little restraint is a virtue, not a vice. Greed is good.

Highly questioning of this conclusion are almost all religious moral traditions. Christianity, for example, follows ancient Hebrew ethics in defining greed as one of the seven deadly sins. The predictable outcome of selfishness and blind dedication to personal financial gain over other values such as altruistic love and compassion for the community of humankind is a certain path to ruin and to sin. In this sense,

For the love of money is the root of all evil.
—Timothy 6:10, the Bible

religious traditions join some of the thinking underlying radical Marxist theorizing (see Chapter 2). These streams of thoughts argue that concern for the welfare of all provides happiness and benefits because only if community interests are protected can individuals realize their most precious personal interest in advancing such common values as the opportunity for maintaining a clean and sustainable environment.

Ecopolitics forces you to weigh rival perspectives and to evaluate competing values. Do you want income and prosperity? Of course, but at what intended and unintended costs? Countries and companies all seek wealth. Does this mean that their quest for profits justify allowing them to dump toxic wastes into lakes, rivers and oceans and overfish, and let others bear the burden of their actions for personal profit? Does the value of freedom mean that tobacco businesses should have the right to market their product freely, and advertise the claim that smoking is a personal choice that may even be good for your health? To maximize their gain, should smokers be free to blow smoke into the air without restraints, and with disregard for the effects on the health of nonsmokers and children in public places? Do you think that the corporate right to seek profits justifies asking you and everyone else to bear the costs of health care for victims of lung cancer?

These and other ethical questions are directly in the crossfire of debate about what is causing the threats to the planetary commons and what if anything should be undertaken to contain them, and at what costs. Your interpretation can be best informed by looking selectively at the presumed causes of today and tomorrow's likely environmental dangers. Beyond the role of human motivation and the causes traced to human values and choices at the *individual level of analysis*, consider some trends that are best classified at the *global level of analysis*. Patterns in the consumption and production of fossil fuel energy and its transfer across state boundaries figure most prominently as the prime contribution to global warming.

The Globalization of Planetary Dangers

The 2007 IPCC report, written and reviewed by one thousand scientists, concluded that "global warming was unequivocal and that human activity was the main cause." To be sure, human activities both individually and in groups *are* fueling the problem, because the choices made about what resources to consume and what products to use are a big part of the equation. What is more, the report stressed that climate changes are contributing to the other international threats to the global environment, such as the destruction of forests and global biodiversity and the creation of dust bowls. That report thus concluded that "changes in climate are now affecting physical and biological systems on every continent."

As a consequence, humanity faces enormous challenges of unprecedented scope and danger: arresting global climate change, preserving biodiversity, providing clean water, restoring forests, fisheries, and other overly exploited renewable resources. The looming threat is nowhere more dramatically illustrated than the fight between countries over carving up the Arctic in order to reap economic payoffs from exploitation of the resources that lie beneath the polar icecap. "As global warming melts the Arctic ice, dreams of a short sea passage to Asia—and riches beneath the surface—have been revived. With Russia planting a flag on the ocean floor at the North Pole, Canada talking tough and Washington wanting to be a player, who will win the world's new Great Game?" (Graff 2007). Climate change affects the Arctic intensely, because the average temperature there has risen about twice the rate of the rest of the planet (*Futurist*, September/October 2007, 33). This trend is paving the way for a geopolitical struggle over ecopolitics among the five countries already laying claim to the resource-rich central zone (Russia, Norway, Canada, the United States, Denmark). The primary motive: possession of as much as one-fourth of the world's remaining oil and gas reserves buried beneath the seabed under Arctic ice (Woodard 2007, 4). A "cold rush" is underway in the battle for the melting north (Funk 2007). None of this international friction would have materialized had global warming not made competition for control of this geostrategic arena possible. The globalization of planetary dangers raises questions about the primary causes of climate change.

Climate-Change Culprits As already observed, the human-made pollution from burning oil, coal, and gas is increasing and their production is creating the greenhouse effect that is causing global temperatures to rise. These emissions of carbon dioxide from the burning of fossil fuels have climbed steadily and risen fourfold since 1950.

Not all countries are contributing to the threat at the same rate. The high-income Global North states contribute more than half of global carbon emissions in large measure because of their big buildings, millions of cars, and relatively inefficient industries. The United States emits more of these gases into the atmosphere than any other state (23 percent) (www.worldwatch.org). However the Global East dynamos China and India have rapidly increased their emissions as their economies have grown and generated increasing demands for fossil fuel energy. Some scientists believe that China has already surpassed the United States as the world's top emitter of greenhouse gases. The International Energy Agency forecasts that the increase of greenhouse-gas emissions from 2000 to 2030 from China alone will nearly equal the increase from the entire industrialized world. India, though behind its Global East rival, could see greenhouse-gas emissions that rise 70 percent by 2025 (Walsh, 2006, 61).

Compare the existing and new industrial giants' consumption of energy and production of greenhouse gases with the low-income Global South countries. They, too, are growing rapidly (see Chapter 5) and their appetite for fossil fuel energy sources is growing along with their economic development. The Global South produces 60 percent of global energy and is responsible for half of the world's energy use (WDI 2007, 152). So all countries in all regions are contributing, at different rates, to the global trend in the growing level of carbon added to the atmosphere, 27 percent higher than at any point since the start of the Industrial Revolution (*Vital Signs 2006–2007*, 42–43). World energy-related carbon-dioxide emissions are predicted to increase 57 percent by 2030 as energy consumption rises (*Economist*, May 21, 2007, 9).

The burning of fossil fuels for energy extracts a heavy environmental price. For example, add into the equation the use of coal, a major source of atmospheric sulfur and nitrogen oxides. These pollutants return to Earth, usually after traveling long distances, in the form of **acid rain**, which adds to the acidification of lakes, the corrosion of materials and structures, and the impairment of ecosystems. These trends in greenhouse-gas emissions, as well as the changing percentage of world greenhouse-gas emissions by sector, suggests that the energy picture will change but that global warming and the environmental damage it causes are problems that are not likely to change (see Figure 12.3).

■ **acid rain**

precipitation that has been made acidic through contact with sulfur dioxide and nitrogen oxides.

The winds of change are blowing faster and faster, producing more and more hot air. This has made the energy-supply energy-consumption equation an increasingly hot issue in world politics.

The Global Politics of Energy Supplies and Consumption   Throughout the twentieth century, demand for and consumption of oil—the primary fossil fuel supplying energy—spiraled upward. An abundant supply of oil at low prices facilitated the recovery of Western Europe and Japan from World War II and encouraged consumers to use energy-intensive technologies, such as the private automobile. An enormous growth in the worldwide demand for and consumption of energy followed. Oil consumption hit a new all-time high of ninety million barrels each day in 2006. The International Energy Agency predicts that by 2030 the world will be using 50 percent more oil as demand grows to 120 million barrels a day, and it warns that the world will need to spend many trillions of dollars over the next twenty-five years to meet this runaway global oil demand.

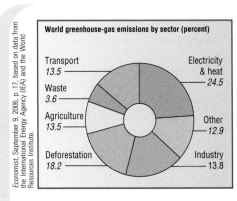

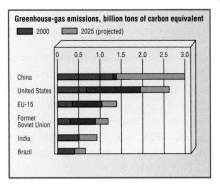

FIGURE 12.3

TOURING TRENDS OF THE GREENHOUSE Energy consumption throughout the world is big and growing fast. International trade in the carbon market was valued at $15 billion in the first half of 2006, which was five times more than in the same period in 2005 (*Economist*, September 9, 2006, 17). The figure on the left charts the sources of greenhouse-gas emissions by each major sector. The figure on the right monitors changes in the distribution of carbon-equivalent greenhouse-gas emissions for major users in the distribution in 2000 and that projected in the year 2025.

The industrialization of many emerging Global East and now Global South economies has contributed to the growing demand, and the global shift to oil has been propelled by the aggressive production and promotion of a small group of MNCs. Their operations encompass every aspect of the business, from exploration to the retail sales of products at their gas stations. Their search for, production of, and marketing of low-cost oil was largely unhindered for decades. Concessions from countries in the oil-rich Middle East and elsewhere were easy to acquire, and incentives for creating technologies for alternate energy sources, such as coal, were virtually nonexistent. Eventually, to maximize profits, the Organization of Petroleum Exporting Countries (OPEC) emerged as an important IGO cartel. Because the resources OPEC controls cannot be easily replaced, it has monopoly power. In March 1999, OPEC began to flex its economic muscles by cutting production to limit supplies. Oil prices tripled within a year, showing that OPEC could still make oil a critical global political issue—as it has again since 2004 in an effort to use oil prices as an instrument of *coercive diplomacy* to influence, by the use of threats, the course of the unfolding war on terrorism, particularly between Palestine and Israel.

Oil supplies assume great importance in world politics because oil is not being discovered at the same rate it is being used. For every two barrels pumped out of the ground, the giant oil companies discover only one new barrel. Production in the United States peaked thirty years ago, and Russia peaked in 1987. About 70 percent of the oil consumed today was found twenty-five years ago or longer. Meanwhile demand for oil keeps escalating, and the era of cheap and abundant oil is ending (Deffeyes 2005; Klare 2008).

What strikes fear in the minds of those who study oil supplies against rising demand is the widespread "illusion" of petroleum plenty. Future petroleum scarcities are certain to come, sooner or later. Even if there are no major supply disruptions caused by wars in the Middle East or bullying tactics by oil exporters, "the world may have arrived at Peak Oil: that condition when dwindling oil reserves no longer permit much, if any, annual increase in production" (Samuelson 2008, 39).

This alarming predicament suggests that a "new geopolitics of oil" has arisen over how the oil producers will use their supplies in international bargaining with those oil-importing countries that are dependent and vulnerable to supply disruptions. The world today does not face the immediate threat of running out of oil; it faces instead the problem that over half of the proven oil reserves are now concentrated in a small number of OPEC countries that are drawing down their reserves at half the average global rate. It seems almost inevitable that OPEC's share of the world oil market will grow. This means that OPEC is critical to global oil supply, the Middle East is critical to OPEC, and countries that depend on oil imports from this volatile, unstable source are highly vulnerable to disruptions. "As the center of gravity of world oil production shifts decisively to OPEC suppliers and state-centric energy producers like Russia, geopolitical rather than market factors will come to dominate the marketplace" (Klare 2008, 19). Indeed, the war between Russia and Georgia is seen by Michael Klare, an expert on peace and world security, "as an intense geopolitical contest over the flow of Caspian Sea energy to markets in the West."

The United States, the world's biggest oil consumer and importer, is especially vulnerable. It now depends on foreign oil suppliers for nearly three-fifths of its oil. In 2008, America's oil inventories hit their lowest levels in thirty years, and it imported about 58 percent of its oil from other countries. This has led to renewed debate about drilling for oil offshore and in the protected Arctic National Wildlife Refuge, which is thought to hold 25 billion barrels of undiscovered crude oil (*Newsweek*, July 7/14 2008, 44–45). Jeffrey Rubin, an economist with CIBC World Markets, predicts that gasoline will reach $7 a gallon and oil $225 a barrel by 2012. By 2025, world energy consumption is likely to double, and oil production is likely to peak. China, the world's second-largest consumer of oil, now at 10 percent of world oil consumption, is expected to see its demand for oil rise by 119 percent by 2025, accelerating the rapid drain on diminishing oil supplies.

> *We are nearing the end of the Petroleum Age and have entered the Age of Insufficiency.*
> —Michael Klare, security analyst

This trend of rising demand and decreasing supply places the oil-producing OPEC countries in a powerful bargaining position. A cutoff of OPEC exports to the United States, Japan, China, or Europe would be catastrophic, and this dependence seemingly puts OPEC in control.

Or does it? OPEC's finances and political clout depend on factors outside its control —changes in international demand (consumption) and supply. And in response to the threat of future shortages, the Global North may be on the verge of a potentially historic juncture that would overturn the pivotal place of oil in the global political economy. Never underestimate the capacity for necessity to become the mother of innovation! In 2008, Russia and Bulgaria agreed to build a new "South Stream" gas pipeline across the Black Sea, and China and Japan ended a long-time dispute by

Keeping America competitive requires affordable energy. And here we have a serious problem: America is addicted to oil, which is often imported from unstable parts of the world. The best way to break this addiction is through technology.

—George W. Bush, U.S. President

agreeing to jointly develop two natural gas fields in the East China Sea. In hopes to break dependence on fossil fuels, efforts have begun to develop alternative potential fuel sources. Seaweed fields of algae are touted as a potential wave of the future as "algal oil can be processed into biodiesel or nonpetroleum gasoline, the carbohydrates into ethanol, and the protein into animal feed or human nutritional supplements. The whole biomass can generate methane, which can be combusted to produce electricity" (Gies 2008, 3). Indonesia and the Philippines, located within the "Pacific Ring of Fire," are looking to harness volcanic power in developing geothermal power. Indonesia has at least 130 active volcanoes, and according to Lester Brown, president of the Earth Policy Institute, "Indonesia could run its economy entirely on geothermal energy and has not come close to tapping the full potential" (Davies and Lema 2008, 13). And while presently too expensive for most people, Honda Motor has begun production of the world's first hydrogen-powered fuel-cell car. Says Takeo Fukui, president of Honda, "This is a must-have technology for the future of the earth" (Fackler 2008, 16). Technological, economic, cultural, and environmental changes suggest that the early stage of a major energy transformation is under way, forced by supply scarcities and demand increases.

GAS GUZZLING IN SHANGHAI **Shown here is one example of what happens when a country's economy rapidly grows and causes demand for oil to grow nearly 200 percent since 1990 (Friedman 2007, A9) and the costs exceed 18 percent of China's gross domestic product: the landscape in Shanghai, dominated by superhighways.**

Stuart Isett/Polaris Images

TOWARD SUSTAINABILITY?

"Overall, there are considerable signs that the capacity of ecosystems to continue to produce many of the goods we depend on is declining," the World Resources Institute summarizes (www.wri.org, January 10, 2008). "This is not a sprint, it's a marathon," is how former U.S. Secretary of State Colin Powell described the race toward sustainable development. Although the goal of sustainable development remains distant and frustrations about lost opportunities high, government and nonstate actors' acceptance of the concept continues to inspire creative, environmentally sensitive responses. No one wants to live in an unhealthy polluted environment; quality of life matters, and matters a lot, for rich and poor alike. Think about your dreams—where you would like to visit, perhaps even live. Not in a place where environmental disaster is likely, the number of which is sadly increasing. At least twenty-five million people became "environmental refugees" ten years ago, "fleeing from hopelessly unlivable environments, and the number is expected to double by 2010, to nearly 8,500 each day" (*Vital Signs Facts*, from www.worldwatch.org). Want to be a tourist in those locations? What about the United States, if you are not already a U.S. citizen? It is also "suffering from many environmental problems. Most Americans have become aware of more crowding and stress . . . living in large American cities and encountering increased commuting delays because the number of people and hence cars is increasing faster than the number of freeway lanes." The environment is collapsing with the possibility that a civilization as most have known it is ending.

Environmental decay seems to recognize few borders; it is a worldwide problem, for both poor and rich countries. That transformation makes protection of the planetary environment a necessity, but the solutions are hard to find when many people put their personal advantage ahead of those of all humanity. Recommended changes to protect and preserve the planet Earth's ecology may be expensive. But it is prudent to

> *Earth provides enough to satisfy every man's need, but not every man's greed.*
> —Mohandas Gandhi, Indian peace activist

try. What approaches are underway? A number stand out. In the first category are solutions at the *global level of analysis*. Taking their point of departure from the adage "Think globally, act locally," there are underway movements to save planet Earth at the state and individual levels of analysis.

Global Solutions

A new and less-destructive source of energy could emerge because of the advent of revolutionary new technologies that derive energy from the sun, wind, and other abundant and renewable sources of energy such as hydrogen.

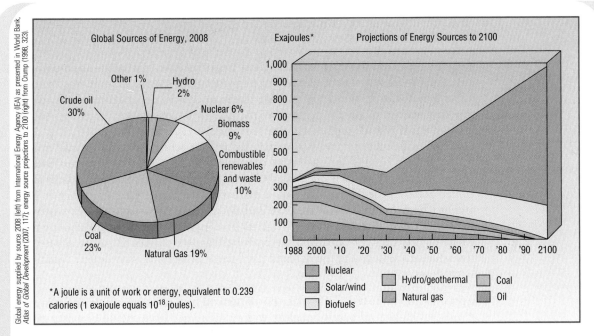

Global energy supplied by source, 2008 (left) from International Energy Agency (IEA) as presented in World Bank; energy source projections to 2100 (right) from Crump (2007; 117); energy source projections to 2100 (right) from Crump. *Atlas of Global Development* (2007; 117); energy source projections to 2100 (right) from Crump (1998; 323).

FIGURE 12.4

PHASING OUT FOSSIL FUELS? THE POTENTIAL FOR RENEWABLE ENERGY TO SUPPLY THE WORLD'S ENERGY NEEDS BY THE YEAR 2100. **The global economy's need for energy continues to rise, requiring more energy than is ultimately available from nonrenewable resources. Rising demand (60 percent from 2005 to 2015) is likely to change the current distribution of resources on which the world relies to meet its energy needs (left), because 70 percent of the world's energy supply presently comes from fossil fuels, and that share cannot continue. As a fossil-free energy supply becomes increasingly probable (see forecast, right), it might become possible to tap renewable sources to meet the world's entire energy needs by the end of the twenty-first century.**

Converting to Renewable Sources of Energy The impact of such a global transformation would be huge, overturning the past 125-year pattern in world energy development and consumption. Could the era of "big oil" really be ending? That could be the case. Together, widely fluctuating but rising oil prices and public alarm about global warming are pushing the world, however haltingly, toward cleaner and cheaper energy systems. The supply of fossil fuels will not run out anytime soon, but the *externalities* or consequences of environmental and health threats make the burning of fossil fuels excessively dangerous. The combustion of oil and coal are traced to lung cancer and many other health hazards. And what is more, it leads to air pollution, urban smog, and acid rain that damage forests, water quality, and soil. There are powerful incentives to harness technology to shift to renewable sources of energy. Solar, tidal, and wind power, as well as geothermal energy and bioconversion, are among the alternatives to oil most likely to become technologically and economically viable, as Figure 12.4 shows.

Advocates of reliance on environmentally friendly, renewable energy supplies picture a radically different twenty-first century. They urge immediate planning for a new global "eco-economy, one that satisfies today's need without jeopardizing the prospects of future generations to meet theirs by altering how we light our homes, what we eat, where we live, how we use our leisure time, and how many children we have. It will give us a world where we are part of nature, instead of estranged from it" (Brown 2002).

Among known technologies, nuclear energy has often been championed as the leading alternative to fossil fuel dependence. For that reason, the United States is now spending billions of dollars to build new nuclear plants to ease its dependence on the foreign suppliers who provide 29 percent of the energy it consumes. Currently, existing nuclear plants provide only 20 percent of America's electricity (WDI 2007, 152, 160). However, safety and financial costs may reduce this scheduled surge toward nuclear power; these problems have led some countries to reduce (or, like Germany, Sweden and Spain, phase out) their nuclear programs. Well-publicized nuclear accidents in the United States at the Three Mile Island nuclear power plant in Pennsylvania in 1979 and at Chernobyl in Ukraine in 1986 and no less than five major accidents between 1995 and 1999 at Japan's fifty-two nuclear power plants (which supply about a third of Japan's electricity) dramatized the potential dangers of nuclear power. Since then, fears have decreased, and the demand for nuclear power has risen despite continuing safety fears.

Concerns about the risks of nuclear power extend beyond safety. How and where to dispose of highly radioactive nuclear waste that comes from the 443 nuclear plants around the world (and the thirty-five additional reactors under construction in thirteen countries in 2008) is an unresolved issue virtually everywhere. For example, at least fifty nuclear weapons are on the ocean's floor out of reach as a result of U.S. and Soviet accidents (*Harper's*, March 2004, 11). There are no safe procedures for handling the fifty-two thousand tons of toxic radioactive nuclear waste (*USA Today*, July 18, 2005, 13A), some of which will remain dangerous for hundreds of thousands of years. "Not in my back yard" (NIMBY) is a divisive cry on the global ecopolitical agenda; the Global North prefers to dump waste outside its own territory, and the Global South would prefer not to be the dump—but often is.

A related fear is that countries that currently do not possess nuclear know-how might develop nuclear weapons. Most nuclear-energy-generating facilities continue to produce weapons-grade material, specifically highly enriched uranium and pluto-nium, which is a national security concern because "with the underlying technical infrastructure able to support both weapons and electrons, there is no clear way to ensure nuclear energy can be developed without also building capabilities for weapons" (*Vital Signs 2006–2007*, 34). This dilemma was highlighted in a debate over North Korea's nuclear development program, which North Korea announced in June 2008 that it would end.

In a political world in which growing population means growing demand for energy, food, and other resources only the environment and technology can provide, the politics of scarcity becomes central. Declining global supplies and soaring demand for crude oil in China, India, and other *newly industrialized countries (NICs)* have forced the United States, Europe, and Japan to compete with them to obtain energy supplies and develop alternative biofuels. What countries do to try to meet their needs has consequences for everyone everyplace. The United States, which daily consumes ten million barrels of imported oil, was politically powerless in bargaining to deter China, India, and Russia from strengthening their relations with Iran, an oil-rich country that has the globe's second largest supply of proven oil reserves (after Saudi Arabia). These new relationships undercut U.S. efforts to halt Iran's nuclear ambitions. This is the vulnerability created by interdependent globalization. Moreover, how countries meet their growing demand for energy directly influences the evolution and preservation of the global commons. Let us look at the concerns raised by the link between energy use and environmental damage.

Conversion to renewable sources of energy represents a possible avenue away from global environmental degradation. Many believe this will not happen soon enough. They propose another path to reduce the dangers: forging international treaties among countries that provide for the protection of the environment and establish compliance mechanisms.

International Treaties for Environmental Protection The 1992 Earth Summit in Stockholm was precedent-setting. From it, a separate treaty set forth a comprehensive agreement for the preservation of biodiversity throughout the world. It committed state governments to devise national strategies for conserving

Yanin Arthus Bertrand/CORBIS

THE UNFORGIVING COST OF NUCLEAR POWER FAILURE **Shown here is the town of Pripyat, Ukraine, which was abandoned after the Chernobyl nuclear accident. Rather than learning from this lesson, and despite strong opposition from the public, Russia opened its borders to become the largest international repository for radioactive nuclear wastes, in the hope of earning billions of dollars over the next two decades.**

habitats, protecting endangered species, expanding protected areas, and repairing damaged ones. Since then, the world has attempted to cooperate through increasingly concerted efforts to reach agreements and to back them with ratified treaties to protect the sustained global commons.

Success breeds success. The *Biodiversity Treaty* was followed by other international efforts to deal with environmental problems by agreements globally. A big example was the Kyoto protocol of 2005 in which 156 countries accounting for at least 55 percent of global greenhouse emissions pledged to cut emissions of gases linked to global warming below 1990 levels by the year 2012. Only the United States refused to cooperate. But even that resistance is likely to change. In 2007, the U.S. Supreme Court rendered a decision condemning President George W. Bush's indifference to the dangers of carbon emissions and global warming. Forced to reverse his position, Bush reluctantly agreed to take the danger of global warming seriously, and the world's heavy-weight polluter, the United States, pledged to make changes to contain the dangers before it is too late. In December 2007, 190 countries met in Bali Indonesia and agreed to negotiate by 2009 a new pollution treaty to fight global warming. This tentative step inspired hope that still other global protection treaties might be created.

Given the growing threats to environmental protection that are now recognized, this collective response is understandable. The question facing the world is whether the response to date is adequate. International environmental treaties have grown exponentially in the last 130 years. However, many skeptics fear that these efforts are too little, too late, and that not enough is being done to save the global commons for future generations. To be seen in the long term is whether the global ecological environment is in peril. Many question the ability of today's existing treaties to manage the environmental dangers they are meant to address. Some are weak and introduce expressions of concern without commanding necessary policy changes to remedy the various problems they identify. Of particular concern is the reluctant backing of the globe's superpower, the United States. Of the UN's thirty-one major global environmental agreements, the United States has only ratified ten. Environmental protection activists worry that if the American hegemon refuses to lead, the prospects for strengthening the rules of the environmental preservation regime are dim.

Trade, the Environment, and Sustainable Development   Multinational corporations are a key player in the ecopolitics game being played that will determine the Earth's fate. Corporations rule globally, and they are strong advocates with powerful lobbyists of free trade. Is their power and quest supportive, or detrimental, to sustainable development? The question is especially pertinent in a rapidly globalizing world in which trade increasingly links politics, economics, ecology, and societies and cultures in webs of ever-tightening interdependencies.

Beyond the issue of the gains from and the costs of trade, environmentalists and liberal economists differ in their assessments of the wisdom of using trade to promote environmental standards. Liberal economists see such efforts as market distortions, whereas environmentalists view them as useful instruments for correcting market failures, such as markets' inability to compensate for the externalities of environmental exploitation (for example, atmospheric pollution by chemical companies). Some countries, however, particularly in the Global South, view the use of trade mechanisms to protect the environment as yet another way the rich states block entry into lucrative Global North markets to keep the Global South permanently disadvantaged.

Trade-offs must sometimes be made between goals that, in principle, all seem designed to increase human well-being and security. However, another interpretation maintains that trade encourages states to live beyond their means. According to some ecologists, trade magnifies the damaging ecological effects of production and

> *The economic case for pursuing the process of trade liberalization is an overwhelming one. But it is impossible to ignore the fact that . . . there are widespread fears of the social and environmental consequences of the combination of liberalization and globalization.*
>
> —Leon Brittan, EU Commissioner for External Trade

consumption by expanding the market for commodities beyond state borders. Countries that have depleted their resource bases or passed strict laws to protect them can easily look overseas for desired products, in ways that shift the environmental stress of high consumption to other states' backyards.

Ruth Fremson/The New York Times/Redux Pictures

Playing in the "Poison Pond" Children play in the shadow of the former Union Carbide factory in Bhopal, India, the site of one of the worst industrial accidents in history. The "pond" in which they are playing was originally a sludge pit containing chemical byproducts from the former pesticide plant, and the actual color of the "water" was closer to black. Though the chemical leakage at Bhopal, which resulted in over 3,000 deaths, occurred in 1984, the area—which still contains over 400 tons of toxic waste—has yet to be cleaned up. The picture is a stark reminder of how environmental crises can long outlive the political will necessary to resolve them.

The tragedy of the commons suggests a bleak future. Is ruin the destination toward which humanity must rush? A more optimistic scenario is possible. A trend is underway in the culture of corporate global finance that bodes well for the potential for global corporations to begin to recognize that their profits will improve if they invest in and develop products for which there is rising consumer demand worldwide because they are environmentally green and popular among consumers.

Cutting down on greenhouse-gas emissions is neither anti-business nor anti-growth. The benefits from curtailing emissions can be realized in lower health care costs, which often make up a substantial portion of a company's operating costs and retiree population benefits. In India and China, lower emissions implies lower pollution and hence lower costs associated with environmental cleanup. Therefore in both these situations having control over emissions would actually help, not hurt, the economy.

—Venkat Lakshmi, geophysicist

Consider Wal-Mart. In 2007 this mega-corporation shifted its marketing strategy by seeking to attract still new customers, promising to cut its energy consumption and to sell products that are environmentally friendly. This was a response to global demand. Another telling sign was the April 2007 transformation that allowed Toyota Motors to surpass General Motors as the leader in the sale of automobiles. Why? Many suspect that Toyota's willingness to produce energy-efficient cars that averaged thirty-five miles to the gallon catapulted it ahead of Detroit's General Motors' line of cars whose gas mileage averaged less than twenty-eight miles to the gallon. Environmentally concerned and financially astute consumers may have recognized a good deal when they saw it; their motives seemed to have mattered. What these and other changes suggest is that newly "green" corporations are beginning to realize financial payoffs. Producing products which planetary citizens value may make profits. In the context of "green" industries seeking to sell environmentally protective products, a new "code of corporate responsibility" is gaining acceptance that could spawn a new era of changes in the development of new products for sale that are designed to protect the environment, rather than seeking to realize short-term financial gains by selling products that contaminate the planetary condition.

The possibility that the international political economy will provide economic incentives for producing products that can contribute to global environment sustainability has inspired hope that the dangers to environmental preservation may be contained. That hope is rising because some governments and individuals are seeking local solutions to environmental sustainability.

National and Local Solutions

A huge concern is that some very powerful states, advantageously positioned in the global hierarchy, are selfishly resisting making painful and costly adjustments now. They are resisting reforms of their own existing environmental protection policies that can allow them in the long run to engineer their own sustainable development and that of the world at large. There are exceptions to the response to the environmental degradation of some of these great powers, especially the United States. A number of countries have managed to take the risk of short-term economic loss in the expectation of long-term economic growth by investing in renewable and costly programs that can enable them to experience sustainable growth with development. Countries differ. Look at Figure 12.5. It charts the rankings of countries according to an "environmental performance index." The score measures their investments in efforts to protect their future environments. Clearly, some countries see environmental sustainability as a priority that protects their interest more so than others, which fail to do so. When the consensus spreads that these national interests can insure future prosperity, there are many reasons to predict that more and more countries will get on the bandwagon and increase their regulations to protect their environment at home and abroad.

Many people worldwide are dissatisfied with the tardy reaction of state governments to the appalling dangers to protection of the global ecology. Another solution is rapidly materializing. In the United States, many of the fifty states have joined the lead pushed by Governor Arnold Schwarzenegger of California. He proclaimed in his inaugural address, "We all breathe the same air. Let's get our act together, fix this problem, and fight global warming." In September 2006, the respected "Governator" signed the *Global Warming Solutions Act* requiring California to reduce its greenhouse-gas emissions 25 percent by 2020, and in 2008 he stood firm in his support for the moratorium against new off-shore drilling. "Everybody recognized that it was so important that we should not argue over philosophy. I am a business-

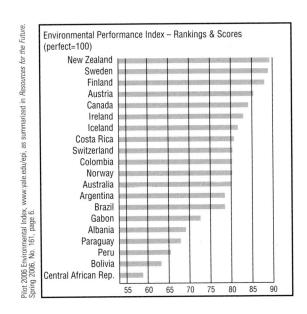

FIGURE 12.5

MEASURING NATIONAL COMMITMENTS TO ENVIRONMENTAL SUSTAINABILITY
Measures of environmental protection performance suggest that some countries are doing much more than many others to assure that their environments are protected. This index gauges the relative performance of selected countries that illustrate these differences.

friendly guy. I'm all about economic growth. I am not here to harm businesses. I am here to make businesses boom, but let's also protect our environment. Let's make our air clear. Let's make our water clean. And let's fight global warming because we know now that this is a major danger, that this is not a debate anymore," Governor Schwarzenegger explained. Since then, three-fifths of American states have taken initiatives to also make rules in their home states to protect their local environments. What is more, since 2007 more than one hundred fifty American cities followed these initiatives by enacting environment-protection legislation to combat the threats in their urban locales.

It is hard to determine whether this reaction was a result of pressure from huge numbers of private citizens who believe that it is crucial to set limits on climate-changing greenhouse emissions because they feel that this was the right thing to do. Whatever the incentives, the pressure from citizens and even corporations for better laws to protect the global environment is growing. They are voicing their preferences in numbers too large to ignore. Within the United States, in March 2007, thirteen corporations joined with fifty-two institutional investors ($4 trillion under management) to lobby the U.S. government for limits on carbon emissions that come from burning fossil fuels. They were joined at the same time by fifteen other state governors who ordered limits of their own, encouraged by the decision of the U.S. Supreme Court that affirmed the right of Environmental Protection Agency to regulate auto emissions and emissions from power plants (*Newsweek*, April 23, 2007, 63).

What should you do as a global citizen? Should you join the thousands on thousands of people worldwide who are demanding changes in existing practices and policies to curtail the threats to planet Earth that they perceive certain to destroy their future if

> *Our entire planet, its land and water areas, the Earth's surface and its subsoil provide today the arena for a worldwide economy, the dependence of whose various parts upon each other has become indissoluble.*
>
> —Leon Trotsky, Russian radical communist theoretician

protective measures are not taken soon? If so, ecologists will tell you quickly that you can make a difference, all by yourself, or more powerfully, by joining a NGO that shares your concerns and is pressuring governments to take the perceived needed urgent steps for changes. The opportunities for participation in this debate are many. Environmentalists recommend many alternative steps that you might take. In *An Inconvenient Truth*, former U.S. presidential candidate Al Gore (www.climatecrisis.net) recommended five simple things you can do to help stop global warming:

- Change a light. Replacing one regular light bulb with a compact fluorescent light bulb will save 150 pounds of carbon dioxide a year.

- Recycle more. You can save 2,400 pounds of carbon dioxide per year by recycling just half of your household waste.

- Use less hot water. It takes a lot of energy to heat water. Use less hot water by installing a low-flow showerhead and washing your clothes in cold or warm water.

- Drive less. Walk, bike, carpool, or take mass transit more often. You'll save one pound of carbon dioxide for every mile you don't drive.

- Conserve electricity. Simply turning off your TV, DVD player, stereo, and computer when you're not using them will save you thousands of pounds of carbon dioxide a year.

There are, of course, many other actions that individuals can undertake that might affect the planetary future. There is such a long list of things that could be done and that should be done that the options are about as unlimited as are the multiple threats to the planetary ecological predicament. Efforts to develop alternative fuels, reduce greenhouse-gases, and resurrect the auto industry by producing environmentally friendly, energy-efficient vehicles are high on everybody's list. The entire world stands at a critical juncture. The path humanity takes will affect human security far into the future. Evidence of serious ecological problems is getting harder and harder to ignore. Because the stakes are so high, all the pieces in the puzzle—population growth, natural resources, technology, and changing preferences in lifestyles—must be worked on simultaneously.

If necessity really is the mother of invention, there is hope. The planet *must* be saved, or all other opportunities will be closed, the global environment will face certain doom, and human history will end. Therefore, the stakes are so high that perhaps solutions will be found. As the world struggles, the debate about solutions is likely to continue on two tracks: between those who think humankinds' concentration should be geared to trying to reverse environmental deterioration, and those who prefer to concentrate on creating new technologies to contain environmental damage.

Both strategies appear to be urgently needed. If environmental sustainability is not preserved, it is certain that future armed conflicts are likely to arise and be fought over access to and supplies of diminishing natural resources.

Throughout history, humanity has faced another kind of global threat: devastation through armed aggression. Rapid population growth alongside the economic expansion driving excessive energy demands and shrinking supplies of natural resources is leading to "resource wars." That prediction invites you to consider another arena of world politics on the global agenda that poses a different kind of, but equally alarming, threat—the global character of armed aggression and its consequences.

Key Terms

the global commons
carrying capacity
ecopolitics
politics of scarcity
environmental security
genetic engineering
transgenetic crops

neo-Malthusians
cornucopians
sustainable development
greenhouse effect
ozone layer
United Nations Environment
    Programme (UNEP)

biodiversity
deforestation
desertification
enclosure movement
tragedy of the commons
acid rain

CHAPTER 13
THE THREAT OF ARMED AGGRESSION TO THE WORLD

Mankind must put an end to war or war will put an end to mankind.

—John F. Kennedy, U.S. President

Khalid Mohammed/AP Photo

The Fog of War. In 2003, the United States invaded Iraq in a lightening conquest and expected jubilant Iraqis to thank the superpower for their liberation. Instead, occupation was followed by a guerrilla and then a civil war, and within five years efforts intensified to find an exit strategy to limit the disaster and destruction. Shown here: the burning aftermath of an attack in central Baghdad.

■ **war**

a condition arising within states (civil war) or between states (interstate war) when actors use violent means to destroy their opponents or coerce them into submission.

■ **conflict**

discord, often arising in international relations over perceived incompatibilities of interest.

In the calm summer of 2001, complacency had taken hold in the zone of peace and prosperity in the Global North, where many thoughtful observers, noting the disappearance of interstate war among the economic giants, began to ask if war was becoming obsolete. That mood and conclusion was shattered shortly thereafter on September 11, 2001, when international terrorists destroyed New York's World Trade Center. The 9/11 attack and the U.S. war in Afghanistan, the terrorist attacks in Madrid in 2004 and London in 2005, the continuing U.S.-led military struggle against insurgents in Iraq, the 2006 Israeli-Hezbollah War in Lebanon, and a wave of civil wars dashed all prior hopes for peace. Violence seemingly could hurt anyone, anywhere, anytime. Violence remains frequent. As 2008 began, there were thirty-two armed conflicts underway throughout the world in twenty-three locations (Harbom and Wallensteen 2007, 632). It is understandable why so many people think that armed aggression is the essence of world politics.

In *On War*, Prussian strategist Karl von Clausewitz advanced his famous dictum that war is merely an extension of diplomacy by other means—"a form of communication between countries," albeit an extreme form. This insight underscores the realist belief that **war** is a policy instrument transnational actors use to resolve their conflicts. War, however, is the deadliest instrument of conflict resolution, and its onset usually means that persuasion and negotiations have failed.

In international relations, **conflict** regularly occurs when actors interact and disputes over incompatible interests arise. In and of itself, conflict (like *politics*—activities aimed at getting another actor to do something it would not otherwise do) is not

TERRORISM'S PAINFUL LEGACY **To** some observers, the terrorists of 9/11 transformed world politics, and ensured that the world would never be the same. Shown here is one example of rising religion-inspired terrorism: Palestinians praying during a funeral for jihadist militants who died while waging a holy war fighting for their cause.

Musa Al-Shaer/AFP/Getty Images

necessarily threatening, because war and conflict are different. Conflict may be seen as inevitable and occurs whenever two parties perceive differences between themselves and seek to resolve those differences to their own satisfaction. Some conflict results whenever people interact and may be generated by religious, ideological, ethnic, economic, political, or territorial issues; therefore, we should not regard it as abnormal. Nor should we regard conflict as necessarily destructive. Conflict can promote social solidarity, creative thinking, learning, and communication—all factors critical to the resolution of disputes and the cultivation of cooperation (Coser 1956). However, the costs of conflict do become threatening when the parties take up arms to settle their perceived irreconcilable differences or use force to settle old scores. When that happens, violence occurs, and we enter the separate sphere of warfare.

This chapter presents information and ideas so you can explore the nature of **armed aggression** in your world—its types, frequency, and changing characteristics and causes. And you will be forced to confront the ethical dilemmas that these military threats create—about when it is moral or immoral to take up arms. *World Politics*

■ armed aggression

combat between the military forces of two or more states or groups.

> *Wars occur because people prepare for conflict, rather than for peace.*
> —Trygve Lie, UN Secretary General

puts into the spotlight three primary ways that armed aggression today most often occurs: wars between states, civil wars within states, and terrorism. And you will have the opportunity to review the leading theories that explain the causes of these three types of armed aggression in world politics.

CHANGES IN INTERSTATE WAR AND ARMED AGGRESSION

In a world seemingly experiencing constant change, one grim continuity stands out: war and violence, or, in the words of former UN Secretary-General Boutros Boutros-Ghali, a "culture of death." The description remains apt. Since 1900, at least 750 armed conflicts have been waged, killing millions, creating hordes of refugees, and costing trillions of dollars of lost revenues as well as untold human misery. The belief that "only the dead will see the end of war" is based on the fact that warfare has been an ugly, almost constant factor in a changing world. In the past thirty-four hundred years, Chris Hedges (2003) calculates, "humans have been entirely at peace for 268 of them, or just 8 percent of recorded history."

Scientists who study war quantitatively through the scientific methodologies of *behavioralism* have attempted to estimate the frequency of armed conflicts and to measure trends and cycles in the global system's level of violent conflicts. Different definitions and indicators produce somewhat different pictures of variations over time (as *constructivism* emphasizes they will; see Gleditsch 2004). Nonetheless, various measures converge on the basic trends and patterns, from different periods of measurement. In the long term (over the past six hundred years), armed aggression has been continual, with a general trend toward rising incidence. In the relative short

USAF/Landow Media

THE WAGES OF WAR **On March 20, 2003, U.S. President Bush ordered thousands of American soldiers to wage a war against Iraq. Since then thousands of American soldiers and tens of thousands of Iraqi civilians had paid the ultimate sacrifice. As violence continued, the *Iraq Study Group Report* grimly concluded that "The situation in Iraq is grave and deteriorating." Shown here in April 2004 is an American official unloading coffins of soldiers killed in Iraq.**

term (since 1950), however, the pattern has shown fewer, but more deadly, armed conflicts. Figure 13.1 records the continuities and changes for comparative purposes from these two observation periods. These inventories report in different ways what the mass media tell us—that violence and global insecurity are entrenched properties of world politics.

The wars in Afghanistan, Iraq, and Georgia, and the December 2007 terrorist killing of opposition leader Benazir Bhutto in Pakistan cast a dark shadow. In the past, when people thought about armed conflicts, they thought primarily about wars *between* states and secondarily about civil wars *within* existing sovereign states. Both types of wars were frequently underway at similar rates each year between 1816 and World War II. However, that began to change thereafter, with internal wars increasingly defining the global landscape. This new pattern of civil wars and armed conflicts that does not involve government forces on at least one side has become especially entrenched since 1990. Indeed, between 1989 and 2008, only seven of all 124 active armed conflicts worldwide, or six percent, were interstate wars between countries (Harbom, Melander, and Wallensteen 2008).

Until 9/11, most security analysts expected civil wars to remain the most common type of global violence. However, they have had to revise their strategies and thinking to accommodate changing realities. Today, military planners face two unprecedented security challenges. As described by Henry Kissinger, these challenges are "terror caused by acts until recently considered a matter for internal police forces rather than international policy, and scientific advances and proliferation that allow

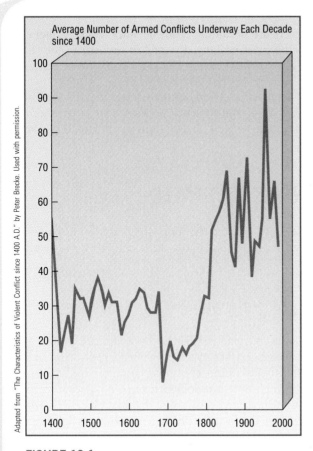

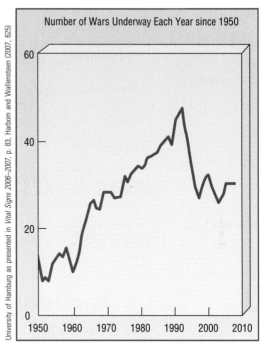

FIGURE 13.1

TWO PICTURES OF THE CHANGING FREQUENCY OF ACTS OF ARMED AGGRESSION **The chart on the left illustrates the trends in the 2,566 total wars fought in the decades between 1400 and 2000. Measuring the frequency of *active* armed conflicts each year since 1950 by different criteria for what constitutes armed conflict, the trend on the right records a gradual increase in the frequency of conflicts until the peak in 1992, after which a decline has taken root.**

the survival of countries to be threatened by developments entirely within another state's territory." This suggests that many future acts of armed aggression are probable, fought by irregular militia and private or semiprivate forces (such as terrorist networks) against the armies of states, or by "shadow warriors" commissioned by states as "outsourced" mercenaries or paid militia.

The characteristics of contemporary warfare appear to be undergoing a major *transformation*, even though many of the traditional characteristics of armed conflict between states and within them, and global terrorism, continue. The general trends show the following:

- The proportion of countries throughout the globe engaged in wars has declined.

- Most wars now occur in the Global South, which is home to the highest number of states, with the largest populations, the least income, and the least stable governments.

■ The goal of waging war to conquer foreign territory has ceased to be a motive.

■ Wars between the great powers are becoming obsolete; since 1945 the globe has experienced a **long peace**—the most prolonged period in modern history (since 1500) in which no wars have occurred between the most powerful countries.

■ **long peace**

long-lasting periods of peace between any of the militarily strongest great powers.

Although the disappearance of armed aggression *between* states may be possible in the long-term future, armed aggression and violence persist and is growing *inside* established states. Next we examine this second face of military threats to the world: armed aggression *within* states.

ARMED AGGRESSION WITHIN STATES

■ **civil wars**

wars between opposing groups within the same country or by rebels against the government.

Civil wars—wars within states—have erupted far more frequently than have wars between states. It is these armed struggles that most often capture news headlines worldwide.

The Characteristics of Civil War

There is a basis in fact for the assertion made earlier in this chapter. Between 1989 and the start of 2009, internal armed conflict over government (civil wars) or over territory (state-formation conflicts) have been the most common by far. In this period, about ninety new civil wars erupted in comparison to only seven between states. As 2008 began, thirty-four armed conflicts were raging in 25 locations around the world, with some of the intrastate conflicts involving a government fighting with more than one rebel group at a time (Harbom, Melander, and Wallensteen 2008).

Civil wars resulting in at least one thousand civilian and military deaths per year occurred 236 times between 1816 and 2008 (Small and Singer 1982; J. Singer 1991, 66–75; see also SIPRI 2007, 78). Their outbreak has been somewhat irregular. Although at least one civil war began in eighty-seven of these years, civil war has become increasingly frequent over time (see Table 13.1). Of the civil wars since 1816, 70 percent began after 1946, with a steadily climbing frequency each decade, until 2005, after which the level has been fairly constant. However, this accelerating trend is, in part, a product of the increased number of independent states in the global system, which makes the incidence of civil war statistically more probable.

Civil wars share defining characteristics (Collier 2005; Sambanis 2004) and center around several salient issues:

■ Ethnic groups seeking greater autonomy or striving to create an independent state for themselves (such as the Kurds in Turkey and Chechens in Russia)

■ Internal battles fought to gain control of an existing state

■ Religious conflicts involving especially intrareligious armed disputes between two or more sects of the same religion (Bakke 2005)

▨ Failed states, where the authority of a national government has collapsed and armed struggle has broken out between the competing ethnic militias, warlords, or criminal organizations seeking to obtain power and establish control of the state

▨ Impoverished states, where there exists "a situation of individual hardship or severe dissatisfaction with one's current situation [and] the absence of any nonviolent means for change" (Walter 2004). As the World Bank (2003, 46) describes the syndrome, "Low-income countries, where about a billion people live, face greatest risk of civil war—about 15 times that of high-income countries."

Additionally, there is a tendency for countries that have experienced one civil war to undergo two or more subsequent civil wars (Quinn, Mason and Gurses 2007), and this pattern is even more pronounced for conflicts characterized by an **enduring internal rivalry (EIR)**. Empirical evidence shows that "76% of all civil war years from 1946 to 2004 took place in the context of EIRs," and that such civil wars were more likely to recur and to be followed by shorter peace spells (DeRouen and Bercovitch 2008, 55). Moreover, the average duration of civil wars once they erupt has increased; one study estimates that 130 civil wars fought worldwide since World War II lasted an average of eleven years (*Harpers,* February, 2007, 98). This means that the number of civil wars *underway* has exceeded the rate of civil war initiation.

■ **enduring internal rivalry (EIR)**

protracted violent conflicts between governments and insurgent groups within a state.

War upon rebellion is messy and slow, like eating soup with a knife.

—T.E. Lawrence, British commander in Arabia

Civil wars dominate the global terrain because they start and re-ignite at a higher rate than they end, and they last longer (Alley 2004; Hironaka 2005). Consider examples of long-lasting and resumed civil wars in Afghanistan, Burundi, Chad, Colombia, Congo, Indonesia, Iran, Iraq, Ivory Coast, Lebanon, Liberia, Myanmar, Peru, the Philippines, Rwanda, Somalia, Sri Lanka, Sudan, Turkey, and Uganda.

Another noteworthy characteristic of civil wars is their severity. The number of lives lost in civil violence has always been very high, and casualties from civil wars since World War II have increased at alarming rates. Children are major participants and victims caught in the crossfire. The most lethal civil wars in history have erupted recently. The cliché that "the most savage conflicts occur in the home" captures the ugly reality, as genocide and mass slaughter aimed at depopulating entire regions have become commonplace in recent civil wars.

That grim reality was illustrated in Rwanda, where the Hutu government orchestrated a genocidal slaughter resulting in the murder of about eight hundred thousand predominantly Tutsi and moderate Hutu people in a matter of weeks. Sudan provides another horrifying example of the mass slaughter of civilians that often occurs when governments seek to keep power by destroying minority opposition groups. The Arab-controlled Sudanese government (and government-backed Janjaweed militia) that seized power in 1989 suspended democracy and undertook a divide-and-destroy campaign of **state-sponsored terrorism** against the black Christian and animist peoples living in the southern Darfur region. By 2008, at least 2.5 million were slaughtered and another 4 million became displaced refugees.

■ **state-sponsored terrorism**

formal assistance, training, and arming of foreign terrorists by a state in order to achieve foreign policy goals.

Table 13.1   213 Civil Wars across Six Periods, 1816–2008

Period	Key System Characteristics	System Size (average number of states)	Number of Civil Wars Begun	Number of Civil Wars Internationalized Through Large-Scale Military Intervention
1816–1848	Monarchies in Concert of Europe suppress democratic revolutions	28	12	3
1849–1881	Rising nationalism and civil wars	39	20	1
1882–1914	Imperialism and colonialization	40	18	3
1915–1945	World wars and economic collapse	59	14	4
1946–1988	Decolonialization and independence for emerging Global South countries during Cold War	117	60	14
1989–2008	Age of failed states and civil wars	198	89	27
1816–2008			213	49

Data for 1816–1988 courtesy of the Correlates of War project under the direction of J. David Singer and Melvin Small; data from 1989 to 2008 based on SIPRI (2007, 79) and Harbom and Wallensteen (2007, 624).

The bloodbath and mass exodus made this tragic place of death the worst since World War II, but the great powers—preoccupied with the Iraq and Afghanistan wars were very late in authorizing UN or African peacekeepers in late 2007 to intervene to stop the killing.

Note also that another salient characteristic of civil wars is their resistance to negotiated settlement. Making peace is difficult among rival factions that are struggling for power, driven by hatred and poisoned by the inertia of prolonged killing that has become a way of life. Few domestic enemies fighting in a civil war have succeeded in ending the combat through negotiated compromise at the bargaining table. Most civil wars end on the battlefield (Walter 1997) but rarely with a decisive victory of one faction over another. This is why fighting often resumes after a temporary cease-fire. Evidence shows that "the longer peace can be sustained, the less likely civil war is to recur," and that the prospects for lasting peace improve when peace agreements are supported by external peacekeeping forces and post-war economic development (Quinn, Mason and Gurses 2007, 167).

A. Yagobzadeh/SIPA Press

ETHNIC WARFARE AND CHILDREN Children have often been the major victims of civil strife. Here we see children caught in the ethnic and religious civil war in Beirut, Lebanon. The fledgling Lebanese government's experiment with democracy will be severely challenged after the deadly 2006 Israeli-Hezbollah war unless the 15,000 UN peacekeepers can preserve the cease-fire.

As trends in world politics have unfolded, especially since the end of the Cold War, a new destabilizing menace has begun to stalk the world. This is the rapidly increasing number of countries that have collapsed from within and left the people residing in them facing anarchy and bloodshed. For that reason, civil war has taken on a new coloration and is often seen as synonymous with what are termed failed states.

Failed States Large-scale civil strife is bred by the failure of state governments to effectively govern within their territorial borders. Mismanagement by governments lacking authority and unable to meet the basic human needs of their citizens is a global trend. Governmental incompetence has led to an epidemic of failed states throughout the globe. Today as many as sixty state governments are under stress and vulnerable to civil war (see Map 13.1). Sometimes the armed aggression is confined to local regions that seek secession and independence, and other times failing states are victims of widespread but episodic fighting by insurgents and warlords. Within five years after a fragile state succeeds in restoring domestic order, more than half collapse, and civil unrest resumes (*Foreign Policy*, July/August 2005, 58). The proliferation of failing states is a growing global danger, because the civil wars percolated by state failure lead to waves of immigrants, famine, disease, drug trafficking, environmental degradation, and terrorism.

The causes of state failure and civil disintegration are multiple, but failed states share some key characteristics that make them vulnerable to disintegration and civil war. In general, studies of this global trend (Collier 2007; Zimmerman 1996; *Foreign Policy*, July/August 2008, 64–73) suggest the following:

- A strong predictor of state failure is poverty, but extreme income and gender inequality within countries are even better warning signs.

- The failing states most vulnerable to internal rebellion are ruled by corrupt governments widely regarded as illegitimate and ineffective.

- Democracy, particularly with a strong parliament, generally lowers the risk of state failure; autocracy increases it.

- Poor democracies, however, are more unstable than either rich democracies or poor nondemocracies, and poor democracies that do not improve living standards are exceptionally vulnerable.

- Population pressures, exacerbated by internally displaced people, refugees, and food scarcity, contribute to state failure and civil unrest.

- Governments that fail to protect *human rights* are especially prone to fail.

- State failure and civil war are particularly evident in the high-risk, weak, and impoverished states in Africa.

- So-called petrostates relying on oil and gas for income are shaky, especially if the governing authority is weak and permissive of huge gaps in the distribution of political power and wealth.

- States with governments that do not protect freedom of religion are especially likely to fail.

- States that have strong rules protecting free international trade gain stability; states with high inflation are prone to fail.

- The stronger a country's capacity to prevent environmental deterioration, the more likely it is to remain stable.

- The existence of a "youth bulge"—a large proportion of young adults in the population—increases the risk of state failure through war because large pools of underemployed youths are easily mobilized into military action.

Inasmuch as most of the sovereign states in the world have one or more of these attributes, it is likely that failed states will grow as a problem in the globalized twenty-first century. The globe is speckled with many dangerous civil war flashpoints where countries are highly vulnerable to dissolution as a result of state failure, mismanagement, and civil revolt. To add to the grim picture, there are a number of disputed regions poised to declare independence. Among them are the Kurdish region of Turkey on the Iraqi border, Nagaland in India, the Cabinda exclave in Angola, and Baida in southern Somalia. In 2008, Kosovo declared its independence from Serbia. In a foreshadowing of the war to come between Russia and Georgia, Russia's Vladimir Putin asked of Georgia's two breakaway enclaves, "If people believe that Kosovo can be granted full independence, why then should we deny it to Abkhazia and South Ossetia?"

The International Dimensions of Internal War The rise of failing states and their frequent fall into civil war may make it tempting for you to think of civil war as stemming exclusively from conditions within countries. However, external factors often influence internal rebellions.

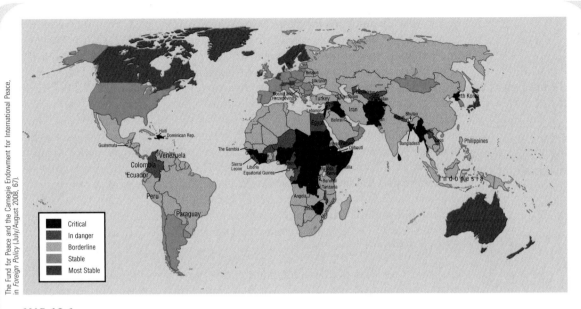

Map of the world showing failed states with legend:
- Critical
- In danger
- Borderline
- Stable
- Most Stable

Countries labeled include: Belarus, Ukraine, Bosnia and Herzegovina, Turkey, Azerbaijan, Iran, Bhutan, North Korea, Philippines, Lebanon, Bahrain, Egypt, Eritrea, Djibouti, Bangladesh, Laos, Indonesia, Haiti, Dominican Rep., Guatemala, Venezuela, Colombia, Ecuador, Peru, Paraguay, The Gambia, Sierra Leone, Liberia, Equatorial Guinea, Cameroon, Uganda, Kenya, Somalia, Burundi, Tanzania, Angola, Zimbabwe, Mozambique

MAP 13.1

THE THREAT OF FAILED STATES This map identifies the world's sixty weakest countries whose governments are most in danger of failing and most likely to collapse in civil war and anarchy. These potential "failed states" threaten the progress and stability of the other stable countries.

Every war has two faces. It is a conflict both between and within political systems; a conflict that is both external and internal. [It is undeniable that] internal wars affect the international system [and that] the international system affects internal wars.

—George Modelski, political scientist

Because the great powers have global interests, they have been historically prone to intervene militarily in civil wars to support friendly governments and to overthrow unfriendly ones. When they have, wars within states became internationalized. But today it is often difficult to determine where an internal war ends and another begins. As Table 13.1 reveals, outside intervention in civil wars has been fairly common. Such intervention has occurred in almost one of every four civil wars (49 of 213) between 1816 and 2008, and almost a third (27 of 89) of all civil wars since 1989. In the aftermath of external intrusions, the targets' domestic societies have been transformed. At times, external actors (states and IGOs) have sent interventionary armed forces into failed states to contain and control the civil war causing violence and attempt to reestablish governing authority. A recent exception to the usual tendency for intra-state wars to become internationalized by foreign intervention is the U.S.-led invasion of Iraq: "In a reversal of the classic spillover of conflict from intra- to inter-state, developments in Iraq during 2004 raised the prospect of an international conflict creating a fully fledged civil war" rather than restoring peace (www.sipri.org).

The Fund for Peace and the Carnegie Endowment for International Peace, in *Foreign Policy* (July/August 2008, 67).

■ diversionary theory of war

the hypothesis that leaders initiate conflict abroad as a way of increasing their citizens' approval of them and national cohesion at home.

There is another dimension to the internationalization of civil wars. Many analysts believe that domestic insurrections become internationalized when leaders experiencing internal opposition within their state intentionally seek to provoke an international *crisis* in the hope that their citizens will become less rebellious if their attention is diverted to the threat of aggression from foreign countries. This proposition has become known as the **diversionary theory of war**. This theory draws a direct connection between civil strife and foreign aggression. It maintains that when leaders sense their country is suffering from conflict at home, they are prone to attempt to contain that domestic strife by waging a war against foreigners—hoping that the international danger will take citizens' attention away from their dissatisfaction with their home leadership. "To put it cynically, one could say that nothing helps a leader like a good war. It gives him his only chance of being a tyrant and being loved for it at the same time. He can introduce the most ruthless forms of control and send thousands of his followers to their deaths and still be hailed as a great protector. Nothing ties tighter the in-group bonds than an out-group threat" (Morris 1969).

It is logical for leaders to assume that national unity will rise when a foreign rivalry exists (Lai and Reiter 2005; Mitchell and Prins 2004). This creates strong temptations for them to seek to manage domestic unrest by initiating foreign adventures and demonstrating their competence (Tarar 2006). Indeed, many political advisers have counseled this strategy, as the realist theorist Niccolò Machiavelli did in 1513 when he advised leaders to undertake foreign wars whenever turmoil within their state became too great.

> *Voice or no voice, the people can always be brought to do the bidding of the leaders. That is easy. All you have to do is tell them they are being attacked and denounce the pacifists for lack of patriotism.*
>
> —Hermann Goering, the Nazi adviser to German dictator Adolf Hitler

Similarly, in 1939, John Foster Dulles recommended before he became U.S. Secretary of State that "the easiest and quickest cure of internal dissension is to portray danger from abroad."

Whether leaders actually start wars to offset domestic conflict and heighten public approval remains a subject of debate. We cannot demonstrate that many leaders intentionally undertake diversionary actions to defend themselves against domestic opposition, even in democracies during bad economic times or to influence legislative

> *In times of social upheaval, the ability to wrap one's own ambitions in the mantle of justified violence may be the only thing that separates perpetrators from victims. The good pupils become the former, the poor ones become the latter.*
>
> —Thucydides, realist theoretician in fourth century BCE Athens after the Peloponnesian War

outcomes (Oneal and Tir 2006). Unpopular leaders may instead be highly motivated to exercise caution in foreign affairs and to avoid the use of force overseas in order to cultivate a reputation as a peacemaker. It may be better for leaders facing opposition to avoid further criticism that they are intentionally manipulative by addressing domestic problems rather than engaging in reckless wars overseas—especially unpopular wars that trigger protest demonstrations and reduce leaders' public opinion approval ratings. Hence, there is reason to question the link between civil unrest and the initiation of interstate war. "The linkage depends," Jack Levy (1989b) observes, "on the kinds of internal conditions that commonly lead to hostile external actions for diversionary purposes." Diversionary wars are undertaken by desperate leaders in desperate times, such as in an economic recession or a reelection that the opposition appears likely to win. In noncrisis times, however, when people take to the streets to protest a leader's domestic policies, most leaders are more inclined to concentrate on the internal disturbances than to manufacture threats of a foreign war.

Civil wars can become internationalized through both (1) the tendency for them to incite external intervention as well as (2) the propensity for leaders of governments that are failing to wage wars abroad in order to try to control rebellion at home. These two trends both are making for the globalization of armed aggression. And that globalization is evident in yet another, third type of armed aggression that brings violence to world politics: the threat of global terrorism that knows no borders and that is spreading worldwide.

TERRORISM

Since the birth of the modern state system some three and a half centuries ago, national leaders have prepared for wars against other countries. Throughout this period, war has been conceived as large-scale organized violence between the regular armies of sovereign states. Although leaders today still ready their countries for such clashes, increasingly they are faced with the prospect of **asymmetric warfare**—armed conflict between terrorist networks and conventional military forces.

Terrorism was well known even in ancient times, as evident in the campaign of assassinations conducted by the Sicarii (named after a short dagger, or sica) in Judea during the first century BCE. Today it is practiced by a diverse group of movements. In 2008 the U.S. National Counter-Terrorism Center (NCTC) identified dozens of different transnational actors as worldwide terrorist groups. Political terrorism is the deliberate use or threat of violence against noncombatants, calculated to instill fear, alarm, and ultimately a feeling of helplessness in an audience beyond the immediate victims. Because perpetrators of terrorism often strike symbolic targets in a horrific manner, the psychological impact of an attack can exceed the physical damage. A mixture of drama and dread, terrorism is not senseless violence; it is a premeditated political strategy that threatens people with a coming danger that seems ubiquitous, unavoidable, and unpredictable.

Terrorism can be employed to support or to change the political status quo. Repressive terror, which is wielded to sustain an existing political order, has been utilized by governments as well as by vigilantes. From the Gestapo (secret state

■ asymmetric warfare

armed conflict between belligerents of vastly unequal military strength, in which the weaker side is often a nonstate actor that relies on unconventional tactics.

police) in Nazi Germany to the "death squads" in various countries, establishment violence attempts to defend the prevailing political order by eliminating opposition leaders and by intimidating virtually everyone else.

Dissidents who use terrorism to change the political status quo vary considerably. Some groups, like the MPLA (Popular Movement for the Liberation of Angola), used terrorism to expel colonial rulers; others, such as ETA (Basque Homeland and Liberty), adopt terrorism as part of an ethnonational separatist struggle; still others, including the Islamic Jihad, the Christian Identity Movement, the Sikh group Babbar Khalsa, and Jewish militants belonging to Kach, place terror in the service of what they see as religious imperatives. Finally, groups such as the Japanese Red Army and Italian Black Order turn to terrorism for left- or right-wing ideological reasons. Dissident terror may be grounded in anticolonialism, separatism, religion, or secular ideology.

Although the ultimate goals of individuals and groups that employ terrorism differ, they seek similar intermediate objectives as a means of attaining their goals. The following objectives are the most common:

■ The *agitational* objectives of terrorism include promoting the dissident group, advertising its agenda, and discrediting rivals. Shocking behavior frightens people, especially when performed at a time and place imbued with symbolism. Nineteenth-century anarchists were among the first to emphasize the propaganda value of terrorism. One stunning act, they believed, would draw more attention than a thousand leaflets.

■ The *coercive* objectives of terrorism include disorienting a target population, inflating the perceived power of the dissident group, wringing concessions from authorities, and provoking a heavy-handed overreaction from the police and military. Launching vicious, indiscriminate attacks at markets, cafés, and other normally tranquil locations can create a paralyzing sense of foreboding within the general public and goad political leaders into adopting repressive policies, which terrorists hope will drive the population to their side of the struggle.

■ The *organizational* objectives of terrorism include acquiring resources, forging group cohesion, and maintaining an underground network of supporters. Robbing banks, obtaining ransom for hostages, and collecting protection money from businesses can finance training and logistical support for field operations. Moreover, because high initiation costs tend to lower group defections, these activities can increase allegiance when recruits are required to participate in violent acts.

To accomplish these objectives, terrorists use a variety of tactics, including bombing, assault, hijacking, and taking hostages. Bombing alone accounts for roughly one third of all recorded terrorist incidents. Hijacking and hostage taking generally involve more complex operations than planting a bomb in a crowded department store or gunning down travelers in a train station. An example of such careful planning can be seen in the September 1970 coordinated hijacking of five airliners by Palestinians, which eventually led to one airliner being blown up in Cairo and three others in Jordan. To be successful, these kinds of seizures require detailed preparation and the capacity to guard captives for long periods of time. Among the payoffs of such efforts is the opportunity to articulate the group's grievances. The

Lebanese group behind the 1985 hijacking of TWA Flight 847, for instance, excelled at using U.S. television networks to articulate their grievances to the American public, which reduced the options that the Reagan administration could consider while searching for a solution to the crisis.

Beyond the conventional tactics of bombings, assaults, hijacking, and hostage taking, two other threats could become part of the terrorist repertoire. First, dissidents may acquire weapons of mass destruction to deliver a mortal blow against detested enemies. Nuclear armaments are the ultimate terror weapons, but radiological, chemical, and biological weapons also pose extraordinary dangers. Crude radiological weapons can be fabricated by combining ordinary explosives with nuclear waste or radioactive isotopes, stolen from hospitals, industrial facilities, or research laboratories. Rudimentary chemical weapons can be made from herbicides, pesticides, and other toxic substances that are available commercially. Biological weapons based on viral agents are more difficult to produce, although the dispersal of anthrax spores through the mail during the fall of 2001 illustrated that low-technology attacks with bacterial agents in powder form are a frightening possibility.

The second tactical innovation on the horizon is cyberterrorism. Not only can the Internet be used by extremists as a recruiting tool and a means of coordinating their activities with like-minded groups, but it also allows them to case potential targets by hacking into a foe's computer system. Viruses and other weapons of **information warfare** could cause havoc if they disabled financial institutions.

■ **information warfare**

attacks on an adversary's telecommunications and computer networks to degrade the technological systems vital to its defense and economic well-being.

Consider also how estimates of terrorism's threat are influenced by how terrorism is defined, often for the political goal of promoting an actor's view. Think, for example, about the seemingly simple question of whether global terrorism has increased in frequency since the 1960s. On the surface, this appears to be an easy question. Yet estimates vary considerably. Indices select, screen, and filter what is perceived about the volume of international terrorism. For instance, the U.S. Department of State's Office of Counter-Terrorism—which employs the broad definition for international terrorism as any "premeditated, politically motivated violence perpetrated against noncombatant targets by subnational groups or clandestine agents, usually intended to influence an audience involving the citizens or territory of more than one country"—began to inventory the frequency of terrorist acts after terrorism first emerged as a significant global problem in the 1960s and grew to epidemic proportions in the 1970s and 1980s. By their counting procedures, the yearly number of acts of international terrorism increased steadily from 174 in 1968 to a peak of 666 in 1987, but then began to decline just as steadily to 200 acts in 2002. After the U.S. broadened its definitional criteria, the estimates of the number of global terrorist acts rose dramatically (see Figure 13.2). Many experts believe that the presence of U.S. soldiers on Islamic soil in Iraq counterproductively ignited a new wave of deadly terrorist activity throughout the world; 91 percent of the most respected terrorist experts believe that the world is becoming increasingly dangerous for Americans and the United States and that the globe is growing more dangerous (*Foreign Policy*, September/October 2007, 64).

The waves of terrorist suicide-bombings in Iraq and the resurgence of the Taliban and Al Qaeda in Afghanistan and the neighboring Pakistani border area cast doubts about the wisdom of the U.S. military occupation in these global hot spots. Though Al Qaeda is now greatly weakened in Iraq, the invasion of Iraq is widely credited with reviving Al Qaeda following its eviction from Afghanistan in 2001. As concluded

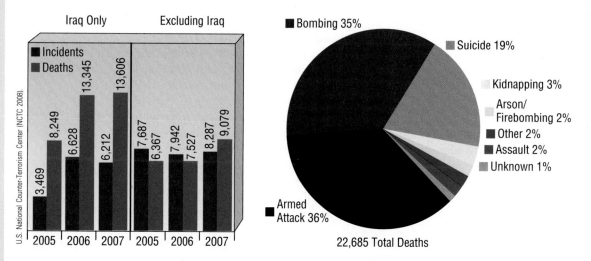

FIGURE 13.2

THE GROWING THREAT OF GLOBAL TERRORISM **Terrorist attacks worldwide shot up more than 30 percent since 2005, killing 40 percent more people (particularly in Iraq where extremists used chemical weapons and suicide bombers to target crowds). Altogether, the U.S. reported that 14,499 terrorist attacks occurred in 2007, and these strikes claimed a total of 22,685 lives (60 percent in Iraq). The figure on the right records the major methods used by terrorists worldwide in 2007, and the percentage of deaths caused by each.**

The war is helping, not hurting, the terrorists.
Before the war, opponents warned that it could strengthen, not weaken, terrorism. And so it has: a C.I.A. report warns that since the U.S. invasion Iraq has become a magnet and training ground for Islamic extremists, who will eventually threaten other countries.

—*Paul Krugman, political journalist*

in 2006 by the U.S.'s National Intelligence Assessment on terrorism, the Iraq conflict was "breeding a deep resentment of U.S. involvement in the Muslim world and cultivating supporters for the global jihadist movement." A shift occurred in 2008, with the resurging strength of the Taliban in Afghanistan and the growth of Al Qaeda in Pakistan's bordering tribal belt. With security conditions deteriorating, for the first time in five years more soldiers died in Afghanistan than in Iraq (Baker and Olya 2008; Gall 2008; *Economist* July 19th 2008).

The New Global Terrorism

The conventional view of terrorism as a rare and relatively remote threat was challenged by the events of September 11, 2001. The horrors visited on the World Trade Center, the Pentagon, and the crash victims in Pennsylvania forced the world to confront a grim new reality: Terrorists were capable of executing catastrophic attacks almost anywhere, even without an arsenal of sophisticated weapons. Not only did groups like Al Qaeda have global reach, but stealth, ingenuity, and meticulous planning could compensate for their lack of firepower. "America is full of fear," proclaimed a jubilant Osama bin Laden. "Nobody in the United States will feel safe."

Osama bin Laden has come to symbolize the new types of global terrorists. He is regarded as a true terrorist mastermind after his strategy succeeded in orchestrating the 9/11 terrorist attacks. A wealthy Saudi expatriate and zealous Islamic revolutionary, bin Laden got his start leading Afghan resistance against the Soviet Union in the 1980s, where he was widely suspected of being helped by the U.S. Central Intelligence Agency (CIA) (Bergen 2006).

> *The United States created the Monster known as Osama bin Laden. Where did he go to terrorist school? At the CIA.*
> —Michael Moore, American documentary film producer

What arguably made 9/11 a symbolic watershed was that it epitomized a deadly new strain of *terrorism,* although arguably politicians are prone to overreact and exaggerate the threat to national security (Mueller 2007). Previously, terrorism was regarded as political theater, a frightening drama where the perpetrators wanted a lot of people watching, not a lot of people dead. Now there seems to be a desire to kill as many people as possible. Driven by searing hatred, annihilating enemies appears more important to global terrorists than winning sympathy for their cause.

The rise of global terrorism is connected to the *globalization* of world politics. This trend has made it easier for clandestine terrorist groups to cross borders. As stateless transnational actors without a territory of their own to defend, terrorists can travel wearing no uniforms to penetrate any existing territorial state.

> *Just as this new terrorist violence doesn't have a front, it doesn't have a face. It doesn't have boundaries.*
> —Yaron Ezrahi, political theorist

Another feature of this new strain of terrorism is its organizational form. Instead of having a hierarchical command structure, Al Qaeda possesses a decentralized, horizontal structure. Loosely tied together by the Internet, e-mail, and cellular telephones, Al Qaeda originally resembled a hub-and-spoke organization: Osama bin Laden and a small core of loyalists provided strategic direction and aid to a franchise of affiliated terrorist cells. Rather than serving as a commander, bin Laden

TERRORISTS BEHIND MASKS Shown here is the faceless militia that target armies in uniforms: Looking like self-funded criminal gangs with no ranks and uncertain allegiances, many terrorist groups hide their identity and report to no superiors.

functioned as a coordinator who, in addition to planning dramatic, high-casualty attacks, provided financial and logistical support to extremist groups fighting those whom he perceived as archenemies.

Following the demise of the Taliban regime in Afghanistan after the U.S.-led military intervention, Al Qaeda underwent a structural change. Combined with its loss of a safe haven in Afghanistan, the killing or capture of roughly one-third of Al Qaeda's leadership transformed the organization into an entity that resembled a chain. Bin Laden and his close associates continued offering ideological inspiration to small, disparate cells scattered around the world, but they no longer were directly involved in the planning and execution of most of the attacks undertaken in Al Qaeda's name. Operating independently, without the training, financing, and logistical infrastructure previously available through a central headquarters, Al Qaeda's diffuse underground cells concentrate on "soft" targets, sometimes attacking in conjunction with sympathetic local forces. Though Al Qaeda did not claim responsibility, some point to the December 2007 assassination of former Pakistan Prime Minister Benazir Bhutto as illustration of this pattern of activity (though others blame the attack on political rival Perez Musharraf).

What makes the new breed of terrorists who belong to organizations such as Al Qaeda more lethal than previous terrorists is their religious fanaticism, which allows them to envision acts of terror on two levels. At one level, terrorism is a means to change the political status quo by punishing those culpable for felt wrongs. At another level, *terrorism* is an end in itself, a sacrament performed for its own sake in an eschatological confrontation between good and evil (Juergensmeyer 2003). Functioning only on the first level, most secular terrorist groups rarely employ suicide missions. Operating on both levels, religious terrorist groups see worldly gain as well as transcendent importance in a martyr's death (Bloom 2005; Pape 2005).

SUICIDAL DEATH AS A WAY OF LIFE Suicide bombings are now routine terrorist tactics carried out by people willing to kill enemy targets with methods such as wearing a concealed vest carrying explosives or driving a car bomb, despite the fact that to be successful the terrorist must die. Suicide bombing is effective, fast, cheap, and difficult to deter, but questions remain about why suicide terrorists are willing to die (Gambetta 2005). Shown here (left) is Raed Abdul Hamid Misk and his children days before he blew himself up on a Jerusalem bus, and (right) is another symptom of terrorism's fury—Sunni Muslim insurgents celebrating their attack of an American military convoy outside Fallujah, Iraq.

Ramadan Shalah of the Palestinian Jihad explained the military logic of suicide tactics through asymmetric warfare by asserting: "Our enemy possesses the most sophisticated weapons in the world. . . . We have nothing . . . except the weapon of martyrdom. It is easy and costs us only our lives."

Counterterrorism

The threat facing civilization after September 11, 2001, was described by then U.S. President George W. Bush as a network of terrorist groups and rogue states that harbored them. Efforts to combat this threat, he insisted, "will not end until every terrorist group of global reach has been found, stopped, and defeated." In what was subsequently called the **Bush Doctrine**, the president declared that each nation had a choice to make: "Either you are with us, or you are with the terrorists."

As you learned in Chapter 7, terrorist groups are a type of transnational nonstate actor (or global NGO) distinguished by the fact that they use violence as their primary method of exercising influence. States have often financed, trained, equipped, and provided sanctuary for terrorists whose activities serve their foreign policy goals. The practice of such *state-sponsored terrorism* is among the charges that the United States leveled against Iraq prior to toppling Saddam Hussein in 2003, and continues to apply to Cuba, Iran, Sudan, and Syria (NCTC 2008). However, disagreement about the character and causes of global terrorism remain pronounced, and, without agreement on these preliminaries, a consensus on the best response is unlikely. Much like a disease that cannot be treated until it is accurately diagnosed, so the plague of the new global terrorism cannot be eradicated until its sources are understood. Those persuaded by one image of terrorism are drawn to certain

■ **Bush Doctrine** the declaration that the United States intended to behave globally in terms of its perceived national self-interests, without the necessary approval of others and, as a corollary, would consider taking unilateral preemptive military action against any perceived security threat (such as Iraq) to defeat it before it could attack the United States.

counterterrorism policies, whereas those holding a different image recommend contrary policies. As constructivist theorists remind us, what we see depends on what we expect, what we look at, and what we wish to see.

Consider the diametrically opposed views of whether repression or conciliation is the most effective counterterrorist policy. Those advocating repression see terrorism springing from the cold calculations of extremists who should be neutralized by preemptive surgical strikes. In contrast to this coercive counterterrorism approach, those who see terrorism rooted in frustrations with a society lacking in civil liberties and human rights (Krueger 2007) or widespread poverty and poor education (Azios 2007) urge negotiation and cooperative nonmilitary approaches (Cortright and Lopez 2008). Rather than condoning military strikes aimed at exterminating the practitioners of terrorism, they endorse conciliatory policies designed to reduce terrorism's appeal.

The debate about how to deal with the new global terrorism has provoked serious concerns about strategies for combating this global threat (see Controversy: Can The War Against Global Terrorism Be Won?). The debate revolves around a series of interconnected issues: Are repressive counterterrorist policies ethical? Are they compatible with democratic procedures? Do they require multilateral (international) backing to be legal, or can they be initiated unilaterally? Is conciliation more effective than military coercion? What are the relative costs, risks, and benefits of these contending approaches to combat terrorism?

Although most experts would agree that while "it is not possible to extirpate terrorism from the face of the globe," they share faith in the more modest goal—that "it should be possible to reduce the incidence and effectiveness of terrorism" (Reinares 2002) and contain it (Shapiro 2007). Accomplishing this goal while maintaining a proper balance between undertaking resolute action and upholding civil liberties will be difficult for multiple reasons. First, today's borderless world makes terrorism easy to practice. Second, numerous *failed states* offer out-of-the-way places for terrorist groups to locate and train. Third, the growing possibility that terrorists will obtain weapons of mass destruction will create unprecedented opportunities for them to commit unspeakable atrocities. Fourth, "technology allows modern-day terrorism to assume insidious forms. The extreme advantage that terrorism provides to the weak against powerful governments means that terrorism is here to stay" (Sandler and Enders 2007). Moreover, the tolerant virtual environment of the Internet provides an online breeding ground for a new generation of terrorists—essentially a self-recruited leaderless jihad, inspired by Al Qaeda's ideology, but lacking any formal connections. It is composed largely of young people seeking an outlet for their frustrations and a sense of significance and belonging in their lives (Sageman 2008). Finally, contemporary terrorists have become extremely violent, holding few reservations about inflicting heavy casualties and causing enormous physical destruction.

The history of terrorism indicates that there is no single counterterrorist orthodoxy on strategic questions, no canon with strict guidelines running from ultimate goals to intermediate objectives to specific tactics. Strategic thinking about the use of terrorism in asymmetric warfare has evolved in response to new technologies, new targets of opportunity, and new counterterrorist policies. The perpetrators of terrorism are not mindless; they have shown that they have long-term aims and rationally calculate how different operations can accomplish their purposes. Indeed, it is their ability to plan, execute, and learn from these operations that makes today's terrorists so dangerous.

CONTROVERSY:

CAN THE WAR AGAINST GLOBAL TERRORISM BE WON?

In the wake of 9/11, a new conventional wisdom arose—as then U.S. Secretary of Defense Donald Rumsfeld put it, "if the [United States] learned a single lesson from 9/11, it should be that the only way to defeat terrorists is to attack them. There is no choice. You simply cannot defend in every place at every time against every technique. All the advantage is with the terrorist in that regard, and therefore you have no choice but to go after them where they are." This statement reflects the view that even if appeasement is tempting, the only way to respond is relentlessly and thoroughly.

Exactly what to do to control the new global terrorism remains controversial. Many experts question the U.S. characterization of the problem and the ambitious crusade it undertook, including skeptical allies on whom the United States depends if the antiterror war is to be won. To conduct a worldwide war requires an enduring commitment at high costs. That is why proposals for an effective and just response to the new global terrorism differ, as do recommendations about how the world can most effectively reduce the probability that 9/11 will be repeated.

What makes counterterrorism so problematic is that strategists often fail to distinguish different types of terrorist movements and their diverse origins. Therefore they construct counterterrorist strategies in the abstract —with a single formula—rather than tailoring approaches for dealing with terrorism's alternate modes. As one expert advises, "One lesson learned since 9/11 is that the expanded war on terrorism has created a lens that tends to distort our vision of the complex political dynamics of countries" (Menkhaus 2002).

What do you think? If terrorism is the problem, and the goal is its complete eradication, how should those pursuing that quest proceed? In evaluating proposed controls in the fight against the latest wave of global terrorism, you will need to confront a series of incompatible clichés and conclusions: "concessions only encourage terrorists' appetite for further terrorism" as opposed to "concessions can redress the grievances that lead to terrorism," or "terrorism requires a long-term solution" as opposed to the claim that "terrorism cannot be cured but it can be prevented by preemption." Your search for solutions will necessarily spring from incompatible assumptions you make about terrorism's nature and sources, and these assumptions will strongly affect your conclusions about the wisdom or futility of contemplated remedies.

Keep in mind that what may appear to be policy around which an effective counterterrorist program might be constructed could potentially only make the problem worse by provoking the very result your preferred plan was designed to solve: future terrorist actions. Counterterrorism is controversial because one person's solution is another person's problem, the answers are often unclear, and the ethical criteria for applying just-war theory to counterterrorism need clarification (Patterson 2005). A counterterrorist program that may succeed in one location may backfire in another. Because promise and/or peril may result when the same countermeasure is deployed, what would you advise governments about the best methods of fighting terrorism?

Armed aggression poses a threat of huge proportions to the global future. It extracts a terrible toll on human life. Having examined trends in the frequency and changing

> *There's nothing quite like a protracted war to shift the landscape of existence. When policy makers start a war, do they realize they have dragged heavy hands across the map of the world and altered the details of daily life?*
>
> —Anna Quindlen, political journalist

character of armed aggression between states, within them, and in global terrorism, it is difficult not to recognize that warfare in all its forms is an extremely dangerous threat to the world.

The magnitude of armed aggression raises questions about *why* wars occur. What ends motivate human beings to continue to resort to armed aggression, given the unspeakable casualties? The question provokes a more fundamental set of related questions about the causes of aggression generally. Accordingly, consider some of the major contending hypotheses and theories about the sources from which armed conflicts arise.

WHAT CAUSES ARMED AGGRESSION?

Throughout history, efforts have been made to explain why people engage in organized violence. Inventories of war's origins (see Cashman and Robinson 2007; Midlarsky 2000; Vasquez 2000; Geller and Singer 1998) generally agree that hostilities are rooted in multiple sources found at various *levels of analysis* (recall Chapters 1 and 3). Some causes directly influence the odds of war; others are remote and indirect, creating explosive background conditions that enable any one of a number of more proximate factors to trigger violence. The most commonly cited causes of armed agression are customarily classified by three broad categories: (1) aggressive traits found in the human species, (2) detrimental national attributes that make some states likely to engage in aggression, and (3) volatile conditions within the global system that encourage disputes to become militarized.

The First Level of Analysis: Individuals' Human Nature

In a sense, all wars originate from the decisions of the leaders of states or transnational nonstate actors such as terrorist organizations. Leaders' choices ultimately determine whether armed aggression will occur (see Chapter 3). So a good starting point for explaining why warfare occurs is to consider the relationship of armed aggression to the choices of individual leaders. For this category of theorizing, questions about human nature are central.

The repeated outbreak of war has led some, such as psychiatrist Sigmund Freud, to conclude that aggression is an instinctive part of human nature that stems from humans' genetic psychological programming. Identifying *homo sapiens* as the deadliest species, ethologists (those who study animal behavior) such as Konrad

Lorenz (1963) similarly argue that humans are one of the few species practicing **intraspecific aggression** (routine killing of their own kind), in comparison with most other species which practice **interspecific aggression** (killing only other species, except in the most unusual circumstances—cannibalism in certain tropical fish being one exception). Ethologists are joined in their interpretation by adherents of realist theory who believe that all humans are born with an innate drive for power that they cannot avoid, and that this instinct leads to competition and war. They therefore accept the sociological premise suggested by Charles Darwin's theories of evolution and natural selection. Life entails a struggle for survival of the fittest, and natural selection eliminates the traits that interfere with successful competition. To sociological realists, **pacifism** is counterproductive because it rejects the right of people to kill in order to obtain power.

Many question these theories on both empirical and logical grounds. If aggression is truly an inevitable impulse deriving from human nature, then should not all humans exhibit this genetically determined behavior? Most people, of course don't; they ethically reject killing as evil and neither murder nor accept others' killing on behalf of the state or any other cause. In fact, at some fundamental genetic level human beings are wired to seek consensus, not conflict.

> *People feel intensely uncomfortable if they live in a society that doesn't have moral rules.*
> —Francis Fukuyama, international theorist

In addition, liberal theory and behavioral social science research suggest that genetics fails to explain why individuals may be belligerent only at certain times. Social Darwinism's interpretation of the biological influences on human behavior can be countered by examining why people cooperate and act morally. As James Q. Wilson (1993) argues, Darwinian **survival of the fittest** realist theory overlooks the fact that "the moral sense must have adaptive value; if it did not, natural selection would have worked against people who had such useless traits as sympathy, self-control, or a desire for fairness in favor of those with the opposite tendencies."

Although the **nature versus nurture** debate regarding the biological bases of aggression has not been resolved (Ridley 2003; Kluger 2007), most social scientists now strongly disagree with the realist premise that because humans are essentially selfish, they are also aggressive and murder and kill because of their innate genetic drives to act aggressively. Instead, they interpret war as a learned cultural habit. Aggression is a propensity acquired early in life as a result of **socialization**. Therefore, aggression is a learned rather than a biologically determined behavior.

> *Violent human nature is a myth.*
> —Timothy Murithi, peace scientist

Individuals' willingness to sacrifice their lives in war out of a sense of duty to their leaders and country is one of history's puzzles. "The fog of war" is what the Russian author Leo Tolstoy and others have called the fact that people will give their lives in

■ intraspecific aggression

killing members of one's own species.

■ interspecific aggression

killing others that are not members of their own species.

■ pacifism

the liberal idealist school of ethical thought that recognizes no conditions that justify the taking of another human's life, even when authorized by a head of state.

■ survival of the fittest

a realist concept derived from Charles Darwin's theory of evolution that advises that ruthless competition is ethically acceptable to survive, even if the actions violate moral commands not to kill.

■ nature versus nurture

the controversy over whether human behavior is determined more by the biological basis of "human nature" than it is nurtured by the environmental conditions that humans experience.

■ socialization

the processes by which people learn to accept the beliefs, values, and behaviors that prevail in a given society's culture.

struggles, large and small, even when the importance and purpose of those struggles are not understood. Clearly, this self-sacrifice stems from learned beliefs that some convictions are worth dying for, such as loyalty to one's own country.

> *It has been widely observed that soldiers fight—and noncombatants assent to war—not out of aggressiveness but obedience.*
> —William R. Caspary, political psychologist

But this does not make human nature a cause of war, even if learned habits of obedience taught in military training are grounds for participation in aggression authorized by others, and even if at times the mass public's chauvinistic enthusiasm for aggression against foreign adversaries encourages leaders to start wars.

Human nature is not a direct cause of armed conflict. How then do we explain the enduring rivalries and the repetitive recourse to genocide in some areas? It is the bloody history of territories such as the Balkans that inspires anthropologists to inquire if territoriality drives human aggression. Could it be that the continuing genocides in Sudan and the Ivory Coast stem from "an innate human aggression, inherited from our animal ancestors, to possess territory believed to be one's own?" Robert Ardrey (1966), the playwright turned anthropologist, advanced the proposition of human territorial aggression in *The Territorial Imperative*. The controversial best-seller argued that the territorial instincts of animals apply equally to humans, who, like animals, are compelled by instinct to conquer and defend territory they think belongs to them exclusively. The **territorial imperative** has been resurrected as a theory to account for the ethnic wars that rage across the globe in so many regions today, especially the war-ravaged Middle East and the explosive Balkans.

■ territorial imperative

the term coined by anthropologist Robert Ardrey to popularize the proposition that people and countries will defend to the death their territory, just like animals instinctively do.

Also to be questioned is that **national character** drives certain nationalities to aggression. Countries sharing cultural values and identity can express these in different ways and can change. For example, Sweden and Switzerland, once warlike, have managed conflicts without warfare since 1809 and 1815, respectively. In fact, since 1500, one in five countries never experienced war (Sivard 1991, 20). This achievement suggests that other factors beyond the inborn collective traits of particular peoples better explain why certain countries tend to engage in organized violence. Rather, armed aggression occurs most often as a result of the choices leaders make, and not because of the popular preferences of their entire societies. As English Statesman Saint Thomas More (1478–1535) put this hypothesis, "The common people do not go to war of their own accord, but are driven to it by the madness of kings."

■ national character

the collective characteristics ascribed to the people within a state.

> *There are no warlike people—just warlike leaders.*
> —Ralph Bunche, American diplomat

This idea introduces an important analytic problem. Can the characteristics of cultures and populations within countries in the aggregate, the sum of the parts, predict the behaviors of the individuals within those groups? No. To generalize from the whole to the part is to commit what demographers and statisticians call a logical **ecological fallacy**. Why? Because, unless all members of the same group are exactly alike, the characteristics of the collectivity (the entire state or culture, for example) do not safely predict the beliefs and behaviors of the individuals in the grouping. Do all Americans think alike? All Muslims? All Japanese or Chinese? Hardly. This is racial and cultural stereotyping at its worst. Rarely can we safely generalize from groups to individuals. Likewise, the opposite, what logicians call the **individualistic fallacy**, is also a mental error. We cannot generalize safely about the beliefs or behavior of individual leaders (Adolf Hitler of Nazi Germany, Joseph Stalin of the Soviet Union, Barack Obama of the United States, or Dmitry Medvedev of Russia) and ascribe them to the prevailing preferences of the collective cultures and states that each of them headed. These individuals are symbols, not samples. Their actions do not tell us much about the opinions and values of the pluralistic populations for whom they spoke or speak. Individual guilt is not collective guilt.

What should be obvious is that some of the foreign policy decisions by leaders are immoral. Moreover, many of those decisions by countries' leaders are, in hindsight, less wise than mistaken; they fail to form to the *rational choice* model of foreign policy decision making that operates from the assumption that decision makers make choices through cool-headed calculations of cost and benefits in order to select the option that has the best chance of accomplishing preferred goals. In addition, even intelligent and moral leaders are sometimes prone to make unnecessarily high-risk decisions to wage war because they are pressured through *groupthink* by influential advisers within their decision-making group rather than acting on what they personally believe would be the most rational choice.

This observation about the determinants of leaders' choices about war and peace directs attention to the domestic factors that encourage some states to engage in foreign aggression.

The Second Level of Analysis: States' Internal Characteristics

Conventional wisdom holds that variations in states' governments, sizes, ideologies, geographical locations, population dynamics, ethnic homogeneity, wealth, economic performance, military capabilities, and level of educational attainment influence whether they will engage in war. Drawing on the possibility suggested by the historical evidence that preparations to wage war has contributed to the rise of the sovereign state (Kegley and Raymond 2002a), we next examine some theories about the internal characteristics of states that influence leaders' choices regarding the use of force.

■ ecological fallacy

the error of assuming that the attributes of an entire population —a culture, a country, or a civilization—are the same attributes and attitudes of each person within it.

■ individualistic fallacy

the logical error of assuming that an individual leader, who has legal authority to govern, represents the people and opinions of the population governed, so that all citizens are necessarily accountable for the vices and virtues (to be given blame or credit) of the leaders authorized to speak for them.

The word state is identical with the word war.

—Prince Peter Kropotkin, nineteenth-century Russian political theorist

Implicit in this approach to explaining armed aggresion at the *state level of analysis* is the assumption that differences in the types or categories of states determine whether they will engage in war. Arguing that the prospects for war are influenced most heavily by national attributes and the types of leaders making policy decisions for states challenges the premise of *neorealism* that war is inevitable and that global circumstances not domestic factors are the most important determinants of warfare.

Secessionist Revolts and Independence

The seeds of civil strife are often sown by national independence movements. Most rebellions have been driven by the quest through guerrilla warfare to escape the bonds of an existing authority and create through force a new state. "More than two-thirds of all armed combat in the world between 1945 and 1995 were manifestations of the state-creation enterprise" (K. Holsti 1995, 22). This means that armed aggression has often been an instrument through which states have been given—or denied—birth. However, statehood does not guarantee peace. New states, not long-lasting ones, are the most likely to experience civil wars and also to initiate foreign wars. Newly independent countries usually go through a period of political unrest following their acquisition of sovereignty and independence as members in the community of states. They then are likely to seek to resolve long-standing internal grievances and take up arms over contested territories with their neighboring enemies (Rasler and Thompson 2006). Such foreign disputes frequently expand into larger wars because throughout history they have frequently provoked great power *intervention* or external interference by other states or nonstate IGOs into the opposed countries' internal affairs. The high levels of civil wars and wars between neighboring states throughout the Global South may be explained by the fact that nearly all these less-developed countries have recently gained independence from colonialism, many through revolutions.

Cultural Determinants, Feminist Theory, and the Decay of Moral Constraints

Countries' behavior is strongly influenced by the cultural and ethical traditions of their peoples. In the state system, governed by the rules championed by realism, moral constraints on the use of force do not command wide acceptance (Hensel 2006). Instead, most governments encourage their populations to glorify the state and to accept whatever decisions their leaders claim are necessary for national security, including warfare against adversaries. Many scholars believe that these kinds of cultural beliefs make violence more probable.

Advocates of the cultural origins of war argue that most people in most societies live an everyday experience of disengagement, or "numbness," that disinclines them to oppose their leaders' decisions to wage war. The modern state thus organizes its society to accept war and "builds a culture that affirms death" and accepts senseless carnage (Caspary 1993). In contrast, critics operating from the perspective of feminist theories of international relations argue that the foundation of war worldwide, alongside cultural numbing, is rooted in the masculine ethos of realism, which prepares people to accept war and to respect the warrior as a hero (see Enloe 2000 and 2004; Tickner 2002). Gender roles supported by realist values, *feminist* theory contends, contribute to the prevalence of militarism and warfare:

> According to feminist critics, international relations theory as it has evolved incorporates "masculinist" prejudices at each of its three levels of analysis: man, the state, and war. Realists are "androcentric" in arguing that the propensity for conflict is universal in

human nature ("man"); that the logic and the morality of sovereign states are not identical to those of individuals ("the state"); and that the world is an anarchy in which sovereign states must be prepared to rely on self-help, including organized violence ("war"). Feminist theorists would stress the nurturing and cooperative aspects—the conventionally feminine aspects—of human nature; they would expose the artificiality of notions of sovereignty, and their connection with patriarchy and militarism; and they would replace the narrow realist emphasis on security, especially military security, with a redefinition of security as universal social justice. (Lind 1993, 37)

To feminists and other constructivist theorists who embrace a cultural interpretation, the penchant for warfare does not evolve in a vacuum but is produced by the ways in which societies shape their populations' beliefs and norms. Many governments, through the educational programs they fund in schools and other institutions, indoctrinate militaristic values in their political culture that condone the practice of war. Ironically, in a world of diverse national cultures, the messages of obedience and of duty to make sacrifices to the state through such **cultural conditioning** are common. States disseminate the belief that their right to make war should not be questioned and that the ethical principles of religious and secular philosophies prohibiting violence should be disregarded. Consequently, critics stress the existence of powerful institutions that prepare individuals to subconsciously accept warfare as necessary and legitimate.

■ **cultural conditioning**
the impact of national traditions and societal values on the behavior of states, under the assumption that culture affects national decision making about issues such as the acceptability of aggression.

Feminist theory extends this explanation of armed aggression. It accounts for the fact that the probability of violence increases in cultures in which gender discrimination, inequality, and violence toward women are an accepted way of life. Where cultural norms condone the mistreatment of women and deny them opportunities for education and employment, the outbreak of civil war is high (Caprioli 2005; Melander 2005).

Poverty and Relative Deprivation   A country's level of economic development effects the probability of its involvement in war and armed revolution. Indeed, "underdevelopment is a statistically significant predictor of war" (Lemke 2003), and discontent with globalization and foreign economic liberalization can result in violent protest and civil war (Bussmann and Schneider 2007).

Armed aggression, often a angry response to frustration, is a product of **relative deprivation** —people's perception that they are unfairly deprived of the wealth and status that they rightly deserve in comparison with advantaged others. Violence erupts so frequently because hundreds of millions "belong to groups that face some form of cultural exclusion and are disadvantaged or discriminated against relative to others in their country," the United Nations observes. The same is true for national images of relative deprivation between countries. This is why the probability of armed aggression is the highest in the Global South, where peoples' expectations of what they deserve are rising more rapidly than their material rewards and the existing gap in the distribution of wealth and opportunities is widening.

■ **relative deprivation**
inequality between the wealth and status of individuals and groups, and the outrage of those at the bottom about their perceived exploitation by those at the top.

To establish a more peaceful, prosperous, and secure world, poverty must be eliminated and income differentials reduced.
—Sadaka Ogata, UN High Commissioner for Refugees

Before concluding that poverty always breeds armed aggression, note that the *most* impoverished countries have been the least prone to start wars with their neighbors. The poorest countries cannot vent their frustrations aggressively because they lack the military or economic resources to do so. This does not mean that the poorest countries will always remain peaceful. If the past is a guide to the future, then impoverished countries that develop economically will be the most likely to acquire arms and engage in future external wars. In particular, states are likely to initiate foreign wars *after* sustained periods of economic growth—that is, during periods of rising prosperity, when they can afford them (Cashman and Robinson 2007). This signals looming dangers if the most rapidly growing Global South economies direct their growing resources toward armaments rather than investing in sustainable development. The decision in 1998 by both Pakistan and India to acquire nuclear weapons could be followed by other restless countries, such as oil-rich Iran.

Geopolitical Environmental Factors   "Location, location, location"—the geographical roots of armed aggression are now increasingly recognized as a powerful influence on the probability of instability and warfare (Flint 2004). Territorial issues and the stability of international borders are important because the setting and location of states and their distances from one another influence the likelihood of disputes and war (Gibler 2007; Starr 2006). Indeed, the likelihood that a country will undergo armed aggression is strongly affected by key characteristics of its geographic circumstances, such as low supplies of cropland, fresh water, and treasured natural resources such as oil and gas reserves. In addition, topography was signaled as a primary cause of war in 2002 when the UN designated that year as the *International Year of the Mountains* because 23 of the 27 armed conflicts underway then were fought in mountainous areas. In particular, "if a country is mountainous and has a large, lightly populated hinterland, it faces an enhanced risk of rebellion [and] when valuable natural resources are discovered in a particular region of a country, the people living in such localities suddenly have an economic incentive to succeed violently if necessary. Conflict is also more likely in countries that depend heavily on natural resources for their export earnings, in part because rebel groups can extort the gains from this trade to finance their operations" (Collier 2005).

Demographic Stress   A number of demographic factors contribute to the onset of armed aggression. Map 13.2 shows that the risk of civil war is the greatest in those countries in which population dynamics impact heavily on living conditions. For example, such variables as the rate of urban population growth and the rate of death among working-age adults are predictors to the outbreak of armed rebellion. Particularly influential as a demographic catalyst to civil war is the presence of a large proportion of young males in the population: "young men—out of school, out of work, and charged with hatred—are the lifeblood of deadly conflict. Countries with a high proportion of adults under thirty have two and a half times the probability of experiencing a new outbreak of civil conflict as do those more mature age structures relative to population size" (Cincotta and Engleman 2004, 18). So the future faces an increasing threat—"a clash of generations"—"as youth bulges increase the risk of internal armed conflict and violence" (Urdal 2006).

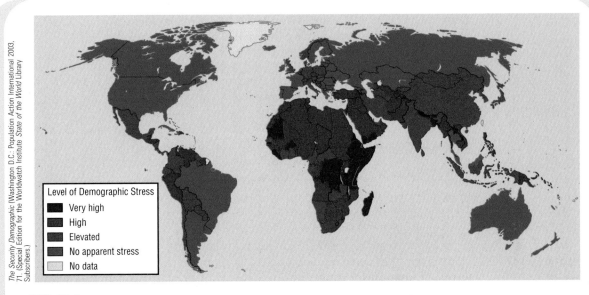

The Security Demographic (Washington D.C.: Population Action International 2003, 71. (Special Edition for the Worldwatch Institute State of the World Library Subscribers.)

Level of Demographic Stress

- Very high
- High
- Elevated
- No apparent stress
- No data

MAP 13.2

DEMOGRAPHIC STRESS AND THE LIKELIHOOD OF CIVIL WAR **Where there are large numbers of unemployed youth concentrated in large cities and a lack of environmentally sustainable growth, the odds of civil war increase dramatically. Shown here are the projected locations of such demographic stress where the likelihood of civil war is expected to be high through the year 2010.**

Militarization "If you want peace, prepare for war," realism counsels. It is questionable whether the acquisition of military power leads to peace or to war, but clearly most Global South countries agree with the realists' thesis that weapons contribute to their security. They have been among the biggest customers in the robust global trade in arms and have built huge armies to guard against their neighboring states' potential aggression and to control their own citizens (see HDR 2008, 294–297; Blanton 1999; and Chapter 14).

As Global South countries concentrate their budgets on equipping their militaries, many worry that war will become more frequent before it becomes less so. Militarization has *not* led to peace in the Global South. Will the curse of violence someday be broken there?

One clue comes from examination of the relationship between changes in military capabilities and war that occurred over centuries in Europe. During its transition to the peak of development, Europe was the location of the world's most frequent and deadly wars. The major European states armed themselves heavily and were engaged in warfare about 65 percent of the time in the sixteenth and seventeenth centuries (Wright 1942). Between 1816 and 1945, three-fifths of all interstate wars took place in Europe, with one erupting about every other year (J. Singer 1991, 58). Not coincidentally, this happened when the developing states of Europe were most energetically arming in competition with one another. Perhaps as a consequence, the great powers—those with the largest armed forces—were the most involved in, and most often initiated, war. Since 1945, however, with the exception of war among the now-independent units of the former Yugoslavia, interstate war has not occurred in Europe. As the European countries moved up the ladder of development, they moved away from war with one another (internal conflict is another matter).

In contrast, the developing countries now resemble Europe before 1945. If, in the immediate future, the Global South follows the model of Europe before 1945, we are likely to see a sea of Global South violence surrounding a European (and Global North) island of peace and prosperity.

Economic System Does the character of states' economic systems influence the frequency of warfare? The question has provoked controversy for centuries. Particularly since Marxism took root in Russia following the Bolshevik Revolution in 1917, communist theoreticians claimed that capitalism was the primary cause of imperialistic wars and colonialism. They were fond of quoting Vladimir Lenin's 1916 explanation of World War I as a war caused by imperialistic capitalists' efforts "to divert the attention of the laboring masses from the domestic political crisis" of collapsing incomes under capitalism. According to the **communist theory of imperialism**, capitalism produces surplus capital. The need to export it stimulates wars to capture and protect foreign markets. Thus *laissez-faire economics* —based on the philosophical principle of free markets with little governmental regulation of the marketplace—rationalized militarism and imperialism for economic gain. Citing the demonstrable frequency with which wealthy capitalist societies militarily intervened on foreign soil for capital gain, Marxists believed that the best way to end international war was to end capitalism.

■ **communist theory of imperialism**

the Marxist-Leninist economic interpretation of imperialist wars of conquest as driven by capitalism's need for foreign markets to generate capital.

Contrary to Marxist theory, *commercial liberalism* contends that free market systems promote peace, not war. Defenders of capitalism have long believed that free market countries that practice free trade abroad are more pacific. The reasons are multiple, but they center on the premise that commercial enterprises are natural lobbyists for world peace because their profits depend on it. War interferes with trade, blocks profit, destroys property, causes inflation, consumes scarce resources, and necessitates big government and counterproductive regulation of business activity and high taxes. By extension, this reasoning continues, as government regulation of internal markets declines, prosperity increases and fewer wars will occur.

The evidence for these rival theories is, not surprisingly, mixed. Conclusions depend in part on perceptions regarding economic influences on international behavior, in part because alternative perspectives focus on different dimensions of the linkage. This controversy was at the heart of the ideological debate between East and West during the Cold War, when the relative virtues and vices of two radically different economic systems—communism and capitalism—were uppermost in people's minds.

The end of the Cold War did not end the historic debate about the link between economics and war. This basic theoretical question commands increasing interest, especially given the "shift in the relevance and usefulness of different power resources, with military power declining and economic power increasing in importance" (Huntington 1991).

Globalization, through which the growing economic interdependence of countries has tightly linked states' growth rates, has intensified the debate about the relationship between trade and international armed conflict. Although "most leaders still cling to the long-standing belief that expanding economic ties will cement the bonds of friendship between and within nations that make resort to arms unfathomable," as Katherine Barbieri and Gerald Schneider observe (1999), "in contrast, realist and Marxist critics reject the liberal view" that the opening of free market economies within states and increased levels of trade between them will produce peace (see Chapter 10). Even though substantial evidence exists to support "the liberals' belief that economic interdependence [and economic and political freedom] have important pacific benefits" (Oneal and Russett 1999), that conclusion is not widely accepted by the many poor Global South countries who maintain that under interdependent globalization the wealthy profit disproportionately from trade, at their expense. This *relative gains* argument insists that conflict is produced because the benefits of economic exchanges are distributed unequally (the rich get richer and the poor get poorer), and trade-war disputes and even wars are likely to undermine world peace.

The future will tell if free markets and free trade will generate international conflict or cooperation. In the meantime, the effects of economic changes (such as the globalization of the sale of products worldwide) on peace continue to provoke interest. For instance, in a tongue-in-cheek extension of this neoliberal logic, political journalist Thomas Friedman advanced the "Golden Arches Theory of Conflict Prevention"—that no two countries have fought a war once McDonald's was present in both countries. Friedman "attributes the phenomenon to the growth of a peaceable middle class. 'People in McDonald's countries don't like to fight wars anymore. . . . They prefer to wait in line for burgers'" (Stross 2002).

Type of Government Realist and especially neorealist theories discount the importance of government type as an influence on war and peace. Not so with liberalism, especially neoliberal theories. As noted in Chapter 2, *liberal theory* assigns great weight to the kinds of political institutions that states create to make policy decisions, and it predicts that the spread of "free" democratically ruled governments will promote peaceful interstate relations. As Immanuel Kant in 1795 argued in *Perpetual Peace,* when citizens are given basic human rights such as choosing their leaders through ballots as well as civil liberties such as free speech and a free press, these democracies would be far less likely to initiate wars than would countries ruled by dictators and kings. This is because a government accountable to the people would be constrained by public opinion from waging war. Kant was joined by other liberal reformers, such as Thomas Jefferson, James Madison, and Woodrow Wilson in the United States. They all believed that an "empire of liberty" (as Madison pictured a growing community of liberal democracies) would be one freed of the curse of war and that, if democratic institutions spread throughout the world, the entire past pattern of belligerent international relations would be replaced by a new pacific pattern.

These liberal and neoliberal predictions have been fulfilled by the passage of time since they were first advanced. "We now have solid evidence that democracies do not make war on each other" (Russett 2001). Much research demonstrates that democracies resolve their differences with one another at the bargaining table rather than the battlefield and that they are more likely to win wars than nondemocracies

(Choi 2004; Souva 2004). This pattern provides the cornerstone for the *democratic peace* proposition (Ray 1995; Sobek 2005) holding that, as Bruce Russett summarizes:

> Democracies are unlikely to engage in any kind of militarized disputes with each other or to let any such disputes escalate into war. They rarely even skirmish. Pairs of democratic states have been only one-eighth as likely as other kinds of states to threaten to use force against each other, and only one-tenth as likely actually to do so. Established democracies fought no wars against one another during the entire twentieth century.
>
> The more democratic each state is, the more peaceful their relations are likely to be. Democracies are more likely to employ "democratic" means of peaceful conflict resolution. They are readier to reciprocate each other's behavior, to accept third-party *mediation* or *good offices* in settling disputes, and to accept binding third-party *arbitration* and *adjudication*. Careful statistical analyses of countries' behavior have shown that democracies' relatively peaceful relations toward each other are not spuriously caused by some other influence such as sharing high levels of wealth, or rapid growth, or ties of alliance. The phenomenon of peace between democracies is not limited just to the rich industrialized states of the Global North. It was not maintained simply by pressure from a common adversary in the Cold War, and it has outlasted that threat. (Russett 2001, 235; see also 2005)

The growing recognition that ballots serve as a barrier against the use of bullets and bombs by one democracy against another has been inspired by the growth of democratic governance over the past three centuries (see Figure 13.3). Yet there is no certainty that liberal democracy will become universal or that the continued growth of democracy will automatically produce a peaceful world order (Rasler and Thompson 2005). Emerging democracies in fact are prone to fight wars (Mansfield and Snyder 2005a). The fact that leaders in elective democracies are accountable to public approval and electoral rejection does not guarantee that they will not use force to settle disputes with other democracies:

> It was, after all, the democratization of conflict in the nineteenth century that restored a ferocity to warfare unknown since the seventeenth century. And even when modern liberal democracies go to war they do not necessarily moderate the scope of the violence they apply; indeed, sensitivity to their own casualties sometimes leads to profligate uses of firepower or violent efforts to end wars quickly. Shaky democracies fight each other all the time. . . . We must remind ourselves just how peculiar the wealthy and secure democracies of the [Global North] are and how painful their evolution to stability and the horror of war with each other has been. (E. Cohen 1998, 39)

In 2008 the fragility of democratic institutions was illustrated by the sham election of President Mugabe in Zimbabwe, the military coup in Mauritania that ousted the country's first freely elected president, and the token parliamentary election that allowed former Russian president Vladimir Putin to retain power after being appointed Prime Minister.

Nationalism   *Nationalism*—love of and loyalty to a nation—is widely believed to be the cauldron from which wars often spring (Van Evera 1994). "The tendency of the vast majority of people to center their supreme loyalties on the nation-state," Jack Levy explains, is a powerful catalyst to war. When people "acquire an intense commitment to the power and prosperity of the state [and] this commitment is strengthened by national myths emphasizing the moral, physical, and political

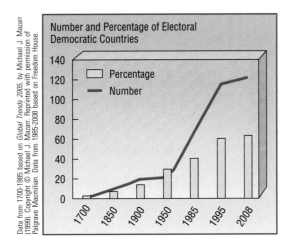

Data from 1700-1985 based on *Global Trends 2005*, by Michael J. Mazarr (1999). Copyright © Michael J. Mazarr. Reprinted with permission of Palgrave Macmillan. Data from 1985-2008 based on Freedom House.

FIGURE 13.3

THE ADVANCE OF ELECTORAL DEMOCRACY, 1700–2008 **For 250 years since 1700, most choices about war were made by monarchs, despots, dictators, and autocrats. That has changed in a major global** *transformation,* **occurring in three "waves" in the growth of "electoral democracy" worldwide, with competitive and regular multi-party elections conducted openly without massive voting fraud (see Cederman and Gleditsch 2004), as this figure shows. In 1974 only one in four countries were electoral democracies; today, the number has grown to 121 countries, or 62 percent (Freedom House 2008). Whether this dramatic transformation will produce peace is being tested.**

strength of the state and by individuals' feelings of powerlessness and their consequent tendency to seek their identity and fulfillment through the state, . . . nationalism contributes to war" (Levy 1989a).

The connection between nationalism and war has a long history. It began as a serious force in Europe three-hundred and fifty years ago when monarchical rulers such as Ferdinand and Isabella of Spain engaged in "state building" by forcibly constructing nationalism to mobilize and manage the population, which bred religious and political intolerance, the repression of minorities, and war (Marx 2003). The linkage between nationalism and war has since grown over time (Woodwell 2008).

The English essayist Aldous Huxley saw nationalism as "the religion of the twentieth century"—when history's most destructive interstate wars were fought. This leads many to critique nationalism, although many defend it as a virtue that makes for unity and solidarity within a country (see Controversy: Does Nationalistic Love of Country Cause War with Foreign Nations?). Whatever its consequences, nationalism is widely seen as perhaps the most powerful force in today's world, an idea and *ideology* that animates the constructed images of many. This is why many behavioral social scientists (recall Chapter 2) conclude that nationalistic sentiments promote the outbreak of war.

CONTROVERSY:

DOES NATIONALISTIC LOVE OF COUNTRY CAUSE WAR WITH FOREIGN NATIONS?

What does *patriotism* mean? The most familiar definition is popularly expressed as "love for one's country." Often, it involves "love for the nation or nationality of the people living in a particular state," especially when the population of that state primarily comprises a single ethnonational racial or linguistic group.

Because "love" for valued objects of affection, such as a person's homeland, is widely seen as a virtue, it is understandable why governments everywhere teach young citizens that love for country is a moral duty—it fosters a sense of political community. Nationalism encourages internal harmony and political stability, thereby making a positive contribution to civic solidarity and domestic peace. Though based on a sense of selective altruism, nationalism is credited with creating wealth, fighting corruption, and reducing crime (de las Casas 2008). On these grounds, nationalism is not controversial.

However, critics of nationalism find patriotism to be potentially dangerous in its extreme form. Superpatriots, these critics warn, are hypernationalists who measure their patriotism by the degree of hatred and opposition exhibited toward foreign countries and by the blind approval of every policy and practice of the "patriot's" own country. In this sense, nationalistic patriotism can ignore transcendent moral principles such as love for all humanity (Etzioni 2005). Nationalism rejects *cosmopolitan values* that put the interests of all above the interests of a national subgroup and is seen as an obstacle to human rights and international harmony in a borderless world (O'Sullivan 2005; Grosby 2006). And nationalism runs counter to the admonition that love should be extended even toward one's enemies, as preached by Jesus Christ in the Sermon on the Mount and other religious leaders such as Muhammad, the founder of Islam, and the legendary King Solomon in Judaism. If so, then is nationalistic superpatriotism sometimes a cause of war between nations? What do you think?

Contemplate your opinion about this controversial issue over values—about whether nationalism and cosmopolitan globalism are mutually exclusive and whether nationalism creates war by undermining justice under law for the world. Take into consideration the view of Karl Deutsch, a German-born immigrant to the United States and famous scholar who taught for many years at Harvard University. Deutsch, an authority on nationalism, described nationalism's linkage to armed conflict in these moving words:

> *Nationalism* is an attitude of mind, a pattern of attention and desires. It arises in response to a condition of society and to a particular stage in its development. It is a predisposition to pay far more attention to messages about one's own people, or to messages from its members, than to messages from or about any other people. At the same time, it is a desire to have one's own people get any and all values that are available. The extreme nationalist wants his people to have all the power, all the wealth, and all the well-being for which there is any competition. He wants his people to command all the respect and deference from others; he tends to claim all rectitude and virtue for it, as well as all enlightenment and skill; and he gives it a monopoly of his affection. In short, he totally identifies himself with his nation. Though he may be willing to sacrifice himself for it, his nationalism is a form of egotism written large. . . .
>
> Even if most people are not extreme nationalists, nationalism has altered the world in many ways. Nationalism has not only increased the number of countries on the face of the earth, it has helped to diminish the number of its inhabitants. All major wars in the twentieth century [were] fought in its name. . . .
>
> Nationalism is in potential conflict with all philosophies or religions—such as Christianity—which teach universal standards of truth and of right and wrong, regardless of nation, race, or tribe. Early in the nineteenth century a gallant American naval officer, Stephen Decatur, proposed the toast, "Our country! In her intercourse

with foreign nations, may she be always in the right, but our country, right or wrong." Nearly one hundred and fifty years later the United States Third Army, marching into Germany following the collapse of the Nazi regime, liberated the huge concentration camp at Buchenwald. Over the main entrance to that place of torture and death, the Nazi elite guard had thoughtfully written, "My Country, Right or Wrong." (Deutsch 1974, 124–25)

In confronting the impact of nationalism on armed conflict, we need to recognize its dual character. It is a force that (1) binds nations and nationalities together in common bonds and (2) divides nation against nation, nationality against nationality, and is used to justify armed conflicts against other countries. Whatever the form and impact of nationalism on world politics, there is one certainty—nationalism "will continue to shape the world in the twenty-first century" (Muller 2008, 20).

NATIONALISM'S DARK AND DEADLY PAST Under the fascist dictatorship of Adolf Hitler (left) the Nazi government glorified the state and claimed that the German people were a superior race. What followed from this extreme form of nationalism was a ruthless German world war and campaign of genocide that exterminated six million Jews and other ethnic minorities. U.S. troops under the command of General George Patton (right) liberated the concentration camp at Buchenwald in May 1945, but not in time to save the lives of the prisoners whom the Nazi guards had put to death in the gas chambers.

Most armed conflicts today are fed by nationalist sentiments and the threat of nationalism to world order could escalate. Former Soviet President Mikhail Gorbachev has warned that "the demons of nationalism are coming alive again, and they are putting the stability of the international system to the test. Even the United States itself is not immune from dangerous nationalism."

This discussion of the characteristics of states that influence their proclivity for war does not exhaust the subject. Many other potential causes internal to the state exist. But, however important domestic influences might be as a source of war, many believe that the nature of the *global system* is even more critical.

Militant ethnic nationalism is on the rise, transforming the healthy pride of nations, tribes, religions, and ethnic groups into cancerous prejudice, eating away at states and leaving their people addicted to the political painkillers of violence and demagoguery.

—Bill Clinton, U.S. President

The Third Level of Analysis: Cycles of War and Peace in the Global System

Realism emphasizes that the roots of armed conflict rest in human nature. In contrast, *neorealism* sees war springing from changes at the global level of analysis, that is, as a product of the decentralized character of the global system that requires sovereign states to rely on *self-help* for their security:

> Although different realist theories often generate conflicting predictions, they share a core of common assumptions: The key actors in world politics are sovereign states that act rationally to advance their security, power, and wealth in a conflictual international system that lacks a legitimate governmental authority to regulate conflicts or enforce agreements.
>
> For realists, wars can occur not only because some states prefer war to peace, but also because of unintended consequences of actions by those who prefer peace to war and are more interested in preserving their position than in enhancing it. Even defensively motivated efforts by states to provide for their own security through armaments, alliances, and deterrent threats are often perceived as threatening and lead to counteractions and conflict spirals that are difficult to reverse. This is the **security dilemma**—the possibility that a state's actions to provide for its security may result in a decrease in the security of all states, including itself. (Levy 1998b, 145)

■ **security dilemma**

the tendency of states to view the defensive arming of adversaries as threatening, causing them to arm in response, so that all states' security declines.

International *anarchy* or the absence of institutions for global governance may promote war's outbreak. However, anarchy fails to provide a complete explanation of changes in the levels of war and peace over time or why particular wars are fought. To capture war's many global determinants, consider also how and why global systems change. This requires exploring the impact of such global factors as the distribution of military capabilities, balances (and imbalances) of power, the number of alliances and international organizations, and the rules of international law. At issue is how the system's characteristics and institutions combine to influence changes in war's frequency. You can examine many of these factors in Chapters 15, 16, and 17. Here you can focus on cycles of war and peace at the global level.

Whenever and wherever the anarchy of armed states exists, war does become inevitable.

—G. Lowes Dickinson, English philosopher

Does Violence Breed Violence? Many interpreters of world history have noted that the seeds of future wars are often found in past wars (see Walter 2004). For example, World War II was an outgrowth of World War I, the U.S. attack of Iraq in 2003 was an extension of the 1990 Persian Gulf War, and the successive waves of terrorism and war in the Middle East were little more than one war, with each battle stimulated by its predecessor. Because the frequency of past wars is correlated with the incidence of wars in later periods, war appears to be contagious and its future

> *Violence only begets conditions that beget future violence.*
>
> —U.S. President Jimmy Carter, acceptance speech
> of the 2002 Nobel Peace Prize

outbreak inevitable. If so, then something within the dynamics of global politics—its anarchical nature, its weak legal system, its uneven distribution of power, inevitable destabilizing changes in the principal actors' relative power, or some combination of structural attributes—makes the global system centered on states a war system.

Those believing in war's inevitability often cite the historical fact that war has been so repetitive. As 2008 began, all the active thirty-two armed aggressions "had a history, many of them a long one. In such entrenched conflicts, the warring parties are more likely to show little interest in negotiation" (Harbom and Wallensteen 2007, 625). However, it is not safe to infer that past wars *cause* later wars. The fact that a war precedes a later one does not mean that it caused the one that followed. Thus, many scholars reject the deterministic view that history is destiny, with outcomes caused by previous events. Instead, they embrace the **bargaining model of war**, which sees war as a product of *rational choice* weighing anticipated costs against benefits. The decision to engage in warfare is part of the bargaining process that occurs between adversaries to settle disputes and disagreements "over scarce goods, such as the placement of a border, the composition of a national government, or control over national resources" (Reiter 2003; see also Filson and Werner 2002; Smith and Stam 2004).

■ **bargaining model of war**

an interpretation of war's onset as a choice by the initiator to bargain through aggression with an enemy in order to win on an issue or to obtain things of value, such as territory or oil.

War's recurrence throughout history does not necessarily mean we will always have it. War is not a universal institution; some societies have never known war and others have been immune to it for prolonged periods. Moreover, since 1945 the outbreak of armed aggression *between* states has greatly declined, despite the large increase in the number of independent countries. This indicates that armed conflict is not necessarily inevitable and that historical forces do not control people's freedom of choice or experiences.

Power Transitions These trends notwithstanding, when changes have occurred in the major states' military capabilities, war has often resulted. Although not inevitable, war has been likely whenever competitive states' power ratios (the differentials between their capabilities) have narrowed. As Monica Toft (2007) concludes "Peace is clearly a value most states share, but not always, and not always above all other values. . . . Shifts in the distribution of power go a long way toward explaining the likelihood of violence."

■ power transition theory

the theory that war is likely when a dominant great power is threatened by the rapid growth of a rival's capabilities, which reduces the difference in their relative power.

This hypothesis is known as the **power transition theory**. This theoretical explanation of armed aggression is a central tenant of *structural realism*—the neorealist theory that emphasizes that changes in the great powers military capabilities relative to their closest rivals is a key determinant of the behavior of states within the global system and of the probability of warfare (see Palmer and Morgan 2007, Zagare 2007). The theory posits that:

> an even distribution of political, economic, and military capabilities between contending groups of states is likely to increase the probability of war; peace is preserved best when there is an imbalance of national capabilities between disadvantaged and advantaged nations; the aggressor will come from a small group of dissatisfied strong countries; and it is the weaker, rather than the stronger, power that is most likely to be the aggressor. (Organski and Kugler 1980, 19)

During the transition from developing to developed status, emergent challengers can achieve through force the recognition that their newly formed military muscles allow them. Conversely, established powers ruled by risk-acceptant leaders are often willing to employ force to put the brakes on their relative decline. Thus, when advancing and retreating states seek to cope with the changes in their relative power, war between the rising challenger(s) and the declining power(s) has become especially likely. For example, the rapid changes in the power and status that produced the division of Europe among seven great powers nearly equal in military strength are often (along with the alliances they nurtured) interpreted as the tinderbox from which World War I ignited.

Rapid shifts in the global distribution of military power *have* often preceded outbursts of aggression, especially when the new distribution nears approximate equality and thereby tempts the rivals to wage war against their hegemonic challengers. According to the power transition theory, periods in which rivals' military capabilities are nearly balanced create "the necessary conditions for global war, while gross inequality assures peace or, in the worst case, an asymmetric, limited war" (Kugler 2001). Moreover, transitions in states' relative capabilities can potentially lead the weaker party to start a war in order to either overtake its rival or protect itself from domination. Presumably, the uncertainty created by a rough equilibrium prompts the challenger's (usually unsuccessful) effort to wage war against a stronger opponent. Equally persistent is the power transition theory's observation that advantages have shifted from the attacker to the defender: "In earlier centuries the aggressor seemed to have a 50–50 chance of winning the war, but this no longer holds. The chances of the starter being victorious are shrinking. In the 1980s only 18 percent of the starters were winners" (Sivard 1991, 20). As in the past (e.g., Japan's attack and subjugation of China in 1931 and 1937), there are notable exceptions where the initiator had advantages (such as the Vietnam, the Six-Day, Bangladesh, Yom Kippur/Ramadan, Falklands, and Persian Gulf wars).

Cyclical Theories   If war is recurrent but not necessarily inevitable, are there other global factors besides power transitions that might also explain changes over time in its outbreak? The absence of a clear trend in its frequency since the late fifteenth century, and its periodic outbreak after intermittent stretches of peace, suggest that world history seesaws between long cycles of war and peace. This provides a third global explanation of war's onset.

The more recent formal analysis of such cycles is known as *long-cycle theory*. As noted in Chapter 4, its advocates argue that cycles of world leadership and global war have existed over the past five centuries, with a "general war" erupting approximately once every century, although at irregular intervals (Hopkins and Wallerstein 1996; Wallerstein 2005; Modelski 1987b; Modelski and Thompson 1996). Long-cycle theory seeks to explain how an all-powerful invisible hand built into the global system's dynamics causes such peaks and valleys in the frequency with which major wars have erupted periodically throughout modern history.

Long-cycle theory draws its insights from the observation that a great power has risen to a hegemonic position about every eighty to one hundred years. Using as a measure of dominance the possession of disproportionate sea power, we observe the rise of a single hegemon regularly appearing after particular hegemonic wars (see Figure 13.4). Portugal and the Netherlands rose at the beginning of the sixteenth and seventeenth centuries, respectively; Britain climbed to dominance at the beginning of both the eighteenth and nineteenth centuries; and the United States became a world leader at the end of World War II and regained its position of global supremacy after the Cold War ended in 1991.

During their reigns, these hegemonic powers monopolized military power and trade and determined the system's rules. Yet no previous hegemonic power has retained its top-dog position perpetually (see Table 4.1, pp. 88–89). In each cycle, over-commitments, the costs of empire, and ultimately the appearance of rivals led to the delegitimation of the hegemon's authority and to the deconcentration of power globally. As challengers to the hegemon's rule grew in strength, a "global war" has

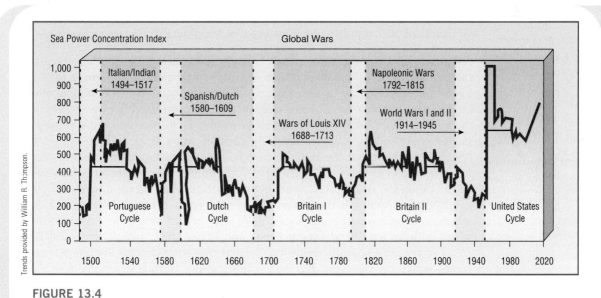

FIGURE 13.4

THE LONG CYCLE OF GLOBAL LEADERSHIP AND GLOBAL WAR, 1494–2020 **Over the past five hundred years, five great powers have risen to control the global system, but in time each former hegemonic leader's top status eventually slipped and a new rival surfaced and waged a global war in an effort to become the next global leader. The troubling question is whether this long cycle of war can be broken in the future when U.S. leadership is eventually challenged by a rising military rival such as China.**

erupted after a long period of peace in each century since 1400. At the conclusion of each previous general war, a new world leader emerged dominant, and the cyclical process began anew. As Brock Tessman and Steve Chan summarize and explain:

> The theory of power cycles contends that the growth and decline of national power holds the key to understanding the occurrence of extensive wars. Certain critical points in a state's power trajectory are especially dangerous occasions for such armed clashes [from which we can] derive expectations about the risk propensity of states during different periods in their power cycle. . . . Critical points tend to incline states to initiate deterrence confrontations and escalate them to war. . . . Changes in national power tend to follow a regular pattern of ascendance, maturation, and decline and . . . these trajectories reflect the major states' relative competitiveness in the international system. When these states encounter an unexpected reversal in the direction or rate of change in their power trajectory, they are subject to various psychological impulses or judgmental challenges that increase the danger of extensive wars. The larger the number of major states that find themselves under the duress of such reversals, the greater the tendency for *their disputes to become extensive wars*. (Tessman and Chan 2004, 131)

Such deterministic theories have intuitive appeal. It seems plausible, for instance, that just as long-term downswings and recoveries in business cycles profoundly affect subsequent behaviors and conditions, wars will produce aftereffects that may last for generations. The idea that a country at war will become exhausted and lose its enthusiasm for another war, but only for a time, is known as the **war weariness hypothesis** (Blainey 1988). The Italian historian Luigi da Porto expresses one version: "Peace brings riches; riches bring pride; pride brings anger; anger brings war; war brings poverty; poverty brings humanity; humanity brings peace; peace, as I have said, brings riches, and so the world's affairs go round." Because it takes time to move through these stages, alternating periods of enthusiasm for war and weariness of war appear to be influenced by learning and forgetting over time.

A true test for the presence of a cycle in major war outbreaks is difficult because of the increase in states' numbers over time, from about twenty-five during the 1816–1848 Concert of Europe to more than two hundred today. The ballooning number of independent states in the global system increases the probability of wars. However, the number of interstate wars between 1816 and 1990 has been fairly stable. This suggests that there is *not* a clear cycle operative in war's onset, and, given that, there is reason to doubt that the global system has properties that automatically produce recurrent cycles in wars (J. Singer 1981). The trends suggest, rather, that since the 1815 Congress of Vienna, war between states has been underway almost continuously. Although there were eighty-two years between 1816 and 1990 in which no new interstate wars began, there were in that period only twenty years in which no wars were being fought (Small and Singer 1982, 149; J. Singer 1991, 60–75). The available scientific evidence "suggests not so much that discrete wars come and go with some regularity, but that, with some level of such violence almost always present, there may be certain periodic fluctuations in the amount of that violence" (Small and Singer 1982). This characteristic draws attention to an abrupt recent development: since 1990 war *between* states has nearly disappeared from the global scene. As 2008 began, of the thirty-two armed conflicts underway, only seven were interstate wars and only six of these were civil wars internationalized by foreign troops sent to support one of the warring parties (Harbom and Wallensteen 2007, 623). Today civil wars dominate the global arena.

■ **war weariness hypothesis**

the proposition that fighting a major war is costly in terms of lost lives and income, and these costs greatly reduce a country's tolerance for undertaking another war until enough time passes to lose memory of those costs.

ARMED AGGRESSION AND ITS FUTURE

You have now inspected three trends in the major types of armed aggression in the world: wars between states, civil wars within states, and global terrorism. Some of these trends, you have noticed, are promising. War between states is disappearing, and this inspires hope among optimists that it will vanish from human history.

> *War may well be ceasing to commend itself to human beings as a desirable or productive, let alone rational, means of reconciling their discontents. Unlike breathing, eating or sex, war is not something that is somehow required by the human condition or by the forces of history. Accordingly, war can shrivel up and disappear, and it seems to be in the process of doing so.*
>
> —John Mueller, the Woody Hayes Chair of National Security Studies at the Ohio State University

However, that threat remains, and because another major war between states could occur again, all of humanity is endangered. War inside states is increasing in frequency and death rates, and this trend in the growth and expansion of civil wars threatens everyone in the borderless globalized world. And, of course, the specter of international terrorism casts a very dark shadow over the world's future.

There is no sure guide to what the future will hold. But the sad news is that your life and livelihood are certain to be threatened by the continuing onset of armed aggression. That threat imperils the future as does the threat of environmental destruction facing planet Earth (Chapter 12). And the threat of armed aggression affects *all* other aspects of world politics, which is why much of world history is written about its causes and consequences from the vantage point of all peoples' and professions' perspectives. As the British poet Percy B. Shelley framed it:

War is the statesman's game, the priest's delight,
The lawyer's jest, the hired assassin's trade,
And, to those royal murderers, whose mean thrones
Are brought by crimes of treachery and gore,
The bread they eat, the staff on which they lean.

You also have been given the opportunity to examine the many leading causes of armed aggression that theorists have constructed to explain why armed aggression in its various forms erupts. These rival theories of causation also can be harnessed to develop possible cures for the contagion. The correlates of war also speak to the correlates of peace.

> *Of war men ask the outcome, not the cause.*
>
> —Lucius Annaeus Seneca , Roman statesman and philosopher in the first century CE

It is the alternative potential paths to peace, security, and world order that you will next consider. In Part V, you will look at the rival ideas presented in the realist road to national and international security, and in Part VI you will look at the liberal paths to peace. Both theoretical traditions speak to each other because they are forced to be in conversation with each other as theorists grapple with the challenge of finding solutions to the threat of armed aggression.

> *Peace, like war, can succeed only where there is a will to enforce it and where there is available power to enforce it.*
> —Franklin D. Roosevelt, U.S. President

Because the world future depends on traveling both of these twin routes, we turn next to examine the vision realism advances about dealing with the threat of war.

Key Terms

war
conflict
armed aggression
long peace
civil wars
enduring internal rivalry (EIR)
state-sponsored terrorism
diversionary theory of war
asymmetric warfare
information warfare

Bush Doctrine
intraspecific aggression
interspecific aggression
pacifism
survival of the fittest
nature versus nurture
socialization
territorial imperative
national character
ecological fallacy

individualistic fallacy
cultural conditioning
relative deprivation
communist theory of imperialism
security dilemma
bargaining model of war
power transition theory
war weariness hypothesis

CORBIS

WEAPONS FOR WAR AND PEACE. Shown here is a U.S. test of a nuclear bomb in 1954, when only the United States and the Soviet Union had nuclear capabilities. Today the capacity to wage war with weapons of mass destruction has spread to many countries, and the diffusion is transforming the global balance of power. What to do with such weapons for war and for peace is the central concern of realist theorizing, which looks on the acquisition of military power and its consequences as the most important dimension of world politics.

Part 5

REALIST ROADS TO NATIONAL AND
INTERNATIONAL SECURITY

"If you want peace, prepare for war."

— *Flavius Vegetius Renatus, General in the Roman Empire*

WHEN YOU THINK ABOUT WORLD POLITICS, WHAT IS THE FIRST IMAGE THAT RACES TO YOUR MIND? For many people, world politics is about arms, armies, alliances, military power, and the exercise by military means of political influence over rivals and other actors on the global stage. Indeed, many people equate world politics with war and its threat to their nation, city, and the world at large. This preoccupation is as old as recorded history itself. And for understandable reasons: An attack by an enemy is the most dangerous direct threat to survival, and preventing such death and destruction is a precondition for the attainment of all other important values, such as food, water, freedom and the possession of a territory on which to live safely and without foreign domination.

It is the theoretical traditions of *realism*, and now, *neorealism*, that speak most directly to the problems of military power in international politics—to the opportunities they create for those who have attained advantages in military capabilities and to the dangers and vulnerabilities weapons create when their rivals and enemies possess superior military capabilities. In this part, you will have the opportunity to explore the many contending ideas about military power that realist theories advance. In Chapter 14, the pursuit of national interest defined in terms of military power is examined through the lens of realist approaches to national and international security. The place of power in international politics, the factors believed important to contribute to power, and the changing character of power are examined. Also provided are surveys of trends in rates of national and global military spending, trends in the arms trade across borders, and trends in the various types of weapons technology. This sets the stage for your consideration of alternative military strategies and different military methods of coercive diplomacy (such as military intervention). Chapter 15 provides an overview of the various roles that realists envision for alliances in international politics, including the attractive purposes that realists ascribe to alliances as a method for increasing the power of a state against its competitors and their allies, as well as an account of the risk and costs that realists warn can result from the formation of alliances. The impact of alliance formation and disintegration on the shifting balance of global power, in the past, today, and in the future is also examined, again through the theoretical viewpoint of realist thinking about these subjects. The entire discussions are nested within the larger range of thinking that realist theory provides about the preconditions for and obstacles to national and international security.

CHAPTER 14
THE MILITARY PURSUIT OF POWER THROUGH ARMS AND MILITARY STRATEGY

The adversaries of the world are not in conflict because they are armed. They are armed because they are in conflict and have not yet learned peaceful ways to resolve their conflicting interests.

— *Richard M. Nixon, U.S. President*

AP Photo

Bullets and Bombs to Bully. Throughout history, countries have been beguiled by bombs as a method for backing their enemies into surrender. Realists regard the prudent use of armed force as a powerful instrument for waging war and projecting military power in world politics. Shown here is one example: the use of air power to compel an adversary without waging a ground war. This method was successfully used by the United States and NATO against Serbia in 1999 and unsuccessfully by Israel in its 2006 war against Hezbollah terrorists in Lebanon.

I magine yourself someday becoming the next Secretary-General of the United Nations. You would face the awesome responsibility for fulfilling the UN's Charter to preserve world peace. But looking at the globe, you would likely see that many countries are experiencing armed aggression, and that those wars are highly destructive of life and property. Moreover, you undoubtedly would be distressed by the fact that many countries and possibly some transnational terrorist groups now have the capacity to annihilate their enemies with new weapons of mass destruction. And you shudder at the realization that many states are living in constant fear of threats to their security while at the same time these armed actors are increasing the military power in their arsenals.

As a result of the escalating destructive power of modern weapons, you cannot help but to wonder about a globe in which the UN members that are most feverishly arming to increase their capacity to resist external and internal threats to their physical survival and core values are the same countries whose *national security* or psychological freedom from fear of foreign aggression seems to be the most rapidly declining. Taking a picture of the pregnant fears circulating the globe, you conclude that as a consequence a true *security dilemma* has been created: The armaments amassed by each state for what they claim to be defensive purposes is seen by others as threatening, and this has driven the alarmed competitors to undertake, as counter-measures, additional military buildups—with the result that the arming states' insecurities are increasing even though their arms are increasing. What course should you counsel the UN's members to pursue in order to escape the dilemma of rising insecurity in which they have imprisoned themselves?

Alas, your options may be limited and your advice ignored. Why? Because when the topic of war and peace is debated, and in periods when international tension is high, policy makers (and theorists) turn to realist theory for guidance.

REALIST APPROACHES TO WAR AND PEACE

Nearly all states continue to conclude that the anarchical global system requires them, of necessity, to rely on *self-help* to depend only on themselves for security.

They have been schooled in the lessons constructed from *realism*—the school of thought that teaches that the drive for power and the domination of others for self-advantage is a universal and permanent motive throughout world history. For this reason, most states follow the realist roads to national and international security. This worldview or *paradigm* for organizing perceptions pictures the available and practical choices for states primarily among three, time-honored options: (1) arming themselves, (2) forming or severing alliances with other countries, or (3) constructing strategies for controlling their destinies through military approaches and *coercive diplomacy* such as acts of military intervention that target their enemies.

In this chapter, you will explore states' efforts to follow the realist recipes for reducing threats to their national security. It introduces the major trends in military spending, the arms trade, and weapons technology that countries are relying on to militarily exercise influence and deter attacks from potential enemies.

The place to begin is to underscore the high place of *power* that realists put in the equation that they believe has, throughout history, driven world politics. National security is truly a paramount priority for the policy makers responsible for constructing their country's foreign policy agendas. Because the threat of armed aggression is ever present, realism recommends that war be placed at the very top of a state's concerns, and that to contain dangers the pursuit of power must be prioritized above all others. As Table 14.1 demonstrates, this emphasis is part and parcel of a much broader range of foreign policy recommendations realists embrace to chart what this theoretical tradition believes to be the safest routes to national and international security. Keep this larger menu for choice and the premises on which it rests in mind as you consider the military methods that realists emphasize in this chapter (and the premium adherence that realists place on alliances and the balance of power considered in Chapter 15).

Table 14.1 Realist Roads to Security: Policy Recommendations and Premises

Realist Policy Prescriptions	Premises
Prepare for war:	If you want peace, prepare for war.
Remain vigilant:	No state is to be trusted further than its national interest.
Avoid moralism:	Standards of right and wrong apply to individuals but not states; in world affairs amoral actions are sometimes necessary for security.
Remain involved and actively intervene:	Isolationism is not an alternative to active global involvement.
Protect with arms:	Strive to increase military capabilities and fight rather than submit to subordination.
Preserve the balance of power:	Do not let any other state or coalition of states become predominant.
Prevent arms races from resulting in military inferiority with rivals:	Negotiate agreements with competitors to maintain a favorable military balance.
The Realist Picture of the Global Environment	
Primary global condition:	Anarchy; or the absence of authoritative governing institutions
Probability of system change/reform:	Low, except in response to extraordinary events such as 9/11

(continues)

Table 14.1 Realist Roads to Security: Policy Recommendations and Premises *(continued)*

The Realist Picture of the Global Environment	
Primary transnational actors:	States, and especially great powers
Principal actor goals:	Power over others, self-preservation, and physical security
Predominant pattern of actor interaction:	Competition and conflict
Pervasive concern:	National security
Prevalent state priorities:	Acquiring military capabilities
Popular state practice:	Use of armed force for coercive diplomacy

POWER IN WORLD POLITICS

Realist theorists far back in antiquity have based their thinking and policy recommendations on the belief that all people and states seek power. This is understandable, because as the Bible observes and warns, people seem born to sin, and one of their inalterable compulsions is the drive for power to dominate those with whom they come into contact. That said, this abstraction called *power,* which realists assume to be humans' and states' primary objective, defies precise definition. Constructivists recognize that in the broadest sense power is usually interpreted as the political capacity of one actor to exercise influence over another actor to the first actor's benefit.

Most leaders follow *realpolitik* and operate from the traditional construction that conceives of power as a combination of factors that give states the capability to promote national interests, to win in international bargaining, and to shape the rules governing interaction in the global system. However, beyond the semantic definition of power as *politics*—the exercise of influence to control others—power is an ambiguous concept (see Claude 1962; Kadera and Sorokin 2004), and difficult to measure. A dictionary definition begs the question: What factors most enable an actor to control or coerce another?

If we view power as the means to control when *conflict* or disputes over incompatible interests occur, it is reasonable to ask: Who is stronger and who is weaker? The answer to this question may predict which party will get its way and which will be forced to make concessions. These considerations invite the more fundamental question, "What empowers states to achieve their goals?"

The Elements of State Power

To estimate the comparative power of states, analysts usually rank countries according to the capabilities or resources presumed necessary to achieve influence over others. For such purposes, multiple factors (most significantly, military and economic capability) measure countries' relative **power potential**. If we could compare each state's total capabilities, according to this logic, we could then rank them by their relative ability to draw on these resources to exercise influence. Such a ranking would reveal the global system's hierarchy of power, differentiating the strong from the weak, the great from the marginal.

■ **power potential**

the capabilities or resources held by a state that are considered necessary to its asserting influence over others.

> *Throughout history, the decisive factor in the fates of nations has usually been the number, efficiency, and dispositions of fighting forces. Military influence bears a direct relationship to gross national strength; without that, the most exquisite statesmanship is likely to be of limited use.*
>
> —F. Clifton German, social scientist

Of all the components of state power potential, realists see military capability as the central element. Realist theory maintains that the ability to coerce militarily is more important than the ability to reward favors or to buy concessions. Realists therefore reject the view of neoliberal strategic thinkers who maintain that under conditions of *globalization* linking countries economically, politically, and culturally in webs of interdependence, economic resources are increasingly more critical to national strength and security than are military capabilities (Nye 2008).

Following traditional thinking, one way to estimate the power potential of states is to compare the extent to which they spend money on acquiring military capabilities. On this index, the United States is the undisputed military powerhouse in the world, spending for defense at a feverish pace that is leaving all other countries far behind. Figure 14.1 shows the trend in U.S. defense budgets over six decades that has made America unsurpassed in military spending: "The USA's military spending accounted for 45 percent of the world total in 2007, followed by the UK, China, France and Japan, with 4–5 percent each" (SIPRI 2008, 10).

Money is not the measure of a person or of a country. Yes, a state can try to spend without apparent concern for costs in an effort to reach the elusive goal of obtaining complete national security. But there is never a guarantee that bucks will translate into bangs. In the U.S. case, it is uncertain whether the White House base budget of $515.4 *billion* for military spending in 2009, an increase of almost 74% since 2001 (www. whitehouse.gov, December 9, 2008), will automatically increase U.S. security or reach the fighting men and women in the field. The size of the defense budget is not as important as how wisely it is spent and whether it goes to the needs that really matter,

> *Power is nothing unless you can turn it into influence.*
>
> —Condoleezza Rice, former U.S. Secretary of State

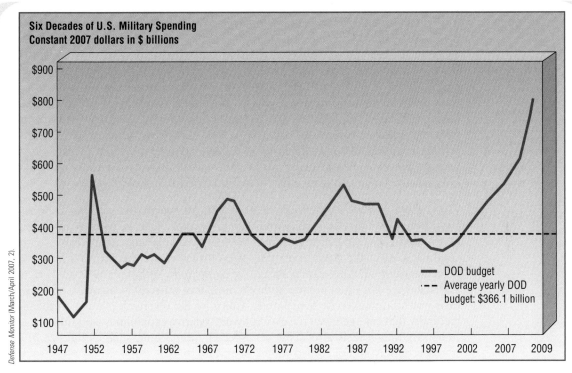

Six Decades of U.S. Military Spending
Constant 2007 dollars in $ billions

— DOD budget
- - - Average yearly DOD
budget: $366.1 billion

Defense Monitor (March/April 2007, 2).

FIGURE 14.1

SIX DECADES OF U.S. MILITARY SPENDING **America's military expenditures have been rising rapidly since 2001, putting the United States far ahead of all other powers. This commitment to militarization is the principle reason the United States is regarded as a true hegemonic superpower, without rival. "Since 2001 US military expenditure has increased by 59 percent in real terms, principally because of massive spending on military operations in Afghanistan and Iraq, but also because of increases in the 'base' defence budget (SIPRI 2008, 10). In 2009, U.S. military spending is scheduled to climb again, and includes over $515 billion in base budget expenditures plus billions more in supplemental appropriations for the war in Iraq and Afghanistan plus security-related spending for such programs as Homeland Security, foreign military aid, and international peacekeeping.**

such as protecting citizens from terrorist attacks. For the United States, the issue is critical. What are the returns for the investment? It is estimated that it costs the average American household over $525 *each month* to finance war, and the U.S. $482 billion *increase* budgeted for military activities in 2009 exceeds the gross national income of ninety-eight of the globe's countries (WDI 2007, 14-16). These huge expenditures do not appear to be paying large dividends, especially in America's war on terrorism: the huge U.S. defense budget did not stem the number of attacks and deaths from terrorism; they rose almost 30 percent and 40 percent in 2007 above the levels in 2005 (NCTC 2008).

Power potential also derives from factors other than military expenditures. Among the so-called elements of power, analysts also consider such capabilities as the relative size of a state's economy, its population and territorial size, geographic position, raw materials, lack of dependence on foreign sources of materials, technological capacity, political culture and values, ideology, efficiency of governmental decision making, industrial productivity, volume of trade, savings and investment, educational level, national morale and internal solidarity, and especially "advances in technology and increases in social and economic transactions [that can] lead to a new world in which states, and their control of force, will no longer be important" (Keohane and Nye 2001b). For example, if power potential is measured by territorial size, Russia, twice as large as its closest rivals (Canada, China, the United States, Brazil, and Australia, in that order), would be the globe's most powerful country. Likewise, if power is measured by the UN's projections for countries' populations by the year 2025, China, India, the United States, Indonesia, Pakistan, Nigeria, and Brazil, in that order, would be the most powerful. In a similar comparison, the rankings of countries' expenditures on research and development (as a percentage of GDP) to fund future economic growth and military strength would rank Israel, Sweden, Finland, Japan, the United States, South Korea, Switzerland, Denmark, and Germany as the countries with the brightest future (WDI 2008, 312–314). Clearly, strength is relative. The leading countries in some dimensions of power potential are not leaders in others because power comes in many forms. The global spread of technology makes it increasingly difficult to distinguish between powerful and weak states.

Thus, there is little consensus on how best to weigh the various factors that contribute to military capability and national power. That is, there is no agreement as to what their relative importance should be in making comparisons, or what conditions affect the power potential of each factor (or whether total measures or percentages of GDP per capita should be compared). Although most analysts agree that states are not equal in their ability to influence others, few agree on how to rank their potential to exercise their power. Consider the divergent pictures of the global hierarchy that emerge when the great powers' relative capabilities are ranked in other categories that realists also define as especially important, such as the size of each state's economy and/or armed forces (see Map 14.1).

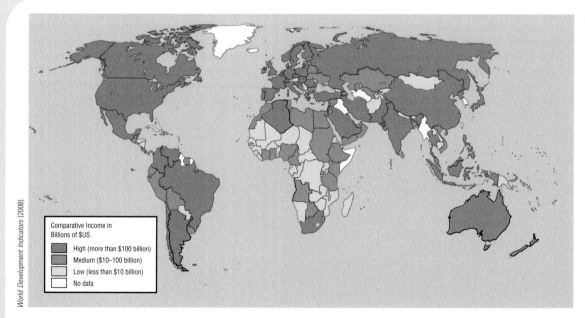

World Development Indicators (2008).

Comparative Income in
Billions of $US

- High (more than $100 billion)
- Medium ($10–100 billion)
- Low (less than $10 billion)
- No data

MAP 14.1

TWO MEASURES OF MILITARY POWER POTENTIAL: STATE WEALTH AND SIZE OF NATIONAL ARMIES **The map above measures gross national income (GNI) across countries to estimate the differences in national wealth that contribute to state power, and the distribution categorizes differences in the size of states' economies that separate the rich from the poor (and the strong from the weak). Another measure of power projection is the number of uniform personnel in states' armies, navies, and air forces. The map on the facing page classifies the varying size of each country's armed forces available for military operations.**

Distinguishing Power from Capabilities

Part of the difficulty of defining the elements of power is that their potential impact depends on the circumstances (in a bargaining situation between conflicting actors, for example) and especially on how leaders perceive those circumstances. Such judgments are subjective, as power ratios are not strictly products of measured capabilities. Perceptions also matter.

In addition, power is not a tangible commodity that states can acquire. It has meaning only in relative terms. Power is relational: A state can have power over some other actor only when it can prevail over that actor. Both actual and perceived strength determine who wins a political contest. To make a difference, an adversary must know its enemy's capabilities and its willingness to mobilize those capabilities for coercive purposes. Intentions—especially perceptions of them—are critically important when making threats. The mere possession of weapons does not increase a state's power if its adversaries do not believe it will use them or if they are willing to suffer huge damages to prevail.

Historically, those with the largest arsenals have not necessarily triumphed in political conflicts. Weaker states often successfully resist pressure from their military superiors. In fact, since 1950 weak states have won more than half of all *asymmetric wars* between belligerents of vastly unequal military strength. This is in part because the weaker party has a greater interest in surviving and that greater interest, not relative military capabilities, is the major deciding factor in wars between the strong and weak (Arreguín-Toft 2006).

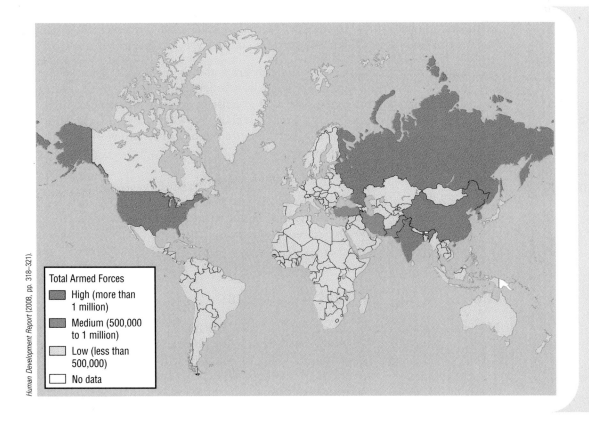

Human Development Report (2008, pp. 318–321).

Total Armed Forces
- High (more than 1 million)
- Medium (500,000 to 1 million)
- Low (less than 500,000)
- No data

There are many examples of weak transnational actors prevailing in armed conflicts with significantly stronger opponents. Although Vietnam was weak in the conventional military sense, it succeeded against a vastly stronger France and, later,

> *The basic presumption that power trumps all other factors in determining who is victorious in battle is historically untenable. With increasing frequency, the weak have been defeating the strong.*
>
> —Michael A. Jensen, political scientist

United States. Similarly, U.S. superior military power did not prevent North Korea's seizure of the USS *Pueblo* in 1968, Iran's taking of American diplomats as hostages a decade later, or the Al Qaeda terrorist network's 9/11 attack. Indeed, after June 2004, the capacity of a quasi-sovereign Iraq to move in directions that the U.S. superpower objected to but could not control underscored the weakness of superior military force in interstate bargaining (L. Diamond 2005). The Soviet Union's inability, prior to its disintegration, to control political events in Afghanistan, Eastern Europe, or even among its own constituent republics (despite an awesome weapons arsenal) shows that the impotence of military power is not particular to the United States. History is replete with examples of small countries that won wars or defended their independence against much more militarily powerful enemies. For example, in the seventeenth century think of Switzerland against the Hapsburg Empire, the Netherlands against Spain, and Greece against the Ottomans. In each case, intangible factors such as the will of the target population to resist a more powerful army and their willingness to die to defend the homeland were key elements in the capacity of each of these weaker countries to defend itself against a much stronger military force. Great Britain reluctantly recognized this factor in 1781 when it concluded that the price of reclaiming the far-weaker American colonies was too great.

■ **coercive diplomacy**

the use of threats or limited armed force to persuade an adversary to alter its foreign and/or domestic policies.

Nonetheless, the quest for security through arms and the realist belief in military force remain widespread. Most security analysts believe that this is because military capability is a prerequisite to the successful exercise of **coercive diplomacy** through the threat of limited force. Perhaps this conviction is what inspired former U.S. President George W. Bush to assert that "a dangerous and uncertain world requires America to have a sharpened sword."

> *While it could be a mistake to assume that political influence is proportional to military strength, it would be an even bigger mistake to deny any connection between the two.*
>
> —Akhtar Majeed, political analyst

The Changing Character of Power

Military power is central in leaders' concepts of national security. As noted in previous chapters, however, many analysts now argue that "the sources of power are, in general, moving away from the emphasis on military force and conquest that marked earlier eras. In assessing international power today, factors such as technology, external respect and reputation, education, and economic growth are becoming more important, whereas geography, population, and raw materials are becoming less important" (Nye 2008). In part, this shift is because military force has often proven ineffectual, notably against revisionist states and violent transnational terrorist groups resisting pressure from abroad. The usefulness of superior military capabilities is especially questionable in wars against mobilized terrorists energized to repel foreign occupation forces from their homeland; people will take up arms against an invading army, even when that army is larger and armed with vastly superior weapons. Arguably, intelligence and communications are more critical in fighting counterterrorism than our military capabilities. Moreover, awareness of trade competitiveness and environmental protection to national standing has directed increasing attention to the nonmilitary underpinnings of national security. In an era of globalization, many policy makers are coming to see policies emphasizing economics and trade as increasingly important to the acquisition of national power.

Trends in Military Spending

Even though the end of the Cold War reduced tensions worldwide and therefore the need for military preparations, world military spending has risen since 1998 by 45 percent, to $1,339 billion. This staggering all-time high is equal to 2.5 percent of global gross domestic product, or $202 for each person in the world (SIPRI 2008, 10). The world is spending over $190,000 each *minute* for military preparations.

Global military spending has increased 60 percent since 1960, and has been growing since 2001 at an average yearly rate of 5.4 percent (SIPRI 2007, 268). This growth rate exceeds that of world population, the rate of expansion of global economic output, and expenditures for public health to protect people from disease.

Historically, rich countries have spent the most money on arms acquisitions, and this pattern has continued. As 2008 began, the Global North was spending $1000 billion for defense, in contrast with the developing Global South's $204 billion. Thus, the high-income developed countries' share of the world total was about 85 percent. However, when measured against other factors, the differences became clearer. The Global North spent an average of 2 percent of their GDPs on weapons, whereas the Global South spent an average 2.5 percent (at a relatively greater sacrifice of funding needed to promote human development and economic growth among the poor where it is most needed (SIPRI 2007, 272).

In addition, these two groups' military spending levels are converging over time. Figure 14.2 reveals that the Global South's military expenditure in 1961 was about 7 percent of the world total, but by 2005 its share had more than tripled (SIPRI 2006, 326–327). This trend indicates that poor states are copying the past costly military budget habits of the wealthiest states.

Since 1945 only a handful of states have borne crushing military costs. The others have gained a relative competitive edge by investing in research on the development of goods to export abroad while conserving resources by relying on allies and global institutions to provide defense against potential threats. The United States is an exception. While accounting for 45 percent of world military expenditures in 2007, America spends most of its research and development funds on military preparations; in contrast, European countries invest heavily in the development of new technologies for consumers and civilians at home and abroad, and Japan

FIGURE 14.2

CHANGES IN THE LEVEL OF MILITARY EXPENDITURES SINCE 1960, GLOBAL NORTH AND GLOBAL SOUTH **Global military budgets have fluctuated since 1960, with total expenditures worldwide peaking in 1987, after which they fell about a third until the 9/11 terrorist attacks. As the trend shows, the military budget of the Global South's developing countries peaked in a 1982–1986 plateau, then declined before rising again to about 15 percent of the world total.**

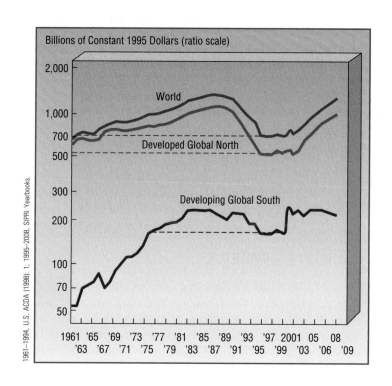

concentrates almost all its research expenditures on the development of products that have very little to do with military capabilities (SIPRI 2007). In comparative terms, the United States is slipping by not keeping up with its great power competitors and is now facing a "creativity crisis" (Florida 2007; Friedman 2005b) in education and science.

Military expenditures also incur other *opportunity costs*—when what is gained for one purpose is lost for other purposes—so that any particular choice means that the cost of some lost opportunity must be paid. Military spending, for example, retards economic growth and creates fiscal deficits. The substantial costs of defense can

> *States can afford more "butter" if they need fewer "guns."*
> *The two objectives sometimes represent trade-offs: The achievement*
> *of one may diminish the realization of the other.*
>
> —Richard Rosecrance, social scientist

erode national welfare—what policy makers hope to defend with military might. Conversely, commercial clout and trade competitiveness for national exports may contribute more than military might to national power in a globalized marketplace without barriers to trade. In that setting, trade bloc competition replaces the military and diplomatic struggles of the past (see Controversy: Does High Military Spending Lower Human Security?). In addition, "political leaders and philosophers have long understood that power comes from setting the agenda and determining the

> *The problem in defense spending is to figure out how far you should go without destroying from within what you are trying to defend from without.*
>
> —Dwight D. Eisenhower, U.S. President

framework of a debate. The ability to establish preferences tends to be associated with intangible power resources such as culture, ideology, and institutions" (Nye 2008). These intangible resources provide what is known as **soft power**—the ability to exercise international influence that is increased when a country's values and conduct are respected throughout the world. Unlike so-called **hard power** associated with military capabilities, soft power is "the ability to achieve goals through attraction rather than coercion . . . by convincing others to follow or getting them to agree to norms and institutions that produce the desired behavior" (Keohane and Nye 2001b). In today's so-called information age, the relative importance of soft power is growing.

■ **soft power**

the capacity to command global influence when a country's culture, ideas and institutions are valued by most other countries.

■ **hard power**

the ability to exercise international influence by means of a country's military capabilities.

CONTROVERSY:

DOES HIGH MILITARY SPENDING LOWER HUMAN SECURITY?

Politics requires making hard choices about priorities and about how public funds should be spent. One such difficult choice is between "guns versus butter"—how to allocate scarce finances for military preparedness as opposed to meeting the human needs of citizens and enabling them to live a secure and long life. The former category looks to arms for *national security,* and the latter stresses *human security.* Neither goal can be pursued without making some sacrifice for the realization of the other.

"Guns versus butter" is a serious controversy in every country, and different countries deal with it in different ways. That difference is captured by the range in states' willingness to pay a heavy burden for defense —by grouping states according to the share of gross domestic product (GDP) they devote to the military and then juxtaposing this relative burden with their GDP. The **relative burden of military spending**, the ratio of defense spending to GDP, is the customary way to measure the sacrifices required by military spending. The global trend shows that the share of resources used for military purposes has increased steadily since 2000, and, on average, the military burden now corresponds to 2.5 percent of world GDP (SIPRI 2008, 10). As the map shows, wide variations exist with many countries allocating high proportions of their total GDP to defense and others spending their wealth to enhance human security.

Indeed, some comparatively wealthy states (Kuwait, Israel, and Brunei) bear a heavy burden, whereas other states that provide a high average income for their citizens (Japan, Austria, and Luxembourg) have a low defense burden. Likewise, the citizens of some very poor countries (Sierra Leone, Mozambique, and Chad) are heavily burdened, whereas those of others (Bhutan and Zaire) are not. It is therefore difficult to generalize about the precise relationship between a country's defense burden and its citizens' standard of living, human development, or stage of development. That said, a simple look at this map reveals that the majority of the countries with the highest military burden are also the countries that are experiencing the highest levels of armed aggression, or are located in regions with huge security problems, such as the Middle East and Africa (recall Chapter 13).

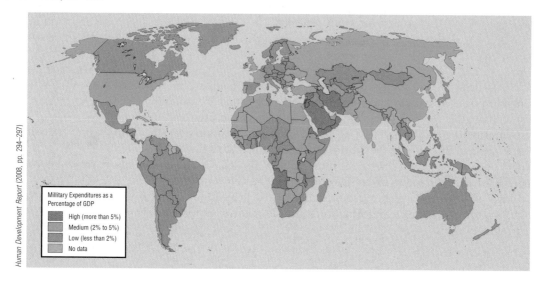

Human Development Report (2008, pp. 294–297)

How much should a country sacrifice for national security? To many realists, the price is never too high. However, others caution that leaders should take heed of U.S. President Dwight Eisenhower's warning: "The world in arms is not spending money alone. It is spending the sweat of its children." These skeptics of high military spending believe the high costs can easily reduce citizens' human security. "Government policy makers will always have to choose how to allocate their scarce resources and whether to prioritize security or social goals. At least in the short term, however, there seems to be little chance of there being a rapid decline in world military expenditure, which could allow governments to give higher priority to social expenditure. A decline in military expenditure is a possibility in some regions, but a strong upward trend in the world total is unlikely to be reversed while the world's largest military spender remains at war. The world trend is likely to be driven for the foreseeable future by the defense and security choices and policies pursued by the United States" (SIPRI 2007, 297).

The consequences for the United States are not encouraging. Consider how, given the U.S. choice to prioritize military spending, the United States ranks on various nonmilitary measures of human security.

How the U.S. Ranks in the World

Indicator	Rank	Indicator	Rank
GDP for each person	9	Life expectancy	40
Cost of living	19	Environmental performance	28
Index of economic freedom	12	Under five mortality rate	15
Largest current account fiscal deficit	1	Number of physicians per person	27
Human development (HDI)	12	Public education expenditures for each person	14
Gender empowerment	14		
Total prison population	1	Public health expenditures (% of GDP)	35

Source: Economist *Pocket World In Figures* (2007); *Human Development Report* (2008); *World Development Indicators* 2007

These rankings raise serious questions about the true costs of national security. Who really pays for defense? If you were a head of state, what budget priorities would you propose for your country's national security and your citizens' human security?

How would you reconcile the need for defense with the need to provide for the common welfare? The choices you would make would be difficult, because they entail a necessary trade-off between competing values. For this reason military-spending decisions are highly controversial everywhere.

> *World leaders must stop viewing*
> *militaristic investment as a measure of national well-being.*
> *The sad fact is that half the world's governments invest more in*
> *defense than in health programs. If we channeled just $40 billion each*
> *year away from armies and into antipoverty programs, in ten years all*
> *the world's population would enjoy basic social services—education,*
> *health care and nutrition, potable water and sanitation.*
>
> —Oscar Arias, Nobel Peace laureate and
> president of Costa Rica

■ **relative burden of military spending**

a measure of the economic burden of military activities calculated by the share of each state's gross domestic product allocated to military expenditures.

How people spend their money reveals their values. Similarly, how governments allocate their revenues reveals their priorities. Examination of national budgets discloses an unmistakable pattern: Although the sources of global political power may be changing, many states continue to seek security by spending substantial portions of their national treasures on arms.

CHANGES IN MILITARY CAPABILITIES

The growing militarization of the United States, the other great powers, and now mobilized nonstate terrorist movements has altered the global distribution of military capabilities. Part of the reason is that weapons production capabilities are more widespread than ever, with even Global South countries and terrorist organizations participating in the business of manufacturing modern aircraft, tanks, and missiles. A parallel change in the open and clandestine (secret) arms market and in the destructiveness of modern weapons has accelerated the spread of military capabilities around the world. Furthermore, as a trend in the arms industry, which has increased dramatically as a result of the Iraq war, the growth of **private military services** enhances military capabilities as it allows governments to conduct operations with fewer troops than would otherwise be needed.

■ **private military services**

the outsourcing of activities of a military-specific nature to private companies, such as armed security, equipment maintenance, IT services, logistics, and intelligence services.

Trends in the Weapons Trade

During the Cold War, many states sought to increase their security through the purchase of arms produced by suppliers eagerly seeking allies and profits from exports. In 1961, the world arms trade was valued at $4 billion. Thereafter, the traffic in arms imports climbed rapidly and peaked in 1987 at $82 billion (U.S. ACDA 1997, 10, 100). The end of the Cold War did not end the arms trade,

FIGURE 14.3

ARMS DELIVERIES TO THE
GLOBAL NORTH AND THE
GLOBAL SOUTH,
1999–2006 **The continuing global
arms trade has led to the globalization of
military capabilities throughout the
Global North and especially the Global
South. Between 2000 and 2007, arms
shipments worldwide were a staggering
$279 billion, but as this figure shows, the
total value of all arms deliveries by all
suppliers has modestly declined since
2004. In 2007, arms deliveries to the
Global South accounted for 56 percent of
all worldwide arms deliveries (CRS 2008,
33).**

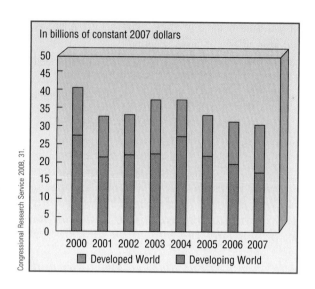

however. Since 1991, when the Cold War ended, and continuing throughout the era of global terrorism that began on 9/11, the total value of all international arms deliveries was $485 billion (CRS 2007, 4).

A noteworthy characteristic of the arms trade is the extent to which the less-developed Global South receives global arms (Figure 14.3). Between 2004 and 2007 the Global South was the recipient of 65 percent of global arms deliveries (CRS 2008, 33). A persistent trend in a changing world, therefore, has been for the least stable Global South states to spend the largest percentages of their relatively small economies for the purchase of weapons of war.

The global arms trade has fueled the dispersion of military capability worldwide. Weapons delivered by major suppliers to developing countries between 2004 and 2007 included 2,462 tanks and self-propelled cannons, 2,689 artillery pieces, 547 supersonic combat aircraft, 6,647 surface-to-air missiles, and a large number of warships, submarines, antishipping missiles, and other technologically advanced weapons systems (CRS 2008, 57).

The major recipients of all global arms shipments remain heavily concentrated in a subset of Global South arms purchasers. In 2007, weapon deliveries to the top ten recipients accounted for two-thirds of all deliveries in the Global South. India heads the list, followed in rank order of the value of their arms imports by Israel, Egypt, Saudi Arabia, Pakistan, South Korea, Venezuela, South Africa, Taiwan, and China (CRS 2008, 55). The stream of weapons to these insecure and eager buyers with money to spend is not likely to end soon. To promote what it called a "security dialogue" in the Persian Gulf, the United States proposed transferring $63 billion in new arms sales to the Middle East over the next ten years (*The Nation*, September 10–17, 2007, 8).

The regional distribution of arms deliveries seems to follow trends in the location of the world's flash points. With its numerous pairs of competitive states, the Near East is experiencing an intense **arms race**. Countries in the Middle East accounted for only 11 percent of world arms imports in 1967, but that share rose to 46 percent between 2004 and 2007. The increasing arms shipments this area has received are due in part to the U.S. global "war on terrorism" in Afghanistan and Iraq and heightened fears about national security throughout the troubled region, as in Pakistan, Turkey, Israel, and elsewhere. However, the Middle East is not alone as a troubled and insecure region. Asia is also living in a shadow of fear, and it is not surprising that it now ranks second in the value of arms imports, accounting for 42 percent of all Global South shipments between 2004 and 2007 (CRS 2008, 15–16).

Each state's proportionate share of total weapons purchases is likely to change, depending on the location of the globe's next hot spots and each country's involvement in them. Similarly, aggregate levels of world arms imports are likely to be influenced by the performance of each state in the global economy. Weapon imports fluctuate sharply from year to year—not only in unstable regions where the risks of civil war and terrorism are high and where pairs of enemy states are engaged in arms races but also in countries where periods of economic growth make financial resources available for arms purchases.

Along with changing demands of arms importers, changes in the activities of arms suppliers are also important. During the Cold War, the superpowers dominated the arms export market. Between 1975 and 1989, the U.S.–Soviet share of global arms exports varied between one-half and three-fourths, and the United States alone had cornered 40 percent of the world arms export market when the Cold War ended (U.S. ACDA 1997, 19). In that period, the two superpowers together "supplied an estimated $325 billion worth of arms and ammunition to the Third World" (Klare 1994, 139). In the post–9/11 global war on terrorism, the United States increased its worldwide supply of weapons to countries that agreed to be partners in the "coalition of the willing" in wars in Afghanistan and Iraq. Emerging as the unrivaled "arms merchant of the world," the United States ranked first among all suppliers in arms deliveries between 2000 and 2007, when it sold $63 billion of arms to the Global South (CRS 2008, 45–46).

The threat of terrorists acquiring nuclear, ballistic missile, and chemical weapons of mass destruction on the black market through covert suppliers poses a real danger. The extent of the threat is impossible to gauge, however, because this flow of the arms trade is invisible. Nonetheless, the absence of evidence is not evidence of absence. Terrorists are widely believed to be actively searching for weapons of mass destruction.

Another development in the post-Cold War era, which has been likened to modern-day mercenaries, is the growth in companies that provide private military services for hire on the global market. Between 1996 and 2006, the number of companies in the top 100 arms-producing companies that specialize in military services grew by 80 percent (SIPRI 2008). While the outsourcing of military-like activities enables governments "to maintain high levels of military operations with relatively small numbers of troops," relying on private contractors in war zones may compromise democratic accountability and the state's monopoly on the use of force, and it may also raise issues about legal status (SIPRI 2008). This dilemma was evident during the war in Iraq when employees of the Blackwater security firm killed seventeen Iraqi civilians and did not appear to be subject to either Iraqi, U.S., civilian, or military law.

■ **arms race**
the buildup of weapons and armed forces by two or more states that threaten each other, with the competition driven by the conviction that gaining a lead is necessary for security.

Alain McLaughlin Photography

THE INTERNATIONAL TRAFFICKING OF SMALL ARMS GOES GLOBAL **The sale of arms is a big trans-border business and it is growing. Part of this growth is because the line between legal and illegal trades is blurred and arms brokers are selling to terrorists in the huge underground black market. Shown here is an example of the thriving international trade in weapons: buyers at one of the many "arms bazaars" in the global weapons marketplace. Small arms kill about 300,000 people each year and an estimated 1,000,000 light weapons are stolen or lost each year (Stohl 2005, 60–62).**

> *The brakes are off. . . . There is no coherent policy on the transfer of arms. It has become a money game; an absurd spiral in which [the United States] exports arms only to have to develop more sophisticated ones to counter those spread out all over the world. . . . It is a frightening trend that undermines American moral authority.*
>
> —Lawrence Korb, Assistant Defense Secretary under U.S. President Ronald Reagan

Motives for the Arms Trade   Economic gain is an important rationale for foreign military sales because producers sell arms abroad to subsidize their arms production at home. For example, the United States uses arms exports to offset its chronic balance-of-trade deficits and to ensure its lead in the lucrative arms business. The U.S. government routinely assigns thousands of full-time federal employees to promote U.S. arms deals, spending half a billion dollars annually to assist U.S. arms dealers. To cement its share of the arms trade, one-fourth "of all U.S. foreign aid

THE PROBLEM IS PLANE: THE "FLYING SHAME" IN WEAPONS ACQUISITIONS
The United States has increased its weapons acquisition plans, from seventy-one major programs costing $790 billion in 2001 to eighty-five new programs costing $1,585 billion in 2005 (SIPRI 2007, 279). The concern: Who benefits—the American military, the corporate profits of weapons manufacturers, or American taxpayers? Shown here is one widely cited example of weapons procurement abuse: "After an investment of $20 billion, 25 years and 30 lives, the *V-22 Osprey* aircraft arrives in Iraq to make its combat debut—lacking both firepower and the ability to land safely if it loses power at low altitudes" (Thompson 2007).

goes to helping the recipients buy U.S.-produced weapons, equipment, or services" (*Harper's,* October 2005, 11). The *military-industrial complex* is widely believed to exercise enormous power over U.S. defense budgets and arms sales agreements. One symptom of the influence of defense contractors is their ability to charge the Pentagon inflated prices for their products. The U.S. government is estimated to overpay by 20 percent for military goods through the Pentagon's prime vendor procurement program, which greased the sale of a deep fat fryer for $5,919, a waffle iron for $1,781, and a toaster for $1,025 (Markoe and Borenstein 2005; Borenstein 2006). It is hardly surprising that arms manufacturers seek to increase their profits, but their corporate greed alarms critics, who worry about the manufacturers' success in lobbying Congress and the Pentagon for high military spending to gain government permission to sell new weapons worldwide.

The same kind of pressures from military-industrial coalitions are operative in many other countries, and globalization has not weakened established national security practices (Ripsman and Paul 2005). What is more, as a sign of the globalization of arms transfers, defense contractors increasingly sell their products everywhere and push their production into other countries' markets as they consolidate their operations and ownership. As an example, the world's second largest aerospace firm, which sells everything from ballistic missiles to mobile medical units (the European Aeronautic Defense and Company), operates from Columbus, Mississippi, to penetrate the U.S. military market. Another example: *Marine One,* the U.S. president's helicopter, is produced in Britain and Italy in partnership with Lockheed Martin (Donnelly 2005).

The Strategic Consequences of Arms Sales   The transfer of arms across borders has produced some unattended and counterproductive consequences. For example, during the Cold War the United States and the Soviet Union thought they could maintain peace by spreading arms to pivotal recipients. Between 1983 and 1987, the United States provided arms to fifty-nine less-developed countries, whereas the Soviet Union supplied arms to forty-two (Klare 1990, 12). Yet many of the recipients went to war with their neighbors or experienced internal rebellion. Of the top twenty arms importers in 1988, more than half "had governments noted for the frequent use of violence" (Sivard 1991, 17). The toll in lives from the wars in the Global South since 1945 exceeds tens of millions of people.

Undoubtedly, the import of such huge arsenals of weapons aided this level of destruction. As the arms exporters "peddle death to the poor," they seldom acknowledge how this scouting for customers contradicts other proclaimed foreign policy goals. For example, while seeking to promote democratization, less democratic countries receive the greatest amounts of U.S. arms (Blanton 2005, 660). Since 2001, less than three-fifths of U.S. arms have been exported to governments classified by Freedom House as "free" (O'Reilly 2005, 11), and now four-fifths of the countries that receive U.S. arms are classified by the U.S. State Department as either being undemocratic or having a poor human rights record (Jackson 2007, A9).

■ **blowback**

the propensity for actions undertaken for national security to have the unintended consequence of provoking retaliatory attacks by the target when relations later sour.

The inability of arms suppliers to control the uses to which their military hardware will be put is troubling. Friends can become foes and supplying weapons can backfire —generating what the CIA calls **blowback** to describe what can happen when foreign activities such as covert shipments of arms are later used in retaliations against the supplier (C. Johnson 2004). The United States learned this painful lesson the hard way. The weapons it shipped to Iraq when Saddam Hussein was fighting Iran in the 1980s were later used against U.S. forces in the Persian Gulf War (Timmerman 1991). This also happened when the Stinger missiles the United States supplied to Taliban forces resisting the Soviet Union's 1979 invasion in Afghanistan fell into the hands of terrorists later opposing the United States. Likewise, in 1982 Great Britain found itself shipping military equipment to Argentina just eight days before Argentina's attack on the British-controlled Falkland Islands, and in 1998 U.S. military technology sold to China was exported to Pakistan, making possible its nuclear weapons test. America's creation of a whole range of robotic armed forces to carry out dangerous missions and do the fighting without risk of soldiers being killed is heralded as a breakthrough in the way weapons are being used. But it seems that every advance in military technology brings with it the strong possibility of blowback because these new fighting machines are likely to be acquired by enemies. It is only a matter of time before the world's conventional armed forces will face, not suicide bombers, but a far more insidious and elusive enemy: robots of death which have no fear. It is naïve, critics warn, to imagine that there will be no trafficking in these technologically revolutionary tools of combat.

Trends in Weapons Technology

The widespread quest for armaments has created a potentially "explosive" global environment. The description is especially apt when we consider not only trends in defense expenditures and the arms trade but also in the destructiveness of modern weapons.

Nuclear Weapons   Technological research and development has radically expanded the destructive power of national arsenals. The largest "blockbuster" bombs of World War II delivered the power of ten tons of TNT. The atomic bomb that leveled Hiroshima had the power of over 15,000 tons of TNT. Less than twenty years later, the Soviet Union built a nuclear bomb with the explosive force of 57,000,000 tons of TNT. Since 1945, more than 130,000 nuclear warheads had been built, all but 2 percent by the U.S. (55 percent) and the U.S.S.R. (43 percent). Most have been dismantled since the 1986 peak, but 10,183 worldwide remain operational at the start of 2008—with a combined explosive force of at least 1,300,000 Hiroshima atomic bombs (SIPRI 2008, 16).

The use of such weapons could not only destroy entire cities and countries but also, conceivably, the world's entire population. Albert Einstein, the Nobel Prize–winning physicist whose ideas were the basis for the development of nuclear weapons, was alarmed by the threat they posed. He professed uncertainty about the weapons that would be used in a third world war but was confident that in a fourth war they would be "sticks and stones." He warned that inasmuch as "the unleashed power of the atom has changed everything save our modes of thinking we thus drift toward unparalleled catastrophe."

As 2008 began, eight states deployed more than 10,183 operational nuclear warheads. The United States possessed 4,075; Russia, 5,189; China, 176; France, 348; Great Britain, 185; Israel, 80; Pakistan, 60; and India, 60–70 (SIPRI 2008, 16).

In addition, as many as twenty-one other states (such as Iran and Brazil) or NGO terrorist organizations are widely believed to be seeking to join the nuclear club. The **proliferation** of arms is a serious global concern, because the so-called **Nth country problem** (the addition of new nuclear states) is expected to become an increasing likelihood. Both **horizontal nuclear proliferation** (the increase in the number of nuclear states) and **vertical nuclear proliferation** (increases in the capabilities of existing nuclear powers) are probable.

The obstacles to increased proliferation are weak. Consider the successful acquisition of nuclear weapons by India and Pakistan, the collapse of the Comprehensive Test Ban Treaty, and Iran and Syria's self-proclaimed aims to acquire nuclear weapons. The incentives to join the nuclear club and acquire missiles and bombers for their delivery are strong, which is why the threat exists that Argentina, Brazil, Libya and Taiwan, which have active nuclear development programs, could use these capabilities to manufacture nuclear weapons (see Map 14.2). Nuclear proliferation could accelerate for additional reasons.

First, the materials needed to make a nuclear weapon are widely available. This is partly because of the widespread use of nuclear technology for generating electricity. Today, almost 450 nuclear-power reactors are in operation in seventy countries throughout the world. The number of new operational nuclear reactors is certain to increase because almost eighty new nuclear reactors are now under construction or planned. In addition to spreading nuclear know-how, states could choose to reprocess the uranium and plutonium, which power plants produce as waste, for clandestine nuclear weapons production. Commercial reprocessing reactors are producing enough plutonium to make as many as 40,000 nuclear weapons.

■ **proliferation**
the spread of weapon capabilities from a few to many states in a chain reaction, so that an increasing number of states gain the ability to launch an attack on other states with devastating (e.g., nuclear) weapons.

■ **Nth country problem**
the expansion of additional new nuclear weapon states.

■ **horizontal nuclear proliferation**
an increase in the number of states that possess nuclear weapons.

■ **vertical nuclear proliferation**
the expansion of the capabilities of existing nuclear powers to inflict increasing destruction with their nuclear weapons.

Second, the scientific expertise necessary for weapons development has spread with the globalization of advanced scientific training. Almost all past technology is accessible and can be duplicated.

Third, export controls designed to stop technology transfer for military purposes are weak. Conversion of peacetime nuclear energy programs to military purposes can occur either overtly or, as in the case of India and Pakistan, covertly. The safeguards built into the **nonproliferation regime** are simply inadequate to detect and prevent secret nuclear weapons development programs.

■ **nonproliferation regime**

rules to contain arms races so that weapons or technology do not spread to states that do not have them.

Fourth, nonnuclear weapons states have strong incentives to develop weapons similar to those of the existing nuclear club. They voice the complaint of French President Charles de Gaulle, who argued that without an independent nuclear capability France could not "command its own destiny." Similarly, in 1960 Britain's Aneurin Bevan asserted that without the bomb Britain would go "naked into the council chambers of the world." And since 1993, North Korea tried to prevent monitoring of its five nuclear-power facilities and vowed to convert its uranium for nuclear weapons. But in 2007 it promised to permit external monitoring in exchange for financial assistance and in 2008 it blew up the cooling tower of its nuclear complex at Yongbyon as a symbolic gesture of its commitment to halt its nuclear program.

James Hill/Contact Press Images

IRAN'S NUCLEAR-BOMB AMBITIONS? **The U.N. has sought to prohibit Iran from exploiting its sophisticated uranium enrichment program so it can make fissile material for nuclear weapons. "Our answer to those who are angry about Iran obtaining the full nuclear cycle is one phrase," Mahmoud Ahmadinejad, Iran's President, in 2006 bellowed, "we say: Be angry, and die of this anger." President Ahmadinejad boasted that soon the world would have "no choice but to live with a nuclear Iran." Though the U.S. National Intelligence Estimate reported that in fact Iran had suspended its nuclear weapons program in 2003, the United States remained fearful that Iran could not be trusted to stay disarmed. Shown here are Iranian soldiers and citizens raising hands to support a banner proclaiming Iran's right to develop nuclear capabilities.**

Nuclear weapons serve as a symbol of status and power. Because of the widespread conviction rooted in realism that military power confers political stature, many countries, such as Iran and North Korea, regard the **Nuclear Nonproliferation Treaty (NPT)** as hypocrisy because it provides a seal of approval to the United States, Russia, China, Britain, and France for possessing nuclear weapons while

> *There's not a snowball's chance in hell we'll eliminate all nuclear weapons from the face of the earth. That genie is long since out of the bottle and there's no chance of ever getting him back in.*
> —Matthew Bunn, arms control expert

denying it to all others. The underlying belief that it is acceptable to develop a nuclear capacity for deterrence, political influence, and prestige was expressed in 1999 by Brajesh Mishra, India's national security adviser, when he justified India's acquisition of nuclear weapons by asserting that "India should be granted as much respect and deference by the United States and others as is China today." It is very unlikely that the nuclear threat will disappear (see Map 14.2).

Weapons Delivery Capabilities   Another trend that is making the weapons of war increasingly deadly has been the rapidity of technological refinements that increase the capacity of states to send their weapons great distances with ever-greater accuracy. Missiles can now send weapons from as far away as 11,000 miles to within 100 feet of their targets in less than thirty minutes. One example was the development by the United States and Russia of the ability to equip their ballistic missiles with **multiple independently targetable reentry vehicles (MIRVs)**. This allows these Cold War enemies to launch many warheads on a single missile toward different targets simultaneously and accurately. One MIRV U.S. MX Peacekeeper missile could carry ten nuclear warheads—enough to wipe out a city and everything else within a fifty- mile radius. Because the superpowers achieved MIRV capability before completing the START II treaty to ban them, the world's combined nuclear inventory grew nearly three times larger than the number of nuclear warheads previously in existence in spite of ongoing efforts to limit it.

Other technological improvements have led to steady increases in the speed, accuracy, range, and effectiveness of weapons. Laser weapons, nuclear-armed tactical air-to-surface missiles (TASMs), stealth air-launched cruise missiles (ACMs), and antisatellite (ASAT) weapons that can project force in and wage war from outer space have become a part of the military landscape.

For decades, a **firebreak** separated conventional and nuclear wars. The term comes from the barriers of cleared land that firefighters use to keep forest fires from racing out of control. In the context of modern weaponry, it is a psychological barrier whose purpose is to prevent even the most intensive forms of conventional combat from escalating into nuclear war. The danger is growing that the firebreak is being crossed from both directions—by a new generation of near-nuclear conventional weapons capable of levels of violence approximating those of a limited nuclear warhead and by a new generation of near-conventional **strategic weapons** capable of causing destruction similar to that of the most powerful weapons of mass destruction.

Nuclear Nonproliferation Treaty (NPT) an international agreement that seeks to prevent horizontal proliferation by prohibiting further nuclear weapons sales, acquisitions, or production.

multiple independently targetable reentry vehicles (MIRVs) a technological innovation permitting many weapons to be delivered from a single missile.

firebreak the psychological barrier between conventional wars and wars fought with nuclear weapons as well as weapons of mass destruction.

strategic weapons weapons of mass destruction that are carried on intercontinental ballistic missiles (ICBMs), submarine-launched ballistic missiles (SLBM)s, or long-range bombers and are capable of annihilating an enemy state.

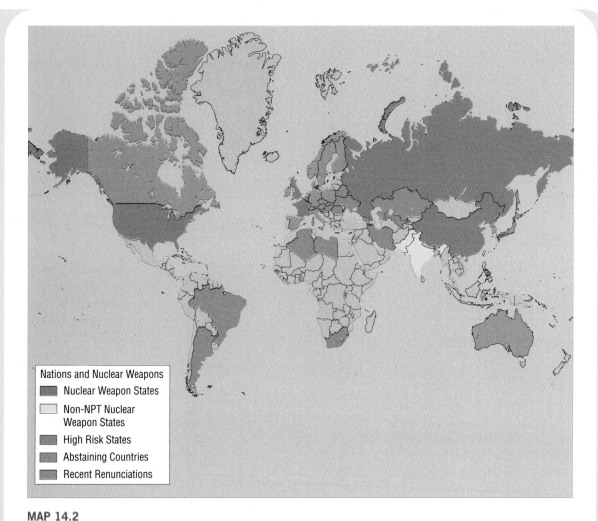

MAP 14.2

NUCLEAR-WEAPON ARMED COUNTRIES, TODAY AND TOMORROW Nuclear proliferation is a growing trend with eight countries already holding 10,183 nuclear warheads and many others poised to join the club of nuclear weapon powers, as this map shows. Nuclear proliferation means that nuclear weapons will continue as a key ingredient of national security strategies.

The Revolution in Military Technology The global terrain is being transformed by another sea change in the kinds of arms being developed to wage war: the new high-tech **nonlethal weapons (NLWs)** made possible by the **revolution in military technology (RMT)**. The new generation includes sounds, shocks, and stinks to disperse or incapacitate crowds. One example is the Long Range Acoustic Device (LRAD) that blasts sounds at a deafening 150 decibels to incapacitate everyone within 300 meters by giving them an instant headache. Another example is the Air Force's "active denial technology" using electromagnetic radiation that penetrates clothing, causing water molecules to vibrate and burn skin tissue. And it's humorous, but true, that the Pentagon has considered various nonlethal chemical weapons to disrupt enemy discipline and morale, including an "aphrodisiac chemical weapon that would make enemy soldiers sexually irresistible to each other" (www.Newscientist.com). More seriously, NLWs already now deploy information-warfare squadrons to protect military computer networks from electronic sneak attacks; energy pulses to knock out or take down enemies without necessarily killing them; biofeedback, beamed electromagnetic and sonic wavelengths that can modify the human behavior of targets (for example, putting people to sleep through electromagnetic heat and magnetic radiation); and underground **smart bombs**, which at a speed of 1,000 feet per second can penetrate a buried bunker and, at the proper millisecond, detonate five hundred pounds of explosive to destroy an adversary's inventory of buried chemical and biological weapons. Robot soldiers that can think, see, and react like humans are based on nanotechnology (the science of very small structures) and are scheduled to become the U.S. Army's major fighting force, financed by a $127 billion contract called *Future Combat Systems*. The Pentagon is enthusiastic, in part because weapons that are symbols of military might like stealth bombers and nuclear submarines are of little use in today's "asymmetric" conflicts, in which individual soldiers equipped with the latest technologies are needed for search-and-destroy missions against guerrilla militias. Technological advances thus may make obsolete orthodox ways of classifying weapons systems as well as prior equations for measuring power ratios.

The precision and power of today's conventional weapons have expanded exponentially, at precisely the moment when the revolution in military technology is leading to "the end of infantry" in the computer age. Even as the nuclear powers

> *The sky has eyes, bullets have brains, and victory will belong to the country whose military has the better data network.*
>
> —Philip E. Ross, military technologist

retain the capacity to turn cities into glass, they (and now, terrorist groups) increasingly rely on a variety of new cyberstrategies using information technological innovation to deter and demobilize enemies (see Dombrowski and Gholz 2007). They are turning to **virtual nuclear arsenals** for **deterrence** of an adversary's attack. Examples include such futuristic weapons as the electromagnetic pulse (EMP) bomb, which can be hand-delivered in a suitcase and can immobilize an entire city's computer and communications systems; computer viruses of electronic-seating microbytes that can eliminate a country's telephone system; and logic bombs that can confuse and

■ nonlethal weapons (NLWs)
the wide array of "soft kill," low-intensity methods of incapacitating an enemy's people, vehicles, communications systems, or entire cities without killing either combatants or noncombatants.

■ revolution in military technology (RMT)
the sophisticated new weapons technologies that make fighting war without mass armies possible.

■ smart bombs
precision-guided military technology that enables a bomb to search for its target and detonate at the precise time it can do the most damage.

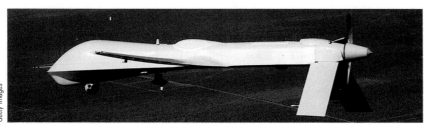

Getty Images

REMOTE-CONTROL WARFARE? **The United States is building a new generation of technologically sophisticated weapons. Shown here is one example: the U.S. unmanned *Predator* search drone used by the CIA in its hunt for Osama bin Laden.**

virtual nuclear arsenals

the next generation of "near nuclear" military capabilities produced by the revolution in military technology that would put strategic nuclear weapons of mass destruction at the margins of national security strategies by removing dependence on them for deterrence.

deterrence

preventive strategies designed to dissuade an adversary from doing what it would otherwise do.

infowar tactics

attacks on an adversary's telecommunications and computer networks to penetrate and degrade an enemy whose defense capabilities depend heavily on these technological systems.

redirect traffic on the target country's air and rail system. Also planned are **infowar tactics** that deploy information-age techniques "to disrupt the enemy's economy and military capabilities without firing a shot." One example of these is the U.S. Air Force's Commando Solo psychological operations plane, which can disrupt signals and insert in their place a "morphed" TV program, in which the enemy leader makes unpopular announcements on the screen to alienate the leader from the population.

Biological and Chemical Weapons   Biological and chemical weapons pose a special and growing threat, particularly in the hands of terrorists aiming for mass destruction rather than influencing public opinion. These unconventional weapons of mass destruction (WMD) are sometimes regarded as a "poor man's atomic bomb" because they can be built at comparatively little cost and cause widespread injury and death. Chemical weapons proliferation is of worldwide concern. In addition to the American hegemon, which led the way in building these weapons, twelve other states have declared past production of chemical weapons; still others are suspected of secret production (SIPRI 2008), and many terrorists claim they intend to acquire and use them. Following the 9/11 terrorist attacks on the United States, for example, there were fears that the spread of anthrax through the U.S. mail system was the first step in an endless series of future biological warfare by terrorist networks.

International law prohibits the use of chemical weapons. The 1925 Geneva Protocol banned the use of chemical weapons in warfare, and the Chemical Weapons Convention, now signed by four-fifths of the world's countries, requires the destruction of existing stocks. However, Iran and Iraq's use of gas in their eight-year 1980s war against each other, and Iraq's 1989 use of chemical weapons against its own Kurdish population, demonstrate the weaknesses of these legal barriers. In addition, many radical extremists, often beyond the control of weak state governments, see chemical and biological weapons as a cheaper and efficient terrorist method. The firebreak has been breached.

Pervasive insecurity haunts much of the world because there do not exist real supranational controls over the proliferation of biological and chemical weapons. The twenty-first century has not become the peaceful and prosperous period many people expected. In December 2008 the famous "Doomsday Clock" of the *Bulletin of the Atomic Scientists* estimated that the world was only five minutes from nuclear Armageddon—two minutes closer than when the clock was originally set in 1947 when the threat of the end of the world loomed large.

The world is *not* a safer place. In response to military dangers, many leaders today still adhere to the realist axiom that "if you want peace prepare for war." Security, realists insist, requires military capabilities. However, because the possession of overpowering military capabilities does not automatically result in their wise use, realists council that what matters greatly in the pursuit of national security are the *methods* on which states rely to use the capabilities they have acquired. How can weapons most effectively be used to promote national interests and exercise international influence? This question underscores the vital importance that choices about the types of military strategies that are devised. What are the primary strategic approaches that the realist road to national security regards as available and effective options?

Military Strategies

The dropping of the atomic bomb on Japan on August 6, 1945, is the most important event distinguishing pre- from post-World War II world politics. In the blinding flash of a single weapon and the shadow of its mushroom cloud, the world was transformed from a "balance of power" to a "balance of terror" system. In the following decades, policy makers in the nuclear states had to grapple with two central policy questions: (1) whether they should use nuclear weapons, and (2) how to prevent others from using them. The search for answers was critical because the immediate and delayed effects of a nuclear war were terrifying to contemplate. Even a short war using a tiny fraction of any great power's nuclear arsenal would destroy life as we know it. The planet would be uninhabitable, because a **nuclear winter** would result, with devastating consequences: "Fires ignited in such a war could generate enough smoke to obscure the sun and perturb the atmosphere over large areas, [lowering] average planetary temperatures [and darkening] the skies sufficiently to compromise green plant photosynthesis" (Sagan and Turco 1993). It has been estimated that "the missiles on board a single [U.S.] SLBM submarine may be enough to initiate nuclear winter" (Quester 1992)—enough to end human existence.

Weapons of mass destruction have grown since World War II, and strategies have changed with changes in technologies, defense needs, capabilities, and global conditions. For analytical convenience, those postures can be divided into three periods: compellence, deterrence, and preemption. The first began at the end of World War II and lasted until the 1962 Cuban Missile Crisis. U.S. nuclear superiority was the dominant characteristic of this period. The second then began and lasted until the 1991 collapse of the Soviet Union. Growing Soviet military capability was the dominant characteristic of this period, which meant that the United States no longer stood alone in its ability to annihilate another country without fear of its own destruction. The third phase began after the break up of the Soviet Union that ended the Cold War, after which the great powers began to revise their strategic doctrines in the light of new global threats.

Compellence Countries that possess military preeminence often think of weapons as instruments in diplomatic bargaining. The United States, the world's first and for many years unchallenged nuclear power, adopted the strategic doctrine of compellence (Schelling 1966) when it enjoyed a clear-cut superiority over the Soviet Union. Military capabilities did not have to be used for them to be useful; the United States could exercise influence over enemies simply by demonstrating the existence of its powerful weapons and signalling its willingness to use those weapons. The U.S. doctrine of compellence used nuclear weapons as tools of political influence, not for fighting but for convincing others to do what they might not otherwise do.

The United States sought to gain bargaining leverage by conveying the impression that it would actually use nuclear weapons. This posture was especially evident during the Eisenhower administration, when Secretary of State John Foster Dulles practiced **brinkmanship**, deliberately threatening U.S. adversaries with nuclear destruction so that, at the brink of war, they would concede to U.S. demands. Brinkmanship was part of the overall U.S. strategic doctrine known as **massive retaliation**. To contain communism and Soviet expansionism, this doctrine called for

■ **nuclear winter**
the expected freeze that would occur in the Earth's climate from the fallout of smoke and dust in the event nuclear weapons were used, blocking out sunlight and destroying the plant and animal life that survived the original blast.

■ **compellence**
a method of coercive diplomacy usually involving an act of war or threat to force an adversary to make concessions against its will.

■ **brinkmanship**
the intentional, reckless taking of huge risks in bargaining with an enemy, such as threatening a nuclear attack, to compel its submission.

■ **massive retaliation**
the Eisenhower administration's policy doctrine for containing Soviet communism by pledging to respond to any act of aggression with the most destructive capabilities available, including nuclear weapons.

■ **countervalue targeting strategy**

a bargaining doctrine that declares the intention to use weapons of mass destruction against an enemy's most valued nonmilitary resources, such as the civilians and industries located in its cities.

■ **counterforce targeting strategy**

targeting strategic nuclear weapons on particular military capabilities of an enemy's armed forces and arsenals.

■ **nuclear deterrence**

dissuading an adversary from attacking by threatening retaliation with nuclear weapons.

a **countervalue targeting strategy**, that is, aiming U.S. nuclear weapons at what the Soviets most valued—their population and industrial centers. The alternative is a **counterforce targeting strategy**, which targets an enemy's military forces and weapons, thus sparing civilians from immediate destruction.

Massive retaliation heightened fears in the Kremlin that a nuclear exchange would destroy the Soviet Union but permit the survival of the United States. In addition to responding by increasing their nuclear capabilities, Soviet leaders accelerated their space program and successfully launched the world's first space satellite (*Sputnik*). This demonstrated Moscow's ability to deliver nuclear weapons beyond the Eurasian landmass. Thus, the superpowers' strategic competition took a new turn, and the United States for the first time faced a nuclear threat to its homeland.

Deterrence   As U.S. nuclear superiority eroded, American policy makers began to question the usefulness of weapons of mass destruction as tools in political bargaining. They were horrified by the destruction that could result if compellence should provoke a nuclear exchange. The nearly suicidal Cuban Missile Crisis of 1962 brought about a major change in American strategic thought, shifting strategic policy from compellence to **nuclear deterrence**.

Whereas *compellence* relies on an offensive coercive threat aimed at persuading an adversary to relinquish something without resistance, *deterrence* seeks to dissuade an adversary from undertaking some future action. At the heart of deterrence theory is the assumption that the defender has the ability to punish an adversary with unacceptably high costs if it launches an attack. The key elements of deterrence are: (1) *capabilities*— the possession of military resources that signal to the adversary that threats of military retaliation are possible; (2) *credibility*—the belief that the actor is willing to act on its declared threats; and (3) *communication*—the ability to send a potential aggressor the clear message that the threat will be carried out. Ironically, the shift from a strategy of compellence to deterrence sped rather than slowed the

NUCLEAR TESTING
Pictured here is a French atomic test in the South Pacific of a nuclear bomb smaller than the U.S. hydrogen bomb that, in 1952, created a three-mile fireball 1,000 times more powerful than each of the bombs the United States dropped on Hiroshima and Nagasaki. More than 2,000 nuclear-weapons tests have occurred since 1945, and testing is certain to resume following the U.S. announcement that it would resume production of plutonium 238 to rebuild its stockpile for nuclear power.

Roger Ressmeyer/CORBIS

Deterrence will succeed if threatened costs can be communicated to the challenger, assessed by the challenger, and believed by the challenger.

—Richard J. Harknett, strategic theorist

arms race. A deterrent strategy depends on obtaining the unquestionable ability to inflict intolerable damage on an opponent. This means that an arming state seeking to deter an enemy must build its weapons to acquire a **second-strike capability**—sufficient destructive weapons to ensure that the country can withstand an adversary's first strike and still retain the capacity to retaliate with a devastating counterattack. To guarantee that an adversary was aware that a second-strike capability existed, deterrence rationalized an unrestrained search for sophisticated retaliatory capabilities. Any system that could be built was built.

■ **second-strike capability**
a state's capacity to retaliate after absorbing an adversary's first-strike attack with weapons of mass destruction.

"Only when arms are sufficient beyond doubt can we be certain without doubt that they will never be employed."

—John F. Kennedy, U.S. President

The phrase **mutual assured destruction (MAD)** was coined to describe the strategic balance that emerged between the United States and the Soviet Union after the Cuban Missile Crisis. Regardless of who struck first, the other side could destroy the attacker. Under these circumstances, initiating a nuclear war was not a *rational choice*; the frightening costs outweighed any conceivable benefits. As Soviet leader Nikita Khrushchev put it, "If you reach for the push button, you reach for suicide." Safety, in former British Prime Minister Winston Churchill's words, was "the sturdy child of terror and survival the twin brother of annihilation."

As U.S.–Soviet relations evolved, another shift in strategic thinking occurred in 1983 when U.S. President Reagan proposed building a space-based defensive shield against ballistic missiles. The **Strategic Defense Initiative (SDI)**, or "Star Wars" as it is now labeled, called for the development of a defense against ballistic missiles using advanced space-based lasers to destroy weapons launched in fear, anger, or by accident. The goal, as President Reagan defined it, was to make nuclear weapons "impotent and obsolete." Thus, SDI sought to shift U.S. nuclear strategy away from mutual assured destruction, which President Reagan deemed "morally unacceptable." However, the United States never managed to build a reliable ballistic missile defense, which Reagan's own Secretary of State George Shultz called "lunacy." As Philip Coyle, former director of Operational Test and Evaluation for the Department of Defense, noted in 2006, there has been "no demonstrated capability to defend the United States against enemy attack under realistic conditions." Nevertheless, the United States continues to aggressively pursue antiballistic missile defense, having spent by 2008 more than $150 billion—with a budget request in 2008 of "some $12 billion, or nearly three times what the United States spent on antimissile systems during any year of the Cold War" (Cirincione 2008, 68). Despite protest from Russia, in 2008 the United States moved forward with a controversial plan in which Poland agreed to host ten U.S. two-stage ground-based missile defense interceptors and the Czech Republic agreed to host a ballistic missile defense radar site.

■ **mutual assured destruction (MAD)**
a condition of mutual deterrence in which both sides possess the ability to survive a first strike with weapons of mass destruction and launch a devastating retaliatory attack.

■ **Strategic Defense Initiative (SDI)**
the so-called Star Wars plan conceived by the Reagan administration to deploy an antiballistic missile system using space-based lasers that would destroy enemy nuclear missiles before they could enter Earth's atmosphere.

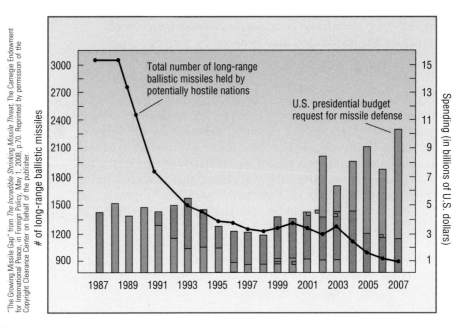

FIGURE 14.4

AN EXPANDING MISSILE GAP The United States plans to spend in excess of $60 billion on missile defense over the next six years. This is an unprecedented sum, the wisdom of which is questionable as the direct threat of ballistic missiles is limited and far less than it was twenty years ago. "The number of long-range missiles fielded by China and Russia has decreased 71 percent since 1987. The number of medium-range ballistic missiles pointed at U.S. allies in Europe and Asia has fallen 80 percent. Most of the twenty-eight countries that have any ballistic missiles at all have only short-range Scud missiles—which travel less than 300 miles and are growing older and less reliable every day" (Cirincione 2008, 68).

Threats and fears animate realists' preoccupation with strategies based on weapons. The strategy of compellence conceived of arms as a means for putting enemies in a defensive position and pushing them to make changes in their policies that they did not want to undertake; the strategy of deterrence conceived of using weapons for defense to prevent an attack. Both strategies worked in some ways but failed in others, and both dealt with the problem of armed force by preserving the reliance on arms rather than trying to eliminate the threat. This is why the search continues for ways to move beyond compellence and deterrence in order "to counteract as well as reduce the negative effects of miscalculation and misperception, practices that are partially responsible for unpredicted and unwanted outcomes in international politics" (Sperandei 2006, 253).

Preemption The end of the Cold War and with it the huge reduction in the total number of nuclear warheads today has not spelled a relaxation of tension. Strategic planning continues to find new ways of dealing with the constant danger of emergent military threats. As in the past, the U.S. hegemon has led the way in forging new strategies to deal with the post-9/11 threats of global terrorism and belligerent enemies. From that threat has come the radical new strategy of preemptive warfare.

"We face a threat with no precedent," U.S. President George W. Bush insisted in 2002. On the one hand, modern technology allows shadowy terrorist networks to launch catastrophic attacks against the United States. On the other hand, these networks cannot be dissuaded by the threat of punishment because they have no fixed territory or populace to protect. "We must take the battle to the enemy," Bush exhorted, "and confront the worst threats before they emerge."

Bush's call for acting preemptively against terrorists and the rogue states that harbor them became the major and most controversial cornerstones of the *U.S. National Security Strategy* (NSS). Building on the proposition that "nations need not suffer an attack before they can lawfully take action to defend themselves against forces that present an imminent danger," the strategic document argued that the acquisition of weapons of mass destruction by global terrorists provided the United States with a compelling case for engaging in anticipatory self-defense. "Traditional concepts of deterrence will not work against a terrorist enemy whose avowed tactics are wanton destruction and the targeting of innocents; whose so-called soldiers seek martyrdom in death; and whose most potent protection is **statelessness**." This requires, the 2006 NSS security strategy reaffirmed, the case for **preemptive war**—to coerce rather than deter enemies. The strategy called for striking a potential enemy before it undertakes armed aggression, either with or without the support of allies and international institutions.

> *This isn't about punishment. We've got the wrong models in our minds if we're thinking about punishment. We're not. This isn't retaliation or retribution.*
>
> —Donald Rumsfeld, former U.S. Secretary of Defense

The 2002 national security strategy was the most sweeping reformulation of U.S. defense policy since the 1947 National Security Act at the start of the Cold War. Although under international law states have a legal right to defend themselves against aggression as well as imminent attacks, critics charge that beneath the language of military preemption lies a more radical policy of preventive war. A *preemptive* military attack entails the use of force to quell or mitigate an impending strike by an adversary. A *preventive* attack entails the use of force to eliminate any possible future strike, even if there is no reason to believe that the capacity to launch an attack currently exists. Whereas the grounds for preemption lie in evidence of a credible, imminent threat, the basis for prevention rests on the suspicion of an incipient, contingent threat (Kegley and Raymond 2004). Indeed, ethicists and legal experts, ever mindful of **just war theory**, question the morality and legality of preemptive war for preventive purposes. The U.S. posture has generated a heated debate (see Controversy: Is It Ethical to Wage Preemptive War to Prevent an Adversary's Potential Aggression?).

According to critics of this radical new strategy, preventive uses of military force set a dangerous precedent. Predicting an adversary's future behavior is difficult because its leadership's intentions are hard to discern, information on long-term goals may be shrouded in secrecy, and signals of its policy direction may be missed in an over-supply of unimportant intelligence information. If suspicions about an adversary become a justifiable cause for military action, then every truculent leader would have a rough-and-ready pretext for ordering a first strike. In rebuttal, the Bush administration argued that waiting for military threats to fully materialize is waiting far too long. In December 2007, Bush echoed his position, announcing he had no intention to halt his preemptive threats against Iran despite his own intelligence agencies' finding that Tehran had halted its nuclear weapons program in 2003, because Iran "could restart it."

■ statelessness

the growing band of people who have no citizenship rights in any country and are forced out of one country and not accepted in any other.

■ preemptive war

a quick first-strike attack that seeks to defeat an adversary before it can organize an initial attack or a retaliatory response.

■ just war theory

the theoretical criteria under which it is morally permissible, or "just," for a state to go to war and the methods by which a just war might be fought.

CONTROVERSY:

IS IT ETHICAL TO WAGE PREEMPTIVE WAR
TO PREVENT AN ADVERSARY'S POTENTIAL AGGRESSION?

From the first recorded use of weapons by one society against another in human history, people have debated the ethical criteria by which a *just war* can be waged without violating the principle that it is morally wrong to kill. That debate has continued worldwide without a consensus emerging about the conditions under which it is morally acceptable to use armed force for political purposes. Experts in both defense and moral ethics remain divided as to the just means for containing aggression. International law also is divided (see Chapter 17).

Can war be stopped by waging it? Some hard-core neoconservative realists believe so, arguing there are no moral limits: The ends justify the terrible means; might makes right; evil must be resisted; you can't negotiate with aggressors, so their aggression must be prevented. But other self-described realists, such as former U.S. National Security Advisor Brent Scowcroft, counsel against the use of force for purposes other than the consequences for international order (Goldberg 2005), and other realists maintain that war cannot be waged ethically if it is undertaken in violation of moral rules (Wesley 2005).

Andrea Comas/Reuters/CORBIS

Protestors in Madrid, Spain, demonstrate against the U.S. led preemptive strike against Iraq.

To neoliberal critics, the moral conditions under which a first-strike military intervention is justified are few (Russsett 2005; Judt 2007). Critics argue that such strategies overlook the traditional right of innocent noncombatants to protection from genocide, violate international law, and are crimes against humanity. Classic Christian and other pacifist theologians also condemn the extreme realist position that accepts evil methods, maintaining that a right intention does not automatically justify any means to achieve it.

The debate over the conditions justifying waging war to preserve peace heated up in 2002. At that time, the Bush administration spelled out its grievances against Iraqi leader Saddam Hussein in an attempt to justify why the United States planned a preemptive first strike to prevent Iraq from using weapons of mass destruction against the United States. The United States invaded, asserting that Hussein was too irrational for deterrence. "We do not have the luxury of doing nothing," National Security Adviser Condoleezza Rice claimed. Critics questioned the logic and the morality. Germany's Chancellor Gerhard Schroeder barked that attacking an enemy simply because of what it might intend to do, to prevent its later aggression, was the same faulty argument Adolf Hitler had used in starting World War II. A preemptive attack also violates the established U.S. ban on assassination of foreign leaders, and the UN Charter's prohibition against waging war except in defense against an actual armed attack by an aggressor—not to remove another state's military capabilities. "Who can possibly argue that there is anything moral about killing other people's children?" the outraged British Labour MP Alice Mahon added. In planning a preemptive attack, critics claimed the Bush administration was ignoring the just war restraints against first strikes for either deterrence or revenge, and overturning 150 years of international law (Patterson 2005).

What do you think? Should the United States expect support for its radical new policy? If the U.S. actions are judged as justifiable, also ask what this means for others if they follow the same logic as that of the globe's reigning superpower. In the "categorical imperative," the German philosopher Immanuel Kant argued that when evaluating the morality of a decision, the question to ask is: What would happen if everyone else acted on the same basis? What will the world be like if preemptive strikes become a universal norm and *all* states base their peace strategies on the claimed right to make war for preemptive purposes?

> *If you recognize a clear and present threat that is undeterrable by the means you have at hand, then you must deal with it. You do not wait for it to strike, you do not allow future attacks to happen before you take action.*
>
> —Colin Powell, former U.S. Secretary of State

The strategy of anticipatory self-defense raises anew timeless questions about the conditions under which, and the purposes for which, military force is justifiable. What does prudent precaution require when ruthless countries and nameless, faceless enemies pursue indiscriminate, suicidal attacks against innocent noncombatants? How can force be used to influence an adversary's decision-making calculus? What conditions affect the success of coercive diplomacy?

COERCIVE DIPLOMACY THROUGH MILITARY INTERVENTION

The strategy of *coercive diplomacy* is used in international bargaining to threaten or use limited force to persuade an opponent to stop pursuing an activity they are already undertaking. Often, threats to use arms are made to force an adversary to reach a compromise or, even better, to reverse its policies. The goal is to alter the target state's calculation of costs and benefits, so that the enemy is convinced that acceding to demands will be better than defying them. This result may be accomplished by delivering an **ultimatum** that promises an immediate and significant escalation in the conflict, or by issuing a warning and gradually increasing pressure on the target (Craig and George 1990).

Coercive diplomacy's reliance on the threat of force is designed to avoid the bloodshed and expense associated with traditional military campaigns. Orchestrating the mix of threats and armed aggression can be done in various ways. The methods range from traditional **gunboat diplomacy** to threaten an enemy by positioning navies and/or armies near its borders to "tomahawk diplomacy" by striking an adversary with precision-guided cruise missiles. These are among the instruments

■ **ultimatum**

a demand that puts a time limit for the target to comply and a threat of punishment for resistance.

■ **gunboat diplomacy**

a show of military force, historically naval force, to intimidate an adversary.

> *Coercive diplomacy seeks to resolve without violence,*
> *or with only minimal violence, those conflicts that are too severe*
> *to be settled by ordinary diplomacy and that in earlier times would*
> *have been settled by war.*
>
> —Glenn H. Snyder and Paul Diesing, security strategy theoreticians

of coercive diplomacy in the arsenal of military options envisioned by realist policy makers to pursue power. To explore this strategy, this chapter looks next at *military intervention*, the oldest and most widely used approach to military coercion.

■ covert operations

secret activities undertaken by a state outside its borders through clandestine means to achieve specific political or military goals with respect to another state.

Intervention can be practiced in various ways. States can intervene physically through direct entry of their armies into another country, indirectly by broadcasting propaganda to the target's population, or through **covert operations**. States also can intervene either alone or in league with other states. Overt military intervention is the most visible method of interference inside the borders of another country. For that reason, it is also the most controversial and costly.

Altogether, nearly 1,000 individual acts of military intervention were initiated between 1945 and 2001, resulting in 2.4 million fatalities (Tillema 2006). Interventionary acts have been frequently if episodically occurring since World War II (see Figure 14.5). This fluctuation in the rate of intervention suggests that military interventions rise and fall in response to both changing global circumstances and also in response to shifting perceptions of the advantages and disadvantages of intervention as an effective method of coercive diplomacy.

> *Military intervention involves operations undertaken openly by a*
> *state's regular military forces within a specific foreign land in such a*
> *manner as to risk immediate combat.*
>
> —Herbert K. Tillema, international behavioral scientist

■ nonintervention norm

a fundamental international legal principle, now being challenged, that traditionally has defined interference by one state in the domestic affairs of another as illegal.

Each act of military intervention had a different rationale and produced different results. Past cases raise tough questions about the use of military intervention for coercive diplomacy. Does the record show that the actions met the goals of the intervening states, such as successfully punishing countries so that they no longer violated their citizens' human rights? Have they for the most part restored order to war-torn societies? Or, on the whole, have they made circumstances worse?

These questions are hotly debated international issues now because of the wave of failed states. The great powers have not reached a consensus about the need to intervene in sovereign states when innocent civilians are victimized by tyrants. Why? Primarily because such interventions undercut the principles of state sovereignty and the **nonintervention norm** in international law. The UN's call for a "new commitment to intervention" stirred up the percolating existing debate about military intervention, even in the name of morality, justice, and human rights.

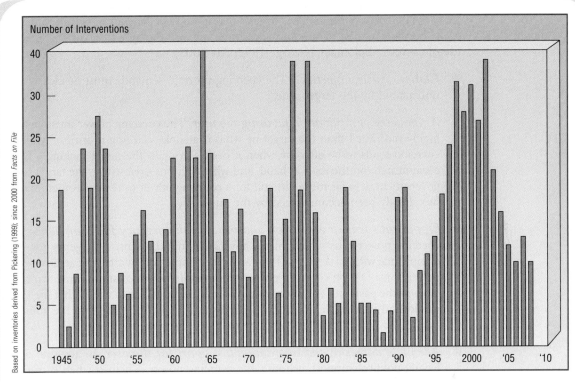

FIGURE 14.5

THE CHANGING INCIDENCE OF UNILATERAL MILITARY INTERVENTION FOR COERCIVE DIPLOMATIC PURPOSES SINCE 1945 **As this evidence shows, states have frequently sent their troops into the sovereign territory of other states in order to influence the target, even though military intervention has been traditionally prohibited by international law. The frequency of this forceful coercive diplomacy fluctuates from year to year, and suggests that the fluctuations are dependent on the personal choices of the leaders authorizing their country's use of national armed forces for military engagement outside their borders.**

Few question the necessity to stand up to genocide and intervene to protect the lives of persecuted peoples. However, many great powers remain reluctant to unconditionally pledge their willingness to uphold human rights anywhere they are violated. Instead, they practice *selective engagement*, by picking and choosing when and where they will intervene. Regardless of humanitarian considerations, the great powers have usually not undertaken bold and dangerous acts of military intervention overseas except when their self-perceived security interests have been at stake. This, of course, was the reason cited by the United States in 2003 when it undertook its "preventive war of choice [which the U.S. claimed] would avenge 9/11, clean up Iraq, stifle Islamic terrorism, spread shock, awe and democracy across the Middle East and reaffirm the credentials of a benevolently interventionist America" (Judt 2007). However, countries have sometimes intervened in other country's territories for impulsive and emotional reasons. Consider Turkey's 2008 bombing of targets in northern Iraq to wipe out guerrillas of the Kurdistan Workers' Party (PKK).

Today, policy makers disagree about the appropriate use of military coercion. Research on coercive diplomacy suggests that its success depends upon the context of each specific situation. The following conditions are thought to favor the effective use of coercive diplomacy (George 1992; Art 2005):

- *Clarity of user objectives.* The coercing power's demands must be clearly understood by the target state.

- *Asymmetry of motivation favoring the user.* The coercing power must be more highly motivated than the target by what is at stake. Timing is critical. Military coercion tends to be effective when it occurs prior to the target making a firm commitment on the issue at hand, and when factions exist within the target state's government. It is far more difficult for a coercing power to reverse something that has already been accomplished by the target state.

- *Opponent's fear of escalation and belief in the urgency for compliance.* The coercing power must create in the adversary's mind a sense of urgency for compliance with its demand. Two factors are important in affecting an adversary's perceptions: (1) the coercing power's reputation for successfully using armed force in the past, and (2) its capability to increase pressure to a level that the target would find intolerable. Coercion generally fails when the target has the ability to absorb the punishment delivered by the coercing state.

- *Adequate domestic and international support for the user.* In addition to having political support at home, the coercing power is helped when it can also count on support from key states and international organizations.

- *Clarity on the precise terms of settlement.* The coercing power must be able to articulate the specific conditions for ending the crisis, as well as to give assurances that it will not formulate new demands for greater concessions once the target capitulates.

Although these conditions improve the odds of successful coercive diplomacy, they do not guarantee success. History teaches that leaders who rely on military intervention for coercive diplomacy often start a process which they later find they cannot control.

> *Every nation is caught in the moral paradox of refusing to go to war unless it can be proved that the national interest is imperiled, and of continuing in the war only by proving that something much more than national interest is at stake.*
>
> —Reinhold Niebuhr, famed Lutheran theologian and realist theoretician

Given the uncertainties surrounding the use of armed force, many a state that has ventured down this military path has come to regret it. Even the meaning of victory in war (especially against terrorists and desperadoes) befuddles politicians and military commanders (Martel 2008). In the aftermath of unsuccessful interventions, confidence in this military method of coercive diplomacy has frequently vanished, and the search for other means to exercise power in world politics has intensified.

RIVAL REALIST ROADS TO SECURITY

Since the beginning of history, preparations for war often have been chosen as a path to security. The realist call for "peace through strength" is certainly understandable in a world where states alone remain responsible for their own self-defense.

> *Until war is eliminated from international relations, unpreparedness for it is well nigh as criminal as war itself.*
> —Dwight Eisenhower, U.S. president

Fear of national vulnerability in an anarchic, self-help environment requires defense planners to assume the worst about other states' capabilities and intentions. Even if the military capabilities accumulated by an enemy are defensively motivated, they usually trigger a strong reaction. The state "always feels itself weak if there is another that is stronger," observed the eighteenth-century French political philosopher Jean-Jacques Rousseau. "Its security and preservation demand that it make itself more powerful than its neighbors. It can increase, nourish, and exercise its power only at their expense. ... It becomes small or great, weak or strong, according to whether its neighbor expands or contracts, becomes stronger or declines."

State power, Rousseau reminds us, is relative. Efforts to obtain absolute security by one state tend to be perceived as creating absolute insecurity for others, with the result that everyone becomes locked into an upward spiral of countermeasures that diminish the security of all. Scholars refer to this as a *security dilemma*, a condition that results when each state's increase in military capabilities is matched by the others, and all wind up with no more security than when they began arming.

Many scholars (Jervis 1976; Snyder 1984) also describe the dynamics of this arms competition as the **spiral model**. The imagery captures the tendency of defense-enhancing efforts to result in escalating arms races that diminish the security of all. Sir Edward Grey, British foreign secretary before World War I, described this process well:

> The increase in armaments, that is intended in each nation to produce consciousness of strength and a sense of security, does not produce these effects. On the contrary, it produces a consciousness of the strength of other nations and a sense of fear. Fear begets suspicion and distrust and evil imaginings of all sorts, 'til each government feels it would be criminal and a betrayal of its own country not to take every precaution, while every government regards every precaution of every other government as evidence of hostile intent.

■ **spiral model**
a metaphor used to describe the tendency of efforts to enhance defense to result in escalating arms races.

Although the security dilemma confronts all states' decisions, most leaders still refuse to accept vulnerability. Searching for strength, they often proceed from the assumptions that: (1) security is a function of power; (2) power is a function of military capability; and (3) military might is a measure of national greatness. Each of these suppositions is, of course, consistent with realpolitik.

Asking whether military preparedness endangers, rather than ensures, national security raises an uncomfortable question that challenges the most actively promoted realist approach to national security throughout much of the world's history: acquiring arms to pursue power. Yet many experts believe questioning is needed.

To their way of thinking, the battles now are less interstate and more transnational, criss-crossing all states. If so, this requires rethinking how military threats can best be managed. To be determined is whether new ways of organizing perceptions of national security will gain greater acceptance, or whether old approaches will be applied to changing global realities.

The critical questions in your age of vulnerability of annihilation persist: How can states escape the danger of destruction? How can they meet such emergent nonmilitary threats as global warming and environmental deterioration when the threat of warfare and destruction by transnational terrorists seem to be more and more dangerous?

The security situation in your future is unlikely to provide much room for maneuvering. Many states are building weapons of attack for deterrence despite the fact that strategies of deterrence have frequently failed in the past, and the premise that successful defense requires the continuing vulnerability of all states appears illogical. Nonetheless, most realists and many others continue to believe that the threat system must be preserved to counter the threat, and they put lasting faith in the realist belief that it is safer to rely on the force of arms than on the force of arguments to successfully resolve disputes.

Security may depend as much on the control of force as on its pursuit. At issue is whether traditional realist emphasis on arms and military strategies that require either the threat or actual use of weapons for coercive diplomacy is the best and safest route to national and international security. To be sure, the traditional realist reliance on military capabilities to increase national security continues to resonate in world capitals. However, other realists recommend an alternative path—one that sees national interests served most, not by the acquisition and use of arms, but rather by the acquisition of allies in order to maintain a balance of power among rivals that will prevent any transnational actor from the temptation to use force against the others. This, these other realists believe, provides the safest path to security. Are they right? The next chapter reviews realist ideas about alliances and their impact in creating a balance of power to keep the peace. So you can evaluate next the prospects, payoffs, and pitfalls of this other primary realist road to international and national security.

Key Terms

power potential
coercive diplomacy
soft power
hard power
relative burden of military
  spending
private military services
arms race
blowback
proliferation
Nth country problem
horizontal nuclear proliferation
vertical nuclear proliferation
nonproliferation regime
Nuclear Nonproliferation Treaty
  (NPT)

multiple independently targetable
  reentry vehicles (MIRVs)
firebreak
strategic weapons
nonlethal weapons (NLWs)
revolution in military technology
  (RMT)
smart bombs
virtual nuclear arsenals
deterrence
infowar tactics
nuclear winter
compellence
brinkmanship
massive retaliation
countervalue targeting strategy

counterforce targeting strategy
nuclear deterrence
second-strike capability
mutual assured destruction (MAD)
Strategic Defense Initiative (SDI)
statelessness
preemptive war
just war theory
ultimatum
gunboat diplomacy
covert operations
nonintervention norm
spiral model

CHAPTER 15
ALLIANCES AND THE BALANCE OF POWER

As nature abhors a vacuum, so international politics abhors unbalanced power. Faced by unbalanced power, states try to increase their own strength or they ally with others to bring the international distribution of power into balance.

—Kenneth N. Waltz, *neorealist theoretician*

Agreeing to Align: In Mecca, a fledgling alliance plans to form a united front on Middle East wars and U.S. intervention. Shown is Saudi Arabia's King Abdullah (third from left) with (from left) Crown Prince Sultan Hashem, Mahmoud Abbas, Khaled Meshaal (the exiled leader of Hamas), Ismail Haniyeh, and Meshaal's deputy, Mussa Abu Marzuk. Illustrated is the historical tendency for countries to come together in alliances in order to counter common security threats.

D o you know who your true friends are? Is there anyone who seems to dislike you and act in opposition to you? What if this foe happens to be a friend of your best friend? How should you then behave toward them?

Now stretch the scenario. What if there is a real bully who likes to push and shove you around? But what if that stronger person also chooses to pick on your foe, and that otherwise troublesome enemy asks you to join him for mutual protection? Are your interests served by such an unlikely alliance? Is an enemy of your biggest enemy now a possible friend? If so, can you count on that former adversary to stand by you, as promised, if the going gets tough? Or might you be deserted?

Complicate this situation still further. You make the sad discovery that the person you thought was your best friend has been flirting with your girlfriend or boyfriend. But given the bully's threat, should you overlook this insult and call upon your "friend" for support? What if your request is denied? And you are aware that it might be. You recall hearing "a friend in need is a friend indeed" but that a self-serving and fearful so-called friend may reject you because when friendship is tested he concludes that "a friend in need is a pest!" Some friend!

Strange as it may seem, these kinds of hypothetical circumstances and choices for people have a powerful parallel in the real world of international politics. Countries, like individuals, make decisions that create friends and enemies. These decisions are based on converging and clashing interests and values. As the realist theoretician Thucydides counseled, "One has to behave as friend or foe according to the circumstances," and these choices are made on a complex geo-strategic playing field in which today's enemy may be tomorrow's ally and where fears of entrapment, abandonment or betrayal are ever present. Moreover, the game is played by actors unequal in strength, but with similar needs: to find allies as a means to self-protection when threats from another actor or opposed coalition appear on the scene. Alliances,

> *Warfare is not a question of brute strength, but rather of winning and losing friends.*
> —Count Diego Sarmiento Gondomar, Spanish Ambassador to London in 1618

like some personal friendships, are often *against* rather than *for* someone or something. And when relationships and conditions change, new alliances form and established alliances dissolve as transnational actors—all obsessed with the power of their rivals—realign.

Alliances in world politics require agreements by the parties to them to cooperate. For that reason, it may seem that *liberal theory*, with its emphasis on the possibility of self-sacrifice for mutual gain, might provide a key to understanding why and how states join together in alliances. However, realist theorizing provides the primary lens through which the dynamics of alliance formation and decay, and the impact of these dynamics on global security, are most often interpreted. Realism, you have learned, portrays world politics as a struggle for power in anarchy by competitive rivals acting for their own self-interests (and *not* for moral principles and global ideals such as improving the security and welfare of *all* throughout the globe). International politics to realism is a war of all against all, fought to increase national power and national security by preparing for war and seeking advantages over rivals such as by acquiring superior military capabilities.

Realists picture alliances as temporary, expedient experiments to cooperate in order to compete with and hold in check the dangerous ambitions of others. Realism provides the most compelling explanation of the coldly calculating motives underlying decisions about alliances, which realists see driven first and foremost as a method for protecting allies from threats posed by predatory common enemies. Most policy makers find this convincing because it speaks to their own experiences (just like the hypothetical scenario about friendships and foes that you may experience introduced the basic politics of human interaction and the factors that may influence such personal choices about with whom to ally and whom to regard as an adversary). Realist theory is the best paradigm for organizing thinking about the calculations behind considerations of security and how it might be maximized. Moreover, realism advances a rational choice account of alliance decisions, based on the observation that military partnerships have rarely been built to express friendship or agreements about ideas and ideals (Owen 2005). Instead, realist theory posits that military alliances are forged when the parties perceive the advantages of an alliance to outweigh the disadvantages.

This chapter looks at alliances in world politics from the account of realist theory, because realism is above all an interpretation of the preconditions for global security, or how military threats to international stability are best managed. As you shall see, realism maintains that alliances are the mechanism by which a "balance of power" can be maintained to prevent an aspiring hegemon from waging imperial wars to achieve world domination.

You might have already guessed that the basis for international stability and security is more complicated than this introduction implies. Realpolitik may be the most compelling theory of alliances discussed in government chambers, but the realist perspective has within its adherents disagreements about the role of alliances in world politics. So take a look at the leading hypotheses before considering the balance of power that is affected by alliance politics in theory and how that theory applies to trends in contemporary global circumstances.

REALIST INTERPRETATIONS OF ALLIANCES IN WORLD POLITICS

When threats to international peace surface, policy makers adhering to the liberal theoretical tradition recommended, almost as a knee-jerk reaction, that the disputants open negotiations to settle their differences at the bargaining table. To liberals, war represents the failure of diplomacy, the failure of countries to resolve their differences through cooperative negotiations to reach compromises (see Chapter 16). However, those abiding by realist foreign policy recommendations see countries' interests best served when they have not unilaterally armed themselves sufficiently to contain an emergent threat (recall Chapter 14), to combine their

> *It is the existence of an enemy that gives rise to the need for allies, and it is for the advantageous conduct of fighting that alliances are formed.*
>
> —Steven Rosen, realist policy maker

strength with the other threatened states in an alliance to contain and combat the common danger. Through that time-honored approach, the danger to all these threats can be contained and, if necessary, combated in a war.

Look at the process of alliance formation and decay from the realist worldview. To this frame of mind, **alliances** predictably come into being when two or more states face a common security threat.

■ **alliances**

coalitions that form when two or more states combine their military capabilities and promise to coordinate their policies to increase mutual security.

Alliances are formal agreements among states to coordinate their behavior by heeding realism's first rule of statecraft: to increase military capabilities. By acquiring allies, states increase their mutual armaments: When facing a common threat, alliances provide their members with the means of reducing their probability of being attacked (*deterrence*), obtaining greater strength in case of attack (defense), and precluding their allies from alliance with the enemy (Snyder 1991).

These advantages notwithstanding, realists often see a downside and counsel against forming alliances, as Britain's Lord Palmerston did in 1848 when he advised that states "should have no eternal allies and no perpetual enemies." Their only duty is to follow their interests and whenever possible to rely on *self-help* by depending only on their own state for defense because under anarchy no state can really count on allies to come to its defense if attacked.

The greatest risk to forming alliances is that they bind a state to a commitment that may later become disadvantageous. Because conditions are certain to change sooner or later and the usefulness of all alliances is certain to change once the common

> *Wise and experienced statesmen usually shy away from commitments likely to constitute limitations on a government's behavior at unknown dates in the future in the face of unpredictable situations.*
>
> —George Frost Kennan, realist American foreign policy maker

threat that brought the allies together declines, the realist tradition advises states not to take a fixed position on temporary convergences of national interests and instead to forge alliances only to deal with immediate threats.

When considering whether a new alliance is a *rational choice* in which the benefits outweigh the costs, heads of state usually recognize that allies can easily do more harm than good (see Controversy: Do the Advantages of Alliances Outweigh the Disadvantages?).

CONTROVERSY:

DO THE ADVANTAGES OF ALLIANCES OUTWEIGH THE DISADVANTAGES?

When states make decisions about forging alliances, they must keep in mind the many risks of sharing their fate with other states. Although realists generally see alliances as potentially beneficial, they caution that making a defense pact with an ally will also carry a heavy price (Weitsman 2004). Creating alliances will:

- foreclose options

- reduce the state's capacity to adapt to changing circumstances

- weaken a state's capability to influence others by decreasing the number of additional partners with which it can align

- eliminate the advantages in bargaining that can be derived from deliberately fostering ambiguity about one's intentions

- provoke the fears of adversaries

- entangle states in disputes with their allies' enemies

- interfere with the negotiation of disputes involving an ally's enemy by preventing certain issues from being placed on the agenda

- preserve existing rivalries

- stimulate envy and resentment on the part of friends who are outside the alliance and are therefore not eligible to receive its advantages

These potential dangers explain why alliance decisions are so controversial, even when advocates enthusiastically propose that another state be sought as an ally for mutual defense. The posture of leaders about the advantage or disadvantage of alliances has depended on their personal philosophy and the country's circumstances.

What do you think? What are the advantages of having alliance partners? In considering your options, look at the 1796 painting picturing George Washington, the first president of the United States, advising other leaders in American government that it should be the foreign policy of the United States to "steer clear of permanent alliances." He felt that whereas a state "may safely trust to temporary alliances for extraordinary emergencies" it is an "illusion . . . to expect or calculate real favors from nation to nation." Yet, almost every state is insecure in one way or another and is tempted to recruit allies to bolster its defense capabilities and protect its power in a united coalition opposed to adversaries that threaten it.

The Granger Collection

Many realists advise states against forming alliances for defense, basing their fears on five fundamental flaws:

■ Alliances enable aggressive states to combine military capabilities for war.

■ Alliances threaten enemies and provoke the creation of counteralliances, which reduces the security for both coalitions.

■ Alliance formation may draw otherwise neutral parties into opposed coalitions.

■ Once states join forces, they must control the behavior of their own allies to discourage each member from reckless aggression against its enemies, which would undermine the security of the alliance's other members.

■ The possibility always exists that today's ally might become tomorrow's enemy.

Despite their uncertain usefulness, many states throughout history have chosen to ally because, the risks notwithstanding, the perceived benefits to security in a time of threat justified that decision.

To best picture how alliances affect global security, it is instructive to move from the state level of analysis, which views alliance decisions from the perspective of an individual state's security, to the global level of analysis (recall Chapter 1) by looking at the impact of alliances on the frequency of interstate war. This view focuses attention on the possible contribution of alliance formation to maintaining the balance of power.

REALISM AND THE BALANCING OF POWER

■ **alignments**

the acceptance by a neutral state threatened by foreign enemies of a special relationship short of formal alliance with a stronger power able to protect it from attack.

The concept of a balance of power has a long and controversial history. Supporters envision it as an equilibrating process that maintains peace by counterbalancing any state that seeks military superiority, distributing global power evenly through **alignments** or shifts by nonaligned states to one or the other opposed coalitions. Critics deny the effectiveness of the balance of power, arguing that it breeds jealousy, intrigue, and antagonism. Part of the difficulty in evaluating these rival claims lies in the different meanings attributed to the concept (see Vasquez and Elman 2003; Claude 1962). Whereas "balance of power" may be widely used in everyday discourse, there is confusion over precisely what it entails.

At the core of nearly all the various meanings of "balance of power" is the idea that national security is enhanced when military capabilities are distributed so that no one state is strong enough to dominate all others. If one state gains inordinate power, balance-of-power theory predicts that it will take advantage of its strength and attack weaker neighbors, thereby giving compelling incentive for those threatened to align and unite in a defensive coalition. According to the theory, the threatened states' combined military strength would deter (or, if need be, defeat) the state harboring expansionist aims. Thus, for realists, laissez-faire competition among states striving to maximize their national power yields an international equilibrium, ensuring the survival of all by checking hegemonic ambitions.

Balance-of-power theory is also founded on the realist premise that weakness invites attack and that countervailing power must be used to deter potential aggressors. Realists assume that the drive for expanded power guides every state's actions. It follows that all countries are potential adversaries and that each must strengthen its military capability to protect itself. Invariably, this reasoning rationalizes the quest for military superiority, because others pursue it as well. The reasons spring from the realist belief that a system revolving around suspicion, competition, and anarchy will breed caution; uncertainty creates restraints on the initiation of war. Why? Because

> *It is a maxim founded on the universal experience of mankind that no nation is to be trusted farther than it is bound by its interest.*
>
> —George Washington, first U.S. president

when all states are independent and, as sovereign actors, free to make rational choices designed to protect their national security interests in a climate of fear and mistrust, they have powerful incentives to realign and form coalitions that would lead to an approximately even distribution of power, curbing the natural temptation of any great power to imperialistically attempt to conquer the others. In classic balance-of-power theory, fear of a third party will encourage alignments, because those threatened would need help to offset the power of the common adversary. An alliance would add the ally's power to the state's own and deny the addition of that power to the enemy. As alliances combine power, the offsetting coalitions would give neither a clear advantage. Therefore, aggression would appear unattractive and would be averted.

To deter an aggressor, counteralliances are expected to form easily, because *free riders*, states sitting on the sidelines, cannot, as rational actors, risk **nonalignment**. If they refuse to ally, their own vulnerability will encourage an expansionist state to attack them sooner or later. The result of these individual calculations, to avoid sharing benefits and limit payoffs to other participants, will be the creation of minimal winning coalitions. This is in accordance with what is known as the **size principle**—the formation of coalitions only sufficient in size to produce victory, resulting in offsetting coalitions that are roughly equal in size (Riker 1962).

To balance power against power in opposed coalitions approximately equal in strength, realists recognize that what is required is for national actors to see the value of rapidly shifting alliances. This requires adherence to decision rules.

Rules for Rivals in the Balancing Process

Although balancing is occasionally described as an automatic, self-adjusting process, most realists see it as the result of deliberate choices undertaken by national leaders to maintain an equilibrium among contending states. They see the balancing of power as being produced by adherence to rules of action and reaction that states must follow. It is necessary for all leaders to constantly monitor changes in states' relative capabilities so policies about arms and allies can be adjusted to rectify imbalances of power. Choices must be made by rational, self-interested actors that recognize the trade-off of costs and benefits between strategic options. For example,

■ **nonalignment**
a foreign policy posture in which states do not participate in military alliances with either of two rival blocs for fear that alliance will lead to involvement in an unnecessary war.

■ **size principle**
the propensity for competitors to form coalitions among a number of partners only sizable enough to ensure victory, even if by a narrow margin, with the result that opposed alliances tend to remain roughly equal to one another over time.

some options, such as expanding military capabilities through armaments and alliances, attempt to add weight to the lighter side of the international balance. Others, such as negotiating limits on weaponry and on a great power's sphere of influence to reduce the size of the geographical region under the domination of a great power, attempt to decrease the weight of the heavier side.

Various theorists have attempted to specify a set of rules that must be heeded in this constructed *security regime* in order for the balancing process to function effectively. These rules include:

1   *Stay vigilant.* Constantly watch foreign developments in order to identify emerging threats and opportunities. Because international anarchy makes each state responsible for its own security and because states can never be sure of one another's intentions, self-interest encourages them to maximize their relative power. As Morton Kaplan (1957) wrote: "Act to increase capabilities but negotiate rather than fight. . . . [At the same time, states should] fight rather than pass up an opportunity to increase capabilities."

2   *Seek allies whenever your country cannot match the armaments of an adversary.* States align with each other when they adopt a common stance toward some shared security problem. An alliance is produced when they formally agree to coordinate their behavior under certain specified circumstances. The degree of coordination may range from a detailed list of military forces that will be furnished by each party in the event of war to the more modest requirement that they will consult with one another should hostilities erupt. According to balance-of-power theory, alliances are the primary means of compensating for an inability to keep up with a rival's arms acquisitions.

3   *Remain flexible in making alliances.* Formed and dissolved according to the strategic needs of the moment, alliances must be made without regard to similarities of culture or ideological beliefs (Owen 2005). Because alliances are instrumental, short-term adjustments aimed at rectifying imbalances in the distribution of military capabilities, past experiences should not predispose states to accept or reject *any* potential partner. Nowhere is this better seen than in the **balancer** role Great Britain once played in European diplomacy. From the seventeenth through the early twentieth centuries, the British shifted their weight from one side of the continental balance to the other, arguing that they had no permanent friends and no permanent enemies, just a permanent interest in preventing the balance from tipping either way (Dehio 1962). As described by Winston Churchill, Britain's goal was to "oppose the strongest, most aggressive, most dominating power on the continent. . . . [It] joined with the less strong powers, made a combination among them, and thus defeated and frustrated the continental military tyrant whoever he was, whatever nation he led."

■ **balancer**
under a balance-of-power system, an influential global or regional great power that throws its support in decisive fashion to a defensive coalition.

4   *Oppose any state that seeks hegemony.* The purpose of engaging in balance-of-power politics is to survive in a world of potentially dangerous great powers. If any state achieves absolute mastery over everyone else, it will be able to act freely. Under such circumstances, the territorial integrity and political autonomy of other states will be in jeopardy. By joining forces with the weaker side to prevent the stronger side from reaching preponderance, states can preserve their independence.

Balance of power is a policy of helping the underdog because if you help the top dog, it may eventually turn around and eat you.

—Joseph Nye, U.S. policy maker and scholar

For this reason, when a single superpower attains preponderant status, the usual reaction at first of other major powers is to engage in "soft balancing" by using "nonmilitary tools to delay, frustrate, and undermine" the hegemon's "military policies. Soft balancing using international institutions, economic statecraft, and diplomatic arrangement," Richard A. Pape (2005b) observes, are "already a prominent feature of the international opposition to the U.S. war against Iraq." He predicts that the major powers now engaging in the early stages of balancing behavior against the United States might follow by turning to "traditional hard-balancing measures, such as military buildups, war-fighting alliances, and transfers of military technology to U.S. opponents," especially if and when the "major powers become confident that members of a balancing coalition will act in unison."

5   *Be charitable in victory.* "An equilibrium," argues Edward Gulick (1955), "cannot perpetuate itself unless the major components of that equilibrium are preserved." In the event of war, the winning side should not eliminate the defeated. Looking forward rather than backward, it should do as little damage as possible to those it has vanquished because yesterday's enemy may be needed as tomorrow's ally. Victors that couple firmness regarding their own interests with fairness toward the interests of others encourage defeated powers to work within the postwar balance of power. Similarly, states that win at the bargaining table can stabilize the balance of power by granting the other side compensation in return for its concessions.

These realist policy prescriptions urge states to check the ambitions of any great power that threatens to amass overwhelming power, because aspiring hegemons are a potential threat to everyone. Human beings and states, they argue, are by nature selfish, but balancing rival interests stabilizes their interactions. Weakness, realists insist, invites aggression. Thus, when faced with unbalanced power, leaders of states should mobilize their domestic resources or ally with others to bring the international distribution of power back into equilibrium (Schweller 2004; Waltz 1979). The alarmed response by China and Russia after the U.S. 2002 *National Security Strategy (NSS)*, which announced that the United States would do everything within its power to preserve forever America's supreme global primacy, illustrates the balancing process. Also illustrative was the resistance of Germany, France, and many other countries to the 2003 U.S. decision to launch a war of preemption to prevent Iraq from acquiring and using weapons of mass destruction—especially because evidence of Iraq's possession of such weapons, ties to the 9/11 terrorist attacks, or intention to wage war did not exist.

Difficulties with the Maintenance of a Balance of Power

Can balancing power help to preserve world order, as most realists believe? Critics of balance-of-power theory raise several objections to the proposition that balancing promotes peace. First, scholars argue that the theory's rules for behavior are contradictory (Riker 1962). On the one hand, states are urged to increase their power. On the other hand, they are told to oppose anyone seeking preponderance. Yet sometimes **bandwagoning** with (rather than balancing against) the dominant state can increase a weaker country's capabilities by allowing it to share in the spoils of a future victory. History suggests that states that are most content with the status quo tend to balance against rising powers more than do dissatisfied states.

■ **bandwagoning**

the tendency for weak states to seek alliance with the strongest power, irrespective of that power's ideology or type of government, in order to increase their security.

A second objection to balance-of-power theory is that it assumes policy makers possess accurate, timely information about other states. As discussed in the previous chapter, the concept of "power" has multiple meanings. Tangible factors are hard to compare, such as the performance capabilities of the different types of weapons found in an adversary's arsenal. Intangible factors, such as leadership skills, troop morale, or public support for adventuresome or aggressive foreign policies, are even more difficult to gauge. Without a precise measure of relative strength, how can policy makers know when power is becoming unbalanced? Moreover, in an environment of secret alliances, how can they be sure who is really in league with whom? An ally who is being counted on to balance the power of an opponent may have secretly agreed to remain neutral in the event of a showdown. Consequently, the actual distribution of power may not resemble the constructed distribution imagined by one side or the other.

Problems in determining the strength of adversaries and the trustworthiness of allies leads to a third objection to balance-of-power theory: the uncertainty of power balances frequently causes defense planners to engage in worst-case analysis, which can spark an arms race. The intense, reciprocal anxiety that shrouds balance-of-power politics fuels exaggerated estimates of an adversary's strength. This, in turn, prompts each side to expand the quantity and enhance the quality of its weaponry. Critics of realism warn that if a serious dispute occurs between states locked in relentless arms competition under conditions of mutually assured suspicions, the probability of war increases.

A fourth objection is that balance-of-power theory assumes that decision makers are risk averse—when confronted with countervailing power, they refrain from fighting because the dangers of taking on an equal are too great. Yet, as prospect theory (see Chapter 3) illuminates, national leaders evaluate risks differently. Some are risk-acceptant. Rather than being deterred by equivalent power, they prefer gambling on the chance of winning a victory, even if the odds are long. Marshaling comparable power against adversaries with a high tolerance for risk will not have the same effect as it would on those who avoid risks.

Finally, many analysts object to balance-of-power theory because its past performance is checkered. If the theory's assumptions are correct, historical periods during which its rules were followed should also have been periods in which war was less frequent. Yet a striking feature of those periods is their record of warfare. After the 1648 Peace of Westphalia created the global system of independent territorial states, the great powers participated in a series of increasingly destructive general wars that threatened to engulf and destroy the entire multistate global system. As Inis

L. Claude (1989) soberly concludes, it is difficult to consider these wars "as anything other than catastrophic failures, total collapses, of the balance-of-power system. They are hardly to be classified as stabilizing maneuvers or equilibrating processes, and one cannot take seriously any claim of maintaining international stability that does not entail the prevention of such disasters." Indeed, the historical record has led some theorists to construct *hegemonic stability theory* as an alternative to the balance of power. This theory postulates that a single, dominant hegemon can guarantee peace better than a rough equality of military capabilities among competing great powers (Ferguson 2004a; Mandelbaum 2006a; Organski 1968).

Managing the Balance through a Concert of Great Powers

A significant problem with the balance-of-power system is its haphazard character. To bring order to the global system, the great powers have occasionally tried to institutionalize channels of communication. The Concert of Europe that commenced with the Congress of Vienna in 1815 exemplified this strategy. In essence, it was a club exclusively for the great powers.

The idea behind a *concert* is "rule by a central coalition" of great powers (Rosecrance 1992). It is predicated on the belief that the leading centers of power will see their interests advanced by collaborating to prevent conflict from escalating into war in those regions under their collective jurisdiction. Although it is assumed that the great powers share a common outlook, concerts still allow "for subtle jockeying and competition to take place among them. Power politics is not completely eliminated; members may turn to internal mobilization and coalition formation to pursue divergent interests. But the cooperative framework of a concert, and its members' concern about preserving peace, prevent such balancing from escalating to overt hostility and conflict" (Kupchan and Kupchan 1992).

A common sense of duty is the glue that holds great-power concerts together. When belief in mutual self-restraint fades, concerts unravel. "Friction tends to build as each state believes that it is sacrificing more for unity than are others," notes Robert Jervis (1985). "Each will remember the cases in which it has been restrained, and ignore or interpret differently cases in which others believe they acted for the common good." Overcoming this friction requires continuous consultation in order to reinforce expectations of joint responsibilities. Concert members should not be challenged over their vital interests, nor should they suffer an affront to their prestige and self-esteem (Elrod 1976). A "just" equilibrium among contending great powers bound together in a concert means more than an equal distribution of military capabilities; it includes recognition of honor, rights, and dignity (Schroeder 1989).

Although a concert framework can help manage relations among counterpoised great powers, the normative consensus underpinning this arrangement is fragile and can erode easily. And this potential for great power harmony to be replaced by great power rivalry is what alarms many realist observers. This scenario is especially threatening to those concerned by the possibility that after the Iraq war the United States could retreat into isolationistic withdrawal from working with the other great powers to keep international peace "We might be getting a glimpse of what a world without America would look like. It will be free of American domination, but perhaps also free of leadership," warns the realist analyst Fareed Zakaria (2007). And a dangerous power vacuum could result as the world witnesses "the end of alliances" when formal military ties fade away and are replaced by informal shifting alignments among the competitors (Menon 2007).

Is there another realist road out of such a threatening development? One avenue of possible escape recommended by realists is to look beyond concerts and/or hegemonic leadership for global stability. To steady precarious power balances, some realists advocate arms control agreements to stabilize the great powers' level of military arsenals.

STABILIZING POWER BALANCES THROUGH ARMS CONTROL?

Liberal reformers have often attacked the theory that power can be balanced to preserve world order (see Chapter 17). Instead, they have advocated the Biblical prescription that states should beat their swords into plowshares.

The destructiveness of today's weapons has inspired many people once again to take this tenet of liberal theory seriously. But this approach is not solely a liberal preserve. Many realists also see arms limitation as a way of stabilizing the balance of power. In fact, most policy makers who have negotiated such agreements have been realists who perceived these treaties as a prudent tool to promote their country's security.

Actually, realists generally favor arms control over disarmament to reduce or eliminate weapons. Realists point to the ability of the United States and Russia to negotiate a series of arms control agreements that have limited their stockpiles of nuclear weapons and restricted how those that remain might be used (see Figure 15.1). This set of agreements did succeed in reducing the two military superpowers' tensions and helped two rivals to maintain a meaningful balance of power between them to increase their mutual security. Arguably, realist policy makers in both countries envisioned self-interests to be served by controlling the arms race that otherwise might have unfolded.

Realists are quick to recommend the acquisition of more and more arms in their own arsenal to increase their country's security, and are understandably fearful of losing ground to a rival's attainment of superior military capabilities. That said, realists also appreciate the risk of a run-away action-reaction sequence when rival states rapidly increase their military capabilities in response to one another. And realists are sobered by their recognition that the probability of war increases when competitive states locked in relentless arms competition find themselves engaged in a serious dispute with each other. Therefore, limiting an arms race can pay dividends.

Nevertheless, realists are also very distrustful of arms control agreements. They warn that the prospects for cooperation between rivals are very dim. States are naturally prone to seek military superiority, even if this requires them to cheat on their prior commitments in arms control treaties. Indeed, to realists, states acting in what they perceive to be their rational self-interest will always be tempted to defect from treaty commitments to restrain their arms buildups "despite the fact that through cooperation [the parties to an arms control agreement] can achieve the collectively

FIGURE 15.1

CAGING THE NUCLEAR THREAT: THE NEGOTIATED CONTROL AND REDUCTION OF DEPLOYED STRATEGIC U.S. AND RUSSIAN WARHEADS **Following the Strategic Arms Limitation Talks (SALT) that produced arms control agreements in 1972 and 1979, the United States and Russia concluded the Strategic Offensive Reduction Treaty (SORT) that through arms control seeks to distance the former superpower adversaries even further from the brink of nuclear destruction. Shown here are trends in their nuclear arsenals between 1946 and 2012.**

A treaty rests and must rest upon moral obligation. No doubt a great power can cast aside a moral obligation if it sees fit and escape from the performance of the duty which it promises. The pathway of dishonor is always open.

—Henry Cabot Lodge, U.S. Senator

rational outcome that results in higher payoffs for all" (Brams 1985). Realists are pessimists about faithful adherence to agreements because they see human behavior driven by sinful self-regard and the search for power over others; this leads people and countries alike to break their promises when they believe they can get ahead of others at their competitor's expense.

As a result, realists recognize that states play a game that paradoxically imprisons them to their disadvantage. There is little hope that the dilemma created by the *zero-sum* competitive pursuit of self-advantage can be overcome. So to realism cooperation is trumped by competition. Arms control cannot be relied upon as a method to preserve power balances. The **Prisoner's Dilemma** is a game that explains why realists are mistrustful of negotiated arms control agreements as a route to international stability. The obstacles realists see to international cooperation also rest in the global circumstances that reduce countries' pursuit of *absolute gains* that could make all the cooperating parties better off. Realists see the players in the game of arms control trapped in a prison of their own making—a dilemma from which they

■ **Prisoner's Dilemma**

from game theory, a non-zero-sum situation in which two prisoners have incentives to cooperate and if they do they will both benefit, so that is the rational decision to make; however, if one defects to maximize personal gain at the expense of the other prisoner, both will suffer—a dilemma that raises questions about what is the prudent or rational course of action in circumstances of distrust.

seldom escape because of their competitive drive to seek *relative gains* or advantages for themselves over their rivals. Realist theory urges policy makers to recognize the strategic imperatives of zero-sum logic that commands avoiding losses by pursuing gains over others (see Controversy: Arms Races and the Prisoner's Dilemma).

These difficulties in preserving the balance of power through efforts to contain arms races by cooperative agreements lead most realists to conclude that international conflict and competition is permanent in world politics, and, therefore, that the best hope is to count on the emergence of a stable balance of power to preserve peace. Next, take a look at trends in the historical record and projections for the future about how the balance of power is likely to function.

BALANCING POWER IN THE CONTEMPORARY GLOBAL SYSTEM

The use of alliances and arms control to balance power has shifted over time in a series of redistributions. At one extreme have been periods in which a powerful state has tried to prevail over another state, which in response usually has built additional arms or sought allies to offset its adversary's strength. Over time, each increase in military capability by one side has provoked an increase by the other. If neither side yields, at times they have managed the spiraling crisis by negotiating arms control agreements. At the other extreme, at times a more fluid competition has emerged, with encroachments by one state against another also precipitating a quest for arms and allies. But rather than resulting in the formation of rigid, counterbalanced blocs, this kind of military confrontation has triggered many shifts by others to produce a kaleidoscope of overlapping alliances—a checkerboard of multiple great powers competing in balance-of-power politics.

■ global structure

the defining characteristics of the global system—such as the distribution of military capabilities —that exist independently of all actors but powerfully shape the actions of every actor.

Having examined how the balance of power is supposed to operate, the chapter next considers how it actually has functioned in world politics. To visualize these potential types of **global structure** and their causes and consequences, the chapter now considers several models of balance-of-power distributions that have arisen since World War II, with an eye to the kinds of power divisions that may develop in the twenty-first-century's age of globalization now dominated by American military supremacy.

Models of the Balance of Power—Past and Present

Military power can be distributed around one or more power centers in different ways—an idea scholars call *polarity*. Historically, these have ranged from highly concentrated power on one end of the continuum to highly dispersed power distributions on the other. The former has included regional empires (e.g., the Roman Empire), and an example of the latter is the approximate equality of power held by the European powers at the conclusion of the Napoleonic Wars in 1815. Using the conventional ways historians separate turning points from one type of balance-of-power system to another, four distinct periods of polarity are observable. This evolution displays a cycle, because the transformations went through four

CONTROVERSY:

ARMS RACES AND THE PRISONER'S DILEMMA

Realists and liberal theorists both agree that the world could be a better place if countries would see their self-interests served by international cooperation. But realists and liberals hold differing views about the prospects for cooperation. The two schools of thought have been engaged in a controversial debate about why competition often trumps cooperation. What do you think?

One way to address this question is to examine the logic underlying the well-known "Prisoner's Dilemma" game. It illuminates the circumstantial barriers to international cooperation among distrustful transnational actors across many arenas of international politics, and is especially relevant to arms control and arms races.

Imagine two suspects following an armed robbery are taken into police custody and placed in separate cells by the district attorney, who is certain that they are guilty but only has sufficient evidence to convict them on an illegal weapons charge. The district attorney tells prisoner A and prisoner B that there are two choices: confess to the robbery, or remain silent. If one prisoner confesses and the other doesn't, he will be given immunity from prosecution for turning state's evidence whereas his accomplice will get a sentence of ten years in the state penitentiary. If both confess, they will be given a reduced sentence of five years in the penitentiary. If neither confesses, they will be convicted on the weapons charge and serve only six months in the county jail. Because both prisoners want to spend as little time incarcerated as possible, their preferences are rank ordered from the best to the worst outcomes as follows: (1) immunity from prosecution; (2) six months in the county jail; (3) five years in the state penitentiary; and (4) ten years in the penitentiary. The matrix below depicts the results that will occur depending on whether each prisoner chooses to cooperate with his accomplice by remaining silent or defect by confessing to the district attorney.

Faced with this situation, what should each prisoner do? Remember that they both want as little time behind bars as possible, and they are being interrogated separately so they cannot communicate. Furthermore, neither prisoner is sure that he can trust the other.

Although the optimal strategy for both prisoners would be to tacitly cooperate with each other and keep quiet so each receives only a six-month sentence (the payoff of 2, 2 in the matrix), the structural properties of this situation are such that there are powerful incentives to defect from your partner and give state's evidence to the district attorney. First, there is an offensive incentive to defect based on the prospect of getting immunity by confessing. Second, there is a defensive incentive to defect grounded in the fear of being double-crossed by an accomplice who squeals. If one prisoner refuses to talk but the other confesses, the one who tried to cooperate with his accomplice to get a mutually beneficial result would receive the worst possible payoff (4, or ten years in the penitentiary), whereas the prisoner who defected to the district attorney would receive the best payoff (1, or immunity). Not wanting be a "sucker" who spends a

	A	
	cooperate	**defect**
cooperate	2, 2	4, 1
defect	1, 4	3, 3

B (label at left)

NOTE: The first number in each cell of this matrix is A's payoff; the second number is B's payoff. The number 1 represents the most preferred outcome, whereas 4 represents the least preferred outcome.

decade incarcerated while his partner in crime goes free, both prisoners conclude that it is their self-interest to defect and testify against one another; consequently, they both receive a worse result (the payoff 3, 3 in the matrix, or five years in prison) than if they had tacitly cooperated by remaining silent. The dilemma is that seemingly rational calculations by each individual actor can yield collectively worse results for both than had they chosen other strategies.

Many theorists liken arms races to the Prisoner's Dilemma game. Consider two countries (A and B) that are approximately equal in military capability, uncertain of whether they can trust one another, and currently facing two choices: cooperate in lowering arms spending or defect by increasing arms spending. Suppose that each country prefers to have a military advantage over the other and fears being at a serious disadvantage, which would happen if one increased arms spending while the other reduced expenditures (the payoffs 4, 1 and 1, 4 in the matrix above). By cooperating to lower arms spending they could devote more resources to other national needs such as education and health care (the payoff 2, 2), but given offensive and defensive incentives that are similar to those tempting the two prisoners in our earlier example, they both conclude that it is in their individual self-interest to play it safe and arm. As a result of their joint defection (payoff 3, 3), they end up worse off by locking themselves into an expensive arms race that may destabilize the prevailing balance of power.

Although this version of the Prisoner's Dilemma game is a simplification that does not take into account what might happen in repeated plays over time (see Axelrod 1984), it highlights for you some of the difficulties in reaching mutually beneficial arms control agreements among self-interested actors who distrust their peers. Do you see any practical methods for escaping the "prison" posed by this dilemma?

---

phases that conclude today the same way the system began: (1) unipolarity, 1945–1949; (2) bipolarity, 1949–1991; (3) multipolarity 1991–2001; and (4) another unipolar system today with the United States again an unchallenged hegemon.

Unipolarity—The United States Most countries were devastated by World War II. The United States, however, was left in a clearly dominant position, with its economy accounting for about half the world's combined gross national product (GNP). The United States was also the only country with the atomic bomb and had demonstrated its willingness to use the new weapon. This underscored to others that it was without rival and incapable of being counterbalanced. The United States was not just stronger than *anybody*—it was stronger than *everybody*.

In the period immediately following World War II, a unipolar distribution of power materialized, because power was concentrated in the hands of a single hegemon able to exercise overwhelming influence over all other states, either through leadership or through domination. So supremely powerful was the United States at that time that people spoke of a new "American Empire" ruling over an impoverished world ravaged by war. That hegemonic status was short lived, however, as an ascendant challenger to U.S. preponderance, the Soviet Union, soon began to undermine America's supremacy and hegemonic status.

The U.S. capacity to act unilaterally in pursuit of its interests and ideals underwent a decline over the next four decades, as the U.S. grip on global developments and its ability to influence others eroded.

Bipolarity—The United States and Russia The recovery of the Soviet economy, the growth of its military capabilities, its maintenance of a large army, and growing Soviet–U.S. rivalry less than five years after the end of World War II gave rise to a new distribution of world power. The Soviets broke the U.S. monopoly on atomic weapons in 1949 and exploded a thermonuclear device in 1953, less than a year after the United States. This achievement symbolized the creation of global *bipolarity*— the division of the balance of power into two coalitions headed by rival military powers, each seeking to contain the other's expansion. Military capabilities became concentrated in the hands of two competitive "superpowers," whose capacities to massively destroy anyone made comparisons with the other great powers meaningless.

Power combined to form two opposing blocs or coalitions through **polarization** when states joined counterbalanced alliances. In interpreting these dynamics, it is important not to use the concepts of polarity and polarization interchangeably. They refer to two distinct dimensions of the primary ways in which military power is combined (or divided) at any point in time in the global system. When states independently build arms at home, their differential production rates change the global system's *polarity*, or the number of power centers (poles). In contrast, when states combine their arms through alliance formation, the aggregation of power through *polarization* changes the system's balance of power. A system with multiple power centers can be said to be moving toward a greater degree of polarization if its members form separate blocs whose external interactions are characterized by increasing levels of conflict while their internal interactions become more cooperative (Rapkin and Thompson with Christopherson 1989). Polarization increases when the number of cross-cutting alignments declines. The concept of polarization is especially apt in this context because a *pole* suggests the metaphor of a magnet—it both repels and attracts.

■ **polarization**
the degree to which states cluster in alliances around the most powerful members of the global system.

The formation of the **North Atlantic Treaty Organization (NATO)**, linking the United States to the defense of Western Europe, and the Warsaw Pact, linking the former Soviet Union in a formal alliance with its Eastern European clients, were produced by this polarization process. The opposing blocs formed in part because the superpowers competed for allies and in part because the less powerful states looked to one superpower or the other for protection. Correspondingly, each superpower's allies gave it forward bases from which to carry on the competition. In addition, the involvement of most other states in the superpowers' struggle globalized the East–West conflict. Few states remained outside the superpowers' rival alliance networks as neutral or nonaligned countries.

■ **North Atlantic Treaty Organization (NATO)**
a military alliance created in 1949 to deter a Soviet attack on Western Europe that since has expanded and redefined its mission to emphasize not only the maintenance of peace but also the promotion of democracy.

By grouping the system's states into two blocs, each led by a superpower, the Cold War's bipolar structure bred insecurity among all. The balance was constantly at stake. Each bloc leader, fearing that its adversary would attain hegemony, viewed every move, however defensive, as the first step toward world conquest. Zero-sum conflict prevailed as both sides viewed what one side gained as a loss for the other. Both superpowers attached great importance to recruiting new allies. Fear that an old ally might desert the bloc was ever present. Bipolarity left little room for compromise or maneuver and worked against the "normalization" of cooperative superpower relations (Waltz 1993).

Bipolarity first began to disintegrate in the 1960s and early 1970s when the opposed coalitions' internal cohesion eroded and new centers of power emerged. At the same time, weaker alliance partners were afforded more room for maneuvering, as illustrated by the friendly relations between the United States and Romania and between France and the Soviet Union. The superpowers remained dominant militarily, but this less rigid system allowed other states to act more independently.

■ **doctrines**

the guidelines that a great power or an alliance embraces as a strategy to specify the conditions under which it will use military power and armed force for political purposes abroad.

■ **extended deterrence**

the protection received by a weak ally when a heavily militarized great power pledges to "extend" its capabilities to it in a defense treaty.

Rapid technological innovation in the superpowers' major weapons systems was a catalyst in the dissolution of the Cold War blocs and the national strategy **doctrines** that the adversaries had constructed. Intercontinental ballistic missiles (ICBMs), capable of delivering nuclear weapons through space from one continent to another, lessened the importance of forward bases on allies' territory for striking at the heart of the adversary. Furthermore, the narrowed differences in the superpowers' arsenals loosened the ties that had previously bound allies to one another. The European members of NATO in particular began to question whether the United States would, as it had pledged, protect Paris or London by sacrificing New York. Under what conditions might Washington or Moscow be willing to risk a nuclear holocaust? The uncertainty became pronounced as the pledge to protect allies through **extended deterrence** seemed increasingly insincere.

The movement toward democracy and market economies by some communist states in the late 1980s further eroded the bonds of ideology that had formerly helped these countries face their security problems from a common posture. The 1989 dismantling of the Berlin Wall tore apart the Cold War architecture of competing blocs. With the end of this division, and without a Soviet threat, the consistency of outlook and singularity of purpose that once bound NATO members together disappeared. Many perceived the need to replace NATO. However, NATO has proven itself to be an adaptive alliance (see Map 17.3, p. 536), although disagreements among these leading members compromise NATO decision making and are likely to do so in the future.

The United States: Dominant Superpower or Hobbled Hegemon?   Following the collapse of the Soviet Union in 1991, a *power transition*—a change in the ratio of military capabilities between great power rivals that produces tensions and increases the probability of war between them—occurred. This prompted many analysts to conclude that a new era of unipolarity had arisen, with the United States emerging as the world's only superpower. A decade after the collapse of communism in Europe, columnist Charles Krauthammer (2002) proclaimed that "no country has been as dominant culturally, economically, technologically, and militarily in the history of the world since the Roman Empire." Others, however, perceived the emergence of a hybrid "uni-multipolar" system with the United States as the sole superpower, but with other states not easily dominated and collaboration required for the resolution of key international issues (Huntington 2005).

The question remains as to whether U.S. predominance will prove beneficial or damaging. Recall that to hegemonic stability theorists a unipolar concentration of power allows the global leader to police chaos and maintain international peace. Their faith in America as a well-intentioned peacekeeper was bolstered by then President George W. Bush's pledge in 2001 that the U.S. role in the world would be "the story of a power that went into the world to protect but not possess, to defend but not to conquer."

Against this optimistic view runs a strong suspicion about the future stability of a unipolar world under U.S. management. Fears rose in reaction to the assertive Bush Doctrine pledging that the United States would unilaterally act however it wishes abroad, without the approval of others. This stimulated criticism and backlash. Throughout the world, U.S. leadership was condemned for its shortsightedness and

> *It is virtually universal in history that when countries become hegemons they tend to want everything their own way, and it never works.*
>
> —Jessica T. Mathews, analyst for the Carnegie Endowment for International Peace

willingness to put narrow self-interests ahead of ideals by seeking to preserve America's position as world leader without working through multilateral cooperation with others for peace and prosperity. However, according to a BBC poll conducted in 2008, the global public is optimistic that under President Barack Obama, U.S. relations with the rest of the world will improve.

Will the optimists, or the pessimists, be proven more accurate in their predictions about the future consequences of the hierarchical structure of world power? Time will tell, but one trend is certain to influence what unfolds: the eventual erosion of today's U.S. preponderance. That unipolar distribution is unlikely to last long. The toll of imperial overstretch from the extraordinary costs of global management in conjunction with the inevitability of differential economic growth rates that favor fast-growing challengers assures that China and India as well as the European Union will overtake U.S. supremacy economically (NIC 2004). This power transition will occur sooner rather than later (Ikenberry 2008) if the United States fails to reduce the heavy financial burden of the American global empire.

> *A great power must maintain its objectives and its power in equilibrium, its purposes within its means and its means equal to its purposes.*
>
> —Walter Lippmann, American policy analyst

U.S. primacy and global domination contain within itself the seeds of U.S. decline. A strong possibility is that as U.S. power recedes relative to rising great power challengers, America's global ambitions will prove counterproductive (Smith 2007). As Figure 15.2 suggests, power transitions breed turmoil and global instability when rising powers, dissatisfied with their subordination by the reigning hegemon, are prone to disrupt the prevailing global hierarchy in their favor. Other countries during this power shift away from U.S. domination can be expected to "obstruct American purposes whenever and in whatever way they can, and the pursuit of American interests will have to be undertaken through coercion rather than consensus. Anti-Americanism will become the global language of political protest— the default ideology of opposition—unifying the world's discontents and malcontents, some of whom can be very dangerous" (Zakaria 2002c; see also Rothkopf 2005).

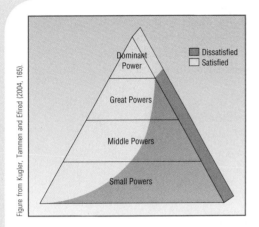

FIGURE 15.2

A POWER TRANSITION IN THE GLOBAL HIERARCHY **Where countries sit in the world pyramid of power predicts their posture toward global change. As this figure suggests, the more favorable a country's position is in the world hierarchy, the more satisfied it is with the international status quo; conversely, states lower in the hierarchy are more dissatisfied and therefore promote change. As the figure on the left suggests, the power transition theory provides leverage for "anticipating when and where great power and regional wars most likely will occur. With a warning well ahead of time comes the opportunity to construct current policies that can manage the events that lead to future disputes" (Kugler, Tammen and Efired 2004). The photo on the right captures the cross-cutting combination of anger and allegiances that surface during power transitions—a mural with a ghostly Statue of Liberty on a wall facing the U.S. Embassy in Tehran.**

Signs of the emergence of an anti-American bloc anchored by other great powers are already evident in the "subtle challenge to Pax Americana—the first stirrings of what might become an anti-American coalition involving at least two great powers. Hegemonic powers, such as Napoleonic France and imperial Nazi Germany, tend almost inevitably to spur the creation of great powers to oppose and contain them" (Krauthammer 2005).

Continuing U.S. dominance in a unipolar distribution of world power is certain to breed resistance, especially if America mismanages its special opportunity to lead by altering the course of history for the benefit of all humanity (Haass 2005; Chua 2008). For example, some (Bowring 2005) fret that the heavy-handed U.S. presence in Asia "has clearly helped to incite [the 2005 and 2007 joint military shows] of force and friendship by Russia and China."

What Lies Ahead?

Sooner or later, America's unipolar period in the sun will inevitably fade, and some new distribution of power will develop. The probable consequences of such a transformation in world politics are not clear. Some forecast the return of a bipolar pattern of direct opposition, with a new Sino-Russian bloc, European-Russian entente, or Sino-Japanese alliance countering the United States (Brzezinski 2004). Others see the emergence of a more complex multipolar pattern of balance-of-power competition, where the United States, China, Japan, Russia, and the European Union would constitute five centers of global power. According to this image of the future,

AFP/Getty Images

ALLIANCES: RIVALRY AND MUTUAL NEED Relations within NATO have long been marked by disputes. U.S. actions in Iraq and plans for missile defense systems in the region have generated a great degree of controversy within many European societies. Shown above is a demonstration in Europe against the United States, which illustrates that even Washington's close allies are looking for ways to tame U.S. power (Walt 2005). However, the resurgence of Russia, as demonstrated by its actions in Georgia, has driven some of the new NATO members even closer toward the United States. As explained by Polish Prime Minister Donald Tusk, "Poland wants to be in alliances where assistance comes in the very first hours of—knock on wood—any possible conflict."

as power becomes more equally distributed, each player will be increasingly assertive, independent, and competitive, leading to confusion about the identity of friends and foes.

The search for the capacity to compete on an equal footing with the other centers of power is characteristically strong when power becomes spread across three or more poles. With the effort by the European Union to enter the playing field alongside the United States, China, Japan, Russia, and other regional players like Brazil and India, the game of rivalry and balancing is becoming much different from the strategies and alignments that tend to materialize in unipolar and bipolar systems. As power becomes increasingly equally distributed, each leading power suspiciously confronts the other; diplomacy displays a nonideological, chesslike character; and conflict intensifies as each contender fears the power of its rivals. An enlarged global chessboard of multiple geostrategic relationships develops. A congested landscape leads to uncertainty about other's allegiances. To make this setting even more confusing, in multipolar systems, the interplay takes place simultaneously on two playing fields—the first military and the second economic (recall Table 4.2 p.117). The major players align together against others on particular issues, as their interests

Manish Swarup/AP Photo

A NEW GLOBAL DANCE CARD? **At the UN General Assembly in 2005, the United States declared its intent to build multilateral alliances instead of acting unilaterally. Yet the call of a powerful state for multilateralism does not prevent counterbalancing by other states. The above picture—taken at that same UN meeting—is one example of such "soft balancing." In it, Prime Minister Manmohan Singh of India and Premier Wen Jiabao of China shake hands to signal their countries' coalition to stymie American and European efforts to impose sanctions against Iran.**

dictate. Behind the diplomatic smiles and handshakes, one-time friends and allies begin to grow apart, formally "specialized" relations begin to dissolve, and former enemies forge friendly ties and begin making common cause against other centers of power that threaten them.

This competition under conditions of multipolarity is already unfolding. It is evident in the growing trade-bloc rivalry between the United States, the European Union, and China and Japan in the Far East on the economic battlefield (see Chapter 10). In addition, much counterbalancing and shifting in flexible and fluid alliances are occurring. For example, at times the United States can be observed casting itself in the role of *balancer* positioned in the middle of disputes between China and Russia. At other times, the United States finds itself opposed by these two neighboring great powers, such as when in August 2007 China and Russia signed a new friendship treaty calling for a new "multipolar world" to oppose American global domination and cemented their alleged allied solidarity by creating the Shanghai Cooperation Organization and staging joint military exercises with four other bordering states.

Alignments shifted again when friction grew between the United States and its closest allies over how to pursue the war on terrorism after former U.S. President Bush condemned North Korea, Iran, and Iraq as an "axis of evil" (though in 2008 North Korea was removed from the list). As a measure of how sensitive particular issues can be among great powers, both the European Union's foreign affairs commissioner, Christopher Pattern, and the German foreign minister, Joschka Fischer, castigated President Bush for treating America's coalition partners as subordinate "satellites,"

> *Those who scoff at "balance of power diplomacy" should recognize that the alternative to a balance of power is an imbalance of power—and history shows us that nothing so drastically escalates the danger of war as such an imbalance.*
>
> —Richard M. Nixon, U.S. President

and Russia's Vladimir Putin quickly joined their criticism of unilateral U.S. disregard of the interests of America's would-be partners in the antiterrorist coalition. This challenge to American leadership is not surprising to some analysts. For example, Chalmers Johnson (2004) argued in *Blowback: The Costs and Consequences of American Empire* that America had produced so much death and destruction in other peoples' countries that it was only a matter of time before the United States would feel the wrath of these countries' vengeance. (*Blowback* is the U.S. Central Intelligence Agency's term for the tendency for great power hardline actions to later provoke retaliatory attacks by the targets.) Johnson (2007) has been joined by other critics such as U.S. policy maker Dennis Ross (2007) who believe that U.S. arrogance and assertiveness toward other countries has increased the risk of blowback by endangering the American superpower physically, sacrificing America's standing in the world, and bankrupting the U.S. financially and morally. These concerns speak to the probability that in a multipolar system, alignments are usually fragile. And already they are fraying. "The new consensus holds that the U.S. invasion of Iraq was a calamity that has reduced America's standing in the world and made the United States less, not more, secure" (Freedland 2007).

Another indicator of continuing balance-of-power jockeying for global position and independence typical of emergent multipolarity was the decision by the European Union to create its own *Eurocorps* rapid deployment force so it can undertake military actions on its own, without the approval of the United States. The European reaction was a response to the growing recognition that U.S. power had grown so dramatically that it overshadowed everyone else combined. In short, history had cyclically begun to move toward the resurrection of a previous condition, as the second era of American unipolarity has begun to show signs that, sooner or later, the unipolar era of U.S. domination will end and a new multipolar era will begin (Hoge 2006).

However, it is difficult to confidently predict what the twenty-first century will look like and whether it will be chaotic or stable. Should a new multipolar world develop in the mid-twenty-first century, the probable consequences are here again unclear. Three different schools of thought on the relationship between polarity and global stability contend with one another (see Controversy: Is a Unipolar, Bipolar, or Multipolar System the Most Stable?, pp. 482–483). Because there is no real consensus on whether systems with a certain number of poles are more war prone than others, it would be imprudent to conclude that a new multipolar system will necessarily produce another period of warfare or of peace. But if the past is truly a reliable guide to the future, the distribution of global power will exert a strong influence on what kind of global system the world will experience.

UNIPOLARITY MAKES FOR UNLIKELY STRATEGIC ALLIANCES AGAINST THE REIGNING HEGEMON

Shown on the left is an example of an attempt to counter the threat of U.S. hegemonic domination. Iranian President Mahmoud Ahmadinejad and Venezuela's President Hugo Chávéz met in July 2006 in Tehran to underscore their joint opposition to America and to sign investment agreements. A month later, Chávéz traveled to Beijing to cement another "strategic alliance" by signing joint projects, such as exporting 500,000 barrels of oil a day to China. Shown on the right is another example of counterbalancing: Russia's Vladimir Putin visiting Iran's Mahmoud Ahmadinejad in Tehran in October 2007 to cement a new friendship in order to isolate the American superpower. Russia is building a $1 billion nuclear reactor in Iran.

Realists insist that the tragic struggle for security among great powers will continue (Mearsheimer 2001). Their expectations have been strengthened by China's rapid rise toward becoming the globe's biggest economy and the growing fears that this coming financial primacy will translate into Chinese *hard power* and a military threat, possibly even a new Chinese unipolar period. If the future belongs to China, counterbalancing by the other great powers in an anti-Chinese coalition is likely (Kugler 2006), possibly culminating in plans to contain and fight China (Kaplan 2005a). Likewise, realists think that great power competition will continue because the American military giant is unlikely to gracefully accept a reduction of its stature. Thus, realists believe that the U.S. quest to run a global empire will guarantee efforts to counterbalance American domination in hostile reaction (Walt 2005).

Other realists anticipate rising great power competition if, as they expect, the European Union grows to superpower status and begins flexing its muscles to counterbalance U.S. supremacy (McCormick 2007; Leonard 2005). In that scenario, the trans-Atlantic divide will widen, and so will economic struggles with China, India, and Japan as those rising powers begin to exert external pressure to contain European hegemony (Van Oudernaren 2005). Likewise, Russia is toughening its hardline opposition to the United States and NATO, and its rejection of any military strike on Iran from any base in a Caspian Sea is one expression of the straining relations.

Although the trajectories in the rise and fall of the great powers' relative position in the global hierarchy are much in doubt, a global shift is clearly in the making. As realists warn, if the past history of power transitions in the global balance of power is prologue, the global future may be a very dangerous future.

A SHIFTING BALANCE OF POWER? **The Caucasus region** "has become the arena for competition between the Americans and Europeans on one hand, and Russia on the other, over how to bring these countries into their respective spheres of influence" (Dempsey 2008, 3). Shown here are blindfolded Georgians atop a Russian personnel carrier. With Russia's show of strength in Georgia, its opposition to the expansion of NATO, and its perception of the missile defense agreement between the United States and Poland as a direct threat to Russian security, many felt a Cold War chill in the air and speculated about a changing tide of strength and strategic interest. At the very least, as Ukrainian Prime Minister Hryhoriy Nemyria observed, "This crisis makes crystal clear that the security vacuums that have existed in the post-Soviet space remain dangerous."

> *Major shifts of power between states occur infrequently and are rarely peaceful.*
>
> —James Hoge, *political scientist*

When American primacy does wane, the American "hobbled hegemon" will no longer remain in position to play its self-described role of global peacekeeper. This power transition will create a new multipolar system (Palmer and Morgan 2007). The probable consequences are certain to prove disquieting.

All kinds of possibilities can be imagined. For example, the British diplomatic historian Niall Ferguson speculates that "the end of the American hegemony might not fuel an orderly shift to a multipolar system but a descent into a world of highly fragmented powers, with no one exercising any global leadership. He calls this 'apolarity.' Apolarity could turn out to mean an anarchic new Dark Age, an era of waning empires and religious fanaticism, of economic plunder and pillage in the world's forgotten regions, of economic stagnation, and civilization's retreat into a few fortified enclaves" (Zakaria 2007).

> *The strongest nation in the history of the world [sees itself] besieged and overwhelmed. In a new global survey, most nations polled believed that China would act more responsibly in the world than the United States. The problem isn't that America is too strong, but that it's seen as too arrogant and insensitive.*
>
> —Fareed Zakaria, *realist American geostrategic analyst*

CONTROVERSY:

IS A UNIPOLAR, BIPOLAR, OR MULTIPOLAR SYSTEM THE MOST STABLE?

In the early twenty-first century, a long-standing debate has intensified about which type of polarity distribution—unipolar, bipolar, or multipolar—is the most capable of preventing large-scale war. What do you think? Consider the divided opinions about this issue, as represented by the arguments in three contending schools of thought.

One interpretation holds that peace will occur when one hegemonic state acquires enough power to deter others' expansionist ambitions. This view maintains that the concentration of power reduces the chances of war because it allows a single superpower to maintain peace and manage the global system. The long peace under Britain's leadership in the 1800s (the Pax Britannica) and earlier, under the Roman Empire (the Pax Romana), offered support for the idea that unipolarity brings peace, and therefore inspires the hope that the twenty-first century under a Pax Americana will be stable as long as U.S. dominance prevails (Ferguson 2006; Mandelbaum 2006b).

In contrast, a second school of *neorealist* thought (e.g., Waltz 1964) maintains that bipolar systems are the most stable. According to this line of reasoning, stability, ironically, results from "the division of all nations into two camps [because it] raises the costs of war to such a high level that all but the most fundamental conflicts are resolved without resort to violence" (Bueno de Mesquita 1975). Under such stark simplicities and balanced symmetries, the two leading rivals have incentives to manage crises so that they do not escalate to war.

Those who believe that a bipolar world is inherently more stable than either its unipolar or multipolar counterparts draw support from the fact that in the bipolar environment of the 1950s, when the threat of war was endemic, major war did not occur. Extrapolating, these observers (e.g., Mearsheimer 1990) reason that because a new multipolar distribution of global power makes it impossible to run the world from one or two centers, disorder will result:

> It is rather basic. So long as there [are] only two great powers, like two big battleships clumsily and cautiously circling each other, confrontations—or accidents—[are] easier to avoid. [With] the global lake more crowded with ships of varying sizes, fueled by different ambitions and piloted with different degrees of navigational skill, the odds of collisions become far greater. (House 1989, A10)

A third school of thought argues that multipolar systems are the least war prone. Although the reasons differ, advocates share the belief that polarized systems that either concentrate power, as in a unipolar system, or that divide the world into two antagonistic blocs, as in a bipolar system, promote struggles for dominance (Thompson 1988; Morgenthau 1985). The peace-through-multipolarity school perceives multipolar systems as stable because they encompass a larger number of autonomous actors, giving rise to more potential alliance partners. This is seen as pacifying because it is essential to counterbalancing a would-be aggressor, as shifting alliances can occur only when there are multiple power centers (Deutsch and Singer 1964). Also, multipolar distributions of world power reduce the temptations of a great power to pursue a global imperial empire, because the effort to do so is likely to make it weaker and less secure as it becomes encircled by the threatened states (Kennedy 2006) and because multipolarity limits the usefulness of self-help strategies to expand global influence (Rosecrance 2005).

Abstract deductions and historical analogies can lead to contradictory conclusions, as the logic underlying these three inconsistent interpretations illustrates. The future will determine which of these rival theories is the most accurate. However, based on your estimates of the possibilities of war and peace under these conditions, what do you predict?

Let us hope that these kinds of conditions will not materialize. But whatever ensues, a crucial question is certain to command attention at the center of debate: whether international security is best served by states' military search for their own national security or whether, instead, the military pursuit of security through arms, alliances, and the balance of power will sow the seeds of the world's destruction. In the next part of this book, turn your attention away from the balance of power politics of realism to examine proposals by liberal theorists to engineer institutional reforms in order to create a more orderly world order.

Key Terms

alliances
alignments
nonalignment
size principle
balancer
bandwagoning

Prisoner's Dilemma
global structure
polarization
North Atlantic Treaty
    Organization (NATO)

doctrines
extended deterrence

NEGOTIATING WITH A NEGOTIATOR ABOUT NEGOTIATION. **U.S. President George H. W. Bush meets with Charles Kegley, one of the authors of** *World Politics*. **The major topics they discussed: the uses and limits of methods of dispute settlement without the use of military force. These include diplomatic negotiations, international courts, collective security, economic sanctions, and other methods of conflict resolution that are advocated by policymakers whose image of world politics is informed by liberal theory.**

Part 6

LIBERAL PATHS TO WORLD ORDER

"What can war beget except war? But good will begets goodwill, equity, equity."

— *Erasmus of Rotterdam, Renaissance moral philosopher and theologian*

WAR—WHAT IS IT GOOD FOR? If you can think of few benefits, and you agree with the American revolutionary and diplomat Benjamin Franklin that "There never was a good war or a bad peace," then you are probably open to the premise of liberal international theory that war is a problem, not a solution, and that changes are required in the practices of states toward one another in order to control armed aggression by seeking reforms that might reduce its frequency and destructiveness.

Liberal paths to peace are predicated on the assumption that progress is possible through reforms of the existing rules and customs of contemporary world politics. To adherents to the liberal theoretical tradition, war and armed aggression are not an inevitable product of evil people, but rather of the institutions and anarchical structure of the prevailing global system that encourage wars to erupt. So liberalism is predicated on the belief that a transformation in world politics can be engineered through human choices that will put the tragedy of death and destruction from warfare into the dustbin of history and replace the war system with a peace system.

Liberalism is an alternative to the realist roads to national and international security, although it shares with it the belief that the threat of warfare is the globe's most dangerous problem. In this part you will look at the major ideas advanced by liberal theory for improving the global condition and meeting the threat of war. Unlike realism, liberalism is a *reform* program for bringing about an end to warfare rather than accepting it as a permanent condition. Yet you will discover that within this tradition many paths are proposed to this same end. In Chapter 16, for example, you will look at liberal ideas for negotiating at the bargaining table rather than fighting on the battlefield to settle international disputes, as well as subjecting inter-state relations to a true system of international law with strong sanctions for noncompliance with rules. Similarly, Chapter 17 introduces the liberal proposal to "beat swords into plowshares" through disarmament of the weapons of war, empowering international organizations for maintaining the collective security of all countries, and the use of economic sanctions as a non-military method of punishment for aggressors.

CHAPTER 16
NEGOTIATED CONFLICT RESOLUTION AND INTERNATIONAL LAW

Diplomacy mediates not between right and wrong but between conflicting interests. It seeks to compromise not between legal equities but between national aspirations.

—Charles W. Thayer, American foreign policy maker

Rina Castelnuovo/UPI Photo/Landov Media

Diplomacy Dialogues. To liberal reformers, direct negotiations between adversaries are a crucial step on the path to make peace a possibility. Talks allow both sides to put their interests on the bargaining table and discuss issues openly—far better than resolving them on the battlefield. Shown here: baby steps toward a "grand bargain" to negotiate ending the Israeli-Palestine conflict by establishing an independent Palestine state: Palestinian President Mahmoud Abbas, then U.S. Secretary of State Condoleezza Rice, and Israel's Prime Minister Ehud Olmert open peace negotiations in December 2007. Regrettably, the negotiations were largely symbolic as lasting peace in this area remains elusive.

Y ou overlook the incredibly low chances, purchase a lottery ticket, and hit an enormous jackpot. You are now very, very rich! What next? Remembering your pledge to try to make the world a better place before you die, you decide to put your ethical principles above power. To make a difference, you decide to invest your newfound wealth in projects that will "give peace a chance." Congratulations! You are joining Andrew Carnegie, Bill Gates, Warren Buffet, and other exceptionally wealthy philanthropists who generously chose to give large portions of their fortunes to causes that try to change the world for the better. You and they are following Carnegie's motto: "Private money for public service."

On what ventures should you prioritize the distribution of your fortune? The menu for choice is large. You could seek, for example, to strengthen human rights law, provide humanitarian relief for refugees, fight worldwide poverty and disease, join others in seeking to stem the threat of global warming, or subsidize a global campaign to educate all youth throughout the world. The needs are endless. Sorting through your moral values, however, you conclude that the greatest threat to the world is the awesome danger of armed aggression. Recalling what the American

With nations as with individuals our interests soundly calculated will ever be found inseparable from our moral duties.

—Thomas Jefferson, U.S. President

statesman John Randolph wrote in 1806, "The surest way to prevent war is not to fear it," you disagree because you believe there really are many reasons to fear war. Acting on this conviction, you see your mission to be helping others find better ways than military methods for preventing war. Reliance on weapons of war and balances of power has been tried since the beginning of time, but never with lasting success. So now you have found your cause—finding peaceful methods for controlling armed aggression. Alas, you must now go another difficult step in your attempt to clarify your values. You must evaluate by rational choice the best means for realizing your chosen primary goal.

It is time for you to do some homework and draw lessons from policy makers and philosophers who have spent their lifetime probing the same questions you are now asking yourself about—how to do good in a wicked world. Your Internet search directs you to thinkers who have values compatible with your own. The search engine directs you for insight to the knowledge of those theorists who call themselves liberals or liberal idealists.

LIBERAL ROUTES TO INTERNATIONAL PEACE

Scanning a long list of great books and then consulting them, you digest a vast literature and then reconstruct the principal approaches to the control of armed aggression. Most are rooted in the liberal theoretical tradition. You then construct a table summarizing your understanding of the primary liberal paths to international security, and display them for review in an outline of premises and policy prescriptions for preventing war. These paths differ greatly in their approach to world order, but they all share your great fear of states' historic propensity to wage war. Table 16.1 presents your condensation of this received liberal wisdom.

Table 16.1 Liberal Paths to International Security

Policy Prescriptions	Premises
Provide states rules of international law to regulate competition.	Interstate cooperation can be encouraged by creating rules for peaceful interaction.
Participate in the creation of international organizations.	If you want peace, prepare global institutions to keep it.
Practice collaboration to bind independent states together in integrated security communities.	Interdependence makes it imperative to unite states and build a transnational civil society.
Promote the spread of democratic governance.	Countries that protect their own citizens' civil liberties do not wage war against other governments that also protect their citizens' human rights.
Provide education.	The pen is mightier than the sword, and education prepares people for democratic governance.
Prepare rules to facilitate free trade.	Trade protectionism is counterproductive to prosperity and peace.
Produce agreements to reduce armaments to levels that discourage war.	States get what they plan for—beat swords into plowshares.
Provide humanitarian assistance to the impoverished.	Rich states can help themselves only by helping poor people also.
Value ethical principles more than power.	Principled moral behavior ultimately reaps higher rewards for all because fair treatment toward others promotes their fair behavior.

Keep this multiple list of rival liberal routes to international security in mind as you contemplate the benefits and liabilities of alternative roads to peace. Here, rivet your focus on the hypotheses that the best way to prevent armed aggression is to either (1) settle through diplomatic negotiations international disputes before they escalate to warfare or (2) bring the use of armed force under meaningful legal controls that restrict the purposes for which armed aggression can be legally conducted, so that the likelihood of taking up arms will decline.

Both of these approaches are at the top of the liberal program for creating world order. Why? The main reason is that severe crises have often erupted and have greatly increased the threat of armed aggression; had past crises been successfully managed through diplomatic negotiations between the disputing sides, war would never have occurred. This sad but instructive international historical record

> *To win without fighting is best.*
> —Sun Tzu, strategist in ancient China

underscores the importance of diplomatic negotiations between conflicting adversaries to resolve their differences at the bargaining table before they go to the battlefield for resolution. So first look closely at this liberal approach to peacemaking before then considering if and how international law is addressing the challenge of controlling wars of choice.

INTERNATIONAL CRISES AND THE NEGOTIATED SETTLEMENT OF DISPUTES

Recall the strategy realism strongly recommended: *coercive diplomacy*—a method of bargaining between states in which threats to use arms or the actual use of limited armed force are made to persuade an opponent to change its foreign policy and force it to make undesired concessions and compromises. The goal here is *political*—to exercise influence over an enemy in order to convince that enemy that acceding to an opposing state's demands will be less costly than defying those demands. This result, realists advise, can be accomplished by delivering an *ultimatum* that threatens the target with an immediate threat in order to increase pressure and make it comply with the coercive state's request.

The major problem with coercive diplomacy's reliance on the threat of armed force is that such acts usually create a **crisis** that escalates to war. And crises have been very frequent in modern history, and now "talk of crisis is everywhere in contemporary international relations" (Clark and Reus-Smit 2007) (see Figure 16.1). The problem that liberal reformers identify is that these crises and armed conflicts could potentially have been settled by diplomatic negotiations had that avenue for dispute settlement been attempted.

When a crisis erupts, the capacity for reaching coolheaded rational decisions is reduced. The threat to use force causes stress and reduces the amount of time available to reach decisions that might successfully end the crisis peacefully. Consider the 1962 Cuban Missile Crisis, which occurred when the Soviet Union installed medium-range nuclear missiles in Cuba and the United States responded to the emergent threat with a naval blockade. The danger of a total nuclear war quickly rose; in the aftermath U.S. President John F. Kennedy estimated that the odds were fifty-fifty that a nuclear exchange could have destroyed the entire world. And, often, such crises resulting from coercive military diplomacy *have* escalated to the use of force when bargaining failed and the adversaries took up arms. The Suez Crisis of 1956 is an often-cited example of the inherent dangers.

■ **crisis**
a situation in which the threat of escalation to warfare is high and the time available for making decisions and reaching compromised solutions in negotiations is compressed.

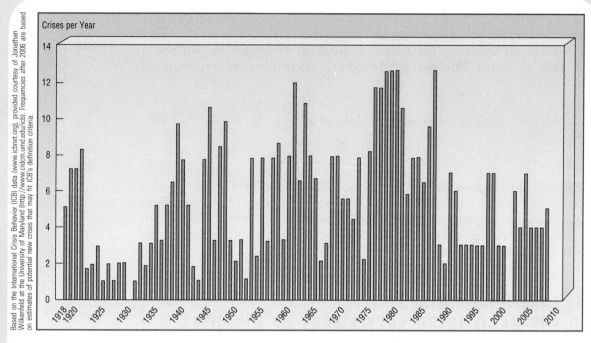

FIGURE 16.1

THE ANNUAL FREQUENCY OF NEW INTERNATIONAL CRISES SINCE WORLD WAR I | **More than 980 states have been involved in 451 international crises between 1918 and 2008. The frequency has varied over time, but its recurrence attests to states' compulsion to make threats to use military force to get their way and demonstrates that efforts to resolve disputes through negotiations have frequently either failed or were not pursued.**

■ **negotiation**

diplomatic dialogue and discussion between two or more parties with the goal of resolving through give-and-take bargaining perceived differences of interests and the conflicts they cause.

■ **reciprocity**

the return of favors for favors or punishment for punishment between parties in a mutual exchange relationship.

To liberals, it is always better to talk about percolating divisive issues at a negotiating table than to let anger and anxieties sizzle and tempt the disputants to take up arms. Only through discussion and bargaining can positions be clarified and, possibly, concession and compromises reached that terminate the threat of warfare. **Negotiation** is the process of bargaining in an effort to deal with an issue or situation in order to reach an agreement that settles the dispute. At a basic, elementary level, negotiation entails an exchange of communications, with discussion flowing back and forth between the bargaining parties (recall the "directed dyad" conception of interrelationships in Chapter 1, which captures what actor A says to actor B and the responses of actor B to actor A). Moreover, negotiations seek to communicate the parties' intentions and goals, and these communications can range from offering rewards ("carrots") for cooperation or threaten punishment ("sticks") for refusals to comply with requests. In the give-and-take required to negotiate a compromised solution, there is a strong propensity for some level of **reciprocity** to emerge from the action-and-reaction sequence of communications—to return in kind or degree the kind of friendly or hostile communication received from the other party.

If the enemy fights deceitfully it should be paid back in its own coin.

—*The Mahabharata*

THE SUEZ CRISIS: A COLLISION TOO PAINFUL TO FORGET On July 26, 1956, the president of Egypt, Gamal Abdul Nasser, ordered the Egyptian army to seize and nationalize the Suez Canal, and the inability to manage the crisis peacefully brought the great powers (Britain, France, the United States, and Russia) and Israel into a serious military confrontation, which the United Nations was unable to prevent. Shown here in a collage are some of the key players in this epic crisis that underscores the importance of peacefully managing disputes before the threat of recourse to arms emerges.

Note that, for this reason, reciprocated communications can produce greater cooperation *or* greater conflict. The Chinese translation of the word "*crisis*" means both "opportunity" and "danger," and efforts to negotiate compromises provide an opportunity to produce a positive agreement or to produce a dangerous negative outcome that heightens threats and tensions. That is why negotiation is not a sure cure-all for the resolution of interstate conflicts and crises. Still, negotiations make possible the settlement of disputes, providing the offers of concessions freely given are reciprocated by the target with the same level of similar concessions.

> *Today to be successful, one must be able to reach agreements. The ability to compromise is not a diplomatic politeness but rather taking into account and respecting your partner's legitimate interests.*
>
> —Vladimir Putin, Russian Prime Minister

■ **tit-for-tat strategy**

a bargaining approach that consistently reciprocates in kind the offers or threats made by the other party in a negotiation, with equivalent rewards returned and equivalent punishing communications returned in retaliation.

Reciprocated gestures of goodwill and empathy for the opponent's situation pave the way for a compromised agreement. Indeed, a common bargaining approach to induce the other party to reach agreements is through a **tit-for-tat strategy** that responds to any cooperative offer by immediately reciprocating it with an equal offer; the reward through repetitive concessions can facilitate a mutually satisfactory agreement.

Sir Harold Nicolson, the British diplomatic historian, defined diplomacy as "the management of the relations between independent states by the process of negotiation." Diplomacy is aimed at resolving international disputes peacefully, which is why diplomacy is favored by liberals. That said, realists stress that diplomacy can be used for the pursuit of power through war, not peace. Marxism takes a similarly pessimistic view of diplomatic approaches to peace, declaring that "when equal rights collide, force decides" (Carty 2008, 122). The Chinese Foreign Minister Zhou Enlai spoke to this view when he stated his cynical conviction that "all diplomacy is the continuation of war by other means."

Even when pursued for the prevention of armed aggression and the peaceful settlement of conflicts, diplomatic negotiations require for success great intelligence, information, imagination, flexibility, ingenuity, and honesty. To quell controversies, manage quarrels without resort to force, and lessen tensions and promote mutual understanding between rivals is a huge challenge in world politics. Convincing adversaries that their interests are served by forging cordial and durable relations and engaging them in a web of mutual interests is fraught with difficulties.

No wonder that negotiations between disputants often fail. Compounding the challenge is the common liability that a diplomat sent to negotiate for his or her country, no matter what their skill or sincerity, cannot succeed unless they have the full backing of their government's authority, and the leadership is willing to accept public criticism for partially backing down to an adversary. In addition, sometimes secrecy is necessary to make concessions and reach compromises without losing face; "unless covenants are arrived at secretly," warned U.S. President Richard M. Nixon, "there will be none to agree to openly."

> *The best results of negotiation cannot be achieved in international life any more than in our private world in the full glare of publicity with current debate of all moves, unavoidable misunderstandings, inescapable freezing of positions due to considerations of prestige and the temptation to utilize public opinion as an element integrated into the negotiation itself.*
> —Dag Hammarskjöld, UN Secretary-General

■ **mediation**

a conflict-resolution procedure in which a third party proposes a nonbinding solution to the disputants.

These problems, potholes, and pitfalls notwithstanding, liberals regard negotiation as a preferred method for fostering international peace. The alternative—the coercive use of military power—is ethically unacceptable to people seeking to avoid war.

Fortunately, those playing the game of international politics have been inventive in creating supplementary methods to enable negotiations to reduce the threat of war. Several types of approaches are available for opponents facing dangerous relations and the threat of war. All are now nested in the laws of nations accepted by the global community. Among such conflict resolution procedures, **mediation** by third-party intermediaries to assist in negotiated settlements display the best track record in terminating international crises (Frazier and Dixon 2006). Mediation occurs when an outside actor, either another state or a group of states in an intergovernmental organization (IGO), participate directly in negotiations between the parties to a dispute to aid them in recognizing their shared interests and proposing solutions based on these common interests. Three modes of mediation are practiced: "*manipulation* (in which the third party employs leverage in a carrot-and-stick approach to manipulate the parties toward a particular conclusion), *facilitation* (in which the third party takes on the noncoercive, facilitative role of communicator), and *formulation* (in which the mediator makes substantive suggestions as to what solutions might be possible)" (Grussendorf 2006, summarizing Wilkenfeld, Young, Quinn, and Asal, 2005). Mediation works best, history shows, when IGOs perform the negotiating service and when the mediators are involved in asymmetric crisis situations between disputants unequal in their relative power (Quinn, Wilkenfeld, Smarick, and Asal, 2006). More pessimistically, the mediation of international crises has proven less successful when ethnic groups have been a player in the crisis that led to armed aggression (Ben-Yehuda and Mishali-Ran, 2006).

In addition, to reach agreements and settle disputes peacefully, several other conflict resolution procedures are practiced. They include:

- **Good offices**—when a third party offers a location for discussions among disputants but does not participate in the actual negotiations

- **Conciliation**—when a third party assists both disputing sides but does not offer any solution

- **Arbitration**—when a third party gives a binding decision about the disputant's claims through an ad hoc forum

- **Adjudication**—when a third party offers a binding decision about a conflict through an institutionalized tribunal such as a court

All of these methods for crisis management and dispute settlement are embedded in the international laws pertaining to negotiation. Liberals have long advocated that international law be strengthened in order to police armed aggression between states and to more capably provide for world order. Next the chapter will consider the place of international law in world politics and the rules that have been fashioned to control by legal methods armed international aggression.

LAW AT THE INTERNATIONAL LEVEL

When you think about law, it is very likely that you construct an image of how law functions within the country in which you are residing. In this constructed image, when a society perceives a particular type of behavior to be harmful, a law is predictably passed to prohibit it. The emergent consensus in many countries that underage drinking and smoking in public places are harmful led, for example, to new laws to regulate and prohibit these practices. So war—the attack by choice by one state of another without imminent threat and therefore not in self-defense—would seem to likewise be an evil and dangerous practice that the global community would automatically prohibit, right? Actually, no, or at least not until relatively recently in the modern saga of world history.

good offices
provision by a third party to offer a place for negotiation among disputants but does not serve as a mediator in the actual negotiations.

conciliation
a conflict-resolution procedure in which a third party assists both parties to a dispute but does not propose a solution.

arbitration
a conflict-resolution procedure in which a third party makes a binding decision between disputants through a temporary ruling board created for that ruling.

adjudication
a conflict-resolution procedure in which a third party makes a binding decision about a dispute in an institutional tribunal.

International law has been conceived by and written mostly by realists, who place the privileges of the powerful as their primary concern and have historically advocated that war should be an acceptable practice to protect a dominant state's position in the global hierarchy. As William Bishop (1902) wrote, international law is not violated "when a state resorts to war for any reason it felt proper." This view then echoed the opinion of Henry Wheaton (1846), that "every state has a right to

> *In the conflict of arms, laws must be silent.*
> —Hugo Grotius, seventeenth century Dutch legal scholar and philosopher, widely proclaimed the founder of international law

force." If murder and killing have been condemned in the precepts of your religion and prohibited by the laws of your country, you may be shocked to learn that the military drive for power has been legal in most historical phases of international law. Next the chapter will look at the evolution of international law and how that situation came to be.

How to Think about the Formation and Decay of International Legal Rules

Start with the basics. Constructivism (see Chapter 2) provides a lens on how international rules are created. That theory informs us that leading ideas have meaningful consequences, and that when a favorable climate of opinion crystallizes about the preferred conduct for relations between states, those constructed images influence perceptions about the rules by which the game of nations should be played. International law communicates the prevailing international consensus about the rules to govern international relations. Consistent with constructivist theory, for this reason many experts see international law mirroring changes in the most popular constructions of images about the ways in which states are habitually acting or should act toward one another in any particular period of history.

Moreover, the rules that are globally accepted are created at the global level by the most powerful countries, to protect their parochial self-interests. The great powers alone have the capacity to promote wide acceptance and then enforce the **transnational norms** of statecraft they favor—the accepted rules for interstate interaction.

transnational norms

the regular customs widely practiced by countries in their relations with other countries and the kinds of behavior that the international community accepts as what *ought* to be practiced.

Again, as constructivist theory elucidates, transnational norms historically change in conjunction with each major transformation in world politics—with fundamental changes in prevailing global conditions, such as shifts in the primary foreign policy goals that states are pursuing. According to this constructivist interpretation, throughout history the rules of international statecraft have changed in the aftermath of changes in the customary practices of how states are mostly behaving. This is different from law formation *within* countries. Internally, a country has a legislature that makes and revises existing laws, an executive branch of government that enforces those laws, and a judiciary that interprets when the enacted laws apply. Not so at the global level. How, then, are *international* legal rules created, enforced, and judged?

The Characteristics of International Law

In 1984, the United States announced that it would unilaterally withdraw from the World Court's jurisdiction. This move followed Nicaragua's accusation that the U.S. Central Intelligence Agency (CIA) had illegally attempted to "overthrow and destabilize" the elected Sandinista government. Nicaragua charged that the United States had illegally mined its ports and supplied money, military assistance, and training to the rebel *contra* forces. The United States denied the tribunal's authority. In so doing, however, it was not acting without precedent; others had done so previously. Nonetheless, by thumbing its nose at the court and the rule of law it represents, had the United States, as some claimed, become an "international outlaw"? Or, as others asserted, had it acted within its rights?

The World Court supported the former view. In 1984, the court ruled against the United States as follows:

> The right to sovereignty and to political independence possessed by the Republic of Nicaragua, like any other state of the region or of the world, should be fully respected and should not in any way be jeopardized by any military and paramilitary activities which are prohibited by the principles of international law, in particular the principle that states should refrain in their international relations from the threat or the use of force against the territorial integrity or the political independence of any state, and the principle concerning the duty not to intervene in matters within the domestic jurisdiction of a state. (*New York Times*, May 11, 1984, 8)

Yet this ruling had little effect, as neither the court nor Nicaragua had any means to enforce it.

Events such as this have led many critics to conclude that international law is "weak and defenseless" (Fried 1971). Indeed, many experts—whether they are realists or liberals—skeptically ask whether international law is really law. Radical theory shares this skepticism, holding that "the form of international law consists of the struggle between states' view of legal right, and the view that prevails will depend on which state happens to be stronger" (Carty 2008, 122; Meiville, 2006). Yet there are many reasons to have confidence in the rule of law. Although international law is imperfect, actors regularly rely on it to redress grievances (see Joyner 2005). Most global activity falls within the realm of **private international law**—the regulation of the kinds of transnational activities undertaken every day in such areas as commerce, communications, and travel. Although largely invisible to the public, private international law is the location for almost all international legal activities. It is where the majority of transnational disputes are regularly settled and where the record of compliance compares favorably with that achieved in domestic legal systems.

In contrast, **public international law** covers issues of relations between governments and the interactions of governments with intergovernmental organizations (IGOs) and nongovernmental organizations (NGOs) such as multinational corporations. Some believe that we should use the phrase *world law* to describe the mixture of public and private, domestic and international transactions that public international law seeks to regulate in an increasingly globalized world. However, it is the regulation of government-to-government relations that dominates the headlines in discussion of public international law. This area of activity also receives most of the

■ **private international law**

law pertaining to routine transnational intercourse between or among states as well as nonstate actors.

■ **public international law**

law pertaining to government-to-government relations as well as countries' relations with other types of transnational actors.

International law is that law which the wicked do not obey and the righteous do not enforce.

—Abba Eban, Israeli ambassador

criticism, for here, failures—when they occur—are conspicuous. This is especially true with respect to the breakdown of peace and security. When states engage in armed conflict, criticism of its shortcomings escalate.

Without a doubt, the inability of public international law to control armed aggression is regarded as its greatest weakness. To cut deeper into the characteristics of contemporary international law, the chapter will next look briefly at some of its other salient characteristics. Among these attributes are the processes by which international law is created and revised, and the institutional mechanisms available for the interpretation and enforcement of the global system's rules. It is these characteristics that liberal critics are seeking to reform to strengthen international law and convert it from a law between nations to a truly authoritative system of world law above states by equipping it to promote peace.

The Sources and Limitations of the International Legal System

Sovereignty is the foundation of modern international law and its most important transnational norm. Ever since the 1648 Treaties of Westphalia, states have tried to reserve the right to perform within their territories in any way the government chooses.

This is a severe problem for liberal reformers. Sovereignty and the legal principles derived from it shape and reinforce international anarchy. This means that world politics is reduced to the level of interaction without meaningful regulation or true global governance; international politics is legally dependent on what governments choose to do with one another and the kinds of rules they voluntarily support. Throughout most of modern history, international law as constructed by realists was designed by states to protect the state and thereby made sovereignty the core principle to ensure states' freedom to act in terms of their perceived national interests.

To liberal theoreticians, putting the state ahead of the global community was a serious flaw that undermined international law's potential effectiveness. Many theorists consider the international legal system institutionally defective due to its dependence on states' willingness to participate. Because formal legal institutions (such as those within states) are weak at the global level, critics make the following points.

First, in world politics, no legislative body is capable of making binding laws. Rules are made only when states willingly observe or embrace them in the treaties to which they voluntarily subscribe. There is no systematic method of amending or revoking treaties.

Article 38 of the Statute of the International Court of Justice (or World Court) affirms this. Generally accepted as the authoritative definition of the "sources of international law," it declares that international law derives from (1) custom; (2)

international treaties and agreements; (3) national and international court decisions; (4) the writings of legal authorities and specialists; and (5) the "general principles" of law recognized since the Roman Empire as part of "natural law" and "right reason."

Second, in world politics, no judicial body exists to authoritatively identify and record the rules accepted by states, interpret when and how the rules apply, and identify violations. Instead, states are responsible for performing these tasks themselves. The World Court does not have the power to perform these functions without states' consent, and the UN cannot speak on judicial matters for the whole global community (even though it has recently defined a new scope for Chapter VII of the UN Charter that claims the right to make quasi-judicial authoritative interpretations of global laws).

Finally, in world politics there is no executive body capable of enforcing the rules. Rule enforcement usually occurs through the unilateral self-help actions of the victims of a transgression or with the assistance of their allies or other interested parties. No centralized enforcement procedures exist, and compliance is voluntary. The whole system rests, therefore, on states' willingness to abide by the rules to which they consent and on the ability of each to enforce through retaliatory measures violations of the norms of behavior they value.

Consequently, states themselves—not a higher authority—determine what the rules are, when they apply, and how they should be enforced. This raises the question of greatest concern to liberal advocates of world law: When all are above the law, are any truly ruled by it? It is precisely this problem that prompts reformers to restrict the sovereign freedom of states and expand their common pursuit of shared legal norms in order to advance collective global interests over individual state's interests.

Beyond the barriers to legal institutions that sovereignty poses, still other weaknesses reduce confidence in international law:

- *International law lacks universality.* An effective legal system must represent the norms shared by those it governs. According to the precept of Roman law, *ubi societas, ibi jus* (where there is society, there is law), shared community values are a minimal precondition for forming a legal system. Yet the contemporary international order is culturally and ideologically pluralistic and lacks consensus on common values, as evidenced by the "clash of civilizations" (Berger and Huntington 2002) and the rejection by terrorists and others of the Western based international legal order. The simultaneous operation of often incompatible legal traditions throughout the world undermines the creation of a universal, *cosmopolitan* culture and legal system (Bozeman 1994).

- *International law justifies the competitive pursuit of national advantage without regard to morality or justice.* As in any legal system, in world politics what is legal is not necessarily moral. In fact, international law legitimizes states' right to take self-help measures to pursue power and hegemony by any means, however amoral, such as launching an offensive armed first strike against a potential enemy that does not pose an immediate military threat (Lissitzyn 1963). In so doing, international law adheres to realists' "iron law of politics"—that legal obligations must yield to the national interest (Morgenthau 1985).

> *In international law the enforcement of rules is left to the vicissitudes of the distribution of power between the violator of the law and the victim of the violation. This makes it easy for the strong both to violate the law and to enforce it, and consequently puts the rights of the weak in jeopardy.*
>
> —Hans J. Morganthau, realist theoretician

■ *International law is an instrument of the powerful to oppress the weak.* In a voluntary consent system, the rules to which the powerful willingly agree are those that serve their interests. These rules therefore preserve the existing global hierarchy (Friedheim 1965; Goldsmith and Posner 2005). For this reason, some liberal theorists claim that international law has bred the so-called **structural violence** resulting from the hierarchical global system in which the strong benefit at the expense of the weak (Galtung 1969).

■ *International law is little more than a justification of existing practices.* When a particular behavior pattern becomes widespread, it becomes legally obligatory; rules *of* behavior become rules *for* behavior (Hoffmann 1971). Eminent legal scholar Hans Kelsen's contention that "states ought to behave as they have customarily behaved" (in Onuf 1982) and E. Adamson Hoebel's dictum (1961) that "what the most do, others should do" reflect the **positivist legal theory** that when a type of behavior occurs frequently, it becomes legal. In fact, highly regarded positivist legal theorists stress states' customary practices as the most important source from which laws derive in the absence of formal machinery for creating international rules. When the origins of international law are interpreted in this way, the actions of states shape law, not vice versa.

■ *International law's ambiguity reduces law to a policy tool for propaganda purposes.* The vague, elastic wording of international law makes it easy for states to define and interpret almost any action as legitimate. This ambivalence makes it possible for states to exploit international law to get what they can and to justify what they have obtained (Wright 1953).

■ **structural violence**

the condition defined by the Norwegian peace researcher Johan Galtung as the harm and injury caused by the global system's unregulated structure, which gives strong states great opportunities to victimize weak states that cannot protect themselves.

■ **positivist legal theory**

a theory that stresses states' customs and habitual ways of behaving as the most important source of law.

> *The lack of clarity and coherence enables international law to be easily stretched, to be a flexible fig leaf or a propaganda instrument.*
>
> —Samuel S. Kim, international legal authority

The Abiding Relevance of International Law

Although international law has deficiencies, this should not lead to the conclusion that it is irrelevant or useless. States themselves find international law useful and expend much effort to shape its evolution. States' actual behavior demonstrates that countries interpret international law as real law and obey it most of the time (Joyner 2005).

The major reason that even the most powerful states usually abide by international legal rules is that they recognize that adherence pays benefits that outweigh the costs of expedient rule violation. International reputations are important. They contribute to a state's *soft power*. Those that play the game of international politics by recognized rules receive rewards, whereas states that ignore international law or opportunistically break customary norms pay costs for doing as they please. Other countries will be reluctant to cooperate with them. Violators also must fear retaliation by those victimized, as well as the loss of prestige. For this reason, only the most ambitious or reckless state is apt to flagrantly disregard accepted standards of conduct.

A primary reason why states value international law and affirm their commitment to it is that they need a common understanding of the "rules of the game." Law helps shape expectations, and rules reduce uncertainty and enhance predictability in international affairs. These communication functions serve every member of the global system.

> *International law is an institutional device for communicating to the policymakers of various states a consensus on the nature of the international system.*
>
> —William D. Coplin, international legal theoretician

Similarly, every breakdown of international law does not prove the existence of general lawlessness. Conditions of crisis strain *all* legal systems, and few, when tested severely, can contain all violence. Since 1500, more people have died from civil wars than from wars between sovereign states (Sivard 1991). Today, with street crime in cities worldwide at epidemic proportions and ethnic and religious warfare *within* countries exacting a deadly toll against hundreds of minority groups, states' domestic legal systems are clearly failing to prevent killing. This suggests that even when strong formal institutions for rule enforcement are in place, they do not and can not guarantee compliance. No legal system can deter all of its members from breaking existing laws. Consequently, it is a mistake to expect a legal system to prevent all criminal behavior or to assert that any violation of the law proves the inadequacy of the legal structure. Law is designed to deter crime, but it is unreasonable to expect it to prevent it. Thus, the allegedly "deficient" international legal system may perform its primary task—inhibiting interstate violence—even more effectively than supposedly more-sophisticated domestic systems. Perhaps, then, the usual criteria by which critics assess legal systems are dubious. Should critics be less concerned with structures and institutions and more concerned with performance?

To evaluate how international law is performing the functions that states have authorized it to perform, the chapter next looks at the most important existing international legal rules that are applicable to international relations today.

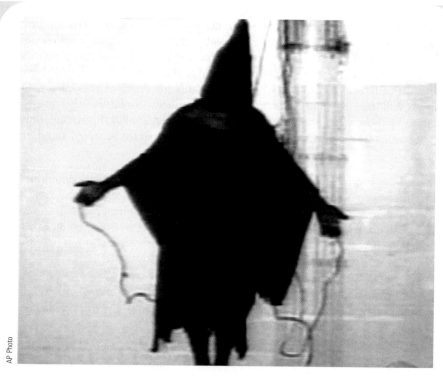

AP Photo

WAR CRIMES AND THE LOSS OF GLOBAL LEGITIMACY **In May 2004, the United States was scandalized when more than one thousand graphic photos taken at the Abu Ghraib prison in Baghdad were televised worldwide, ostensibly showing U.S. personnel preparing to use electric shocks to torture Iraqi prisoners. Claiming that the United States "does not torture people," then President Bush nonetheless defended his government's interrogation of terrorist suspects at the Guantánamo detainee prison by using such methods as frigid tempatures and simulated drowning. By November 2005 (at which point the United States had detained more than eighty-three thousand foreigners), the U.S. Senate voted 90–2 to outlaw the U.S. use of torture that violated the Geneva Conventions.**

Core Principles of International Law Today

Public international law is usually defined as the rules that govern the conduct of states in their relations with one another. The *corpus juris gentium* (the body of the law of nations) has grown considerably during the past four centuries, changing in response to transformations in world politics. An inventory of the basic legal principles relevant to the control of war helps to define the contemporary character of the global system.

As we have seen, no principle of international law is more important than state sovereignty. That norm is the basis for all other legal rules; the key concepts in international law all speak to the rules by which sovereign states say they wish to abide. Sovereignty means that no authority is legally above the state, except that which the state voluntarily confers on the international organizations it joins. In fact, as conceived by theoreticians schooled in the realist tradition since the seventeenth century, all the rules of international law express codes of conduct that protect states' freedom. Each state is given "a complete freedom of action" (Parry 1968) to do whatever it takes to preserve their sovereign independence.

Nearly every legal doctrine supports and extends the cardinal principle that states are the primary subjects of international law. Although the *Universal Declaration of Human Rights* in 1948 expanded concern about states' treatment of individual people, states remain supreme. Accordingly, the vast majority of rules address the

> *Laws are made to protect the state from the individual and not the individual from the state.*
> —Gidon Gottlieb, international legal scholar

rights and duties of states, not people. For instance, the principle of **sovereign equality** entitles each state to full respect by other states as well as equal protection by the system's legal rules. The right of independence also guarantees states' autonomy in their domestic affairs and external relations, under the logic that the independence of each presumes that of all. Similarly, the doctrine of **neutrality** permits states to avoid involvement in others' conflicts and coalitions.

Furthermore, the noninterference principle forms the basis for the *nonintervention norm*—requiring states' to refrain from uninvited activities within in another country's territory. This sometimes-abused classic rule gives governments the right to exercise jurisdiction over practically all things on, under, or above their bounded territory. (There are exceptions, however, such as **diplomatic immunity** for states' ambassadors from the domestic laws of the country where their embassies are located and **extraterritoriality**, which allows control of embassies on other states' terrain.)

In practice, domestic jurisdiction permits a state to enact and enforce whatever laws it wishes for its own citizens. In fact, international law was so permissive toward the state's control of its own domestic affairs that, prior to 1952, "there was no precedent in international law for a state to assume responsibility for the crimes it committed against a minority within its jurisdiction" (Wise 1993). A citizen was not protected against the state's abuse of human rights or **crimes against humanity**. Also, international law permits states to set their own rules for citizenship. Two basic principles govern the way nationality and citizenship are conferred: under *jus soli* (such as in the United States), citizenship is determined by the state in whose territory the birth took place; under *jus sanguinis*, citizenship is acquired by descent from a parent who is already a citizen of a state.

In addition, in earlier periods of modern international law, states were permitted to create whatever form of government they desired without regard to its acceptability to other states. This principle was expressed in the realpolitik language of the Treaty of Augsburg (1555) and the Westphalian treaties (1648), which made states all-powerful by recognizing the **divine right of kings**. This doctrine was reaffirmed in the 1943 Atlantic Charter's pledge of "the right of all people to choose the form of government under which they will live." However, the right of people to live under the liberties of democracy is increasingly being defined as an "entitlement" or a basic human right. At Geneva, in 1999, states proclaimed that all individuals have a right to democracy, thereby revising international law through a United Nations resolution and by the same vote dealing "a severe blow to those countries which

■ sovereign equality
the principle that states are legally equal in protection under international law.

■ neutrality
the legal doctrine that provides rights for states to remain nonaligned with adversaries waging war against each other.

■ diplomatic immunity
the legal doctrine that gives a country's officials when abroad (e.g., diplomats and ambassadors) release from the local legal jurisdiction of the state when they are visiting or stationed abroad to represent their own government.

■ extraterritoriality
the legal doctrine that allows states to maintain jurisdiction over their embassies in other states.

■ crimes against humanity
a category of activities, made illegal at the Nuremberg war crime trials, condemning states that abuse human rights.

■ **divine right of kings**

the realist doctrine that kings and sovereign monarchs have the right to rule their subjects authoritatively and are not accountable to the public because their rule is claimed to be ordained by God.

■ **statehood**

the legal criteria by which a country and its government become a state in the global community.

■ **diplomatic recognition**

the formal legal acceptance by one existing sovereign state of another state's official status as an independent country.

■ **de facto recognition**

a government's acknowledgment of the factual existence of another state or government short of full recognition.

■ **de jure recognition**

a government's formal, legal recognition of another sovereign government or state.

continue to deny their citizens not only democracy but other fundamental human rights" (Rubin 1999; see also Slaughter 2004a). International law still gives states the complete freedom to regulate economic transactions within their boundaries and empowers the state to draft those living on its soil into its armed forces to fight—and die, if necessary—to defend the state.

The 1933 *Montevideo Convention on the Rights and Duties of States* summarizes the major components of **statehood**. A state must possess a permanent population, a well-defined territory, and a government capable of ruling its citizens and of managing formal diplomatic relations with other states. Essentially, the acquisition of statehood depends on a political entity's recognition as such by other states. Whether a state legally exists thus rests in the hands of other states; that is, preexisting states must extend **diplomatic recognition** to another entity. **De facto recognition** is provisional and capable of being withdrawn in the event that the recognized government is replaced by another. It does not carry with it the exchange of diplomatic representatives or other legal benefits and responsibilities. **De jure recognition**, by contrast, extends full legal and diplomatic privileges from the granting state. This distinction emphasizes that recognition is a political tool of international law through which approval or disapproval of a government can be expressed.

Other rules specify how treaties are to be activated, interpreted, and abrogated. International law holds that treaties entered into voluntarily are binding (*pacta sunt servanda*). However, it also reserves for states the right to unilaterally terminate treaties previously agreed to, by reference to the escape clause known as *rebus sic stantibus*. This is the principle that a treaty is binding only as long as no fundamental change occurs in the circumstances that existed when the treaty went into effect.

THE LEGAL CONTROL OF ARMED AGGRESSION

Liberal reformers often complain that international law is the weakest in controlling armed aggression—the realm of behavior most resistant to legal control. If under international law, as fashioned by realist leaders, states are "legally bound to respect each other's independence and other rights, and yet free to attack each other at will" (Brierly 1944), international law may actually encourage war. The ethical and jurisprudential **just war doctrine** from which the laws of war stem shapes discussions of contemporary public international law (Wills 2004). Throughout history, changes in international law have followed changes in the moral consensus about the ethics of using armed force in interstate relations. Therefore, it is important to understand the origins of just war theory and the way it is evolving today, before reviewing contemporary changes in the legal rules of warfare that have led to the formation of *security regimes*—sets of rules to contain armed aggression.

Just War Doctrine: The Changing Ethics Regarding the Use of Armed Force

Many people are confused by international law because it both prohibits and justifies the use of force. The confusion derives from the just war tradition in "Christian realism," in which the rules of war are philosophically based on **morals** (principles of behavior) and *ethics* (explanations of why these principles are proper). In the fourth century, St. Augustine questioned the strict view that those who take another's life to defend the state necessarily violate the commandment "Thou shalt not kill." He counseled that "it is the wrong-doing of the opposing party which compels the wise man to wage just wars." The Christian was obligated, he felt, to fight against evil and wickedness. To St. Augustine, the City of Man was inherently sinful, in contrast to the City of God. Thus, in the secular world, it was sometimes permissible to kill—to punish a sin by an aggressive enemy (while still loving the sinner) to achieve a "just peace." This realist logic was extended by Pope Nicholas I, who in 866 proclaimed that any defensive war was just.

The modern just war doctrine evolved from this perspective, as developed by such humanist reformers as Hugo Grotius. He challenged the warring Catholic and Protestant Christian powers in the Thirty Years' War (1618–1648) to abide by humane standards of conduct and sought to replace the two "cities," or ethical realms of St. Augustine, with a single global society under law. For Grotius, a just war was only one fought in self-defense to punish damages caused by an adversary's blatant act of armed aggression: "No other just cause for undertaking war can there be excepting injury received." For war to be moral it must also be fought by just means without harm to innocent noncombatants. From this distinction evolved the modern version of just war doctrine, consisting of two categories of argument, *jus ad bellum* (the justice of a war) and *jus in bello* (justice in a war). The former sets the legal criteria by which a leader may wage a war. The latter specifies restraints on the range of permissible tactics to be used in fighting a just war.

■ **just war doctrine**

the moral criteria identifying when a just war may be undertaken and how it should be fought once it begins.

■ **morals**

principles clarifying the difference between good and evil and the situations in which they are opposed.

Mierevelt, Michiel van. Jansz (1567-1641) Hugo Grotius (1583-1645), father of international law, 1631. Stedelijk Museum Het Prinsenhof, Delft, The Netherland/Erich Lessing/Art Resource, Inc.

WAR AND THE BIRTH OF MODERN INTERNATIONAL LAW **Enraged by inhumane international conditions that he witnessed during his lifetime, Dutch reformer Hugo Grotius (1583–1645) wrote *De Jure Belli et Pacis (On the Law of War and Peace)* in 1625 in the midst of the Thirty Years' War. His treatise called on the great powers to resolve their conflicts by judicial procedures rather than on the battlefield and specified the legal principles he felt could encourage cooperation, peace, and more humane treatment of people.**

These distinctions have been hotly debated since their inception. Drawing the line between murder and just war is a controversial task. Yet just war theory seeks to define these boundaries. According to this legal tradition, some circumstances in which lethal force may be justifiable are recognized under international law, which also provides guidelines for sanctioned coercive methods.

At the core of the just war tradition is the conviction that the taking of human life may be a "lesser evil" when it is necessary to prevent further life-threatening aggression (Ignatieff 2004b). The Christian theologian St. Thomas More (1478–1535) contended that the assassination of an evil leader responsible for starting a war was justified if it would prevent the taking of innocent lives. From this premise, a number of other principles now follow. The criteria today include ten key ideas:

1 All other means to a morally just solution of conflict must be exhausted before a resort to arms can be justified.

2 War can be just only if employed to defend a stable political order or a morally preferable cause against a real threat or to restore justice after a real injury has been sustained.

3 A just war must have a reasonable chance of succeeding in these limited goals.

4 A just war must be proclaimed by a legitimate government authority.

5 War must be waged for the purpose of correcting a wrong rather than for malicious revenge.

6 Negotiations to end a war must be in continuous process as long as fighting continues.

7 Particular people in the population, especially noncombatants, must be immune from intentional attack.

8 Only legal and moral means may be employed to conduct a just war.

9 The damage likely to be incurred from a war may not be disproportionate to the injury suffered.

10 The final goal of the war must be to reestablish peace and justice.

These ethical criteria continue to color thinking about the rules of warfare and the circumstances under which the use of armed force is legally permissible. However, the advent of nuclear and chemical or biological weapons of mass destruction that would violate many of these principles has created a crisis of relevance in just war doctrine (Hensel 2007). Fuzzy circumstances have materialized with the innovations of the revolution in military technology (RMT). For example, insurgent terrorists and now the armies fighting them are increasingly relying on Improvised Explosive Devices (IEDs) planted on animal carcasses, mobile cell phones, or human cadavers in addition to IEDs left in the open in order to kill without risk of death to the killers. Today's IEDs, first invented by the United States and now on the global black market for purchase by any transnational extremist, are cheap and easy-to-make gadgets like garage-door openers used to detonate bombs. How can international law control such innovative new ways of carrying out armed aggression, when the aggressors using them are not humans that can be treated as criminals? Because containment and prevention of violence have become the chief purposes of arms and armies today, leaders and scholars are struggling to revise just war doctrine to deal with the new strategic realities of contemporary weapons and warfare (J. Johnson 2005).

As Figure 16.2 shows, since World War I the international community has increasingly rejected the traditional legal right of states to use military force to achieve their foreign policy objectives. Just war theory reflects the continuing quest to place legal constraints on the use of armed force in order to create a moral consensus about the conditions under which ends justify means, even though today disagreements continue about the criteria that should be accepted. These differences became especially evident in the heated debate after the U.S. preemptive invasion of Iraq. Many condemn the U.S. attack as a legal breach of international law (Paust 2007) and argue that the U.S. counterterror war in general violates many principles of just war theory (Crawford 2003), making the American hegemon a "rogue nation" (Gareau 2004) and outlaw state (Hathaway 2007). Others (Elsthain 2003) disagree. The 2003 U.S. invasion of Iraq has made the legality of the use of force a hot topic. Even famous realists (Mearsheimer and Walt 2003) have joined liberals in labeling the U.S. attack on Iraq "an unnecessary war" (see Controversy: Was the War in Iraq a Just War?).

■ **preventive war** strictly outlawed by international law, a war undertaken by choice against an enemy to prevent it from suspected intentions to attack sometime in the distant future—if and when the enemy might acquire the necessary military capabilities.

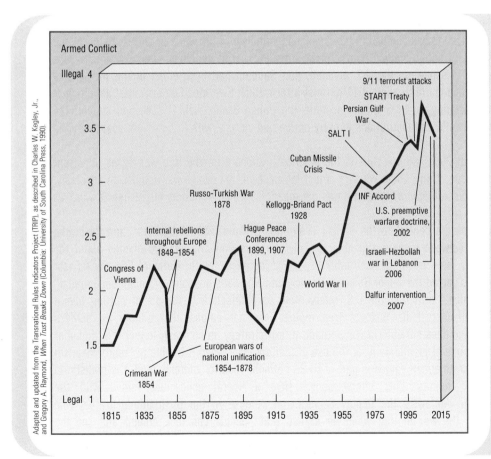

FIGURE 16.2

THE LEGAL PROHIBITION AGAINST INITIATING WARS, 1815–2008 **Legal restraints on the historic right of states to start a war have fluctuated over time, but have increased steadily since World War I when that carnage prompted the global community to make wars of conquest illegal. Since 9/11, these legal prohibitions have been questioned in the aftermath of the U.S. efforts to promote *preemption* as a legal right to repel the *potential* aggression of another state or nonstate terrorist network even before its threat of attack is imminent, which blurs the distinction between preemptive war and preventive war.**

CONTROVERSY:

WAS THE WAR IN IRAQ A JUST WAR?

Before the March 2003 U.S. invasion of Iraq, U.S. President Bush claimed to have solid evidence that Iraqi dictator Saddam Hussein possessed and was concealing "some of the most lethal weapons ever devised." Bush warned that Saddam would "stop at nothing until something stops him." The Bush administration further claimed that Saddam had close ties with the Al Qaeda terrorist network that orchestrated the 9/11 attack on the United States. The United States undertook a massive attack to overthrow the rogue Hussein dictatorship. The preemptive strike to attack Saddam's country before he could attack the United States resulted in a quick and overwhelming intervention that drove the Iraqi leader into hiding (and later, death by hanging).

On May 1, 2003, President Bush, dramatically dressed in an Air Force uniform, spoke from the flight deck of the *USS Abraham Lincoln* behind a flying banner that declared, "Mission Accomplished." However, that was not to be the case; more than six years later, American troops remained locked in deadly fighting with Iraqi insurgents and suicide terrorist bombers seeking to drive the United States from occupied Iraq, Afghanistan and Islamic holy lands. Expecting to be welcomed with rice and rose petals, according to the U.S. Coalition Provisional Authority polls when the U.S. attack occurred, 80 percent of the Iraqi population saw the American troops as an invading army rather than their liberators.

As the body toll of American troops climbed in the thousands, criticism of the war's purposes, conduct, and strategy mounted in American public opinion. Furthermore, after exhaustive searches, even U.S. intelligence agencies could uncover no evidence, as the U.S. claimed, that Saddam had been either hiding weapons of mass destruction or had supported Al Quada's 9/11 terrorist attack. Bush then modified his initial definition of the Iraq war's mission, declaring in 2005 that henceforth the United States would "seek and support the growth of democratic movements and institutions in every nation and culture, with the ultimate goal of ending tyranny in our world."

This "liberal-hawk" (Judt 2007) abrupt shift in the American rationale for the Iraq war raises important questions about the conditions, if any, under which it is just for any country to wage war against an adversary. When is warfare justified (*jus ad bellum*)? What are the just means by which a military might fight a war (*jus in bello*)?

These types of questions are central to the ethical evaluation of international behavior, and lie at the intersection of the debate between realists and liberals. Policy makers and analysts are divided about the purposes for which military force might be justifiably used. For instance, former National Security Advisor General Brent Scowcroft who served the senior Bush presidency, and who calls himself an "enlightened realist" as well as a "cynical idealist," criticized the U.S. intervention as a misguided example of putting liberal idealism over national self-interest because "a true realist does not employ the military for selfless humanitarian operations" and does not enter a war without an exit strategy. In contrast, former U.S. diplomat Richard Holbrooke voiced a liberal justification for the use of military force when it is able to "marry idealism and realism. . . . Support for American values is part of [U.S.] national-security interests, and it is realistic to support humanitarian and human-rights interventions." Here a liberal policymaker sided with the neoconservative realist Paul Wolfowitz, the Deputy Secretary of Defense in the Bush administration who most vigorously advocated the war in Iraq when he argued that "people can look around and see the overwhelming success of representative government."

To illustrate the spectrum of opinion about the war further, many neoliberals complain that the Bush administration abused "liberal democratic peace theory" and applied it inappropriately to justify an illegal preventive war against an enemy that posed no real threat (Russett 2005). To fight a war to overthrow a tyrant and establish by force democratic regimes in the Middle East are "rationales that strain the traditional understanding of humanitarian intervention" (Nardin 2005). In this context, George W. Bush's claim that "the advance of freedom leads to peace" has empirical merit (Rasler and Thompson 2005), but critics can agree with the warning of Jürgen Habermas that "bad consequences can discredit good intentions." To fight for noble causes and risk waging an unjust war can become a form of "humanitarian imperialism" (Nardin 2005). These viewpoints suggest an ethical principle about the politics of military intervention argued by the famed realist Lutheran theologian Reinhold Niebuhr: "Every nation is caught in the moral paradox of refusing to go to war unless it can be proved that the national interest is imperiled, and of continuing in the war only by proving that something much more than national interest is at stake."

What do you think? Drawing on the criteria proposed by just war theorists (e.g., Wills 2004; Johnson 2005; Patterson 2005; Wesley 2005), would you characterize the 2003 U.S. war against Iraq as a just war? Was it initiated for a just cause and with the right intentions? Was it undertaken as a last resort with the appropriate authorization? Did the good toward which the war aimed outweigh the harm caused by the fighting?

Until 9/11, legal injunctions increasingly restricted states' rights to resort to war. The doctrine of **military necessity** still accepts the use of military force as legal, but only as a last recourse for defense (Raymond 1999). However, even though the initiation of war is no longer licensed and the intention to make war is still a crime (making those who start a war "criminals"), the posture of a hegemonic superpower has the capacity to challenge this norm and change international law (Byers and Nolte 2003).

■ **military necessity**

the legal principle that violation of the rules of warfare may be excused for defensive purposes during periods of extreme emergency.

Throughout history dominant states have shaped international law.

—*Richard N. Cooper, U.S. diplomat*

The Bush Doctrine defending the legality of preemptive military strikes to prevent possible anticipated wars could pave the way for the legalization of preventive war for all countries (Caldwell and Williams 2006; Kegley and Raymond 2004, 2007).

New Rules for Military Intervention

International law has recently begun to fundamentally revise its traditional prohibition against military intervention in the wake of the recent wave of terrorism by states against their own people. For humanitarian purposes, the belief that governments have a right, even an obligation, to intervene in the affairs of other states has won advocates. Today international law has defined military intervention as a right and duty to alleviate human suffering, stop genocide and ethnic cleansing, and prevent the repression by states of basic human rights and civil liberties (Feinstein and Slaughter 2004; Finnemore 2003). The result has been the collapse of the Westphalian principle that what a state does within its own boundaries was its own business. International law has relaxed its restrictive definition of when the global community can legally use military intervention to make it increasingly permissive (see Figure 16.3). The world has made a choice on genocide, declaring organized savagery illegal: "The last fifty years have seen the rise of universally endorsed principles of conduct," defining humanitarian intervention as a legal right to protect *human rights*—political rights and civil liberties now recognized by the global community as inalienable and valid for all individuals in all countries. This rule change permits states and international organizations to punish acts of genocide by re-interpreting the traditional rule against external interference in the internal affairs of another state and making outside intervention permissible. This includes even the right to military invasion and occupation.

This sea change suggests that international law develops and changes most rapidly when global problems arise that require collective solutions and legal remedies. The spread of genocide and atrocities in failed states and countries ruled by tyrants has spawned new sets of legal rules to arrest these dangers. Likewise, the rising frequency of global terrorism has pushed efforts to rewrite international law to permit interventions within countries providing terrorists a secure base of operations, in order to contain criminal terrorist acts of violence.

Attention to terrorism has led to increased cooperation and spawned new branches of international law. Terrorism has prompted states to step up their mutual cooperation on criminal matters based on common interest, both to prevent terrorist groups from attacking innocent civilians or state officials, and, in case such attacks are carried out, to arrest the culprits and bring them to justice. Treaties which demand that states either

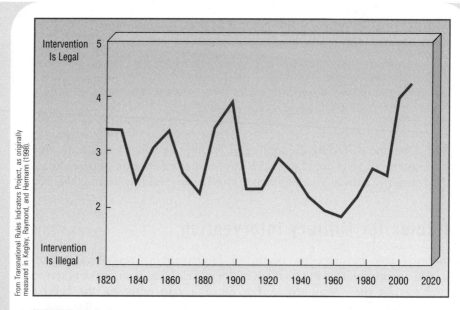

FIGURE 16.3

THE CHANGING STATUS OF THE NONINTERVENTION NORM IN INTERNATIONAL LAW SINCE 1820 **Over time, the illegality of intervening in sovereign states has changed, as measured by changes in international law about the prevailing consensus regarding rules for international conduct. Since 1960, international law has adopted an increasingly permissive posture toward this form of coercive diplomacy for a variety of purposes including humanitarian aid, preventing genocide, protecting civil liberties, promoting democracy through "reform interventions," and combating global terrorism.**

extradite or prosecute those accused of terrorism committed outside their territory have multiplied and are now copied in fields such as money laundering, corruption, and drug trafficking. (Cassese and Clapham 2001, 411)

The Rules for War's Conduct and the Expansion of Human Rights Legislation

Laws regulating the methods that states may use in war (*jus in bello*) have also grown. These restraints include the principles of discrimination and **noncombatant immunity**, which attempt to protect innocent civilians by restricting military targets to soldiers and supplies. The laws of retaliation specify conditions under which certain practices are legitimate. One category of **coercive power**, **reprisals** (hostile and illegal acts permitted only if made in proportionate response to a prior hostile and illegal act), stipulates procedures for military occupations, blockades, shows of force, and bombardments. Another category, **retorsion** (hostile but legal retaliatory acts made in response to similar legal acts initiated by other states), provides rules for embargoes, boycotts, import quotas, tariffs, and travel restrictions to redress grievances.

The advent of a new set of legal justifications for military intervention to protect civilians is explained by the fact that noncombatants have become the primary victims in warfare. "World War I was a mass-conscription, democratic war with a vengeance, but it still was limited in its direct effect on civilians. The ratio of soldiers to civilians killed between 1914 and 1918 was about 90 to 10. In World War II, the ratio was 50-to-50. In recent years, it has been 90 civilian casualties to every 10 military losses—a reversal of the World War I ratio" (Pfaff 1999, 8).

To prevent the horror of civilian casualties and contain the mass slaughter that has increasingly taken place, the global community has radically revised international law. For the first time, it holds leaders of countries accountable for war crimes as war criminals. International law now prohibits leaders from allowing their militaries to undertake actions in violation of certain principles accepted by the international community, such as the protection of innocent noncombatants. Formerly, when violations occurred, little could be done except to condemn those acts because international law then failed to hold government leaders to the same standards it held soldiers and military officers who committed atrocities against enemy civilians and captured soldiers. Previously, international law exempted leaders from legal jurisdiction under the doctrine of "sovereign immunity," even when their commands ignored the laws of war. Although they might behave as criminals, leaders traditionally were treated with respect (perhaps because they were the only people with whom negotiations could be held to settle disputes). This tradition has now been legally rejected.

> *Crimes against international law are committed by men, not by abstract entities, and only by punishing individuals who commit such crimes can the provisions of international law be enforced.*
>
> — *The Nuremberg International Military Tribunal established to try World War II German Nazi war criminals*

■ **noncombatant immunity**

the legal principle that military force should not be used against innocent civilians.

■ **coercive power**

the use of threats and punishment to force the target to alter its behavior.

■ **reprisals**

the international legal practice of resorting to military force short of war in retaliation for losses suffered from prior illegal military actions.

■ **retorsion**

retaliatory acts (such as economic sanctions) against a target's behavior that is regarded as objectionable but legal (such as trade restrictions) to punish the target with measures that are legal under international law.

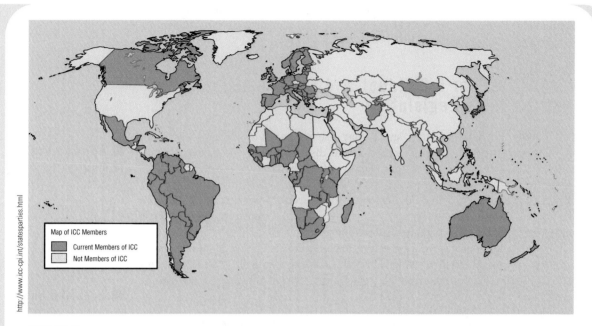

MAP 16.1

WHICH WORLD COURT? In 1945, the International Court of Justice (ICJ), which is known as the World Court, was established by the UN Charter. It is the primary judicial body of the United Nations, with global jurisdiction to settle legal disputes between states and provide advisory opinions to international agencies and the UN General Assembly. Also commonly referred to as a "world court," the International Criminal Court (ICC) is an independent court of last resort that tries those accused of committing the most horrendous of mass crimes, such as war crimes and genocide. Founded through ratification of an international treaty in 2002, it is legally independent of the United Nations. As 2009 began, 108 countries had joined the ICC (see map), though the United States, Russia and China have not. Separate from the ICJ and ICC, criminal tribunals are established by the United Nations for a limited time period and jurisdiction.

■ international criminal tribunals

special tribunals established by the United Nations to prosecute those responsible for wartime atrocities and genocide, bring justice to victims, and deter such crimes in the future.

The formation of **international criminal tribunals** in 1993 signaled to would-be perpetrators the global community's intolerance for these atrocities. The International Criminal Tribunal for the former Yugoslavia (ICTY) was established in 1993, followed by the International Criminal Tribunal for Rwanda (ICTR) in 1994. One of the most famous tribunal detainees was Slobodan Milosevic, the former Yugoslav president and architect of four wars in the 1990s that killed more than 250,000 and tore the Balkans apart, who died in March 2006 in his Hague prison cell while facing trial. Both the ICTY and the ICTR were set up by the United Nations on an ad hoc basis for a limited time period and a specific jurisdiction, and underscored the need for a permanent global criminal court. With the ratification of the Rome Statute by sixty countries, the **International Criminal Court (ICC)** was launched in 2002 as an independent court of last resort that investigates and prosecutes terrible mass crimes such as genocide, crimes against humanity, and war crimes that have been committed since the court's inception. The ICC only pursues a case when a state's courts are unwilling or unable to do so. To date, the ICC has opened investigations into atrocities in Uganda, the Democratic Republic of Congo, the Central African Republic, and Darfur—and in July 2008 sought to indict Sudanese President Omar al-Bashir for genocide. The criminalization of rulers' **state-sponsored terrorism** raises the legal restraints on the initiation and conduct of war to an all-time high, widening the scope of acts now classified as **war crimes**.

LAW'S CONTRIBUTION TO PEACE

To be sure, liberal reformers have a long way to travel to fulfill their wish to see international law strengthen so that it can more effectively police international armed aggression. The institutional weaknesses remain. However, much progress has been made toward the goal of bringing armed aggression under more potent legal controls. This progress inspires liberal hopes for the future.

A just war is in the long run far better for a nation's soul than a most prosperous peace obtained by acquiescence in wrong and injustice.

—Theodore Roosevelt, U.S. President

Despite its deficiencies, liberal reformers take heart from the trends that have recently enabled international law to increase its capacity to manage the threat of war within states, between states, and through global terrorism. They point with confidence to these steps. And they question those cynics who still contend that international law is and should remain irrelevant to states' use of armed force. Liberals argue that:

- International law is not intended to prevent *all* warfare. Aggressive war is illegal, but defensive war is not. It is a mistake, therefore, to claim that international law has broken down whenever war breaks out.

- Instead of doing away with war, international law preserves it as a sanction against breaking rules. Thus, war is a method of last resort to punish aggressors and thereby maintain the global system's legal framework.

- International law is an institutional substitute for war. Legal procedures exist to resolve conflicts before they erupt into open hostilities. Although law cannot prevent war, legal procedures often make recourse to violence unnecessary by resolving disputes that might otherwise escalate to war.

The demonstrable capacity of legal methods to reduce the frequency of war does not mean that international adjudicative machinery is well developed or functionally effective. Nowhere is this more evident than with the International Court of Justice (ICJ), known as the World Court, which was created after World War II as the highest judicial body on the earth—the only international court with universal scope and general jurisdiction. The court is highly regarded in principle: 191 states are party to the statute of the court, and 64 have made declarations that they accept the court's compulsory jurisdiction. (This number includes the EU members but not the United States.) In addition, more than three hunded bilateral or multilateral treaties provide for the World Court to have jurisdiction in the resolution of disputes arising from their application for a legal interpretation.

A weakness in the World Court is that it can make rulings only on disputes freely submitted by states exercising their sovereign rights; the court cannot rule on cases that states do not bring to it. State sovereignty is protected, and many states have traditionally been hesitant to use the court because ICJ decisions are final—there is no opportunity to appeal. This is why between 1946 and 2008 states granted the court permission to hear only 104 cases, about one-fourth of which the disputants

■ **International Criminal Court (ICC)**

a court established by international treaty for indicting and administering justice to people committing war crimes.

■ **state-sponsored terrorism**

formal assistance, training, and arming of foreign terrorists by a state in order to achieve foreign policy and/or domestic goals.

■ **war crimes**

acts performed during war that the international community defines as crimes against humanity, including atrocities committed against an enemy's prisoners of war, civilians, or the state's own minority population.

withdrew before the court could make a ruling. In 76 of those cases that the ICJ heard, the judges ruled on substantive questions. Border disputes have been the most common issues (31), followed by cases about the legality of uses of military force (22), property (14), and aerial violations of alleged territorial space (14).

The trends in the World Court's activity are not encouraging to advocates of world law. Whereas the number of sovereign states since 1950 has tripled, the court's caseload has not increased at the same rate. It is instructive that two-thirds of today's states have never appeared before the ICJ, and only the Global North liberal democracies have most actively agreed to litigate disputes before the court (the United States, 21 cases; Britain, 15; France, 11; Germany, 7; and Belgium and Iran, 5 each). Once the court has ruled on these 104 cases, the disputants have complied with ICJ judgments only 60 percent of the time. This record suggests that while approval for using the court of law to resolve international conflicts is increasingly voiced, most states remain reluctant to voluntarily use judicial procedures to settle their most important international disputes.

World order will depend to a considerable extent on the future uses to which states put international law. Alleged shortcomings of international law do not lie with the laws but with their creators—states and their continuing realpolitik dedication to preserving sovereignty as a legal right in order to protect states' independence and autonomy.

The crucial factor in determining the future role of international law depends on which trend prevails. Will states choose to strengthen international law or, instead, insist on continuing to resist the compulsory jurisdiction to the World Court and other international tribunals? One path is displayed by the United States, which in 2002 pledged that it would continue to act in accordance to its so-called Connally amendment that reserves the U.S. right to determine which cases it will permit the World Court to hear. The U.S. preference is to try cases in U.S. courts and to let others use U.S. courts as global arbiters of global rights and wrongs. The latter use of American courts by foreigners to sue for human rights violations stems from the 1789 *Alien Tort Claims Act* (which was written to fight piracy). It now enables victims of torture, genocide, slavery, and war crimes throughout the world to try to get justice in U.S. courts. This trend toward the use of U.S. courts to conduct criminal prosecutions of foreign terrorists captured abroad is accelerating as the United States transforms itself from "global policeman" to "global attorney" (Glaberson 2001; Slaughter 2004a). An example of this occurred in 2001 when five Chinese civilians sued Chinese Prime Minister Li Peng in an American court for his role in the 1989 crackdown in Beijing's Tiananmen Square, which killed hundreds of civilians. The U.S. Supreme Court in 2004 upheld this old law by allowing victims of the Abu Ghraib prison abuses to sue U.S. contractors.

> *It is better to lose a point now and then in an international tribunal and gain a world in which everyone lives at peace under the rule of law.*
> —Dwight D. Eisenhower, U.S. President

The international climate of opinion is changing. Now at the regional level the EU's twenty-seven members give the European Court of Human Rights the power to exercise authoritative jurisdiction, and in South America the Inter-American Court on Human Rights routinely makes binding decisions.

The global community could, in principle, follow Europe's and South America's lead and strengthen international law's capacity. Still, many barriers remain to creating, as John F. Kennedy expressed liberal theory's hope, "a new world of law, where the strong are just and the weak secure and the peace preserved."

In this chapter, you have inspected two of the major liberal paths to peace: procedures for the negotiated settlement of international disputes and the legal control of armed aggression. Both routes have pitfalls but promising prospects for a more just and stable world order. Liberal theory is a road map to the future that has many other routes to the same objective. In the next chapter, you will consider other liberal avenues to collective security and international peace.

Key Terms

crisis
negotiation
reciprocity
tit-for-tat strategy
mediation
good offices
conciliation
arbitration
adjudication
transnational norms
private international law
public international law
structural violence

positivist legal theory
sovereign equality
neutrality
diplomatic immunity
extraterritoriality
crimes against humanity
divine right of kings
statehood
diplomatic recognition
de facto recognition
de jure recognition
just war doctrine
morals

preventive war
military necessity
noncombatant immunity
coercive power
reprisals
retorsion
international criminal tribunals
International Criminal
    Court (ICC)
state-sponsored terrorism
war crimes

514

CHAPTER 17
LIBERAL APPROACHES
TO COLLECTIVE SECURITY

The road followed by the authors of the Preamble of the United Nations Charter begins with the recognition of the threat under which we all live, speaking as it does of the need to save succeeding generations from the scourge of war which has brought untold sorrow to mankind. It ends with a promise to practice tolerance and live together in peace with one another as good neighbors and to unite our strength to maintain peace.

—Dag Hammarskjöld, *former Secretary General of the United Nations*

Global Change Through Global Connections. Liberals are dissatisfied with the world and would like to change it. They have mobilized to exert pressure to contain arms races, global warming, warfare, and world poverty, among other causes. Shown here: A crowd in London presses for humanitarian aid to fight African poverty at one of ten demonstrations organized on the same day around the world.

David Silpa/UPI Photo/Landov Media

Many global trends are sweeping the world. Most of them appear to be moving at accelerating rates. Major transformations may be in store in your future world. But not all trends are converging, and some are pulling against others in opposite directions. Whatever their collective synergistic impact on one another, it seems certain that your future world will be different from the one that now exists.

Another certainty: Your own values are clashing. Some values can only be achieved at the expense of others. The things you desire cannot all be obtained, and so you will confront making trade-offs among incompatible choices about how to set priorities and best help forge a better world.

Many of your value preferences lie at the vortex of the contest between realist and liberal thought, and they defy easy reconciliation. Sure, you want your country to be militarily powerful for defense, but you do not want other countries to build their military capabilities and you must dread the prospect of a world darkened by the worldwide proliferation of weapons. Yes, you would like to see your country's economy grow, but what if it can't unless your country accepts free trade, which spells a potential loss of your employment opportunities at home and the rise of other countries' economies at rates that exceed that of your own country? To be sure, you would prefer your country to have the capacity to unilaterally make foreign policy decisions independently without foreign approval, but what if many of the dangers you foresee—global warming, the spread of contagious diseases across borders, the protection of innocents from genocide or starvation or tyranny—cannot be solved without the collective cooperation of other countries? Ouch! Many of the things you value can only be served by some sacrifice of other values.

Liberal theory wrestles with these dilemmas and paradoxes as it strives to reconcile its values and policy preferences with those advocated by realists' premises about what is prudent, possible, and productive for international security.

In this chapter, focus your attention on some of the major ways in which liberal international thought directly challenges the assumptions underlying realist thinking about world politics. This will require you to contemplate the consequences that are likely to result if three major roads to world order promoted by liberalism are pursued: disarmament, collective security through international organizations, and the building of a single world culture through the promotion of norms supporting free trade and free governments worldwide. All three are questioned and are opposed by the dominant strains of thought in the realist theoretical tradition.

BEATING SWORDS INTO PLOWSHARES THROUGH DISARMAMENT

The realist road to national security counsels, "if you want peace prepare for war." On the surface this makes intuitive sense. If your country is militarily stronger than its rivals, it is not very likely to be attacked. Using *counterfactual* logic by asking what would be the likely consequences if all countries adhered to this advice, and what would happen if your country did *not* build bigger and better weapons capabilities, you might arrive at another conclusion. Your country may become less secure, not more, as it builds its military might. That is the deduction of liberal thought. In this construction, the *security dilemma* figures prominently—when a country builds armaments, alarmed neighbors mistrust its claims that the weapons are for defensive purposes, and in fearful reaction begin to vigorously arm themselves also. An *arms race* results, with no arming state more secure. All the arming parties are now more vulnerable; wanting peace, war preparations increase the likelihood of war.

This liberal conviction goes back to antiquity. Jesus Christ warned "for all those who take up the sword perish by the sword" (Matthew 26:52). Centuries earlier, the Hebrew prophet Isaiah voiced in the same spirit a recommendation that is inscribed on the United Nations headquarters in New York City: "the nations shall beat their swords into plowshares" (Isaiah 2:4).

This liberal axiom and advice has been echoed many times. For example, Sir John Frederick Maurice wrote in his memoirs, "I went into the British Army believing that if you want peace you must prepare for war. I now believe that if you prepare thoroughly for war you will get it." The same liberal conviction was expressed by the French political philosopher Charles de Montesquieu when he observed that the quest for a preponderance of power in relation to rivals "inevitably becomes a contagious disease; for, as soon as one state increases what it calls its forces, the others immediately increase theirs, so that nothing is gained except mutual ruination."

This proposition is the foundation of one major liberal road to peace. It is based on the counterintuitive prediction that states that build awesome arms arsenals become more endangered, not more secure. The liberal program for reform therefore concludes that reducing the weapons of war can increase the prospects for global peace. This conclusion is advanced even while liberal policy makers accept the conclusion with realists that it is morally defensible to use constrained and proportional armed force to repel an imminent military attack by an adversary (Mapel 2007).

Where will this disarmament road, if taken, lead the world? We do not have much available evidence with which to test this liberal tenet because this path is not very well beaten. The infrequency with which countries have chosen to unilaterally disarm throughout history makes it difficult to draw valid inferences about what might have happened had that avenue been more often traveled and a better record existed about the payoffs and pitfalls of such efforts. That lack of evidence does not reduce the confidence of liberal reformers about one of their preferred methods for reducing armed aggression.

Liberals are sobered by the long history of arming states that experienced war—a history which in their constructed images convincingly alerts the world to the dangers of relying on military superiority for protection. The strongest states *have* been the ones most frequently involved in warfare. So liberals are inspired by hopes that their proposed alternative can lead to a safer and more secure world.

"I would rather be defeated in a cause that will ultimately triumph, than to win in a cause that will ultimately be defeated," the liberal U.S. president Woodrow Wilson proclaimed. It was this faith that underscored his conviction in Point IV of his famous Fourteen Points Address at the end of World War I that "the programme of the world's peace [requires that] national armaments be reduced to the lowest point consistent with domestic safety."

The destructiveness of today's weapons has inspired many people to embrace this tenet of liberal theory seriously. But in thinking about disarmament, keep in mind that many realists also see arms limitations as a useful way for stabilizing the global balance of power (see Chapter 15). Indeed, most policy makers who have negotiated agreements to limit arms have been realists who perceived such treaties as prudent tools to promote security by balancing military power with power to maintain the threat of war.

> *Arms control is not a substitute for defense. It is defense conducted by diplomatic means: the mutually agreed rules of the road in the arms race—rules that make the competition somewhat more predictable that set limits on the most dangerous kinds of weapons and help advert the sudden appearance of new weapons systems that might upset the balance.*
>
> —Strobe Talbott, U.S. National Security Advisor

Where liberalism and realism part ways is on their respective posture toward the advantages of disarmament in contrast to arms control. Liberals are more willing to take a heroic leap of faith and consider disarmament as a workable possibility for peace. Realists are much more inclined to accept arms control as a method for maintaining military balances between competitive states.

Disarmament versus Arms Control as Routes to Peace

Several distinctions must be made in any consideration of this approach to international security. The first is between the terms "disarmament" and "arms control." Sometimes the terms are used interchangeably. They are not, however, synonymous. **Disarmament** is ambitious. It aims to reduce or eliminate armaments or classes of armaments completely, usually by a negotiated reciprocal agreement between two or more rivals, in efforts to prevent the use of those weapons in warfare. **Arms control** is less ambitious. Arms control is designed to regulate arms levels either by limiting their growth or by restricting how they might be used. It results from agreements from potential enemies to cooperate in order to reduce the probability that conflicting interests will erupt in warfare, and to reduce the scope of violence in any armed conflict which may nonetheless occur. Because arms control is based on recognition that a true conflict of interest between rivals exists, it is favored by realists who see a positive contribution potentially made when enemies negotiate an agreement to balance their weapons and through that balancing build mutual confidence.

Controlling war by reducing weapons inventories is hardly a novel idea. Yet, until recently, few states have negotiated disarmament agreements. True, some countries in the past did reduce their armaments. For example, in 600 BCE the Chinese states formed a disarmament league that produced a peaceful century for the league's members. Canada and the United States disarmed the Great Lakes region through the 1817 Rush-Bagot Agreement. Nonetheless, these kinds of achievements have

■ **disarmament**
agreements to reduce or destroy weapons or other means of attack.

■ **arms control**
multilateral or bilateral agreements to contain arms races by setting limits on the number and types of weapons states are permitted.

been relatively rare in history. Most disarmament has been involuntary, the product of reductions imposed by the victors in the immediate aftermath of a war, as when the Allied powers attempted to disarm a defeated Germany after World War I.

■ **bilateral agreements**

exchanges between two states, such as arms control agreements negotiated cooperatively to set ceilings on military force levels.

In addition to differentiating between arms control and disarmament, you should also distinguish between **bilateral agreements** and **multilateral agreements**. Because the former involves only two countries, they are often easier to negotiate and to enforce than are the latter, which are agreements among three or more countries. As a result, bilateral arms agreements tend to be more successful than multilateral agreements.

By far the most revealing examples are the superpower agreements to control nuclear weapons. This chapter will look briefly at the record of Soviet-American negotiations before examining the checkered history of multilateral arms control and disarmament.

■ **multilateral agreements**

cooperative compacts among many states to ensure that a concerted policy is implemented toward alleviating a common problem, such as levels of future weapons capabilities.

Bilateral Arms Control and Disarmament

The Cold War between the Soviet Union and the United States never degenerated into a trial of military strength. One of the reasons was the series of more than twenty-five arms control agreements that Moscow and Washington negotiated in the wake of the Cuban Missile Crisis. Beginning with the 1963 Hot Line Agreement, which established a direct radio and telegraph communications system between the two governments, Soviet and American leaders reached a series of modest agreements aimed at stabilizing the military balance and reducing the risk of war. Each of these bilateral treaties lowered tensions and helped build a climate of trust that encouraged efforts to negotiate further agreements.

■ **Strategic Arms Reduction Treaty (START)**

the U.S.–Russian series of negotiations that began in 1993 and, with the 1997 START-III agreement ratified by Russia in 2000, pledged to cut the nuclear arsenals of both sides by eighty percent of the Cold War peaks, in order to lower the risk of nuclear war.

The most important agreements between the superpowers were the *Strategic Arms Limitation Talks (SALT)* of 1972 and 1979; the **Strategic Arms Reduction Treaty (START)** of 1991, 1993, and 1997; and the **Strategic Offensive Reductions Treaty (SORT)** of 2002. The first two agreements stabilized the nuclear arms race, and the remaining agreements reduced the weapons in each side's inventories (recall Figure 15.1). When the Cold War ended in 1991, the United States still had more than ninety-five hundred nuclear warheads and Russia had about eight thousand. Then disarmament began in earnest. After decades in which the two rivals engaged in a rapidly expanded arms race that increased the size of their nuclear arsenals, the United States and Russia reached a series of historic disarmament agreements that has cut the number of new nuclear warheads in their stockpiles dramatically. Since its 1986 peak, the size of the two superpowers' nuclear arsenals have declined by nearly ninety percent, and it will decline much further by 2012 as a result of the 2002 Strategic Offensive Reductions Treaty.

This disarmament achievement has inspired most of the other nuclear powers to not increase the number of warheads they have deployed. That said, threatened states are always tempted to rearm, and therefore fears that disarmament will not continue are rising. Provoking concerns was the U.S. decision to store rather than to destroy its remaining Cold War warheads and to continue developing its "Star Wars" missile defense from outer space. Also dispelling disarmament hopes was Russia's successful test in August 2008 of a new long-range nuclear missile. Designed to dodge defense systems, the Topol intercontinental stealth rocket has a range of 6,125 miles, and poses a threat to peace in Europe. The record of successful bilateral arms control and even disarmament between the United States and Russia attests to the possibilities for rival military powers to contain by agreement a dangerous arms race. But the fragility of these agreements underscores the difficulties.

Multilateral Arms Control and Disarmament

History provides many examples of multilateral arms control and disarmament efforts. As early as the eleventh century, the Second Lateran Council prohibited the use of crossbows in fighting. The 1868 St. Petersburg Declaration prohibited the use of explosive bullets. In 1899 and 1907, International Peace Conferences at The Hague restricted the use of some weapons and prohibited others. The leaders of the United States, Britain, Japan, France, and Italy signed treaties at the Washington Naval Conferences (1921–1922) agreeing to adjust the relative tonnage of their fleets.

Nearly thirty major multilateral agreements have been signed since the second world war (see Table 17.1). Of these, the 1968 Nuclear Nonproliferation Treaty (NPT), which prohibited the transfer of nuclear weapons and production technologies to nonnuclear weapons states, stands out. This twenty-four-hundred-word contract that some say saved the world, is historically the most symbolic multilateral arms control agreement, with 189 signatory countries. In 2005, painstaking negotiations sought to renew and preserve the NPT, which promotes the nonproliferation that had stopped the spread of nuclear weapons of mass destruction (WMD) until 1998 when India and Pakistan broke the NPT's barriers to become nuclear-weapon states. This set the precedent for North Korea and Iran (which remain outside the NPT) to join Israel and others who some believe have already secretly produced nuclear weapons (see Chapter 14). The final consensus documents to the 2005 NPT renewal conference are considered politically binding, giving a boost to nonproliferation. But the heart of the contract seems to grow weaker year by year. Cheaters are found on the inside, nuclear bombs on the outside. Some states that signed the original agreement are wondering whether the deal they were handed by the "nuclear club" in 1968 was a raw one. They observe the failure of the original nuclear powers to honor their pledge to disarm, the U.S. talk of building new nuclear weapons and using them against nonnuclear states, and the U.S. rejection of the nuclear test-ban treaty. The original NPT goal—"three No's to prevent nuclear catastrophe: no 'loose' smuggled nukes for sale on the black market, no nascent nuclear states, no new nuclear weapon states" (Allison 2004)—is in jeopardy. More than ten thousand nuclear war heads remain (SIPRI 2008, 15), and more and more countries are acquiring the means to produce them. The forty-six countries that launched the *International Nuclear Fuel Cycle Evaluation* negotiations in 2005 to sever the link between nuclear energy and nuclear proliferation took a step toward nuclear arms control. But further nuclear nonproliferation remains much in doubt.

■ **Strategic Offensive Reductions Treaty (SORT)**
the U.S.–Russian agreement to reduce the number of strategic warheads to between 1,700 and 2,200 for each country by 2012.

Much of the established multilateral disarmament machinery has started to rust.

—Kofi Annan, former Secretary-General of the United Nations

Table 17.1 Major Multilateral Arms Control Treaties since 1945

Date	Agreement	Number of Parties (signed, 2008)	Principle Objectives
1959	Antarctic Treaty	45	Prevents the military use of the Antarctic, including the testing of nuclear weapons
1963	Partial Test Ban Treaty	136	Prohibits nuclear weapons in the atmosphere, outer space, and underwater
1967	Outer Space Treaty	134	Outlaws the use of outer space for testing or stationing any weapons, as well as for military maneuvers
1967	Treaty of Tlatelolco	33	Creates the Latin American Nuclear Free Zone by prohibiting the testing and possession of nuclear facilities for military purposes
1968	Nuclear Nonproliferation Treaty	189	Prevents the spread of nuclear weapons and nuclear-weapons-production technologies to nonnuclear weapons states
1971	Seabed Treaty	115	Prohibits the development of weapons of mass destruction and nuclear weapons on the seabed beyond a twelve-mile coastal limit
1972	Biological and Toxic Weapons Convention	171	Prohibits the production and storage of biological toxins; calls for the destruction of biological weapons stockpiles
1977	Environmental Modifications Convention (Enmod Convention)	87	Bans the use of technologies that could alter Earth's weather patterns, ocean currents, ozone layer, or ecology
1980	Protection of Nuclear Material Convention	132	Obligates protection of peaceful nuclear material during transport on ships or aircraft
1981	Inhumane Weapons Convention	108	Prohibits the use of such weapons as fragmentation bombs, incendiary weapons, booby traps, and mines to which civilians could be exposed

(continues)

Table 17.1   Major Multilateral Arms Control Treaties since 1945
(continued)

Date	Agreement	Number of Parties (signed, 2008)	Principle Objectives
1985	South Pacific Nuclear Free Zone (Roratonga) Treaty	19	Prohibits the testing, acquisition, or deployment of nuclear weapons in the South Pacific
1987	Missile Technology Control Regime (MTCR)	34	Restricts export of ballistic missiles and production facilities
1990	Conventional Forces in Europe (CFE)	30	Places limits on five categories of weapons in Europe and lowers force levels
1990	Confidence- and Security Building Measures Agreement	53	Improves measures for exchanging detailed information on weapons, forces, and military exercises
1991	UN Register of Conventional Arms	101	Calls on all states to submit information on seven categories of major weapons exported or imported during the previous year
1992	Open Skies Treaty	35	Permits flights by unarmed surveillance aircraft over the territory of the signatory states
1993	Chemical Weapons Convention (CWC)	181	Requires all stockpiles of chemical weapons to be destroyed
1995	Protocol to the Inhumane Weapons Convention	135	Bans some types of laser weapons that cause permanent loss of eyesight
1995	Treaty of Bangkok	10	Creates a nuclear-weapon-free zone in Southeast Asia
1995	Wassenaar Export-Control Treaty	40	Regulates transfers of sensitive dual-use technologies to nonparticipating countries
1996	ASEAN Nuclear Free Zone Treaty	10	Prevents signatories in Southeast Asia from making, possessing, storing, or testing nuclear weapons
1996	Comprehensive Test Ban Treaty (CTBT)	177	Bans all testing of nuclear weapons

(continues)

Table 17.1 Major Multilateral Arms Control Treaties since 1945
(continued)

Date	Agreement	Number of Parties (signed, 2008)	Principle Objectives
1996	Treaty of Pelindaba	21	Creates an African nuclear-weapon-free zone
1997	Antipersonnel Landmines Treaty (APLT)	155	Bans the production and export of land-mines and pledges plans to remove them
1999	Inter-American Convention on Transparency in Conventional Weapons Acquisitions	34	Requires all thirty-four members of the Organization of American States (OAS) to annually report all weapons acquisitions, exports, and imports
2005	Nuclear Nonproliferation Treaty Review Conference	(123 delegates)	Final communiqué voices approval to continue support for the NPT treaty
2007	Treaty on Nuclear Free Zone in Central Asia (Treaty of Semipolinsk)	5	Obligates parties not to acquire nuclear weapons

SIPRI Yearbook (2007, 667-689).

Similar problems plague other multilateral agreements. The 1993 Chemical Weapons Convention (CWC), for example, required all stockpiles of chemical weapons to be destroyed within ten years. However, the agreement lost some of its authority in 2001 when the Bush administration refused to accept the enforcement measures.

The Problematic Future of Arms Control and Disarmament

The obstacles to arms control and disarmament are formidable. Critics complain that these agreements frequently only regulate obsolete armaments or ones that the parties to the agreement have little incentive for developing in the first place. Even when agreements are reached on modern, sophisticated weapons, the parties often set ceilings higher than the number of weapons currently deployed, so they do not have to slash their inventories.

A second pitfall is the propensity of limits on one type of weapon system to prompt developments in another system. Like a balloon that is squeezed at one end but expands at the other, constraints on certain parts of a country's arsenal can lead to enhancements elsewhere. An example can be seen in the 1972 SALT I agreement, which limited the number of intercontinental ballistic missiles possessed by the

United States and Soviet Union. Although the number of missiles was restricted, no limits were placed on the number of nuclear warheads that could be placed on each missile. Consequently, both sides developed *multiple independently targeted reentry vehicles* (MIRVs). In short, the quantitative freeze on launchers led to qualitative improvements in their warhead delivery systems.

Also reducing faith in future meaningful arms control is the slow, weak, and ineffective ability of the global community to ban some of the most dangerous and counterproductive weapons. Consider the case of **antipersonnel landmines (APLs)**, which cannot discriminate between soldiers and civilians. More than one hundred to three hundred million landmines are believed to be scattered on the territory of more than seventy countries (with another one hundred million in stockpiles). It is estimated that about one mine exists for every fifty people in the world and that each year they kill or maim more than twenty-six thousand people—almost all of them civilians. In 1994, not a single state would endorse a prohibition on these deadly weapons. It took a peace activist, Jody Williams, to organize the International Campaign to Ban Landmines, which opened for signature in December 1997 the *Convention on the Prohibition of the Use, Stockpiling, Production and Transfer of Antipersonnel Mines.* For her efforts, Williams received the Nobel Peace Prize. But the United States, Russia, and other great powers stubbornly resisted the APL convention until a coalition of NGO peace groups mounted sufficient pressure for them to produce this epic treaty (still without U.S. acceptance). The challenge of enforcing the ban, now signed by 155 states, and the task of removing APLs, remains staggering. The same challenge faces efforts to produce "biosecurity" through treaties controlling biological weapons (Fidler and Gostin 2008).

■ **antipersonnel landmines (APLs)** weapons buried below the surface of the soil that explode on contact with any person—soldier or citizen—stepping on them.

A final problem facing those advocating arms control and disarmament is continuous innovation. By the time that limits are negotiated on one type of weapon, a new generation of weapons has emerged. Modern technology is creating an ever-widening range of novel weapons—increasingly smaller, deadlier, and easier to conceal.

Why do states often make decisions to arm that apparently imprison them in the grip of perpetual insecurity? On the surface, the incentives for meaningful arms control seem numerous. Significant controls would save money, reduce tension, decrease environmental hazards, and diminish the potential destructiveness of war. However, most countries are reluctant to limit their armaments because of the self-help system that requires each state to protect itself. Thus, states find themselves caught in a vicious cycle summarized by two basic principles: (1) "Don't negotiate when you are behind. Why accept a permanent position of number two?" and (2) "Don't negotiate when you are ahead. Why accept a freeze in an area of military competition when the other side has not kept up with you?" (Barnet 1977).

Here policy makers read from the realist script, which insists that national security is best protected by developing military capabilities and not by reducing armaments or military spending. Realists regard treaties to be dangerous in an anarchical world in which the promises of self-interested rivals cannot be trusted (recall the *Prisoner's Dilemma*, Chapter 15). They counsel against putting faith in arms control treaties, because deception and broken promises are to be expected by ruthless leaders in the global jungle. Thus, instead of holding commitments to arms control agreements that cannot be enforced, realists advise reliance on unilateral self-help through military preparedness.

That realist mind-set was very evident in U.S. decisions at the turn of the century to reject an array of international treaties designed to control the threat of nuclear weapons. During 2001 alone, the United States decided to abrogate the 1972 Anti-Ballistic Missile (ABM) Treaty, withdraw from a UN conference to impose limits on illegal trafficking of small arms, and reject proposed enforcement measures for the 1972 Biological Weapons Convention. This disregard for arms control set a standard for other states to follow. Especially troubling was the U.S. repudiation of the 1972 ABM treaty, which was regarded by many as the cornerstone of nuclear arms

> *We are spending billions of dollars on missile defense.*
> *And I actually believe that we need missile defense... but I also believe*
> *that, when we are only spending a few hundred million dollars on*
> *nuclear proliferation, then we're making a mistake.*
>
> —Barack Obama, U.S. President

control, as that announcement was the first time in modern history that the United States had renounced a major international accord, and it ignited fears that a global chain reaction of massive repudiations of arms control agreements by other states would follow. For example, in 2007 Russia threatened to quit the INF missile treaty and to place a moratorium on the CFE treaty.

The tendency of states to make improving their weapons a priority over controlling them is illustrated by the example of nuclear testing (see Map 17.1). The eight known nuclear states have conducted a total of 2,056 nuclear explosions in twenty-four different locations since 1945—an average of one test every ten days. Both China and the United States regularly conduct so-called zero-yield nuclear experiments and are suspected of conducting explosive tests so small that they can't be detected. Moreover, the partial test ban treaty of 1963, which prohibited atmospheric and underwater testing but not underground explosions, did not slow the pace of testing. Three-fourths of all nuclear tests took place after the ban went into effect.

The past record of arms control and disarmament has dispirited liberal reformers whose hopes for negotiated compromises to curtail the global arms race have not been fulfilled. It appears that realists, and their abiding emphasis on peace through military preparations, are trumping those liberals who counsel that weapons acquisitions are not a safe road toward world order. Someday, Woodrow Wilson's cause of world disarmament may yet triumph, as he hoped and prayed. As long as the threat of armed aggression haunts the world, leaders are unlikely to think it prudent to disarm. Liberals perceive other paths to peace as more promising. The construction of international organizations for collective security benefits from a more encouraging history, in part because so many military crises require multilateral cooperation to be peacefully managed.

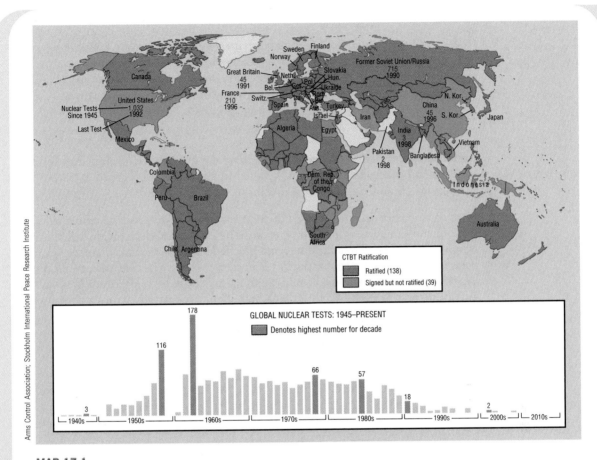

MAP 17.1

TRICK OR TREATY? CAN ARMS-CONTROL TREATIES ARREST THE PROLIFERATION OF WEAPONS? Since the dawn of the nuclear age, the eight known nuclear powers have conducted 2,057 documented tests of their weapons. As the timeline at the bottom of the map shows, testing declined since the 1960s, but following North Korea's tests since 2006 fear of a wave of new testing has accelerated (SIPRI 2007, 689).

MAINTAINING COLLECTIVE SECURITY THROUGH INTERNATIONAL ORGANIZATIONS

International organizations throughout history have all advanced the preservation of peace as one of the prime rationales for their formation. The United Nations Charter, for example, identifies maintaining international peace and security through multilateral cooperation as its primary purpose. International organizations have usually come into being in the aftermath of major wars to help prevent warfare from re-occurring.

This institutional pathway to international peace is sculpted in liberal thinking and especially neoliberalism. It is an approach voiced as an alternative to the balance of power advocated by realist thinkers to maintain peace by redistributing power through the free-floating mechanism of shifting alliances and alignments. The global

My first axiom: The quest for international security involves the unconditional surrender by every nation, in a certain measure, of its liberty of action, its sovereignty that is to say, and it is clear beyond all doubt that no other road can lead to such security.

—Albert Einstein, scientist

community has usually trodden down the liberal path to peace through international organization when each previous balance of power has collapsed in large-scale warfare (as all past balances of power have sooner or later).

Note that reliance on international organization so enthusiastically recommended by most liberal thinkers is opposed vigorously by classical realist thinking. Realism, it should be recalled, prizes the sovereign independence of states as a core value, and berates international organization as a barrier to states' foreign policy autonomy, and freedom and flexibility of unilateral action. Indeed, realists traditionally have religiously abided by the dictum that states should "constrain actors who subscribe to supranational organizational principles" (Kaplan 1957).

Liberal prescriptions for the global community to "get organized" by creating institutions *above* states as a route to global stability are rejected by realist thought. The only exception to this realist posture is when great powers have elected to create supranational multilateral institutions for the management of military power in international relations, and this *only* when the great powers forming them were certain that the organizations would be managed authoritatively *by* them for their own self-interests (Claude 1962).

For liberal reformers, *collective security* is conceived as an alternative to balance of power politics favored by realists. By definition, collective security requires collective decisions for collective purposes to contain international armed aggression, guided by the principle that an active aggression by any state will be met with a unified response from the rest. Next the chapter will take a deeper look at this second liberal path to peace.

The League of Nations and Collective Security

Perhaps more than any other event, World War I discredited the realist argument that peace was a by-product of a stable balance of power. Citing arms races, secret treaties, and competing alliances as sources of acute tension, many liberals viewed power balancing as a *cause* of war instead of as an instrument for its prevention. U.S. President Woodrow Wilson voiced the strongest opposition to balance of power politics; Point XIV of his Fourteen Points proposals for postwar peace called for "a general association of nations for the purpose of preserving the political independence and territorial integrity of great and small states alike." This plea led to the formation of the League of Nations to replace the balance of power with a global governance system for world order in which aggression by any state would be met by a united response.

The Logic of Collective Security Long before Wilson and other liberal reformers called for the establishment of a League of Nations, the idea of collective security had been expressed in various peace plans. Between the eleventh and thirteenth centuries, for example, French ecclesiastic councils held in Poitiers (1000), Limoges (1031), and Toulouse (1210) discussed rudimentary versions of collective security. Similar proposals surfaced in the writings of Pierre Dubois (1306), King George Podebrad of Bohemia (1462), the Duc de Sully (1560–1641), and the Abbé de Saint-Pierre (1713). Underlying these plans was the belief that an organized "community" of power would be more effective in preserving peace than shifting alliances aimed at balancing power.

Collective security is based on the creed voiced by Alexandre Dumas's d'Artagnan and his fellow Musketeers: "One for all and all for one!" In order for collective security to function in the rough-and-tumble international arena, its advocates usually translate the Musketeer creed into the following rules of statecraft:

1 *All threats to peace must be a common concern to everyone.* Peace, collective security theory assumes, is indivisible. If aggression anywhere is ignored, it eventually will spread to other countries and become more difficult to stop; hence, an attack on any one state must be regarded as an attack on all states.

2 *Every member of the global system should join the collective security organization.* Instead of maneuvering against one another in rival alliances, states should link up in a single "uniting" alliance. Such a universal collectivity, it is assumed, would possess the international legitimacy and strength to keep the peace.

> *Collective security assumes that every nation perceives every challenge to the international order in the same way, and is prepared to run the same risk to preserve it.*
> —Henry Kissinger, former U.S. Secretary of State

3 *Members of the organization should pledge to settle their disputes through pacific means.* Collective security is not wedded to the status quo. It assumes that peaceful change is possible when institutions are available to resolve conflicts of interest. In addition to providing a mechanism for the *mediation* of disagreements, the collective security organization would also contain a judicial organ authorized to issue binding judgments on contentious disputes.

4 *If a breach of the peace occurs, the organization should apply timely, robust sanctions to punish the aggressor.* A final assumption underpinning the theory holds that members of the collective security organization would be willing and able to give mutual assistance to any state suffering an attack. Sanctions could range from public condemnation to an economic boycott to military retaliation.

> *The paradox is that men of liberal mind, who would be offended by the idea that the police are the most important factor in a sharing social cohesion, do not hesitate to become fierce police enthusiasts when they discuss the international system.*
>
> —Abba Eban, Israeli diplomat

Putting the pieces of these premises together, this liberal approach to international peace through collective security organizations aims to control national self-help warfare by guaranteeing states' defense through collective regulation. Ironically, therefore, liberal reformers accept the use of military might—not to expand state power, but rather to deter potential aggressors by confronting them with armed force organized by the united opposition of the entire global community. Might *can* be used to fight for right.

The Limitations of Collective Security   As discussed in Chapters 2 and 4, the League of Nations was constructed according to the blueprint of collective security. To the disappointment of its advocates, the League was not endorsed by the United States, the very power that had most championed it in the waning months of World War I. Other problems for the League arose when its members disagreed over how to define "aggression," as well as how to share the costs and risks of mounting an organized response to aggressors. In the final analysis, collective security theory's central fallacy was that it expected states to be as anxious to see others protected as they were to protect themselves. That assumption did not prove true in the years preceding World War II; consequently, the League of Nations never became an effective collective security system.

The United Nations and Peacekeeping

Like the League, the United Nations was established to promote international peace and security after a gruesome world war. The architects of the United Nations were painfully aware of the League's disappointing experience with collective security. They hoped a new structure would make the United Nations more effective than the defunct League. Recall from Chapter 6 that the UN Charter established a Security Council of fifteen members, a General Assembly composed of representatives from all member states, and an administrative apparatus (or Secretariat) under the leadership of a Secretary-General. Although the UN's founders voiced support for collective security, they were heavily influenced by the idea of a *concert* of great powers. The UN Charter permitted any of the Security Council's five permanent members (the United States, the Soviet Union, Great Britain, France, and China) to veto and thereby block proposed military actions. Because the Security Council could approve military actions only when the permanent members fully agreed, the United Nations was hamstrung by great power rivalries, especially between the United States and the Soviet Union.

To further enhance the great powers' authority relative to the UN, the Charter severely restricted the capacity of the General Assembly to mount collective action, authorizing it only to initiate studies of conflict situations, bring perceived hostilities to the attention of the Security Council, and make recommendations for initiatives to keep the peace. Moreover, in deciding wheather the Secretary-General should be a secretary or a general (Chesterman 2007), the charter chose to make the Secretary-General only a chief administrative officer. Article 99 confined the Secretary-General to alerting the Security Council to peace-threatening situations and to providing administrative support for the operations that the Security Council approved.

Because the UN's structure limited its ability to function as a true collective security organization, the United Nations fell short during the Cold War of many of the ideals its more ambitious founders envisioned, principally because its two most powerful members in the Security Council, the United States and the Soviet Union, did not cooperate. More than 230 Security Council vetoes were cast, stopping action of any type on about one-third of the UN's resolutions. Nevertheless, the United Nations found other ways to contribute to world order.

Like any adaptive institution, the UN found other ways to overcome the compromising legal restrictions and lack of great power cooperation that inhibited its capacity to preserve world order. For example, in contrast to peace enforcement as

Kofi Annan, 1996–2006
He had a quiet charisma, but the Iraq war and the oil-for-food scandal marred his second term.

Dag Hammarskjold, 1953–1961
The U.N.'s most effective leader. Hammarskjold died on a peacekeeping mission to Congo.

Boutros Boutros-Ghali, 1992–1996 The United States dumped the acerbic and undiplomatic Egyptian after one turbulent term.

Kurt Waldheim, 1972–1981
An effective bureaucrat, Waldheim is now remembered mainly for his Nazi past.

Javier Perez de Cuellar, 1982–1991 He quietly guided the organization out of Cold War paralysis and back into business.

Trygve Lie, 1946–1952
The gruff politician helped create the organization but accomplished little in office.

U Thant, 1961–1971
The placid Thant had a low profile but got flak for pulling U.N. peacekeepers from Sinai.

BOSSES OF THE UN'S BLUE HELMET PEACEKEEPERS The Secretary-Generals of the UN have had a big influence in shaping UN peacekeeping operations. Shown here are the seven Secretary Generals who have preceded the present Secretary General, Ban Ki-Moon, and a profile of their administrative philosophies while holding what U.S. President Franklin D. Roosevelt called "the most important job in the world."

■ **peacekeeping**

the efforts by third parties such as the UN to intervene in civil wars and/or interstate wars or to prevent hostilities between potential belligerents from escalating, so that by acting as a buffer a negotiated settlement of the dispute can be reached.

■ **preventive diplomacy**

diplomatic actions taken in advance of a predictable crisis to prevent or limit violence.

■ **peacemaking**

the process of diplomacy, mediation, negotiation, or other forms of peaceful settlement that arranges an end to a dispute and resolves the issues that led to conflict.

■ **peace building**

postconflict actions, predominantly diplomatic and economic, that strengthen and rebuild governmental infrastructure and institutions in order to avoid renewed recourse to armed conflict.

in the Korean War, the UN undertook a new approach, termed **peacekeeping**, that aimed at separating enemies. The UN Emergency Force (UNEF), authorized in 1956 by the *Uniting for Peace Resolution* in the General Assembly in response to the Suez crisis, was the first of many other peacekeeping operations. In addition, in 1960, Secretary-General Dag Hammarskjöld sought to manage security through what he termed **preventive diplomacy** by attempting to resolve conflicts before they reached the crisis stage, in contrast to ending wars once they erupted. Likewise, in 1989, Secretary-General Javier Pérez de Cuéllar, frustrated with the superpowers' prevention of the UN to "play as effective and decisive a role as the charter certainly envisaged for it," pursued what was called **peacemaking** initiatives designed to obtain a truce to end the fighting so that the UN Security Council could then establish operations to keep the peace. UN Secretary-General Kofi Annan concentrated the UN's efforts on **peace building** by creating the conditions that make renewed war unlikely, while at the same time working on peacemaking (ending fighting already underway) and managing the UN's **peace operations** to police those conflicts in which the threat of renewed fighting between enemies is high. These endeavors have emphasized **peace enforcement** operations, relying on UN forces that are trained and equipped to use military force if necessary without the prior consent of the disputants.

For more than four decades, the UN was a victim of superpower rivalry. However, the end of the Cold War removed many of the impediments to the UN's ability to lead in preserving peace. For example, in 1999, the Security Council swung into action to authorize military coercion to force Iraq to withdraw from Kuwait, which it had invaded. This successful collective security initiative jump started optimism for and use of the UN for peacekeeping leadership. After 1990, the UN launched five times as many peacekeeping missions as it had in its previous forty years of its existence. On average, since 1990 it has managed seventeen operations each year (see Map 17.2).

When inspecting the UN's record at peacekeeping, opposing images surface. Popular perceptions of peacekeeping frequently include noble, blue-helmeted soldiers hailing from a cross-section of the world's countries and representing the powerful will of the international community determined to end a conflict and rebuild a state. The ugly reality of modern peacekeeping operations belies that image. . . . Peace operations have shown decidedly mixed results in recent years, frequently suffering from underfunding, understaffing, and horrific financial and sex scandals. And they are always tormented by the "ad-hocery" that inevitably characterizes large-scale international military cooperation. Largely devoid of superior Western military forces, most international peace operations make do with sundry odd table scraps for troops and resources. Analysts familiar with the turmoil of modern peace operations are often amazed they enjoy any success at all. . . . The United Nations can be both astonishingly incompetent and surprisingly capable at addressing international conflicts and crises, but both its most ardent supporters and its harshest critics largely misunderstand its nature. The organization's successes and failures can best be explained by looking into a mirror; UN missions are only as good as the UN members that support those missions with their own citizens. Western nations, to the detriment of UN peacekeeping, have largely abrogated this responsibility.

In fact, roughly 50 percent of peacekeeping missions simply fail, a schizophrenic record of success that is too often ignored when advocates call for yet more peacekeeping missions. Nevertheless, the UN has several features that continue to make it the first option to launch international peace operations. First, it brings political legitimacy. There is no other international organization with such authority and recognition. Second, it spreads the cost of such missions among its members. And third,

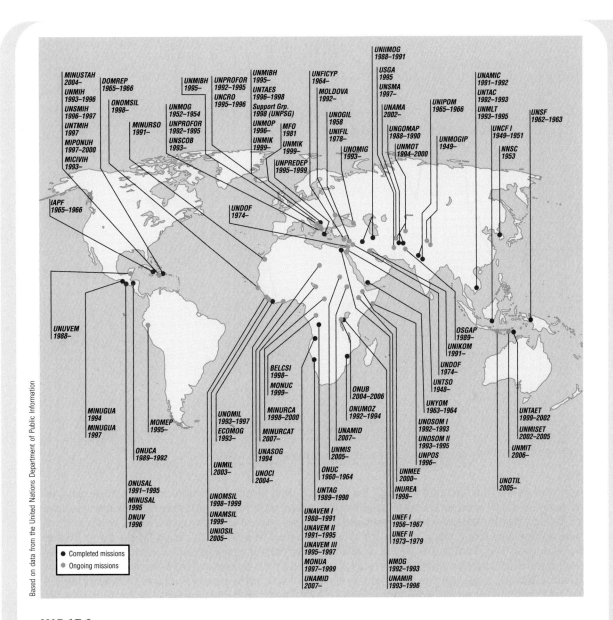

MAP 17.2

UN PEACE MISSIONS SINCE 1948 In its first forty years, the United Nations undertook a mere thirteen peacekeeping operations. But since 1986, the UN has been much more active, sending Blue Helmet peacekeepers to forty-eight flash points. Since 1989, on average, the UN has had seventeen operations underway each year, and as the following figure shows, most of the sixty-three missions between 1948 and 2009 have been in operation for at least a decade.

it brings some surprising capabilities to drive humanitarian relief, peacemaking, and state-building. In general, the UN's benefits far outweigh its faults, and it remains a useful organization (Brooks and Laroia 2005, 121–22).

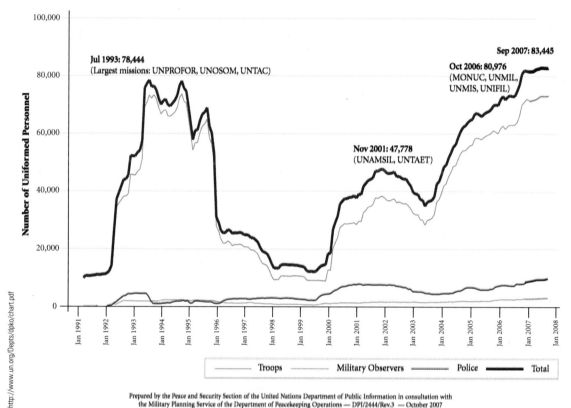

Uniformed Personnel in UN Peacekeeping: 1991- present

Jul 1993: 78,444
(Largest missions: UNPROFOR, UNOSOM, UNTAC)

Sep 2007: 83,445

Oct 2006: 80,976
(MONUC, UNMIL, UNMIS, UNIFIL)

Nov 2001: 47,778
(UNAMSIL, UNTAET)

— Troops   — Military Observers   — Police   ■ Total

Prepared by the Peace and Security Section of the United Nations Department of Public Information in consultation with
the Military Planning Service of the Department of Peacekeeping Operations — DPI/2444/Rev.3 — October 2007

http://www.un.org/Depts/dpko/chart.pdf

THE INCREASING DEMAND FOR "PEACE" The above chart shows a clear trend in the demand for peacekeepers over time, as the total number of personnel involved in peacekeeping missions has increased fivefold since 1999. The other trend lines show two of the other key functions increasingly performed by these personnel: military observers (who monitor conditions on the ground and have no mandate to engage militarily) and police. Unfortunately, as argued by UN analysts Thorsten Benner, Stephan Mergenthaler, and Philipp Rotmann (2008, 6), "UN peacekeeping is the victim of its own success," as the increased demand for peacekeepers, as well as the increasingly diverse nature of their missions, has not been matched by increases in infrastructure and training. Moreover, troops have been dispatched in an injudicious manner and have been put into areas (such as Somalia and Chad) in which the basic mission of peacekeeping is simply not applicable to conditions on the ground—put another way, the "UN is sending peacekeepers to places where there simply is no peace to keep."

■ peace
operations

a general category
encompassing both
peacekeeping and
peace enforcement
operations
undertaken to
establish and
maintain peace
between disputants.

Despite these advantages, those advocating an active peacekeeping role for the UN still encounter resistance. The UN seems to have many critics because many countries make demands on the organization that cannot be met with existing resources and that other countries oppose. Countries call on the UN in times of need but attack it when it fails to comply with the requests made.

The office of the Secretary-General is seeking to fulfill the UN's humanitarian and security mandate, especially through intervention to stop horrific atrocities wherever and whenever they occur. However, critics voice concerns that the UN is inclined to practice selective engagement in sending peacekeeping forces primarily to those trouble spots where the Security Council's great powers have economic interests in securing access to resources such as oil and other products. There is "some evidence of a regional bias in the UN's selection of missions" but the UN nonetheless has attempted to "balance between the dictates of power and concerns of principle [because] one of the best predictors of UN interventions is the number of deaths in a conflict [which] speaks well of the UN's mission to address costly human suffering. By contrast, the UN has not been evenhanded in how it responds to deaths. The UN acts more swiftly when the deaths occur in Europe than in Africa, and it acts more swiftly in Africa than in Asia" (Gilligan and Stedman 2003).

Perhaps this selective peacekeeping focus is a product of limited financial restraints as much as it is the priorities of the Security Council's great powers. For the UN's sixty-one peacekeeping operations since 1948, expenditures have totaled more than $53 billion, and for the period between July 2007 and June 2008, the budget support to 82,868 UN peacekeeping personnel was $5.3 billion, and outstanding contributions were running $1.54 billion. UN peacekeeping operations remain understaffed, underfunded, and overwhelmed in responding where "Blue Helmet" participation is needed.

The UN is not empowered to achieve the high purposes for which it was created, and the aim of global collective security for all humanity cannot be met with inadequate capabilities. This weakness accounts for the UN's growing reliance on regional organizations and multiparty state alliances to step in the breach in situations where UN forces have not been given the support necessary to provide assistance.

■ **peace enforcement**
the application of military force to warring parties, or the threat of its use, normally pursuant to international authorization, to compel compliance with resolutions or with sanctions designed to maintain or restore peace and order.

■ **selective engagement**
a state's or an IGO's choosing to intervene militarily in some situations but declining to do so in others.

> *The business of peacekeeping has been getting a lot tougher. Rich nations are putting their muscle where their immediate interests lie, leaving the job of patrolling in hardscrabble territory to their less financially capable UN colleagues.*
>
> —Laura Neack, foreign policy expert

For the UN to succeed, the world community must match the demands made on it with the means given to it. The organization must strike a balance between realism and liberalism. As with other intergovernmental organizations (IGOs), the UN in the realist image *reflects* more than it *affects* world politics and, in the liberal image, promotes peace—especially when it has a strong consensual support with the full cooperation of its largest and most important members.

Although less than perfect, the United Nations is the only global institution effective at organizing international collaboration to meet security crises in situations where states are unwilling or unprepared to act alone. As a seasoned UN official, Brian Urquhart, concludes:

> In the great uncertainties and disorders that lie ahead, the United Nations, for all its shortcomings, will be called on again and again, because there is no other global institution, because there is a severe limit to what even the strongest powers wish to take on themselves. . . . Either the UN is vital to a more stable and equitable world and should be given the means to do its job, or peoples and governments should be encouraged to look elsewhere. But is there really an alternative?

Actually, there is a conspicuous alternate. Although the great powers are often reluctant in equipping the United Nations to contain civil wars, the use of regional security organizations is rising. Regional IGOs are stepping into the breach in those situations where UN Blue Helmets have not been given the support necessary to do the job.

> *Important issues are being taken care of by regional organizations, with the United Nations giving its blessings.*
> —Karel Kovanda, Czech Republic Ambassador to the United Nations

Regional Security Organizations and Collective Defense

If the UN reflects the lack of shared values and common purpose characteristic of a divided global community, perhaps regional organizations, whose members already share some interests and cultural traditions, offer better prospects. The kinds of wars raging today do not lend themselves to control by a worldwide body because these conflicts are now almost entirely civil wars. The UN was designed to manage only international wars *between* states; it was not organized or legally authorized to intervene in internal battles *within* sovereign borders.

Regional IGOs are different. Regional IGOs see their security interests vitally affected by armed conflicts within countries in their area or adjacent to it, and historically they have shown the determination and discipline to police bitter civil conflicts "in their backyards." The "regionalization" of peace operations is a global trend. As 2008 began, no less than sixty-one peace missions served by 169,467 military and civilian personnel were carried out by regional organizations and UN-sanctioned coalitions of states (SIPRI 2008). Hence, regional security organizations can be expected to play an increasingly larger role in the future security affairs of their regions.

The North Atlantic Treaty Organization (NATO) is the best-known regional security organization. Others include the Organization for Security and Cooperation in Europe (OSCE), the ANZUS pact (Australia, New Zealand, and the United States), and the Southeast Asia Treaty Organization (SEATO). Regional organizations with somewhat broader political mandates beyond defense include the Organization of American States (OAS), the League of Arab States, the Organization of African Unity (OAU), the Nordic Council, the Association of Southeast Asian Nations (ASEAN), and the Gulf Cooperation Council.

■ **regional collective defense regimes**

collective security agreements by members of a geographic region to join together to prevent armed aggression by an expansionist state.

Whereas Article 51 of the UN Charter encourages the creation of regional organizations for collective self-defense, it would be misleading to describe NATO and the other regional organizations as a substitute collective security instrument for the UN. They are not. More accurately, **regional collective defense regimes** are designed to deter a potential common threat to the region's peace, one typically identified in advance. The exception in NATO, which in 2007 took over command of 31,000 troops from thirty-seven countries in Afghanistan—NATO's first ground war in sixty years.

Many of today's regional security organizations face the challenge of preserving consensus and solidarity without a clearly identifiable external enemy or common threat. Cohesion is hard to maintain in the absence of a clear sense of the alliance's

A LIBERAL MILITARY INTERVENTIONIST ROAD TO PEACE? Although many states and IGOs have been reluctant to intervene militarily to keep peace in civil wars outside their spheres of influence, NATO's 1999 humanitarian intervention in Kosovo proves an exception. Here, a British tank heading to the Kosovo border in 1999 is greeted by jubilant Islamic Albanian Kosovars, thankful that NATO's KFOR (Kosovo Force) peacekeepers appeared on the scene to rescue them from the state-sponsored campaign of terror against them.

mission. Consider NATO. The ambiguous European security setting is now marked by numerous ethnic and religious conflicts that NATO was not originally designed to handle. Its original charter envisioned only one purpose—mutual self-protection from external attack. It never defined policing civil wars as a goal. Consequently, until 1995, when NATO took charge of all military operations in Bosnia-Herzegovina from the UN, it was uncertain whether the alliance could adapt to a broadened purpose. Since that intervention, NATO *has* redefined itself, and in March 1999, it undertook an interventionary peacemaking assignment to police the civil violence in Kosovo.

Today, NATO is an enlarged alliance, with seven new members joining in 2002 (see Map 17.3, p. 536), and has transformed itself to become both a *military* alliance for security between states and within them and for containing the spread of global terrorism, as well as a *political* alliance for encouraging the spread of democracy. That said, the primary purpose remains putting NATO's twenty-six members under a security umbrella, with the promise that an attack on one would be considered an attack on all.

Likewise, in other regional mutual security systems, controversies among the coalition partners about the identity of "the enemy" and the conditions warranting intervention raise doubts about their capacity to engineer collective defense projects. These doubts are fueled by the history of regional organizations in peacemaking efforts. Between 1945 and 1984, of 291 high-intensity armed conflicts involving military units, less than one-fourth, or only sixty-eight, were handled by regional organizations (K. Holsti 1992, 353). This record suggests that although regional collective defense institutions were, to some extent, created to overcome the deficiencies of global institutions, they may not be able to perform that task any better than global institutions.

The barriers to collective security faced by regional organizations are similar to those faced by the United Nations. Liberal reformers are well aware of these obstacles and are seeking to strengthen global and regional institutions for collective defense to help overcome the weaknesses standing in the way of their peacekeeping performance.

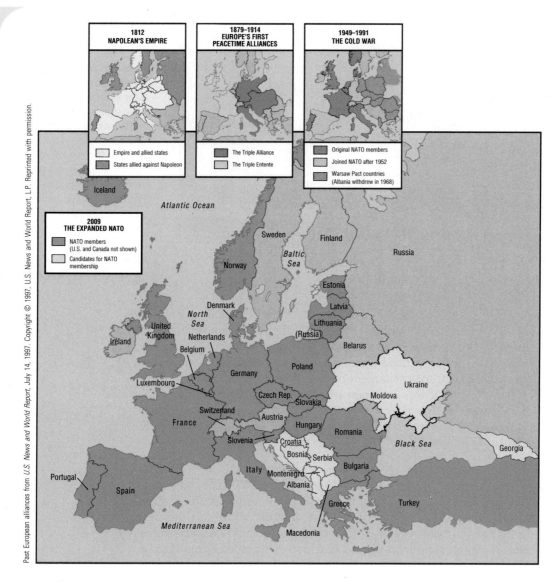

Past European alliances from *U.S. News and World Report*, July 14, 1997. Copyright © 1997. U.S. News and World Report, L.P. Reprinted with permission.

MAP 17.3

THE ENLARGED NATO IN THE NEW GEOSTRATEGIC BALANCE OF POWER **The twenty-first century geostrategic landscape has been transformed by NATO's expansion to twenty-six full members. An additional thirty-eight countries now work as Partners for Peace in the Euro-Atlantic Partnership Council (EAPC). As shown in this map, NATO now casts its security umbrella across and beyond Europe in its endeavor to create a collective security regime including states that were once its enemies. NATO has redefined itself as a coalition of liberal democracies fighting tyranny, terrorism, and other economic and environmental problems.**

The recent record indicates that there are several key preconditions that must be met for collective security organizations to work both globally and regionally. First, these security organizations are most capable of creating successful peacekeeping operations only when their most powerful members reach agreement about the benefits of any proposed operation. Second, such third-party peacekeeping operations have been most successful in those cases when the target is neither a great power nor has a military alliance with a major power. Third, the success rate of peace missions improves when the operations are aimed at a target country where (1) a great power or (2) the United Nations or (3) a regional IGO has previously intervened to contain a civil war or a secessionist movement (Mullenbach 2005). Finally, past cases indicate that security organizations' capacity to control controversial conflicts depends on pressure from world public opinion to mobilize international organizations to take action. The absence of some of these preconditions accounts for the frequent failure of IGOs to engineer a timely response to tragic situations where slaughter and genocide occur; the slow and insufficient reaction to stop the bloodshed in the Darfur region of Sudan and Somalia in the Horn of Africa are the most recent examples of inadequate collective global action.

Will a true global security sometime emerge to create a future world in which the expectation of peace exceeds the expectation of armed aggression? The collective security dreamed of by liberal reformers remains just that—a dream—without institutional backing to make the dream a reality. World politics remains far removed from world government and global governance.

The processes through which such transformations might be engineered require the formation of a global consensus about the core values from which a common or *cosmopolitan* (cosmos = world; polity = governing unit) world culture might emerge, as liberals hope. Are global trends unfolding that increase the prospects for such a *transformation* in world politics as long envisioned by liberal reformers?

> *There is no salvation for civilization, or even the human race, other than the creation of a world government.*
> —Albert Einstein, scientist and liberal peace activist

UNITING ONE WORLD IN A COMMON CULTURE OF SHARED MORAL VALUES

Liberal convictions about war and peace, armed aggression, and international security are fundamentally derived from the utmost importance liberals attach to ethics and morality in world politics. The liberal road to peace begins with a dedication to doing what is right and not doing what is wrong. This differs greatly from much realist theorizing that "opens the door to a purely amoral foreign policy" (Gordis 1984) and that "holds international politics to be beyond the concern of morality" (Suganami 1983). At the extreme, realism concludes that "might makes right." In contrast, liberalism places the power of principle over the principle of power (see Kegley 1992) because it is based on the conviction that peace depends on acting by moral motives.

> *Blessed are the peacemakers, for they shall be called sons of God.*
> —Jesus Christ, Matthew 5:9

Ethics is about the criteria for evaluating right and wrong behavior and motives; *morality* is about the norms for behavior that should govern actors' interactions. Liberals understandably focus on humanitarian concerns and human rights when they emphasize the importance of normative values as factors shaping global conditions. One of the greatest moral ethicists who grappled with war and peace in an immoral world was the German philosopher Immanuel Kant. In 1798, Kant wrote "the character of the human race . . . is that of a multitude of persons living one after another and one beside another, unable to *do without* peaceful coexistence, yet also unable to *avoid* being constantly hateful to one another . . . ; a coalition always threatened with dissolution, but on the whole progressing towards a worldwide *civil society*." A global civil society is one in which institutions are created to protect civil liberties and use peaceful methods for conflict resolution. The world does not yet benefit from either these institutions or agreement about the **mores** or normative convictions that should guide international decision making. However, liberals believe that these ethical standards can gain acceptance and create a civil society at the global level of analysis.

■ **mores**

the customs of a group accepted as morally binding obligations.

In 1795, Kant wrote a famous essay titled *Perpetual Peace*. In it, he asked how enduring peace might be created. He advanced two liberal ideas that were revolutionary at the time. Picturing war as a consequence of illogical reasoning because its practice works against states' long-term interests, Kant proposed using humans' capacity to reason rationally to discover paths that would truly serve their real long-term interests in living in an orderly and just world. He emphasized two pathways that form the bedrock of liberal approaches to world peace: free trade and free governments.

These were both radical ideas in Kant's time. Most powerful states in his era were then (1) great powers practicing narrow *mercantilism* to expand their national economies at others' expense through imperialism and colonialism and (2) monarchies ruled by kings opposed to democratic liberties for the subjects under their absolute reign. Needless to say, Kant was repelled by the acceptance and frequent use of warfare by these realist rulers to increase by military means the power of their states. So Kant advocated a total transformation of the realist values on which world politics was then functioning, replacing that chaotic global environment with a new and more secure one based on liberal free trade and citizens' freedom to choose their leaders through democratic elections.

These radical ideas resonated in the ears of other innovators in liberal thought, such as Adam Smith, Thomas Jefferson, and James Madison. And they later were made pillars of the peace program that Woodrow Wilson proposed in his Fourteen Points Address. Point III advocated free trade through the abolition of protective tariffs: "the removal, so far as possible, of all economic barriers and the establishment of an equality of trade conditions among the nations [seeking] peace and associating themselves for its maintenance." Likewise, Wilson echoed Kant when Wilson opined "making the world safe for democracy" would make "the world fit and safe to live in." These twin highways to peace require the global acceptance of the norms for international conduct that together capture the third major liberal path to international security.

Trade Ties to Avoid War by Binding Countries Together

As you learned in Chapter 9, *commercial liberalism* is based on the proposition that when barriers to trade between and among countries are reduced through cooperative agreements, the prosperity of the trading parties will rise. Recall also that much evidence supports this hypothesis. However, there exists another expanding side-payoff to free trade: When it increases, it ties the trading partners together in an expanding web of interdependence from which all the trading parties to the free trade agreement benefit. It is therefore rational, according to liberal economic theory, to promote free trade. Over the long run, the benefits outweigh the short-term costs. Self-interests are served by trade cooperation, not competition.

To liberal reformers, there is an even-more important *political* and *military* consequence of free trade: Parties to active free exchanges of goods across borders increasingly need each other for the growth of their wealth, and therefore are less and less tempted to go to war with one another. Armed aggression would end the cooperation that makes their mutual prosperity grow.

In this regard, global economic trade interdependence among nations is, as liberal theory argues, a strong underpinning for peace. *Interdependence* (when the behavior of states greatly affects the others with whom they come into frequent contact, and the parties to such active exchanges become increasingly mutually vulnerable to each others' actions), the trade-interdependent countries will then need each other for their own welfare. Accordingly, when free trade increases, the incentives for war decline: Why attack another country on which your own state's economy is dependent for growth? In this construction, therefore, trade interdependence is a financial path to peace.

The global trend for the past six decades has been a profound progress for the reduction of barriers to free trade such as tariffs and import quotas (see Chapter 9). This expansion of free trade worldwide has witnessed alongside it a drastic reduction in the number of armed conflicts *between* states; inter-state wars have almost now vanished from the global scene (recall Chapter 13).

Free trade! What is it? Why, breaking down the barriers that separate nations; those barriers behind which nestle the barriers of pride, revenge, hatred and jealousy, which every now and then burst their bounds and deluge whole countries with blood; those barriers which nourish the poison of war and conquest.

—Richard Cobden, British liberal political economist

Liberals are celebrating this correlation between free trade and the absence of interstate warfare that they champion. A global consensus of opinion has been constructed that liberal policy makers' core premise about the pacifying impact of trade ties has been vindicated.

To liberals, increasing interconnections among countries and peoples on the economic front can thus reduce their historic tendency to wage war with one another. For this liberal nonmilitary path to global security to truly arrive at its preferred pacific destination, the global community must accept the norms for behavior on which this approach is predicated. The *Liberal International Economic Order (LIEO)* rests on a normative value consensus. Realists warn that it could collapse if and when economic conditions deteriorate and countries are then likely to return to ruthless economic competition and trade protectionism to gain at others' expense. Liberal reformers agree with realist pessimism; they also see a liberal civil society with peace dependent on the preservation of normative values and mores that must retain global acceptance. Should such a free-trade liberal climate of global world opinion decay, so will the prospects for world order.

That said, the far distance the global community has journeyed down the free-trade avenue toward prosperity and peace has instilled growing faith that this progress will persist, so long as countries continue to recognize that their interests are advanced through peace and economic interdependence. Will the majority of countries accept this construction? Time will tell. But, in the meantime, note how far the economic underpinnings of international security have traveled in international thinking. This is why noncoercive methods of bargaining have become so important in international diplomacy, and why the use of economic sanctions is so popular at a time when another global trend is evident: The declining popularity of military coercion and intervention traditionally relied on by realist policy makers.

economic sanctions

the punitive use of trade or monetary measures, such as an embargo, to harm a targeted adversary's economy in order to exercise influence over the target's policies.

Economic sanctions—deliberate actions against a target country to deprive it of the benefits of continuing economic relations—is increasingly common in world politics as a nonmilitary method of diplomatic bargaining. Withholding foreign aid, placing tariffs and quotas on imports from the targeted state, and imposing **sanctions** through **boycotts** of purchases of the products that the targeted state attempts to sell in the international marketplace are all advocated by liberals as a preferred method to avoid the dangers and costs of using armed force. A global trend is underway: Economic sanctions have been used with increasing frequency since World War II. A major force behind this trend is the globalization of international trade, which has heavily integrated state economies. It is also due, "in part, from the movement toward international organization and collective security communities, which have viewed non-violent forms of coercion as preferable to direct military action" (Allen 2008, 256; Cortright and Lopez 2000). All of these factors have contributed to the rise in the use of sanctions to affect behavior, what Thomas Jefferson termed "peaceable coercion."

sanctions

punishment by one state against another to retaliate for its objectionable behavior and to make the target change its policies and practices.

Despite the increasing use of sanctions as an instrument of statecraft, the historical record raises questions about whether they are an efficient nonmilitary tool of coercive diplomacy. "Sanctions are seldom effective in impairing the military potential of an important power," an important empirical study concludes (Hufbauer, Schott and Elliot 1990). In fact, sanctions are rarely successful in preventing warfare: A study of 200 cases of sanctions found that when sanctions were used to punish a government without resorting to armed aggression, military conflict actually became "as much as six times more likely to occur between two countries than if sanctions had not been imposed" (Foreign Policy, July/August 2007, 19). Yet, the effectiveness of sanctions may vary depending upon the regime type of the target. Democracies are much more constrained in their policy response and hence more susceptible to sanctions pressure as the "threat that a shrinking pie caused by sanctions could compromise a democrat's ability to create favorable policy outcomes is a threat to his or her political survival" (Allen 2008, 260). Conversely,

boycotts

concerted efforts, often organized internationally, to prevent transactions such as trade with a targeted country in order to express disapproval or to coerce acceptance of certain conditions.

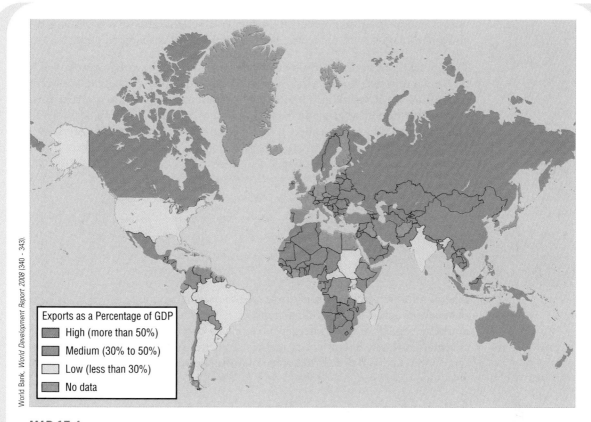

World Bank, *World Development Report 2008* (340 - 343).

Exports as a Percentage of GDP

High (more than 50%)

Medium (30% to 50%)

Low (less than 30%)

No data

MAP 17.4

COUNTRIES DEPENDENT ON TRADE AND VULNERABLE TO SANCTIONS **Many states find themselves subject to external coercion and vulnerable to manipulations by states that impose sanctions on them, especially if they are highly dependent on trade for their economic prosperity. "Without imports many products that consumers want would be unavailable or more expensive [and] without exports many jobs would be eliminated" (S. Allen 2006). In the globalized marketplace the level of states' dependence on exports for economic prosperity is growing. This map shows the great extent to which many countries are today dependent on trade.**

autocratic states can "resist sanctions, as they can shunt the costs of sanctions off into the general public, who have little influence over policy outcomes or leadership retention" (Allen 2008; 255). When economic sanctions are used, the targeted state "gains greater control of a smaller pie and shifts resources in the country toward groups that support the state and away from those that oppose it," (Pape 2007, 39).

The evidence largely underscores why many realist critics see economic instruments for influencing foreign leaders' choices a weak bargaining tool (Shiffman 2006). Critics therefore conclude that economic sanctions are imposed primarily to let a government play a *two-level game* to symbolically demonstrate to their domestic citizens that they are punishing the unacceptable behavior of other states. What is worse, when sanctions are imposed to accomplish higher moral purposes, they usually backfire because most often the sanctions hurt the endangered people they claim to be helping—the targeted country's average suffering citizens. Sanctions also often fail because widespread and collective sustained cooperation from the international community and international organizations seldom materialize when drastic action is most needed, and unilateral actions almost never succeed in a globalized market with many competitive suppliers of embargoed goods.

These limitations underscore why the use of sanctions is very often questioned when they are proposed. Nonetheless, the impulse to use this bargaining tool remains strong because it serves an ulterior goal domestically—enabling a leader to show leadership without suffering the harsh criticism that usually follows decisions to use military force. As long as leaders feel that flexing economic muscles against enemies abroad can win public approval at home, economic sanctions are likely to remain common in foreign policy making.

> *Sanctions are like the Energizer Bunny of foreign policy.*
> *Despite a dismal record, they just keep on ticking.*
> —Fareed Zakaria, international journalist

Liberal reformers acknowledge these weaknesses in economic sanctions to exercise political influence in bargaining noncoercively. They also are well aware of the potential fragility of trade interdependence as a condition for fostering international security. However, liberal policy makers see better payoff to an alternative route to cement international peace: the spread of liberal norms supporting democratic values.

A Democratic Peace Pact

What is now widely known as the *democratic peace* is the theory that, because democratic states almost never fight wars with one another, the spread of democratic governance throughout the world will reduce greatly the probability of war. This is not a new theory or approach to international security. In 1792 James Madison, president of the United States, voiced this proposition when he argued that "in the advent of republican governments would be found not only the prospect of a radical decline in the role played by war but the prospect as well of a virtual revolution in the conduct of diplomacy." Three short years later, Immanuel Kant advanced the same liberal speculation in his more famous *Perpetual Peace*, when he, too, hypothesized that giving peace-loving citizens the right to vote could stop violence—that allowing ballots for citizens could become a sturdy barrier against authoritarian rulers' habitual use of bullets and bombs.

History demonstrates that there are sound reasons for accepting this liberal proposition. Many scholarly quantitative studies of modern international history have convincingly shown that "well established democracies have never made war on one another [and] republics and only republics have tended to form durable, peaceful leagues" (Weart 1994; see also Choi and James 2005; Rasler and Thompson 2005).

This lesson was not lost on leaders of democratic states seeking to find a principle on which to ground their national security policies. "Ultimately the best strategy to insure our security and to build a durable peace is to support the advance of democracy elsewhere," the 1994 *U.S. National Security Strategy* concluded. That doctrine was officially endorsed earlier by the other major EU and NATO liberal democracies whose members insisted on states being democratically ruled as a condition for membership. In addition, the major international organizations have also endorsed the promotion of democracy as a policy priority, including the *Group of Eight (G-8)*, the World Bank, the International Monetary Fund (IMF), the Organization for Economic Cooperation and Development (OECD), and the Organization of American States (OAS).

Democratic reforms over the past four decades have produced impressive results worldwide. Since the mid-1970s, freedom and civil liberties within countries have expanded through a series of liberalizing governmental reforms in many new countries. Throughout the world, countries that were formerly ruthlessly ruled by autocratic military dictators practicing political repression have collapsed, as the "quiet revolution" in South America's successful deepening of democratic institutions and civil liberties attests (Fukuyama 2007). Today the community of liberal democracies (countries ruled by "free" or "partially free" governments) has now spread to more than three-fourths of the globe's states (see Figure 17.1).

Some realist skeptics question whether democracies should really be counted upon to put their liberal ideals ahead of their narrow national interests by resisting the natural temptation to use armed force when serious disputes surface. And both realists and liberals are very worried about the possibility that a democratic great power will abuse this liberal principle by forcing "democracy at gunpoint" (Pickering and Peceny

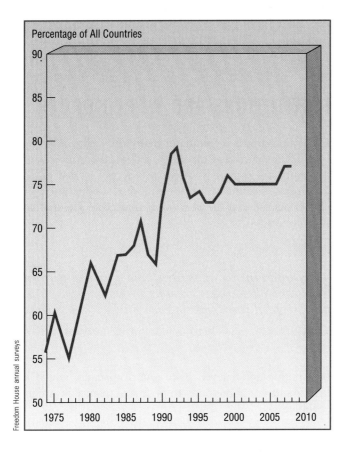

FIGURE 17.1

WILL A FREEDOM FENCE RESULT FROM THE GLOBAL GROWTH OF DEMOCRATIC GOVERNANCE? **This figure shows that as the year 2009 began, seventy-eight percent of the countries in the world were either fully or partially democratic, according to Freedom House. This inspires liberals' hopes that a global peace among democracies will continue to spread and deepen, even in difficult times of terrorism and tension.**

2006; O'Reilly and Renfro 2007). What if other liberal powers do as the United States did in 2003 when it invaded and occupied Iraq, and they also dispatch soldiers to foreign lands for "regime change" to push countries toward democracy (or accepting their religious preferences)? If the export of democratic institutions for state-building is mismanaged, the basis for resting global security on the growth of democracy is likely to lead to more wars, not fewer (Coyne 2007).

These doubts about a lasting "democratic peace pact" not withstanding, liberal reformers are heartened by past trends. These provide strong evidence to support the liberal tenet that democracy produces many beneficial moral values, including freedom, human rights, civil liberties, prosperity, and especially an increased

> *If we fail to nurture democracy—the most fundamental political project—we will never be able to realize our goals and the responsibilities which the future will call for.*
> —Ingvar Carlsson, former Swedish Prime Minister

capacity to deter wars within and between members of the democratic community of states. Therefore, providing that democratic states continue to abide by their past record of dealing with conflicts through negotiation, mediation, arbitration, and adjudication, the existing liberal democracies' efforts to enlarge their community could usher in a major transformation of world politics. Pope John Paul II's expressed hopes could make an ancient dream a reality: "No more war, war never again." However, promise dictates neither performance nor destiny.

LIBERAL INSTITUTIONS AND WORLD ORDER

Liberal and neoliberal theorists recommend many different paths to the control of armed aggression. These pathways all are based on the conviction that war and international instability are primarily caused by deeply rooted global institutional deficiencies that reduce incentives for international cooperation (Barrett 2007). Neoliberal reformers believe that the prevailing anarchical global conditions are the problem, not the solution.

> *Military intervention, hostilities, and war can neither be predicted nor controlled unless account is taken of the circumstances which preceded them within each of the states involved.*
> —James T. Russell and Quincy Wright, pioneering behavioral scientists

Weak institutions at the global level make security scarce, which is why liberals advocate legal and institutional methods to pool sovereignty in order to collectively manage global problems.

Liberal institutionalists have appropriately raised various concerns about the capacity of independent and competing sovereign states to engineer a hopeful future for humanity. On balance, sovereign states have not used their foreign policies to create a safe and secure global environment. Instead, states historically have been

> *During the coming decades global challenges will continue and may increase. There is more and more of an overlap between national interests and global responsibilities. The task of multilateral diplomacy is to cope with new issues, new demands and new situations [through] "shared responsibilities" and "strengthened partnerships."*
>
> —J.N. Kinnis, liberal international relations scholar

constructed to make war with others (Wagner 2007), and, as constructivist international theory instructs, great powers have persistently been primarily "predator and parasite" agents of transnational harm (Löwenheim 2007). Moreover, it is a paradox that despite their continuing power, the governments of sovereign states' governments have proven to be very weak at either preventing civil wars within their borders or commanding widespread citizen loyalty and respect. The disintegration of many failed states does not support the conclusion that states are necessarily strong.

To liberal reformers, the global agenda facing the world is huge, with one inventory ranking no less than twenty-seven of the biggest problems facing humanity (Lomborg 2008). All of these are transnational; none can be solved effectively with a unilateral national response. A multilateral approach is required. However, the number of global problems that now require peaceful management through collective solutions are staggering. They cannot *all* be managed at once, and this is creating a serious debate about how resources should be allocated for each global problem (see Controversy: How Should the World's Problems Be Prioritized?).

CONTROVERSY:

HOW SHOULD THE WORLD'S PROBLEMS BE PRIORITIZED?

Many of the world's environmental and security problems are projected to become more severe in the decades ahead. Yet even if the international community decides not to follow a business-as-usual course and chooses instead to tackle pressing world problems, which ones should it take on, and in what order? Arresting global climate change, preserving biodiversity, combating communicable diseases, providing clean water, alleviating poverty, fighting malnutrition and hunger, and restoring forests, fisheries, and other overexploited renewable resources are just some of the environmental challenges humanity faces. Equally challenging are many security problems, such as deterring terrorism, stabilizing failed states, stopping genocide, and preventing the spread of weapons of mass destruction.

Whereas there are numerous global problems, financial resources to deal with them are limited. When it is impossible to address every major need at once, priorities must be set. But how should they be established? Faced with multiple competing demands and complicated trade-offs, how should the international community determine which problems warrant the most attention?

One approach focuses on cost–benefit ratios. Bjørn Lomborg, a Danish political scientist known for his skepticism about many of the ecological threats emphasized by environmental scientists, adopted this method when he convened a panel of eminent economists during May 2004 in Copenhagen and asked them how they would allocate a hypothetical $50 billion to advance global welfare. The exercise resulted in a consensus on spending funds on projects that would yield high benefits for low costs. For example, the panelists strongly supported spending money on such things as promoting condom use to prevent the spread of HIV and AIDS, distributing vitamin and mineral supplements to reduce malnutrition, and providing chemically treated mosquito netting for beds to reduce the incidence of malaria. Conversely, steps to avert climate change, such as carbon taxes and mandatory targets for lowering greenhouse gas emissions, were not given high priorities, allegedly because of their enormous expense relative to distant and uncertain benefits. A similar exercise involving UN diplomats from seven non-European countries was directed in 2006 by John Bolton, the U.S. ambassador to the United Nations. Once again, inexpensive approaches to health care and nutrition were given higher priorities over mitigating climate change.

The so-called "Copenhagen Consensus" has been criticized on several grounds. First, critics complained that cost–benefit analysis was an inappropriate method for setting global priorities. Although it may be a valuable instrument for making narrow, technical choices between different ways of achieving an agreed-upon goal (such as whether to build a road along proposed route A or proposed route B), they denied that it could determine what goal should receive the highest priority (such as whether to spend funds on building a road or hiring more teachers for the local school). Second, by giving the panel members a small sum to allocate (roughly one-sixth of the cost of the war in Iraq as of the end of fiscal year 2006), the exercise was biased in favor of low-cost projects, like distributing vitamin A supplements to prevent blindness. Finally, critics charged that the panelists did not receive sufficient background information on the state of scientific knowledge in each problem area they attempted to prioritize, which, in particular, led them to overlook existing, affordable technologies that can help in climate stabilization (see Pacala and Socolow 2004). Operating from the assumption that curbing such seemingly intractable problems as failed states, armed aggression, and climate change were costly and uncertain ventures, they discounted the planet's longer-term future and chose to center efforts on more immediate and managable global problems such as health and nutrition.

To avoid emerging disasters it is necessary to set priorities. But how should that be done? Is cost–benefit analysis the best method for establishing global funding priorities? Or are there too many difficulties in calculating and comparing costs and benefits for it to be a useful tool for setting priorities among the world's many problems? What do you think? How would you go about prioritizing the world's pressing security, humanitarian, and environmental challenges?

> *Liberal internationalists see a need for international rules to solve states' problems, proclaim the end of the nation-state, [and see] transgovernmentalism rapidly becoming the most widespread and effective mode of international governance.*
>
> —Anne-Marie Slaughter, neoliberal international theorist

Whether multilateral IGOs such as the United Nations, the democratically driven European Union, and the liberal community of peace-loving states can organize a collective response through multilateral action to the multitude of needs will shape how liberal pathways to world order will likely be judged by future generations.

What is clear is that countries *are* making bold *efforts* to unite in a common civic culture behind common values to create global institutions to jointly protect themselves against the many problems they face in common. They appear to increasingly accept the once radical liberal view that, as Kofi Annan argues, "a new, broader definition of national interest is needed" which would unify states to work on common goals that transcend national interests.

Human progress is neither automatic nor inevitable. We are faced now with the fact that tomorrow is today. We are confronted with the fierce urgency of now. In this unfolding conundrum of life and history there is such a thing as being too late... We may cry out desperately for time to pause in her passage, but time is deaf to every plea and rushes on. Over the bleached bones and jumbled residues of numerous civilizations are written the pathetic words: Too Late.

—The Reverend Dr. Martin Luther King Jr.,
peace activist and civil rights leader

Borders and oceans cannot isolate or insulate states from these threats to security; they can only be controlled in the global commons by a collective effort. It is for this reason that many IGOs originally came into being, and it is the persistence of collective threats produced by an increasingly globalized world that makes IGOs durable. As the globe shrinks and borders prove to be increasingly ineffective as barriers, we can predict that liberal paths to peace and prosperity will continue to find favor and policy makers will take seriously the call to help create what former Swedish Foreign Minister Anna Lindh described as "a global culture of conflict prevention."

If the paths you have explored in this and the previous chapter are pursued, will acceptance of the liberal belief that peace is best preserved through ethical policies break the violent historical pattern? The world awaits an answer.

Key Terms

disarmament
arms control
bilateral agreements
multilateral agreements
Strategic Arms Reduction Treaty
  (START)
Strategic Offensive Reductions
  Treaty (SORT)

antipersonnel landmines (APLs)
peacekeeping
preventive diplomacy
peacemaking
peace building
peace operations
peace enforcement
selective engagement

regional collective defense regimes
mores
economic sanctions
sanctions
boycotts

GLOBAL DESTINY: DELIGHT OR DESPAIR? The possible types of future global environment you will inherit are captured by this photo of a changing city that could be almost anyplace—part populated by rising prosperity, part living in desperate squalor. Both conditions are products of prevailing trends in world politics. In which world are most people in the future likely to live?

Part 7

ENVISIONING YOUR ALTERNATIVE GLOBAL FUTURES AND PREDICTING GLOBAL TRANSFORMATIONS

"The statesman is like a man wandering in a forest who knows his general direction, but not the exact point at which he will emerge from the wood."

— *Otto von Bismarck, realist Prussian strategist*

"Trend is not destiny."

— *Rene Dubos, French futurist*

Most conjectures about the global future are based on some extrapolation from earlier events and experiences. People usually speculate about future prospects based on their understanding of prevailing trends. What makes prediction so difficult is the sheer complexity of uncertainties surrounding world politics; some trends move forward seemingly in the same direction; others change direction; some trends intersect, others diverge over time; some trends increase the speed of other trends; still different global trends reduce the impact of the others. Your challenge in deciphering the meaning of prevailing but diverse trends is twofold: (1) to distinguish between those that are transient and those that are likely to have a significant and lasting impact on world politics, and (2) to project the configuration of the most important trends, rather than become preoccupied with any single trend in isolation.

How will the combination of major trends unfolding in world politics today influence your global future? Will the twenty-first century find previous efforts to construct world order useful, or will it reject past approaches as new issues arise on the global agenda?

Part 7 of *World Politics* poses in a concluding chapter *not* answers or predictions, but instead some important, thought-provoking questions for you to contemplate about the prospects for the twenty-first century. When thinking about the issues raised by these questions, ask yourself how they might be addressed to create a more peaceful and just global future.

CHAPTER 18

THINKING ABOUT GLOBAL TRENDS, TRANSFORMATIONS, AND THE FUTURE OF WORLD POLITICS

Statesmen stand or fall on their perception of trends.

—Henry A. Kissinger, *former U.S. Secretary of State*

A Time for Change? In front of a crowd of an estimated 200,000 Germans at the Victory Column at Tiergarten Park in Berlin in July 2008, Barack Obama called for global cooperation and purpose. "Now is the time to build new bridges across the globe as strong as the one that bound us across the Atlantic. Now is the time to join together, through constant cooperation, strong institutions, shared sacrifice, and a global commitment to progress, to meet the challenges of the 21st century."

Opposing global trends are unfolding. Some point toward integration, and others to fragmentation; the world looks like it is coming together and at the same time it is coming apart. A new global system is on the horizon, but it is one whose characteristics have yet to develop definition. Understandably, uncertainty and unpredictability are today's prevailing mood. But one thing is certain: seismic shifts underway are challenging the wisdom of old beliefs and orthodox visions. Because both turmoil and turbulence describe contemporary international affairs, they require asking unconventional questions about conventional ideas. They push us to think four-dimensionally in order to understand the political, military, market, and environmental pressures that are increasingly being brought to bear on the countries of the world, the people who reside in them, and their interactions.

In facing the future, you face an awesome investigative challenge: anticipating and interpreting the probable future contours of world affairs and constructing compelling theoretical explanations of their causes. To do so, you must consider a number of unusual and controversial questions that are rising to the top of the global agenda for public debate throughout the world.

Those caught up in revolutionary change rarely understand its ultimate significance.

—Boutros Boutros-Ghali, former UN Secretary–General

Experts whose profession it is to help you may be somewhat informative. However, the rival conclusions boldly advanced by would-be prophets are not likely to be very definitive, and they diverge wildly.

GLOBAL TRENDS AND FORECASTS

A bewildering array of problems and challenges are expected to confront humanity in the future. The UN's report, *A More Secure World*, concludes:

> We face a world of extraordinary challenges—and of extraordinary interconnectedness. We are all vulnerable to new security threats, and to old threats that are evolving in complex and unpredictable ways. ...Six clusters [stand out]: economic and social threats, including poverty and deadly infectious disease; interstate conflict and rivalry; internal violence, including civil war, state collapse and genocide; nuclear, radiological, chemical, and biological weapons; terrorism; and transnational organized crime.

Consider another inventory of global trends that constructs another set of predictions about what the world will be like in the year 2020. It forecasts a world markedly different from today's.

On the cusp of epochal change, a new world seems to be emerging to dwarf even our most recent expectations, for better and for worse.

—Jim Hoagland, international journalist

The National Intelligence Council (2004, 25) predicts that the globe's most significant characteristics will include:

- Globalization's contradictory consequences

- Rising powers and a changing geopolitical landscape

- New challenges to governance

- A more pervasive sense of *in*security

- An expanding global economy

- An accelerating pace of scientific change and dispersion of dual-use technologies

- Lingering social inequalities

- Emerging new powers

- A global aging phenomenon

- Halting democratization

- A spreading radical Islamic ideology

- A potential for catastrophic terrorism

- A proliferation of weapons of mass destruction

- Increased pressures on international institutions

Given this complex and potentially dangerous changing global environment with many complex crises to manage (Boin, 't Hart, Stern and Sundelius 2007), it is important to probe additional probable scenarios. A scenario is a logical, compelling story that traces a timeline of events from the present to some point in the future in order to identify the characteristics that the future is likely to display.

To construct your own images of the future of world affairs, begin by thinking about what key questions are likely to dominate international relations in the coming decades. The questions you identify will determine which scenarios and theories

> *A man may fulfill the object of his existence by asking a question he cannot answer, and attempting a task he cannot achieve.*
> —Oliver Wendell Holmes, American legal scholar

better inform your understanding of your global future. To assist you, *World Politics* concludes this chapter (and this book) with some additional questions to consider, and those questions will require you to weigh plausible contending interpretations to further prepare you intellectually to interpret the problematic future of world politics.

HOW TO THINK ABOUT HOW PEOPLE THINK ABOUT THE WORLD

As you construct your scenarios about what kinds of global futures are possible, probable, and preferable, begin by keeping in mind that your images, like those of everyone, are shaped heavily by our prior perceptions of reality and the inherited values and expectations that underlie them (this would be a good place to review the discussion in Chapter 1 of how perceptions influence beliefs about world politics). So proceed cautiously and with an open mind to views that may be different from those you now hold. Take the insight and received wisdom about how people think, as expressed in the following observations:

■ "Any frontal attack on ignorance is bound to fail because the masses are always ready to defend their most precious possession—their ignorance."

> —Hendrik Willem van Loon, Dutch-American journalist

■ "The most fatal illusion is the settled point of view. Since life is growth and motion, a fixed point of view kills anybody who has one."

> —Brooks Atkinson, American drama critic

■ "Fanaticism consists in redoubling your effort when you have forgotten your aim."

> —George Santayana, Spanish philosopher

■ "Men are more apt to be mistaken in their generalizations than in their particular observations."

> —Niccoló Machiavelli, seventeenth century Italian realist theoretician

■ "One of the sources of pride in being a human being is the ability to bear present frustrations in the interests of longer purposes."

> —Helen Merrel Lynd, American sociologist

■ "The philosophies of one age have become the absurdities of the next, and the foolishness of yesterday has become the wisdom of tomorrow."

> —Sir William Osler, Canadian physician and educator

■ "It is better to know some of the questions than all of the answers."

> —James Thurber, American writer

Armed with an understanding about how ideas about international relations form and are retained, rejected, or replaced, imagine yourself at the end of a semester preparing to take a final exam in your course about international relations. Your entire grade, your instructor tells you, will be determined by an essay exam with only one question. Sitting nervously, you open your blue book and are astonished at the instructions: "(1) define the question which you wish had been asked in this exam for this course, and (2) then answer it; you will be graded on both the understanding you display in the kind of question you ask and the answers you provide." How would you respond?

Believe it or not, this kind of question is not altogether fictional. It has been used to sort out candidates on exams for entry into the foreign service of several countries. In them, and for your exams, there really are no right or wrong questions about international relations. Indeed, there is little agreement about the trends and issues that are the most important in international affairs, and no scholarly consensus among experts and policy makers exists about the questions most deserving of attention today.

To stimulate your thinking, how would you make a preliminary list, based on what you now know after reading *World Politics*, of what you believe will be the crucial questions to ask when you make predictions about the future of the world? How would you go about interpreting your own questions? What rival theories (refer to Chapter 2) would you rely on to frame your analyses? This mental exercise will sharpen your evaluative skills and will tell you as much about yourself and your reasoned perspective as it does about your capacity to describe the present global condition, predict its future course, and explain *why* world politics is changing and also displaying continuities with the past.

Rather than leave you in the lurch, *World Politics* puts itself to the same test. It concludes now by identifying a series of questions about the global future that are high on the agenda for debate. As a further catalyst to framing your own thinking, look critically at them, for how they are answered is widely expected to give shape to world politics throughout the remainder of the twenty-first century.

THE GLOBAL PREDICAMENT: KEY QUESTIONS ABOUT A TURBULENT WORLD

Throughout, *World Politics* has argued that international relations are subject to recurring patterns and regularities. Despite changes and chaos, behavior by transnational actors on the planet is not random. It is governed by patterned propensities, and this makes it possible to uncover "laws" or generalized patterns of action-and-reaction. As the realist theoretician Hans J. Morganthau argued in his classic text *Politics Among Nations*, the past historical record speaks with sufficient continuity to make the scientific study of international politics a meaningful intellectual endeavor. There are some lessons about how countries interact that are constant across time and place. It is the purpose of scholarship to uncover these patterns and make sound policy decisions based on the lessons history provides.

Under certain conditions, it can be assumed that certain types of transnational actors respond the same way to the same kinds of stimuli. Yet, there are exceptions. Sometimes similar actors in similar situations make different decisions. Thus despite the existence of regularities in world politics, social scientists cannot draw on a body

The more things change, the more they remain the same.

—widely attributed to Alphonse Karr, French journalist

of uniform, deterministic laws to predict the global future precisely. Instead, they make contingent forecasts about what is likely to happen, other things being equal (Singer, 2000).

Another factor that makes it difficult to predict what will come to pass is the role of happenstance in world politics. History is replete with what the Greek philosopher Aristotle called accidental conjunctions—situations in which things come together by chance. Consider, for example the outbreak of World War I. Recall from Chapter 4 that one of the proximate causes of the war was Austrian Archduke Franz Ferdinand's assassination in Sarajevo on June 28, 1914. Earlier that day, several would-be assassins had failed to find an opportunity to kill the archduke and apparently gave up in frustration. When Ferdinand's motorcade made a wrong turn en route to visit patients in a city hospital, it stopped briefly in front of a café where Gavrilo Pincip, one of the frustrated assassins, coincidentally had gone to get something to eat. Astonished to find the archduke's open-air car just five feet away, Princip fired two shots, killing the archduke and his wife. Given the political climate in Europe at the time, if Franz Ferdinand had not been assassinated, something else might have precipitated the war. But as political scientist Stuart Bremer (2000) asks, "Who can say whether a different triggering event, a day, a month, or a year later, would have led to the same chain of events that produced World War I?"

Myriad possible futures lie ahead. Some are desirable; others, frightening. Although we cannot predict with certainty which one will materialize, we can narrow the range of possibilities by forecasting how current trends will probably develop and how steps might be taken to channel the course of events toward a global future we prefer.

Thinking in the future tense does not demand prophecy or divination; rather it requires anticipating how today's activities will most likely affect generations yet unborn. In other words, it approaches inquiry by forecasting alternative futures to improve policy decisions in the present.

What follows are seven questions designed to help you think about the future of world politics. Each question is based on information presented in previous chapters. When pondering the long-term implications of these questions, you are encouraged to (1) imagine what conceivable global futures are possible, (2) estimate which are the most probable, and (3) consider what policies would be of the most help to bring about the global future you prefer.

Is Globalization a Cure, or a Curse?

Why does it now appear that the world and the states within it are spinning out of control? One answer is ascribed to "globalization," a widely accepted socially constructed code word understood as a transforming force that is creating sweeping governance crises in a new age of increasing interdependent complexity. *Globalization* captures the idea that everything on the planet is now more closely connected than ever before, but on an institutional foundation that is shaky and unprepared for managing the massive adjustments brought on by accelerating worldwide changes. The communications and technology revolution has spread the flow of information, capital, people, and jobs across state boundaries, and the impact has provoked much debate within globalization theory (see Martell 2007).

The integration of the globe in this transformed, interconnected, borderless world and common *cosmopolitan* culture (Appiah 2006) has reduced old feelings of independence, identity, and autonomy, and driven many states to surrender some of their sovereignty in order to benefit from collaborative participation in a competitive global marketplace. The message has been heard everywhere: borders and barriers cannot be revived in a nationalistic effort to close off a country in solitary isolation. "Join the world or become irrelevant" is the way that Edouard Balladur, a former French prime minister, described "the end of nationalism."

From an optimistic perspective, an awareness of the common destiny of all, alongside the declining ability of many sovereign states to cope with global problems through unilateral *self-help* approaches, will energize efforts to put aside interstate competition. According to this reasoning, conflict will recede as humanity begins to better recognize that national borders and oceans provide little protection against the multiple challenges arising from the global revolution in travel, communications, and trade. These shared problems can only be managed through collective, multilateral cooperation (Barrett 2007). Globalization is creating a strong web of constraints on the foreign policy behavior of those who are plugged into the network of global transactions. Consequently, because globalization makes it imperative that states cooperate, this continued tightening of interstate linkages should be welcomed.

> *The glorious thing about the human race is that it does change the world—constantly. It is the human being's capacity for struggling against being overwhelmed which is remarkable and exhilarating.*
>
> —Lorraine Hansberry, American author

What is especially favorable about globalization is that when everyone depends on everyone else, all *must* work together. Global interdependence makes it imperative for states to renounce their competition because they increasingly have a shared interest in cooperation and fewer and fewer incentives to fight. Globalization, optimists argue, is an irreversible motor for unity and progress, and ought to be promoted because ultimately it will increase the wealth of everyone everywhere (Norberg 2006).

From a more pessimistic perspective, the current era of globalization that now seems unstoppable could be passing its peak (Abdelal and Segal 2007). Even if the present period of globalization continues to create ever-increasing interconnectedness rather than ending, as the previous 1870–1914 era of globalization disastrously did, pessimists fret, as well they should, about how to cope with our "flat" earth (Friedman 2007). Globalization may not lead to greater transnational cooperation, but instead to cut-throat competition. Regardless of how compelling the need or how rewarding the benefits, increased contact and the trend toward an integrated single society of states may breed enmity, not amity. According to this view, globalization empowers advantaged states but constrains the prospects of weak states, producing new inequalities as the gap between the wealthy and the poor widens. "The problem," writes James Surowiecki (2007), "is that the number of countries that have dramatically improved their standard of living in the era of globalization is surprisingly small. It is not surprising that people are made unhappy by the sight of others getting richer while they stay the same or actually get poorer." Because its benefits will not be distributed equally, globalization will likely generate conflict between winners and losers. Intertwined economies will sour relations more than sweeten them. Under conditions of fierce competition, scarcity, and resurgent

Interdependence promotes war as well as peace.
—Kenneth Waltz, neorealist theoretician

nationalism, the temptation to seek isolation from the assault of globalization on national autonomy by creating barriers to trade and other transactions may be irresistible. The temptation to achieve political benefits by military force will also continue. Thus, the tightening web of globalization could lead to either danger or to opportunity.

Adding to growing concerns about escalating levels of globalization is the recognition that it is reducing states' control over their national futures and fates. States' capacities to govern themselves is eroding. Their sovereign ability to manage their economies, politics, environment, and even security (in the era of globalized terrorism) *within* their territories is slipping (Rudolph 2005). As states lose their grip on coping with pressures and problems originating outside their borders, they fret about the loss of influence and identity.

Globalization may have emasculated the sovereign power of states, but this same force has strengthened many governments (Lentner 2004; Opello and Rosow 2004). The question for the future is whether humanity can count on relatively powerless but growing nongovernmental organizations (NGOs) at the grassroots level seeking to assume responsibility for engineering human progress through global public policy networks. If states do not respond to the challenge, can the world's people expect a new global architecture to crystallize with accepted supranational global governance and global norms and *mores* or values obligating moral compliance with established customs? This arguably is one of the most important issues facing twenty-first-century world politics.

Will Technological Innovation Solve Pressing Global Problems?

The surge in globalization that followed on the heels of late-twentieth-century discoveries in microelectronics and information processing has unleashed revolutionary changes. "Biotechnology will dominate our lives during the next fifty years," predicts physicist philosopher Freeman Dyson (2007), "at least as much as computers have dominated our lives during the previous fifty years." The consequences of the technological revolution, however, are not certain. Technological innovations solve some problems but cause others. "Like any irrepressible force," observes the Nobel laureate economist Wassily Leontief, "technology can bestow on us undreamed benefits but also inflict irreparable damage." It can increase productivity and economic output, but it can also displace workers and trigger social unrest and environmental damage.

Although acknowledging that there is often a significant time lag between the diffusion of new technology and the adjustment of society to the changes it fosters, some people assert that technological innovation promises humanity a more secure and bountiful future (Fidler and Gostin 2008). Indeed, the most optimistic members of this group believe that because of promising developments in such fields as biotechnology and digital software, humanity is entering the most innovative period in history. From their perspective, sufficient resources exist to fuel continued progress. With patience, technological solutions eventually will be found to ease the most serious problems facing the world today. Malnutrition and disease, they note as an example, may still exist, but, as a result of technological advances in agriculture and medicine, many people are alive today who might have perished in previous centuries.

In contrast to those who envision technological innovation as a way to increase economic growth and alleviate social welfare problems, others remain concerned that some proposed technological solutions will compound current problems. Whereas genetically modified crops are seen by members of the former group as a way to reduce famine, members of the latter group worry about the public health consequences. Even the so-called green revolution had its drawbacks, they argue. Although fertilizers, pesticides, and herbicides initially increased crop yields in various Global South countries, they eventually spawned new problems, such as contaminated water supplies. Without wise management, technological advances can have detrimental side effects. Consider the case of the world's fisheries. At first, larger ships and improvements in maritime technology resulted in increases in the amount of fish harvested from the world's oceans. Over time, however, many fisheries were depleted. Applying more technology could not increase catches once the ecosystem had collapsed. As one member of this school of thought has put it: "Many of our new technologies confer upon us new power without automatically giving us new wisdom" (Gore 2006).

What do you think? Is the customary way of seeing technological discoveries as the engines of progress really valid? Or is the tendency to overrate the positive impact of new technology based on wishful thinking (Edgerton 2007)? It is sobering to remember that the world was once promised that "nuclear power would provide electricity too cheap to meter, eliminating pollution, forestalling energy crises, alleviating world poverty and putting an end to war. . . . The 'paperless office' was celebrated as long ago as 1975, but since we've had avalanches of the stuff: global consumption of paper has tripled in the last three decades and the average American worker now goes through 12,000 sheets of paper every year. Learning how to make new technology is one thing; learning how to use it is another" (Shapin 2007, 146). So, when you look at new technologies (stem cells, nanotechnology, human genomes, etc.), think counterfactually and imagine how things might turn out if new technologies had not been previously invented or how new ones might influence life on planet earth for better or for worse.

What Types of Armed Aggression Will Become the Major Fault Line in the Geostrategic Landscape?

Prevalent practices tend to wither away when they cease to serve their intended purpose, as the examples of slavery, dueling, and colonialism illustrate. Trends point toward the possibility that this may happen as well for war between states, which have declined nearly to the vanishing point. Even more impressively, the period since 1945 has been the longest span of great power peace since the sixteenth century. This achievement is raising expectations that large-scale warfare between countries will disappear and armed aggression between countries will become obsolete. Part of the confidence in that prediction is based on the assumption that no sane national leader would dare to wage war against another state because any conceivable rewards would be greatly exceeded by the cost of mass destruction.

> *The choice is either nonviolence or nonexistence.*
> —The Reverend Dr. Martin Luther King, Jr., peace activist and civil rights leader

To be sure, most leaders are still preparing for traditional kinds of warfare against other states, and are convinced by the abiding wisdom of the philosopher Aristotle in ancient Greece: "A people without walls is a people without choice." That said, the use of traditional weapons of warfare against the emergent threats that now haunt the globe are of questionable usefulness. How can countries combat effectively with the weapons in their arsenals the dangers presented by faceless and invisible nonstate terrorists willing to die in suicide bombings for their causes? Can these movements' attacks be deterred when there is not a territory to target? How does a state destroy an enemy with preemptive strikes when those adversaries have neither a location or things of value to attack? The old forms of military power still used by states today may be becoming impotent, and no level of military might can guarantee a state's invulnerability. When countries' primary security problem is no longer an attack by another country but instead the threat of internal aggression (a civil war) or an attack by a transnational terrorist network such as Al Qaeda, the question is how to fight wars against the major military threats in today's globe.

The conduct of war has undergone several "generational" changes since the Thirty Years' War drew to a close and gave birth to the modern state system. In what has been called the "first generation of modern warfare," which extended from the Peace of Westphalia to the American Civil War, soldiers armed with smooth-bore muskets were normally deployed in tight linear formations to coordinate volleys from relatively inaccurate weapons. Once weapons with greater accuracy and rates of fire became available, line-and-column tactics on open ground lost their effectiveness, which led to a new generation of tactics that emphasized massive firepower to annihilate fixed-fortification defenses.

The second generation of modern land warfare substituted massed artillery for massed infantry. During World War I, machine guns, barbed wire, minefields, and entrenched defenses strung along continuous fronts stymied the precise, geometric lines of attack typical of early modern warfare. In response, artillery barrages from the rear were used to breach fortified positions, allowing infantry units to overrun crippled defenses.

Although lengthy preparatory barrages could shatter fixed positions, they alerted the other side to where the subsequent infantry assault would occur. By extending defenses in greater depth and maintaining significant reserve forces, defenders could counterattack before advancing foot soldiers were able to break through. However, improvements in transportation and communication technology provided a way to deal with these tactics. Drawing on their country's experience of combining suppressive firepower with movement during the spring offenses of 1918, German officers such as Heinz Guderian and Erich von Manstein envisioned a third generation of warfare that accentuated speed and surprise rather than firepower and attrition. Tracked-armored vehicles and tactical air power, they reasoned, enabled an attacker to concentrate mobile forces at a decisive point along the front, penetrate deep into enemy territory, and roll the opposition up from the rear in battles of encirclement.

Whereas third-generation thinking has influenced most countries since World War II, today the threat of being attacked by the military forces of another country has receded, particularly in the Global North. Instead, a "fourth generation" of warfare has emerged in which states are pitted against nonstate actors in hostilities that lack front lines and clear distinctions between soldiers and civilians (Hammes 2004). Unable to defeat conventional armies on the field of battle, irregular forces using unconventional tactics focus on their adversary's will, using patience, ingenuity, and gruesome acts of violence to compel their opponent to weigh the mounting costs of

> *The military does not prepare for the last war; it prepares for the last war it liked.*
> —Jeffrey D. McCausland, U.S. General

continuing a long, drawn-out struggle. Some political and military leaders, however, continue to think of warfare in third-generational terms, dismissing this new face of war as an annoyance that detracts from preparations for decisive, large-scale engagements (Woodward 2006). Do the current wars in Afghanistan and Iraq provide a glimpse into the future? Will most military clashes in the early twenty-first century follow their pattern?

Will the Great Powers Intervene to Protect Human Rights?

Conflicts within countries are raging throughout the world. Many civilians are targets of overt oppression and violence by governments presumably created to preserve law and order in courts and through ballots. Of great concern is whether the moral outrage of the globe's major powers will be sufficient for them to make concerted peacekeeping and peacemaking interventions to end human rights abuses in those countries where standards of conduct accepted in international law have been blatantly disregarded. Atrocities in many failed states each year force a mass exodus of tens of millions of refugees and displaced people from their homes to seek safety. The global community is being put to a test of its true ideals and its capacity to defend them, at potentially high costs. Will a humanitarian concern for the victims targeted for extermination crystallize into a response? Or will the victims perish in a sea of indifference?

Human rights law in principle now provides unprecedented protection for people everywhere to live in freedom without fear. The traditional legal rule of state sovereignty and its corollary—the *nonintervention norm* prohibiting external interference in the internal affairs of states—has been revised. Former UN Secretary-General Kofi Annan described well the redefinition when he noted that "states are now widely understood to be instruments at the service of their people, and not vice versa."

Principle is one thing; the reality of human suffering is another. Will the great powers in the globalized community back their expressed convictions with action to free humanity from the oppression of mass murder? Can the great powers agree on rules for humanitarian intervention that define when it is legitimate to militarily respond

> *Injustice anywhere is a threat to justice everywhere.*
> —The Reverend Dr. Martin Luther King, Jr., peace activist and civil rights leader

to gross violations of "human rights, wherever they take place, and also on ways of deciding what action is necessary, and when, and by whom"? The challenge, UN Secretary-General Kofi Annan elaborated, is to transcend traditional notions of sovereignty. Those old ideas remain an "obstacle to effective action in humanitarian crises" that still encourages states "to stand idly by while the horror unfolds," instead of taking military action to enforce international human rights law.

If the global community truly recognizes that all people have rights that transcend state borders and defines those human rights as the core of the community's "common global interests," then it will have to answer and act on essential unresolved questions: What is the common interest? Who shall define it? Who shall defend it? Under whose authority? And by what means of intervention?

Karel Prinsloo/AP Photo

IGNORING SYSTEMATIC SLAUGHTER IN SUDAN? **Shown here is a Sudanese refugee after she and her family reached sanctuary on the Chad border after hiding for a year in a cave in Sudan's Darfur region. Called the worst genocide since the World War II Holocaust, this slaughter (like the simmering conflicts in Congo and Somalia that have killed millions) raises deep concerns that the world's great powers will intervene only when vital security interests or needed resources such as oil are threatened.**

Is the World Preparing for the Wrong War?

To preserve peace, one must prepare for war. That remains the classical realist formula for national security. But would states not be wiser to prepare to conquer the conditions that undermine prosperity, freedom, and welfare? "War for survival is the destiny of all species," observes philosopher Martin J. Siegel (1983). "In our case, we are courting suicide [by waging war against one another]. The world powers should declare war against their common enemy—the catastrophic and survival-of-the-fittest forces that destroyed most of the species of life that came before us."

Leaders have long been loath to fall prey to the single-mindedness of preparing to compete with other states. As France's former President Francois Mitterand once urged, "together we must urgently find the solutions to the real problems at hand—especially unemployment and underdevelopment. This is the battlefield where the outlines of the [future] will be drawn." India's former Prime Minister Indira Gandhi warned that "either nuclear war will annihilate the human race and destroy the Earth, thus disposing of any future, or men and women all over must raise their voices for peace and for an urgent attempt to combine the insights of different civilizations with contemporary knowledge. We can survive in peace and goodwill only by viewing the human race as one, and by looking at global problems in their totality." These prescriptions adhere to a fundamental premise, as expressed by Martti Ahtisaari, then president of Finland: "To deal with the great security challenges of our time, including population growth, the spread of weapons of mass destruction, crime, environmental degradation, and ethnic conflicts, we must resolutely adopt new methods of managing change and building global security."

These rhetorical positions doubtless reflect the problems and self-interests these leaders faced at home and abroad. Nonetheless, they reveal a minority view. The war of people against people goes on. Human security remains precarious.

A large percentage of humanity faces famine, poverty, and a denial of basic human rights. Millions are threatened by genocide and terrorism sponsored by their own governments. Humankind may consequently self-destruct, not because it lacks opportunities, but because of its collective inability to see and to seize them. "Perhaps we will destroy ourselves. Perhaps the common enemy within us will be too strong for us to recognize and overcome," the eminent astronomer Carl Sagan lamented. "But," he continued, "I have hope. . . . Is it possible that we humans are at last coming to our senses and beginning to work together on behalf of the species and the planet?"

We look forward to the time when the power of love will replace the love of power, then will our world know the blessings of peace.

—William Ewart Gladstone, former British Prime Minister

Is This the "End of History" or the End of Happy Endings?

To many observers, the history of world affairs is the struggle between tyranny and liberty. The contest has taken various forms since antiquity: between kings and mass publics, despotism and democracy, ideological principle and pragmatic politics. Labels are misleading and sometimes dangerous. However, they provide the vocabulary of diplomacy and inform theoretical discussion of governance and statecraft (Rousseau 2006). History, in this image, is a battle for hearts and minds. It is an ideological contest for the allegiance of humanity to a particular form of political, social, and economic organization.

With the defeat of fascism in World War II and the collapse of the international communist movement a generation later, it has become fashionable to argue that the world had witnessed the end of a historic contest of epic proportions—and thus the triumph of liberalism and what Francis Fukuyama called the *end of history:*

> The twentieth century saw the developed world descend into a paroxysm of ideological violence, as liberalism contended first with the remnants of absolutism, then bolshevism and fascism, and finally an updated Marxism that threatened to lead to the ultimate apocalypse of nuclear war. But the [twentieth] century that began full of self-confidence in the ultimate triumph of Western liberal democracy [seemed] at its close to be returning full circle to where it started: . . . to the unabashed victory of economic and political liberalism. (Fukuyama 1989, 3)

The abrupt repudiation of communism raised expectations that history had indeed "ended," in the sense that liberal democratic capitalism had triumphed throughout most of the world. Liberals, inspired by the belief that "liberal democracy and a market-oriented economic order are the only viable options for modern societies" (Fukuyama 1999b; see also Fukuyama 2004), are heartened by the doubling since the mid-1980s of the number of countries practicing multiparty elections and capitalism at home and in foreign trade. World order, they believe, can best be created by free governments practicing free trade. As Woodrow Wilson argued, making the world "safe for democracy" would make the world itself safe. From this liberal perspective, the diffusion of democratic capitalism bodes well for the future of world politics.

A less reassuring possibility is that history has not "ended" and that the battle between totalitarian and democratic governance is not truly over. "The continued spread of democracy in the twenty-first century is no more inevitable than it is impossible" (Mandelbaum 2007). There are signals that the march of democracy's spread is stalling, and many democracies remain ruled by one-party despots who, although elected, disregard constitutional limits on their power and deny their citizens basic political freedoms and religious and economic human rights. What is more, *new* democracies often lack the rule of law, political parties, or a free news media and as a consequence are unstable and warlike (Mansfield and Snyder 2005). This persistence of leaders not accountable to the electorate suggests that we may *not* be witnessing history's end. Like previous turning points in history, tomorrow may signal history's resumption: the return to the ageless search for barriers against the resurgence of tyranny, nationalism, and terrorism and war. Especially to followers of *realpolitik*, the most salient feature of world politics—the relentless competitive struggle for power under global anarchy—is permanent. They take as evidence the continuing efforts of terrorist movements to use violence against such despised targets as the United States and the republic for which it stands. There is no assurance that the global community has moved beyond tyranny or interstate competition and militarized conflict. As the former Soviet president Mikhail Gorbachev said, "A major international effort will be needed to render irreversible the shift in favor of a democratic world—and democratic for the whole of humanity, not just half of it."

Is There a Reordered Global Agenda?

The paradox of contemporary world politics is that a world no longer haunted by the paralyzing fear of a looming all-out war between great powers now faces a series of challenges every bit as threatening and as potentially unmanageable. Globalization has simultaneously enlarged the responsibilities and expanded the issues to be confronted. In a prosperous and stable period of history, when confidence in peace and economic growth was high, and his administration was still in office, U.S. President Bill Clinton found it necessary to warn that "profound and powerful forces are shaking and remaking our world. And the urgent question of our time is whether we can make change our friend and not our enemy."

The changes in recent years have spawned transnational threats to world order, in addition to the resurgence of nationalism, ethnic conflict, failed states, and separatist revolts. These include acid rain, AIDS, bird flu, other contagious diseases, drug trafficking, international organized crime, ozone depletion, climate change, obstacles to gender equality, energy and food scarcities, desertification and deforestation, financial crises and collapsing economies, and neomercantile trade protectionism.

The potential impact of these additional threats is formidable, as emerging trends suggest that nonmilitary dangers will multiply alongside the continuing threat of arms and armed aggression in civil wars, as well as interstate wars in particular regions and terrorism almost any place and at any time in the world. The distinction between *high politics* (geostrategic issues of national and international security that pertain to matters of war and peace) and *low politics* (the category of global issues related to the economic, social, demographic, and environmental aspects of relations between governments and people) may disappear. As distance and borders cease to be barriers in the global village, low politics is becoming high politics. At the same time, whenever bombs and bullets are fired, killing people and degrading the environment, high politics becomes low politics. How will humanity set priorities for action on a planet crowded with so many interrelated issues and problems, all of which require attention if peace and prosperity with justice is to prevail?

A NEW WORLD ORDER OR NEW WORLD DISORDER?

Previously established patterns and relationships have been obliterated. Something revolutionary, not simply new, appears to be unfolding. This book has focused on global change. It has identified the most important changes underway that are potentially leading to transformations in world politics.

Change, as we have seen, can be abrupt or slow. It moves constantly, but at its own pace, and history reminds us that the evolutionary direction of global change is uncertain. Many trends are unfolding at the same time, and their impact in combination can move the world along an unexpected trajectory. In addition, trends can reverse themselves, and each trend that moves forward advances at its own rate. Some trends move incredibly slowly in an evolutionary process that can only result in dramatic transformations over many centuries, whereas others exhibit short bursts of rapid change, interrupted by long periods without much change. Many examples of reversible, interrupted, and constant trends exist, as you have learned in this book. It is in their mix that the future will be shaped.

Global, overarching forces such as modernization and widespread interconnectivity are converging to reshape our lives. These "metatrends" are transformational or transcendent phenomena, not simply big, pervasive ones. A meta-trend implies multidimensional or catalytic change, as opposed to a linear or sequential change. ... But human adaptability—itself a meta-trend—will help keep our future from spinning out of control.

—David Pearce Snyder, futurologist

NASA

PICTURING GLOBAL DESTINY **This view of a globe without borders is captured by the photo taken of the eastern Mediterranean from the Earth-orbiting space shuttle *Columbia*. It pictures an integrated world community, in which humanity shares a common destiny. It also captures the kinds of environmental threats confronting humanity in a globalized world, where problems do not stop at borders. Note the difference in visibility in this panorama, which scientists believe is the result of pollution contaminating the atmosphere over the Black Sea.**

To appreciate the diverse ways trends may combine to affect each other, it is helpful for you to construct your images by both using memories of the past and by being inspired by visions of the future. In 1775, an American revolutionary, Patrick Henry, underscored the importance of history, observing that he had "but one lamp by which my feet are guided, and that is the lamp of experience. I know of no way of judging the future but by the past." Decades later, in 1848, another patriot, the Italian political leader Guiseppe Mazzini, stressed the importance of futurist thinking when he observed, "great things are achieved by guessing the direction of one's century." All of us need both perspectives, constructed with keen awareness that our images of history and of the future must avoid the temptation to see ourselves and our own country as we wish to be seen without taking into account how differently others might view us and our state.

It now appears that the collective impact of the divergent trends under way is signaling a major transformation in world politics. Yet, juxtaposed against the revolutionary is the persistent—the durability of enduring rituals, existing rules, established institutions, and entrenched customs that resist the pull of the momentous recent changes in world politics. Persistence and change coexist uneasily, and it is this mixture that makes the future so uncertain. The twin forces of integration and disintegration, continuity and change, create a mood of both confidence and disorientation. As Australia's former Prime Minister John Howard put it, "In one sense, you are a remarkably lucky generation, but in another sense you have been born into a period of social and technological change . . . and economic evolution."

A civilization has the same fragility as a life.
—Paul Valéry, French philosopher

The outcomes of two races will determine the difference between the world that is and the world that will be. The first is the race between knowledge and oblivion. Ignorance stands in the way of global progress and justice. Advances in science and technology far outpace the resolution of the social and political problems they generate. Building the knowledge to confront these problems may therefore present the ultimate challenge. "The splitting of the atom," Albert Einstein warned, has "changed everything save our modes of thinking, and thus we drift toward unparalleled catastrophe. Unless there is a fundamental change in [our] attitudes toward one another as well as [our] concept of the future, the world will face unprecedented disaster."

"Knowledge is our destiny," the philosopher Jacob Bronowski declared. If the world is to forge a promising future, it must develop more sophisticated knowledge. Sophistication demands that we see the world as a whole, as well as in terms of its individual parts; it does not permit picturing others according to our self-images or projecting onto others our own aims and values. We must discard belief in a simple formula for a better tomorrow and resist single-issue approaches to reform. Toleration of ambiguity, even the pursuit of it, is essential.

The future of world politics also rests on the outcome of a race between states' ability to cooperatively act together and their historic tendency to compete and fight. Only concerted international cooperation stands in the way of slipping back into military conflicts and ruthless competition. To meet the global challenges of the future, and to make wise decisions to implement needed changes for bringing about a world that is more secure and just, vision is required.

> *If our image of the future were different, the decisions of today would be different. [An inspiring vision] will impel us to action. But if there is no commonly held image of what is worth striving for, [global] society will lack both motivation and direction.*
>
> —Willis Harman, policy analyst

The future is not fixed, and headlines are not trend lines. So we can overcome threatening present dangers by making wise and ethical choices. How, then, should we proceed? "In times like these," the futurologist David Pearce Snyder (2006) counsels, "the best advice comes from ancient ideas that have withstood the test of time." The Greek philosopher Heraclitus observed twenty-five thousand years ago that "nothing about the future is inevitable except change." Two hundred years later, the mythic Chinese general Sun Tzu advised that "the wise leader exploits the inevitable." Their combined message is clear: "The wise leader exploits change." Therefore, rather than fear the global future, we should welcome its opportunities as we strive to build a more peaceful and just world. The moving words of President John F. Kennedy thus describe a posture we might well assume: "However close we sometimes seem to that dark and final abyss, let no man of peace and freedom despair. For he does not stand alone. . . . Together we shall save our planet or together we shall perish in its flames. Save it we can, and save it we must, and then shall we earn the eternal thanks of mankind."

glossary

A

absolute gains Conditions in which all participants in exchanges become better off.

acid rain Precipitation that has been made acidic through contact with sulfur dioxide and nitrogen oxides.

acquired immune deficiency syndrome (AIDS) An often fatal condition that can result from infection with the human immunodeficiency virus (HIV).

actor An individual, group, state, or organization that plays a major role in world politics.

adjudication A conflict-resolution procedure in which a third party makes a binding decision about a dispute in an institutional tribunal.

agency The capacity of actors to harness power to achieve objectives.

agenda setting The thesis that by their ability to identify and publicize issues, the communications media determine the problems that receive attention from governments and international organizations.

alignments The acceptance by a neutral state threatened by foreign enemies of a special relationship short of formal alliance with a stronger power able to protect it from attack.

alliances Coalitions that form when two or more states combine their military capabilities and promise to coordinate their policies to increase mutual security.

anarchy A condition in which the units in the global system are subjected to few if any overarching institutions to regulate their conduct.

antidumping duties Taxes placed on another exporting state's alleged selling of a product at a price below the cost to produce it.

antipersonnel landmines (APLs) Weapons buried below the surface of the soil that explode on contact with any person—soldier or citizen—stepping on them.

appeasement A strategy of making concessions to another state in the hope that, satisfied, it will not make additional claims.

arbitrage The selling of one currency (or product) and purchase of another to make a profit on changing exchange rates; traders ("arbitragers") help to keep states' currencies in balance though their speculative efforts to buy large quantities of devalued currencies and sell them in countries where they are more highly valued.

arbitration A conflict-resolution procedure in which a third party makes a binding decision between disputants through a temporary ruling board created for that ruling.

armed aggression Combat between the military forces of two or more states or groups.

arms control Multilateral or bilateral agreements to contain arms races by setting limits on the number and types of weapons states are permitted.

arms race The buildup of weapons and armed forces by two or more states that threaten each other, with the competition driven by the conviction that gaining a lead is necessary for security.

Asian Tigers The four Asian NICs that experienced far greater rates of economic growth during the 1980s than the more advanced industrial societies of the Global North.

asylum The provision of sanctuary to safeguard refugees escaping from the threat of persecution in the country where they hold citizenship.

asymmetric warfare Armed conflict between belligerents of vastly unequal military strength, in which the weaker side is often a nonstate actor that relies on unconventional tactics.

atrocities Brutal and savage acts against targeted citizen groups or prisoners of war, defined as illegal under international law.

autocratic rule A system of authoritarian or totalitarian government in which unlimited power is concentrated in a single leader.

B

balance of power The theory that peace and stability are most likely to be maintained when military power is distributed to prevent a single superpower hegemon or bloc from controlling the world.

balancer Under a balance-of-power system, an influential global or regional great power that throws its support in decisive fashion to a defensive coalition.

bandwagoning The tendency for weak states to seek alliance with the strongest power, irrespective of that power's ideology or type of government, in order to increase their security.

bargaining model of war An interpretation of war's onset as a choice by the initiator to bargain through aggression with an enemy in order to win on an issue or to obtain things of value, such as territory or oil.

barter The exchange of one good for another rather than the use of currency to buy and sell items.

behavioralism The methodological research movement to incorporate rigorous scientific analysis into the study of world politics so that conclusions about patterns are based on measurement, data, and evidence rather than on speculation and subjective belief.

bilateral Interactions between two transnational actors, such as treaties they have accepted to govern their future relationship.

bilateral agreements Exchanges between two states, such as arms control agreements, negotiated cooperatively to set ceilings on military force levels.

biodiversity The variety of plant and animal species living in the Earth's diverse ecosystems.

bipolarity A condition in which power is concentrated in two competing centers so that the rest of the states define their allegiances in terms of their relationships with both rival great-power superstates, or "poles."

blogs Online diaries, which spread information and ideas worldwide in the manner of journalists.

blowback The propensity for actions undertaken for national security to have the unintended consequence of provoking retaliatory attacks by the target when relations later sour.

bounded rationality The concept that decision maker's capacity to choose the best option is often constrained by many human and organizational obstacles.

boycotts Concerted efforts, often organized internationally, to prevent transactions such as trade with a targeted country in order to express disapproval or to coerce acceptance of certain conditions.

brinkmanship The intentional, reckless taking of huge risks in bargaining with an enemy, such as threatening a nuclear attack, to compel its submission.

bureaucracies The agencies and departments that conduct the functions of a central government or of a nonstate transnational actor.

bureaucratic politics model A description of decision making that sees foreign policy choices as based on bargaining and compromises among competing government agencies.

Bush Doctrine The unilateral policies of the George W. Bush administration proclaiming that the United States will make decisions only to meet America's perceived national interests, not to concede to other countries' complaints or to gain their acceptance.

C

capital mobility hypothesis The proposition that the massive movement of investment capital across state borders has led to the globalization of finance.

carrying capacity The maximum number of humans and living species that can be supported by a given territory.

cartel A convergence of independent commercial enterprises or political groups that combine for collective action, such as limiting competition, setting prices for their services, or forming a coalition to advance their groups interests.

Carter Doctrine President Jimmy Carter's declaration of U.S. willingness to use military force to protect its interests in the Persian Gulf.

caucuses Informal groups that individuals in governments and other groups join to promote their common interests.

civil society A community composed of citizens that create institutions to protect civil liberties (such as free speech and freedom from arbitrary governmental interference) and that use peaceful methods for conflict resolution.

civil wars Wars between opposing groups within the same country or by rebels against the government.

clash of civilizations Political scientist Samuel Huntington's controversial thesis that in the twenty-first century the globe's major civilizations will conflict with one another, leading to anarchy and warfare similar to that resulting from conflicts between states over the past five hundred years.

classical liberal economic theory A body of thought based on Adam Smith's ideas about the forces of supply and demand in the marketplace, emphasizing the benefits of minimal government regulation of the economy and trade.

coercive diplomacy The use of threats or limited armed force to persuade an adversary to alter its foreign and/or domestic policies.

coercive power The use of threats and punishment to force the target to alter its behavior.

cognitive dissonance The general psychological tendency to deny discrepancies between one's preexisting beliefs (cognitions) and new information.

Cold War The 42-year (1949–1991) rivalry between the United States and the Soviet Union, as well as their competing coalitions, which sought to contain each other's expansion and win worldwide predominance.

collective good A public good, such as safe drinking water, from which everyone benefits.

collective security A security regime agreed to by the great powers that set rules for keeping peace, guided by the principle that an act of aggression by any

state will be met by a collective response from the rest.

colonialism The rule of a region by an external sovereign power.

commercial domino theory The proposition that under conditions of globalization, the depletion of one country's currency reserves panics investors worldwide and spreads like a contagious disease to other countries, which witness the decline of their own currency reserves as the flight of capital also reduces the value of their currency.

commercial liberalism An economic theory advocating free markets and the removal of barriers to the flow of trade and capital as a locomotive for prosperity.

communications technology The technological means through which information and communications are transferred, such as through the World Wide Web.

communism The radical ideology maintaining that if society is organized so that every person produces according to his or her ability and consumes according to his or her needs, a community without class distinctions will emerge, sovereign states will no longer be needed, and imperial wars of colonial conquest will vanish from history.

communist theory of imperialism The Marxist-Leninist economic interpretation of imperialist wars of conquest as driven by capitalism's need for foreign markets to generate capital.

comparative advantage The concept in liberal economics that a state will benefit if it specializes in those goods it can produce comparatively cheaply and acquires through trade goods that it can only produce at a higher cost.

compellence A method of coercive diplomacy usually involving an act of war or threat to force an adversary to make concessions against its will.

complex interdependence A model of world politics based on the assumptions that states are not the only important actors, security is not the dominant national goal, and military force is not the only significant instrument of foreign policy. This theory stresses cross-cutting ways in which the growing ties among transnational actors make them vulnerable to each other's actions and sensitive to each other's needs.

concert A cooperative agreement in design and plan among great powers to manage jointly the global system.

conciliation A conflict-resolution procedure in which a third party assists both parties to a dispute but does not propose a solution.

conflict Discord, often arising in international relations over perceived incompatibilities of interest.

consequentialism An approach to evaluating moral choices on the basis of the results of the action taken.

constitutional democracy Government processes that allow people, through their elected representatives, to exercise power and influence the state's policies.

constructivist theory A theoretical approach advocated by Alexander Wendt that sees self-interested states as the key actors in world politics; their actions are determined not by anarchy but by the ways that states socially construct and then accept images of reality and later respond to the meanings given to power politics. As consensual definitions change, it is possible for either conflictual or cooperative practices to evolve.

containment A strategy to prevent a great power rival from using force to alter the balance of power and increase its sphere of influence.

cornucopians Optimists who question limits-to-growth analyses and contend that markets effectively maintain a balance between population, resources, and the environment.

cosmopolitan An outlook that values viewing the cosmos or entire world as the best polity or unit for political governance and personal identity, as opposed to other polities such as one's local metropolis or city of residence (e.g., Indianapolis or Minneapolis).

counterfactual reasoning Speculations about historical events and developments that ask how the world might have changed had certain momentous foreign policy choices not been taken or had other conditions prevailed by inquiring "what would have happened if . . . "

counterforce targeting strategy Targeting strategic nuclear weapons on

particular military capabilities of an enemy's armed forces and arsenals.

countervailing duties Government tariffs to offset suspected subsidies provided by foreign governments to their producers.

countervalue targeting strategy A bargaining doctrine that declares the intention to use weapons of mass destruction against an enemy's most valued nonmilitary resources, such as the civilians and industries located in its cities.

covert operations Secret activities undertaken by a state outside its borders through clandestine means to achieve specific political or military goals with respect to another state.

crimes against humanity A category of activities, made illegal at the Nuremberg war crime trials, condemning states that abuse human rights.

crisis A situation in which the threat of escalation to warfare is high and the time available for making decisions and reaching compromised solutions in negotiations is compressed.

cultural conditioning The impact of national traditions and societal values on the behavior of states, under the assumption that culture affects national decision making about issues such as the acceptability of aggression.

cyberspace A metaphor used to describe the global electronic web of people, ideas, and interactions on the Internet, which is unencumbered by the borders of the geopolitical world.

cycles The periodic reemergence of conditions similar to those that existed previously.

D

de facto recognition A government's acknowledgment of the factual existence of another state or government short of full recognition.

de jure recognition A government's formal, legal recognition of another sovereign government or state.

decolonization The achievement of sovereign independence by countries that were once colonies of the great powers.

deconstructivism The postmodern theory that the complexity of the world system renders precise description

impossible and that the purpose of scholarship is to understand actors' hidden motives by deconstructing their textual statements.

deforestation The process of clearing and destroying forests.

democratic peace The theory that although democratic states sometimes wage wars against nondemocratic states, they do not fight one another.

demography The study of population changes, their sources, and their impact.

dependency A condition of retarded economic growth believed to result from the Global South's subordination and structural exploitation by the Global North's advanced capitalistic market economies, making the Global South especially vulnerable to the Global North's business cycles of expansion and contraction.

dependency theory A theory hypothesizing that less developed countries are exploited because global capitalism makes them dependent on the rich countries that create exploitative rules for trade and production.

dependent development The industrialization of peripheral areas within the confines of the dominance-dependence relationship between the Global North and the Global South, which enables the poor to become wealthier without ever catching up to the core Global North countries.

desertification The creation of deserts due to soil erosion, overfarming, and deforestation, which converts cropland to nonproductive, arid sand.

détente In general, a strategy of seeking to relax tensions between adversaries to reduce the possibility of war.

deterrence Preventive strategies designed to dissuade an adversary from doing what it would otherwise do.

developed countries A category used by the World Bank (WDR 2008) to identify Global North countries, with a GNI per capita of $11,116 or more annually.

developing countries A category used by the World Bank to identify low income Global South countries with a 2008 GNI per capita below $905 and middle income countries with a GNI per capita of more than $905 but less than $11,116.

development The processes, economic and political, through which a country develops to increase its capacity to meet its citizens' basic human needs and raise their standard of living.

devolution States' granting of political power to minority ethnic groups and indigenous people in particular national regions under the expectation that greater autonomy will curtail the groups' quest for independence as a new state.

diasporas The migration of religious or ethnic groups to foreign lands despite their continuation of affiliation with the land and customs of their origin.

digital divide The division between the Internet technology-rich Global North and the Global South in the proportion of Internet users and hosts.

digital world economy A system based largely on globalized electronic debt and credit transfers.

diplomatic immunity The legal doctrine that gives a country's officials (e.g., diplomats and ambassadors) release from the local legal jurisdiction of the state when they are visiting or stationed abroad to represent their own government.

diplomatic recognition The formal legal acceptance by one existing sovereign state of another state's official status as an independent country.

directed dyadic A perception of foreign policy in which the actor's foreign policy refers to specific goals with respect to another actor or target in particular.

disarmament Agreements to reduce or destroy weapons or other means of attack.

diversionary theory of war The hypothesis that leaders sometimes initiate conflict abroad as a way of increasing national cohesion at home by diverting national public opinion away from controversial domestic issues and internal problems.

divine right of kings The realist doctrine that kings and sovereign monarchs have the right to rule their subjects authoritatively and are not accountable to the public because their rule is claimed to be ordained by God.

doctrines The guidelines that a great power or an alliance embraces as a strategy to specify the conditions under which it will use military power and armed force for political purposes abroad.

domino theory A metaphor popular during the Cold War that predicted that if one state fell to communism, its neighbors would also fall in a chain reaction, like a row of falling dominoes.

dualism The separation of a country into two sectors, the first modern and prosperous centered in major cities, and the second at the margin, neglected and poor.

E

ecological fallacy The error of assuming that the attributes of an entire population—a culture, a country, or a civilization—are the same attributes and attitudes of each person within it.

economic sanctions The punitive use of trade or monetary measures, such as an embargo, to harm a targeted adversary's economy in order to exercise influence over the target's policies.

ecopolitics How political actors influence perceptions of, and policy responses to, changing environmental conditions, such as the impact of carbon dioxide emissions on the temperature of the Earth.

enclosure movement The claiming of common properties by states or private interests.

end of history Francis Fukuyama's thesis that an end-point in the ideological debate about the best form of government and economy had been reached, with liberal capitalism and democracy prevailing throughout the world without serious competition from advocates of either communism or autocracy.

enduring internal rivalries Protracted violent conflicts between governments and insurgent groups within a state.

enduring rivalries Prolonged competition fueled by deep-seated mutual hatred that leads opposed actors to feud and fight over a long period of time without resolution of their conflict.

entente An agreement between states to consult one another and take a common course of action if one is attacked by another state.

environmental security A concept recognizing that environmental threats to global life systems are as dangerous as the threat of armed conflicts.

epistemic communities Scientific experts on a subject of inquiry such as global warming that are organized internationally as NGOs to communicate with one another and use their constructed understanding of "knowledge" to lobby for global transformations.

epistemology The philosophical examination of the ways in which knowledge is acquired and the analytic principles governing the study of phenomena.

ethics Criteria for evaluating right and wrong behavior and the motives of individuals and groups.

ethnic cleansing The extermination of an ethnic minority group by a state, in violation of international law.

ethnic groups People whose identity is primarily defined by their sense of sharing a common ancestral nationality, language, cultural heritage, and kinship.

ethnic nationalism Devotion to a cultural, ethnic, or linguistic community.

ethnicity Perceptions of likeness among members of a particular racial grouping leading them to prejudicially view other nationality groups as outsiders.

ethnocentrism A propensity to see one's nationality or state as the center of the world and therefore special, with the result that the values and perspectives of other groups are misunderstood and ridiculed.

European Commission The executive organ administratively responsible for the European Union.

European Union (EU) A regional organization created by the merger of the European Coal and Steel Community, the European Atomic Energy Community, and the European Economic Community (called the European Community until 1993) that has since expanded geographically and in its authority.

exchange rate The rate at which one state's currency is exchanged for another state's currency in the global marketplace.

export quotas Barriers to free trade agreed to by two trading states to protect their domestic producers.

export-led industrialization A growth strategy that concentrates on developing domestic export industries capable of competing in overseas markets.

extended deterrence The protection received by a weak ally when a heavily militarized great power pledges to "extend" its capabilities to it in a defense treaty.

externalities The unintended side effects of choices that reduce the true value of the original decision, such as trade protectionism against foreign imports increasing the costs of goods to consumers and stimulating inflation.

extraterritoriality The legal doctrine that allows states to maintain jurisdiction over their embassies in other states.

extreme militant religious movements Politically active organizations based on strong religious convictions, whose members are fanatically devoted to the global promotion of their religious beliefs.

F

failed states Countries whose governments have so mismanaged policy that their citizens, in rebellion, threaten revolution to divide the country into separate independent states.

fascism A far-right ideology that promotes extreme nationalism and the establishment of an authoritarian society built around a single party with dictatorial leadership.

feminist theory Body of scholarship that emphasizes gender in the study of world politics.

fertility rate The average number of children born to a woman (or group of women) during her lifetime.

firebreak The psychological barrier between conventional wars and wars fought with nuclear weapons as well as weapons of mass destruction.

First World The relatively wealthy industrialized countries that share a commitment to varying forms of democratic political institutions and developed market economies, including the United States, Japan, the European Union, Canada, Australia, and New Zealand.

fixed exchange rates A system under which states establish the parity of their currencies and commit to keeping fluctuations in their exchange rates within narrow limits.

floating exchange rates An unmanaged process in which governments neither establish an official rate for their currencies nor intervene to affect the value of their currencies, and instead allow market forces and private investors to influence the relative rate of exchange for currencies between countries.

foreign aid Economic assistance in the form of loans and grants provided by a donor country to a recipient country for a variety of purposes.

foreign direct investment (FDI) A cross-border investment through which a person or corporation based in one country purchases or constructs an asset such as a factory or bank in another country so that a long-term relationship and control of an enterprise by nonresidents results.

foreign policy The decisions governing authorities make to realize international goals.

Fourth World A term used to recognize the native national groups residing in many so-called united states who, although often minorities, occupied the state's territory first and refuse to accept domination, seeking instead as noncentral governments (NGCs), regional governments, and subnational entities (SNEs) to govern themselves or to create a new state for themselves by separating from existing states.

Free Trade Area of the Americas (FTAA) A set of rules to promote free trade among thirty-four democracies in North and South America.

free-riders Those who obtain benefits at others' expense without the usual costs and effort.

functionalism The theory advanced by David Mitrany and others explaining how people can come to value transnational institutions (IGOs, integrated or merged states) and the steps to giving those institutions authority to provide the public goods (for example, security) previously, but inadequately, supplied by their own state.

G

game theory An approach to the analysis of making rational decisions based on observation of how opposing players with conflicting interests react to the kinds of

situations such as in business or military strategy to calculate gains and losses in order to achieve desired outcomes.

Gender Empowerment Measure (GEM) The UN Development Programme's attempt to measure the extent of gender equality across the globe's countries, based on estimates of women's relative economic income, high-paying positions, and access to professional and parliamentary positions.

gender inequalities Differences between men and women in opportunity and reward that are determined by the values that guide states' foreign and domestic policies.

General Agreement on Tariffs and Trade (GATT) An UN affiliated IGO designed to promote international trade and tariff reductions, replaced by the World Trade Organization.

genetic engineering Research geared to discover seeds for new types of plant and human life for sale and use as substitutes for those produced naturally.

genocide The attempt to eliminate, in whole or in part, an ethnic, racial, religious, or national minority group.

geo-economics The relationship between geography and the economic conditions and behavior of states that define their levels of production, trade, and consumption of goods and services.

geopolitics The theoretical postulate that states' foreign policies are determined by their location, natural resources, and physical environment.

Global commons The physical and organic characteristics and resources of the entire planet—the air in the atmosphere and conditions on land and sea—on which human life depends and which is the common heritage of all humanity.

Global East The rapidly growing economies of East and South Asia that have made those countries competitors with the traditionally dominant countries of the Global North.

global level of analysis Analyses that emphasize the impact of worldwide conditions on foreign policy behavior and human welfare.

global migration crisis A severe problem stemming from the growing number of people moving from their home country to another country, straining the ability of the host countries to absorb the foreign emigrants.

Global North A term used to refer to the world's wealthy, industrialized countries located primarily in the Northern Hemisphere.

Global South A term now often used instead of "Third World" to designate the less-developed countries located primarily in the Southern Hemisphere.

global structure The defining characteristics of the global system—such as the distribution of military capabilities—that exist independently of all actors but powerfully shape the actions of every actor.

global system The predominant patterns of behaviors and beliefs that prevail internationally to define the major worldwide conditions that heavily influence human and national activities.

global village A popular cosmopolitan perspective describing the growth of awareness that all people share a common fate because the world is becoming an integrated and interdependent whole.

globalization The integration of states, through increasing contact, communication, and trade, to create a common global culture for all humanity.

globalization of finance The increasing transnationalization of national markets through the world-wide integration of capital flows.

globally integrated enterprises MNCs organized horizontally with management and production located in plants in numerous states for the same products they market.

good offices Provision by a third party to offer a place for negotiation among disputants but does not serve as a mediator in the actual negotiations.

great powers The most powerful countries, militarily and economically, in the global system.

greenhouse effect The phenomenon producing planetary warming when gases released by burning fossil fuels act as a blanket in the atmosphere, thereby increasing temperatures.

gross national income (GNI) A measure of the production of goods and services within a given time period, which is used

to delimit the geographic scope of production. GNI measures production by a state's citizens or companies, regardless of where the production occurs.

Group of 77 (G-77) The coalition of Third World countries that sponsored the 1963 calling for reform to allow greater equality in North–South trade.

groupthink The propensity for members of a group to accept and agree with the group's prevailing attitudes, rather than speaking out for what they believe.

gunboat diplomacy A show of military force, historically naval force, to intimidate an adversary.

H

hard power The ability to exercise international influence by means of a country's military capabilities.

heavily indebted poor countries (HIPCs) The subset of countries identified by the World Bank's Debtor Reporting System whose ratios of debt to gross national product are so substantial they cannot meet their payment obligations without experiencing political instability and economic collapse.

hegemon A preponderant state capable of dominating the conduct of international political and economic relations.

hegemonic stability theory A body of theory that maintains that the establishment of hegemony for global dominance by a single great power is a necessary condition for global order in commercial transactions and international military security.

hegemony The ability of one state to lead in world politics by promoting its worldview and ruling over arrangements governing international economics and politics.

high politics Geostrategic issues of national and international security that pertain to matters of war and peace.

history-making individuals model An interpretation that sees foreign policy decisions that affect the course of history as products of strong-willed leaders acting on their personal convictions.

horizontal nuclear proliferation An increase in the number of states that possess nuclear weapons.

Human Development Index (HDI) An index that uses life expectancy, literacy, average number of years of schooling, and income to assess a country's performance in providing for its peoples' welfare and security.

human immunodeficiency virus (HIV) A virus that can lead to the lethal acquired immune deficiency syndrome (AIDS).

human needs Those basic physical, social, and political needs, such as food and freedom, that are required for survival and security.

human rights The political rights and civil liberties recognized by the international community as inalienable and valid for individuals in all countries by virtue of their humanity.

human security A measure popular in liberal theory of the degree to which the welfare of individuals is protected and promoted, in contrast to realist theory's emphasis on putting the state's interests in military and national security ahead of all other goals.

humanitarian intervention The use of peacekeeping troops by foreign states or international organizations to protect endangered people from gross violations of their human rights and from mass murder.

hypotheses Speculative statements about the probable relationship between independent variables (the presumed causes) and a dependent variable (the effect).

I

ideology A set of core philosophical principles that leaders and citizens collectively construct about politics, the interests of political actors, and the ways people ought to behave.

imperial overstretch The phrase coined by Paul Kennedy to capture the historic tendency for past hegemons to sap their own strength through costly imperial pursuits and military spending that weaken their economies in relation to the economies of their rivals.

imperialism The policy of expanding state power through the conquest and/or military domination of foreign territory.

import quotas Nontariff barriers to free trade that limit the quantity of particular products that can be imported.

import-substitution industrialization A strategy for economic development that centers on providing investors at home incentives to produce goods so that previously imported products from abroad will decline.

indigenous peoples The native ethnic and cultural inhabitant populations within countries ruled by a government controlled by others, referred to as the "Fourth World."

individual level of analysis An analytical approach that emphasizes the psychological and perceptual variables motivating people, such as those who make foreign policy decisions on behalf of states and other global actors.

individualistic fallacy The logical error of assuming that an individual leader, who has legal authority to govern, represents the people and opinions of the population governed, so that all citizens are necessarily accountable for the vices and virtues (to be given blame or credit) of the leaders authorized to speak for them.

infant industry Newly established industries ("infants") that are not yet strong enough to compete against mature foreign producers in the global marketplace until in time they develop and can then compete.

information age The era in which the rapid creation and global transfer of information through mass communication contributes to the globalization of knowledge.

information technology (IT) The techniques for storing, retrieving, and disseminating through computerization and the Internet recorded data and research knowledge.

information warfare Attacks on an adversary's telecommunications and computer networks to degrade the technological systems vital to its defense and economic well-being.

infowar tactics Attacks on an adversary's telecommunications and computer networks to penetrate and degrade an enemy whose defense capabilities depend heavily on these technological systems.

instrumental rationality A conceptualization of rationality that emphasizes the tendency of decision makers to compare options with those previously considered and then select the one that has the best chance of success.

intellectual property Inventions created by the use of human intelligence in publications, art, and design by individuals that are often illegally used for commercial purposes without credits or royalties to their creators in violation of GATT's agreement.

interdependence A situation in which the behavior of international actors greatly affects others with whom they have contact, making all parties mutually sensitive and vulnerable to the others' actions.

intergovernmental organizations (IGOs) Institutions created and joined by states' governments, which give them authority to make collective decisions to manage particular problems on the global agenda.

International Criminal Court (ICC) A court established by the UN for indicting and administering justice to people committing war crimes.

international criminal tribunals Special tribunals established by the UN prosecute those responsible for war time atrocities and genocide, bring justice to victims, and deter such crimes in the future.

international liquidity Reserve assets used to settle international accounts in the form of dollars.

International Monetary Fund (IMF) A financial agency now affiliated with the UN, established in 1944 to promote international monetary cooperation, free trade, exchange rate stability, and democratic rule by providing financial assistance and loans to countries facing financial crises.

international monetary system The financial procedures used to calculate the value of currencies and credits when capital is transferred across borders through trade, investment, foreign aid, and loans.

international political economy (IPE) The study of the intersection of politics and economics that illuminates why changes occur in the distribution of states' wealth and power.

international politics The study of how global actors' activities entail the exercise of influence to achieve and defend their goals and ideals, and how it affects the world at large.

international regime A concept constructed to explain the benefits to actors supporting particular rules to regulate a specific international problem, such as disposal of toxic wastes.

international relations Relationships that exist between pairs or among groups of global actors.

international terrorism The threat or use of violence as a tactic of terrorism against targets in other countries.

interspecific aggression A biological category of species having common characteristics that kill species other than members of their own species.

intraspecific aggression Killing members of one's own species comprising related organisms or populations potentially capable of cross-breeding.

irredentism A movement by an ethnic national group to recover control of lost territory by force so that the new state boundaries will no longer divide the group.

isolationism A policy of withdrawing from active participation with other actors in world affairs and instead concentrating state efforts on managing internal affairs.

J

just war doctrine The moral criteria identifying when a just war may be undertaken and how it should be fought once it begins.

just war theory The theoretical criteria under which it is morally permissible, or "just," for a state to go to war and the methods by which a just war might be fought.

K

Kellogg-Briand Pact A multilateral treaty negotiated in 1928 that outlawed war as a method for settling interstate conflicts.

L

laissez-faire From a French phrase (meaning literally "let do") that Adam Smith and other commercial liberals in the eighteenth century used to describe the advantages of free-wheeling capitalism without government interference in economic affairs.

laissez-faire economics The philosophical principle of free markets and free trade to give people free choices with little governmental regulation.

least developed of the less developed countries (LLDCs) The most impoverished countries in the Global South.

levels of analysis The different aspects of and agents in international affairs that may be stressed in interpreting and explaining global phenomena, depending on whether the analyst chooses to focus on "wholes" (the complete global system and large collectivities) or on "parts" (individual states or people).

Liberal International Economic Order (LIEO) The set of regimes created after World War II, designed to promote monetary stability and reduce barriers to the free flow of trade and capital.

liberalism A paradigm predicated on the hope that the application of reason and universal ethics to international relations can lead to a more orderly, just, and cooperative world; liberalism assumes that anarchy and war can be policed by institutional reforms that empower international organization and law.

"linkage" strategy A set of assertions claiming that leaders should take into account another country's overall behavior when deciding whether to reach agreement on any one specific issue so as to link cooperation to rewards.

long peace Long-lasting periods of peace between any of the militarily strongest great powers.

long-cycle theory A theory that focuses on the rise and fall of the leading global power as the central political process of the modern world system.

low politics The category of global issues related to the economic, social, demographic, and environmental aspects of relations between governments and people.

M

macroeconomics The study of aggregate economic indicators such as GDP, the money supply, and the balance of trade that governments monitor to measure changes in national and global economies

such as the rates of economic growth and inflation or the level of unemployment.

Marxist-Leninism Communist theory as derived from the writings of Karl Marx, Vladimir Lenin, and their successors, which criticizes capitalism as a cause of class struggle, the exploitation of workers, colonialism, and war.

massive retaliation The Eisenhower administration's policy doctrine for containing Soviet communism by pledging to respond to any act of aggression with the most destructive capabilities available, including nuclear weapons.

matchpolitik The German realist philosophy in statecraft that sees the expansion of state power and territory by use of armed force as a legitimate goal.

mediation A conflict-resolution procedure in which a third party proposes a nonbinding solution to the disputants.

mercantilism A government trade strategy for accumulating state wealth and power by encouraging exports and discouraging imports.

military intervention Overt or covert use of force by one or more countries that cross the borders of another country in order to affect the target country's government and policies.

military necessity The legal principle that violation of the rules of warfare may be excused for defensive purposes during periods of extreme emergency.

military-industrial complex A combination of defense establishments, contractors who supply arms for them, and government agencies that benefit from high military spending, which act as a lobbying coalition to pressure governments to appropriate large expenditures for military preparedness.

mirror images The tendency of states and people in competitive interaction to perceive each other similarly—to see others the same hostile way others see them.

modernization A view of development popular in the Global North's liberal democracies that wealth is created through efficient production, free enterprise, and free trade, and that countries' relative wealth depends on technological innovation and education more than on natural endowments such as climate and resources.

monad A conception of foreign policy that the political actor's foreign policy is undifferentiated to the target, and that it acts under a presupposed generalized characteristic.

monetary policy The decisions made by states' central banks to change the country's money supply in an effort to manage the national economy and control inflation, using fiscal policies such as changing the money supply and interest rates.

monetary system The processes for determining the rate at which each state's currency is valued against the currency of every other state, so that purchasers and sellers can calculate the costs of financial transactions across borders such as foreign investments, trade, and cross-border travel.

money supply The total amount of currency in circulation in a state, calculated to include demand deposits, such as checking accounts in commercial banks, and time deposits, such as savings accounts and bonds, in savings banks.

morality Principles about the norms for behavior that should govern actors' interactions.

morals Principles clarifying the difference between good and evil and the situations in which they are opposed.

mores The customs of a group accepted as morally binding obligations.

most-favored-nation principle (MFN) The central GATT principle of unconditional nondiscriminatory treatment in trade between contracting parties underscoring the WTO's rule requiring any advantage given by one WTO member to also extend it to all other WTO members.

muddling through The tendency for leaders to make foreign policy decisions by trial-and-error adjustments in an attempt to cope with challenges.

multilateral agreements Cooperative compacts among many states to ensure that a concerted policy is implemented toward alleviating a common problem, such as levels of future weapons capabilities.

multilateralism Cooperative approaches to managing shared problems through collective and coordinated action.

multinational corporations (MNCs) Business enterprises headquartered in one state that invest and operate extensively in many other states.

multiple advocacy The concept that better and more rational choices are made when decisions are reached in a group context, which allows advocates of differing alternatives to be heard so that the feasibility of rival options receives critical evaluation.

multiple independently targetable reentry vehicles (MIRVs) A technological innovation permitting many weapons to be delivered from a single missile.

multipolarity The distribution of global power into three or more great-power centers, with most other states allied with one of the rivals.

mutual assured destruction (MAD) A condition of mutual deterrence in which both sides possess the ability to survive a first strike with weapons of mass destruction and launch a devastating retaliatory attack.

N

nation A collectivity whose people see themselves as members of the same group because they share the same ethnicity, culture, or language.

national character The collective characteristics ascribed to the people within a state.

national interest The goals that states pursue to maximize what they perceive to be selfishly best for their country.

national security A country's psychological freedom from fears that the state will be unable to resist threats to its survival and national values emanating from abroad or at home.

nationalism A mind set glorifying a particular state and the nationality group living in it, which sees the state's interest as a supreme value.

nature versus nurture The controversy over whether human behavior is determined more by the biological basis of "human nature" than it is nurtured by the environmental conditions that humans experience.

negotiation Diplomatic dialogue and discussion between two or more parties with the goal of resolving through give-and-take bargaining perceived differences of interests and the conflicts they cause.

neo-Malthusians Pessimists who warn of the global ecopolitical dangers of uncontrolled population growth.

neocolonialism (neoimperialism) The economic rather than military domination of foreign countries.

neofunctionalism The revised functional theory explaining that the IGOs created by states to manage common problems provide benefits that exert new pressures by political means for further political integration, the creation of additional IGOs, and the globalization of international relations in an expanding network of independence that reduces states' incentives to wage war.

neoliberalism The "new" liberal theoretical perspective that accounts for the way international institutions promote global change, cooperation, peace, and prosperity through collective programs for reforms.

neomercantilism A contemporary version of classical mercantilism that advocates promoting domestic production and a balance-of-payment surplus by subsidizing exports and using tariffs and nontariff barriers to reduce imports.

neorealism A theoretical account of states' behavior that explains it as determined by differences in their relative power within the global hierarchy, defined primarily by the distribution of military power, instead of by other factors such as their values, types of government, or domestic circumstances.

neutrality The legal doctrine that provides rights for states to remain non-aligned with adversaries waging war against each other.

New International Economic Order (NIEO) The 1974 policy resolution in the UN that called for a North–South dialogue to open the way for the less-developed countries of the Global South to participate more fully in the making of international economic policy.

New World Information and Communication Order (NWICL) The controversial Global South effort to combat what was termed "cultural imperialism" by limiting the news and information disseminated by the Western transnational news agencies.

newly industrialized countries (NICs) The most prosperous members of the Global South, which have become important exporters of manufactured goods as well as important markets for the major industrialized countries that export capital goods.

no first use The doctrine that a nuclear state would not be the first to use its strategic weapons in the event of a military attack by another state.

Nonaligned Movement (NAM) A group of more than one hundred newly independent, mostly less-developed, states that joined together as a group of neutrals to avoid entanglement with the superpowers' competing alliances in the Cold War and to advance the Global South's primary interests in economic cooperation and growth.

nonaligned states Countries that do not form alliances with opposed great-powers and practice neutrality on issues that divide great powers.

nonalignment A foreign policy posture that rejects participating in military alliances with rival blocs for fear that formal alignment will entangle the state in an unnecessary involvement in war.

noncombatant immunity The legal principle that military force should not be used against innocent civilians.

nondiscrimination rule A rule accepting both most-favored-nation and nondiscrimination as principles for free trade, stipulating that goods produced at home and abroad are to be treated the same for import and export agreements.

nongovernmental organizations (NGOs) Transnational organizations of private citizens maintaining consultative status with the UN; they include professional associations, foundations, multinational corporations, or simply internationally active groups in different states joined together to work toward common interests.

nonintervention norm A fundamental international legal principle, now being challenged, that traditionally has defined interference by one state in the domestic affairs of another as illegal.

nonlethal weapons (NLWs) The wide array of "soft kill," low-intensity methods of incapacitating an enemy's people, vehicles, communications systems, or entire cities without killing either combatants or noncombatants.

nonproliferation regime Rules to contain arms races so that weapons or technology do not spread to states that do not have them.

nonstate nations National or ethnic groups struggling to obtain power and/or statehood.

nontariff barriers (NTBs) Measures other than tariffs that discriminate against imports without direct tax levies and are beyond the scope of international regulation.

norms Generalized standards of behavior that, once accepted, shape collective expectations about appropriate conduct.

North American Free Trade Agreement (NAFTA) An agreement that brings Mexico into the free-trade zone linking Canada and the United States.

North Atlantic Treaty Organization (NATO) A military alliance created in 1949 to deter a Soviet attack on Western Europe that since has expanded and redefined its mission to emphasize not only the maintenance of peace but also the promotion of democracy.

Nth country problem The expansion of additional new nuclear weapon states.

nuclear deterrence Dissuading an adversary from attacking by threatening retaliation with nuclear weapons.

Nuclear Nonproliferation Treaty (NPT) An international agreement that seeks to prevent horizontal proliferation by prohibiting further nuclear weapons sales, acquisitions, or production.

nuclear utilization theory (NUTs) A body of strategic thought that claimed deterrent threats would be more credible if nuclear weapons were made more usable.

nuclear winter The expected freeze that would occur in the Earth's climate from the fallout of smoke and dust in the event nuclear weapons were used, blocking out sunlight and destroying the plant and animal life that survived the original blast.

O

official development assistance (ODA) Grants or loans to countries from donor countries, now usually channeled through multilateral aid institutions such as the World Bank for the primary purpose of promoting economic development and welfare.

opportunity costs The kinds of sacrifices that sometimes result when the decision to select one option means that the opportunity to realize gains from other options is lost.

orderly market arrangements (OMAs) Voluntary export restrictions through government-to-government agreements to follow specific trading rules.

outsourcing The transfer of jobs by a corporation usually headquartered in a Global North country to a Global South country able to supply trained workers at lower wages.

ozone layer The protective layer of the upper atmosphere over the Earth's surface that shields the planet from the sun's harmful impact on living organisms.

P

pacifism The liberal idealist school of ethical thought that recognizes no conditions that justify the taking of another human's life, even when authorized by a head of state.

paradigm Derived from the Greek, meaning an example, a model, or an essential pattern; a paradigm structures thought about an area of inquiry.

peace building Postconflict actions, predominantly diplomatic and economic, that strengthen and rebuild governmental infrastructure and institutions in order to avoid renewed recourse to armed conflict.

peace enforcement The application of military force to warring parties, or the threat of its use, normally pursuant to international authorization, to compel compliance with resolutions or with sanctions designed to maintain or restore peace and order.

peace operations A general category encompassing both peacekeeping and peace enforcement operations undertaken to establish and maintain peace between disputants.

peaceful coexistence Soviet leader Nikita Khrushchev's 1956 doctrine that war between capitalist and communist states is not inevitable and that inter-bloc competition could be peaceful.

peacekeeping The efforts by third parties such as the UN to intervene in civil wars and/or interstate wars or to prevent hostilities between potential belligerents from escalating, so that by acting as a buffer a negotiated settlement of the dispute can be reached.

peacemaking The process of diplomacy, mediation, negotiation or other forms of peaceful settlement that arranges an end to a dispute and resolves the issues that led to conflict.

podcasting To Thomas Friedman, "the technology that enables individuals to produce their own poetry and songs, videos and photos, and upload them onto a podcasting Web site, and then offer this content to anyone who wants to sample it."

polarity The degree to which military and economic capabilities are concentrated in the global system that determines the number of centers of power, or "poles."

polarization The formation of competing coalitions or blocs composed of allies that align with one of the major competing poles, or centers, of power.

policy agenda The changing list of problems or issues to which governments pay special attention at any given moment.

policy networks Leaders and organized interests (such as lobbies) that form temporary alliances to influence a particular foreign policy decision.

political economy A field of study that focuses on the intersection of politics and economics in international relations.

political efficacy The extent to which policy makers' self-confidence instills in them the belief that they can effectively make rational choices.

political integration The processes and activities by which the populations of many or all states transfer their loyalties to a merged political and economic unit.

politics To Harold Lasswell, the study of "who gets what, when, how, and why."

politics of scarcity The view that the unavailability of resources required to sustain life, such as food, energy, or water, can undermine security in degrees similar to military aggression.

pooled sovereignty Legal authority granted to an IGO by its members to make collective decisions regarding specified aspects of public policy heretofore made exclusively by each sovereign government.

population density The number of people within each country, region, or city, measuring the geographical concentration of the population as a ratio of the average space available for each resident.

population implosion A rapid reduction of population that reverses a previous trend toward progressively larger populations; a severe reduction in the world's population.

positivist legal theory A theory that stresses states' customs and habitual ways of behaving as the most important source of law.

postmodern terrorism To Walter Laqueur, the terrorism practiced by an expanding set of diverse actors with new weapons "to sow panic in a society to weaken or even overthrow the incumbents and to bring about political change."

power The factors that enable one actor to manipulate another actor's behavior against its preferences.

power balance A division of global military and economic capabilities among more than one center or dominant superpower.

power potential The capabilities or resources held by a state that are considered necessary to its asserting influence over others.

power transition A narrowing of the ratio of military capabilities between great-power rivals that is thought to increase the probability of war between them.

power transition theory The theory that war is likely when a dominant great power is threatened by the rapid growth of a rival's capabilities, which reduces the difference in their relative power.

preemption A quick, first-strike military attack in self defense to prevent an aggressor from launching a war of aggression, for which there is overwhelming evidence that the aggressor's threat is real and imminent or about to be undertaken.

preemptive war A quick first-strike attack that seeks to defeat an adversary before it can organize an initial attack or a retaliatory response.

preventive diplomacy Diplomatic actions taken in advance of a predictable crisis to prevent or limit violence.

preventive war Strictly outlawed by international law, a war undertaken by choice against an enemy to prevent it from suspected intentions to attack sometime in the distant future—if and when the enemy might acquire the necessary military capabilities.

Prisoner's Dilemma From game theory, a non-zero-sum situation in which two prisoners have incentives to cooperate and if they do they will both benefit, so that is the rational decision to make; however, if one defects to maximize personal gain at the expense of the other prisoner, both will suffer—a dilemma that raises questions about what is the prudent or rational course of action in circumstances of distrust.

private military services The outsourcing of activities of a military-specific nature to private companies, such as armed security, equipment maintenance, IT services, logistics, and intelligence services.

private international law Law pertaining to routine transnational intercourse between or among states as well as non-state actors.

proliferation The spread of weapon capabilities from a few to many states in a chain reaction, so that an increasing number of states gain the ability to launch an attack on other states with devastating (e.g., nuclear) weapons.

prospect theory The social psychological theory that international decision making is constrained by formed opinions and tendencies to overreact in crises, that decisions tend to be made based on the perceived prospects of choices to fulfill objectives, and that for policy makers, a crucial consideration in taking risks is the perceived prospects for avoiding losses and realizing big gains.

protectionism Barriers of foreign trade, such as tariffs and quotas, that protect local industries from competition for the purchase of products local manufacturers produce.

public international law Law pertaining to government-to-government relations as well as countries' relations with other types of transnational actors.

purchasing power parity (PPP) An index that calculates the true rate of exchange among currencies when parity—when what can be purchased is the same—is

achieved; the index determines what can be bought with a unit of each currency.

R

rapprochement In diplomacy, a policy seeking to reestablish normal cordial relations between enemies.

rational choice Decision-making procedures guided by careful definition of situations, weighing of goals, consideration of all alternatives, and selection of the options most likely to achieve the highest goals.

Reagan Doctrine A U.S. promise to support anticommunist insurgents attempting to overthrow governments backed by the Soviet Union.

realism A paradigm based on the premise that world politics is essentially and unchangeably a struggle among self-interested states for power and position under anarchy, with each competing state pursuing its own national interests.

realpolitik The theoretical outlook prescribing that countries should increase their power and wealth in order to compete with and dominate other countries.

reciprocity The return of favors for favors or punishment for punishment between parties in a mutual exchange relationship.

refugees People who flee for safety to another country because of a well-founded fear of political persecution, environmental degradation, or famine.

regimes The rules agreed upon by states to work together to manage shared problems, because long term benefits to all are expected even though short-term relative losses may be encountered.

regional collective defense regimes Collective security agreements by members of a geographic region to join together to prevent armed aggression by an expansionist state.

regional currency union The pooling of sovereignty to create a common currency (such as the EU's euro) and single monetary system for members in a region, regulated by a regional central bank within the currency bloc to reduce the likelihood of large-scale liquidity crises.

regional trade agreements (RTAs) Sometimes called preferential trade agreements, RTAs are treaties among members of a trade bloc that establish special advantageous reductions of trade barriers to members but permit discrimination tariffs against nonmembers.

relative burden of military spending Measure of the economic burden of military activities calculated by the share of each state's gross domestic product allocated to military expenditures.

relative deprivation Inequality between the wealth and status of individuals and groups, and the outrage of those at the bottom about their perceived exploitation by those at the top.

relative gains The benefits some participants in an exchange receive that are larger than the benefits of the other participants.

remittances The money earned by immigrants working in rich countries (which almost always exceeds the income they could earn working in their home country) that they send to their families in their country.

rents Higher-than-normal financial returns on investments that are realized from governmental restrictive interference or monopolistic markets.

replacement-level fertility One couple replacing themselves on average with two children so that a country's population will remain stable if this rate prevails.

reprisals The international legal practice of resorting to military force short of war in retaliation for losses suffered from prior illegal military actions.

retorsion Retaliatory acts (such as economic sanctions) against a target's behavior that is regarded as objectionable but legal (such as trade restrictions) to punish the target with measures that are legal under international law.

revolution in military technology (RMT) The sophisticated new weapons technologies that make fighting war without mass armies possible.

roles The constraints written into law or custom that predispose decision makers in a particular governmental position to act in a manner and style that is consistent with expectations about how the role is normally performed.

S

sanctions Punitive actions (short of military force) by one global actor against another to retaliate for its previous objectionable behavior.

sanctuary A place of refuge and protection.

satisficing The tendency for decision makers to choose the first satisfactory option rather than searching further for a better alternative.

schematic reasoning The process of reasoning by which new information is interpreted according to a memory structure, a schema, which contains a network of generic scripts, metaphors, and simplified characterizations of observed objects and phenomena.

secession, or separative revolts A religious or ethnic minority's efforts, often by violent means, to gain independent statehood by separating territory from an established sovereign state.

Second World During the Cold War, the group of countries, including the Soviet Union, its (then) Eastern European allies, and China, that embraced communism and central planning to propel economic growth.

second-strike capability A state's capacity to retaliate after absorbing an adversary's first-strike attack with weapons of mass destruction.

security community A group of states whose high level of institutionalized or customary collaboration results in the settlement of disputes by compromise rather than by military force.

security dilemma The tendency of states to view the defensive arming of adversaries as threatening, causing them to arm in response, so that all states' security declines.

security regime Norms and rules for interaction agreed to by a set of states to increase security.

selective engagement A state's or an IGO's choosing to intervene militarily in some situations but declining to do so in others.

self-determination The liberal doctrine that people should be able to determine the government that will manage their affairs.

self-fulfilling prophecy The tendency for one's expectations to evoke behavior that helps to make the expectations become true.

self-help The principle that because in international anarchy all global actors are independent, they must rely on themselves to provide for their security and well-being.

semiperiphery To world-system theorists, countries midway between the rich "core" or center, and the poor "periphery" in the global hierarchy, at which foreign investments are targeted when labor wages and production costs become too high in the prosperous core regions.

size principle The propensity for competitors to form coalitions among a number of partners only sizable enough to ensure victory, even if by a narrow margin, with the result that opposed alliances tend to remain roughly equal to one another over time.

smart bombs Precision-guided military technology that enables a bomb to search for its target and detonate at the precise time it can do the most damage.

socialization The processes by which people learn to accept the beliefs, values, and behaviors that prevail in a given society's culture.

soft power The capacity to co-opt through such intangible factors as the popularity of a state's values and institutions, as opposed to the "hard power" to coerce through military might.

sovereign equality The principle that states are legally equal in protection under international law.

sovereignty The legal doctrine that states have supreme authority to govern their internal affairs and manage their foreign relations with other states and non-state actors.

sphere of influence A region of the globe dominated by a great power.

spillaround The stagnation or encapsulation of regional integration as the costs of integration in one cooperative venture reduce efforts to try integration in other spheres of transaction.

spillback The reversal of previous steps toward integration, reducing the number of sectors in which integrating states are engaged in cooperative exchanges.

spillover The propensity for successful integration across one area of collaboration between states to propel further integration in other areas.

spiral model A metaphor used to describe the tendency of efforts to enhance defense to result in escalating arms races.

standard operating procedures (SOPS) Rules for reaching decisions about particular types of situations.

state An independent legal entity with a government exercising exclusive control over the territory and population it governs.

state level of analysis An analytical approach that emphasizes how the internal attributes of states influence their foreign policy behaviors.

state sovereignty A state's supreme authority to manage internal affairs and foreign relations.

state-sponsored terrorism Formal assistance, training, and arming of foreign terrorists by a state in order to achieve foreign policy and/or domestic goals.

statehood The legal criteria by which a country and its government become a state in the global community.

statelessness The growing band of people who have no citizenship rights in any country and are forced out of one country and not accepted in any other.

states' attributes State characteristics that shape foreign policy behavior, such as its size, wealth, and the extent to which its leaders are accountable to its citizens in comparison with other states:

Strategic Arms Limitation Talks (SALT) Two sets of agreements reached during the 1970s between the United States and the Soviet Union that established limits on strategic nuclear delivery systems.

Strategic Arms Reduction Treaty (START) The U.S.–Russian series of negotiations that began in 1993 and, with the 1997 START-III agreement ratified by Russia in 2000, pledged to cut the nuclear arsenals of both sides by 80 percent of the Cold War peaks, in order to lower the risk of nuclear war.

strategic corporate alliances Cooperation between multinational corporations and foreign companies in the same industry, driven by the movement of MNC manufacturing overseas.

Strategic Defense Initiative (SDI) The so-called Star Wars plan conceived by the Reagan administration to seek to deploy an antiballistic missile system using space-based lasers that would destroy enemy nuclear missiles before they could reenter the Earth's atmosphere.

Strategic Offensive Reductions Treaty (SORT) The U.S.–Russian agreement to reduce the number of strategic warheads to between 1,700 and 2,200 for each country by 2012.

strategic trade policy Government subsidies for particular domestic industries to help them gain competitive advantages over foreign producers.

strategic weapons Weapons of mass destruction that are carried on intercontinental ballistic missiles (ICBMs), submarine-launched ballistic missiles (SLBM)s, or long-range bombers and are capable of annihilating an enemy state.

structural realism The neorealist theory postulating that the structure of the global system determines the behavior of transnational actors within it.

structural violence The condition defined by the Norwegian peace researcher Johan Galtung as the harm and injury caused by the global system's unregulated structure, which gives strong states great opportunities to victimize weak states that cannot protect themselves.

structuralism The neorealist proposition that states' behavior is shaped primarily by changes in the properties of the global system, such as shifts in the balance of power, instead by individual heads of states or by changes in states' internal characteristics.

summed dyads The dyadic relationships between various actors that is based upon their foreign policies and toward each other and the acts that are a result of those relationships.

survival of the fittest A realist concept derived from Charles Darwin's theory of evolution that advises that ruthless competition is ethically acceptable to survive, even if the actions violate moral commands not to kill.

sustainable development Economic growth that does not deplete the resources needed to maintain life and prosperity.

T

tariffs Tax assessed on goods as they are imported into a country.

territorial imperative The term coined by anthropologist Robert Ardrey to popularize the proposition that people and countries will defend to the death their territory, just like animals instinctively do.

terrorism Premeditated violence perpetrated against noncombatant targets by subnational or transnational groups or clandestine agents, usually intended to influence an audience.

the singularity A future phenomenon that will occur when machine intelligence surpasses human intelligence.

theocracy A country whose government is organized around a religious dogma.

theory A set of hypotheses postulating the relationship between variables or conditions advanced to describe, explain, or predict phenomena and make prescriptions about how positive changes ought to be engineered to realize particular goals and ethical principles.

Third Way An approach to governance advocated primarily by many European leaders who, while recognizing few alternatives to liberal capitalism, seek to soften the cruel social impact of free-market individualism by progressively allowing government intervention to preserve social justice and the rights of individuals to freedom from fear of the deprivations caused by disruptions in the global economy.

Third World A Cold War term to describe the less-developed countries of Africa, Asia, the Caribbean, and Latin America.

tit-for-tat strategy A bargaining approach that consistently reciprocates in kind the offers or threats made by the other party in a negotiation, with equivalent rewards returned and equivalent punishing communications returned in retaliation.

trade integration The difference between gross rates in trade and gross domestic product.

tragedy of the commons A metaphor, widely used to explain the impact of human behavior on ecological systems, that explains how rational self-interested behavior by individuals may have a destructive collective impact.

transformation A change in the characteristic pattern of interaction among the most active participants in world politics of such magnitude that it appears that one "global system" has replaced another.

transgenetic crops New crops with improved characteristics created artificially through genetic engineering that combine genes from species that would not naturally interbreed.

transnational banks (TNBs) The globe's top banking firms, whose financial activities are concentrated in transactions that cross state borders.

transnational norms The regular customs widely practiced by countries in their relations with other countries and the kinds of behavior that the international community accepts as what is to be practiced.

transnational relations Interactions across state boundaries that involves at least one actor that is not the agent of a government or intergovernmental organization.

transnational religious movements A set of beliefs, practices, and ideas administered politically by religious organizations to promote the worship of their conception of a transcendent deity and its principles for conduct.

Truman Doctrine The declaration by President Harry S. Truman that U.S. foreign policy would use intervention to support peoples who allied with the United States against communist external subjugation.

two-level games A concept referring to the growing need for national policy makers to make decisions that will meet both domestic and foreign goals.

U

ultimatum A demand that puts a time limit for the target to comply and a threat of punishment for resistance.

underemployment A condition critics trace to trade globalization in which a large portion of the labor force only works part time at low pay in occupations below its skill level.

unilateralism An approach that relies on self-help, independent strategies in foreign policy.

unipolarity A condition in which the global system has a single dominant power or hegemon capable of prevailing over all other states.

unitary actor A transnational actor (usually a sovereign state) assumed to be internally united, so that changes in its domestic opinion do not influence its foreign policy as much as do the decisions that actor's leaders make to cope with changes in its global environment.

United Nations Environment Programme (UNEP) A UN agency that studies environmental deterioration and proposes regulations to protect the global environment.

V

vertical nuclear proliferation The expansion of the capabilities of existing nuclear powers to inflict increasing destruction with their nuclear weapons.

virtual corporations Agreements between otherwise competitive MNCs, often temporary, to join forces and skills to coproduce and export particular products in the borderless global marketplace.

virtual nuclear arsenals The next generation of "near nuclear" military capabilities produced by the revolution in military technology that would put strategic nuclear weapons of mass destruction at the margins of national security strategies by removing dependence on them for deterrence.

virtuality Imagery created by computer technology of objects and phenomena that produces an imaginary picture of actual things, people, and experiences.

voluntary export restrictions (VERs) A protectionist measure popular in the

1980s and early 1990s, in which exporting countries agree to restrict shipments of a particular product to a country to deter it from imposing an even more burdensome import quota.

W

war A condition arising within states (civil war) or between states (interstate war) when actors use violent means to destroy their opponents or coerce them into submission.

war crimes Acts performed during war that the international community defines as crimes against humanity, including atrocities committed against an enemy's prisoners of war, civilians, or the state's own minority population.

war weariness hypothesis The proposition that fighting a major war is costly in terms of lost lives and income, and these costs greatly reduce a country's tolerance for undertaking another war until enough time passes to lose memory of those costs.

Washington consensus The view that Global South countries can best achieve sustained economic growth through democratic governance, fiscal discipline, free markets, a reliance on private enterprise, and trade liberalization.

World Bank Also known as the International Bank for Reconstruction and Development (IBRD), the World Bank is the globe's major IGO for financing economic growth and reducing poverty through long-term loans.

world federalism A reform movement proposing as a path to peace combining many or all previously independent countries into a single federal institution for global governance.

World Trade Organization (WTO) A multilateral agency that monitors the implementation of trade agreements and settles disputes among trade partners.

world-system theory A theory claiming that the perpetual and widening inequality among states is explained by capitalism's international division of labor and production, which over time allows the wealthy core countries to become richer while the peripheral states that supply raw materials and cheap labor become poorer.

X

xenophobia The suspicious dislike, disrespect, and disregard for members of a foreign nationality, ethnic, or linguistic group.

Y

Yalta Conference The 1945 summit meeting of the Allied victors to resolve postwar territorial issues and to establish voting procedures.

Yoshida Doctrine Japan's traditional security policy of avoiding disputes with rivals, preventing foreign wars by low military spending, and promoting economic growth through foreign trade.

Z

zeitgeist The "spirit of the times," or the dominant cultural norms assumed to influence the behavior of people living in particular periods.

zero-sum An exchange in a purely conflictual relationship in which what is gained by one competitor is lost by the other.

references

Aaronson, Susan Ariel. (2002) *Taking Trade to the Streets: The Lost History of Public Efforts to Shape Globalization.* Ann Arbor: University of Michigan Press.

Aaronson, Susan, and Jamie Zimmerman. (2007) *Trade Imbalance: The Struggle to Weigh Human Rights Concerns in Trade Policymaking.* Cambridge: Cambridge University Press.

Abdelal, Rawi, and Adam Segal. (2007) "Has Globalization Passed Its Peak?" *Foreign Affairs* 86 (January/February): 103–114.

Abouharb, Rodwan, and David Cingranelli. (2007) *Human Rights and Structural Adjustment.* New York: Cambridge University Press.

Abramowitz, Morton. (2002) "The Bush Team Isn't Coping," *International Herald Tribune* (August 20): 6.

Addo, Michael K. (ed.). (2005) *International Human Rights Law.* Burlington, Ver.: Ashgate.

Adelman, Kenneth L., and Norman R. Augustine. (1992) "Defense Conversion," *Foreign Affairs* 71 (Spring): 26–47.

Adler, Emanuel. (2002) "Constructivism and International Relations," pp. 95–118 in Walter Carlsnaes, Thomas Risse, and Beth Simmons (eds.), *Handbook of International Relations.* London: Sage.

Adler, Jerry. (2005) "How Big a Threat is the Avian Flu to the U.S.?" *Newsweek* (October 31): 38–45.

Agnew, John. (2007) "Know-Where: Geographies of Knowledge of World Politics," *International Political Sociology* 1 (June): 138–148.

Albert, Mathias. (2007) "'Globalization Theory': Yesterday's Fad or More Lively Than Ever?" *International Political Sociology* 1 (June): 165–182.

Albright, David. (1993) "A Proliferation Primer," *Bulletin of the Atomic Scientists* 49 (June): 14–23.

Albright, Madeleine K. (2005) "United Nations," pp. 219–23 in Helen E. Purkitt (ed.), *World Politics 04/05.* Dubuque, Iowa: McGraw-Hill/Dushkin.

———. (2000) "Time to Renew Faith in the Nonproliferation Treaty," *International Herald Tribune* (March 7): 8.

Alesina, Alberto, and Enrique Spolaore. (2003) *The Size of Nations.* Cambridge, Mass.: MIT Press.

Allen John L. (2006) *Student Atlas of World Politics,* 7th ed. Dubuque, Iowa: McGraw-Hill.

———. (2002) *Student Atlas of World Politics,* 5th ed. New York: Dushkin/McGraw-Hill.

———. (2001) *Student Atlas World Geography,* 2nd ed. New York: McGraw-Hill.

———. (2000) *Student Atlas of World Politics,* 4th ed. New York: Dushkin/McGraw-Hill.

Allen, John L., and Elizabeth J. Leppman. (2004) *Student Atlas of World Politics,* 6th ed. Guilford, Conn.: Dushkin/McGraw-Hill.

Allen, Susan Hannah. (2008) "Political Institutions and Constrained Response to Economic Sanctions," Foreign Policy Analysis (July): 255–274.

———. (2005) "The Determinants of Economic Sanctions Success and Failure," *International Interactions* 31 (April-June): 117–38.

Alley, Roderic. (2004) *Internal Conflict and the International Community: Wars Without End?* Burlington, Ver.: Ashgate.

Allison, Graham T. (2004) *Nuclear Terrorism: The Ultimate Preventable Catastrophe.* New York: Henry Holt.

———. (1971) *Essence of Decision: Explaining the Cuban Missile Crisis.* Boston: Little, Brown.

Allison, Graham T., and Philip Zelikow. (1999) *Essence of Decision: Explaining the Cuban Missile Crisis,* 2nd ed. New York: Longman.

Al-Samarrai, Bashir. (1995) "Economic Sanctions against Iraq," pp.133–39 in David Cortwright and George A. Lopez (eds.), *Economic Sanctions.* Boulder, Colo.: Westview.

Altman, Daniel. (2005) "China: Both a Powerhouse and a Pauper," *International Herald Tribune* (October 8–9): 16.

Altman, Lawrence K. (2002) "AIDS Is Called a Security Threat," *International Herald Tribune* (October 2): 1, 10.

Altman, Roger C., and C. Bowman Cutter. (1999) "Global Economy Needs Better Shock Absorbers," *International Herald Tribune* (June 16): 7.

Amoore, Louise (ed.). (2005) *The Global Resistance Reader: Concepts and Issues.* New York: Routledge.

Andreas, Peter. (2005) "The Criminalizing Consequences of Sanctions," *International Studies Quarterly* 49 (June): 335–60.

Angell, Norman. (1910) *The Grand Illusion: A Study of the Relationship of Military Power in Nations to Their Economic and Social Advantage.* London: Weidenfeld & Nicholson.

Annan, Kofi. (2006) "Courage to Fulfill Our Responsibilities," pp. 205–09 in Helen E. Purkitt (ed.), *World Politics 05/06.* Dubuque, Iowa: McGraw-Hill/Dushkin.

———. (1999) "Two Concepts of Sovereignty," *Economist* (September 18): 49–50.

Appiah, Kwame Anthony. (2006) *Cosopolitanism: Ethics in a World of Strangers.* New York: Norton.

Ardrey, Robert. (1966) *The Territorial Imperative: A Personal Inquiry into the Animal Origins of Property and Nations.* New York: Atheneum.

Ariely, Dan. (2008) *Predictably Irrational: The Hidden Forces that Shape our Decisions.* New York: Harper.

Arreguín-Toft, Ivan. (2006) *How the Weak Wins Wars: A Theory of Asymmetric Conflict.* New York: Cambridge University Press.

Art, Robert J. (2005) "Coercive Diplomacy," pp. 163–77 in Robert J. Art and Robert Jervis (eds.), *International Politics*, 7th ed. New York: Pearson Longman.

Ash, Timothy Garton. (2004) *Free World: America, Europe, and the Surprising Future of the West.* New York: Random House.

Auguste, Byron G. (1999) "What's So New about Globalization?" pp. 45–47 in Helen E. Purkitt (ed.), *World Politics 99/00*, 20th ed. Guilford, Conn.: Dushkin/McGraw-Hill.

Axelrod, Robert M. (1984) *The Evolution of Cooperation.* New York: Basic Books.

Ayoob, Mohammed. (2004) "Third World Perspectives on Humanitarian Intervention," *Global Governance* 10 (January-March): 99–18.

———. (1995) *The Third World Security Predicament.* Boulder, Colo.: Lynne Rienner.

Azios, Tony. (2007) "What Is It That Drives Terrorism?" *Christian Science Monitor* (August 28): 1, 17.

Babai, Don. (2001) "International Monetary Fund," pp. 412–18 in Joel Krieger (ed.), *The Oxford Companion to Politics of the World*, 2nd ed. Oxford: Oxford University Press.

Babones, Jonathan, and Jonathan H. Turner. (2004) "Global Inequality," pp. 101–20 in George Ritzer (ed.), *Handbook of Social Problems.* London: Sage.

Bacevich, Andrew J. (2005). *The New American Militarism: How Americans Are Seduced by War.* New York: Oxford University Press.

———. (ed.). (2003) *The Imperial Tense.* Chicago: Ivan R. Dee/Rowman & Littlefield.

———. (2002) *American Empire.* Cambridge, Mass.: Harvard University Press.

Badey, Thomas J. (ed.). (2005) *Violence and Terrorism 05/06*, 8th ed. Guilford, Conn.: Dushkin/McGraw-Hill.

Baines, Erin K. (2004) *Vulnerable Bodies: Gender, the UN, and the Global Refugee Crisis.* Burlington, Ver.: Ashgate.

Bakke, Kristen M. (2005) "Clash of Civilizations or Clash of Religions?" *International Studies Review* 7 (March): 87–89.

Baker, Aryn, and Kajaki Olya. (2008) "A War That's Still Not Won," *Time* (July 7): 37–43.

Baldwin, David A. (2000) "The Sanctions Debate and the Logic of Choice," *International Security* 24 (Winter): 80–107.

———. (ed.). (1993) *Neorealism and Neoliberalism: The Contemporary Debate.* New York: Columbia University Press.

Baldwin, David A. (1989) *Paradoxes of Power.* New York: Basil Blackwell.

Bamford, James. (2005) *A Pretext for War: 9/11, Iraq, and the Abuse of America's Intelligence Agencies.* New York: Anchor Vintage.

Bandy, Joe, and Jackie Smith. (2004). *Coalitions Across Borders: Transnational Protest and the Neoliberal Order.* Lanham, Md: Rowman & Littlefield.

Baratta, Joseph Preston. (2005) *The Politics of World Federation.* New York: Praeger.

Barber, Benjamin R. (2003) *Fear's Empire.* New York: Norton.

———. (1995) *Jihad vs. McWorld.* New York: Random House.

Barbieri, Katherine. (2003) *The Liberal Illusion: Does Trade Promote Peace?* Ann Arbor: University of Michigan Press.

Barbieri, Katherine, and Gerald Schneider. (1999) "Globalization and Peace," *Journal of Peace Research* 36 (July): 387–404.

Barboza, David. (2005) "For China, New Malls Jaw-Dropping in Size," *International Herald Tribune* (May 25): 1, 4.

Bardhan, Pranab. (2005) "Giants Unchained? Not So Fast," *International Herald Tribune* (November 3): 6.

Barkin, Samuel. (2003) "Realist Constructivism," *International Studies Review* 5 (September): 328–42.

———. (2001) "Resilience of the State," *Harvard International Review* 22 (Winter): 40–46.

Barnes, Joe, Amy Jaffe, and Edward L. Morse. (2004) "The New Geopolitics of Oil," *National Interest* (Winter/Energy Supplement): 3–6.

Barnet, Michael. (2005) "Social Constructivism," pp. 251–270 in John Baylis and Steve Smith (eds.), The Globalization of World Politics, 3rd ed. New York: Oxford University Press.

Barnet, Richard J. (1980) *The Lean Years.* New York: Simon & Schuster.

———. (1977) *The Giants: Russia and America.* New York: Simon & Schuster.

Barnet, Richard J., and John Cavanagh. (1994) *Global Dreams: Imperial Corporations and the New World Order.* New York: Simon & Schuster.

Barnet, Richard J., and Ronald E. Müller. (1974) *Global Reach: The Power of the Multinational Corporations.* New York: Simon & Schuster.

Barnett, Michael. (2005) "Social Constructivism," pp. 251–70 in John Baylis and Steve Smith (eds.), *The Globalization of World Politics*, 3rd ed. New York: Oxford University Press.

Barnett, Michael, and Martha Finnemore. (2004) *Rules for the World: International Organizations in Global Politics.* Ithaca, N.Y.: Cornell University Press.

Barnett, Thomas P. M. (2004) *The Pentagon's New Map.* New York: G. P. Putnam's Sons.

Bar-On, Tamir, and Howard Goldstein. (2005) "Fighting Violence: A Critique of the War on Terrorism," *International Politics* 42 (June): 225–45.

Baron, Samuel H., and Carl Pletsch (eds.). (1985) *Introspection in Biography.* Hillsdale, N.J.: Analytic Press.

Barrett, Scott. (2007) *Why Cooperate? The Incentive to Supply Global Public Goods.* New York: Oxford University Press.

Baylis, John, and Steve Smith (eds.). (2005) *The Globalization of World Politics*, 3rd ed. New York: Oxford University Press.

Bayne, Nicholas, and Stephen Woolcock (eds.). (2004) *The New Economic Diplomacy.* Burlington, Ver.: Ashgate.

Becker, Elizabeth. (2003) "W.T.O. Rules Against U.S. On Steel Tariff," *The New York Times* (March 27).

Beckman, Peter R., and Francine D'Amico (eds.). (1994) *Women, Gender, and World Politics.* Westport, Conn.: Bergin & Garvey.

Beddoes, Zanny Minton. (2005) "The Great Thrift Shift," *Economist* (September 24): 3.

Begley, Sharon. (2008) "Global Warming is a Cause of This Year's Extreme Weather," *Newsweek* (July 7/14): 53.

———. (2007) "Get Out Your Handkerchiefs," *Newsweek* (June 4): 62.

Behe, Michael J. (2005) "Rationalism and Reform," *First Things* (August-September): 75–79.

Beitz, Charles R. (2001) "Human Rights as a Common Concern," *American Political Science Review* 95 (June): 269–82.

Bell, James John. (2006) "Exploring the 'Singularity'," pp. 207–10 in Robert M. Jackson (ed.), *Global Issues 05/06*. Dubuque, Iowa: McGraw-Hill/Dushkin.

Bellamy, Alex J., and Paul D. Williams. (2005) "Who's Keeping the Peace?" *International Security* 29 (Spring): 157–97.

Benhabib, Seyla. (2005) "On the Alleged Conflict Between Democracy and International Law," *Ethics and International Affairs* 19 (No. 1): 85–100.

Benner, Thorsten, Stephan Mergenthaler, and Philipp Rotman. (2008) "Rescuing the Blue Helmets," International Herald Tribune (July 23): 6.

Bennett, Scott, and Allan C. Stam. (2004) *The Behavioral Origins of War*. Ann Arbor: University of Michigan Press.

Benson, Michelle. (2007) "Extending the Bounds of Power Transition Theory," *International Interactions* 33 (July/September): 211–215.

Ben-Yehuda, Hemda, and Meirav Mishali-Ran. (2006) "Ethnic Actors and International Crises," *International Interactions* 32 (January/March): 49–78.

Berdal, Mats, and Mónica Serrano (eds.). (2002) *Transnational Organized Crime and International Security*. Boulder, Colo.: Lynne Rienner.

Bergen, Peter L. (2006) *The Osama bin Laden I Know*. New York: Free Press.

Berger, Peter L., and Samuel P. Huntington (eds.). (2002) *Many Globalizations: Cultural Diversity in the Contemporary World*. Oxford: Oxford University Press.

Berger, Peter, and Thomas Luckmann. (1967) *The Social Construction of Reality*. New York: Anchor.

Bergesen, Albert, and Ronald Schoenberg. (1980) "Long Waves of Colonial Expansion and Contraction, 1415–1969," pp. 231–77 in Albert Bergesen (ed.), *Studies of the Modern World-System*. New York: Academic Press.

Bergsten, C. Fred. (2005) *The United States and the World Economy*. Washington, D.C.: Institute of International Economics.

———. (2004) "The Risks Ahead for the World Economy," *Economist* (September 11): 63–65.

Bernstein, Richard. (2003) "Aging Europe Finds its Pension is Running Out," *New York Times International* (June 29): 3.

Berthelot, Yves. (2001) "The International Financial Architecture—Plans for Reform," *International Social Science Journal* 170 (December): 586–96.

Bhagwati, Jagdish. (2005) "A Chance to Lift the 'Aid Curse,'" *Wall Street Journal* (March 22): A14.

———. (2004) *In Defense of Globalization*. New York: Oxford University Press.

Bijian, Zheng. (2005) "China's 'Peaceful Rise' to Great-Power Status," *Foreign Affairs* 84 (October): 18–24.

Bishop, William. (1962) *International Law*. Boston Little, Brown.

Blainey, Geoffrey. (1988) *The Causes of War*, 3rd ed. New York: Free Press.

Blake, Mariah. (2008) "Europe Ratchets Up its Pressure on Immigrants," *The Christian Science Monitor* (June 20): 1.

Blanton, Robert G., and Shannon Lindsey Blanton. (2007) "Human Rights and Trade," *International Interactions* 33 (April/June): 97–117.

Blanton, Shannon Lindsey. (2005) "Foreign Policy in Transition? Human Rights, Democracy, and U.S. Arms Exports," *International Studies Quarterly* 49 (December): 647–67.

———. (1999) "Instruments of Security or Tools of Repression? Arms Imports and Human Rights Conditions in Developing Countries," *Journal of Peace Research* 36 (March): 233–244.

Blanton, Shannon Lindsey, and Charles W. Kegley, Jr. (1997) "Reconciling U.S. Arms Sales with America's Interests and Ideals," *Futures Research Quarterly* 13 (Spring): 85–101.

Bloom, Mia. (2005) *Dying to Kill: The Allure of Suicide Terror*. New York: Columbia University Press.

Blum, Andrew, Victor Asal, and Jonathan Wilkenfeld (eds.). (2005) "Nonstate Actors, Terrorism, and Weapons of Mass Destruction," *International Studies Review* 7 (March): 133–70.

Blumenthal, W. Michael. (1988) "The World Economy and Technological Change," *Foreign Affairs* 66 (No 3): 529–50.

Boot, Max. (2006) *War Made New*. New York: Gothan.

Boehmer, Charles, Erik Gartzke, and Timothy Norstrom. (2005) "Do International Organizations Promote Peace?" *World Politics* 57 (October): 1–38.

Boin, Arjen, Paul 't Hart, Eric Stern, and Bengt Sunderlius. (2007) *The Politics of Crisis Management*. Cambridge, U.K.: Cambridge University Press.

Boli, John, Michael A. Elliott and Franziska Bieri. (2004) "Globalization," pp. 389–415 in George Ritzer (ed.), *Handbook of Social Problems*. London: Sage.

Boli, John, and Frank L. Lechner. (2004) *World Culture*. London: Blackwell.

Bolton, M. Kent. (2005) *U.S. Foreign Policy and International Politics: George W. Bush, 9/11, and the Global-Terrorist Hydra*. Upper Saddle River, N.J.: Prentice Hall.

Borenstein, Seth. (2006) "Pentagon Accused of Wasteful Spending," *The Idaho Statesman* (January 24): Main 3.

———. (2005) "Mankind is Using Up the Earth, Scientists Say," Columbia, S.C., *The State* (March 30): A8.

———. (2003) "U.S. to Revive Dormant Nuclear-Power Industry," Columbia, S.C., *The State* (June 16): A5.

Borer, Douglas A., and James D. Bowen. (2007) "Rethinking the Cuban Embargo," *Foreign Policy Analysis* 3 (April): 127–143.

Borgerson, Scott G. (2008) "Arctic Meltdown: The Economic and Security Implications of Global Warming," *Foreign Affairs* 87 (2): 63–77.

Bostdorff, Denise M. (1993) *The Presidency and the Rhetoric of Foreign Crisis.* Columbia: University of South Carolina Press.

Boswell, Terry. (1989) "Colonial Empires and the Capitalist World-Economy," *American Sociological Review* 54 (April): 180–96.

Bowring, Philip. (2005) "Russian-Chinese Maneuvers Send a Message," *International Herald Tribune* (August 21–22): 5.

———. (2004) "Echoes of Panic over Global Disease," *International Herald Tribune* (February 18): 7.

———. (2001) "Thinking at Cross-Purposes about Globalization," *International Herald Tribune* (February 1): 8.

Boyle, Francis A. (2004) *Destroying World Order.* London: Clarity/Zed.

Bozeman, Adda B. (1994) *Politics and Culture in International History.* New Brunswick, N.J.: Transaction.

Brams, Steven J. (1985) *Rational Politics: Decisions, Games, and Strategy.* Washington, D.C.: CQ Press.

Braudel, Fernand. (1973) *The Mediterranean and the Mediterranean World at the Age of Philip II.* New York: Harper.

Braveboy-Wagner, Jacqueline Anne (ed.). (2003) *The Foreign Policies of the Global South.* Boulder, Colo.: Lynne Rienner.

Brecke, Peter. (1999) "The Characteristics of Violent Conflict since 1400 A.D.," paper presented at the annual meeting of the International Studies Association, Washington, D.C., February 17–20.

Breitmeier, Helmut. (2005) *The Legitimacy of International Regimes.* Burlington, Ver.: Ashgate.

Bremer, Ian. (2007) *The J Curve: A New Way to Understand Why Nations Rise and Fall.* New York: Simon and Schuster.

Bremer, Stuart A. (2000) "Who Fights Whom, When, Where, and Why?" pp. 23–36 in John A. Vasquez (ed.), *What Do We Know About War?* Lanham, Md.: Rowman & Littlefield.

Brinkley, Joel. (2005) "As Nations Lobby to Join Security Council, U.S. Resists Giving Them Veto Power," *New York Times International* (May 15): 12.

Broad, Robin (ed.). (2002) *Global Backlash: Citizen Initiatives for a Just World Economy.* Lanham, Md.: Rowman & Littlefield.

Broad, William J. (2005) "U.S. Has Plans to Again Make Own Plutonium," *New York Times* (June 27): A1, A13.

Broder, David. (2002) "Senator Brings Vietnam Experiences to Bear on Iraq," Columbia, S.C., *The State* (September 18): A15.

———. (1999) "Global Forces May Change Balance between States and Federal Government," Columbia, S.C., *The State* (August 11): A9.

Brody, William R. (2007) "College Goes Global," *Foreign Affairs* 56 (March/April): 122–133.

Bronfenbrenner, Urie. (1961) "The Mirror Image in Soviet-American Relations," *Journal of Social Issues* 17 (No. 3): 45–56.

Brooks, David. (2007) "The Entitlements People," Columbia, S.C., *The State* (October 2): A7.

———. (2005a) "Hunch Power," *New York Times Book Review* (January 16): 1, 12–13.

———. (2005b) "Our Better Understanding of Who the Terrorists Are," Columbia, S.C., *The State* (August 6): A11.

Brooks, Doug, and Gaurav Laroia. (2005) "Privatized Peacekeeping," *The National Interest* 80 (Summer): 121–25.

Brown, John. (2006) "Beyond Kyoto," pp. 209–13 in Helen E. Purkitt (ed.), *World Politics 05/06.* Dubuque, Iowa: McGraw-Hill/Dushkin.

Brown, Justin. (1999) "Arms Sales: Exporting U.S. Military Edge?" *Christian Science Monitor* (December 2): 2.

Brown, Lester R. (2006) "Deflating the World's Bubble Economy," pp. 35–38 in Robert M. Jackson (ed.), *Global Issues 05/06.* Dubuque, Iowa: McGraw-Hill/Dushkin.

———. (2002) "Planning for the Eco-economy," *USA Today* (March): 31–35.

Brown, Lester R., and Brian Halweil. (1999) "How Can the World Create Enough Jobs for Everyone?" *International Herald Journal* (September 9): 9.

Brown, Stuart S. (2006) "Can Remittances Spur Development?" *International Studies Review* 8 (March): 55–75.

Brundtland, Gro Harlem. (2003) "The Globalization of Health," *Seton Hall Journal of Diplomacy and International Relations* (Summer-Fall): 7–12.

Brunk, Darren C. (2008) "Curing the Somalia Syndrome: Analogy, Foreign Policy Decision Making, and the Rwandan Genocide," *Foreign Policy Analysis* 4 (July): 301–320.

Brzezinski, Zbigniew. (2005) "George W. Bush's Suicidal Statecraft," *International Herald Tribune* (October 14): 6.

———. (2004) *The Choice: Global Domination or Global Leadership.* New York: Basic Books/Perseus.

Bueno de Mesquita, Bruce. (1975) "Measuring Systemic Polarity," *Journal of Conflict Resolution* 22 (June): 187–216.

Bueno de Mesquita, Bruce, and George W. Downs. (2005) "Development and Democracy," *Foreign Affairs* 84 (September/October): 77–86.

Bueno de Mesquita, Bruce, George W. Downs, and Alastair Smith. (2005) "Thinking Inside the Box: A Closer Look at Democracy and Human Rights," *International Studies Quarterly* 49 (September): 439–57.

Bueno de Mesquita, Bruce, James D. Morrow, Randolph M. Siverson, and Alastair Smith. (2004) "Testing Novel Implications from the Selectorate Theory of War," *World Politics* 56 (April): 363–88.

Bull, Hedley. (2002) *The Anarchical Society: A Study of Order in World Politics,* 3rd ed. New York: Columbia University Press.

Burke, Anthony. (2005) "Against the New Internationalism," *Ethics and International Affairs* 19 (No. 2, Special Issue): 73–89.

Buruma, Ian. (2005) "The Indiscreet Charm of Tyranny," *New York Review of Books* 52 (May 12): 35–37.

Bussmann, Margit, and Gerald Schneider. (2007) "When Globalization Discontent Turns Violent: Foreign Economic Liberalization and Internal War," *International Studies Quarterly* 51 (March): 79–97.

Buzan, Barry. (2005) "The Dangerous Complacency of Democratic Peace," *International Studies Review* 7 (June): 292–93.

Buzan, Barry, and Gerald Segal. (1998) *Anticipating the Future.* London: Simon & Schuster.

Buzan, Barry, and Ole Weaver. (2003) *Regimes of Power.* Cambridge: Cambridge University Press.

Byers, Michael, and George Nolte (eds.). (2003) *United States Hegemony and the Foundations of International Law.* New York: Columbia University Press.

Byman, Daniel. (2005) *Deadly Connections: States That Sponsor Terrorism.* Cambridge: Cambridge University Press.

Caldwell, Christopher. (2004) "Select All: Can You Have Too Many Choices?" *New Yorker* (March): 91–93.

Caldwell, Dan, and Robert E. Williams, Jr. (2006) *Seeking Security in an Insecure World.* Lanham, Md.: Rowman & Littlefield.

Calvocoressi, Peter, Guy Wint, and John Pritchard. (1989) *Total War: The Causes and Courses of the Second World War,* 2nd ed. New York: Pantheon.

Campbell, Ian. (2004) "Retreat from Globalization," *National Interest* 75 (Spring): 111–17.

Canton, James. (2007) *The Extreme Future.* New York Penguin.

Caporaso, James A. (1993) "Global Political Economy," pp. 451–481 in Ada W. Finifter (ed.), *Political Science: The State of the Discipline II.* Washington, D.C.: American Political Science Association.

Caporaso, James A., and David P. Levine. (1992) *Theories of Political Economy.* New York: University Press.

Caprioli, Mary. (2005) "Primed for Violence: The Role of Gender Inequality in Predicting International Conflict," *International Studies Quarterly* 49 (June): 161–78.

———. (2004) "Feminist IR Theory and Quantitative Methodology," *International Studies Review* 6 (June): 253–69.

Carment, David. (1993) "The International Dimensions of Ethnic Conflict," *Journal of Peace Research* 30 (May): 137–50.

Carpenter, R. Charli. (2005) "Women, Children and Other Vulnerable Groups: Genders, Strategic Frames, and the Protection of Civilians as a Transnational Issue," *International Studies Quarterly* 49 (June): 295–334.

Carpenter, Ted Galen. (1991) "The New World Disorder," *Foreign Policy* 84 (Fall): 24–39.

Carpenter, Ted Galen, and Charles V. Peña. (2005) "Re-Thinking Non-Proliferation," *The National Interest* 80 (Summer): 81–92.

Carr, E. H. (1939) *The Twenty-Years' Crisis, 1919–1939.* London: Macmillan.

Carter, Jimmy. (2005) *Our Endangered Values: America's Moral Crisis.* New York: Simon and Schuster.

Carty, Anthony. (2008) "Marxist International Law Theory as Hegelianism," *International Studies Review* 10 (March): 122–125.

Caryl, Christian. (2005) "Why They Do It," *New York Review of Books* 52 (September 22): 28–32.

Casetti, Emilio. (2003) "Power Shifts and Economic Development: When Will China Overtake the USA?" *Journal of Peace Research* 40 (November): 661–75.

Cashman, Greg, and Leonard C. Robinson. (2007) *An Introduction to the Causes of War.* Lanham, Md.: Rowman & Littlefield.

Caspary, William R. (1993) "New Psychoanalytic Perspectives on the Causes of War," *Political Psychology* 14 (September): 417–46.

Cassese, Antonio, and Andrew Clapham. (2001) "International Law," pp. 408–11 in Joel Krieger (ed.), *The Oxford Companion to Politics of the World,* 2nd ed. Oxford: Oxford University Press.

Cassidy, John. (2005) "Always with US?" *New Yorker* (April 11): 72–77.

Cassis, Youssef. (2007) *Capitals of Capital.* New York: Cambridge University Press.

Castles, Stephen, and Mark Miller. (2004) *The Age of Migration,* 3rd ed. London: Palgrave Macmillan.

Cavallo, Alfred. (2004) "Oil: The Illusion of Plenty," *Bulletin of the Atomic Scientists* (January-February): 20–22, 70.

CCEIA (Carnegie Council for Ethics in International Affairs). (2005) *Human Rights Dialogue.* Carnegie Council for Ethics in International Affairs, Series 2 (Spring) 1–34.

Cederman, Lars-Erik, and Kristian Skrede Gleditsch. (2004) "Conquest and Regime Change," *International Studies Quarterly* 48 (September): 603–29.

Center for World Indigenous Studies. (2005) *The State of Indigenous People.* Olympia, Wash.: Center for World Indigenous Studies.

Central Intelligence Agency. (2002) *Global Trends 2015.* Washington, D.C.: Central Intelligence Agency.

———. (2001) *Handbook of International Economic Statistics 2000.* Langley, Va.: Central Intelligence Agency.

Cetron, Marvin J. (2007) "Defeating Terrorism," *The Futurist* (May/June): 17–25.

Cetron, Martin J., and Owen Davies. (2005) *53 Trends Now Shaping the Future.* Bethesda, Md.: World Future Society.

CGD/FP (Center for Global Development/Foreign Policy). (2005) "Ranking the Rich," *Foreign Policy* (September-October): 76–83.

Chaliand, Gérald, and Jean-Pierre Rageau. (1993) *Strategic Atlas,* 3rd ed. New York: Harper Perennial.

Chapman, Dennis. (2005) "US Hegemony in Latin America and Beyond," *International Studies Review* 7 (June): 317–19.

Chase-Dunn, Christopher, and E. N. Anderson (eds.). (2005) *The Historical Evolution of World-Systems.* London: Palgrave.

Checkel, Jeffrey T. (1998) "The Constructivist Turn in International Relations Theory," *World Politics* 50 (January 1998): 324–48.

Chen, Lincoln, Jennifer Leaning, and Vasant Narasimhan (eds.). (2003). *Global Health Challenges for Human Security.* Cambridge, Mass.: Harvard University Press.

Chernoff, Fred. (2008) *Theory and Metatheory in International Relations.* London: Palgrave Macmillan.

———. (2004) "The Study of Democratic Peace and Progress in International Relations," *International Studies Review* 6: 49–77.

Chesterman, Simon, ed. (2007) *Secretary or General?: The UN Secretary-General in World Politics.* New York: Cambridge University Press.

Chesterman, Simon, Michael Ignatieff, and Ramesh Thakur (eds.). (2005) *Making States Work: State Failure and the Crisis of Governance.* Tokyo: United Nations University Press.

Choi, Ajin. (2004) "Democratic Synergy and Victory in Wars, 1816–1992," *International Studies Quarterly* 48 (September): 663–82.

Choi, Seung–Whan, and Patrick James. (2005) *Civil–Military Dynamics, Democracy, and International Conflict.* New York: Palgrave Macmillan.

Chomsky, Noam. (2004) *Hegemony or Survival: America's Quest for Global Dominance.* New York: Metropolitan Books/Henry Holt.

Chua, Amy. (2008) *Day of Empire: How Hyperpowers Rise to Global Dominance—and Why They Fail.* New York: Doubleday.

Cincotta, Richard P., and Robert Engelman. (2004) "Conflict Thrives Where Young Men Are Many," *International Herald Tribune* (March): 18.

Cirincione, Joseph. (2008) "The Incredible Shrinking Missile Threat," *Foreign Policy* (May/June): 68–70.

Clapham, Andrew. (2001) "Human Rights," pp. 368–70 in Joel Krieger (ed.), *The Oxford Companion to Politics of the World*, 2nd ed. New York: Oxford University Press.

Clark, Gregory. (2008) *A Farewell to Alms: A Brief Economic History of the World.* Princeton, N.J.: Princeton University Press.

Clark, Ian, and Christian Reus-Smit. (2007) "Preface," *International Politics* 44 (March/May): 153–156.

Clarke, Richard A. (2004) *Against All Enemies.* New York: Simon & Schuster.

Claude, Inis L., Jr. (1989) "The Balance of Power Revisited," *Review of International Studies* 15 (January): 77–85.

———. (1971) *Swords into Plowshares*, 4th ed. New York: Random House.

———. (1967) *The Changing United Nations.* New York: Random House.

———. (1962) *Power and International Relations.* New York: Random House.

Clemens, Michael A. (2007) "Smart Samaritans," *Foreign Affairs* (September/October): 132–140.

Cline, William. (2004) *Trade Policy and Global Poverty.* Washington D.C.: Institute for International Economics.

Cobb, Roger, and Charles Elder. (1970) *International Community.* New York: Harcourt, Brace & World.

Cohen, Benjamin J. (ed.). (2005) *International Political Economy.* Burlington, Ver.: Ashgate.

———. (2000) *The Geography of Money.* Ithaca, N.Y.: Cornell University Press.

———. (1996) "Phoenix Risen: The Resurrection of Global Finance," *World Politics* 48 (January): 268–96.

———. (1973) *The Question of Imperialism.* New York: Basic Books.

Cohen, Daniel. (2006) *Globalization and its Enemies.* Cambridge, Mass.: MIT Press.

Cohen, Eliot A. (1998) "A Revolution in Warfare," pp. 34–46 in Charles W. Kegley, Jr., and Eugene R. Wittkopf (eds.), *The Global Agenda*, 4th ed. New York: McGraw-Hill.

Cohen, Joel E. (1998) "How Many People Can the Earth Support?" *New York Review of Books* 45 (October 8): 29–31.

Cohen, Roger. (2005) "Next Step: Putting Europe Back Together," *New York Times International* (June 5): Section 4, 3.

———. (2000) "A European Identity," *New York Times* (January 14): A3.

Cohen, Saul Bernard. (2003) *Geopolitics of the World System.* Lanham, Md.: Rowman & Littlefield.

Cole, Juan. (2006) "9/11," *Foreign Policy* 156 (September/October): 26–32.

Coleman, Isobel. (2005) "The Payoff from Women's Rights," pp. 191–96 in Robert J. Griffiths (ed.), *Developing World 05/06.* Dubuque, Iowa: McGraw-Hill/Dushkin.

Collier, Paul. (2007) *The Bottom Billion.* New York: Oxford University Press.

———. (2005) "The Market for Civil War," pp. 28–32 in Helen E. Punkitt (ed.), *World Politics 04/05.* Dubuque, Iowa: McGraw-Hill/Dushkin.

CRS (Congressional Research Service) (2007). *Conventional Arms Transfers to Developing Nations, 1999–2006.* Washington, D.C. Congressional Research Service (September 26; prepared by Richard F. Grimmett).

Cooper, Richard N. (2004) "A False Alarm: Overcoming Globalization's Discontents," *Foreign Affairs* 83 (January-February): 152–55.

Coplin, William D. (1971) *Introduction to International Politics.* Chicago: Markham.

———. (1965) "International Law and Assumptions about the State System," *World Politics* 17 (July): 615–34.

Cornish, Edward. (2004) *Futuring: Re-Exploration of the Future.* Bethesda, Md.: World Future Society.

Cortright, David, and George A. Lopez (eds.). (2008) *Uniting Against Terror.* Cambridge, Mass.: MIT Press.

———. (2002) *Smart Sanctions: Targeting Economic Statecraft.* Lanham, Md.: Rowman & Littlefield.

———. (1995) "The Sanctions Era: An Alternative to Military Intervention," *Fletcher Forum of World Affairs* 19 (May): 65–85.

Coser, Lewis. (1956) *The Functions of Social Conflict.* London: Routledge & Kegan Paul.

Cox, Robert J., with Timothy J. Sinclair. (1996) *Approaches to World Order.* Cambridge: Cambridge University Press.

Coyne, Christopher J. (2007) *After War: The Political Economy of Exporting Democracy.* Palo Alto, Calif.: Stanford University Press.

Craig, Gordon A., and Alexander L. George. (1990) *Force and Statecraft*, 2nd ed. New York: Oxford University Press.

Crawford, Neta C. (2003) "Just War Theory and the U.S. Counterterror War," *Perspectives on Politics* 1 (March): 5–25.

Crenshaw, Martha. (2003) "The Causes of Terrorism," pp. 92–105 in Charles W. Kegley, Jr. (ed.), *The New Global Terrorism*. Upper Saddle River, N.J.: Prentice Hall.

Crook, Clive. (2003) "A Cruel Sea of Capital," *Economist* (May 3): 3–5.

———. (1997) "The Future of the State," *Economist* (September 20): 5–20.

Crump, Andy. (1998) *The A to Z of World Development*. Oxford: New Internationalist.

Daadler, Ivo H., and James M. Lindsay. (2005) "Bush's Revolution," pp. 83–90 in Helen E. Purkitt (ed.), *World Politics 04/05*. Dubuque, Iowa: McGraw-Hill/Dushkin.

———. (2003) *America Unbound: The Bush Revolution in Foreign Policy*. Washington, D.C.: Brookings Institution Press.

D'Amico, Francine, and Peter R. Beckman (eds.). (1995) *Women in World Politics*. Westport, Conn.: Bergin and Garvey.

Danner, Mark. (2005) "What Are You Going to Do with That?" *New York Review of Books* 52 (June 23): 52–57.

Davies, Ed, and Karen Lema. (2008) "Pricey Oil Making Geothermal Projects More Attractive," *International Herald Tribune* (June 30): 13.

Davis, Wade. (1999) "Vanishing Cultures," *National Geographic* (August): 62–89.

de las Casas, Gustavo. (2008) "Is Nationalism Good for You?" *Foreign Policy* (March/April): 51–57.

Deffeyes, Kenneth. (2005) "It's the End of Oil," *Time* (October 31): 66.

Dehio, Ludwig. (1962) *The Precarious Balance*. New York: Knopf.

Dempsey, Judy. (2008) "War Scrambles Strategic Map of Europe," *International Herald Tribune* (August): 1, 3.

Denemark, Robert A., Jonathan Friedman, Barry K. Gills, and George Modelski (eds.). (2002) *World System History: The Social Science of Long-Term Change*. London: Routledge.

Deng, Yong, and Thomas G. Moore. (2006) "China Views Globalization: Toward a New Great-Power Politics," pp. 147–56 in Helen E. Purkitt (ed.), *World Politics 05/06*. Dubuque, Iowa: McGraw-Hill/Dushkin.

DeParle, Jason. (2007) "Migrant Money Flow," *New York Times* (November 18): Week in Review, 3.

DeRivera, Joseph H. (1968) *The Psychological Dimension of Foreign Policy*. Columbus, Ohio: Merrill.

DeRouen, Karl R. Jr., and Jacob Bercovitch. (2008) "Enduring Internal Rivalries: A New Framework for the Study of Civil War." *Journal of Peace Research* 45 (January): 55–74.

Destler, I. M. (2005) *American Trade Politics*, 4th ed. Washington, D.C.: Institute of International Economics.

Deutsch, Karl W. (1974) *Politics and Government*. Boston: Houghton Mifflin.

———. (1957) *Political Community and the North Atlantic Area*. Princeton, N.J.: Princeton University Press.

———. (1953) "The Growth of Nations: Some Recurrent Patterns in Political and Social Integration," *World Politics* 5 (October): 168–95.

Deutsch, Karl W., and J. David Singer. (1964) "Multipolar Power Systems and International Stability," *World Politics* 16 (April): 390–406.

Deutsch, Morton. (1986) "Folie à deux: A Psychological Perspective on Soviet–American Relations," pp. 185–196 in Margaret P. Kearns (ed.), *Persistent Patterns and Emerging Structures in a Waning Century*. New York: Praeger.

Diamond, Jared. (2005) *Collapse: How Societies Choose to Fail or Succeed*. New York: Viking.

———. (2003) "Environmental Collapse and the End of Civilization," *Harper's* (June): 43–51.

Diamond, Larry (2005) *Squandered Victory: The American Occupation and the Bungled Effort to Bring Democracy to Iraq*. New York: Henry Holt.

Dickinson, G. Lowes. (1926) *The International Anarchy, 1904–1914*. New York: Century.

Diehl, Paul F. (ed.). (2005) *The Politics of Global Governance*, 3rd ed. Boulder, Colo.: Lynne Rienner.

Dillon, Dana. (2005) "Maritime Piracy: Defining the Problem," *SAIS Review* 25 (Winter-Spring): 155–65.

DiRenzo, Gordon J. (ed.). (1974) *Personality and Politics*. Garden City, N.Y.: Doubleday-Anchor.

Dobson, William J. (2006) "The Day Nothing Much Changed," *Foreign Policy* 156 (September/October): 22–25.

Dogan, Mattei. (2004) "Four Hundred Giant Cities Atop the World," *International Social Science Journal* 181 (September): 347–60.

Dolan, Chris. (2005) *In War We Trust: The Ethical Dimensions and Moral Consequences of the Bush Doctrine*. Burlington, Ver.: Ashgate.

Dollar, David. (2005) "Eyes Wide Open: On the Targeted Use of Foreign Aid," pp. 80–83 in Robert J. Griffiths (ed.), *Developing World 05/06*. Dubuque, Iowa: McGraw-Hill/Dushkin.

Dollar, David, and Aart Kraay. (2004) "Spreading the Wealth," pp. 43–49 in Robert Griffiths (ed.), *Developing World 04/05*. Guilford, Conn.: Dushkin/McGraw Hill.

Dombrowski, Peter, and Eugene Gholz. (2007) *Buying Military Transformation*. New York: Columbia University Press.

Donnelly, Sally B. (2005) "Foreign Policy," *Time Inside Business* (June): A17–A18.

Dos Santos, Theotonio. (1970) "The Structure of Dependence," *American Economic Review* 60 (May): 231–36.

Dougherty, James E., and Robert L. Pfaltzgraff, Jr. (2001) *Contending Theories of International Relations*, 5th ed. New York: Longman.

Dowd, Maureen. (2004) *Bushworld: Enter at Your Own Risk*. New York: G. P. Putnam's Sons.

Downs, George W. (ed.). (1994) *Collective Security Beyond the Cold War*. Ann Arbor: University of Michigan Press.

Doyle, Michael W. (1997) *Ways of War and Peace*. New York: Norton.

Doyle, Michael W., and G. John Ikenberry (eds.). (1997) *New Thinking in International Relations Theory*. Boulder, Colo.: Westview.

Draper, Robert. (2008) *Dead Certain: The Presidency of George W. Bush*. New York: Free Press.

Drew, Jill. (2008) "Dalai Lama's Envoys in Beijing for Tibet Talks," *Washington Post* (July 1): A07.

Drezner, Daniel W. (2007) *All Politics is Global*. Princeton, N.J.: Princeton University Press.

———. (2000) "Bottom Feeders," *Foreign Policy* (Nov/Dec): 64–70.

Drezner, Daniel W., and Henry Farrell. (2006) "Web of Influence," pp. 12–19 in Helen E. Purkitt (ed.), *World Politics 05/06*. Dubuque, Iowa: McGraw-Hill/Dushkin.

Drucker, Peter F. (2005) "Trading Places," *The National Interest* 79 (Spring): 101–07.

Dunne, Tim. (2005) "Liberalism," pp. 185–203 in John Baylis and Steve Smith (eds.), *The Globalization of World Politics*, 3rd ed. New York: Oxford University Press.

Dupont, Alan. (2002) "Sept. 11 Aftermath: The World Does Seem to Have Changed," *International Herald Tribune* (August 6): 6.

Durch, William J. (2005) "Securing the Future of the United Nations," *SAIS Review* 25 (Winter-Spring): 187–91.

Durning, Alan (1993) "Supporting Indigenous Peoples," pp. 80–100 in Lester A. Brown, et al. (eds.) *State of the World 1993*. New York: Norton.

Dworkin, Ronald. (2001) *Sovereign Virtue*. Cambridge, Mass.: Harvard University Press.

Dykman, Jackson. (2008) "Why the World Can't Afford Food," *Time* (May 19): 34–35.

Dyson, Freeman. (2007) "Our Biotech Future," *The New York Review of Books* 54 (July 19): 4–8.

Easterbrook, Gregg. (2002) "Safe Deposit: The Case for Foreign Aid," *New Republic* (July 29): 16–20.

Easterly, William. (2007) "The Ideology of Development," *Foreign Policy* (July/August): 31–35.

———. (2006) *The White Man's Burden: Why the West's Efforts to Aid the Rest Have Done So Much Ill and So Little Good*. New York: Penguin.

Easton, Stewart C. (1964) *The Rise and Fall of Western Colonialism*. New York: Praeger.

Eberstadt, Nicholas. (2004) "The Population Implosion," pp. 168–77 in Robert J. Griffiths (ed.), *Developing World 04/05*, Guilford, Conn: McGraw-Hill/Dushkin.

Economist. (2008) "Winning or Losing? A Special Report on al-Qaeda," The Economist (July 19): 1–12.

———. (2007) *Pocket World in Figures*, 2007 Edition. London: The Economist.

Economy, Elizabeth C. (2007) "The Great Leap Backward?" *Foreign Affairs* 86 (September/October): 38–59.

Edgerton, David. (2007) *The Shock of the Old: Technology and Global History Since 1900*. New York: Oxford University Press.

Edwards, Stephen R. (1995) "Conserving Biodiversity," pp. 212–65 in Ronald Bailey (ed.), *The True State of the Planet*. New York: Free Press.

Eggen, Dan, and Scott Wilson. (2005) "Suicide Bombs Potent Tools of Terrorists," *Washington Post* (July 17): A1, A20.

Eichengreen, Barry. (2000) "Hegemonic Stability Theories of the International Monetary System," pp. 220–44 in Jeffrey A. Frieden and David A. Lake (eds.), *International Political Economy*. Boston: Bedford/St. Martin's.

Eisler, Riane. (2007) "Dark Underbelly of the World's 'Most Peaceful' Countries," *Christian Science Monitor* (July 26): 9.

Eizenstat, Stuart. (1999) "Learning to Steer the Forces of Globalization," *International Herald Tribune* (January 22): 6.

Ekhoragbon, Vincent. (2008) "Nigeria: Influx of Illegal Immigrants Worries Immigration Service," http://allafrica.com/stories/200808080481.html (accessed August 8, 2008).

Eland, Ivan. (2004) *The Empire Has No Clothes: U.S. Foreign Policy Exposed*. New York: Independent Institute.

Elliott, Kimberly Ann. (1998) "The Sanctions Glass: Half Full or Completely Empty?" *International Security* 23 (Summer): 50–65.

———. (1993) "Sanctions: A Look at the Record," *Bulletin of the Atomic Scientists* 49 (November): 32–35.

Elliott, Michael. (1998) "A Second Federal Democratic Superpower Soon," *International Herald Tribune* (November 24): 8.

Elms, Deborah Kay. (2008) "New Directions for IPE: Drawing From Behavioral Economics," *International Studies Review* 10 (June): 239–265.

Elrod, Richard. (1976) "The Concert of Europe," *World Politics* 28 (January): 159–74.

Elshtain, Jean Bethke. (2003) *Just War against Terror: The Burden of American Power in a Violent World*. New York: Basic Books.

Engelhardt, Henriette, and Alexia Prskawetz. (2004) "On the Changing Correlation between Fertility and Female Employment over Space and Time," *European Journal of Population* 20 (No. 1): 1–21.

Enloe, Cynthia H. (2004) *The Curious Feminist*. Berkeley: University of California Press.

———. (2001) "Gender and Politics," pp. 311–15 in Joel Krieger (ed.), *The Oxford Companion to Politics of the World*, 2nd ed. New York: Oxford University Press.

———. (2000) *Maneuvers: The International Politics of Militarizing Women's Lives*. Berkeley: University of California Press.

Enriquez, Juan. (1999) "Too Many Flags?" *Foreign Policy* 116 (Fall): 30–50.

Etzioni, Amitai. (2005) *From Empire to Community: A New Approach to International Relations*. London: Palgrave Macmillan.

Evans, Peter B. (2001) "Dependency," pp. 212–14 in Joel Krieger (ed.), *The Oxford Companion to Politics of the World*, 2nd ed. New York: Oxford University Press.

Fackler, Martin. (2008) "Honda Rolls Out Hydrogen-Powered Car," *International Herald Tribune* (June 18): 16.

Falk, Richard A. (2001a) "The New Interventionism and the Third World," pp. 189–98 in Charles W. Kegley, Jr., and Eugene R. Wittkopf (eds.), *The Global Agenda*, 6th ed. Boston: McGraw-Hill.

———. (2001b) "Sovereignty," pp. 789–91 in Joel Krieger (ed.), *The Oxford Companion to Politics of the World*, 2nd ed. Oxford: Oxford University Press.

———. (1970) *The Status of Law in International Society.* Princeton, N.J.: Princeton University Press.

Falk, Richard, and Andrew Strauss. (2001) "Toward Global Parliament," *Foreign Affairs* 80 (January-February): 212–18.

Fallows, James. (2005) "Countdown to a Meltdown," *The Atlantic Monthly* 51 (July-August): 51–63.

———. (2002) "The Military Industrial Complex," *Foreign Policy* 22 (November-December): 46–48.

Farber, David (ed.). (2007) *What They Think of Us: International Perceptions of the United States Since 9/11.* Princeton, N.J.: Princeton University Press.

Feingold, David A. (2005) "Human Trafficking," *Foreign Policy* (September-October): 26–31.

Feinstein, Lee, and Anne-Marie Slaughter (2004) "A Duty to Prevent," *Foreign Affairs* 83 (No. 1): 136–50.

Ferencz, Benjamin B., and Ken Keyes, Jr. (1991) *Planet-Hood.* Coos Bay, Ore.: Love Line.

Ferguson, Niall. (2006) "A World Without Power," pp. 62–68 in John T. Rourke (ed.), *Taking Sides.* Dubuque, Iowa: McGrawHill/Dushkin.

———. (2005) "Our Currency, Your Problem," *New York Times Magazine* (March 13): 19–21.

———. (2004) *Colossus: The Price of America's Empire.* New York: Penguin.

———. (2001) *The Cash Nexus.* New York: Basic Books.

———. (1999) *The Pity of War.* New York: Basic Books.

Festinger, Leon. (1957) *A Theory of Cognitive Dissonance.* Evanston, Ill.: Row, Peterson.

Fidler, David P., and Lawrence O. Gostin. (2008) *Biosecurity in the Global Age.* Palo Alto, Calif.: Stanford University Press.

Fieldhouse, D. K. (1973) *Economics and Empire, 1830–1914.* Ithaca, N.Y.: Cornell University Press.

Fields, A. Belden, and Kriston M. Lord (eds.). (2004) *Rethinking Human Rights for the New Millennium.* London: Palgrave.

Filson, Darren, and Suzanne Werner. (2002) "A Bargaining Model of War and Peace," *American Journal of Political Science* 46 (No. 4): 819–38.

Financial Times. (2007) "Why are Food Prices Rising," Interactive video found at http://media.ft.com/cms/s/2/f5bd920c-975b-11dc-9e08-0000779fd2ac.html?from=textlinkindepth (accessed August 2008).

Finnegan, William. (2007) "The Countdown," *New Yorker* (October 15): 70–79.

———. (2002) "Leasing the Rain," *New Yorker* (April 18): 43–53.

Finnemore, Martha. (2003) *The Purpose of Intervention: Changing Beliefs about the Use of Force.* Ithaca, N.Y.: Cornell University Press.

Fishman, Ted C. (2005) *China, Inc.* New York: Scribner.

Flanagan, Stephen J., Ellen L. Frost, and Richard Kugler. (2001) *Challenges of the Global Century.* Washington, D.C.: Institute for National Strategic Studies, National Defense University.

Flavin, Christopher, and Seth Dunn. (1999) "Reinventing the Energy System," pp. 23–40 in Lester R. Brown et al., *State of the World 1999.* New York: Norton.

Flint, Colin (ed.). (2004) *The Geography of War and Peace.* New York: Oxford University Press.

Florida, Richard. (2007) "America's Looming Creativity Crisis," pp. 183–190 in Robert M. Jackson, ed., *Global Issues 06/07.* Dubuque, Iowa: McGraw-Hill Contemporary Learning Series.

———. (2005a) *The Flight of the Creative Class: The New Global Competition for Talent.* New York: HarperBusiness.

———. (2005b) "The World Is Spiky," *Atlantic Monthly* 296 (October): 48–52.

Flynn, Stephen. (2004) *America the Vulnerable.* New York: HarperCollins.

Foreign Policy/A.T. Kerney Inc. (2005) "Measuring Globalization," *Foreign Policy* (May-June): 52–60.

Forero, Juan. (2005) "Bolivia Regrets IMF Experiment," *International Herald Tribune*, (December 14).

Frank, Andre Gunder. (1969) *Latin America: Underdevelopment or Revolution.* New York: Monthly Review Press.

Frankel, Max. (2004) *High Noon in the Cold War: Kennedy, Khrushchev, and the Cuban Missile Crisis.* New York: Random House.

Frazier, Derrick V., and William J. Dixon. (2006) "Third-Party Intermediaries and Negotiated Settlements, 1946–2000," *International Interactions* 32 (December): 385–408.

Frederking, Brian, Michael Artine and Max Sanchez Pagano. (2005) "Interpreting September 11," *International Politics* 42 (March): 135–51.

Freedland, Jonathan. (2007) "Bush's Amazing Achievement," *The New York Review of Books* 54 (June 14): 16–20.

Freedman, Lawrence. (2005) "War," pp. 8–11 in Helen E. Purkitt (ed.), *World Politics 04/05.* Dubuque, Iowa: McGrawHill/Dushkin.

———. (2004) *Deterrence.* Cambridge, Mass: Polity Press.

French, Howard W. (2002) "Japan Considering Nuclear Weapons," *New York Times* (June 9): A12.

Freud, Sigmund. (1968) "Why War," pp. 71–80 in Leon Bramson and George W. Goethals (eds.), *War.* New York: Basic Books.

Fried, John H. E. (1971) "International Law—Neither Orphan nor Harlot, Neither Jailer nor Never-Never Land," pp. 124–76 in Karl W. Deutsch and Stanley Hoffmann (eds.), *The Relevance of International Law.* Garden City, N.Y.: Doubleday-Anchor.

Friedheim, Robert L. (1965) "The 'Satisfied' and 'Dissatisfied' States Negotiate International Law," *World Politics* 18 (October): 20–41.

Friedman, Benjamin M. (2005a) *The Moral Consequences of Economic Growth.* New York: Knopf.

———. (2005b) "Homeland Security," *Foreign Policy* (July-August): 22–28.

Friedman, Thomas L. (2007) "It's a Flat World, After All," pp. 7–12 in Robert M. Jackson, ed., *Global Issues 06/07*. Dubuque, Iowa: McGraw-Hill Contemporary Learning Series.

Friedman, Thomas L. (2007) "Eating Up Energy," Columbia, S.C. *The State* (September 22): A9.

———. (2006) "Looking Ahead from China," Columbia, S.C., *The State* (November 12): A9.

———. (2005a) "Arms Sales Begin at Home," Columbia, S.C., *The State* (March 6): A13.

———. (2005b) "Disarmed in the Science Race," Columbia, S.C., *The State* (April 17): D3.

———. (2005c) "The Revolution Will Be Podcast," Columbia, S.C., *The State* (October 24): A11.

———. (2005d) *The World Is Flat: A Brief History of the Twenty-First Century*. New York: Farrar, Straus, and Giroux.

———. (2004a) "Dreadful Irresponsibility after 9/11," Columbia, S.C., *The State* (December 5): D3.

———. (2004b) "The Third Great Era of Globalization," *International Herald Tribune* (March 5): 9.

———. (2001) "Love It or Hate It, But the World Needs America," *International Herald Tribune* (June 16–17): 6.

———. (1999) *The Lexus and the Olive Tree: Understanding Globalization*. New York: Farrar, Straus, Giroux.

Friedmann, S. Julio, and Thomas Homer-Dixon. (2004) "Out of the Energy Box," *Foreign Affairs* 83 (November-December): 72–83.

Frum, David, and Richard Perle. (2004) *An End to Evil: How to Win the War on Terror*. New York: Random House.

Fukuyama, Francis (ed.). (2008) *Blindside: How to Anticipate Future Events and Wild Cards in Global Politics*. Washington, D.C.: Brookings Institution.

———. (2007) "A Quiet Revolution: Latin America's Unheralded Progress," *Foreign Affairs* 86 (November/December): 177–182.

———. (2004) *State-Building: Governance and World Order in the 21st Century*. Ithaca, N.Y.: Cornell University Press.

———. (2002) "The West May Be Cracking," *International Herald Tribune* (August 9): 4.

———. (1999a) *The Great Disruption: Human Nature and the Reconstitution of Social Order*. New York: Free Press.

———. (1999b) "Second Thoughts: The Last Man in a Bottle," *National Interest* 56 (Summer): 16–33.

———. (1992a) "The Beginning of Foreign Policy," *New Republic* (August 17 and 24): 24–32.

———. (1992b) *The End of History and the Last Man*. New York: Free Press.

———. (1989) "The End of History?" *National Interest* 16 (Summer): 3–16.

Fuller, Graham E. (1995) "The Next Ideology," *Foreign Policy* 98 (Spring): 145–58.

The Fund for Peace and the Carnegie Endowment for International Peace. (2008) "The Failed States Index 2008," *Foreign Policy* (July/August): 64–73.

Funk, McKenzie. (2007) "Cold Rush: The Coming Fight for the Melting North," *Harper's* (September): 45–55.

Gaddis, John Lewis. (2004) *Surprise, Security, and the American Experience*. Cambridge, Mass.: Harvard University Press.

———. (1997) *We Now Know: Rethinking Cold War History*. Oxford: Oxford University Press.

———. (1990) "Coping with Victory," *Atlantic Monthly* (May): 49–60.

———. (1983) "Containment: Its Past and Future," pp. 16–31 in Charles W. Kegley, Jr., and Eugene R. Wittkopf (eds.), *Perspectives on American Foreign Policy*. New York: St. Martin's.

Galeota, Julia. (2006) "Cultural Imperialism: An American Tradition," pp. 18–23 in John T. Rourke (ed.), *Taking Sides*. Dubuque, Iowa: McGraw-Hill/Dushkin.

Gall, Carlotta. (2008) "Afghan Highway Drenched in Blood," *The Commercial Appeal* (August 17): A18.

Galtung, Johan. (1969) "Violence, Peace, and Peace Research," *Journal of Peace Research* 6 (No. 3): 167–91.

Gambetta, Diego (ed.). (2005) *Making Sense of Suicide Missions*. New York: Oxford University Press.

Gardels, Nathan. (1991) "Two Concepts of Nationalism," *New York Review of Books* 38 (November 21): 19–23.

Gardner, Richard N. (2003) "The Future Implications of the Iraq Conflict," *American Journal of International Law* 1997 (July): 585–90.

Gareau, Frederick H. (2004) *State Terrorism and the United States*. London: Clarity/Zed.

Garrett, Geoffrey. (2004) "Globalization's Missing Middle," *Foreign Affairs* 83 (November-December): 84–96.

Garrett, Laurie. (2007) "The Challenge of Global Health," *Foreign Affairs* 86 (January/February): 14–38.

———. (2005) "The Scourge of AIDS," *International Herald Tribune* (July 29): 6.

Garrison, Jean. (2007) "From Stop to Go in Foreign Policy," *International Studies Review* 9 (June): 291–293.

Gazzaniga, Michael S. (2005) *The Ethical Brain*. New York: Dana Press.

Gelb, Leslie H., and Morton H. Halperin. (1973) "The Ten Commandments of the Foreign Affairs Bureaucracy," pp. 250–59 in Steven L. Spiegel (ed.), *At Issue*. New York: St. Martin's.

Gelber, Harry. (1998) *Sovereignty through Interdependence*. Cambridge, Mass.: Kluwer Law International.

Geller, Daniel S., and J. David Singer. (1998) *Nations at War: A Scientific Study of International Conflict*. Cambridge: Cambridge University Press.

George, Alexander L. (2000) "Strategies for Preventive Diplomacy and Conflict Resolution," *PS: Political Science and Politics* 33 (March): 15–19.

———. (1992) *Forceful Persuasion: Coercive Diplomacy as an Alternative to War*. Washington, D.C.: United States Institute of Peace.

———. (1986) "U.S.-Soviet Global Rivalry: Norms of Competition," *Journal of Peace Research* 23 (September): 247–62.

———. (1972) "The Case for Multiple Advocacy in Making Foreign Policy," *American Political Science Review* 66 (September): 751–85.

German, F. Clifford. (1960) "A Tentative Evaluation of World Power," *Journal of Conflict Resolution* 4 (March): 138–44.

Gershman, Carl. (2005) "Democracy as Policy Goal and Universal Value," *The Whitehead Journal of Diplomacy and International Affairs* (Winter-Spring): 19–38.

Gerson, Michael. (2006) "The View From the Top," *Newsweek* (August 21): 58–60.

Gibler, Douglas M. (2007) "Bordering On Peace," *International Studies Quarterly* 51 (September): 509–532.

Giddens, Anthony. (1984) *The Constitution of Society: Outline of the Theory of Structuration.* Cambridge: Polity.

Gies, Erica. (2008) "New Wave in Energy: Turning Algae to Oil," *International Herald Tribune* (June 30): 3.

Gilbert, Alan. (2000) *Must Global Politics Constrain Democracy?* Princeton, N.J.: Princeton University Press.

Gilboa, Eytan. (2005) "Global Television News and Foreign Policy," *International Studies Perspectives* 6 (August): 325–41.

———. (2003) "Foreign Policymaking in the Age of Global Television," *Georgetown Journal of International Affairs* 4 (Winter): 119–26.

———. (2002) "Global Communication and Foreign Policy," *Journal of Communication* 52 (December): 731–48.

Gill, Stephen. (2001a) "Group of 7," pp. 340–41 in Joel Krieger (ed.), *The Oxford Companion to Politics of the World,* 2nd ed. Oxford: Oxford University Press.

———. (2001b) "Hegemony," pp. 354–86 in Joel Krieger (ed.), *The Oxford Companion to Politics of the World,* 2nd ed. Oxford: Oxford University Press.

Gilligan, Michael, and Stephen John Stedman. (2003) "Where Do the Peacekeepers Go?" *International Studies Review* 5 (No. 4): 37–54.

Gilpin, Robert. (2004) "The Nature of Political Economy," pp. 403–10 in Karen A. Mingst and Jack L. Snyder (eds.), *Essential Readings in World Politics,* 2nd ed. New York: Norton.

———. (2001) "Three Ideologies of Political Economy," pp. 269–86 in Charles W. Kegley, Jr., and Eugene R. Wittkopf (eds.), *The Global Agenda,* 6th ed. Boston: McGraw-Hill.

———. (1981) *War and Change in World Politics.* Cambridge: Cambridge University Press.

Glaberson, William. (2001) "U.S. Courts Become Arbiters of Global Rights and Wrongs," *New York Times* (June 21): A1, A20.

Gladwell, Malcolm. (2005) *Blink.* New York: Little, Brown.

Gleditsch, Kristian Skrede. (2004) "A Revised List of Wars Between and Within Independent States, 1816–2002," *International Interactions* 30 (July-September): 231–62.

Glenn, Jerome C., and Theodore J. Gordon. (2008) *2008 State of the Future.* New York: United Nations.

Global Policy Forum. (2006) *UN Finance,* http://www.global policy.org/finance/index.htm.

Goertz, Gary. (2003) *International Norms and Decision Making: A Punctuated Equilibrium Analysis.* Lanham, Md.: Rowman & Littlefield.

Goldberg, Jeffrey. (2005) "Breaking Ranks: What Turned Brent Scowcroft Against the Bush Administration?" *New Yorker* (October 31): 52–65.

Goldsmith, Jack. (2008) *The Terror Presidency: Law and Judgment Inside the Bush Administration.* New York: Norton.

Goldsmith, Jack I., and Eric A. Posner. (2005) *The Limits of International Law.* New York: Oxford University Press.

Goldstein, Joshua S. (2005). *The Real Price of War.* New York: New York University Press.

———. (2002) *War and Gender.* Cambridge: Cambridge University Press.

Gordis, Robert. (1984) "Religion and International Responsibility," pp. 33–49 in Kenneth W. Thompson, ed., *Moral Dimensions of American Foreign Policy.* New Brunswick, N.J.: Transaction Books.

Gordon, John Steele. (2004) *An Empire of Wealth.* New York: HarperCollins.

Gore, Al. (2006) *An Inconvenient Truth: The Planetary Emergency and What We Can Do About It.* Emmaus, Penn.: Rodale.

Gottlieb, Gidon. (1982) "Global Bargaining," pp. 109–30 in Nicholas Greenwood Onuf (ed.), *Law-Making in the Global Community.* Durham, N.C.: Carolina Academic Press.

Graff, James. (2007) "Fight For the Top of The World," *Time* (October 1): 28–36.

Grant, Ruth W., and Robert O. Keohane. (2005) "Accountability and Abuses of Power in World Politics," *American Political Science Review* 99 (February): 29–43.

Greenstein, Fred I. (1987) *Personality and Politics.* Princeton, N.J.: Princeton University Press.

Grey, Edward. (1925) *Twenty-Five Years, 1892–1916.* New York: Frederick Stokes.

Grieco, Joseph M. (1995) "Anarchy and the Limits of Cooperation: A Realist Critique of the Newest Liberal Institutionalism," pp. 151–71 in Charles W. Kegley, Jr. (ed.), *Controversies in International Relations Theory.* New York: St. Martin's.

Griggs, Richard. (1995) "The Meaning of 'Nation' and 'State' in the Fourth World," Occasional Paper No. 18. Capetown, South Africa: Center for World Indigenous Studies.

Grimmett, Richard F. (2007) *Conventional Arms Transfers to Developing Nations, 1999-2006.* Washington, D.C.: Congressional Research Service.

———. (2006) *Conventional Arms Transfers to Developing Nations, 1998-2005.* Washington, D.C.: Congressional Research Service.

Grosby, Steven. (2006) *Nationalism.* New York: Oxford University Press.

Grunwald, Michael. (2008) "The Clean Energy Scam," *Time* (April 7): 40–45.

Grusky, Sara. (2001) "Privatization Tidal Wave: IMF/ World Bank Water Policies and the Price Paid by thePoor," *The Multinational Monitor* 22 (September): http://www. multinationalmonitor.org/mm2001/01september/ sep01corp2.htm.

Grussendorf, Jeannie. (2006) "When the Stick Works: Power in International Mediation," *International Studies Review* 8 (June): 318–320.

Gugliotta, Guy. (2004) "Scientists Say Warming to Increase Extinctions," Columbia, S.C., *The State* (January 8): A6.

Gulick, Edward V. (1999) *The Time Is Now: Strategy and Structure for World Governance.* Lanham, Md.: Lexington.

———. (1967 [1955]) *Europe's Classical Balance of Power.* Ithaca, N.Y.: Cornell University Press.

Gurr, Ted Robert. (2001) "Managing Conflict in Ethnically Divided Societies," pp. 173–86 in Charles W. Kegley, Jr., and Eugene R. Wittkopf (eds.), *The Global Agenda,* 6th ed. Boston: McGraw-Hill.

———. (2000) *Peoples versus States.* Washington, D.C.: United States Institute of Peace Press.

———. (1993) *Minorities at Risk.* Washington, D.C.: United States Institute of Peace Press.

———. (1970) *Why Men Rebel.* Princeton, N.J.: Princeton University Press.

Gvosdev, Nikolas K. (2005) "The Value(s) of Realism," *The SAIS Review of International Affairs* 25 (Winter-Spring) 17–25.

Haass, Richard N. (2005) *The Opportunity: America's Moment to Alter History's Course.* New York: Public Affairs.

———. (1997) "Sanctioning Madness," *Foreign Affairs* 76 (December): 74–85.

Habermas, Jürgen. (1984) *The Theory of Communicative Action,* 2 vols. Boston: Beacon Press.

Hacking, Ian. (1999) *The Social Construction of What?* Cambridge, Mass.: Harvard University Press.

Haffa, Robert P., Jr. (1992) "The Future of Conventional Deterrence," pp. 5–30 in Gary L. Guertner, Robert Haffa, Jr., and George Quester (eds.), *Conventional Forces and the Future of Deterrence.* Carlisle Barracks, Pa.: U.S. Army War College.

Hafner-Burton, Emilie M., Kiyoteru Tsutsui, and John W. Meyer. (2008) "International Human Rights Law and the Politics of Legitimation: Repressive States and Human Rights Treaties," *International Sociology* 23 (January): 115–141.

Haggard, Stephan, and Beth A. Simmons. (1987) "Theories of International Regimes," *International Organization* 41 (Summer): 491–517.

Hall, Anthony J. (2004) *The America Empire and the Fourth World.* Montreal: McGill-Queen's University Press.

Hall, John A. (2001) "Liberalism," pp. 499–502 in Joel Krieger (ed.), *The Oxford Companion to Politics of the World,* 2nd ed. Oxford: Oxford University Press.

Hall, Thomas D. (2004) "Ethnic Conflicts as a Global Social Problem," pp. 139–55 in George Ritzer (ed.), *Handbook of Social Problems.* London: Sage.

Hammes, Thomas X. (2004) *The Sling and the Stone: On War in the 21st Century.* St. Paul, Minn.: Zenith Press.

Hansenclever, Andreas, Peter Mayer, and Volker Rittberger (1996) "Interests, Power, and Knowledge," *Mershon International Studies Review* 40 (October): 177–228.

Hanson, Victor Davis. (2003) *Ripples of Battle.* New York: Doubleday.

Harbom, Lotta, and Peter Wallensteen. (2007) "Armed Conflict, 1989-2006," *Journal of Peace Research* 44 (No 5): 623–634.

Hardin, Garrett. (1993) *Living within Limits.* Oxford: Oxford University Press.

———. (1968) "The Tragedy of the Commons," *Science* 162 (December): 1243–48.

Harknett, Richard J. (1994) "The Logic of Conventional Deterrence and the End of the Cold War," *Security Studies* 4 (Autumn): 86–114.

Hartung, William, and Michelle Ciarrocca. (2005) "The Military Industrial-Think Tank Complex," pp. 103–7, in Glenn P. Hastedt (ed.), *American Foreign Policy 04/05,* 10th ed., Guiford, Conn: Dushkin/McGraw-Hill.

Harries, Owen. (1995) "Realism in a New Era," *Quadrant* 39 (April): 11–18.

Harris, Edward. (2008) "World Chopping Down Trees at Pace That Affects Climate," *The Cincinnati Enquirer* (February 3): A2.

Harvey, David. (2004) *The New Imperialism.* Oxford: Oxford University Press.

Hathaway, Oona A. (2007) "Why We Need International Law," *The Nation* (November 19): 35–39.

Hayden, Patrick. (2005) *Cosmopolitan Global Politics.* Burlington, Ver.: Ashgate.

Haynes, Jeffrey. (2005) *Comparative Politics in a Globalizing World.* Cambridge, U.K.: Polity.

———. (2004) "Religion and International Relations," *International Politics* 41 (September): 451–62.

HDI (2007). *Human Development Indicators.* New York: United Nations Development Programme.

———. (2006) *Human Development Indicators.* New York: United Nations Development Programme.

HDR. (2008). *Human Development Report.* New York: United Nations Development Programme.

———. (2007). *Human Development Report.* New York: United Nations Development Programme.

———. (2005) *Human Development Report.* United Nations Development Programme. New York: Oxford University Press.

Hedges, Chris. (2003) "What Every Person Should Know about War," *New York Times* (July 6): www.nytimes.com.

Hegre, Håvard. (2004) "The Duration and Termination of Civil War," *Journal of Peace Research* 41 (May): 243–52.

Hehir, J. Bryan. (2002) "The Limits of Loyalty," *Foreign Policy* (September–October): 38–39.

Held, David, and Anthony McGrew. (2001) "Globalization," pp. 324–27 in Joel Krieger (ed.), *The Oxford Companion to Politics of the World,* 2nd ed. Oxford: Oxford University Press.

Held, David, and Anthony McGrew, with David Goldblatt, and Jonathan Perraton. (2001) "Managing the Challenge of Globalization and Institutionalizing Cooperation through Global Governance," pp. 136–48 in Charles W. Kegley, Jr., and Eugene R. Wittkopf (eds.), *The Global Agenda*, 6th ed. Boston: McGraw-Hill.

———. (1999) *Global Transformations*. Stanford, Calif.: Stanford University Press.

Hensel, Howard M. (ed.). (2007) *The Law of Armed Conflict*. Burlington, Ver.: Ashgate.

Heredia, Blanca. (1999) "Prosper or Perish? Development in the Age of Global Capital," pp. 93–97 in Robert M. Jackson (ed.), *Global Issues 1999/00*, 15th ed. Guilford, Conn.: Dushkin/McGraw-Hill.

Hermann, Charles F. (1988) "New Foreign Policy Problems and Old Bureaucratic Organizations," pp. 248–65 in Charles W. Kegley, Jr., and Eugene R. Wittkopf (eds.), *The Domestic Sources of American Foreign Policy*. New York: St. Martin's.

Hermann, Margaret G. (ed.). (2008) *Comparative Foreign Policy Analysis*. Upper Saddle River, N.J.: Prentice Hall.

———. (1988) "The Role of Leaders and Leadership in the Making of American Foreign Policy," pp. 266–84 in Charles W. Kegley, Jr., and Eugene R. Wittkopf (eds.), *The Domestic Sources of American Foreign Policy*. New York: St. Martin's.

———. (1976) "When Leader Personality Will Affect Foreign Policy," pp. 326–33 in James N. Rosenau (ed.), *In Search of Global Patterns*. New York: Free Press.

Hermann, Margaret G., and Joe D. Hagan. (2004) "International Decision Making: Leadership Matters," pp. 182–88 in Karen A. Mingst and Jack L. Snyder (eds.), *Essential Readings in World Politics*, 2nd ed. New York: Norton.

Hermann, Margaret G., and Charles W. Kegley, Jr. (2001) "Democracies and Intervention," *Journal of Peace Research* 38 (March): 237–45.

Herrmann, Richard K., and Richard Ned Lebow (eds.). (2004) *Ending the Cold War: Interpretations, Causation, and the Study of International Relations*. London: Palgrave Macmillan.

Hersh, Seymour M. (2005) "The Coming Wars: What the Pentagon Can Now Do in Secret," *New Yorker* (January 24 and 31): 40–47.

Hertsgaard, Mark. (2003) *The Eagle's Shadow: Why America Fascinates and Infuriates the World*. New York: Picador/Farrar, Straus & Giroux.

Herz, John H. (1951) *Political Realism and Political Idealism*. Chicago: University of Chicago Press.

Hiatt, Fred. (1997) "Globalization," *International Herald Tribune* (June 12): 8.

Hilsman, Roger. (1967) *To Move a Nation*. New York: Doubleday.

Hindle, Tim. (2004) "The Third Age of Globalization," pp. 97–98 in the *Economist, The World in 2004*. London: Economist.

Hironaka, Ann. (2005) *Neverending Wars*. Cambridge, Mass.: Harvard University Press.

Hirsh, Michael. (2003) *At War with Ourselves: Why America Is Squandering Its Chance to Build a Better World*. Oxford: Oxford University Press.

Hobson, John A. (1965 [1902]) *Imperialism*. Ann Arbor: University of Michigan Press.

Hodge, Carl Cavanagh. (2005) *Atlanticism for a New Century*. Upper Saddle River, N.J.: Prentice Hall.

Hoebel, E. Adamson. (1961) *The Law of Primitive Man*. Cambridge, Mass.: Harvard University Press.

Hoffman, Eva. (2000) "Wanderers by Choice," *Utne Reader* (July-August): 46–48.

Hoffmann, Stanley. (2005) "Clash of Globalizations," pp. 3–7 in Helen E. Purkitt (ed.), *World Politics 04/05*. Dubuque, Iowa: McGraw-Hill/Dushkin.

———. (1998) *World Disorders*. Lanham, Md.: Rowman & Littlefield.

———. (1992) "To the Editors," *New York Review of Books* (June 24): 59.

———. (1971) "International Law and the Control of Force," pp. 34–66 in Karl W. Deutsch and Stanley Hoffmann (eds.), *The Relevance of International Law*. Garden City, N.Y.: Doubleday-Anchor.

———. (1961) "International Systems and International Law," pp. 205–37 in Klaus Knorr and Sidney Verba (eds.), *The International System*. Princeton, N.J.: Princeton University Press.

Hoffmann, Stanley, with Frédéric Bozo. (2004) *Gulliver Unbound: America's Imperial Temptation and the War in Iraq*. Lanham, Md.: Rowman & Littlefield.

Hoge, James F., Jr. (2006) "A Global Power Shift in the Making," pp. 3–6 in Helen E. Purkitt (ed.), *World Politics 05/06*. Dubuque, Iowa: McGraw-Hill/Dushkin.

Hollander, Jack M. (2003) *The Real Crisis: Why Poverty, Not Affluence, Is the Environment's Number One Enemy*. Berkeley: University of California Press.

Holsti, Kalevi J. (2004) *Taming the Sovereigns: Institutional Changes in International Politics*. Cambridge: Cambridge University Press.

———. (1996) *The State, War, and the State of War*. Cambridge: Cambridge University Press.

———. (1995) "War, Peace, and the State of the State," *International Political Science Review* 16 (October): 319–39.

———. (1992) *International Politics*, 6th ed. Englewood Cliffs, N.J.: Prentice Hall.

———. (1991) *Peace and War*. Cambridge: Cambridge University Press.

———. (1988) *International Politics*, 5th ed. Englewood Cliffs, N.J.: Prentice Hall.

Holsti, Ole R. (2001) "Models of International Relations: Realist and Neoliberal Perspectives on Conflict and Cooperation," pp. 121–35 in Charles W. Kegley, Jr., and Eugene R. Wittkopf (eds.), *The Global Agenda*, 6th ed. Boston: McGraw-Hill.

Holt, Jim. (2005) "Time-Bandits," *New Yorker* (February 28): 80–85.

Homer-Dixon, Thomas. (2006) "The Rise of Complex Terrorism," pp. 214–220 in Thomas J. Badey (ed.), *Violence and Terrorism 06/07*. Dubuque, Iowa: McGraw-Hill.

Hopf, Ted. (1998) "The Promise of Constructivism in International Relations Theory," *International Security* 23 (Summer): 171–200.

Hopkins, Terence K., and Immanuel Wallerstein (eds.). (1996) *The Age of Transitions: Trajectory of World Systems 1945–2025*. London: Zed.

Horkheimer, Max. (1947) *Eclipse of Reason*. New York: Oxford University Press.

Hough, Peter. (2004) *Understanding Global Security*. New York: Routledge.

House, Karen Elliot. (1989) "As Power is Dispersed Among Nations, Need for Leadership Grows," *Wall Street Journal* (February 21): A1, A10.

Howard, Michael E. (1978) *War and the Liberal Conscience*. New York: Oxford University Press.

Howell, Llewellyn D. (2003) "Is the New Global Terrorism a Clash of Civilizations?" pp. 173–84 in Charles W. Kegley, Jr. (ed.), *The New Global Terrorism*. Upper Saddle River, N.J.: Prentice Hall.

———. (1998) "The Age of Sovereignty Has Come to an End," *USA Today* 127 (September): 23.

Hufbauer, Gary Clyde, Jeffrey J. Schott, and Kimberly Ann Elliott. (1990) *Economic Sanctions Reconsidered*, 2nd ed. Washington, D.C.: Institute for International Economics.

Hughes, Emmet John. (1972) *The Living Presidency*. New York: Coward, McCann and Geoghegan.

Hulsman, John C., and Anatol Lievan. (2005) "The Ethics of Realism," *The National Interest* 80 (Summer): 37–43.

Human Rights Dialogue (2005). Series 2 (Spring): 1–34. New York: Carnegie Council for Ethics in International Affairs.

Human Security Centre. (2006) *Human Security Brief 2006*. Vancouver: The University of British Columbia, Canada.

Hume, David. (1817) *Philosophical Essays on Morals, Literature, and Politics*, Vol. 1. Washington, D.C.: Duffy.

Hunt, Swanee, and Cristina Posa. (2005) "Women Making Peace," pp. 212–17 in Robert J. Griffiths (ed.), *Developing World 05/06*. Dubuque, Iowa: McGraw-Hill/Dushkin.

Huntington, Samuel P. (2005) "The Lonely Superpower" pp. 540–550 in G. John Ikenberry (ed.), *American Foreign Policy: Theoretical Essays*. New York: Pearson/Longman.

———. (2004) "The Hispanic Challenge," *Foreign Policy* (March-April): 30–45.

———. (2001a) "The Coming Clash of Civilizations, or the West against the Rest," pp. 199–202 in Charles W. Kegley, Jr., and Eugene R. Wittkopf (eds.), *The Global Agenda*, 6th ed. Boston: McGraw-Hill.

———. (2001b) "Migration Flows Are the Central Issue of Our Time," *International Herald Tribune* (February 2): 6.

———. (1996) *The Clash of Civilizations and the Remaking of World Order*. New York: Simon & Schuster.

———. (1991) *The Third Wave: Democratization in the Late Twentieth Century*. Norman: University of Oklahoma Press.

Hurwitz, Jon, and Mark Peffley. (1987) "How Are Foreign Policy Attitudes Structured?" *American Political Science Review* 81 (December): 1099–1120.

Huth, Paul K., and Todd L. Allee. (2003) *The Democratic Peace and Territorial Conflict in the Twentieth Century*. Cambridge: Cambridge University Press.

Ignatieff, Michael. (2005a) "Human Rights, Power, and the State," pp. 59–75 in Simon Chesterman, Michael Ignatieff, and Ramesh Thakur (eds.), *Making States Work: State Failure and the Crisis of Governance*. Tokyo: United Nations University Press.

———. (2005b) "Who Are the Americans to Think That Freedom is Theirs to Spread?" *New York Times Magazine* (June 28): 40–47.

———. (2004a) "Hard Choices on Human Rights," pp. 54–55 in the *Economist, The World in 2004*. London: Economist.

———. (2004b) *The Lesser Evil: Political Ethics in an Age of Terror*. Princeton, N.J.: Princeton University Press.

———. (2001a) "The Danger of a World Without Enemies," *New Republic* 234 (February 26): 25–28.

———. (2001b) *Human Rights as Politics and Ideology*. Princeton, N.J.: Princeton University Press.

Ikenberry, G. John. (2008) "The Rise of China and the Future of the West," *Foreign Affairs* 87 (January/February): 23–37.

———. (2004) "Is American Multilateralism in Decline?" pp. 262–82 in Karen A. Mingst and Jack L. Snyder (eds.), *Essential Readings in World Politics*, 2nd ed. New York: Norton.

Iklé, Fred Charles. (2007) *Annihilation from Within*. New York: Columbia University Press.

International Labour Office. (2004) *Working Out of Poverty*. Geneva: International Labour Office.

IMF (International Monetary Fund). (2007) *World Economic Outlook*. New York: International Monetary Fund.

Jacobson, Harold K. (1984) *Networks of Interdependence*. New York: Knopf.

Jackson, Derrick Z. (2007) "Spreading Fear, Selling Weapons," Columbia, S.C., *The State* (August 6): A9.

Jaeger, Hans-Martin. (2007) "Global Civil Society and the Political Depoliticization of Global Governance," *International Political Sociology* 1 (September): 257–277.

Jaffe, Greg, and Jonathan Karp. (2005) "Pentagon Girds for Big Spending Cuts," *Wall Street Journal* (November 5): A7.

James, Barry. (2002a) "Summit Aims, Again, for a Better World," *International Herald Tribune* (August 8): 1, 8.

———. (2002b). "Talks to Tackle Threat to Biodiversity," *International Herald Tribune* (August 23): 1, 9.

James, Patrick. (1993) "Neorealism as a Research Enterprise," *International Political Science Review* 14 (No. 2): 123–48.

Janis, Irving. (1982) *Groupthink: Psychological Studies of Policy Decisions and Fiascoes*, 2nd ed. Boston: Houghton Mifflin.

Janowski, Louis. (2006) "Neo-Imperialism and U.S. Foreign Policy," pp. 54–61 in John T. Rourke (ed.), *Taking Sides*. Dubuque, Iowa: McGraw-Hill/Dushkin.

Jensen, Lloyd. (1982) *Explaining Foreign Policy.* Englewood Cliffs, N.J.: Prentice Hall.

Jervis, Robert. (2005) *American Foreign Policy in a New Era.* New York: Routledge.

———. (1992) "A Usable Past for the Future," pp. 257–68 in Michael J. Hogan (ed.), *The End of the Cold War.* New York: Cambridge University Press.

———. (1985) "From Balance to Concert," *World Politics* 38 (October): 58–79.

———. (1976) *Perception and Misperception in World Politics.* Princeton, N.J.: Princeton University Press.

Johansen, Robert C. (1991) "Do Preparations for War Increase or Decrease International Security?" pp. 224–44 in Charles W. Kegley, Jr. (ed.), *The Long Postwar Peace.* New York: HarperCollins.

Johnson, Chalmers. (2007) *Nemesis: The Last Days of the American Republic.* New York: Metropolitan.

———. (2004a) *Blowback: The Costs and Consequences of American Empire.* New York: Henry Holt.

———. (2004b) *The Sorrows of Empire.* New York: Metropolitan Books/Henry Holt.

Johnson, James Turner. (2005) "Just War, As It Was and Is," *First Things* 149 (January): 14–24.

———. (2003) "Just War Theory: Responding Morally to Global Terrorism," pp. 223–38 in Charles W. Kegley, Jr. (ed.), *The New Global Terrorism.* Upper Saddle River, N.J.: Prentice Hall.

Johnston, Michael. (2006) *Syndromes of Corruption.* Cambridge: Cambridge University Press.

Jones, Dorothy V. (2002) *Toward a Just World.* Chicago: University of Chicago Press.

———. (1991) *Code of Peace: Ethics and Security in the World of the Warlord States.* Chicago: University of Chicago Press.

Joyce, Mark. (2005) "From Kosovo to Katrina," *International Herald Tribune* (August 8): 6.

Joyner, Christopher C. (2005) *International Law in the 21st Century.* Lanham, Md.: Rowman & Littlefield.

Judis, John B. (2005) *The Folly of Empire.* New York: Scribner.

———. (2004) "Imperial Amnesia," *Foreign Policy* (July-August): 50–59.

Judt, Tony. (2007) "From Military Disaster to Moral High Ground," *New York Times* (October 7): Week in Review, 15.

———. (2005) "The New World Order," *New York Review of Books* 52 (July 14): 14–18.

Judt, Tony, and Denis Lacurne (eds.). (2005) *With US or Against US: Studies in Global Anti-Americanism.* London: Palgrave Macmillan.

Juergensmeyer, Mark. (2003) "The Religious Roots of Contemporary Terrorism," pp. 185–93 in Charles W. Kegley, Jr. (ed.), *The New Global Terrorism.* Upper Saddle River, N.J.: Prentice Hall.

Kadera, Kelly M., and Gerald L. Sorokin. (2004) "Measuring National Power," *International Interactions* 30 (July-September): 211–30.

Kagan, Robert. (2007) *Dangerous Nation.* New York: Knopf.

Kahneman, Daniel. (2003) "Maps of Bounded Nationality," *American Economic Review* 93 (December):1449–1475.

Kaiser, David. (1990) *Politics and War.* Cambridge, Mass.: Harvard University Press.

Kaminski, Matthew. (2002) "Anti-Terrorism Requires Nation Building," *Wall Street Journal* (March 15): A10.

Kane, Hal. (1995) *The Hour of Departure: Forces That Create Refugees and Migrants.* Washington, D.C.: Worldwatch Institute.

Kant, Immanuel. (1964; 1798). *Anthropologie in Pragmatischer Hinsicht.* Darmstadt, Germany: Werke.

Kaplan, Morton A. (1957) *System and Process in International Politics.* New York: Wiley.

Kaplan, Robert D. (2005a) "How We Would Fight China," *Atlantic Monthly* 295 (May): 49–64.

———. (2005b) "Supremacy by Stealth," pp. 91–100 in Helen E. Purkitt (ed.), *World Politics 04/05.* Dubuque, Iowa: McGraw-Hill/Dushkin.

Kapstein, Ethan B. (2006) "The New Global Slave Trade," *Foreign Affairs* 85 (November/December): 103–115.

———. (2004) "Models of International Economic Justice," *Ethics & International Affairs* 18 (No. 2): 79–92.

———. (1991–92) "We Are Us: The Myth of the Multinational," *National Interest* 26 (Winter): 55–62.

Kapur, Devesh, and John McHale. (2003) "Migration's New Payoff," *Foreign Policy* (November-December): 49–57.

Karns, Margaret P., and Karen A. Mingst. (2004) *International Organizations.* Boulder, Colo: Lynne Rienner.

Kasher, Asa, and Amos Yadlin. (2005) "Assassination and Preventive Killing," *SAIS Review* 25 (Winter-Spring): 41–57.

Kearney, A. T. (2004) "Measuring Globalization" *Foreign Policy* (March-April): 54–69.

———. (2002) "Globalization's Last Hurrah?" *Foreign Policy* (January-February): 38–71.

Keck, Margaret E., and Kathryn Sikkink. (2004) "Transnational Advocacy Networks in International Politics," pp. 222–33 in Karen A. Mingst and Jack L. Snyder (eds.), *Essential Readings in World Politics,* 2nd ed. New York: Norton.

Keegan, John. (1999) *The First World War.* New York: Knopf.

Kegley, Charles W., Jr. (ed.). (1995) *Controversies in International Relations Theory: Realism and the Neoliberal Challenge.* New York: St. Martin's.

———. (1994) "How Did the Cold War Die? Principles for an Autopsy," *Mershon International Studies Review* 38 (March): 11–41.

———. (1993) "The Neoidealist Moment in International Studies? Realist Myths and the New International Realities," *International Studies Quarterly* 37 (June): 131–46.

———. (1992) "The New Global Order: The Power of Principle in a Pluralistic World," *Ethics & International Affairs* 6: 21–42.

Kegley, Charles W., Jr., and Margaret G. Hermann. (2002) "In Pursuit of a Peaceful International System," pp. 15–29 in Peter J. Schraeder (ed.), *Exporting Democracy.* Boulder, Colo.: Lynne Rienner.

———. (1997) "Putting Military Intervention into the Democratic Peace," *Comparative Political Studies* 30 (February): 78–107.

Kegley, Charles W., Jr., and Gregory A. Raymond. (2007a) *After Iraq: The Imperiled American Imperium.* New York: Oxford University Press.

———. (2007b) *The Global Future,* 2nd ed. Belmont, Calif.: Wadsworth/Thomson Learning.

———. (2004) "Global Terrorism and Military Preemption: Policy Problems and Normative Perils," *International Politics* 41 (January): 37–49.

———. (2002a) *Exorcising the Ghost of Westphalia: Building World Order in the New Millennium.* Upper Saddle River, N.J.: Prentice Hall.

———. (2002b) *From War to Peace: Fateful Decisions in World Politics.* Belmont, Calif.: Wadsworth.

———. (1999) *How Nations Make Peace.* Boston: Bedford/ St. Martin's.

———. (1994) *A Multipolar Peace? Great-Power Politics in the Twenty-First Century.* New York: St. Martin's.

———. (1990) *When Trust Breaks Down: Alliance Norms and World Politics.* Columbia: University of South Carolina Press.

Kegley, Charles W., Jr., Gregory A. Raymond, and Margaret G. Hermann. (1998) "The Rise and Fall of the Nonintervention Norm: Some Correlates and Potential Consequences," *Fletcher Forum of World Affairs* 22 (Winter-Spring): 81–101.

Kegley, Charles W., Jr., with Eugene R. Wittkopf. (2006) *World Politics,* 10th ed. Belmont, Calif.: Wadsworth/Thomson Learning.

———. (1982) *American Foreign Policy,* 2nd ed. New York: St. Martin's.

Keller, Jonathan W. (2005) "Leadership Style, Regime Type, and Foreign Policy Crisis Behavior," *International Studies Quarterly* 49 (June): 205–31.

Kellman, Barry. (2007) *Bioviolence.* Cambridge: Cambridge University Press.

Kennan, George F. (1985) "Morality and Foreign Policy," *Foreign Affairs* 64 (Winter): 205–218.

———. (1984a) *The Fateful Alliance.* New York: Pantheon.

———. (1984b) "Soviet-American Relations," pp. 107–20 in Charles W. Kegley, Jr., and Eugene R. Wittkopf (eds.), *The Global Agenda.* New York: Random House.

———. (1967) *Memoirs.* Boston: Little, Brown.

———. (1954) *Realities of American Foreign Policy.* Princeton, N.J.: Princeton University Press.

———. (1951) *American Diplomacy, 1900–1950.* New York: New American Library.

———. ["X"]. (1947) "The Sources of Soviet Conduct," *Foreign Affairs* 25 (July): 566–82.

Kennedy, Paul. (2006) "The Perils of Empire," pp. 69–71 in Helen E. Purkitt (ed.), *World Politics 05/06.* Dubuque, Iowa: McGraw-Hill/Dushkin.

———. (1987) *The Rise and Fall of the Great Powers.* New York: Random House.

Keohane, Robert O. (2002) "Governance in a Partially Globalized World," *American Political Science Review* 94 (March): 1–13.

———. (1989) "International Relations Theory: Contributions from a Feminist Standpoint," *Millennium* 18 (Summer): 245–53.

———. (ed.). (1986a) *Neorealism and Its Critics.* New York: Columbia University Press.

———. (1986b) "Realism, Neorealism and the Study of World Politics," pp. 1–26 in Robert O. Keohane (ed.), *Neorealism and Its Critics.* New York: Columbia University Press.

Keohane, Robert O., and Joseph S. Nye. (2001a) *Power and Interdependence,* 3rd ed. New York: Addison WesleyLongman.

———. (2001b) "Power and Interdependence in the Information Age," pp. 26–36 in Charles W. Kegley, Jr., and Eugene R. Wittkopf (eds.), *The Global Agenda,* 6th ed. Boston: McGraw-Hill.

———. (2000) "Globalization: What's New? What's Not? (And So What?)," *Foreign Policy* 118 (Spring): 104–19.

———. (1977) *Power and Interdependence.* Boston: Little, Brown.

———, (eds.). (1971) *Transnational Relations and World Politics.* Cambridge: Harvard University Press.

Khanna, Parag. (2006) "United They Fall," *Harper's* (January): 31–40.

Kher, Unmesh. (2006) "Oceans of Nothing," *Time* (November 13): 56–57.

Kibbe, Jennifer D. (2004) "The Rise of Shadow Warriors." *Foreign Affairs* 83 (March-April): 102–15.

Kifner, John. (2005) "A Tide of Islamic Fury, and How It Rose," *New York Times* (January 30): Section 4, 4–5.

Kim, Dae Jung, and James D. Wolfensohn. (1999) "Economic Growth Requires Good Governance," *International Herald Tribune* (February 26): 6.

Kim, Samuel S. (1991) "The United Nations, Lawmaking and World Order," pp. 109–24 in Richard A. Falk, Samuel S. Kim, and Saul H. Mendlovitz (eds.), *The United Nations and a Just World Order.* Boulder, Colo.: Westview.

Kindleberger, Charles. (2001) *Manics, Panics, and Crashes: A History of Financial Crises,* 4th ed. Hoboken, NJ: John Wiley and Sons.

———. (1973) *The World in Depression, 1929–1939.* Berkeley: University of California Press.

Kingsbury, Kathleen. (2007) "The Changing Face of Breast Cancer," *Time* (October 15): 36–43.

Kinnas, J. N. (1997) "Global Challenges and Multilateral Diplomacy," pp. 23–48 in Ludwik Dembinski (ed.), *International Geneva Yearbook.* Berne, Switzerland: Peter Lang.

King, Gary, and Langche Zeng. (2007) "When Can History Be Our Guide?", *International Studies Quarterly* 51 (March): 183–210.

Kirkpatrick, David D. (2007) "This War is Not Like the Others—Or is It?" *New York Times* (August 26): The Week in Review, 1, 4.

———. (2005) "Battle Splits Conservative Magazine," *New York Times* (13 March): 12.

Kissinger, Henry A. (2004) "America's Assignment," *Newsweek* (November 8): 32–38.

———. (2001) *Does America Need a Foreign Policy?* New York: Simon & Schuster.

———. (1999) *Years of Renewal.* New York: Simon & Schuster.

———. (1994) *Diplomacy.* New York: Simon & Schuster.

———. (1992) "Balance of Power Sustained," pp. 238–48 in Graham Allison and Gregory F. Treverton (eds.), *Rethinking America's Security.* New York: Norton.

———. (1979) *White House Years.* Boston: Little, Brown.

———. (1969) "Domestic Structure and Foreign Policy," pp. 261–75 in James N. Rosenau (ed.), *International Politics and Foreign Policy.* New York: Free Press.

Klare, Michael. (2008) *Rising Powers, Shrinking Planet.* New York: Metropolitan Books.

———. (2007) "Beyond the Age of Petroleum," *The Nation* 285 (November 12): 17–22.

———. (2004) *Blood and Oil.* New York: Henry Holt.

———. (2002) *Resource Wars: The New Landscape of Global Conflict.* New York: Holtzbrinck Academic.

Klein, Naomi. (2008) "China's All-Seeing Eye," *Rolling Stone* (May 29): 59–66.

———. (2007) *The Shock Doctrine: The Rise of Disaster Capitalism.* New York: Metropolitan Books/Henry Holt.

Klimová-Alexander, Ilona. (2005) *The Romani Voice in World Politics: The United Nations and Non-State Actors.* Burlington, Ver.: Ashgate.

Kluger, Jeffrey. (2007) "What Makes Us Moral," *Time* (December 3): 54–60.

———. (2006) "The Big Crunch," pp. 24–25 in Robert M. Jackson (ed.), *Global Issues 05/06.* Dubuque, Iowa: McGraw-Hill/Dushkin.

———. (2001) "A Climate of Despair," *Time* (April 9): 30–35.

Knickerbocker, Brad. (2007) "Might Warming Be 'Normal'," *Christian Science Monitor* (September 20): 14, 16.

Knight, W. Andy. (2000) *A Changing United Nations.* London: Palgrave.

Knorr, Klaus, and James N. Rosenau (eds.). (1969) *Contending Approaches to International Politics.* Princeton, N.J.: Princeton University Press.

Knorr, Klaus, and Sidney Verba (eds.). (1961) *The International System.* Princeton, N.J.: Princeton University Press.

Knox, MacGregor, and Williamson Murray. (2001) *The Dynamics of Military Revolution: 1300–2050.* Cambridge: Cambridge University Press.

Kober, Stanley. (1990) "Idealpolitik," *Foreign Policy* 79 (Summer): 3–24.

Kohli, Atul. (2004) *State-Directed Development.* Cambridge: Cambridge University Press.

Kolbert, Elizabeth. (2008) "What Was I Thinking? The Latest Reasoning about Our Irrational Ways," *The New Yorker* (February 25): 77–79.

———. (2005) "The Climate of Man-II," *New Yorker* (May 2): 64–73.

Korten, David. (1995) *When Corporations Rule the World.* West Hartford, Conn.: Berrett-Koehler.

Krasner, Stephen P. (2004) "Sharing Sovereignty: New Institutions for Collapsed and Failing States," *International Security* 29 (Fall): 85–120.

———. (2001) "International Political Economy," pp. 420–22 in Joel Krieger (ed.), *The Oxford Companion to Politics of the World,* 2nd ed. New York: Oxford University Press.

Krauthammer, Charles. (2005a) "As Liberty Advances, Opposition Begins to Unite," Columbia, S.C., *The State* (January 21): A9.

———. (2005b) "Door to Power Open to China," Columbia, S.C., *The State* (September 25): D3.

———. (2004) "Democratic Realism: An American Foreign Policy for a Unipolar World." Speech delivered at the American Enterprise Institute (February 10).

———. (2003) "The Unipolar Moment Revisited," *National Interest* 70 (Winter): 5–17.

———. (2002) "NATO Is Dead; We Should Not Work to Revive It," Columbia, S.C., *The State* (May 26): D3.

———. (2001) "The Bush Doctrine," *Time* (March 5): 42.

———. (1993) "How Doves Become Hawks," *Time* (May 17): 74.

Kristof, Nicholas D. (2005) "The Fire Bell in the Night on Climate Change," Columbia, S.C., *The State* (September 28): A11.

———. (2004) "A New Ethnic Cleaning," Columbia, S.C., *The State* (March 25): A9.

———. (1993) "The Rise of China," *Foreign Affairs* 72 (November-December): 59–74.

Krueger, Alan B. (2007) *What Makes a Terrorist.* Princeton, N.J.: Princeton University Press.

Krueger, Anne O. (2006) "Expanding Trade and Unleashing Growth," pp. 4–19 in John T. Rourke (ed.), *Taking Sides.* Dubuque, Iowa: McGraw-Hill/Dushkin.

Krugman, Paul. (2005) "America Held Hostage," Columbia, S.C., *The State* (July 1): A19.

———. (2004) "An Oil-Driven Recession Is Possible," *International Herald Tribune* (May 15–16): 9.

———. (2003) *The Great Unraveling: Losing Our Way in the New Century.* New York: Norton.

———. (1987) "Is Free Trade Passé?" *Journal of Economic Perspectives* 1 (Autumn): 131–144.

Kugler, Jacek. (2006) "China: Satisfied or Dissatisfied, the Strategic Equation," paper presented at the Annual Meeting of the International Studies Association, March 22–25, San Diego.

———. (2001) "War," pp. 894–96 in Joel Krieger (ed.), *The Oxford Companion to Politics of the World.* 2nd ed. New York: Oxford University Press.

Kugler, Jacek, Ronald L. Tammen, and Brian Efird. (2004) "Integrating Theory and Policy," *International Studies Review* 6 (December): 163–79.

Kunzig, Robert. (2003) "Against the Current," *U.S. News & World Report* (June 2): 34–35.

Kupchan, Charles A. (2003) *The End of the American Era: U.S. Foreign Policy and the Geopolitics of the Twenty-First Century.* New York: Knopf.

Kupchan, Charles A., and Clifford A. Kupchan. (1992) "A New Concert for Europe," pp. 249–66 in Graham Allison and Gregory F. Treverton (eds.), *Rethinking America's Security.* New York: Norton.

Kurzweil, Ray. (2005) *The Singularity is Near: When Humans Transcend Biology.* New York: Penguin Group (USA).

Lai, Brian, and Dan Reiter. (2005) "Rally Round the Union Jack?" *International Studies Quarterly* 49 (June): 255–72.

Landes, David S. (1998) *The Wealth and Poverty of Nations: Why Are Some So Rich and Some So Poor?* New York: Norton.

Laqueur, Walter. (2006) "The Terrorism to Come," pp. 229–36 in Thomas J. Badey (ed.), *Violence and Terrorism 06/07.* Dubuque, Iowa: McGraw Hill/Dushkin.

——. (2003) "Postmodern Terrorism," pp. 151–59 in Charles W. Kegley, Jr. (ed.), *The New Global Terrorism.* Upper Saddle River, N.J.: Prentice Hall.

——. (2001) "Terror's New Face," pp. 82–89 in Charles W. Kegley, Jr., and Eugene R. Wittkopf (eds.), *The Global Agenda,* 6th ed. Boston: McGraw-Hill.

Larkin, John. (2005) "India Bets on Nuclear Future," *Wall Street Journal International* (November 4): A12.

Lebovic, James H. (2004) "Uniting for Peace?" *Journal of Conflict Resolution* 48 (December): 910–36.

Lebow, Richard Ned. (2003) *The Tragic Vision of Politics: Ethics, Interests, and Orders.* Cambridge: Cambridge University Press.

——. (1981) *Between Peace and War.* Baltimore: Johns Hopkins University Press.

Legrain, Philippe. (2003) "Cultural Globalization Is Not Americanization," *Chronicle of Higher Education* (May 9): B7–B70.

Legro, Jeffrey W. (2007) *Rethinking the World: Great Power Strategies and International Order.* Ithaca, N.Y.: Cornell University Press.

Legro, Jeffrey W., and Andrew Moravcsik. (1999) "Is Anybody Still a Realist?" *International Security* 24 (Fall): 5–55.

Lemke, Douglas. (2003) "Development and War," *International Studies Review* 5 (December): 55–63.

Lentner, Howard H. (2004) *Power and Politics in Globalization: The Indispensable State.* New York: Routledge.

Leonard, Mark. (2005) *Why Europe Will Run the 21st Century.* New York: Fourth Estate.

Leow, Rachel. (2002) "How Can Globalization Become 'O.K.' for All?" *International Herald Tribune* (February 15): 9.

Levi, Michael. (2008) "Stopping Nuclear Terrorism," *Foreign Affairs* 87 (January/February): 131–140.

Levingston, Steven. (1999) "Does Territoriality Drive Human Aggression?" *International Herald Tribune* (April 14): 9.

Levitt, Peggy. (2007) *God Needs No Passport.* New York: New Press.

Levy, Jack S. (2003) "Applications of Prospect Theory to Political Science," *Syntheses* 135 (May): 215–41.

——. (2001) "War and Its Causes," pp. 47–56 in Charles W. Kegley, Jr., and Eugene Wittkopf (eds.), *The Global Agenda,* 6th ed. Boston: McGraw-Hill.

——. (1998a) "The Causes of War and the Conditions of Peace," *Annual Review of Political Science* 1 (June): 139–65.

——. (1998b) "Towards a New Millennium," pp. 47–57 in Charles W. Kegley, Jr., and Eugene R. Wittkopf (eds.), *The Global Agenda,* 5th ed. New York: McGraw-Hill.

——. (1997) "Prospect Theory, Rational Choice, and International Relations," *International Studies Quarterly* 41 (March): 87–112.

——. (1990–91) "Preferences, Constraints, and Choices in July 1914," *International Security* 15 (Winter): 151–86.

——. (1989a) "The Causes of War: A Review of Theories and Evidence," pp. 209–333 in Philip E. Tetlock, Jo L. Husbands, Robert Jervis, Paul C. Stern, and Charles Tilly (eds.), *Behavior, Society, and Nuclear War.* New York: Oxford University Press.

——. (1989b) "The Diversionary Theory of War," pp. 259–88 in Manus I. Midlarsky (ed.), *Handbook of War Studies.* Boston: Unwin Hyman.

Levy, Jack S., and Katherine Barbieri. (2004) "Trading with the Enemy During Wartime," *Security Studies* 13 (Spring): 1–47.

Lieber, Robert J. (2005) *The American Era.* New York: Cambridge University Press.

Lind, Michael. (1993) "Of Arms and the Woman," *New Republic* (November 15): 36–38.

Lindberg, Todd, (ed.). (2005) *Beyond Paradise and Power: Europe, America, and the Future of a Troubled Relationship.* New York: Routledge.

Lindblom, Charles E. (1979) "Still Muddling, Not Yet Through," *Public Administration Review* 39 (November-December): 517–26.

Lindsay, James M. (1986) "Trade Sanctions as Policy Instruments," *International Studies Quarterly* 30 (June): 153–73.

Lipson, Charles. (1984) "International Cooperation in Economic and Security Affairs," *World Politics* 37 (October): 1–23.

Lissitzyn, Oliver J. (1963) "International Law in a Divided World," *International Conciliation* 542 (March): 3–69.

Little, David. (1993) "The Recovery of Liberalism," *Ethics & International Affairs* 7: 171–201.

Loescher, Gil. (2005) "Blaming the Victim: Refugees and Global Security," pp. 126–29 in Robert J. Griffiths (ed.), *Developing World 05/06.* Dubuque, Iowa: McGraw-Hill/Dushkin.

Lomborg, Bjørn. (2007) *Solutions for the World's Biggest Problems.* New York: Cambridge University Press.

——. (ed.). (2004) *Global Crisis, Global Solutions.* Cambridge: Cambridge University Press.

Longman, Phillip. (2005) "The Global Baby Bust," pp. 173–179 in Robert J. Griffiths (ed.), *Developing World 05/06.* Dubuque, Iowa: McGraw-Hill/Dushkin.

Lopez, George A., and David Cortright. (1995) "Economic Sanctions in Contemporary Global Relations," pp. 3–16 in David Cortright and George A. Lopez (eds.), *Economic Sanctions*. Boulder, Colo.: Westview.

Lorenz, Konrad. (1963) *On Aggression*. New York: Harcourt, Brace & World.

Löwenheim, Oded. (2007) *Predators and Parasites*. Ann Arbor: Pluto Books, University of Michigan Press.

Lumpe, Lora. (1999) "The Lender of the Pack," *Bulletin of the Atomic Scientists* 58 (January-February): 27–33.

Lutz, Wolfgang. (1994) "The Future of World Population," *Population Bulletin* 49 (June): 1–47.

Lynch, Colum. (2008) "U.N. Chief to Prod Nations on Food Crisis," *Washington Post* (June 2): A07.

Lynn, Jonathan. (2008) "Diplomats See Reason for Hope in WTO Talks," *International Herald Tribune* (May 29).

Mackinder, Sir Halford. (1919) *Democratic Ideals and Reality*. New York: Holt.

Mahan, Alfred Thayer. (1890) *The Influence of Sea Power in History*. Boston: Little, Brown.

Mahbulbani, Kishore. (2005) "Understanding China," *Foreign Affairs* 84 (October): 49–60.

Majeed, Akhtar. (1991) "Has the War System Really Become Obsolete?" *Bulletin of Peace Proposals* 22 (December): 419–25.

Malaquias, Assis V. (2001) "Humanitarian Intervention," pp. 370–74 in Joel Krieger (ed.), *The Oxford Companion to Politics of the World*, 2nd ed. New York: Oxford University Press.

———. (2008) "The Benefits of Goliath," pp. 55–64 in Eugene R. Wittkopf and James M. McCormick, eds., *The Domestic Sources of American Foreign Policy*. Lanham, Md.: Rowman and Littlefield.

Mandelbaum, Michael. (2007) "Democracy Without America," *Foreign Affairs* 86 (September/October): 119–130.

———. (2006a) "David's Friend Goliath," *Foreign Policy* (January-February): 49–56.

———. (2006b) *The Case for Goliath: How America Acts as the World's Government in the 21st Century*. New York: Public Affairs.

———. (2002) *The Ideas That Conquered the World: Peace, Democracy, and Free Markets in the Twenty-First Century*. New York: Public Affairs/Perseus.

Mann, Charles C. (2005) "The Coming Death Shortage," *Atlantic Monthly* 295 (May): 92–102.

Mann, James. (2004) *Rise of the Vulcans: The History of Bush's War Cabinet*. New York: Viking.

Mansfield, Edward D., Helen V. Milner, and B. Peter Rosendorff. (2002) "Replication, Realism, and Robust-ness: Analyzing Political Regimes and International Trade," *American Political Science Review* 96 (March): 167–69.

Mansfield, Edward D., and Brian M. Pollins (eds.). (2003) *Economic Interdependence and International Conflict*. Ann Arbor: University of Michigan Press.

Mansfield, Edward D., and Jack Snyder. (2005a) *Electing to Fight*. Cambridge, Mass.: MIT Press.

———. (2005b) "When Ballots Bring Bullets," *International Herald Tribune* (November 29–30): 6.

Mapel, David R. (2007) "The Right of National Defense," *International Studies Perspectives* 8 (February): 1–15.

Markoe, Lauren, and Seth Borenstein. (2005) "We Overpay by 20% for Military Goods," Columbia, S.C., *The State* (October 23): A1, A8.

Marshall, Monty G., and Ted Robert Gurr. (2003) *Peace and Conflict 2003*. College Park, Md.: Center for International Development and Conflict Management.

Martel, William C. (2008) *Victory in War*. New York: Cambridge University Press.

Martell, Luke. (2007) "The Third Wave in Globalization Theory," *International Studies Review* 9 (Summer): 173–196.

Marx, Anthony W. (2003) *Faith in Nation: Exclusionary Origins of Nationalism*. New York: Oxford University Press.

Mathews, Jessica T. (2000) "National Security for the Twenty-First Century," pp. 9–11 in Gary Bertsch and Scott James (eds.), *Russell Symposium Proceedings*. Athens: University of Georgia.

Matlock, Jack F. (2004) *Reagan and Gorbachev: How the Cold War Ended*. New York: Random House.

May, Ernest R. (2000) *Strange Victory*. New York: Hill and Wang.

Mayall, James. (2001) "Mercantilism," pp. 535 and 540 in Joel Krieger (ed.), *The Oxford Companion to Politics of the World*, 2nd ed. New York: Oxford University Press.

Mazarr, Michael J. (1999) *Global Trends 2005*. London: Palgrave.

Mazur, Amy G. (2002) *Theorizing Feminist Policy*. New York: Oxford University Press.

McCormick, John. (2007) *The European Superpower*. London: Palgrave MacMillan.

McGinnis, John O. (2005) "Individualism and World Order," *The National Interest* 28 (Winter): 41–51.

McGranahan, Donald. (1995) "Measurement of Development," *International Social Science Journal* 143 (March): 39–59.

McGrew, Anthony. (2005) "The Logics of Globalization," pp. 207–34 in John Ravenhill (ed.), *Global Political Economy*. New York: Oxford University Press.

McGurn, William. (2002) "Pulpit Economics," *First Things* 122 (April): 21–25.

McKibbin, Bill. (2006) "A Special Moment in History," pp. 3–7 in Robert M. Jackson (ed.), *Global Issues 05/06*. Dubuque, Iowa: McGraw-Hill/Dushkin.

———. (1998) "The Future of Population," *Atlantic Monthly* (May): 55–78.

McNamara, Robert S. (2005) "Apocalypse Soon," *Foreign Policy* (May-June): 29–35.

Mead, Margaret. (1968) "Warfare Is Only an Invention—Not a Biological Necessity," pp. 270–74 in Leon Bramson and George W. Goethals (eds.), *War*. New York: Basic Books.

Mead, Walter Russell. (2008) *God and Gold: Britain, America, and the Making of the Modern World*. New York: Knopf.

————. (2006) "America's Sticky Power," pp. 8–10 in Robert M. Jackson (ed.), *Global Issues 05/06*. Dubuque, Iowa: McGraw-Hill/Dushkin.

Mearsheimer, John J. (2004) "Anarchy and the Struggle for Power," pp. 54–72 in Karen A. Mingst and Jack L. Snyder (eds.), *Essential Readings in World Politics,* 2nd ed. New York: Norton.

————. (2001) *The Tragedy of Great Power Politics*. New York: Norton.

————. (1990) "Back to the Future: Instability in Europe after the Cold War," *International Security* 15 (Summer): 5–56.

Mearsheimer, John J., and Stephen W. Walt. (2003) "An Unnecessary War," *Foreign Policy* (January-February): 50–58.

Meernik, James David. (2004) *The Political Use of Military Force in US Foreign Policy*. Burlington, Ver.: Ashgate.

Melander, Erik. (2005) "Gender Equality and Intrastate Armed Conflict," *International Studies Quarterly* 49 (December): 695–714.

Melloan, George. (2002) "Bush's Toughest Struggle Is with His Own Bureaucracy," *Wall Street Journal* (June 25): A19.

Mendelsohn, Jack. (2005) "America and Russia: Make-Believe Arms Control," pp. 205–9 in Glenn P. Hastedt (ed.), *America Foreign Policy 04/05*, 10th ed. Guilford, Conn.: Dushkin/McGraw-Hill.

Menkhaus, Ken. (2002) "Somalia: In the Crosshairs of the War on Terrorism," *Current History* (May): 210–18.

Menon, Rajan. (2007) *The End of Alliances*. New York: Oxford University Press.

Michael, Marie. (2001) "Food or Debt," pp. 78–79 in Robert J. Griffiths (ed.), *Developing World 01/02*. Guilford, Conn.: Dushkin/McGraw-Hill.

Micklethwait, John, and Adrian Wooldridge. (2001) "The Globalization Backlash," *Foreign Policy* (September-October): 16–26.

Midlarsky, Manus I. (2006) *The Killing Trap: Genocide in the Twentieth Century*. New York: Cambridge University Press.

————. (2003) "The Impact of External Threat on States and Domestic Societies," *International Studies Review* 5 (No. 4): 13–18.

————. (ed.). (2000) *Handbook of War Studies II*. Ann Arbor: University of Michigan Press.

————. (1988) *The Onset of World War*. Boston: Unwin Hyman.

Mieville, China. (2006) *Between Equal Rights: A Marxist Theory of International Law*. Chicago: Haymarket Books.

Miller, Mark Crispin. (2006) "What's Wrong With This Picture?" pp. 115–17 in Robert M. Jackson (ed.), *Global Issues 05/06*. Dubuque, Iowa: McGraw-Hill/Dushkin.

Mintz, Alex. (2007) "Why Behavioral IR?" *International Studies Review* 9 (June): 157–172.

Mitchell, Sara McLaughlin, and Brandon C. Prins. (2004) "Rivalry and Diversionary Uses of Force," *Journal of Conflict Resolution* 48 (December): 937–61.

Mitrany, David. (1966) *A Working Peace System*. Chicago: Quadrangle.

Modelski, George. (ed.). (1987a) *Exploring Long Cycles*. Boulder, Colo.: Lynne Rienner.

————. (1987b) "The Study of Long Cycles," pp. 1–15 in George Modelski (ed.), *Exploring Long Cycles*. Boulder, Colo.: Lynne Rienner.

————. (1964) "The International Relations of Internal War," pp. 14–44 in James N. Rosenau (ed.), *International Aspects of Civil Strife*. Princeton, N.J.: Princeton University Press.

————. (1962) *A Theoretical Analysis of the Formulation of Foreign Policy*. London: University of London.

Modelski, George, and William R. Thompson. (1999) "The Long and the Short of Global Politics in the Twenty-First Century," *International Studies Review*, special issue, ed. by Davis B. Bobrow: 109–40.

————. (1996) *Leading Sectors and World Powers*. Columbia: University of South Carolina Press.

Moens, Alexander. (2005) *The Foreign Policy of George W. Bush*. Burlington, Ver.: Ashgate.

Moisy, Claude. (1997) "Myths of the Global Information Village," *Foreign Policy* 107 (Summer): 78–87.

Møller, Bjørn. (1992) *Common Security and Nonoffensive Defense: A Neorealist Perspective*. Boulder, Colo.: Lynne Rienner.

Moorehead, Caroline. (2007) "Women and Children For Sale," *New York Review of Books* (October 11): 15–18.

Moran, Theodore H., Edward M. Graham, and Magnus Blomström (eds.). (2005) *Does Foreign Direct Investment Promote Development?* Washington, D.C.: Institute for International Economics.

Morgan, Patrick. (2005) *International Security: Problems and Solutions*. Washington, D.C.: CQ Press.

Morgenthau, Hans J. (1985) *Politics Among Nations*, 6th ed. Revised by Kenneth W. Thompson. New York: Knopf.

————. (1948) *Politics among Nations*. New York: Knopf.

Morphet, Sally. (2004) "Multilateralism and the Non-Aligned Movement," *Global Governance* 10 (October-December): 517–37.

Morris, Desmond. (1969) *The Human Zoo*. New York: Dell.

Morse, Edward L., and James Richard. (2002) "The Battle for Energy Dominance," *Foreign Affairs* 81 (March-April): 16–31.

Morton, David. (2006) "Gunning for the World," *Foreign Policy* (January-February): 58–67.

Mowlana, Hamid. (1995) "The Communications Paradox," *Bulletin of the Atomic Scientists* 51 (July): 40–46.

Mueller, John. (2007) *Overblown*. New York: Free Press.

————. (2005) "Simplicity and Spook: Terrorism and the Dynamics of Threat Exaggeration," *International Studies Perspectives* 6 (May): 208–34.

Mullenbach, Mark J. (2005) "Deciding to Keep Peace," *International Studies Quarterly* 49 (September): 529–55.

Muller, Jerry Z. (2008) "Us and Them: The Enduring Power of Ethnic Nationalism," *Foreign Affairs* 87 (March/April): 18–35.

Murdoch, James C., and Todd Sandler. (2004) "Civil Wars and Economic Growth," *American Journal of Political Science* 48 (January): 138–51.

Murithi, Timothy. (2004) "The Myth of Violent Human Nature," *Peace & Policy* 8: 28–32.

Murray, Williamson, and Allan R. Millett. (2000) *A War to Be Won.* Cambridge, Mass.: Harvard University Press.

Naím, Moisés. (2007) "The Free-Trade Paradox," *Foreign Policy* (September/October): 96–97.

———. (2006a) "The Five Wars of Globalization," pp. 61–66 in Robert M. Jackson (ed.), *Global Issues 05/06.* Dubuque, Iowa: McGraw-Hill/Dushkin.

———. (2006b) "The Most Dangerous Deficit," *Foreign Policy* (January-February): 94–95.

Nardin, Terry. (2005) "Humanitarian Imperialism," *Ethics and International Affairs* 19 (No. 2, Special Issue): 21–26.

National Intelligence Council (NIC). (2004) *Mapping the Global Future.* Washington, D.C.: National Intelligence Council.

NCTC. (National Counter-Terrorism Center). (2007) *NCTC Report on Terrorist Incidents.* Washington, D.C.: National Counter-Terrorism Center.

Neack, Laura. (2004) "Peacekeeping, Bloody Peacekeeping," *Bulletin of the Atomic Scientists* 57 (July-August): 40–47.

Nelson, Stephan D. (1974) "Nature/Nurture Revisited: A Review of the Biological Bases of Conflict," *Journal of Conflict Resolution* 18 (June): 285–335.

Neuman, Johanna. (1995–96) "The Media's Impact on International Affairs, Then and Now," *National Interest* 16 (Winter): 109–23.

Neumann, Iver B. (2007) "'A Speech That the Entire Ministry May Stand For,' or: Why Diplomats Never Produce Anything New," *International Political Sociology* 1 (June): 183–200.

Newhouse, John. (2003) *Imperial America: The Bush Assault on World Order.* New York: Knopf.

Newell, Richard G. (2005) "The Hydrogen Economy," *Resources for the Future* 156 (Winter): 20–23.

Newsweek. (2008) "The United States Doesn't Have Any Oil," *Newsweek* (July 7/14): 44–45.

Nichols, John. (2002) "Enron's Global Crusade," *The Nation* (March 4) http://www.thenation.com/doc/20020304/nichols.

Niebuhr, Reinhold. (1947) *Moral Man and Immoral Society.* New York: Scribner's.

9/11 Commission. (2004) *Final Report of the National Commission on Terrorist Attacks upon the United States: The 9/11 Commission Report.* New York: Norton.

Norberg, Johan. (2006) "Three Cheers for Global Capitalism," pp. 52–60 in Robert M. Jackson (ed.), *Global Issues 05/06.* Dubuque, Iowa: McGraw-Hill/Dushkin.

Nossel, Suzanne. (2004) "Smart Power," *Foreign Affairs* 83 (March-April): 31–142.

Nye, Joseph S., Jr. (2008) "Soft Power and American Foreign Policy," pp. 29–43 in Eugene R. Wittkopf and James M. McCormick, eds., *The Domestic Sources of American Foreign Policy.* Lanham, Md.: Rowman and Littlefield.

Nye, Joseph S. (2007) *Understanding International Conflicts,* 6th ed. New York: Pearson Longman.

———. (2005) *Power in the Global Information Age.* New York: Routledge.

———. (2004a) "America's Soft Learning Curve," pp. 31–34 in *The World in 2004,* London: Economist.

———. (2004b) *Soft Power.* New York: Public Affairs.

———. (1990) *Bound to Lead: The Changing Nature of American Power.* New York: Basic Books.

Oatlay, Thomas. (2008) *International Political Economy,* 3rd ed. New York: Pearson Longman.

———. (2004) *International Political Economy.* New York: Pearson Longman.

Oberdorfer, Don. (1991) *The Turn.* New York: Poseidon.

O'Brien, Conor Cruise. (1977) "Liberty and Terrorism," *International Security* 2 (Fall): 56–67.

Obuah, Emmanuel. (2006) "Combating Global Trafficking in Persons," *International Politics* 43 (April): 241–265.

OECD. (2007a) *Trends and Recent Developments in Foreign Direct Investment.* Paris: Organisation for Economic Co-operation and Development.

———. (2007b) *World Investment Report.* Paris: Organisation for Economic Co-operation and Development.

———. (2005) *Distribution of Aid by Development Assistance Committee (DAC) Members.* Paris: Organization for Economic Cooperation and Development.

Oneal, John R., and Bruce Russett. (1999) "Assessing the Liberal Peace with Alternative Specifications: Trade Still Reduces Conflict," *Journal of Peace Research* 36 (July): 423–42.

Oneal, John R., and Jaroslav Tir. (2006). *International Studies Quarterly* 50 (December): 755–779.

Onuf, Nicholas. (2002) "Worlds of Our Making: The Strange Career of Constructivism in International Relations," pp. 119–41 in Donald J. Puchala (ed.), *Visions of International Relations.* Columbia: University of South Carolina Press.

———. (1989) *World of Our Making: Rules and Rule in Social Theory and International Relations.* Columbia: University of South Carolina Press.

———. (1982) "Global Law-Making and Legal Thought," pp. 1–82 in Nicholas Greenwood Onuf (ed.), *Law-Making in the Global Community.* Durham, N.C.: Carolina Academic Press.

Opello, Walter C., Jr., and Stephen J. Rosow. (2004) *The Nation-State and Global Order,* 2nd ed. Boulder, Colo.: Lynne Rienner.

O'Reilly, Kelly. (2005) "U.S. Arms Sales and Purchaser's Governments," Occasional Paper, Walker Institute of International Studies. Columbia: University of South Carolina.

O'Reilly, Marc J., and Wesley B. Renfro. (2007) "Evolving Empire," *International Studies* Perspectives 8 (May): 137–151.

Organski, A. F. K. (1968) *World Politics.* New York: Knopf.

Organski, A. F. K., and Jacek Kugler. (1980) *The War Ledger.* Chicago: University of Chicago Press.

O'Rourke, Lindsey. (2008) "The Woman Behind the Bomb," *International Herald Tribune* (August 5): Op-Ed.

Ostler, Nicholas. (2003) "A Loss for Words," *Foreign Policy* (November-December): 30–31.

Ostry, Sylvia. (2001) Review of *The Challenge of Global Capitalism* by Robert Gilpin, *American Political Science Review* 95 (March): 257–58.

O'Sullivan, John. (2005) "In Defense of Nationalism," *The National Interest* 78 (Winter): 33–40.

Owen, John M., IV. (2005) "When Do Ideologies Produce Alliances?" *International Studies Quarterly* 49 (March): 73–99.

Pacala, Stephen, and Robert Socolow. (2004) "Stabilization Wedges: Solving the Climate Problem for the Next 50 Years with Current Technologies," *Science* 305 (August): 968–972.

Packenham, Robert. (1992) *The Dependency Movement.* Cambridge, Mass.: Harvard University Press.

Palmer, Glenn, and T. Clifton Morgan. (2007) "Power Transition, the Two-Good Theory, and Neorealism: A Comparison with Comments on Recent U.S. Foreign Policy," *International Interactions* 33 (July/September): 329–346.

Panagariya, Arvind. (2003) "Think Again: International Trade," *Foreign Policy* (November-December): 20–28.

Pape, Robert A. (2005a) *Dying to Win: The Strategic Logic of Suicide Terror.* New York: Random House.

———. (2005b) "Soft Balancing Against the United States," *International Security* 30 (Summer): 7–45.

Parker, Owen, and James Brassett. (2005) "Contingent Borders, Ambiguous Ethics: Migrants in (International) Political Theory," *International Studies Quarterly* 49 (June): 233–53.

Parry, Clive. (1968) "The Function of Law in the International Community," pp. 1–54 in Max Sørensen (ed.), *Manual of Public International Law.* New York: St. Martin's.

Patterson, Eric. (2005) "Just War in the 21st Century: Reconceptualizing Just War Theory after September 11," *International Politics* 42 (March): 116–34.

Paul, T. V., G. John Ikenberry, and John A. Hall (eds.). (2003) *The Nation-State in Question.* Princeton, N.J.: Princeton University Press.

Pauly, Louis W. (2005) "The Political Economy of International Financial Crises," pp. 176–203 in John Ravenhill (ed.), *Global Political Economy.* New York: Oxford University Press.

Paust, Jordan J. (2008) *Beyond the Law.* New York: Cambridge University Press.

———. (2007) *Beyond the Law: The Bush Administration's Unlawful Responses in the War on Terror.* New York: Cambridge University Press.

Payne, Richard J. (2007) *Global Issues.* New York: Pearson Longman.

Peirce, Neal R. (2000) "Keep an Eye on 'Citistates' Where Economic Action Is," *International Herald Tribune* (January 11): 8.

———. (1997) "Does the Nation-State Have a Future?" *International Herald Tribune* (April 4): 9.

Pells, Richard. (2002) "Mass Culture Is Now Exported from All Over to All Over," *International Herald Tribune* (July 12): 9.

Peterson, Erik. (1998) "Looming Collision of Capitalisms?" pp. 296–307 in Charles W. Kegley, Jr., and Eugene R. Wittkopf (eds.), *The Global Agenda,* 5th ed. New York: McGrawHill.

Peterson, V. Spike. (2003) *A Critical Rewriting of Global Political Economy: Retrospective, Productive and Virtual Economies.* London: Routledge.

Peterson, V. Spike, and Anne Sisson Runyan. (1993) *Global Gender Issues.* Boulder, Colo.: Westview Press.

Petras, James. (2004) *The New Development Politics.* Williston, Vt.: Ashgate.

Petras, James, and Henry Veltmeyer. (2004) *A System in Crisis: The Dynamics of Free Market Capitalism.* London: Palgrave.

Pettman, Jan Jindy. (2005) "Gender Issues," pp. 669–87 in John Baylis and Steve Smith, (eds.), *The Globalization of World Politics,* 3rd ed. New York: Oxford University Press.

Pfaff, William. (2001a) "Anti-Davos Forum is Another Sign of a Sea Change," *International Herald Tribune* (July 25): 6.

———. (2001b) "The Question of Hegemony," *Foreign Affairs* 80 (January-February): 50–64.

Pfetsch, Frank L. (1999) "Globalization: A Threat and a Challenge for the State," paper presented at the European Standing Conference on International Studies, Vienna, September 11–13.

Pham, J. Peter. (2005) "Killing to Make a Killing," *The National Interest* 81 (Fall): 132–37.

Phillips, Nicola (ed.). (2005) *Globalizing Political Economy.* London: Palgrave.

Piasecki, Bruce. (2007) "A Social Responsibility Revolution in the Global Marketplace," *Christian Science Monitor* (August 9): 9.

Pickering, Jeffrey, and Mark Peceny. (2006) "Forging Democracy At Gunpoint," *International Studies Quarterly* 50 (September): 539–559.

Pipes, Richard. (1977) "Why the Soviet Union Thinks It Could Fight and Win a Nuclear War," *Commentary* 26 (July): 21–34.

Pogge, Thomas. (2005) "World Poverty and Human Rights," *Ethics & International Affairs* 19 (No. 1): 1–7.

Posen, Barry R. (2004) "The Security Dilemma and Ethnic Conflict," pp. 357–66 in Karen A. Mingst and Jack L. Snyder (eds.), *Essential Readings in World Politics,* 2nd ed. New York: Norton.

Powell, Colin L. (1995) *My American Journey.* New York: Random House.

Power, Jonathan. (2004) "United Nations—Much Maligned, But Much Needed," *International Herald Tribune* (February 26): 6.

Powers, Thomas. (1994) "Downwinders: Some Casualties of the Nuclear Age," *Atlantic Monthly* (March): 119–24.

Prakash, Aseem, and Matthew Potoski. (2007) "Investing Up," *International Studies Quarterly* 51 (September): 723–744.

Prempeh, E. Osei Kwadwo, Joseph Mensah, and Senyo B. S. K. Adjibolosoo. (eds.). (2005) *Globalization and the Human Factor.* Burlington, Ver.: Ashgate.

Prestowitz, Clyde. (2005) *Three Billion New Capitalists.* New York: Basic Books.

———. (2003). *Rogue Nation: American Unilateralism and the Failure of Good Intentions.* New York: Basic Books/Perseus.

Price, Richard. (2003) "Transnational Civil Society and Advocacy in World Politics," *World Politics* 55 (July): 519–606.

Price, Richard, and Christian Reus-Smit. (1998) "Dangerous Liaisons? Critical International Theory and Constructivism," *European Journal of International Relations* 4 (3): 259–294.

Putnam, Robert D. (1988) "Diplomacy and Domestic Politics: The Logic of Two-Level Games," *International Organization* 42 (Summer): 427–60.

Quester, George H. (1992) "Conventional Deterrence," pp. 31–51 in Gary L. Guertner, Robert Haffa, Jr., and George Quester (eds.), *Conventional Forces and the Future of Deterrence*. Carlisle Barracks, Pa.: U.S. Army War College.

Quinn, David, Jonathan Wilkenfeld, Kathleen Smarick, and Victor Asal. (2006) "Power Play: Mediation in Symmetric and Asymmetric International Crises," *International Interactions* 32 (December): 441–470.

Quinn, Jane Bryant. (2002) "Iraq: It's the Oil, Stupid," *Newsweek* (September 30): 43.

Quinn, J. Michael, T. David Mason and Mehmet Gurses. "Sustaining the Peace: Determinants of Civil War Recurrence," *International Interactions* 33 (April/June): 167–193.

Quirk, Matthew. (2007) "The Mexican Connection," *The Atlantic* (April) 26–27.

Rabin, Matthew. (1993) "Incorporating Fairness Into Game Theory and Economics," *The American Economic Review* 83 (May): 1281–1302.

Rabkin, Jeremy A. (2005) *Law Without Nations? Why Constitutional Government Requires Sovereign States*. Princeton, N.J.: Princeton University Press.

Raloff, Janet. (2006) "The Ultimate Crop Insurance," pp. 166–68 in Robert J. Griffiths (ed.), *Global Issues 05/06*. Dubuque, Iowa: McGraw-Hill/Dushkin.

Rapkin, David, and William R. Thompson, with Jon A. Christopherson. (1989) "Bipolarity and Bipolarization in the Cold War Era," *Journal of Conflict Resolution* 23 (June): 261–95.

Raslar, Karen A., and William R. Thompson. (2006) "Contested Territory, Strategic Rivalries, and Conflict Escalation," *International Studies Quarterly* 50 (March): 145–167.

Rasler, Karen, and William R. Thompson. (2005) *Puzzles of the Democratic Peace: Theory, Geopolitics, and the Transformation of World Politics*. London: Palgrave Macmillan.

Ravallion, Martin. (2004) "Pessimistic on Poverty?" *Economist* (April 10): 65.

Ravenhill, John (ed.). (2004) *Global Political Economy*. New York: Oxford University Press.

Ray, James Lee. (1995) *Democracy and International Conflict: An Evaluation of the Democratic Peace Proposition*. Columbia: University of South Carolina Press.

Raymond, Gregory A. (2003) "The Evolving Strategies of Political Terrorism," pp. 71–105 in Charles W. Kegley, Jr. (ed.), *The New Global Terrorism*. Upper Saddle River, N.J.: Prentice Hall.

———. (1999) "Necessity in Foreign Policy," *Political Science Quarterly* 113 (Winter): 673–88.

Redfield, Robert. (1962) *Human Nature and the Study of Society*, vol. 1. Chicago: University of Illinois Press.

Regan, Patrick M., and Aida Paskevicute. (2003) "Women's Access to Politics and Peaceful States," *Journal of Peace Research* 40 (March): 287–302.

Reich, Robert B. (2007a) "How Capitalism is Killing Democracy," *Foreign Policy* (September/October) 39–42.

Reich, Robert B. (2007b) *Supercapitalism*. New York: Knopf.

Reid, T. R. (2004) *The United States of Europe: The New Superpower and the End of American Supremacy*. New York: Penguin.

Reinares, Fernando. (2002) "The Empire Rarely Strikes Back," *Foreign Policy* (January/February): 92–94.

Reiter, Dan. (2003) "Exploring the Bargaining Model of War," *Perspectives on Politics* 1 (March): 27–43.

Reuveny, Rafael, and William R. Thompson. (2004) "World Economic Growth, Systemic Leadership and Southern Debt Crises," *Journal of Peace Research* 41 (January): 5–24.

Revel, Jean-Francois. (2004) *Anti-Americanism*. San Francisco: Encounter.

Rich, Frank. (2004) "The Corporate-Military Whiz Kids," *International Herald Tribune* (January 24–25): 8.

Ridley, Matt. (2003) *Nature vs. Nurture: Genes, Experiences and What Makes Us Human*. New York: HarperCollins.

Riedel, Bruce. (2007) "Al Qaeda Strikes Back," *Foreign Affairs* 86 (May/June) 24–40.

Rieff, David. (2005) *At the Point of a Gun: Democratic Dreams and Armed Intervention*. New York: Simon & Schuster.

———. (1999) "The Precarious Triumph of Human Rights," *New York Times Magazine* (August 8): 36–41.

Rifkin, Jeromy. (2004) *The European Dream: How Europe's Vision of the Future is Quietly Eclipsing the American Dream*. New York: Tarcher.

Riggs, Robert E., and Jack C. Plano. (1994) *The United Nations*, 2nd ed. Belmont, Calif.: Wadsworth.

Riker, William H. (1962) *The Theory of Political Coalitions*. New Haven, Conn.: Yale University Press.

Ripsman, Norrin M. (2005) "Two Stages of Transition from a Region of War to a Region of Peace," *International Studies Quarterly* 49 (December): 669–93.

Ripsman, Norrin M., and T. V. Paul. (2005) "Globalization and the National Security State," *International Studies Review* (June): 199–227.

Roche, Douglas. (2007) "Our Greatest Threat," pp. 137–140 in Robert M. Jackson, ed., *Global Issues 06/07*. Dubuque, Iowa: McGraw-Hill Contemporary Learning Series.

Rochester, J. Martin. (2006) *Between Peril and Promise: The Politics of International Law*. Washington, D.C.: CQ Press.

Rodrik, Dani. (1999) *The New Global Economy and Developing Countries*. Washington, D.C.: Overseas Development Council.

Rogoff, Kenneth. (2003) "The IMF Strikes Back," *Foreign Policy* (Jan/Feb): 38–46.

Rose, Gideon. (2005) "The Bush Administration Gets Real," *International Herald Tribune* (August 19): 7.

Rosecrance, Richard. (2005) "Merger and Acquisition," *The National Interest* 80 (Summer): 65–73.

———. (1997) "Economics and National Security," pp. 209–38 in Richard Shultz, Roy Godson, and George Quester (eds.), *Security Studies for the Twenty-First Century*. New York: Brassey's.

———. (1992) "A New Concert of Powers," *Foreign Affairs* 71 (Spring): 64–82.

Rosenau, James N. (1995) "Security in a Turbulent World," *Current History* 94 (May): 193–200.

———. (1980) *The Scientific Study of Foreign Policy*. New York: Nichols.

Rosenberg, Justin. (2005) "Globalization Theory: A Post Mortem," *International Politics* 42 (March): 2–74.

Rosenberg, Shawn W. (1988) *Reason, Ideology and Politics*. Princeton, N.J.: Princeton University Press.

Rosenthal, Elisabeth. (2005) "Global Warming: Adapting to a New Reality," *International Herald Tribune* (September 12): 1, 5.

Rosenthal, Joel H. (1991) *Righteous Realists*. Baton Rouge: Louisiana State University Press.

Ross, Dennis. (2007) *Statecraft and How to Restore America's Standing in the World*. New York: Farrar, Straus and Giroux.

Ross, Michael L. (2004) "What Do We Know about Natural Resources and Civil War?" *Journal of Peace Research* 41 (May): 337–56.

Ross, Philip E. (1997) "The End of Infantry?" *Forbes* (July 7): 182–85.

Rosset, Peter. (1999) "Biotechnology Won't Feed the World," *International Herald Tribune* (September 2): 8.

Rostow, W. W. (1960) *The Stages of Economic Growth*. Cambridge: Cambridge University Press.

Rothkopf, David J. (2005) *Running the World*. New York: Public Affairs.

Rousseau, David L. (2006) *Identifying Threats and Threatening Identities: The Social Construction of Realism and Liberalism*. Stanford, Calif.: Stanford University Press.

Rubenstein, Richard E. (2003) "The Psycho-Political Sources of Terrorism," pp. 139–50 in Charles W. Kegley, Jr. (ed.), *The New Global Terrorism*. Upper Saddle River, N.J.: Prentice Hall.

Rubin, Nancy. (1999) "It's Official: All of the World Is Entitled to Democracy," *International Herald Tribune* (May 18): 8.

Rudolph, Christopher. (2005) "Sovereignty and Territorial Borders in a Global Age," *International Studies Review* 7 (March): 1–20.

Ruggie, John Gerald. (1998) "What Makes the World Hang Together? Neo-Utilitarianism and the Social Constructivist Challenge," *International Organization* 52 (Autumn): 855–885.

———. (1983) "Continuity and Transformation in the World Polity: Toward a Neorealist Synthesis," *World Politics* 35 (January): 261–85.

Rummel, Rudolph J. (1994) *Death by Government*. New Brunswick, N.J.: Transaction.

Russett, Bruce. (2005) "Bushwhacking the Democratic Peace," *International Studies Perspectives* 6 (November): 395–408.

———. (2001) "How Democracy, Interdependence, and International Organizations Create a System for Peace," pp. 232–42 in Charles W. Kegley, Jr., and Eugene Wittkopf (eds.), *The Global Agenda*, 6th ed. Boston: McGraw-Hill.

Rynning, Sten, and Jens Ringsmose. (2008) "Why are Revisionist States Revisionist? Reviving Classical Realism as an Approach to Understanding International Change," *International Politics* 45 (January): 19–39.

Sabastenski, Anna (ed.). (2005) *Patterns of Global Terrorism 1985–2004*. Great Barrington, Mass.: Berkshire.

Sachs, Jeffrey. (2005) *The End of Poverty*. New York: Penguin Press.

Sadowaski. Yahya. (1998) "Ethnic Conflict," *Foreign Policy* 112 (Summer): 12–23.

Sagan, Carl. (1989) "Understanding Growth Rates: The Secret of the Persian Chessboard," *Parade* (February 14): 14.

———. (1988) "The Common Enemy," *Parade* (February 7): 4–7.

Sagan, Carl, and Richard Turco. (1993) "Nuclear Winter in the Post-Cold War Era," *Journal of Peace Research* 30 (November): 369–73.

Sageman, Marc. (2008) *Leaderless Jihad: Terror Networks in the Twenty-First Century*. Philadelphia: University of Pennsylvania Press.

———. (2004) *Understanding Terror Networks*. Philadelphia: University of Pennsylvania Press.

Sambanis, Nicholas. (2004) "What Is Civil War?" *Journal of Conflict Resolution* 48 (December): 814–58.

Samin, Amir. (1976) *Unequal Development*. New York: Monthly Review Press.

Samuelson, Robert J. (2008) "Learning From the Oil Shock." *Newsweek* (June 23): 39.

———. (2007) "The Expanding Power of Capital," Columbia, S.C. *The State* (August 8): A7.

———. (2006) "This Year Could Mark the End of Pax Americana," Columbia, S.C., *The State* (December 19): A9.

———. (2005a) "A Future We Can't Afford," Columbia, S.C., *The State* (April 8): A13.

———. (2005b) "The Dawn of a New Oil Era?" *Newsweek* (April 4): 37.

———. (2002a) "'Digital Divide' Facing Poor Looks Like Fiction," Columbia, S.C., *The State* (April 3): A13.

———. (2002b) "The New Coin of the Realm," *Newsweek* (January 7): 38.

Sandler, Todd and Walter Enders. (2007) "Applying Analytical Methods to Study Terrorism," *International Studies Perspectives* 8 (August): 287–302.

Sands, Phillippe. (2005) *Lawless World: America and the Making and Breaking of Global Rules*. New York: Viking Penguin.

Sang-Hun, Choe. (2008) "Hundreds Injured in South Korean Beef Protest," *International Herald Tribune* (June 29).

Sanger, David E. (2005) "The New Global Dance Card," *New York Times* (September 18): Section 4, 3.

———. (1998) "Contagion Effect: A Guide to Modern Domino Theory," *New York Times* (August 2): Section 1, 4–5.

Saul, John Ralstom. (2004) "The Collapse of Globalism and the Rebirth of Nationalism," *Harper's* 308 (March): 33–43.

Saurin, Julian. (2000) "Globalization, Poverty, and the Promises of Modernity," pp. 204–29 in Sarah Owen Vandersluis and Paris Yeros (eds.), *Poverty in World Politics*. New York: St. Martin's.

Saxton, Gregory D. (2005) "Repression, Grievances, Mobilization, and Rebellion," *International Interactions* 31 (No. 1): 87–116.

Schelling, Thomas C. (2006) *Strategies of Commitment and Other Essays*. Cambridge, Mass.: Harvard University Press.

———. (1978) *Micromotives and Macrobehavior*. New York: Norton.

———. (1966) *Arms and Influence*. New Haven, Conn.: Yale University Press.

Schlesinger, Arthur, Jr. (1997) "Has Democracy a Future?" *Foreign Affairs* 76 (September-October): 2–12.

———. (1986) *The Cycles of American History*. Boston: Houghton Mifflin.

Schneider, Gerald, Katherine Barbieri, and Nils Petter Gleditsch (eds.). (2003) *Globalization and Armed Conflict*. Lanham, Md.: Rowman & Littlefield.

Schraeder, Peter J. (ed.). (2002) *Exporting Democracy*. Boulder, Colo.: Lynne Rienner.

Schroeder, Paul W. (1989) "The Nineteenth-Century System," *Review of International Studies* 15 (April): 135–53.

Schuler, Corinna. (1999) "Helping Children Warriors Regain Their Humanity," *Christian Science Monitor* (October 20): 1, 12–13.

Schulz, William F. (2001) *In Our Own Best Interest: How Defending Human Rights Benefits Us All*. Boston: Beacon Press.

Schwarz, Benjamin. (2005) "Managing China's Rise," *Atlantic Monthly* 295 (June): 27–28.

Schweller, Randall L. (2004) "Unanswered Threats: A Neoclassical Realist Theory of Underbalancing," *International Security* 29 (Fall): 159–201.

———. (1999) Review of *From Wealth to Power* by Fareed Zakaria, *American Political Science Review* 93 (June 1999): 497–99.

Scowcroft, Brent, and Samuel R. Berger. (2005) "In the Wake of War: Getting Serious About Nation-Building," *The National Interest* 81 (Fall): 49–60.

Seck, Manadon Manosour. (1999) "Shrinking Forests," *Christian Science Monitor* (May 3): 9.

Secor, Laura. (2005) *Sands of Empire*. New York: Simon and Schuster.

Selck, Torsten J. (2004) "On the Dimensionality of European Union Legislative Decision-Making," *Journal of Theoretical Politics* 16 (April): 203–22.

Sen, Amartya. (2006) *Identity and Violence: The Illusion of Destiny*. New York: Norton.

Sengupta, Somini. (2005) "Hunger for Energy Transforms How India Operates," *New York Times International* (June 5): Section 4, 3.

Senese, Paul D., and John A. Vasquez. (2008) *The Steps to War*. Princeton, N.J.: Princeton University Press.

Serfaty, Simon. (2003) "Europe Enlarged, America Detached?" *Current History* (March): 99–102.

Sezgin, Yüksel. (2005) "Taking a New Look at State-Directed Industrialization," *International Studies Review* 7 (June): 323–325.

Shah, Timothy Samuel. (2004) "The Bible and the Ballot Box: Evangelicals and Democracy in the 'Global South,'" *SAIS Review of International Affairs* 24 (Fall): 117–32.

Shane, Scott. (2005) "The Beast That Feeds on Boxes: Bureaucracy," *New York Times* (April 10): Section 4, 3.

Shannon, Thomas Richard. (1989) *An Introduction to the World-System Perspective*. Boulder, Colo.: Westview.

Shapin, Steven. (2007) "What Else is New," *The New Yorker* (May 14): 144–148.

Shapiro, Ian. (2007) *Containment: Rebuilding a Strategy Against Global Terrorism*. Princeton, N.J.: Princeton University Press.

Sheehan, Michael. (1996) "A Regional Perspective on the Globalization Process," *Korean Journal of Defense Analysis* 8 (Winter): 53–74.

Sheffer, Gabriel. (2003) *Diaspora Politics: At Home Abroad*. Cambridge: Cambridge University Press.

Shiffman, Gary M. (2006) *Economic Instruments of Security Policy*. Basingstoke, U.K.: Palgrave MacMillan.

Shlapentorkh, Vladmir, Eric Shirae, and Josh Woods (eds.). (2005) *America: Sovereign Defender or Cowboy Nation?* Burlington, Ver.: Ashgate.

Shreeve, Jamie. (2005) "The Stem-Cell Debate," *New York Times Magazine* (April 10): 42–47.

Shultz, Richard H., Jr., Roy Godson, and George H. Quester (eds.). (1997) *Security Studies for the Twenty-First Century*. New York: Brassey's.

Shultz, Richard H., Jr., and William J. Olson. (1994) *Ethnic and Religious Conflict*. Washington, D.C.: National Strategy Information Center.

Siegel, Martin J. (1983) "Survival," *USA Today* 112 (August): 1–2.

Siegle, Joseph T., Michael M. Weinstein, and Morton H. Halperin. (2004) "Why Democracies Excel," *Foreign Affairs* 83 (September-October): 57–71.

Simmons, Beth A., and Zachary Elkins. (2004) "The Globalization of Liberalization: Policy Diffusion in the International Political Economy," *American Political Science Review* 98 (February): 171–89.

Simon, Herbert A. (1997) *Models of Bounded Rationality*. Cambridge, Mass.: MIT Press.

———. (1957) *Models of Man*. New York: Wiley.

Singer, Hans W., and Javed A. Ansari. (1988) *Rich and Poor Countries*, 4th ed. London: Unwin Hyman.

Singer, J. David. (2000) "The Etiology of Interstate War," pp. 3–21 in John A. Vasquez (ed.), *What Do We Know About War?* Lanham, Md.: Rowman & Littlefield.

———. (1991) "Peace in the Global System," pp. 56–84 in Charles W. Kegley, Jr. (ed.), *The Long Postwar Peace*. New York: HarperCollins.

——— (ed.). (1968) *Quantitative International Politics*. New York: Free Press.

Singer, Max. (1999) "The Population Surprise," *Atlantic Monthly* (August): 22–25.

Singer, Max, and Aaron Wildavsky. (1993) *The Real World Order: Zones of Peace/Zones of Turmoil*. Chatham, N.J.: Chatham House.

Singer, Peter. (2004) *One World: The Ethics of Globalization*, 2nd ed. New Haven, Conn.: Yale University Press.

SIPRI (Stockholm International Peace Research Institute). (2008). *SIPRI Yearbook*. New York: Oxford University Press.

_____. (2007) *SIPRI Yearbook*. New York: Oxford University Press.

_____. (2006) *SIPRI Yearbook*. New York: Oxford University Press.

Sivard, Ruth Leger. (1996) *World Military and Social Expenditures 1996*. Washington, D.C.: World Priorities.

———. (1991) *World Military and Social Expenditures 1991*. Washington, D.C.: World Priorities.

Siverson, Randolph M., and Julian Emmons. (1991) "Democratic Political Systems and Alliance Choices," *Journal of Conflict Resolution* 35 (June): 285–306.

Skinner, E. Benjamin. (2008) "A World Enslaved," *Foreign Policy* (March/April): 62–67.

Sklair, Leslie. (1991) *Sociology of the Global System*. Baltimore: Johns Hopkins University Press.

Slackman, Michael. (2008) "Dreams Stifled, Egypt's Young Turn to Islamic Fervor," *The New York Times* (February 17): 1.

Slater, David. (2005) *Geopolitics and the Post-Colonial: Rethinking North–South Relations*. Malden, Mass: Blackwell.

Slaughter, Anne-Marie. (2004a) *A New World Order*. Princeton, N.J.: Princeton University Press.

———. (2004b) "The Clear, Cruel Lessons of Iraq," *Financial Times* (April 8): 15.

———. (1997) "The Real New World Order," *Foreign Affairs* 76 (September-October): 183–97.

Small, Melvin, and J. David Singer. (1982) *Resort to Arms: International and Civil Wars, 1816–1980*. Beverly Hills, Calif.: Sage.

Smith, Alastair, and Allan C. Stam. (2004) "Bargaining and the Nature of War," *Journal of Conflict Resolution* 48 (December): 783–813.

Smith, Jackie, and Timothy Patrick Moran. (2001) "WTO 101: Myths about the World Trade Organization," pp. 68–71 in Robert J. Griffiths (ed.), *Developing World 01/02*, Guilford, Conn.: Dushkin/McGraw-Hill.

Smith, Michael J. (2000) "Humanitarian Intervention Revisited," *Harvard International Review* 22 (April): 72–75.

Smith, Steve, and Patricia Owens. (2005) "Alternative Approaches to International Theory," pp. 271–93 in John Baylis and Steve Smith (eds.), *The Globalization of World Politics*, 3rd ed. New York: Oxford University Press.

Smith, Tony. (2007) *Pact With the Devil: Washington's Bid for World Supremacy and the Betrayal of the American Promise*. New York: Routledge.

Snidal, Duncan. (1993) "Relative Gains and the Pattern of International Cooperation," pp. 181–207 in David A. Baldwin (ed.), *Neorealism and Neoliberalism: The Contemporary Debate*. New York: Columbia University Press.

Snyder, David Pearce. (2006) "Five Meta-Trends Changing the World," pp. 13–17 in Robert M. Jackson (ed.), *Global Issues 05/06*. Dubuque, Iowa: McGraw-Hill/Dushkin.

Snyder, Glenn H. (1991) "Alliance Threats: A Neorealist First Cut," pp. 83–103 in Robert L. Rothstein (ed.), *The Evolution of Theory in International Relations*. Columbia: University of South Carolina Press.

———. (1984) "The Security Dilemma in Alliance Politics," *World Politics* 36 (July): 461–495.

Snyder, Glenn H., and Paul Diesing. (1977) *Conflict Among Nations*. Princeton, N.J.: Princeton University Press.

Snyder, Jack. (2005) "A Perfect Peace," *The Washington Post National Review Weekly Edition* (January 10): 33.

———. (2004) "One World, Rival Theories," *Foreign Policy* (November-December): 53–62.

Sobek, David. (2005) "Machiavelli's Legacy: Domestic Politics and International Conflict," *International Studies Quarterly* 49 (June): 179–204.

Somavia, Juan. (2004) "For Too Many, Globalization Isn't Working," *International Herald Tribune* (February 27): 6.

Somit, Albert. (1990) "Humans, Chimps, and Bonobos: The Biological Bases of Aggression, War, and Peacemaking," *Journal of Conflict Resolution* 34 (September): 553–82.

Sørensen, Georg. (1995) "Four Futures," *Bulletin of the Atomic Scientists* 51 (July-August): 69–72.

Sorensen, Theodore C. (1963) *Decision Making in the White House*. New York: Columbia University Press.

Sorokin, Pitirim A. (1937) *Social and Cultural Dynamics*. New York: American Book.

Soros, George. (2003) *The Bubble of American Supremacy: Correcting the Misuse of American Power*. New York: Public Affairs.

Souva, Mark. (2004) "Institutional Similarity and Interstate Conflict," *International Interactions* 30 (July-September): 263–80.

Sperandei, Maria. (2006) "Bridging Deterrents and Compellence," *International Studies Review* 8 (June): 253–280.

Sprout, Harold and Margaret Sprout. (1965) *The Ecological Perspective on Human Affairs*. Princeton, N. J.: Princeton University Press.

Spykman, Nicholas. (1944) *The Geography of Peace*. New York: Harcourt Brace.

Starr, Harvey. (2006) "International Borders," *SAIS Review* 26 (Winter/Spring): 3–10.

Steele, Brent J. (2007) "Liberal-Idealism: A Constructivist Critique," *International Studies Review* 9 (Spring): 23–52.

Stephenson, Carolyn M. (2000) "NGOs and the Principal Organs of the United Nations," pp. 270–94 in Paul Taylor and R. J. Groom (eds.), *The United Nations at the Millennium*. London: Continuum.

Stiglitz, Joseph. (2006) *Making Globalization Work*. New York: Norton.

————. (2003) *Globalization and Its Discontents*. New York: Norton.

Stohl, Rachel. (2005) "Fighting the Illicit Trafficking of Small Arms," *SAIS Review* 25 (Winter-Spring): 59–68.

Stopford, John. (2001) "Multinational Corporations," pp. 72–77 in Robert J. Griffiths (ed.), *Developing World 01/02*. Guilford, Conn.: Dushkin/McGraw-Hill.

Strang, David. (1991) "Global Patterns of Decolonization, 1500–1987," *International Studies Quarterly* 35 (December): 429–545.

————. (1990) "From Dependence to Sovereignty: An Event History Analysis of Decolonization 1870–1987," *American Sociological Review* 55 (December): 846–60.

Streeten, Paul. (2001) "Human Development Index," pp. 367–68 in Joel Krieger (ed.), *The Oxford Companion to Politics of the World*, 2nd ed. New York: Oxford University Press.

Stross, Randall E. (2002) "The McPeace Dividend," *U.S. News & World Report* (April 1): 36.

Suganami, Hidemi. (1983) "A Normative Enquiry in International Relations," *Review of International Studies* 9: 35–54.

Summers, Lawrence H. (2006) "America Overdrawn," pp. 25–27 in Helen E. Purkitt (ed.), *World Politics 05/06*. Dubuque, Iowa: McGraw-Hill/Dushkin.

Surowiecki, James. (2007) "The Myth of Inevitable Progress," *Foreign Affairs* 86 (July/August): 132–139.

Sutherland, Peter. (2008) "Transforming Nations: How the WTO Boosts Economies and Opens Societies," *Foreign Affairs* 87 (March): 125–136.

Sylvester, Christine. (2002) *Feminist International Relations*. New York: Cambridge University Press.

Talbott, Strobe, and Nayan Chanda (eds.). (2002) *The Age of Terror*. New York: Basic Books.

Tan, Sor-hoon (ed.). (2005) *Challenging Citizenship: Group Membership and Cultural Identity in a Global Age*. Burlington, Ver.: Ashgate.

Tarar, Ahmar. (2006) "Diversionary Incentives and the Bargaining Approach to War," *International Studies Quarterly* 50 (March): 169–188.

Tarrow, Sidney. (2006) *The New Transnational Activism*. New York: Cambridge University Press.

Tellis, Ashley J. (2005) "A Grand Chessboard," *Foreign Policy* (January-February): 51–54.

Teslik, Lee Hudson. (2008) "Council for Foreign Relations Backgrounder: Food Prices," http://www.cfr.org/publication/16662/price_of_food.html?breadcrumb=%2Findex (accessed August 2008).

Tessman, Brock, and Steve Chan. (2004) "Power Cycles, Risk Propensity and Great Power Deterrence," *Journal of Conflict Resolution* 48 (April): 131–53.

Tetlock, Philip. (2006) *Expert Political Judgment*. Princeton, N.J.: Princeton University Press.

Thachuk, Kimberley. (2005) "Corruption and International Security," *SAIS Review* 25 (Winter-Spring): 143–52.

Thakur, Ramesh. (1998) "Teaming Up to Make Human Rights a Universal Fact," *International Herald Tribune* (December 10): 10.

Thakur, Ramesh, and Steve Lee. (2000) "Defining New Goals for Diplomacy in the Twenty-First Century," *International Herald Tribune* (January 19): 8.

Thomas, Ward. (2005) "The New Age of Assassination," *SAIS Review* 25 (Winter-Spring): 27–39.

Thompson, Kenneth W. (1960) *Political Realism and the Crisis of World Politics*. Princeton, N.J.: Princeton University Press.

Thompson, Mark. (2007) "Flying Shame," *Time* (October 8): 34–41.

Thompson, William R. (ed.). (1999a) *Great Power Rivalries*. Columbia: University of South Carolina Press.

————. (1999b) "Why Rivalries Matter and What Great Power Rivalries Can Tell Us about World Politics," pp. 3–28 in William R. Thompson (ed.), *Great Power Rivalries*. Columbia: University of South Carolina Press.

————. (1988) *On Global War: Historical-Structural Approaches to World Politics*. Columbia: University of South Carolina Press.

Thurow, Lester C. (1999) *Building Wealth*. New York: HarperCollins.

————. (1998) "The American Economy in the Next Century," *Harvard International Review* 20 (Winter): 54–59.

Tickner, J. Ann. (2005) "What Is Your Research Program? Some Feminist Answers to International Relations Methodological Questions," *International Studies Quarterly* 49 (March): 1–21.

————. (2002) *Gendering World Politics*. New York: Columbia University Press.

Tilford, Earl H., Jr. (1995) *The Revolution in Military Affairs*. Carlisle Barracks, Pa.: U.S. Army War College.

Tillema, Herbert K. (2008) *Overt Military Intervention in the Cold War Era*. Columbia: University of South Carolina Press.

————. (1994) "Cold War Alliance and Overt Military Intervention, 1945–1991," *International Interactions* 20 (No. 3): 249–78.

Tilly, Charles. (2003) *The Politics of Collective Violence*. Cambridge: Cambridge University Press.

Timmerman, Kenneth. (1991) *The Death Lobby: How the West Armed Iraq*. Boston: Houghton Mifflin.

Tocqueville, Alexis de. (1969 [1835]) *Democracy in America*. New York: Doubleday.

Todaro, Michael P. (2002) *Economic Development*, 8th ed. Reading, Mass.: Addison-Wesley.

————. (2000) *Economic Development*, 7th ed. Reading, Mass.: Addison-Wesley.

————. (1994) *Economic Development in the Third World*, 5th ed. New York: Longman.

Todd, Emmanuel. (2003) *After the Empire: The Breakdown of the American Order*. Translated by C. Jon Delogu. New York: Columbia University Press.

Toft, Monica Duffy. (2007) "Population Shifts and Civil War: A Test of Power Transition Theory," *International Interactions* 33 (July/September): 243–269.

Toner, Robin. (2002) "FBI Agent Gives Her Blunt Assessment," Columbia, S.C., *The State* (June 7): A5.

Toynbee, Arnold J. (1954) *A Study of History*. London: Oxford University Press.

Traub, James. (2005) "The New Hard-Soft Power," *New York Times Magazine* (January 30): 28–29.

Trumbull, Mark and Andrew Downie. (2007) "Great Global Shift to Service Jobs," *The Christian Science Monitor* (September): 1, 10.

Tuchman, Barbara W. (1984) *The March of Folly*. New York: Ballantine.

———. (1962) *The Guns of August*. New York: Dell.

Tures, John A. (2005) "Operation Exporting Freedom," *The Whitehead Journal of Diplomacy and International Relations* 6 (Winter-Spring): 97–111.

Tyler, Patrik E. (2001) "Seeing Profits, Russia Prepared to Become World's Nuclear Waste Dump," *International Herald Tribune* (May 28): 5.

UIA (Union of International Associations). (2006) *Yearbook of International Organizations*. 2005/2006, Edition 42. München: K.G. Saur.

———. (2005) *Yearbook of International Associations 2004/2005*, Vols. 1–5. Munich: K.G. Sauer.

Underhill, Geoffrey R. D., and Xiakoe Zhang (eds.). (2003) *International Financial Governance under Stress: Global Structures versus National Imperatives*. Cambridge: Cambridge University Press.

UNDP. (2008) *Human Development Report 2007/2008*. New York: United Nations Development Programme.

———. (2007) *Human Development Report*. New York: Oxford University Press.

———. (2005a) *Arab Human Development Report 2005*. New York: United Nations Development Programme.

———. (2005b) *Human Development Report 2005*. United Nations Development Programme. New York: Oxford University Press.

———. (2004) *Human Development Report 2004*. New York: Oxford University Press.

———. (2003) *Human Development Report 2003*. New York: Oxford University Press.

———. (2002) *Human Development Report 2002*. New York: Oxford University Press.

———. (2001) *Human Development Report 2001*. New York: Oxford University Press.

UNHCR. 2008. *2007 Global Trends: Refugees, Asylum-seekers, Returnees, Internally Displaced and Stateless Persons*. Geneva: UN High Commissioner for Refugees.

———. (2007). *2006 Global Trends*. Geneva: UN High Commissioner for Refugees.

United Nations Conference on Trade and Development (UNCTAD). (2004) "Global FDI Decline Bottoms Out in 2003," press release.

United Nations Environment Programme (UNEP). (2004) *State of the Environment and Policy Perspective*. New York: United Nations.

———. (2002) *Global Environment Outlook*. New York: Oxford University Press.

United Nations Population Division (UNPD). (2004) *World Population Prospects*. New York: United Nations.

Urdal, Henrik. (2006) "A Clash of Generations? Youth Bulges and Political Violence," *International Studies Quarterly* 50 (September): 607–629.

Urquhart, Brian. (2002) "Shameful Neglect," *International Herald Tribune* (April 25): 12–14.

———. (2001) "Mrs. Roosevelt's Revolution," *New York Review of Books* 49 (April 26): 32–34.

———. (1994) "Who Can Police the World?" *New York Review of Books* 41 (May 12): 29–33.

U.S. Arms Control and Disarmament Agency (ACDA). (2002) *World Military Expenditures and Arms Transfers*. Washington, D.C.: U.S. Government Printing Office.

———. (1997) *World Military Expenditures and Arms Transfers 1995*. Washington, D.C.: U.S. Government Printing Office.

Valentino, Benjamin. (2004) *Final Solutions: Mass Killing and Genocide in the Twentieth Century*. Ithaca, N.Y.: Cornell University Press.

Vandersluis, Sarah Owen, and Paris Yeros. (2000a) "Ethics and Poverty in a Global Era," pp. 1–31 in Sarah Owen Vandersluis and Paris Yeros (eds.), *Poverty in World Politics*. New York: St. Martin's.

——— (eds.). (2000b) *Poverty in World Politics*. New York: St. Martin's.

Van Evera, Stephen. (1999) *Causes of War*. Ithaca, N.Y.: Cornell University Press.

———. (1994) "Hypotheses on Nationalism and War," *International Security* 18 (Spring): 5–39.

———. (1990–91) "Primed for Peace," *International Security* 15 (Winter): 6–56.

Van Oudenaren, John. (2005) "Containing Europe," *The National Interest* 80 (Summer): 57–64.

Vasquez, John A. (2005) "Ethics, Foreign Policy, and Liberal Wars," *International Studies Perspectives* 6 (August): 307–315.

———. (2000) *What Do We Know About War?* Lanham, Md.: Rowman & Littlefield.

———. (1998) *The Power of Power Politics: From Classical Realism to Neotraditionalism*. Cambridge: Cambridge University Press.

———. (1997) "The Realist Paradigm and Degenerative versus Progressive Research Programs," *American Political Science Review* 91 (December): 899–912.

———. (1993) *The War Puzzle*. Cambridge: Cambridge University Press.

———. (1991) "The Deterrence Myth," pp. 205–23 in Charles W. Kegley, Jr. (ed.), *The Long Postwar Peace*. New York: HarperCollins.

Vasquez, John A., and Colin Elman (eds.). (2003) *Realism and the Balancing of Power: A New Debate*. Upper Saddle River, N.J.: Prentice Hall.

Verba, Sidney. (1969) "Assumptions of Rationality and Nonrationality in Models of the International System," pp. 217–31 in James N. Rosenau (ed.), *International Politics and Foreign Policy*. New York: Free Press.

Vidal, Gore. (2004). *Imperial America*. New York: Nation Books.

Vital Signs 2006–2007. New York: Norton, for the Worldwatch Institute.

Vital Signs 2005. New York: Norton, for the Worldwatch Institute.

Vital Signs 2004. New York: Norton, for the Worldwatch Institute.

Vital Signs 2003. New York: Norton, for the Worldwatch Institute.

Vital Signs 2002. New York: Norton, for the Worldwatch Institute.

Vital Signs 2000. New York: Norton, for the Worldwatch Institute.

Voeten, Erik. (2004) "Resisting the Lonely Superpower: Responses of States in the United Nations to U.S. Dominance," *Journal of Politics* 66 (August): 729–54.

von Drehl, David. (2008) "A New Line in the Sand," *Time* (June 30): 28–35.

von Glahn, Gerhard. (1996) *Law Among Nations,* 7th ed. Boston: Allyn & Bacon.

Vreeland, James Raymond. (2003) *The IMF and Economic Development.* Cambridge: Cambridge University Press.

Wagner, R. Harrison. (2007) *War And The State.* Ann Arbor: Pluto Books, University of Michigan Press.

Wallace, Brian. (1978) "True Grit South of the Border," *Osceola* (January 13): 15–16.

Wallerstein, Immanuel. (2005) *World-Systems Analysis.* Durham, N.C.: Duke University Press.

———. (2002) "The Eagle Has Crash Landed," *Foreign Policy* (July-August): 60–68.

———. (1988) *The Modern World-System III.* San Diego: Academic Press.

Walsh, Bryan. (2006) "The Impact of Asia's Giants," *Time* (April 3): 61–62.

Walt, Stephen M. (2005) *Taming American Power.* New York: Norton.

Walter, Barbara F. (2004) "Does Conflict Beget Conflict?" *Journal of Peace Research* 41 (May): 371–88.

———. (1997) "The Critical Barrier to Civil War Settlement," *International Organization* 51 (Summer): 335–64.

Walters, Robert S., and David H. Blake. (1992) *The Politics of Global Economic Relations,* 4th ed. Englewood Cliffs, N.J.: Prentice Hall.

Waltz, Kenneth N. (2000) "Structural Realism after the Cold War," *International Security* 25 (Summer): 5–41.

———. (1995) "Realist Thought and Neorealist Theory," pp. 67–83 in Charles W. Kegley, Jr. (ed.), *Controversies in International Relations Theory.* New York: St. Martin's.

———. (1993) "The Emerging Structure of International Politics," *International Security* 18 (Fall): 44–79.

———. (1979) *Theory of International Politics.* Reading, Mass.: Addison-Wesley.

———. (1964) "The Stability of a Bipolar World," *Daedalus* 93 (Summer): 881–909.

Walzer, Michael. (2004) *Arguing About War.* New Haven, Conn.: Yale University Press.

Ward, Michael D., David R. Davis, and Corey L. Lofdahl. (1995) "A Century of Tradeoffs," *International Studies Quarterly* 39 (March): 27–50.

Watson, Douglas. (1997) "Indigenous Peoples and the Global Economy," *Current History* 96 (November): 389–91.

Wattenberg, Ben J. (2005) *Fewer: How the Demography of Depopulation Will Shape Our Future.* Chicago: Ivan R. Dee.

WDI. (2007) *World Development Indicators 2007.* Washington, D.C.: World Bank.

———. (2006) *World Development Indicators 2006.* Washington, D.C.: World Bank.

———. (2005) *World Development Indicators 2005.* Washington, D.C.: World Bank.

WDR. (2008) *World Development Report 2008.* Washington, D.C.: World Bank.

———. (2007) *World Development Report 2007.* Washington, D.C.: World Bank.

———. (2005) *World Development Report 2006.* Washington, D.C.: World Bank.

Weart, Spencer R. (1994) "Peace among Democratic and Oligarchic Republics," *Journal of Peace Research* 31 (August): 299–316.

Weber, Cynthia. (2005) *International Relations Theory,* 2nd ed. New York: Routledge.

Weidenbaum, Murray. (2004) "Surveying the Global Marketplace," *USA Today* (January): 26–27.

Weiner, Tim. (2005) "Robot Warriors Becoming Reality," Columbia, S.C., *The State* (February 18): A17.

Weir, Kimberly A. (2007) "The State Sovereignty Battle in Seattle," *International Politics* 44 (September): 596–622.

Weisbrot, Mark. (2005) "The IMF Has Lost Its Influence," *International Herald Tribune* (September 23): 7.

Weitsman, Patricia A. (2004) *Dangerous Alliances: Proponents of Peace, Weapons of War.* Stanford, Calif.: Stanford University Press.

Wendt, Alexander. (2000) *Social Theory of International Politics.* Cambridge: Cambridge University Press.

———. (1995) "Constructing International Politics," *International Security* 20 (Summer): 71–81.

———. (1994) "Collective Identity Formation and the International State," *American Political Science Review* 88 (June): 384–396.

Wendzel, Robert L. (1980) *International Relations: A Policymaker Focus.* New York: Wiley.

Wesley, Michael. (2005) "Toward a Realist Ethics of Intervention," *Ethics & International Affairs* 19 (No. 2, Special Issue): 55–72.

Weston, Drew, (2007) *The Political Brain: The Role of Emotion in Deciding the Fate of the Nation.* New York: PublicAffairs.

Western, Jon. (2006) "Doctrinal Divisions: The Politics of U.S. Military Interventions," pp. 87–90 in Glenn P. Hastedt (ed.), *American Foreign Policy,* 12th ed. Dubuque, Iowa: McGraw-Hill/Dushkin.

Wheaton, Henry. (1846) *Elements of International Law.* Philadelphia: Lea and Blanchard.

White, Ralph K. (1990) "Why Aggressors Lose," *Political Psychology* 11 (June): 227–242.

Wilkenfeld, Jonathan, Kathleen J. Young, David M. Quinn and Victor Asal. (2005) *Mediating International Crises*. London: Routledge.

Will, George F. (2005) "Aspects of Europe's Mind," *Newsweek* (May 9): 72.

Wills, Garry. (2004) "What Is a Just War?" *New York Review of Books* (November 18): 32–32.

Wilmer, Franke. (2000) "Women, the State and War: Feminist Incursions into World Politics," pp. 385–395 in Richard W. Mansbach and Edward Rhodes (eds.), *Global Politics in a Changing World*. Boston: Houghton Mifflin.

Wilson, James Q. (1993) *The Moral Sense*. New York: Free Press.

WIR. (2004) *World Investment Report 2004*. New York: United Nations Conference on Trade and Development.

Wise, Michael Z. (1993) "Reparations," *Atlantic Monthly* 272 (October): 32–35.

Wittkopf, Eugene R., Christopher M. Jones and Charles W. Kegley, Jr. (2008) *American Foreign Policy*, 7th edition. Belmont, Calif.: Thomson Wadsworth.

Wittkopf, Eugene R., Charles W. Kegley, Jr., and James M. Scott. (2003) *American Foreign Policy*, 6th ed. Belmont, Calif.: Wadsworth.

Wohlforth, William C. (1999) "The Stability of a Unipolar World," *International Security* 24 (Summer): 5–41.

Wolfe, Tom. (2005) "The Doctrine That Never Died," *New York Times* (January 30): Section 4, 17.

Wolfensohn, James. (2004) "The Growing Threat of Global Poverty," *International Herald Tribune* (April 24–25): 6.

Wolfers, Arnold. (1962) *Discord and Collaboration*. Baltimore: Johns Hopkins University Press.

Wolfers, Arnold, and Laurence Martin (eds.). (1956) *The Anglo-American Tradition in Foreign Affairs*. New Haven, Conn.: Yale University Press.

Wolfsthal, Jon B. (2005) "The Next Nuclear Wave," *Foreign Affairs* 84 (January-February): 156–61.

Wong, Edward. (2005) "Iraq Dances with Iran, While America Seethes," *New York Times* (July 31): Section 4, 3.

Woodard, Colin. (2007) "Who Resolves Arctic Disputes?," *Christian Science Monitor* (August 20): 1, 6.

Woodward, Bob. (2006) *State of Denial*. New York: Simon & Schuster.

———. (2004). *Plan of Attack*. New York: Simon & Schuster.

———. (2002). *Bush at War*. New York: Simon & Schuster.

Woodwell, Douglas. (2008) *Nationalism in International Relations*. London: Palgrave Macmillan.

World Bank. (2008) "World Bank President to G8: 'World Entering a Danger Zone'," http://go.worldbank.org/FXVBH85XS0, July 2 (accessed August 2008).

———. (2007) *Atlas of Global Development*. Washington, D.C.: World Bank.

———. (2005) *World Bank Atlas*. Washington, D.C.: World Bank.

———. (1996) *World Debt Tables 1996*, Vol. 1. Washington, D.C.: World Bank.

World Resources Institute (WRI). (2004) *SDI: Sustainable Development Index*. Washington, D.C.: World Resources Institute.

World Trade. (2002) *World Trade 14* (June): 13–15.

World Trade Organization (WTO) (2003) *World Trade Report 2003*, Geneva: WTO.

Worldwatch Institute. (2000) *The World in 2000*. New York: Norton.

Wright, Quincy. (1953) "The Outlawry of War and the Law of War," *American Journal of International Law* 47 (July): 365–76.

———. (1942) *A Study of War*. Chicago: University of Chicago Press.

Yang, David W. (2005) "In Search of an Effective Democratic Realism," *SAIS Review* 15 (Winter-Spring): 199–205.

Yergin, Daniel. (2006) "Thirty Years of Petro-Politics," pp. 106–7 in Robert M. Jackson (ed.), *Global Issues 05/06*. Dubuque, Iowa: McGraw-Hill/Dushkin.

———. (2005) "An Oil Shortage?" Columbia, S.C., *The State* (August 2): A9.

Youde, Jeremy. (2005) "Enter the Fourth Horseman: Health Security and International Relations Theory," *The Whitehead Journal of Diplomacy and International Affairs* 6 (Winter-Spring): 193–208.

Zacher, Mark W. (1987) "Trade Gaps, Analytical Gaps: Regime Analysis and International Commodity Regulation," *International Organization* 41 (Spring): 173–202.

Zacher, Mark W., and Richard A. Matthew. (1995) "Liberal International Theory: Common Threads, Divergent Strands," pp. 107–49 in Charles W. Kegley, Jr. (ed.), *Controversies in International Relations Theory: Realism and the Neoliberal Challenge*. New York: St. Martin's.

Zagare, Frank C. (2007) "Toward a Unified Theory of Interstate Conflict," *International Interactions* 33 (July/September): 305–327.

———. (2004) "Reconciling Rationality with Deterrence," *Journal of Theoretical Politics* 16 (April): 107–41.

———. (1990) "Rationality and Deterrence," *World Politics* 42 (January): 238–60.

Zakaria, Fareed. (2007) "Preview of a Post-U.S. World," *Newsweek* (February 5). 47.

———. (2005a) "Does the Future Belong to China?" *Newsweek* (May 9): 26–47.

———. (2005b) "The Wealth of More Nations," *New York Times Book Review* (May 1): 10–11.

———. (2004) "The One-Note Superpower," *Newsweek* (February 2): 41.

———. (2002a) "Europe: Make Peace with War," *Newsweek* (June 3): 35.

———. (2002b) "Stop the Babel over Babylon," *Newsweek* (October 16): 34.

———. (2002c) "The Trouble with Being the World's Only Superpower," *New Yorker* (October 14 and 21): 72–81.

———. (1999) "The Empire Strikes Out: The Unholy Emergence of the Nation-State," *New York Times Magazine* (April 18): 99.

———. (1998a) *From Wealth to Power: The Unusual Origins of America's World Role*. Princeton, N.J.: Princeton University Press.

———. (1998b) "The Future of Statecraft," p. 42 in *The World in 1999*. London: Economist.

———. (1992–93) "Is Realism Finished?" *National Interest* 30 (Winter): 21–32.

Zelikow, Philip. (2006) "The Transformation of National Security," pp. 121–27 in Robert M. Jackson (ed.), *Global Issues 05/06*. Dubuque, Iowa: McGraw-Hill/Dushkin.

Ziegler, David. (1995) Review of *World Politics and the Evolution of War* by John Weltman, *American Political Science Review* 89 (September): 813–14.

Zimmerman, Tim. (1996) "CIA Study: Why Do Countries Fall Apart?" *U.S. News & World Report* (February 12): 46.

name index

subject index